SURSUM CORDA!
The Collected Letters of Malcolm Lowry
Volume I: 1926-1946

SURSUM CORDA!

The Collected Letters of Malcolm Lowry
Volume I: 1926–1946

Edited with Introduction and Annotations
by Sherrill E. Grace

JONATHAN CAPE
LONDON

First published 1995

1 3 5 7 9 10 8 6 4 2

Malcolm Lowry's Letters © The Malcolm Lowry Estate 1995
Introductions, annotations and editorial comments © Sherrill E. Grace 1995

Sherrill E. Grace has asserted her right
under the Copyright, Designs and Patents Act, 1988
to be identified as the author of this work

First published in the United Kingdom in 1995 by
Jonathan Cape
Random House, 20 Vauxhall Bridge Road, London SW1V 2SA

Random House Australia (Pty) Limited
20 Alfred Street, Milsons Point, Sydney,
New South Wales 2061, Australia

Random House New Zealand Limited
18 Poland Road, Glenfield,
Auckland 10, New Zealand

Random House South Africa (Pty) Limited
PO Box 337, Bergvlei, South Africa

Random House UK Limited Reg. No. 954009

A CIP catalogue record for this book
is available from the British Library

ISBN 0 224 03290 9

Typeset in Bembo by SX Composing Ltd, Rayleigh, Essex
Printed in Great Britain by Mackays of Chatham plc

For Basil Stuart-Stubbs and Anne Yandle
and as always
for John

'One would think you expected from it the answer to the riddle of the universe,' she said; and I denied the impeachment only by replying that if I had to choose between that precious solution and a bundle of Jeffrey Aspern's letters I knew indeed which would appear to me the greater boon.

Henry James, The Aspern Papers

You know, if you read the collected letters of any writer . . . you will always get a sense that there's something missing, something biographers don't have access to, the real thing, the crucial thing, the thing that really mattered . . . . There are always letters that were destroyed. *The* letters, usually.

A.S. Byatt, Possession

Contents

Illustrations

Figures *(holographs, drawings, etc., with letters)*

The Editor, Dr Sherrill Grace, wishes to thank the following for permission to reproduce the photographs in this book: the Reverend Betty Atwater, 17, 18; K. Chung, 23; Ralph Ellison, 35; E. Grace, 7, 10; The Grieg Collection, Oslo, 14; Anna Walling Hamburger, 25; C. Higgins, 24; Jonathan Cape Ltd., 32; the Leys School governors, 4, 5, 6; Russell Lowry, 1, 2, 3; the Lowry Collection, University of British Columbia, 13, 22, 26, 27, 29, 33, 34, 36, 37, 38; Frank Monaco, 16; Jan Gabrial Singer, 20; James Stern, 15; Paul Tiessen, 31; Vancouver City Archives, 21; Priscilla Bonner Woolfan, 19, 30; Dorothy Yada, 28.

Preface and Acknowledgements

Readers of Malcolm Lowry's masterpiece, *Under the Volcano* (1947), will already be familiar with his epistolary skill. Whether they exist inside or outside his fiction, Lowry's letters are complex in form, intense in feeling, and full of erudite allusions, ironic undertones, and comic (often self-mocking) anecdotes. It is fair to say that Lowry approached the act of letter-writing much as he did the act of writing his novels, stories, and poems – as an act of creation involving the whole man.

Consequently, editing his letters has presented many fascinating problems that have led me on innumerable 'Tooloose Lowrytreks' over a period of several years and across as many countries. At times, I confess, the journey has seemed never-ending; in a sense, preparing a *collected* letters is a voyage that never ends. Only in a few instances, however, have materials or information been withheld, and I discuss this problem further in my introduction. Here it is my sincere pleasure to thank all those institutions and individuals who have helped me along the way.

I have been granted access to collections and been accorded courteous support at all times from university archives and archivists in Canada, the United States, England, Scotland, Norway, Germany, and France. However, the people without whom my research, and that of so many others, could never have taken place are the librarians in charge of Special Collections in the main library of the University of British Columbia. Basil Stuart-Stubbs, who was head of Special Collections from 1960 to 1965 and later University Librarian, had the vision to begin the Lowry collection in the early sixties with the help of Canadian poet Earle Birney, a personal friend of the Lowrys. The development of the collection then fell to Anne

Yandle, head of Special Collections from 1966 to 1991 and a generous friend to avid Lowryans of all ages. Lowry readers, students, and scholars owe an incalcuable debt to Basil and Anne, for which a thank you is scarcely enough.

It is a pleasure as well to extend my warmest thanks to George Brandak and the entire staff of Special Collections at UBC, who have put up with my requests, worries, frantic double-checkings, and occasional shouts of glee with patience and good humour. To librarians and archivists elsewhere I also extend my sincere appreciation, in particular to Geoffrey Houghton, archivist of the Leys School, Cambridge; Sidney Huttner, curator of Special Collections at the McFarlin Library, the University of Tulsa; and Laura Endicott in Special Collections at the Alderman Library, the University of Virginia; and also to Cathy Henderson at the Harry Ransom Humanities Research Center, University of Texas at Austin; Leona Schonfeld and the staff of the Huntington Library; Rodney Dennis and Susan Halpert of the Houghton Library, Harvard University; John Delaney at the Princeton University Library; Philip Cronenwett of the Dartmouth College Library; the librarians at the Beineke Rare Book and Manuscript Library; and Edna Hajnal of the Thomas Fisher Rare Book Library at the University of Toronto; and to the librarians at the Lilly Library, Indiana, Yale University Library, the Bancroft Library of the University of California, Berkeley, the Columbia University Library, and the librairies of the University of Pennsylvania, the University of Alberta, Queen's University, the University of Manitoba, and the University of Saskatchewan; and to Sigbjørn Grindheim of the Royal University Library, Oslo; Michael Bott at the University of Reading; Richard Bell of the Bodleian Library, Oxford; the archivists at Trinity College, Gonville and Caius College, and the University Library, Cambridge; Jean Ayton and David Taylor of the Manchester Central Library; the staff of the British Library, the National Library of Scotland, the Browne, Pictou, and Hornby Libraries of Liverpool, and the National Archives of Canada. I am grateful as well to the many librarians across Canada and the United States who answered my personal requests for specific information.

Over the years I have pestered many of my colleagues in the English Department at UBC for help with innumerable problems, from unscrambling Lowry's Greek to identifying the most obscure or oblique reference. My thanks to you all: John Cooper, Dick Bevis, Richard Cavell, Dick Fredeman, Elliott Gose, Jr, Peter Quartermain, Andrew Busza, Bruce Grenberg, Joel Kaplan, Harriet Kirkley, Kate Sirluck, Warren Stevenson, Ira Nadel, Gernot

Wieland, and Michael Zeitlin. Bill New and Christine Parkin read sections of my work in progress, shared their advice with me, and provided encouragement. Roberto Flores of the Department of Hispanic and Italian Studies helped me with a Cervantes question, William Winder of the Department of French helped me with Flaubert, and Richard Menkis of the Department of Religious Studies advised me on questions concerning the Cabbala. The Lowry network, however, extends far beyond UBC, and I would like to acknowledge the help and support of colleagues from further afield: Rick Asals (University of Toronto), Hallvard Dahlie (University of Calgary), Paul Tiessen (Wilfrid Laurier University), Victor Doyen (Katholieck Universiteit Leuven), Muriel Bradbrook (Cambridge), and Suzanne Kim (Sorbonne), with whom I shared an unforgettable 'Lowrytrek' around Paris in February 1992.

One of the pleasures of this kind of work is that I have met or corresponded with many wonderful people whom I would not otherwise have come to know. Some have become friends, but all have provided valued help: Jan Gabrial, David Markson, Russell and Meg Lowry, Harvey and Dorothy Burt, Bill McConnell, Sheryl and Kirk Salloum, the Reverend Betty Atwater, Peter Matson, J. Howard Woolmer, Albert Erskine, Jonathan Matson, Ben Camardi, Johannes ten Holder, Frank Taylor, Dorothy Yada, Huw Richards, Richard Eberhart, Kenneth Wright, Rabbi Dr Martin Samuel Cohen, Dennis Duffy, Stanley Fox, Bob Clark, Priscilla Woolfan, Betty Moss, Bill Hoffer, James Jaffe, Julien Green, Eva Thoby-Marcelin, Rhoda Jackson, Christian Bourgois, Guillaume Chpaltine, Jay Neugeboren, Brigitte Winter at Klett-Cotta Publishers in Stuttgart, Dorothy Livesay, Ralph Gustafson, Nora Sayre, Roger Davenport, Frank Taylor, Pierre Caizergues, Dr John Aiken, Mrs Robert Pick, Mrs Philip Hamburger (formerly Anna Walling Matson), Charles Scribner III, James Stern, Bette L. Stanton, Professor N.A. Furness. My sincere thanks to you all.

The list of individuals or publishers I have contacted for information is too long to recapitulate here, but I am mindful of the help I have received from so many quarters. I do wish to make special mention of my editor at Cape, Anthony Colwell. Several years ago, when the Jonathan Cape office was still in beautiful Bedford Square, I walked in with the bright idea of editing Lowry's collected letters, and Tony welcomed me with encouragement and enthusiasm. Over the years and months since that day I have been grateful for his patience and sheer faith.

Other innocent people swept up in my obsession also deserve very special thanks: my husband, John, for being a constant source of

good advice and a model objective reader of introductions and annotations; my daughter, Elizabeth, for taking photographs and touring
the Wirral with me in July 1989; my graduate students and research
assistants Kathleen Scherf and Cynthia Sugars, who have gone on to
make their own contributions to Lowry studies; Stefan Haag, who
smoothed my path through the dark forest of technology and took
charge of Lowry's and my German; and Shari Urban, Peter Dickinson, and Carol McConnell, for their help with proofing and
annotations. This is the third time that Susan Kent Davidson has
copy-edited a manuscript into print for me with her usual wisdom,
tact, intelligence, and good cheer. Again, Susan, my thanks; you
are the ideal interlocutor. Another person whose help has been
invaluable to me is my research assistant Kathy Chung. While main-
taining her own graduate work in Theatre and English, she has
provided meticulous sleuthing, with patience, intelligence, enthusiasm, dedication, and good humour. Without your help, Kathy,
this edition would be less accurate and would have taken longer to
prepare.

   Finally, it is a pleasure to thank formally the University of British
Columbia, the Social Sciences and Humanities Research Council
of Canada, and the Isaak Walton Killam Fellowship Trust for the
funding necessary to conduct research, to travel to other archives,
and to prepare what Lowry would have called the 'wholus bolus.'

S.E.G.
Vancouver
1993

Editing Lowry's Letters

An Introduction by Sherrill E. Grace

I

At the end of chapter six of *Under the Volcano* (1947), and at the heart of that complex tale of loss, failure, and miscommunication, lies this quintessential Lowry scene: on their way to Jacques Laruelle's 'mad-house' for a drink, Geoffrey, Yvonne, and Hugh are stopped by the local cartero, the present postman in a family of postmen. 'There is a letter, a letter, a letter . . . a message por el señor,' he cries, searching feverishly in his bag, spreading its contents on to the road. 'It must be. Here. No. This is. Then this one. Ei ei ei ei ei ei.' Failing to find it and disappointed, he moves away, only to come 'trotting back with little yelps of triumph.'[1]

The significance of this scene is twofold: it demonstrates the importance of letters in Malcolm Lowry's world, both the fictional and the real world, and it underscores the apparent ease with which they become lost or mislaid – especially when they are important, as this one is. Moreover, the local cartero is a sympathetic image of the editor because, like him, I know what it is to search feverishly for the missing, the crucial letter, only to find it at last buried somewhere, perhaps in Lowry's working notes, where it is marked for inclusion in the fiction, or amongst the drafts – on the verso of a page, perhaps – or even with the final typescript of a story.

This epistolary link between the life and the fiction is only one, albeit one of the more fascinating, reasons for my decision to prepare this edition of Lowry's letters. It is also a link that Lowry was well aware of, self-consciously exploited, and used to great effect, so that there are times when it is difficult to decide what *is* and *is not* a Lowry letter. For example, in chapter one of *Under the Volcano* Jacques Laruelle finds a letter from the Consul to his estranged wife,

Yvonne. From Laruelle's description, the Consul's handwriting would seem uncannily to resemble Malcolm Lowry's:

> the hand, half crabbed, half generous, and wholly drunken . . . the Greek e's, flying buttresses of d's, the t's like lonely wayside crosses save where they crucified the entire word, the words themselves slanting steeply downhill, though the individual characters seemed as if resisting the descent, braced, climbing the other way. (42)

The writer, Laruelle speculates, probably had neither the intention nor the capability of posting this letter. However, not only is the handwriting or the drunken state of the writer reminiscent of Lowry, but the entire situation is also an ironic, oblique comment upon him because a close study of his letters reveals that, like his Consul, Lowry sometimes wrote eloquent, impassioned letters, in a 'half crabbed, half generous' hand, that he did not post but nevertheless preserved for other purposes. What this letter from *Under the Volcano* does not answer is whether or not it is a *Lowry* letter, and thus whether it belongs in the *Collected Letters*.

I have begun this introduction to Lowry's *Collected Letters* with a brief detour through his fiction because it is, in my view, the best way to set the stage for what follows. At one level it is unwise, indeed impossible, to separate Lowry the novelist, short story writer, and poet from Lowry the man – the man who also wrote letters. The letters constantly take us back to his fiction, just as the fiction constantly alerts us to the nature and importance of his letters. On another level, however, his fiction must be separated from his letters because the letters belong together as a distinct vehicle for expression, a vehicle complete with its own assumptions, conventions, and purposes. But Lowry was always pushing at epistolary boundaries, so that his letters could as easily become fictions, or parts of fictions, as they could become poems.

This conscious, deliberate transgression of traditional generic boundaries complicates interestingly the question of what constitutes a Lowry letter. For example, there are several Lowry letters that were clearly intended for use in his fiction, either at the time of composition or after the act. His December 1937 letter (**80**) to Juan Fernando Márquez was present in *Dark as the Grave* until the page proofs, when, I suspect, it was removed by Margerie Lowry because of its references to Jan Gabrial, and there are several letters from the early fifties that may never have been sent because they were primarily intended for inclusion in his fiction. One surviving letter (**473**) to Margerie has been crumpled up, smoothed out, and labelled, in Lowry's writing, for use in the fiction, and, at the end of one of his March 1952 letters (**508**) to Albert Erskine he asks Erskine to return 'this agonised unbalanced & demoniac missive' because he wants it for a story he is writing. (The story, called 'In the Abyss,' was never written.)

Another factor that complicates this business of defining a Lowry letter is his habit of writing drafts. It is not always clear whether a holograph is merely a draft version of a letter, a final version (or fair copy) that was actually sent, or, possibly, a draft meant for fictional purposes only. Uncertainty arises because of Lowry's habits: he often wrote in pencil; he usually signed what he wrote, be it draft or fair copy, and he was *always* revising and adding to a letter. Thus a given holograph copy-text can appear highly provisional and very much in the process of being written, even when it exists as an incoming letter with the papers of Lowry's correspondent.

Despite this transgression of boundaries, I have decided to respect an arbitrary separation between Lowry's fiction and his letters. They are all, of course, Lowry letters, but the ones in *Under the Volcano* are the characters' letters, not Lowry's, because there is no extant evidence that Lowry copied or adapted them from his own pre-existing personal letters. Otherwise all letters available to date, regardless of how rough a given holograph may appear, are included in these volumes; each holograph is one of Lowry's letters and each captures some of Lowry's most spontaneous, frank, and thoughtful moments.

Whether in his fiction or not, whether rough or polished, holograph or typed, what Lowry's letters always convey is an urgent quality of address. He could not exist without written, verbal communication. Because he was physically inept and often shy and inarticulate in personal encounters, writing was his preferred means of self-expression. Moreover, his letters demonstrate what is also clear from his fiction – that he was obsessed with language and driven by the need to relate to others in and through words. For Lowry writing was a form of dialogue, of communication with others. It should not be surprising, therefore, that writing, especially letter-writing, was central to his art as well as to his life. One only has to listen to his ardent courtship of Jan Gabrial, his editorial confabulations with Albert Erskine, or his daily conversations, in notes or on the pages of his manuscripts, with Margerie (who was, let us remember, only a few feet away from him in their tiny two-room shack) to appreciate the magnitude of this need. On occasion Lowry's readers have bemoaned the fact that he spent so much time writing letters instead of fiction, but I hope that the *Collected Letters* will go some way towards alleviating that regret because, with Lowry, the letters are texts of intrinsic value and interest, and they are central to his *oeuvre*.

Before I look more closely at how the letters participate in the dynamic process of his writing, their position in his biographical and historical context should be briefly considered. (More detailed biographical background is provided with each subdivision of the letters.) Malcolm Lowry wrote interesting letters to a great many interesting people. Among his best friends and correspondents are such writers as Conrad Aiken, James Stern, John Davenport, and David Markson, each of whom comes to life as Lowry addresses him. But other figures from the literary scene of the thirties and forties are also present, among them Sylvia Beach, Whit Burnett, Nordahl Grieg, and Christopher Isherwood. He was fortunate as well in his choice of publishers and editors. Several letters to Jonathan Cape have survived, the most important being Lowry's famous explication of *Under the Volcano* (letter **210**), and there is an important and fascinating group of close to one hundred letters to his editor, Albert Erskine, that span the decade 1946 to 1956. But Lowry's constant, keen discussion, in all his letters, of living writers and contemporary writing demonstrates how widely and eclectically he read and how much this extended literary world meant to him. He had something germane to say about writers as different as Jean Cocteau, Ernst Toller, Julien Green, John Buchan, Ralph Ellison, and James Agee, and he always found time to read and comment upon the work of friends like Gerald Noxon and Harvey Burt.

In addition to what might be called his literary correspondence, Lowry wrote many eloquent personal letters to wives, friends, and family members. These letters reveal a complex man who could best express himself in metaphor, imagery, and literary allusion, regardless of his purpose in writing a letter. Even the personal letters contain allusions to contemporary politics, writing, or the latest film. What is more, the letters to wives and close friends provide fascinating glimpses into Lowry's personality. For example, there are five men with whom Lowry carried on extended correspondences over many years – Conrad Aiken, Harold Matson, Gerald Noxon, Albert Erskine, and David Markson – and his emotional and psychological dependence upon these men was extraordinary. In fact he spent comparatively little time with any of them; Erskine and Markson he met only a few times. His relationship with each was *written*, created in the activity of writing letters, and the dominant theme of the correspondence was writing, especially Lowry's own writing. Lowry needed these men to write to and for; the threatened separation from Erskine in the early fifties, after the latter's move from Reynal & Hitchcock to Random House, nearly brought Lowry to the point of collapse. Lowry allotted each of them a symbolic place in his autobiography – Aiken the father, Matson, Noxon, and Erskine the brothers, and Markson the son – and, to a degree, they replaced the family Lowry believed he had never had.

Lowry signed his letters to these men with 'love,' and it was a love that represented great trust, faith, and his desperate need for support. The extreme vulnerability revealed in these letters led inevitably to his feeling anxious or betrayed when his cries for attention, sympathy, or communication were ignored or received a curt response. By 1930, within a year of meeting Lowry, Aiken, who was serving *in loco parentis* at the time as Lowry's tutor, was exhausted by his pupil's demands. In a 1930 letter to a friend he confessed that Lowry was 'a fine lad, and brilliant . . . but psychologically a good deal of a drain on me. Fearfully dependent, worried about a thousand things, he has to be bolstered up periodically with injections of aiken adrenalin.'[2] Albert Erskine also grew to dread the arrival of Lowry's long, virtually indecipherable letters, pencilled on scraps of paper or postcards. And yet each of these men, and many others besides, acknowledged Lowry's genius and were prepared to offer affection and encouragment.

Lowry's relations with the women in his life are remarkably consistent, and they parallel those with the men. Each woman, with the exception of his mother, was a writer herself, or an artist, and Russell Lowry has recalled that on occasion Evelyn Lowry could be an engaging story-teller. Substantial correspondences survive with three women: Carol Brown, a friend with whom Lowry fancied himself to be in love at seventeen, Jan Gabrial, his first wife, and Margerie Bonner, his second wife. The few letters that survive to other girl-friends (Dolly Lewis and Carol Phillips) and to his mother provide further insight into the role women played in his life and work. In each case he writes to them about writing, usually his own, sometimes theirs, and even at his most passionate (for example, with Jan), he places them as alter egos and receptive, understanding interlocutors. At the same time as he is talking with them about writing, he is courting, flattering, charming, and seducing them.

Receiving the kind of letters Lowry could write – to call them 'love' letters misses the mark – must have been an experience. Jan, Carol Phillips, and Margerie all fell in love with his epistolary prowess; the man himself was another matter. As he did with his major male correspondents, Lowry cast his women in his family drama, but their role was always the same and, if possible, more demanding than those of the men. They were expected to mother him, to nurture him verbally, spiritually, and physically. Jan has described this maternal dependency and its destructive consequences with striking clarity in her short story 'Not with a Bang,' where the hero, Michael, offers his wife a surrogate for himself in the form of a helpless, dying puppy but rejects her attempts to make him grow up and abandons himself to the oblivion of drink.[3] A psychologist might explain Lowry's constant demand for mothering as the need to feel at ease with language, the mother tongue, in order to be able to write. A more traditional literary explanation would be that Lowry made his women into muses, and then turned on them when the inspiration failed.

As a general rule, of course, one must be cautious about conflating an artist's life and work. With Lowry the risk, like the temptation, is especially high because he was always creating fictions of his life and raiding his life for the purposes of his fiction. Russell Lowry has taken pains to expose some of the lies (as he sees them), distortions, and fantasies disseminated by the youngest sibling and black sheep of the family. Nevertheless, Lowry's letters provide invaluable information about his life and about the relationship he saw between his life and his writing. For example, in a March 1952 letter (**512**) to Albert Erskine, Lowry defends at length his interest in the writer as a character in fiction. Such a character, he argues, is not only viable but of more general interest to readers than is usually allowed. 'There is an artist,' Lowry tells Erskine, 'a poet in every man, hence he is a creature easy for anyone to identify themselves with: & his struggles are likely to be universal.' But Lowry's fascination with the fictional writer was not something he discovered in the fifties. As the *Collected Letters* show, he started writing portraits of the artist as early as 1930-31 with 'In Ballast to the White Sea,' and his creation of the writer-protagonist of *The Voyage That Never Ends*, Sigbjørn Wilderness, is the logical extension of that initial idea.

What is perhaps unusual about Lowry's creation of the fictional writer is not that he was interested in such a figure – there is, after all, a tradition of writers creating such heroes, from Goethe to Pirandello and Thomas Wolfe – but that this character came to be his central, indeed obsessive, concern. What is more, Lowry's 'writer' was undeniably autobiographical: 'a very original character, both human and pathetically inhuman at once. I much approve of him as a doppleganger' (letter **512** to Erskine). And, as Lowry knew, his work on *The Voyage That Never Ends* was taking him in the direction of autobiographical fiction. He did not live to complete the *Voyage*, of course (if, indeed, it could have been completed), but his comments in the letters about the writer-as-character and about himself as a writer complement his fictional treatment of the subject, and illuminate his changing concept of the writer and the self.[4]

To a degree, especially in the twenties and thirties, Lowry saw himself as the suffering, romantic masculine artist-outcast (after Eugene O'Neill and D.H. Lawrence) who must experience what Maurice Beebe has described as the 'sacred fount' of life in order to write.[5] This artist, like Joyce's Stephen Dedalus in *A Portrait of the Artist as a Young Man* (1916), aspires to be a godlike originator, creating *sui generis* in the 'smithy of [his] soul,' devouring and superseding his precursors. However, Lowry's temperament, psychology, and poetics gradually pushed him towards a very different image of himself. Because of his capacity for identification with other writers (a capacity he speaks of repeatedly in his letters) and his fierce need to share the creative process with those people in his symbolic family support system (his 'brothers' and 'mothers'), during the forties he came more and more to see himself, and the writer, as part of a process of writing in a shared world of language and texts where the boundaries used to define authorship and to demarcate originality could not be fixed.

Such a view of the artist, characterized by shared contexts, connections with others, collaboration, and confabulation, runs counter to the traditional notion of the artist as an autonomous, creative originator. In recent studies of autobiography and of the figure of the writer as a fictional character this type of artist has been described as representing a more 'feminine' or 'feminist' model of the artist.[6] Just what type of artist Malcolm Lowry was, however, is a question for others to pursue elsewhere. His collected letters provide much useful information for such a study and are constant reminders of how central to Lowry was the problem of creativity.

2

1926: ' – Carol: I am about to otter hunt. Ottiturhunturus sum.' **1928:** 'I have lived only nineteen years and more or less all of them badly.' **1931:** 'I'm in the company of Tomlinson & Coppard. W'ot ho she bumps. You can sell this letter!' **1934:** 'The story is as it were a letter to you; as I am working for you it *is* your letter.' **1937:** 'S.O.S. Sinking fast by both bow and stern.' **1940:** 'My dear Dad: There is a side of the moon always turned away from the earth, and this is like an attempt to get in touch from that quarter.' **1946:** 'Dear Mr Erskine: Well, every man his own Laocoon!' **1948:** 'Courage mon ami, le diable est mort!' **1950:** 'Warning: BEGGING LETTER if couched in golden (and truthful) words.' **1952:** 'Hold that note, Roland.' **1954:** 'Bang!'

1957: 'God damn it Kyd, I didn't know how else to address you but in this verdammit Norwegian.'

How does one summarize the Lowry voice or suggest the delight of reading these letters? It is, perhaps, best not to try; the letters speak for themselves. Some general observations should, nevertheless, be made because there are so many Lowry personae that speak in his letters. One of the most striking qualities of the Lowry voice is its self-consciousness. He was always posing, watching himself address a reader, watching his letter being read. He was always dramatizing himself. Even at his darkest moments, in 1937, for example, he was able to play a part and joke at his own expense. He was also, always, telling stories, narrating his life. It is this histrionic capacity that, in large part, makes these letters at once entertaining as fictions and unreliable as fact. This quintessential Lowryan combination of autobiographical fiction and fact is one quality that links the letters with the novels, stories, and poems. That link becomes an outright overlap, an instance of intertextuality, when Lowry uses a letter in the fiction, as he did, for example, with the December 1937 letter (**80**) to Juan Fernando Márquez. The fact that Lowry's fiction is so auto-biographical, that he was continually writing his life, is the other side of the coin.

Another fascinating quality of these letters is the obvious pleasure Lowry takes in language, whether in a playful note or postcard, or in the serious exegetical letter to Cape. Here, as with the fiction, words – the sound, rhythm, and look of them – are irresistible to Lowry, and this passion for words, together with his voracious, eclectic reading, are the symptoms of his lifelong obsession with plagiarism. Of the many concerns that recur in his letters, plagiarism is one of the most persistent and important because it is central to Lowry's sense of himself as a writer (hence, as a man) and to what can only be described as his poetics.

Stated briefly, Lowry borrowed freely, even ruthlessly, from other writers, indeed from any text that caught his attention. He operated on the principle that words did not belong to anyone but were there for the taking, part of the universe of discourse and the great tradition of writing of which he knew himself to be a part. This is not to say that he was unaware of how his borrowings might be viewed by others. Indeed, he was tormented by anxiety and guilt over this practice. He confesses in his 1939 letter (**85**) to Nordahl Grieg that 'my identity with Benjamin [the hero of Grieg's novel *The Ship Sails On*] eventually led me into mental trouble. Much of *Ultramarine* is paraphrase, plagiarism, or pastiche from you.' After being openly accused of plagiarism by the American writer

Burton Rascoe (see letter **141**), he refused to allow his friends to read
Ultramarine or publishers to reprint it.

Despite his own guilty apologies, however, it seems quite inappropriate to think of Lowry as a plagiarist *tout court*, and these
annotated letters (like the annotations to *Under the Volcano*) show
why. At its richest and most dense Lowry's prose carries a complex
mixture of allusion, paraphrase, parody, pastiche, and quotation that
displays an acute sensitivity to verbal and textual contexts, connections, and significances. This resonant allusiveness that strains to
leave nothing out, to relate everything to everything else, is what
Canadian poet Sharon Thesen calls Lowry's 'confabulations.'[7]
Lowry's 27 October 1930 letter (**25**) to John Davenport is a case in
point. Here nearly every sentence is constructed out of words and
phrases lifted from other (others') con/texts. But it is in his 8 September 1931 letter (**35**) to Nordahl Grieg that Lowry identifies the
literary tradition to which he belongs – the tradition of Herodotus,
Sophocles, Euripides, Virgil, Marston, Webster, Shakespeare,
Montaigne, Molière, Pascal, Sterne, Voltaire, Rousseau, Milton,
Coleridge, Stendhal, Lautréamont, Conrad, Eliot, Aiken, and Joyce
. . . all of them writers who 'reset other people's jewels and re-
doubled their lustre.'[8]

In an interesting study of plagiarism called *Voleurs de mots: Essai sur
le plagiat, la psychanalyse et la pensée*, Michel Schneider questions
modern attitudes towards plagiarism and the contemporary obsession with originality.[9] As far as he is concerned, Lowry was not a
plagiarist so much as a writer obsessed by the image of his own guilt,
an image further complicated by the perceived pressure to create
something new. The profile of the self-styled plagiarist sketched
by Schneider is that of a man suffering from a persecution complex
and terrified by the thought that he is nothing more than someone
else's creation. Such a man, says Schneider, suffers from a psychosis
stemming from troubled relations with his parents, especially his
mother, that signal his inability to separate himself from the other:

> Le plagiaire en apparence prend l'autre en soi. Il fait comme si
> l'autre était lui-même. Mais en fait il projette sa propre créativité
> dans l'auteur-source. (The plagiarist appears to assimilate the
> other into himself. He acts as if the other is himself. But in fact
> he projects his own creativity on to the source-author. [275])

There can be little doubt, I think, that Lowry's fears, creative
methods, practices, and psychology correspond very closely to this
profile. If ever there was a writer terrified of being written by
another and determined to assimilate, rework, and reaccentuate

others' words, and his own, from notebooks, margins, letters, clippings, and documents of all kinds, it was Lowry.

One complaint, if not outright criticism, often levelled at Lowry's fiction is that it is overstuffed and, therefore, uncontrolled, lacking in some prized, classical aesthetic quality called unity. Whether or not one agrees that such unity is important or that Lowry's fiction sometimes lacks it, it is still a fact that he was obsessed with the need to include as much as he could – everything, if possible – in his work. And yet the attempt to do so is absurd, for, as the writer in the story 'Ghostkeeper' realizes, 'nothing is static or can be pinned down . . . everything is evolving or developing into other meanings' (*Psalms and Songs*, 223). Nevertheless, this Lowryan practice of inclusion is evidence of his frequently articulated belief that one thing is inextricably connected with another, one idea, word, or symbol with another, one phenomenon with another. The symbol for this global and cosmic interconnectedness of living things in *Under the Volcano* is the Cabbala; in *Hear us O Lord from heaven thy dwelling place* it is the Tao that Lowry invokes in images of expanding circles of raindrops on water or the eternal ebb and flow of the tide. Like William Blake, Lowry saw eternity in a grain of sand, and it is a vision that speaks immediately and urgently to our damaged and threatened globe.

But as Lowry found, such a vision of inclusiveness and vital interconnectedness could be overwhelming, its psychological consequences devastating. Some of the anxiety of this approach to life and writing manifests itself in the visual appearance of his manuscripts, and this can only be appreciated by looking at the actual document. The sense of tactile, tangible immediacy is regrettably sacrificed in any transcribed material. Even a full facsimile reproduction of a text will not capture the look and feel of a holograph page. One cannot, after all, reproduce the pressure of the pen or pencil on paper and the suggestion such pressure conveys of the writer's emotion or concentration. But a certain amount can be achieved by examining in some detail a reproduction of an exemplary page. Lowry's illustrations to his letters, and other aspects of the copytexts for this edition, are discussed in part 3 of this introduction. For the moment my focus is on the semiotics of a page and what the signs might tell us about Lowry and about editing Lowry.

Letter **83**, written to Conrad Aiken, probably from Oaxaca, Mexico, early in 1938, survives only in a rough pencil draft on the verso of a typescript page for a story called 'China.'[10] Amazingly, given Lowry's state in 1938, it was not lost or destroyed, perhaps *because* it was drafted on the verso of a story typescript (assuming, of course, that this typescript preceded the composing of the letter).

Whether Lowry ever intended to send it or rewrote and actually did send it is unclear. What is clear is that this holograph (see Figure 1) tells us a good deal about the writer and provides a challenge in transcription for the editor.

The most striking visual feature of this text is the way Lowry has filled the space of the page. Scarcely a corner is left empty. Thought after thought is added, squeezed in, appended to the main paragraph that occupies the upper half of the page. Moreover, the added thoughts are connected to, spring from, words, ideas, images, or thoughts already inscribed on the page; the branching out from 'churlish' to 'churchish' to 'Richard Church' captures this process perfectly. It is as if, even from the depths of his despair, Lowry could not (did not want to) finish or end this letter. As long as there was more to say or more empty space to say it in, another link or connection to trace out, he kept working at the text, at the page, holding open the gesture of communication while at the same time rendering it virtually indecipherable. This page demonstrates what is true of so many of Lowry's letters and of all his fiction: he resisted closure, finalization, ending.

What the page also shows us is something of the writer's mood at the time of writing. At first glance it seems a chaotic mapping of his ideas and feelings. It is as if the blank page became a surface on which he could chart zones of thought and emotion that were separate yet related to other parts of the psycho-textual terrain. When this letter is transcribed and transmitted in the standard horizontal, justified, uniform type-face of the professional printer, this emotional texture is erased. Moreover, the drama of the writing is obscured. The holograph page is a performance, as is the 'Caravan of Silence' letter (25) to Davenport or the 1931 letter (35) to Grieg. If one imagines receiving this letter (as Aiken may have done), one can guess at the reader's response to its writerly, expressive nature. Here is a letter whose writer foregrounds the act of writing, the act of writing to *you* – 'the only man I wish to write to' – in the very process of that activity. Something of the importance, the desperation, the need for communication, the impromptu plea, is present in the look of the page. The address, 'A mi padre,' acquires further associations and greater resonance when *seen* in the context of the page.

Although much more might be said about this letter – about Lowry's handwriting, his use of lines, asterisks, brackets, arrows, and emphases that, together, constitute a kind of key to the map – one other feature demands some comment. The top half of this page is comparatively tidy. The signature, albeit in an uncharacteristic position just below the middle of the page, follows logically from the

Figure 1: *Lowry's early 1938 holograph letter (83) to Conrad Aiken was written on the verso of a page for the story 'China' (UBC 8:2).*

closing sentence: 'Please believe in my sincere friendship & if I die, give me sanctuary.' Up to this point the letter is a relatively straight-forward-seeming apology to Aiken. But after this, and occupying the bottom half of the page, is what amounts to another letter, a fragmented, difficult-to-decipher subtext, that makes a palimpsest of the page. The traces of this subtext provide a type of apologia for Lowry, the man who did Aiken dirt, explaining how he has been punished and has suffered and appealing to Aiken's former status, *in loco parentis*, as Lowry's poet-hero, mentor, tutor, and surrogate father. These notes are all struck in the main text of the letter, but the subtext elaborates, expands upon, and substantiates Lowry's position *vis-à-vis* Aiken, their shared past, the present, and so on. The psychological complexity of this letter addressed to the father is, I submit, represented visually in the division and use of the page.

3

Editors, and literary scholars in general, have received a surprising amount of fictional attention of late. David Lodge describes them jet-setting and misbehaving in *Changing Places* (1975) and *Small World* (1984). In *Foucault's Pendulum* (1989) Umberto Eco constructs an elaborate cabbalistic parable about the fatal attraction of texts and words that Malcolm Lowry in particular would have appreciated, but from which all editors should take warning. With a backward glance at that 'publishing scoundrel' in Henry James's masterpiece *The Aspern Papers* (1888), Julian Barnes presents editors in a peculiarly distasteful light in *Flaubert's Parrot* (1984). Here the main character is a pathetic, parasitic middle-aged Englishman whose personal life is incomprehensible – 'stable, yet hopeless.'[11] In *Swann* (1987) Carol Shields portrays editors as voracious villains prepared to commit almost any crime to get their greedy hands on letters, manuscripts, and original documents. But it is A.S. Byatt who comes closest to my composite image of the editor and the editorial enterprise. In her delightful romance *Possession* (1990) Byatt creates a veritable rogues' gallery of editors on both sides of the Atlantic, each with his or her own vested interest, each scrabbling to find the buried treasure: *the* letter that will unlock the secret of their subject's life and art. In a telling confessional moment Dr Maud Bailey, the most sympathetic of Byatt's editors, admits: 'Of course we are mad. And bad. . . . I'm as bad as Cropper and Blackadder. All scholars are a bit mad. All obsessions are dangerous. This one's got a bit out of hand.'[12]

Over several years of work on the *Collected Letters*, my 'Tooloose Lowrytrek' has often threatened to get 'a bit out of hand.' But the need for such a collection was never in doubt. Beyond Lowry's importance as a major twentieth-century writer, several additional factors convinced me to undertake the task. Since 1965 the number of critical monographs, articles, and other studies of Lowry has multiplied at a dizzying rate. As I write, a new biography (the fourth) is about to be published, and critical editions of hitherto unpublished works are in process or being planned. Lowry's influence on other writers continues to grow, and the power of his prose has had an inspiring impact upon such diverse artists as Mexican painter Alberto Gironella, British composer Graham Collier, Canadian playwright Michael Mercer, and German poet Wolf Wondratschek. Since 1965 the amount of original material held in the Malcolm Lowry collection at the University of British Columbia has grown enormously, so that this main source of information about the man and his work has become increasingly valuable to scholars. I note 1965 as an especially important year for Lowry letters because it saw the publication of *Selected Letters of Malcolm Lowry*, edited by Margerie Bonner Lowry and Harvey Breit.

Selected Letters sparked much of the attention Lowry has received over the past thirty years because it allowed readers to sample the richness and variety of his correspondence. However, for all its usefulness, *Selected Letters* is a flawed and misleading volume. It is, in fact, extremely selective. Only a fraction of the total extant correspondence (approximately one-fifth, of what is now known to have survived) was published, and of that many letters were edited to suppress crucial evidence about Lowry's life. All references to Jan Gabrial were silently deleted, for example, and no letters to her or to Gerald Noxon were included. Little attempt was made to annotate the letters, and as a result their literary importance is obscured. However, since 1987, when I began to prepare this edition, other parts of Lowry's correspondence, and a few individual letters, have been published. The most significant publications are Paul Tiessen's *Letters of Malcolm Lowry and Gerald Noxon, 1940-1952* (1988) and Cynthia Sugars's *Letters of Conrad Aiken and Malcolm Lowry, 1929-1954* (1992).

Both the amount of work being done on Lowry and the unreliability of *Selected Letters*, then, underscore the need for a collected, annotated edition, and at this point I should explain briefly how this edition was prepared and how the text itself is laid out.

My research has taken me to dozens of archives in as many countries and has involved the writing of many hundreds of letters to archives and individuals who might possibly have a Lowry letter or information about Lowry. This search has turned up many new letters and not a few surprises. A caveat is in order, however, about the term 'collected.' In fact, and inevitably, the term describes the attempt, the original intention, the editorial desire (if you will, the mad obsession!) rather than the final product. Many letters have eluded me for many different reasons. A few of Lowry's surviving friends and correspondents, themselves of advanced years or in poor health, have been unable to locate their surviving Lowry letters. Most of Lowry's correspondents, however, have died, and in several cases their papers have not been made available to the public or have not yet been catalogued for accurate reference or have simply not survived. In other instances, attempts to locate Lowry's friends or their families have proved fruitless; I have my own collection of dead letters marked 'Return to sender.'

I have already alluded to important gaps in the edition, the most important of which is the absence of many surviving letters to Jan Gabrial; however, the letters she has selected, and given me permission to include, provide invaluable information never before made public and go a considerable way towards clarifying her role in Lowry's life. Unfortunately, some letters used by Lowry's biographers have not been made available in time for their inclusion here. This means that future Lowry readers and scholars will be obliged to put the scattered pieces together as best they can and to imagine a context for them. Perhaps there is a kind of 'strange comfort afforded' by the notion that we inhabit the world of Byatt's Blackadder and Cropper, of Shields' Lang and Jimroy, fiction being, as Lowry knew best, our reality. And as Lowry also knew, it is essential to celebrate hope and to maintain faith; thus I have chosen 'Sursum corda' (lift up your hearts), the phrase with which he closes many letters in the late forties and early fifties, as my title.

In transcribing Lowry's letters, I have adhered to the following principles. Lowry's holographs are transcribed exactly as they appear in order to preserve his idiosyncratic punctuation, erratic spellings, and, in so far as that is possible, the visual form of the letter. Careful transcription of these letters shows that spellings he used as early as 1926, such as 'noone,' recur in letters from 1956 to 1957, and that when writing longhand he often spelt the final syllable of 'disaster' with an English accent: disas*tar*. I have not standardized his paragraph indentation or supplied an opening address or complimentary close or signature (something often done in *Selected Letters*) where none was originally provided.

This business of signatures is interesting, and accurately reproducing the copy-text is important. Lowry had the habit of drafting and revising his letters in pencil, sometimes several times, but he usually signed even a draft letter. Occasionally, the signed, pencil letter was actually sent. On rare occasions, however, the letters (or drafts) are unsigned, and the absence of the signature is meaningful. The letter may have been continued, with additional pages now lost, or he may have simply have broken off without finishing the letter, or he may have felt incapable of signing; in this case the content of the letter makes this clear, and Margerie sometimes takes over. In any of these cases, adding a signature (or supplying a full one where Lowry used an initial instead) gives a false impression of order, formality, and completion to the text.

When the copy-texts are typed (usually by Margerie), I have taken some additional editorial liberties and silently corrected obvious typographical errors. I have provided standardized dating throughout; thus, the inside address and date always appear at the top right of the letter in a consistent form – with the day and month followed by the year. Lowry was haphazard about these details, often omitting the date and address altogether or merely noting the day or occasion ('Sunday' or 'Hallowe'en'), but Margerie provided complete information thus: month, day, and year. *Selected Letters*, however, has a number of errors in dating, and I have pointed these out in editorial notes where needed.

Before turning to the annotations and editorial notes, I should explain the decisions made for incorporating marginalia and illustrations, and for representing other idiosyncratic features of the copy-text. Lowry had the habit of squeezing marginalia and postscripts into any available corner of the page. Sometimes these are clearly marked for inclusion in the main body of the letter or are labelled P.S., but sometimes they are not. At other times the positioning of the marginal comment is unclear, or the comment is so extensive or so peripheral that to insert it in the body of the letter would cause a serious interruption. When this happens, the material carries an asterisked note or is set off in braces: { }; letter **2I** is an example. Throughout the edition all editorial interventions appear within square brackets: [ ].

As my analysis of letter **83** shows, the status and visual appearance of the copy-texts have presented some fascinating problems. If Lowry's use of marginalia and postscripts often raises the problem of where and how to incorporate material so that the reader has a coherent text to examine, his practice of writing draft letters raises a number of still more difficult questions, not the least of which is: when is a draft a letter? On some occasions, what is almost certainly a draft is all that survives of a particular letter; therefore, I have used it as my copy-text. The status of the copy-text is indicated at the top left of each transcribed letter. For example, if the copy-text is a holograph held in the UBC Lowry collection, the provenance line shows: UBC(ms). A key to the full set of abbreviations is provided below. Editorial notes following the annotations describe the particular features of interest on a given copy-text. These notes are used sparingly and only to comment on the copy-text.

Lowry's habit of illustrating his letters presents some special challenges. Sometimes he created full-scale pictures on separate sheets of paper (letter **36**); more often the drawing was part of the page, with the writing surrounding the image on two or three sides (letter **4**). In this case the drawing is an integral part of the text and must be reproduced accordingly. However, Lowry's drawings are quite varied in size and complexity. During the forties he began the practice of decorating certain letters with seagulls: ⌒⌒ . These signs indicate optimism, happiness, and good cheer. In his many love notes, and in the late letters to Margerie, he used numerous little sketches and other graphological adornments, most of which could not be visually represented without prohibitive expense. A selection from the love notes, none of which is dated, is presented in Appendix 1, but the note reproduced in Figure 2 illustrates the type of verbal/visual play that Lowry always enjoyed.

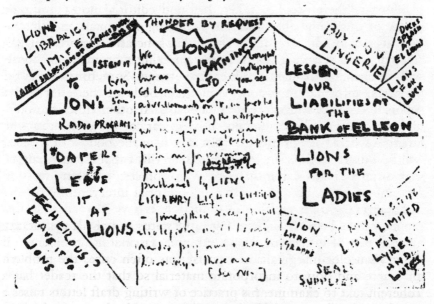

Figure 2: *Undated note to Margerie Bonner Lowry, which she kept with her copy of Under the Volcano; see Appendix 1.*

This small 10-by-15-cm note has been transformed into a mock billboard, or page of advertising, for the various enterprises of 'El Leon,' Lowry's favourite nickname (with a 28 July birthday, he was born under the zodiacal sign of the lion).

This edition of the Lowry letters was deliberately conceived and designed as an annotated edition. The chief argument against annota-

tions is that they intrude upon or interfere with the pleasure and continuity of the actual letters. A second argument against them is that
they can easily become 'much too long and over elaborate' (as the
reader for Cape once said of *Under the Volcano*).[13] To the first objection I can say that the annotations have been buried at the end of the
letter, instead of at the bottom of the page, where the reader can consult or ignore them at will. All that appears within the letter is the
small superscript number indicating that an annotation exists. The
second objection is harder to meet, and an editor must be on guard
against the temptation to indulge in unnecessary annotation, to
duplicate information, or, worst of all, to annotate annotations. In
Lowry's case I believe that the annotations provide important – at
times crucial – information that helps the reader in many ways. But
who is this reader for whom the annotations are intended?

It is not likely that a project of this size will be undertaken again for
many years; therefore, I have kept before me at all times a composite
image of the reader that includes people of different ages, life experiences, and educational backgrounds, living in several different
countries and speaking many languages other than English. Some
will be general readers of literature and biography with little
previous information about Malcolm Lowry; some will be
sophisticated, specialized readers of twentieth-century culture and
history. Others will be students, now in primary school, who will
inherit a world vastly different from Lowry's. And some, of course,
will be Lowry *aficionados*. I cannot know if I have met the needs of
such different readers, but there are other, equally important, reasons
for annotations.

At several points in this introduction I have argued that the
capillary links between and among Lowry's texts make his letters an
integral part of his *oeuvre*. These links are manifest in the quality of
the prose itself, in the vast network of shared allusions, images, and
phrases common to the fiction, poetry, and letters, in the autobiographical common ground occupied by the letters and the fiction,
and in Lowry's use of his letters in his fictions. It is important, therefore, to identify and delineate this complex network of what
amounts to the dense *world* of Malcolm Lowry. There are, of course,
many other reasons for pursuing Lowryan traces, even when, like
Winnie the Pooh hunting wizzles and woozles, they lead me in
circles. Contained in the densely woven texture of Lowry's letters
is a wealth of biographical, literary, and historical information
that, when identified, puts flesh on the bones of the first half of the
twentieth century. The annotations supply a dimensionality, perspective, and context for Lowry, a ground against which to observe

the figures that inhabit his letters. In this age of computers and tele-communications, literary scholars may never again find a letter-writer like Lowry who writes it all out in such nuanced detail. Even for his period he was exceptional in the length and number of his letters and in the serious attention he so often gave to writing them.

Some explanation about when and how I have used annotations is in order. I have attempted to identify all people (some, of course, have eluded me), titles of books, articles, plays, films, songs, and so on the first time they appear. Subsequent references are not anno-tated unless new information is provided or a cross-reference is required. There are, however, many cross-references among the letters because Lowry accumulates favourite allusions or phrases, and their significance grows or changes with each iteration. Where letters exist to an individual, that person is identified fully in the first annotation to the first letter addressed to him or her, even when the name appears in preceding letters to other people. Where incoming correspondence from Lowry's addressee is extant and sheds light on points in Lowry's letter, I have paraphrased or quoted from the in-coming letter in my annotation. To avoid unnecessary duplication, I have not annotated poems that appear in the letters, or those passages in letters to Albert Erskine that concern the editing of *Under the Vol-cano*. Both the poetry and the novel have been annotated elsewhere, and readers should consult *The Collected Poetry of Malcolm Lowry* and *A Companion to Under the Volcano* for details.

It is frustrating, but inevitable, that some of Lowry's allusions, for example to Henry James or Flaubert, have escaped detection. Others, I am sure, have eluded my grasp because I failed to see or hear them in the first place. The process of annotating is intuitive, serendipitous, and often quite unscientific; one finds the sources for Lowry's references in unexpected, indeed uncanny places, but that is another story. If I have explained the obvious at times, I apologize, but there are always some of us for whom much is new. Moreover, Lowry's references to what seems most familiar and culturally acces-sible often derive their full significance from some obscure association or little-known detail embedded in the reference or in the context of the source. Where I am mistaken or have misinterpreted Lowry's intentions, I will no doubt be promptly informed, and cor-rections will be made in a later printing. What I have not done is attempt to annotate every allusion. Lowry's letters, like his poetry and fiction, are spun from a host of intertextual references, but to label them all is both impossible and impractical. At some point the editor must withdraw and leave the reader to listen to Lowry's prose.

Throughout the editing and annotating of these letters I have kept before me, as ideal and goal, D. F. McKenzie's conception of the bibliographic enterprise as a 'sociology of texts.'[14] As McKenzie reminds us in his 1985 Panizzi lectures, *Bibliography and the Sociology of Texts*, 'texts are social products' that exist *in time*. They are created by human beings for other human beings. Lowry's letters are, of course, splendid examples of this complex, dynamic process because, like all letters, they situate their writer in a historical period while capturing the intense, personal moment of composition; they are products, yes, but they are also the living evidence of one of the most essential and fundamental of human activities: communication.

To preserve that fragile quality of living process has been difficult, and I do not claim much success in the endeavour because, in a very real sense, the act of writing, let alone of transcribing, printing, publishing, even photographing the letters stops them, literally, in their tracks. A letter should pass from one pair of living hands and eyes to another; a letter should be answered. As Lowry knew so well, anything written down becomes 'static, a piece of death, fixed, a sort of butterfly on a pin' ('Ghostkeeper,' *Psalms and Songs*, 224). Thus, the writer's (and the editor's) despair is 'occasioned by the patent fact that the universe itself – as the Rosicrucians also held – is in the process of creation. An organic work of art, having been conceived, must grow in the creator's mind, or proceed to perish.'[15]

It is in the attempt to preserve and transmit something of this 'organic' quality that I have found McKenzie's notion of sociology so valuable. By laying bare the editorial process, and by offering as rich a subsoil of annotation as possible, I have tried to transplant Lowry's letters into a ground that will nourish rather than kill them. My whole effort in the annotations, editorial notes, and illustrations has been to trace the living roots of the letters and to describe their foliage without reducing them to the kind of dead artefacts and relics that Lowry describes with such horror in the story 'Strange Comfort Afforded by the Profession.' At its best, and when viewed as part of the bibliographic 'sociology of texts,' editing has, as McKenzie suggests, 'an unrivalled power to resurrect authors in their own time, and their readers at any time.'

Notes on the Introduction

1 *Under the Volcano* (London: Jonathan Cape, 1947), pp. 205-06. All references are to this edition of the novel, and a list of Lowry's works as cited in *Collected Letters* is provided on pages xl-xli.

2 Aiken makes this remark in an unpublished letter, dated 13 September 1930, to Creighton Hill; see the Barrett Papers in Special Collections, Alderman Library, University of Virginia. Aiken wrote this letter when Lowry had just returned to Cambridge after spending several weeks at Jeake's House in Rye.

3 'Not with a Bang,' first published in *Story* 24 (September-October 1946): 44-61, is reprinted in *Swinging the Maelstrom: New Perspectives on Malcolm Lowry* (Montreal: McGill-Queen's University Press, 1992), pp. 21-30.

4 See *Dark as the Grave Wherein My Friend Is Laid,* 'Through the Panama,' and 'Strange Comfort Afforded by the Profession' in *Hear us O Lord from heaven thy dwelling place*, and 'Ghostkeeper,' which was included by Margerie Lowry in *Malcolm Lowry: Psalms and Songs* (1975).

5 See Maurice Beebe, *Ivory Towers and Sacred Founts: The Artist as Hero in Fiction from Goethe to Joyce* (New York University Press, 1964).

6 Two useful studies of this type are *The Private Self: Theory and Practice of Women's Autobiographical Writings*, ed. Shari Benstock (Chapel Hill: University of North Carolina Press, 1988), and *Writing the Woman Artist: Essays on Poetics, Politics, and Portraiture*, ed. Suzanne W. Jones (Philadelphia: University of Pennsylvania Press, 1991).

7 See Sharon Thesen's *Confabulations: Poems for Malcolm Lowry* (Lantzville, B.C.: Oolichan Books, 1984).

8 This description of writers who 'reset other people's jewels' is, in fact, Rupert Brooke's in *John Webster & the Elizabethan Drama* (New York: Russell & Russell, 1967), p. 147. Lowry knew Brooke's book well, and I have discussed Lowry's plagiarism, as well as other theoretical problems in editing Lowry, in the following: '"The Daily Crucifixion of the Post": Editing and Theorizing the Lowry Letters,' in *Challenges, Projects, Texts: Canadian Editing*, ed. John Lennox and Janet Paterson (New York: AMS Press, 1993), pp. 26-53; 'Thoughts towards the Archeology of Editing: "Caravan of Silence",' *Malcolm Lowry Review* 29/30 (1991-92): 64-77; and 'Respecting Plagiarism: Tradition, Guilt and Malcolm Lowry's "pelagiarist pen",' *English Studies in Canada* 28, 4 (1993): 461-82.

9 In his provocative study of plagiarism published by Gallimard in 1985, Schneider uses Freud, Lacan, and Gérard Genette to explore the causes and signs of plagiarism, and in passing he makes many interesting observations about Lowry.

10 'China' first appeared in *Malcolm Lowry: Psalms and Songs*.

11 See Julian Barnes, *Flaubert's Parrot* (London: Jonathan Cape, 1984), pp. 168-69.

12 See A.S. Byatt, *Possession: A Romance* (London: Chatto & Windus, 1990), p. 352.

13 William Plomer had been critical of the *Volcano* manuscript, and it was his criticisms, and Jonathan Cape's invitation to reply, that prompted Lowry to write his 2 January 1946 letter (**210**) to Cape. Lowry mentions some of these criticisms at the beginning of his letter.

14 See D.F. McKenzie, *Bibliography and the Sociology of Texts* (London: The British Library, 1986).

15 *Dark as the Grave Wherein My Friend Is Laid* (New York: New American Library, 1968), p. 154.

Notes on the Text

The Collected Letters of Malcolm Lowry has been divided into two volumes. Volume I covers the period 1926 to 1946 and contains two hundred and seventy letters. Volume II covers the period 1947 to 1957 and contains over four hundred letters and three appendices. The volumes have been divided in this way for several reasons, most importantly because there is a clear division in Lowry's life between the pre- and post-publication of *Under the Volcano* in February 1947, and because several of the letters from the first two decades are extremely long. Each volume has been further subdivided into periods, which are prefaced by short introductions, and there are brief editorial commentaries preceding certain key letters or sequences of letters. The appendices are grouped together in Volume II for the sake of efficiency, even though they are referred to in both volumes.

Each letter is numbered chronologically and carries an identification key in the upper left-hand corner, immediately below the name of the addressee. This key shows the provenance (P), where known, of the original letter, the status of the copy-text (manuscript, typescript, postcard, etc.), the existence (if relevant) of a copy in the Lowry collection at the University of British Columbia, and previous publication (PP). This information is presented in the abbreviated format explained below.

Most letters have a set of annotations immediately following the text of the letter; some have editorial notes as well. The annotations, which provide information on the contents of the letter, are indicated by a small superscript number at the relevant point in the text; the editorial notes, which provide bibliographic information about the copy-text, are indicated by small superscript letters. The sequential letter number, rather than the date, is used for cross-referencing (although a date may also be given) because this number is un-equivocal, whereas dating is often incomplete or potentially confusing. For example, from time to time, there are two or more letters to the same addressee in a given month and year but no way of determining the exact day of writing. All letter numbers appear in bold. An index to names and subjects has been provided for each volume. All editorial additions to and intrusions on the copy-text, whether to suggest a probable date, complete a known address, or clarify some problem of transcription, appear in square brackets.

Citations and Abbreviations

Manuscript Location   *Abbreviation*

The major repository of Lowry's papers is the   UBC 5:3,
Malcolm Lowry Collection in Special Collections of   1-4
the main library at the University of British
Columbia. It is referred to throughout as UBC,
followed by box and folder number, with page
numbers where they exist. Subdivisions of the
collection, such as the Markson or the Templeton
papers, are indicated after UBC.

Conrad Aiken's papers, including incoming letters   H
from Lowry, are held at the Huntington Library,
San Marino, California.

An extensive Lowry file is currently held by the   Matson
Harold Matson Company, New York. All original
material from this file is indicated.

Where material is in private hands, no name is   private
shown.

*The locations of all other original Lowry letters are shown
as follows:*

The University Library, University of Alberta   Alberta
  (Dorothy Livesay Papers)
The University Library, Queen's University (Alan   Queen's
  Crawley Papers; Dorothy Livesay Papers)
The Elizabeth Dafoe Library, University of   Manitoba
  Manitoba (Dorothy Livesay Papers)
The University Library, University of Saskatchewan   Sask
  (Ralph Gustafson Papers)

The McFarlin Library, University of Tulsa (Malcolm Lowry Papers)	Tulsa
The Houghton Library, Harvard University (Malcolm Lowry Papers)	Harvard
The Princeton Library, Princeton University (Sylvia Beach Papers; *Story* Archives)	Princeton
The Harry Ransom Center for the Humanities, University of Texas (Gerald Noxon Papers; James Stern Papers)	Texas
The Lilly Library, Indiana University (Frank Taylor Papers)	Lilly
The Van Pelt Library, University of Pennsylvania (Burton Rascoe Papers)	Penn
The University Library, Columbia University (Matson Company Archives)	Columbia
Beinecke Rare Book and Manuscript Library, Yale University (New World Writing Archives)	Yale
The Nordahl Grieg Collection in the Royal University Library, Oslo	Oslo
The Brown, Pictou and Hornby Libraries, Liverpool (Ayrton and Alderson Smith Files)	Liverpool

Copy-text Abbreviations

provenance	P
previous publication	PP
manuscript	ms
typescript	ts
manuscript carbon	msc
typescript carbon	tsc
photocopy	phc
other form of copy such as typed or transcribed copy	c
postcard	pcard
Christmas or other type of greeting card	card
telegram	telegram

Frequently cited works by and about Lowry

References to Lowry's works are to first editions only, and they are abbreviated as follows, with acronyms reserved for the previous publication line and author's or editor's name or abbreviated title used in the annotations. Editions of Lowry's works present a problem because first editions are often hard to find and subsequent editions are sometimes out of print; therefore, except when citations are essential, references are indicated by position within a chapter rather than by page number.

Works by Lowry

Ultramarine. London: Jonathan Cape, 1933.	U
Under the Volcano. London: Jonathan Cape, 1947.	UV
Hear us O Lord from heaven thy dwelling place. London: Jonathan Cape, 1962.	HUOL
Selected Poems of Malcolm Lowry. San Francisco: City Lights Books, 1962.	SP
Selected Letters of Malcolm Lowry. Philadelphia: Lippincott, 1965.	SL
Letters between Malcolm Lowry & Jonathan Cape about Under the Volcano. London: Jonathan Cape, 1966.	MLJC
Dark as the Grave Wherein My Friend Is Laid. New York: New American Library, 1968.	DAG
Lunar Caustic. London: Jonathan Cape, 1968.	LC
October Ferry to Gabriola. London: Jonathan Cape, 1971.	OF
Psalms and Songs. New York: New American Library, 1975.	PS

Translations

Les Lettres nouvelles 51 (juillet-août 1960)	*Lln*
Malcolm Lowry/Clemens ten Holder Briefwechsel, ed. Wolfgang Rohner-Radegast. Essen: Rigodon-Verlag, 1985.	*Brief*

Annotated editions and secondary studies

Woodcock, George, ed. *Malcolm Lowry: The Man and His Work*. University of British Columbia Press, 1971.	MLMW
Doyen, Victor. 'Fighting the Albatross of Self.' PhD, Leuven, 1973.	Doyen
Kilgallin, Tony. *Lowry*. Erin, Ont.: Porcèpic, 1973.	Kilgallin
Day, Douglas. *Malcolm Lowry: A Biography*. Oxford University Press, 1973.	Day
Bradbrook, Muriel. *Malcolm Lowry: His art and early life*. Cambridge University Press, 1974.	Bradbrook

Grace, Sherrill. *The Voyage That Never Ends.*   Grace
  University of British Columbia Press, 1982.

Woolmer, J. Howard, ed. *Malcolm Lowry: A*   Woolmer
  Bibliography. Revere, Penn.: Woolmer/
  Brotherson, 1983.

Ackerley, Chris and Lawrence Clipper. *A*   *Companion*
  Companion to Under the Volcano. University of
  British Columbia Press, 1984.

Bowker, Gordon, ed. *Malcolm Lowry*   *Malcolm Lowry*
  Remembered. London: Ariel Books, 1985.   *Remembered*

Salloum, Sheryl. *Malcolm Lowry: Vancouver*   MLVD/
  Days. Vancouver: Harbour Publishing, 1987.   Salloum

Tiessen, Paul, ed. *The Letters of Malcolm Lowry*   LLN
  and Gerald Noxon, 1940 to 1952. University of
  British Columbia Press, 1988.

Tiessen, Paul, ed. *Apparently Incongruous Parts:*   *Apparently*
  The Worlds of Malcolm Lowry. Metuchen: N.J.:   *Incongruous Parts*
  Scarecrow Press, 1990.

Scherf, Kathleen, ed. *The Collected Poetry of*   CP/Scherf
  Malcolm Lowry. University of British
  Columbia Press, 1992.

Grace, Sherrill, ed. *Swinging the Maelstrom: New*   *Swinging the*
  Perspectives on Malcolm Lowry. Montreal: *Maelstrom*
  McGill-Queen's University Press, 1992.

Sugars, Cynthia, ed. *The Letters of Conrad Aiken*   LAL/Sugars
  and Malcolm Lowry, 1929-1954. Montreal: ECW
  Press, 1992.

Malcolm Lowry Review, ed. Paul Tiessen   MLR
  Waterloo, Ont.: Wilfrid Laurier University
  Press, 1977–.

★Bowker, Gordon. *Pursued by Furies: A Life of*   Bowker
  Malcolm Lowry. London: HarperCollins, 1993.

---

*This Bowker biography appeared after Volume I of the *Letters* had gone to press
and, thus, too late for extensive citation.

Chronology: 1909 to 1946

1909 – Born Clarence Malcolm Lowry on 28 July at 'Warren Crest,' Liscard, Cheshire, England.

1912 – Family moves to 'Inglewood,' Caldy, on the southern side of the Wirral Peninsula, Cheshire.

1915 to 1923 – Attends school, first Braeside, then Caldicote in Hitchen; summer trips to the Isle of Man.

1923 to 1927 – Attends the Leys School, Cambridge, where he plays sports, writes for the Leys *Fortnightly*, and serves on its editorial committee; acts in *Tilly of Bloomsbury*; April to June 1926, writing to Carol Brown; 15 May 1927, sets sail on ss *Pyrrhus*; writes to Tessa Evans, a girl from New Brighton; 26 September 1927, returns from voyage; spends Christmas at Inglewood.

1928 – January to June, studying for his 'Previous' exams for entry to Cambridge with Jerry Kellett in Blackheath, London; September to October, studying German in Bonn.

1929 – March, accepted to Cambridge; discovers the work of Conrad Aiken and asks Aiken to become his tutor; 28 July to 16 September 1929, with Aiken in Cambridge, Massachusetts; meets Doris ('Dolly') Lewis.

1929 – October, goes up to St Catharine's College, Cambridge; 15 November suicide of fellow student, Paul Fitte; establishes reputation as a heavy drinker.

1930 – Spends birthday at Inglewood, where rift with family deepens; spends from late summer to September with Aiken in Rye, Sussex; continues at Cambridge.

1931 – March to April, with Aiken in Rye, Sussex; August to September, travels to Norway to meet Nordahl Grieg; sees Grieg in Oslo in early September; continues at Cambridge, is writing for *Experiment*, and begins work on 'In Ballast to the White Sea.'

1932 – Easter vacation with John Davenport in Hartland, Devon, working on *Ultramarine*; May, graduates from Cambridge; spends May and June with Aiken in Rye and the summer and fall in and around London; manuscript of *Ultramarine* stolen.

1933 – January, has final fight with Russell and leaves parental home; spends January, February, and March with Julian Trevelyan in Paris; April, travels with Aiken to Granada, where he meets Jan Gabrial; *Ultramarine* published on 12 June; returns to London during the summer and spends time in hospital and in Devon; in fall, travels to Wales with Jan and Tom Forman.

1934 – 6 January, marries Jan in Paris; spends winter in Paris with trip to Chartres; April, Jan returns to New York, where he joins her in August; trip to New England; September, they settle in New York and spend Christmas 1934 with Jan's mother on Long Island.

1935 to 1936 – He and Jan live in the Somerset Hotel, New York, where Lowry works on stories, poems, and 'In Ballast'; they move on 1 May 1936; spring and summer 1936, Lowry living separately from Jan in Greenwich Village; May/June 1936, spends ten days in the psychiatric wing of New York's Bellevue Hospital; September, he and Jan are reunited and leave, by bus, for Los Angeles, where they spend October with John Davenport; 30 October, arrive in Mexico, and 18 November, settle in Cuernavaca; Lowry working on 'The Last Address' (early version of *Lunar Caustic*).

1937 – Begins *Under the Volcano*; June to early July, Aiken visits and Lowry is drinking heavily; October to November, Arthur Calder-Marshall visits; December, their house is robbed and Jan returns to Los Angeles to find work; Lowry goes to Oaxaca, where he spends Christmas in jail.

1938 – Trip into the mountains outside Oaxaca; goes to Acapulco and Mexico City; July, leaves Mexico for Los Angeles, where he is put under the care of attorney Benjamin Parks, is treated for alcoholism, and moves into the Normandie Hotel.

1939 – Begins divorce proceedings with Jan; meets Carol Phillips and resumes work on 'The Last Address,' poetry, and *Under the Volcano*; June, meets Margerie Bonner; 30 July, Benjamin Parks drives him to Vancouver, British Columbia, where he stays in the Hotel Georgia; August, moves in with A.B. Carey, who is in charge of his finances; September, moves to house rented by Maurice Carey, where Margerie joins him on 31 September.

1940 – January, manuscript of *Under the Volcano* arrives from Los Angeles and Lowry begins revising; mid–May, moves to home of J.D. Smith at 1236 Eleventh Avenue, Vancouver; 22 June, sends *Under the Volcano* to Whit Burnett in New York; 15 August, goes to beach shack at Dollarton for a holiday; 1 November, divorce from Jan final; 2 December, marries Margerie Bonner.

1941 – 1 May, he and Margerie move into a shack at Dollarton that they have purchased; 2 June, Canada census day, and they meet Charles Stansfeld-Jones; September, receives letter from Harold Matson that lists twelve publishers who have rejected *Under the Volcano*.

1941 to 1944 – Living at Dollarton, working on poetry and prose and revising *Under the Volcano*; 7 June 1944, fire destroys the shack and most of their manuscripts (*Volcano* is saved); late June, they go east to Oakville, Ontario, to stay with Gerald and Betty Noxon; July, Margerie goes to New York to see publishers and Matson; 1 October, move to Niagara-on-the-Lake.

1945 – Early February, return to Dollarton; 11 February, Arthur Lowry dies; rebuilding the shack and finishing *Volcano*, which is sent to Matson at the end of May or beginning of June; 28 November, Malcolm and Margerie visit Los Angeles en route to Mexico; 11 December, arrive Mexico City; Christmas to New Year's in Cuernavaca, where they receive letter from Jonathan Cape with reader's report on *Volcano*.

1946 – 2 January, Lowry begins famous letter to Cape; February to April, he and Margerie experience increasing trouble with the Mexican authorities; April, *Volcano* accepted by both Jonathan Cape and Reynal & Hitchcock; 4 May, deported from Mexico; 12 May, they leave Los Angeles by bus for Vancouver; June, Lowry begins editing of *Volcano* with Albert Erskine; 30 November, he and Margerie begin trip to Haiti via New Orleans; 6 December, arrive New Orleans; 25 December, set sail for Haiti.

Sursum Corda. Hold that note, Roland!
Love
Malcolm
(22 February 1957)

Beginning: 1926 to 1939

Then at last again to be outward bound, always outward, always
onward, to be fighting always for the dreamed-of harbour, when
the sea thunders on board in a cataract, and the ship rolls and
wallows in the track of the frozen sea's storm – *Ultramarine*, 274

CLARENCE MALCOLM LOWRY was born in Liscard, Cheshire, on 28
July 1909, the youngest of four sons born to Evelyn Boden
Lowry and Arthur Osborne Lowry, a successful Liverpool business
man. He was educated at local schools before being sent to Cambridge, at the age of fourteen, to attend the Methodist public school
called the Leys, where he studied from 1923 to 1927. Most of the
letters that Lowry wrote to his family during these early years have
been lost; many were destroyed in the 1950s when the family home,
'Inglewood,' was sold.

From the earliest surviving letters to a childhood sweetheart, written while he was at the Leys School, we can see and hear something
of the life of an English public school boy in the 1920s for whom the
General Strike, 3-12 May 1926, was a mere fringe annoyance that
slowed down delivery of the mail. Music, cinema, and the stage
were his enthusiasms (as they continued to be throughout his life),
and these early letters bristle with references to the popular tunes,
films, and stage hits of the day. Occasionally something unusual
stands out from among his reports on jaunts to London or his excited
reference to the latest blues recording. His knowledge of and admiration for Luigi Pirandello is one such surprise; his awareness of
expressionist painting is another. The dominant impression one receives from these letters, however, is of a young man utterly in love
with language and fascinated by the prospect of becoming a writer.
Malcolm Lowry seems never to have thought of himself as being
anything else.

Little is known about his life between 1927 and 1929 except what
can be guessed at from the pages of *Ultramarine* or from occasional
reminiscences. The Cambridge University years (1929-32) mark the

I

next documented phase in his life, and the letters from this period show a Lowry involved in extra-curricular life at university, from the magazines *Experiment*, *Cambridge Poetry*, and *Venture*, the 'salon' of Charlotte Haldane, and the ADC and Cambridge Festival theatres to the pubs. It was during the late twenties and early thirties that he discovered Conrad Aiken and Nordahl Grieg, both of whom would be major influences on his life and art, travelled to the United States and to Norway to meet these literary mentors, and established close personal friendships that would support – or haunt – him for the rest of his life. It was at Cambridge that he met John Davenport, Gerald Noxon, Michael Redgrave, Julian Trevelyan, and *lost* Paul Fitte, and it was there that he received his first serious recognition as a writer with the publication, in *Experiment*, of his story 'Punctum Indifferens Skibet Gaar Videre,' which was picked up by E.J. O'Brien for his *Best British Short Stories of 1931*.

The letters that survive from 1929 to 1932 provide glimpses of Lowry's general reading, his work on *Ultramarine*, and the deteriorating relationship with his family. The gulf that opened up between father and son during these years was only partially bridged during the early forties, prior to Arthur Lowry's death. Perhaps the most significant surviving letter from this period is that of 8 September 1931 (**35**) to Nordahl Grieg because this letter allows us to date with certainty Lowry's trip to Norway and his meeting with Grieg in Oslo. The richness of this letter as a piece of prose is further testimony to his gift with language, his intense need to converse, and his imaginative grasp of literature and literary tradition.

It is clear that Lowry had begun drinking while still at the Leys, but this practice became serious during his Cambridge years and immediately after. When he travelled to Spain with Conrad Aiken and his wife, Clarissa Lorenz, in the early summer of 1933, he was rarely sober and often very difficult. His meeting in Granada with a young American woman, Jan Gabrial, marked a sharp about turn for Lowry, at least in the short term. He fell deeply in love with Jan, whom he married six months later after an extraordinary courtship conducted largely through the mail.

The period from the time he met Jan, in the summer of 1933, until his dark night of the soul in Mexico in the winter of 1937-38, is still largely undocumented. Apart from his letters to Jan and the fiction based on this period, relatively little appears to have survived, but the letters Jan has released for inclusion here provide important new information about their relationship and about Lowry. They were both very young in 1933, he twenty-four and hopelessly in love, she twenty-two and ready to believe in his genius. His letters to her highlight the excitement, romance, and idealism of youth.

Otherwise, what does survive from these years, such as the letters to Sylvia Beach and to Whit Burnett (**63, 64**) and the three letters to Alfred Mendes (**65, 66, 67**), allows us to date his arrival in New York as September 1934, and his brief stay in the psychiatric wing of Bellevue Hospital as sometime in the spring or early summer of 1936 (not 1935 as was previously thought). These letters also indicate something of his life at the time. Evidence of what Lowry was doing during most of 1937 is slim, until Jan's departure for Los Angeles in early December triggered several desperate and despairing letters to his friends. The 1937-38 letters give us Lowry at his most maudlin and self-dramatizing. The Consul of *Under the Volcano* owes much to the Lowry of this period.

When Lowry left Mexico in July 1938, he went straight to Los Angeles, where he arrived at Jan's door drunk, with little more than his manuscripts in his bags. During the remainder of the summer and the fall months he spent time 'drying out' in what Jan has described as a place much like Bellevue Hospital in New York, and the two began to drift further and further apart. By this time Lowry's father had entrusted his son's financial affairs to a Los Angeles attorney named Benjamin Parks, who eventually found a room for Lowry in a residential hotel called the Normandie, where he could put everything on the room bill and have no need for cash. Lowry was, in effect, a helpless dependent during that year in Los Angeles.

Again, little information survives from these months. Sometime early in 1939 he was sober enough to resume work on his manuscripts, and this led to his meeting with Carol Phillips, who typed for him and with whom he enjoyed a brief romance. By the spring of 1939, however, divorce proceedings with Jan were under way, and Benjamin Parks, on Arthur Lowry's urging, decided that the troublesome Malcolm should be moved from Los Angeles to the nearest safe location. At the end of July, Parks drove his charge to Vancouver in Canada, where he transferred him to the care of a local business man called A.B. Carey. Lowry was devastated by this turn of events. He found Vancouver and his Canadian guardian utterly objectionable. Moreover, shortly before being forced to leave Los Angeles he had met and fallen in love with Margerie Bonner. In a series of frantic letters to Margerie he described his agonies without her so dramatically that, when his attempt to return to Los Angeles failed, she dropped her work there to join him in Vancouver at the end of September 1939. Her arrival marked the beginning of a period of happiness, work, and comparative stability that would last for the next six years.

Even in his earliest letters Lowry took his art seriously. Here he responds to his fellow students's criticisms of a short story he had published in his school magazine, and he does so with energy and wit. This may be the first time in his life that Lowry felt called upon to defend his prose style, but it was not to be the last. Almost nineteen years later, on 2 January 1945, he wrote to Jonathan Cape explaining exactly why Under the Volcano *was written the way it was. That letter (210) to Cape is justly famous, but the spirit required to write it is first visible in this letter.*

Letter number 1: To The Editor, the Leys *Fortnightly*

P: Leys
PP: *Fortnightly* 50, 877: 157–58; Day 83–84

Leys School,
Cambridge,
26 February 1926

(Our Reporter thanks the Editor for allowing him the opportunity of an immediate reply to the last two letters.)[1]

Sirs,

I have not the time, nor, had I the time, would I take it, to deal with you all in detail, but I am tendering a statement – not an apology, nor yet an explanation – of a state of affairs for which I have not the slightest intention of apologising. I cannot say I read your somewhat childish slating with any interest; your chief objection to my writing I gathered, after some deliberation, to be the fact that I employ those really quite useful little punctuation marks, dots.[2] In fact you almost go the length of describing my story as futile because of their multiplicity; furthermore you say it is degrading (or some such adjective) to the *Fortnightly*. This reasoning is most immature: these things the Editor, a man of infinite experience, is capable of deciding without your help. Furthermore, it is throwing mud, not only at myself, but at the escutcheon of the *Fortnightly* Committee, and the escutcheon of the *Fortnightly* Committee, I may say, is so clear that we shave in it every other Saturday morning.[3] You consider, too, that you have forestalled the only possible reply by making casual reference to the do-your-own-rotten-stories-then form of counter attack. If I may judge by what I take to be your usual style, I should say that the *Fortnightly* would go far before it asked you for a contribution. I do not know how long you have been, or were, at the School. Two years, is it, or was it? or only one? Perhaps then you have not had time to form your style: perhaps (indeed you almost admit it) you are not old enough to write for our excellent magazine. Presumably you are of the School, for you make mention of West House. There seems to be a yet further objection concerning my reports,[4] on which I have attempted to bestow a little sadly needed originality; you ask, 'What can I mean by Pantagruelian?' It is a confession that you yourselves do not know your Rabelais,[5] and perhaps a further confession that you are not old enough to read it: and 'fox' – what can I mean by 'fox'? A fox, I may state for your benefit, is an animal which, in its spare time, foxes. Hence, the verb, to fox.

And dots. I admit (being in a generous mood) on reading through my story, that there were, maybe, just too many of them for some tastes: but this error was partly due to the printers, who are liable to print . . as . . . . (this with all due respect: no offence taken, and none intended, I'm sure – *Tilly of Bloomsbury*).[6] But even so they (the dots) remained much less offensive than your letters. Another point. One of you remarks that I have undoubted talent: you will find me making no such mistake with you. You tell me, and this I expect you considered to be a rather more appropriate last straw than usual, to use my talent in a different vein. This is a matter entirely between the Editor and myself, and an ancient criticism of the sort which Hengist might have made to Horsa. Therefore I say, dots to you, Sirs. And, I may be permitted to add, having, a bad cold, that I shall continue to write as I wish, dotwithstanding. This place is reserved for conventional salutations.

Camel[7]

Annotations:

1 The following two letters to the editor of the *Fortnightly* appeared immediately before Lowry's reply in the 26 February 1926 number.

> Dear Sir,
> The stories over the pen name of 'Camel' which have recently been published in the *Fortnightly* have for some time been a source of amazement and disgust to us. But when in your last number we read 'Satan in a Barrel,' from the same pen, we felt that a point had been reached when some protest was surely necessary.
> We feel sure that you will reply, 'If you can write anything better, do so, and we will publish it.' Our retort to that is simple. By all means, we say, let your contributor

continue with his undoubted talent; but, whatever happens,
let him continue in a different vein.

We are your disgusted
Six West House Readers

Dear Sir,

What is becoming of the *Fortnightly*? Its stories are
written thus . . . . and thus * * * and moreover thus . . . .

And what does the First reporter mean by 'fox';
'Pericles'; 'torpid'; 'Pantagruelian'; and such absurd
words? It might be a second-rate newspaper instead of the
finest School magazine it should be.

Yours, hoping for a better number,
Optimist

2 The six 'disgusted' readers from West House, where Lowry lived during
his years at the school (see photograph 5), were objecting to Lowry's
story 'Satan in a Barrel,' published in the *Fortnightly*, 12 February 1926,
141-43. This story, written when Lowry was only seventeen, is not
accomplished, yet for us, looking back from the perspective of *Under the
Volcano*, it is of considerable interest. Besides an enthusiastic use of dots,
always three at a time, to suggest a break in the *monologue intérieur* of his
character Judge Jeffreys, Lowry dramatizes the struggle of the man's
conscience in a 'voice' that urges him to pray. At first, the Judge prays;
then he forswears drinking so as not to die too soon. But he finally
gives in to despair, curses everything and loses his precious voices:
'"Voices," said Jeffreys. "Oh! my voices, come again!" [. . .] But they
came no more . . . The curtain crashed down. Nineteen clocks chimed
eight unevenly.'

3 Lowry joined the *Fortnightly* editorial committee in the fall of 1926.

4 Lowry's critic is referring to his first reports on school hockey games,
which appeared in the 12 February 1926 issue of the *Fortnightly*. By 26
February his reports were more sedate, and they continued in this vein
through 1926 and 1927. In all he published six short stories, four poems,
one review, sixteen hockey reports and two letters in the *Fortnightly* over
a two-year period, from March 1925 to February 1927.

5 Pantagruel is the huge son of Gargantua in François Rabelais's satirical
novel *Pantagruel* (1532). If something is described as Pantagruelian, it is
very large and characterized by cynical humour.

6 Lowry played the part of Percy in Ian Hay's *Tilly of Bloomsbury* (1919),
which was put on by the school in March 1926. In his review of the performance in the 29 March 1926 *Fortnightly*, W.H. Balgarnie praised it
highly and remarked of Lowry that he 'acted the character of Percy with
a delightful breezy abandon . . .: if he had a fault, it was that he was too
emphatically resolute' (193). See photograph 4.

7 Lowry signed his contributions to the *Fortnightly* 'Camel,' a pseudonym
based on his initials C.M.L. for Clarence Malcolm Lowry.

⌢

The following sequence of seventeen letters (2-18) from Malcolm Lowry to a childhood sweetheart, Carol Brown, is remarkable for several reasons. These letters are among the earliest extant examples of his writing, and they reveal many of the qualities and obsessions that would characterise the man and the writer. Most notable among these are his love of words for their own sake and his hysterical identification with another writer. Even at this early age Lowry is articulate and eloquent, but his darker side is visible in his incipient drinking, his vulnerability, and his intense concern with the self.

Letter **2**: To Carol Brown

P: Tulsa(ms)

> Inglewood,
> Caldy,
> Cheshire[a]
> Letter by installments
> 9.45 am. Saturday [April 1926]

– Carol:[1] I am about to otter hunt. Ottiturhunturus sum.[2] I didn't sleep last night at all: I didn't try, as a matter of fact – I paced up and down the room like a loon, half-blubbing: Then I swore for three quarters of an hour using a different word every time. Then I tried to read 'The Way of All Flesh.'[3] Then I drank some cold coffee Russell[4] had shoved in my room. Then I swore for half an hour further using a different word every time. Then I went on trying to read the 'Way of all Flesh.'

Then I paced up and down, laughing and swearing. Then I tried to go to sleep in a chair: I could'nt[5] bear to get into bed, and finally, having dozed for about half-an-hour, till roughly 4.40 am – I climbed out of the window, on to a balcony, let myself down on to our unused tennis lawn, and walked to Heswall.[6] At Heswall I smoked three* (this * on second thoughts is an exaggeration – I smoked only two) pipes: then I walked back again in time for breakfast. (I had a cold bath before this: detail is the essence of art oh artist) And now I am going to otter hunt. Ottihunturus sum.

> 7 pm.

I've just got in (not the bath) – from the otterhunt: naturally, you will see, the first thing I do is to continue this. It's been on my mind all day – not the letter – you: apologies for 'it.'

Now. Bachelor. I must apologise. There was much truth in what you said so far as concerns yourself: I can see that it must be dashed annoying to tell people cheerfully every other day that they're paying you a superlative compliment but (dot), and (dot), if (dot). But as for me, did *I* tell you to your face that I loved you? I didn't: I do, of course, but ça va: wait a minute: I gave you a note telling you as much, a note which had it not been for a combination of ridiculous circumstances, I would never have given you. Of course I meant every word and much more: but let me say to my credit that if I have written one note to you I have written fifty, or five hundred is perhaps nearer, which I had'nt the cheek to deliver, of course, then: I tore them up sadly railing at the irony of . . . . the strength of notepaper. Wait a moment. I've got to browse upon a chop with considerable gusto. Then on with the dance.

11.30 p.m.

I went to the flicks directly after dinner with Russ to accompany him upon his Saturday evening spree – the only time the poor lad can get off for anything. I tell you, Bach, I was so eaten up with my thoughts that unless I asked him I would'nt know what picturehouse we went

to – much less the picture. Cōntrōvĕrŝy $\begin{cases} \text{surged} \\ \text{raged in my brain.} \\ \text{controversed} \end{cases}$

I *was* an interesting companion, sparkling in epigram and epithet. I'm writing this in bed so excuse the pencil. Now talking about this letter – here was I dying of love for you taking a walk before lunch for no purpose other than just to see the house you live in, and (sentimental blighter) as I walked I dreamed a little dream: I would meet you on the moor, and you would be looking sweeter than ever: you would rate me sardonically-playfully for ill treating the dog, and the dog would look at me so adoringly that you could'nt[b] help but believe that here was the perfect master: the wind would play about with your hair, you would accompany me on my walk, or I on yours, and in a secluded spot I would say 'My God, Carol, I love you'. Just like that. No more, no less. {I would give you the letter to read later.} And you were going to be so impressed, but not impressed enough to make me believe that you had'nt thought I loved you all along, and you would be just discouraging enough for me to see that you not only did'nt mind but were as braced as anything. And in the stage of my mind, a pretty little romance featuring yourself, myself, the dog, and wind (off) – with ripping scenery – was playing its two thousandth performance to an empty house.

12-2am So far so good. And then suddenly my seat in an ethereal upper circle became heather: You were there, a scarf was blowing about. My hat, but did'nt you look sweet, not 'arf you did'nt: You were there, Carol dear, I was there, the dog was there. You looked so fair. Chaucer would have said you were fayre Shakespeare that you were fair. I have said fair. What indeed could be fairer than that? And I came along to you, and I swallowed and looked a complete smidgett, the dog ran away, and as a last resort I gave you the letter as though to convince myself that the dream, had, in a fashion come true. And it had for you were there, and it was the most deliriously happy moment of my life when I saw you. I walked to Greasby[7] looking for the dog which had gone in the other direction – but I sang all the way. Thanks, dear Carol, for whatever you may have done in the ultimate restoration of that canine – awfully. I sang my way into lunch. I sang my way into Hillthorpe to play tennis. I sang my way silently into the drawing room: and sang discordantly into vile drivel I strained out of a wonderful piano, but a piano which must just hate the sight of me in future – poor piano. I sang my way down the drive: but at the bottom – 'You were flattered,' You were a member of a worthy club, You were horrid and you were bitten and you did'nt encourage me in the least: (really you made me love you more 12.30 than ever.) There were others. So with me – but all vanished in the wind. I'd die for you, Carol. I'd sell my soul for you. If you were bitten – I'd sail round the world to make the fellow who bit you apologise to you for it again. Or if you love him, I'd make him marry, you, somehow – dunno how, damn him! I know I'm the sincerest: I'll love you still when you have'nt a tooth or a hair in your head: for you, if I'm in your way, I'll chuck up all my material ambition, such as it is, run away from home, school, toil, kindred (see hymn?), and become an assistant bar tender in Honduras or somewhere without a ½ sou if necessary – I'm not trying to appeal to your sense of romance: I'm endeavouring to be desperately (you will say, 2.45 comically, or pathetically or something – 'the child Malcolm is'nt old enough,' is'nt he though!) sincere.

I'll wait as many years as you like if you'll offer me only hope: I can't believe that I have it in me to write a letter so consistently unappealing and bad as this. Carol, I'm beastly sleepy, you're seeing Raffles to-night are'nt you, hope you have a good time.[8]

Oh Carol will you try and manage to see me *alone* again to-day: if you disdain to dream of me as a too youthful lover, can't you effect a compromise between the idea of a friend and a lover. More than friend – less than lover, a lie – : but a lie of advancement; a sort of frover, not to be confused with plover. Carol, if you won't wait, I'll swear that I'll never marry anybody else, and I'll die of love for you

anyhow, before I could think of such a thing. Carol I'm going to
sleep with the light on I'm too tired to turn it off

Light's still on. I did go to sleep, Carol, but my brain's clear now. I –   2-0a
love – you. A word in eight letters beginning with I and ending with
u. Will you write some sort of note just telling me the worst, telling
me to go to blazes or something, though don't say anything you
don't mean because you're so kind to everything you might easily
Am I a rotter talking like this?
How can I possibly stop loving you when its sort of predestined. I
know I'm rather a smidgett: but I play the average games as aver-
agely badly as the average public school boy: and there's always one
chance in 1 million, twenty thousand, five hundred that I might win
the amateur (pronounced amater {I've just learned that}) Champion-
ships.[9] I'll die of sorrow at school if you don't say something.
Tell me your address at the Art School and I'll write you there from
school if it's only friendly, 'unaccomplished unaccomplishment'.
But I accomplished something to-day. I went to an Otterhunt. I have
otterhunted. Otterhuntavi. Oh my hat, there is nothing like adding
the last touch of bathos.

Yours
'Mr If not exactly right not altogether wrong'

Annotations:

1 Carol Brown and her family lived in Caldy, not far from the Lowrys'
   home, Inglewood, and the two families were good friends. During 1926
   Carol was either at her home, 'Hillthorpe,' in Caldy or at the City
   School of Art in Liverpool. Her letters to Malcolm do not appear to
   have survived, but it would seem that she returned his adolescent infatuation only with friendship. See Bowker (49–55).
2 Perhaps to impress his correspondent, Lowry has Latinized his statement 'I am about to otter hunt': *sum* = I am, *turus* = about to. But why
   otter hunting?
3 *The Way of All Flesh*, a novel by the English writer Samuel Butler (1835–
   1902), was published in 1903.
4 Arthur Russell Lowry (1905–) is Lowry's elder brother, the third of the
   four sons in the family; like Stuart and Wilfrid Lowry, Russell worked
   in Arthur O. Lowry's firm. Contrary to Day (60-61), Malcolm and
   Russell were very close during these early years.
5 Lowry repeatedly misspells his conjunctions in these early letters, and in
   his later holograph letters he reverts to this practice.
6 Heswall is a small town close to Caldy in the Wirral Peninsula of
   Cheshire.
7 Greasby is another small village near Lowry's home in Caldy.

8 'Raffles' is the name of the title character of Ernest William Hornung's very popular crime stories collected in a volume called *Raffles: The Amateur Cracksman* that first appeared in 1906 but went through six printings during the twenties. Raffles is the upper-class English crook and man-about-town who has all sorts of adventures with his sidekick 'Bunny.' Lowry, however, is probably referring to a screening of the 1918 film called *Raffles*, starring John Barrymore in the title role. There was another popular film version made in 1930 starring Ronald Colman.

9 Lowry was a very good golfer as a boy, but he was never a champion, as he implies he was in his 24 June 1947 letter (**310**) to Albert Erskine. According to the records of the Royal Liverpool Golf Club in Hoylake, Lowry won the club's Boys' Medal in 1923 and 1925; see Russell Lowry's 'Brother Malcolm' in *Malcolm Lowry Remembered* (20).

Editorial Notes:

a. Lowry was writing to Brown from the family home, Inglewood, during the Easter holidays, which ran from 24 March to 27 April 1926, when the summer term commenced. The first four pages of the letter are written in black ink and pencil on pink paper with the Inglewood letterhead. In a small poetic flourish on the word 'controversy,' Lowry has tried three possible verbs, and he has marked the syllables of 'controversy' in accordance with British pronunciation.

b. From this point to the end of the letter, Lowry has written in pencil on both sides of two pages of 20-by-26-cm lined binder paper with two holes and a ruled margin on the left. The pages are numbered 5, 6, 2001 and 2002, the latter two perhaps because he is imagining two more performances of his 'pretty little romance,' which is 'playing its two thousandth performance' in his mind. He has noted the hour of each 'installment' of his writing in the margins.

Letter 3: To Carol Brown

P: Tulsa(ms)

[Leys School,]
[Cambridge]
[April 1926][a]

Dearest Carol:

One thing at any rate is proved thoroughly in my mind and I think it ought to be in yours by now and that is that I *do* love you. Can there be any other Explanation for the fact that I think of you in everything I do – I've said it all before so many times Carol, for heaven's sake do something – write and tell me off thoroughly – or something. I can't help this being incoherent. I don't know what I want, except that I love you; I can't read this letter over because I can't see the paper properly – but look here, Carol, if you don't believe that I love you, can't you set me some Herculean labours to prove it – I'd do anything for you Carol, and I can see you shaking with laughter at me and not believing a word I say: is'nt Life wonderful?[1]

Carol I [illegible][b]

VERY INTERESTING DOCUMENT DISCOVERED IN POCKET

FULL PARTICULARS

LINES

WRITTEN IN FRENZY ON NOT RECEIVING LETTER
TIME AND DATE DOUBTFUL. TEMP. 98.4° (below zero)

– Why don't you write? Have I done anything wrong? Carol – I love you so much I don't know what to do: I can't sleep at night for thinking of you, or do anything Carol, don't you like me at all, that you won't write to me?

It's all very well to talk about being heroic in such circumstances Here am I, actually having a perfectly hectic time with Mac & Nick but not enjoying it a bit. I can't understand why. I suppose I'm being selfish wanting you to write, but still it's not the writing I care about so much. Its to know that you're all right. You're not ill are you – for God's sake don't tell me you're ill.

I'm a silly fool talking like this, but its human only to be a silly fool sometimes. Can't you even tell me how you're getting on with your freize or something?

Or how you're playing tennis? Or something. Just to know you're O.K. Speech day, is on the 18th June.[2] A ridiculous, futile, formal, hypocritical day which will be made positively beautiful if you're coming. Even if I don't see you, it will be great to know you're there

This is Mechanics, and I'm working for an exam old girl. I'm keeping an ogle upon Colin with real enthusiasm.[3]

[breaks off unsigned]

Annotations:

1 *Isn't Life Wonderful* is the title of D.W. Griffith's 1924 film about two young lovers who respond to being robbed with the cheerful remark: 'Isn't life wonderful.' They end up living happily married in a pretty cottage. This film stayed in Lowry's mind, and he used it as a thematic

motif in *October Ferry to Gabriola*. See my discussion of the allusion in *The Voyage That Never Ends* (88–89).

2 Speech Day at the Leys was the annual occasion for speeches by the chairman of the school's governing body, by the headmaster and others. There was a concert, an interlude of recitations, and the distribution of prizes, and family members joined their sons for the celebrations.

3 Colin Brown, Carol's younger brother, was a pupil at the Leys.

Editorial Notes:

a. This letter is written in black ink on one badly worn sheet of lined note-pad paper approximately 16.5 by 19 cm; it is undated and unsigned, perhaps because Lowry was writing it in class and was interrupted. This fragment may have been sent to Carol Brown with his 27 April 1926 letter. The salutation, while legible, has been crossed out, something Lowry occasionally did on these letters to Brown. I have included it here nevertheless because it clarifies where the letter begins and it illustrates Lowry's characteristic use of the colon on one of his earliest extant letters. This use of the colon would not have been considered correct by British standards of the day, but it was common in American usage.

b. Lowry breaks off at this point, and the next two lines suggest that his letter-writing may have been interrupted by the more serious concerns of the classroom.

Letter 4: To Carol Brown

P: Tulsa(ms)

[Leys School,]
[Cambridge]
27 April [1926]ᵃ

Dear old Bachelor,

Pardon my execrable manners, but I simply *must* write you immediately: the execrable manners are, I take it, forgiven. Thank you. This is rotten paper, but I can't find any notepaper; if I do, I'll continue on it. However . . . This is continued at tea. The great trouble about this first school tea is that one has'nt salved any of one's friends as yet, one sits where one may find a place, and there is such a clatter of bent tin knives and forks on rancid ham that one can't hear oneself eat if one *would* eat, which one in one case – one – would'nt: the whole thing, believe me, reminding one of the sordidity of the first chapters of a Russian novel by Leonid Andreyev.[1] 'Let me not, though,' said the wicked Sir Guy – lighting a Corona-Corona-Corona, 'talk of trifles.'[2]   I read your topping note through so many times that I know it almost off by heart now. You were so rippingly gentle about it which is after all just what I would expect from the rippingest girl in the world. Of course I'm horribly jealous that two (two of many, said he up his sleeve, one too many, coughing demurely) of your worshippers should use the very phrase predestined etc. Listen. This 'ere age, (said the night-watchman, blowing the foam tentatively off a pint of bitter), is an age of romance, of, let's face it – passion to a curiously developed pitch, said pitch being the pitch to which novelists would have extended it. And, he continued in his best Oxford manner, young lovers of the present generation are helped greatly in awkward situations by the use of words which have been used by their fictional heroes in similarly awkward positions, or position, helpful matter which would have been denied to those who lived before the days of shall we say, Charles Dickens, James Elroy Flecker, and Michael Arlen.[3] Thus 'predestined' is a word which might well have occurred to a lover of, shall we say, you, or if not quite 'predestined' – words or word to that effect. I don't blame him. Predestined, or to that effect, is good. It does not mean for one moment that it *was* predestined. No doubt he loved you and all that, confound him, but I'm jolly sure he said predestined etc because he thought it was an epigramattical phrase calculated to win the heart of any woman. (I'm being thoroughly naughty, old girl, I am forgiven – though.) Now I, although literally dying to show how much more honest a lover I am than everybody else, have little to prove it except that – well it *was* predestined. I did – I mean, rather, that it *was*, really. (Quotation. P.G. Wodehouse)[4] I knew you, in other words before I met you. You were born, obviously, on Christmas day. When I was introduced to you – I had known you for ages. When we eventually spoke, you were the oldest friend I had in the world. This, as they say in Wyomin', is 'sure a curious l'il psychological fact,' which has not prevented me from being nervous in your company till this morning. This morning I could have picked you up in my arms and kissed you in front of the whole station, I felt so gay. This morning I loved you with a new vigour, which almost sent me singing to school in its very exhilaration, you looked so utterly charming, gay, irresponsible and not in the least bachelorlike. I had no earthly right to be feeling braced. My dreams had been shattered. They are. Until the day that god pleases to smile and make you perhaps love me a little. They won't be exactly the same although *I* love *you* ten times as much. Besides, you argue, a lad like me should'nt have dreams. I [don't have] – only of you. You see I like fresh air and games and all that much better than being in. Who would'nt? But it does'nt alter my dreams of you. There's surely nothing healthier than dreaming of what, as you remark, the jolly old future, holds in store. Here I should be down in the mouth. All my friends, (and they were quite a few very good souls) have left: – except about 2 – not in West.[5] I feel distinctly irritated, but I'm inspired, despite a sort of desperate & hopeless misery about it, by my love for you. I feel here, like a new boy, or rather something like the oldest member in a golf club full of uninspiring noise. And I've only two crumpled photos of you & I desire more and I love you & I'll never, never, fall in love or marry anybody else but you – L'il gal. despite your remark about Waterloo. Nowever.   Richard Connell[6]

28 April
P.S. Concerning letting thinking about you interfere with my work. I would try and obey you – but I can't, I don't think: loving you as I do I'm thinking of you always at the back of my mind, however occupied I may be. That's not to say I don't work – although I'm finishing this letter when I should be doing 'Essay.' And concerning sleepless nights. They are not sleepless now for you've given me back hope, though when I go to sleep it is with two crumpled photos (one of you, when a kid, looking like this, more or less,) and another of you much older looking too sweet for words (it was sacrilege for me to attempt to draw it so I tore it out) under my pillow – with one arm under the pillow so that I know they're there all right.

Malcolm

Annotations:

1 Leonid Andreyev (1871-1919), a prolific Russian writer of plays and short stories, is best known in the English-speaking world for his 1922 play *He Who Gets Slapped*.
2 The 'wicked Sir Guy' is probably a character from melodrama, but I have not been able to identify the line or the play. 'Corona' is a brand name of cigar and a word that describes the classic shape of the cigar.
3 Though Lowry's correspondent and readers can be expected to know the fiction of Dickens, they might not recognize the names of the two contemporary writers. James Elroy Flecker (1884-1915), an English writer and contemporary of Rupert Brooke's at Cambridge, was best known for his poetry and the play *Hassan*, produced in 1923-24. Michael Arlen (1895-1956) was a popular English writer in the 1920s, best known for his novel *The Green Hat* (1924) and his short stories, several of which were included in E.J. O'Brien's volumes of *Best Short Stories*.
4 P.G. Wodehouse (1881-1975), the English humorist, is still remembered for his series of 'Jeeves' stories, which were collected in such volumes

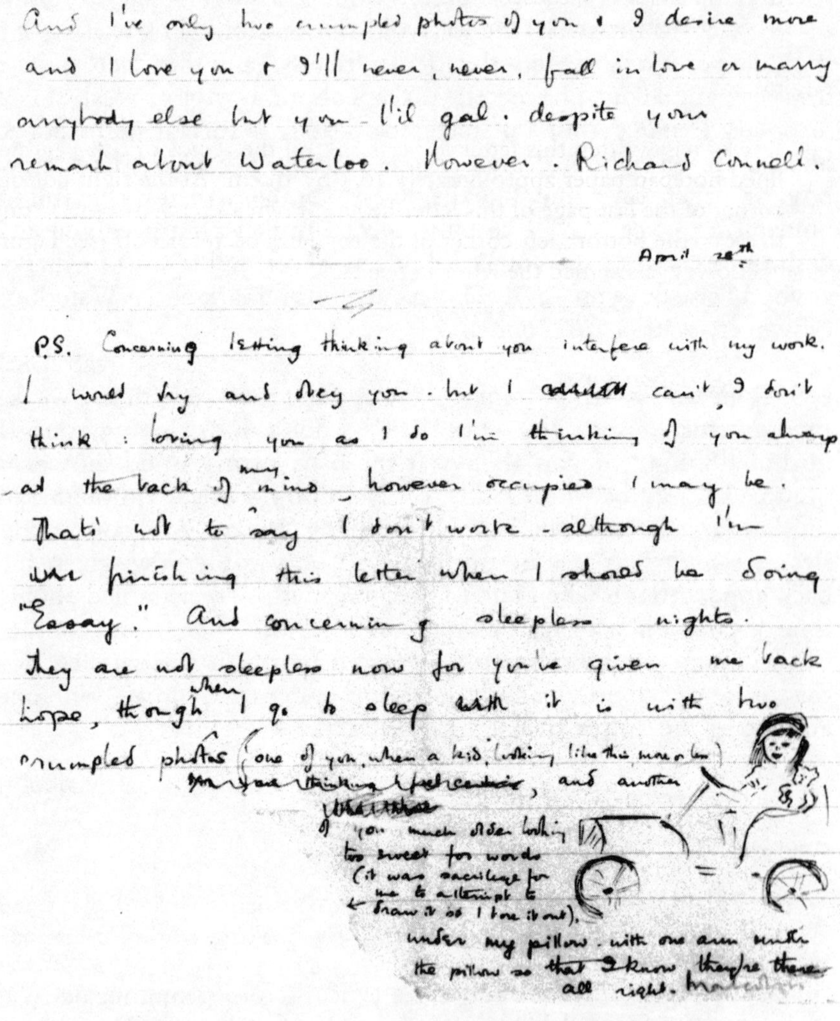

And I've only two crumpled photos of you & I desire more and I love you & I'll never, never, fall in love or marry anybody else but you - l'il gal. despite your remark about Waterloo. However. Richard Connell.

April 20th

P.S. Concerning letting thinking about you interfere with my work. I would try and obey you. but I can't, I don't think: loving you as I do I'm thinking of you always at the back of my mind however occupied I may be. That's not to say I don't work - although I'm was finishing this letter when I should be doing "Essay." And concerning sleepless nights. they are not sleepless now for you've given me back hope, though when I go to sleep with it is with two crumpled photos (one of you when a kid, looking like this more or less) and another of you much older looking too sweet for words (it was sacrilege for me to attempt to draw it as I have it out). under my pillow. with one arm under the pillow so that I know they're there all right. Malc

Figure 3: *Final page of letter 4 showing Lowry's postscript and drawing of Carol.*

as *The Inimitable Jeeves* (1924), and his Mulliner family tales. Lowry may be thinking of a story like 'The Truth about George,' in which the stuttering hero, George Mulliner, cries that his fiancée is 'predestined' to be his. Aspects of Lowry's punctuation, such as the dashes, and his locutions (what, ho! cove, old girl, 'er) strongly resemble the brittle wittiness of Wodehouse.

5 West House was the residence in which he was living.

6 Lowry has concluded this part of his letter with the name of Richard Connell, who was a contemporary American writer. See Lowry's 14

May 1926 letter (**9**) to Brown for further information on Connell and his 25 May 1926 letter (**10**) for his last reference to this name.

Editorial Notes:

a. Lowry has written this letter in black ink on the rectos of five pages of lined notepad paper approximately 16.5 by 19 cm. At the right bottom corner of the last page of this letter he has drawn a sketch of a girl sitting in a car; the bottom left corner of the page has been torn off (see Figure 3). Lowry has signed the letter in pencil.

5: To Carol Brown

P: Tulsa(ms)

> [Leys School,]
> [Cambridge]
> 29, 30 [April],
> 1, 2 May
> [1926][a]

Dear, Carol , (two words which are meant more than you'll ever dream)

Things are better than I thought they would be. Mac (whom I thought had left) has turned up. An excellent fellow, Mac, Carol, so as he's staying with me the first week of next hols. you will probably meet him. If that week is 'on' – we're going up to Scotland afterwards for another weeks intensive golf. His real name, as a matter of fact, is Macmorran,[1] and he just about runs 'B' House, although in no official capacity. I'm afraid that we've both led such unscrupulous and unconventional lives (from the Head's point of view) at this place that authorities would think twice before providing us with sceptres. We formed between us, a sort of stalky & Co: with the third member another Scotchman, Nichol:[2] whom we are going to 'intensive golf with' in his home country, all being well. Mac & I went to France together,[3] spending a week in London beforehand sitting in the pit at all the shows we could. We have never had any secrets from each other, so of course, with my heart bursting really to tell the whole world about it, I told him how desperately in love I was with you. He also, is in love – like me, desperately. ALTHOUGH HE *CANNOT* BE *SO DESPERATELY IN LOVE* So to-day, we sallied forth into the verdant pastureland of Cambridgeshire, armed with our pipes and plenty of navy cut, or in my case Empire grown shag, 'luvly stuff' as Burley of the office, says, and leaning over a gate, we swore that we would, as far as we ourselves were concerned not counting absolutely superlatively extenuating outside interference, one has to be practical, or he said so, marry anybody else: Mac for Pegs: and me for Carol. Further we swore that the man who was not married first would act as best man at the other's wedding. By that we meant that we would not, could not, whatever extenuating outside interference love anybody else but Mac – Pegs: me – Carol. And we were deucedly serious. Honestly, Carol, I never knew I had it in me to love anybody like I love you.[4] I'm afraid those are more or less the words of a comic song, but in that case I take off my hat to the comic song – It expresses exactly my state of mind. I can't believe that anybody ever loved like me.

'For her love I cark and droop.'[5]

Another comic song.

Latin.   Lowry

Look here, am I a beast going on like this – when perhaps it offends you. Let us then, talk of something else. Art, for instance. I don't know how much money you've made out of it already, and what I say I say, with perfect willingness to believe that you know far more about money making than I do. Talent, however, strikes me should be placed always to pecuniary account except where the obvious subjugation of one's art is necessary for the public. You find that in stories and things. One writes a good story with a coherent and even clever plot, for a magazine like 'Short Stories' or 'Lot o' fun' and they'll turn it down on the very grounds that it happens to be a *good* story[6]

'Dear Sir, (They say), or Madam,

Thank you for your story. It is nothing if not interesting: but "Short Stories" (or Lot o' fun) has its public, and that public I may say, sir or madam, does not lap up stories which have coherent or even clever plots. If you are clever enough to lower your art to the writing of a bad enough story for our pages, we should be obliged. If not, not. In the meantime thank you very much for the temporary diversion you have afforded the Editorial staff of "Short Stories" (or Lot o' fun).

I remain,
yours sincerely,
The Editor of "Short Stories" or (Lot o' fun).'

The whole secret of the matter, therefore, is finding your market. The best stories are invariably returned. It is just having the knack of striking the right note of mediocrity that gets the money. That's so with the 'Papers registered as second-class matter in Canada and Czecho-Slovakia' calibre. The Strand, I suppose, Pearsons, and The Grand, and perhaps the London, are all more or less first class magazines with second-rate stories – The 20 story is a second-rate magazine with first-second-third-fourth-fifth, and sometimes tenth rate stories.[7] Thats the beauty of having twenty stories. You are asked for legibility if not typewritten, and an unexpected twist at the end. Style does'nt matter.

An original illustration might 'go' on the cover of the 20 story. Otherwise it has no illustrations. But 'Gaiety' 'The Humorist' 'The Passing Show' 'John O'London's Weekly,' 'John Bull,' and the 'London Opinion' are only too glad to receive and print jokes illustrated artistically.

But they're rather below your mark – these people: therefore: I dunno, old girl: art for your own sweet art's sake. I'm rather inclined to believe, though, that if you invited representatives of the monthly press to the opening of your boudoir, you'd have a lot of offers. But this is rather sordid: you silhouette (whatever you call it, you do it beautifully) for the pleasure of the thing: I write and tear up for pleasure and exercise. Filthy lucre ruins the romance of the thing. But if ever you want (I don't say you have'nt already had five thousand things in papers & what-not) help from me concerning any of these magazines: I am always capable of putting on a tout cap slipping up to Fleet Street or Odham's Press, Longacre and finding out.[8]

Lord, how I love you, Carol: could'nt you forget your feminine misogynism and love me a little. But even if we're friends, I may be able to do an awful lot for you. And you can't dream of what you've already done for me. And you've no idea how I value the very fact that you were kind enough to let me into your friendship. You did it with such an air of – you know, jollity. I shall never, as long as I live, forget that night, by the gate, when I would have sold my soul for a kiss, you took me by the hand, gently and so kindly – and you said.

Malcolm – don't, please. I've been free from that

Friends – yes. But that – that's for Mr Right.

Oh, Mr Right – Mr Right, how I envy you – you priceless old bean. I'm looking forward inexpressibly to half-term even if it's a glimpse only I get of you. And then the hols. Do you know, Carol, you must'nt tell me you're horrid, and that you're not worth it – for you are, you know, I'd do anything, anything, for you – whether you love me or not. – Carol, dear: I was thinking out an ideal house if you ever would marry me years ahead. The idea is so beautiful I dare'nt think of it. You know: first of all – the house, furnished you know – you'd be able to choose that I'd think better than I – far better of course – and decorated chiefly with your pictures, I should think: and our own bathing pool with really decent deep salt water, and a high dive – and a tennis court. A gramophone's playing George Gershwin's 'Rhapsody in Blue' and its reminding me of you awfully. Carol, although I'm serious at heart, and you're seriously opposed to it – could'nt you think on a 'When you and I were seventeen' principle. Because after all, I do love you awfully: and I never want, and I know I won't, ever tell *that* to anybody but you. And I never have, before, you know: I've only just thought about silly people sillily. Thought I was in love, I daresay, but now I know.

Thine

Malcolm

Annotations:

1 In these letters to Brown, Lowry frequently refers to his friends Mac and Nick. Mac was Tom McMorran, a close friend while they were at the Leys and later at Cambridge University. Muriel Bradbrook describes Lowry's connection with the McMorrans in 'Lowry and Some Cambridge Literary Friends,' *Proceedings of the London Conference on Malcolm Lowry*, ed. Gordon Bowker and Paul Tiessen (University of London and *Malcolm Lowry Review*, 1985), pp. 12-13.

2 Lowry's 'Stalky & Co.' is modelled upon the group of three public school boys in Rudyard Kipling's novel *Stalky & Co.* (1897), which was in turn based upon Kipling's own life at Westward Ho! school in Devon. Lowry's friend Nick was probably P.G. Nichol, also of West House, and a reasonably effective member of both hockey and football teams.

3 This trip to France may have been the school's field hockey tour from 2 to 6 April. Lowry, who did not play in any of the four matches, covered them for the Leys *Fortnightly*. His reports appeared in early May, 50, 880 (1926): 228-30.

4 Perhaps unconsciously, Lowry is paraphrasing the words to a popular love song of the day, 'I Never Knew (I could love anybody like I'm loving you)' (1920) by Tom Pitts, Ray Egan and Roy Marsh.

5 'Cark' is an obsolete word meaning 'to be worried, vexed or burdened with care.' The line may have come from a music-hall song of the day.

6 *Short Stories* and *Lot O' Fun* were popular magazines for boys and girls in the United States and England respectively. They specialized in gripping adventure stories with healthy themes.

7 *20-Story Magazine* was an English monthly magazine that began publication in 1922. As Lowry says, they published a mixture of stories, often by regular contributors, that were quite predictable and 'safe,' and the calibre of the stories was not high. See Lowry's 14 May 1926 letter (**9**) to Brown.

8 The address of *20-Story Magazine* was Odhams Press, Long Acre, London WC2. Several other magazines had offices in Fleet Street.

Editorial Notes:

a. This letter is written in black ink on the rectos of five consecutively numbered pages and on the recto and verso of a sixth; the pages have been torn from a lined notepad approximately 16.5 by 19 cm. The small blue envelope with this letter is addressed to Carol Brown at the City School of Art in Liverpool, and the postmark shows Cambridge, 2 May; the year has been torn away. It is probable that this letter and the following separate note (**6**) were mailed together.

6: To Carol Brown

P: Tulsa(ms)

> [Leys School,]
> [Cambridge]
> 2 May [1926]
> Sunday[a]

Dear Carol old gal

Forward my incoherent, and illegible letters to you during the week.

Hope you don't mind my writing like this: but I love you for the thumping good sort you are to let me even be friends.

Please write again

> Malcolm

Editorial Notes:

a. This note, written in black ink on a loose piece of 6.5-by-13-cm paper, may have served as a sort of covering letter for the preceding lengthy epistle begun at the end of April and continued into the beginning of May.

7: To Carol Brown

P: Tulsa(ms)

[Leys School,]
[Cambridge]
[6 May 1926][a]

Geometry   Lowry pr

The tangents from T to a circle whose radius is .7″ are each 2.4″ in length. Read to find distance of T from the center of the circle. Draw the figure and check the result.

I don't know, Mr Osborn, excellent fellow as you are, how you can expect me to think of two things at once: how, I ask you this, hoc te rogo an quaero ex te,[1] (red hot Latin that) can I, do your Geometry and think of Carol at the same time? How have you the coldness of heart to make me mess about with tangents, when I'm playing a set of tennis with Carol in my mind? Did a pencil ever draw an accurate circle when it was being used as an ethereal tennis racket? Very likely not. One does'nt know, of course. Carol, have I done anything wrong? You have'nt written me once since Tuesday. There's no earthly reason why you should, of course, but then you might you know – just once. You see I'm so blindly in love with you (the hypotenuse TO is common, Quite as, OP = OQ, being radii, absolutely yes) that I can't see my way properly, and don't know what I'm writing or what I want, just all I know is that if a quadrilateral is described about a circle, the angles subtended at the center by any two opposite sides are supplementary, which is stated and proved in the converse theorem, and very neatly avoids sentiment, which you must hate from me. But do write, Carol dear, and if you're going to tell me off properly for writing you so much, do it really cruelly, and sarcastically, and sardonically, and cynically, if you must do it at all, because that would be much easier to bear than your usual manner, which I know to be kind – even to animals.

Bow-Wow.

Must do a drop 'o' work.

If any two circles touch one another the centres and the point of contact being in one straight line let two circles centres O and Q touch at point P Join O P Q R – since the given circles touch at P – they have a common tangent at that point . . . . What rot. By the way, Carol, I made 22 at cricket the other day in one over 4.4.4.6.4 caught cover point.[2] Keep fit, old thing, and don't think too *badly* of me.

Malcolm

Annotations:

1 Lowry's 'red hot Latin' translates 'this I ask you or ask from you.'
2 In the parlance of cricket, which any English girl would understand, this means that Lowry had done very well in that particular 'over' (a term that refers to the number of balls, usually six, delivered between successive changes of ends) until the last bowl, when the ball he hit was caught in the air by the boy playing the position of 'cover point.'

Editorial Notes:

a. This letter, written in black ink on the recto and verso of a page of lined 16.5-by-19-cm notepad paper, is undated. It may, however, have been sent, with other material, in the envelope postmarked 6 May 1926 that accompanies it in the Lowry Collection at the McFarlin Library, Tulsa.

8: To Carol Brown

P: Tulsa(ms)

[Leys School,]
[Cambridge]
[early May 1926]ᵃ

Started in Arithmetic
Yes, far more than that,
I am a nincompoop, in fact several types of.
I've *just* received your letter, having forgotten all about this 'ere strike, it's taken 6 days to get here.[1] I hope this is'nt invisible ink, it looks a pretty poisonous sort of mixture.

However, as I say, having forgotten about the strike, I was smitten, struck, and otherwise afflicted with the idea that a wasp was, or had, lurked in your bonnet, prompting you to scorn, cut, or otherwise scathe such epistolary efforts which have flowed from time to time from the old pen. In other words, having so many friends, I feared you had forgotten all about me. Consequently I have been tottering to every post like a swerving snipe to see if there was a letter for me, from you. But no. Again no. Now – yes. Eureka. Oh, thank you. How I thank you.

Mac and Nick, both being in a similar position but with the added advantage of being actually 'loved,' confound them, could not understand my general fatalism: the result being that under their much appreciated coercion to try and brace me up, I have been forced from my Empire Growths to a peculiarly foul tobacco costing at least twice as much. This has not been the only sign of my depression. My pipe is suffering from a chronic sooted up sparking plug: I've written three more unsatisfactory stories, sure sign of depression: and the first act of a rather unsatisfactory play, which by the way I have decided to be the only act: (this play is undergoing a French translation at the hands of Monsieur Georges Yardley,[2] who being a knowing bird, actually entertains hopes of smuggling it into the 'Thêatre du grand guignol' for me: home of 1 act plays. The old bean may entertain vainly: however one waits and – er – sees.) In tennis, further sign of my depression, I can barely reach the net – but I can keep the score quite well. If I was playing golf at all, I would be off my approach shots. And all this, woman, is your fault – therefore, said he, in a burst of eloquence and a change of ink, I do not intend to apologise for writing on this paper: by the way, I'm writing this in dire peril of my life under M. Osborn's nose.

'How are you getting on with those logarithums, Lowry?'

'Number four's a little difficult – otherwise all right. No – I don't want any help, thanks. Thank you. Yes. Priceless day. A little cold. Showers . . .

Don't, old thing, congratulate me on my facial expression. I have no facial expression. One day, however, I will let you see my world renowned imitation of the back of a cat with the old mug. For this, one's ears must be well thrown back, one's . .

Do you know, Carol, you're growing into a cynic, you know. A good fault. I have a reputation for cynicism here: I write cynical letters to the Fortnightly telling the Fortnightly what a rotten, hypocritical school they have to put up with:[3] it's not more rotten or hypocritical than any other public schools, in fact I have a ripping time here, but it amuses me to say so: Bisseker actually phoned Balgarnie[4] for half an hour the other night while I was supping with the latter (via the private master's telephone) telling him the following home truths.

1 that I was a danger to the school.

2 that the Fortnightly would be blasted everlastingly if they published my latest excrescence on the snobbishness of prefects singing out of one corner of their mouth in chapel, and giving punishments with the other.

3 that the Fortnightly would be blasted everlastingly in the after life, for entertaining such an immoral character as myself on their staff.

4 that my works, fairly smart no-doubt, were viper's productions, cheeseparings and hogwash.

5 that he doubted of late whether they were even smart: that they were mere, braggartly, cynicism.

6 that I had been reading Alec Waugh. (which was quite true, rather a hit, that). that not only had I been reading Alec Waugh, but I had been reading Noel Coward, Michael Arlen, Eugene O'Neill, and Samuel Butler.[5]

7 that I was not original, although I thought I was.

8 That it was rot.

9 That I was a disgrace to the school.

10 That I would continue to be a disgrace to the school.

11 that my works were boa-constricterine and adderesque.

12 That they were cheesparings and hogwash.

Here I went out.

When I came back, the great W.H. Barrelorgani was shaking with laughter.

'I don't advise you' he said 'to agitate about the insertion of that particular letter. I gather from the Head's remarks that you are (cough) not much thought of by him. That is the horrible effects of being CYNICAL. Have a meringue?' I had . . .

This all sprang from the fact that I was accusing you of being cynical. You accuse yourself of being a Vamp from Savannah. Why? You ask me to take solace in the fact that nine thousand, five hundred and forty eight people, not including myself, which makes in all nine thousand, five hundred and forty nine are all dying to kiss you. It is not in the least solicitous. I'm all for the jolly old mediaeval 'chivachye,' but what do you expect I'm going to do if the nine thousand, five hundred and forty eight, all turned up to kiss you – at the same time.

I can't fight them all.

And then you fairly rubbed it in about being in love with love and not with me. Do I need telling that? Why, as Stanley Lupino[6] says, Why, Naow. It is thrust upon me. You won't. You can't. You are a bachelor. You never will. I do. I am. Always. But you won't. Not a bit of it. But if you can't do anything else, just be a ripping little pal, and I'll stand by you till Hell freezes. Till Hell freezes? Till Hell freezes.

I've found a good Latin phrase which I'm just tackling with, to suit the 9,548. 'Romanus unam cervicem haberet!'[7] Don't think I know

any Latin – because I don't. But that's apt. You may hazard as to the identity of the people of Rome.
By the way, the sentiment tap is going to be turned on. Mind you don't get splashed. At least you're going to get splashed. Never mind. Shove on the old Burb.[8] Now, don't grin, we're off.

When I think of you I think always of those moors, a smell of bracken, heather and gorse, and the Ecclesian trees over which it seems one may dive into the Dee.[9] And the Dee, on a dark day, looks like a sheet of plate glass with ink, Stephen's Ink preferably, spilled over it. I think also of a certain wood where Trespassers are Prosecuted, and Dogs Dogged. Also of a certain sordid looking but not unromantic pond. And then I dream I'm walking there with you, and I dream and dream and kiss you to my heart's content. Then we go back and play tennis. Beautiful it is. You know, I have a feeling that one day I shall kiss you. I feel it in my bones. Oh – you Sweet Miss Carolina Brown! Now I more than love you if that is possible, and thankyou so much for writing!

I am in love with you all the while. Mac, Nick & I slope about the countryside, have tea at old inns, play tennis and cricket, though not I fear seriously ever, and if ever we want to work we take the book out in the country, weather permitting, and lying down in the fields work 'cum pipo.' A jolly cheery life – Carol old dear – but not serious: never serious: we exclude almost all serious issues. Plenty seriousness later on – that's our energetic motto. However Mac's a third (ex-second) at rugger and a trihouse colour, as well as being an expert on biology and tea, Nick's the best mathematician I ever set eyes on, and the most unscrupulous A.F. Blakiston[10] of a forward that ever disgraced a second rugger team, also a tri-house colour, And I'm a third at rugger, and a tri-house colour: and as we're all fairly high in the school, Nick almost top of it, we're quite useful to the general community.

   Although I fear you will not see me receive a prize: I'm top of the school at essay, but the only prize they give in that line is for answering set questions on a 'Essay Book' – the thing Coll [Colin Brown] was getting hot and bothered about towards the end of the holidays – and I refuse to read what I'm told. So unless they give me a special prize for writing actual essays – I won't get one at all.

   However the Fortnightly always rake up a prize for me at the end of the year: last year they gave me O'Neills 'Anna Christie,' Michael Arlen's 'Mayfair,' and 'The Wrecker' by R.L.S.[11] This year it will probably take the form of hush-money. I say, don't read this letter – I'm talking about myself all the while: how perfectly beastly you must think me. Dam. And I've never done anything worth talking about either. However – to proceed. Perambulating the country with the company you dance before my eyes all the while. You dance in the book I'm reading, in the smoke from my pipe, and when I walk back my mind works: left right Carol left Carol Carol left plod CAROL Carol Carol Carol . . . . . Talking about Hannahs. There's another tune, 'Oh Miss Hannah!' on the other side of 'Collegiate,' sung in the most original manner by the 'Revellers' on H.M.V.[12] It's absolutely the world's best sung tune, and they sing it in Fox Trot Time as though they were a band. They also record 'I'm gonna Charleston back to Charleston' – also priceless. If ever you're going to get a new record there, get 'Oh Miss Hannah!' – great fun, believe me. And think of me while you play it if you can and reflect that it has a better moral than H.H.H.[13] Every time I hear 'Fascinating Rythm' it reminds me of that evening by the gate.[14]

Mac and Nick, sitting near me in prep., seem to know that I'm writing you, and are making divers signs and popping noises that they must not be left out, and that I must send their love to you.

But don't heed them – they're bad old men.

Malcolm

Annotations:

1 The 1926 General Strike in England lasted from 3 to 12 May, and almost brought the country to a standstill. Cambridge University, however, was fairly conservative, so that it is not likely that the Leys, with its close ties to the university, would have been strongly pro-labour. For a good discussion of response to the Strike, see T.E.B. Howarth, *Cambridge Between Two Wars* (London: Collins, 1978), pp. 141-48.

2 G.E. Yardley was a fellow student who lived in North 'B' House.

3 See Lowry's 20 February 1926 letter (1) to the editor of the school newspaper, *Fortnightly*. On 14 December 1926 a second letter (19) to the editor was published.

4 The Reverend Harry Bisseker (1878-1965) was headmaster at the Leys from 1919 to 1934. W.H. Balgarnie, the real-life model for Mr Chips in James Hilton's novel *Goodbye, Mr Chips* (1934) and the 1939 film, was president and treasurer of the Leys *Fortnightly* committee, master from 1900 to 1928 and from 1940 to 1946, and acting headmaster for 1929-30. See Lowry's comments on Balgarnie and on the film in his 24 December 1939 letter (122) to Aiken.

5 Alexander (Alec) Waugh (1898-1981) was popular in England for his stories and novels, and his first novel, *The Loom of Youth* (1917), which mentioned homosexuality in English public schools, caused a sensation. Noel Coward (1899-1973), the English playwright and composer, was

well known in the 1920s and 1930s for his witty plays and revues; Michael Arlen was a popular English short story writer during the 1920s, and Eugene O'Neill was already an important American playwright by 1926 (see annotation 11). Samuel Butler was an English novelist whom Lowry was reading at this time; see his April 1926 letter (2) to Brown.

6 Stanley Lupino (1893-1942) was an English comedian who appeared in pantomimes, revues and musical comedies. The patter that follows is Lowry's imitation of a Lupino routine.

7 Lowry's Latin translates literally as 'The Roman would have one neck,' but it carries the metaphorical association of carrying a burden.

8 A 'Burb' is a Burberry raincoat, still a popular make of coat in England.

9 The Wirral Peninsula is bounded on the north by the busy Mersey River and the city of Liverpool and on the south by the broad, peaceful estuary of the River Dee. The banks of the Dee were an easy walk from the Lowry home in Caldy. The 'Ecclesian' trees may be Lowry's reference to almond trees, which are mentioned in Ecclesiastes, 12:5.

10 Sir Arthur Frederick Blakiston (1892-1974) was a prominent English back-row forward in rugger who played in many matches during the 1920s.

11 *Anna Christie* (1922) is an early play by American playwright Eugene O'Neill (1888-1953), who was one of Lowry's lifelong favourites. Michael Arlen, the English novelist and short story writer, published his collection of stories called *May Fair* in 1925. *The Wrecker* (1892) is a novel by the popular Scottish writer Robert Louis Stevenson (1850-94).

12 'Oh Miss Hannah' (1924) and 'Collegiate' (1925) were popular songs of the day, but I have not been able to find a listing for a recording on His Master's Voice (HMV) by a group called the 'Revellers.'

13 'H.H.H.' is probably 'Hard Hearted Hannah' (1924), with words and music by Jack Yellen, Milton Ager, Bob Bigelow and Charles Bate. The refrain of the song begins: 'They call her Hard Hearted Hannah, the vamp of Savannah / The meanest gal in town.'

14 'Fascinating Rhythm' (1924) was written by George and Ira Gershwin for the popular American musical comedy *Lady, Be Good*, which played at the Empire Theatre in London from 14 April 1926 to 22 January 1927. The song was a favourite of Lowry's, and *Lady, Be Good* is now recognized as marking the rise of American jazz-based musical comedy.

Editorial Notes:

a. This letter is written in black ink on the rectos of nine consecutively numbered pages of 16.5-by-19-cm lined notepad paper. There is no date or envelope for this letter, but judging from Lowry's reference to the General Strike, it must have been written early in May. See annotation 1.

9: To Carol Brown

P: Tulsa(ms)

Leys School,
Cambridge
14 May [1926]
Continued in instalments.[a]

Dearest old thing,

    You terrific letter drove me mad with delight. I received it at tea; I was digging into a jolly old sardine and absent mindedly I shovelled the whole lot off my plate into the stuff that calls itself tea.

I shroke with delight:

    Nick said to Mac.

        'Lobs[1] is mad.'

    Mac said to Nick.

        'Lobs is mad.'

    I said:

        'I am mad.'   I was.

Now – although your letter made me love you so much that I went dippy in the dome, cultivated bats in the belfry, not to mention an owl or two in the outhouse, it also made me slightly sad. It is a minor matter only, but I better confess to it immediately. That is that although 'The D Box,' which I am afraid I thought not at all a bad sort of story, (but which you made no comment on. Tears) *was written by Clarence Malcolm Lowry in the flesh*: I am not the money making Richard Connell who has cultivated quite a fruity sort of market. He is 'Carl.'[2] He is also the biggest liar, the biggest coward, the bravest man, the most immoral and the most puritannical man, the most insipid drunkard, and the worst and the best friend alternately that I hope to have. He drinks to inspire himself, and he goes to church to think out a story about dopes. He is, of course, quite mad – having in that respect a very similar temperament to myself. He is small, insignificant, and brushes his hair like a fifth rate pawnbroker's assistant, and the other day I threw him backwards off the high dive, and he squashed and squelched into the water like a spider with one wing . . . He wears an old double breasted jacket and he stoops: he is 19, with a mind of a man of sixty suffering from senile decay: and he drives a car as though he were Count Zborowski or the Devil himself.[3] Well this 'Man,' whom Stalky & Co adopt occasionally when he's not blind drunk, was born way over the duckpond of an Anglo-Frenchwoman – and during the period of going steadily mad – he has turned out a Pantagruelian amount of writing & drawings. He seems to be W. Bird of 'Punch'[4] – which may be mere drunken raving, but he certainly is, or was when I last met him 'Richard Connell' – although he is the biggest crook journalist that ever sent three of the same stories to three different editors. Some of his exploits in this line do not bear credence – ! but I know for a fact that he has raked in almost enough money to buy himself a Bentley. Well, being more or less a struggling sort of writer myself, I was faintly amused to find myself beating this cove in essay, which for Frank Ives, are stories.[5] And what's more he served up stories as essays which I HAVE SEEN IN PRINT. Consequently we became friends, (of a sort) and the result of it all was, that the man found he had'nt enough brains or time or something to fulfil his 20 story commission for February, so asked me if I could do it for him suggesting my story 'The D Box' – which had been hitherto called 'Doan't try.'[6] (an essay on Disallusionment) This was at the beginning of the Christmas hols – that story was in the February, not the October number: I have a sort of feeling that I told you it was October when I handed it to you – but if you search all over it you may find 'Feb' written on it somewhere. Unfortunately the cover, which, I remember, was Gilbert's drawing of 'The old Summerton Temper' – was not in evidence when I hauled the mag. out of a drawer for your delectation:[7]

(Sorry – the light's gone out – catch up the thread to morrow. Good night, dearest l'il gal)

[breaks off unsigned]

[Lowry has sent the following short story fragment to Carol Brown and presented it as his own. It is, however, a passage copied from 'The Yes-and-No Man' by Richard Connell which appeared in the May number of *20-Story Magazine* 8, 47 (1926): 47-53.][8]

'Don't give up' I counselled 'go after her. Its nonesense' said Tepler morosely, I'm hopeless. Lets talk about something else."

He was in genuine misery. So I said 'very well. Have you heard anything from Myler – the inventor & his trick self playing piano?

From his face I saw that my choice of subject had not been a happy one.

Theres another thing' he groaned. I've been thinking about it day & night when I was'nt thinking about Stella. I told you how Myler wants me to go in with him and help market his invention. He's offered me ½ int. for £5000 £2000 down. I'd be an utter fool to throw away all my savings on a thousand to one shot. Of course, on the other hand, the invention may have possibilities; but I feel sure they are'nt strong enough to warrant my investing on it.

'Then you turn down that offer then?'

'In a word – I think so. I've until to-morrow to decide.

'Eustace, admit it' I said 'this new piano idea interests you. You're playing with it.

Well. I am and I am not" said Tepler. Does'nt cost anything to play with an idea.

'Neither does it make the bank balance plumper.'

'I prefer to be on the safe side' said Tepler Well good night I've got some writing to do.'

At noon next day Eustace stuck an agitated head into my office.

[P.S.] I don't know if this (discovered at the back of my locker) has any intrinsic value to you – but it looks like a bit of the 'Yes & No Man' in its very *raw* state[8]

                                         & I love you

Annotations:

1 'Lobs' was Lowry's nickname at school; see Ronnie Hill's reminiscences, 'The Sophisticated Schoolboy,' in *Malcolm Lowry Remembered* (22-26).

2 'The D Box,' attributed to Richard Connell, *not* Malcolm Lowry, appeared in *20-Story Magazine* 8, 44 (1926): 39-42. Richard Connell (1893-1949) was an American writer. He published over three hundred short stories in a wide range of English and American magazines, and he wrote some novels and screenplays. He appears always to have published under his own name, not under the pseudonym of 'Carl,' as Lowry suggests. Although he made a good deal of money from his clever stories, he never achieved status as an important or serious writer. Connell's stories are frequently listed in O'Brien's best American short story volumes during the 1920s, and two articles on him are cited in the best English short stories for 1926. His story 'The D Box,' first published in *Red Book* for November 1925, is given three stars for quality by O'Brien in *The Best Short Stories of 1926 and the Yearbook of the American Short Story* (New York: Dodd, Mead, 1927), pp. 325, 415.

It would seem that Lowry had created something of a fantasy about Connell and either convinced himself that 'The D Box' was his own story or tried to impress Carol Brown by passing off Connell's story as his own. The Leys School has no record of anyone called Richard Connell or anyone who signed himself 'Carl.' Lowry, of course, signed some of his early work 'Camel,' but why he should have identified with Connell or attributed such unsavory qualities – not to mention being an 'insipid drunkard' – to him is now impossible to know. This letter, however, provides a fascinating glimpse into Lowry's psychology at an early stage. In his 23 May 1926 letter (**10**) to Brown he admits having deceived her 'foully about Richard Connell,' and asks her not to mention Connell's name again.

3 Count Louis Zborowski (or Zborowsky) was a well-known racing motorist who had won many races at Brooklands racetrack during the early 1920s. His death on 19 October 1924, while racing at the Monza track near Milan, was announced in the *Times*, 20 October 1924.

4 'W. Bird' of *Punch* was, in fact, Jack B. Yeats (1871-1957), the well-known illustrator and painter and younger brother of W.B. Yeats. Jack Yeats gained his reputation as a serious modern painter in the 1930s, but his cartoons for *Punch* already displayed his ironic humour. See R.G.G. Price, *A History of Punch* (London: Collins, 1957), pp. 209-11.

5 F.W. Ives was a master at the Leys.

6 'The D Box' is an interesting, well-executed short story about a rather pathetic bachelor called Francis Dawson who lives in a shabby Bloomsbury flat and dines every night, alone, at the Standish Club. He collects his mail at the club in the 'D' box, where another member, Henry Cunningham Doan, also collects his letters. Fascinated by the letters addressed to Doan, Dawson develops an elaborate fantasy about the man, imagining him to be 'everything that Francis Dawson wished to be,' but he never speaks to Doan and thus never realizes the sad truth that Doan is as lonely, bored, and insignificant as he is. The governing idea of the story is Dawson's vicarious identification with the fictitious figure of Doan that he creates for himself. The words 'Doan't try' do not appear in the published story, although one could certainly describe it as being about disillusionment in so far as the *reader* is made aware that Dawson's fantasy has no basis in fact.

7 Albert Thomas Jarvis Gilbert (?-1927), art master at the Leys for close to sixty years, was a member of the Royal Society of British Artists and of the Royal Society of Painters in Oil Colours. He was also a designer of posters and an illustrator; however, the illustration that Lowry remembers for the cover of *20-Story Magazine* 8, 44 (1926) is by the magazine's regular illustrator, Charles Crombie. It does indeed show a picture of two men fighting as an illustration of the lead story by George Weston, 'The Old Summerton Temper,' and the title of this story is prominently displayed on the cover. Information on Gilbert is sparse, and I have not been able to verify what kind of illustrating he did or whether he used a pseudonym for this aspect of his work. Gilbert exhibited regularly with the Royal Academy between 1907 and 1927, but neither they nor the Royal Society for Painters in Oil Colours has any further information on his activities, and his obituary notice in the Leys *Fortnightly* adds nothing new. No archives appear to exist for *20-Story Magazine*, which precludes any chance of confirming or refuting Lowry's claims about Gilbert, Connell or himself. That said, however, it is still just possible that 'Charles Crombie' was Albert Gilbert and that Lowry did submit some of his early work to the magazine under his own name or Connell's.

8 Connell's 'The Yes-and-No Man' is a rather slight story of a young man called Eustace Tepler who is so cautious that he can never speak or act decisively, his habitual response to a question being 'Well, yes and no.' The passage that Lowry is sending to Carol Brown is from near the end of the story (52). If I am correct in assuming that 'The D Box' and 'The Yes-and-No Man' were written by the American writer Richard Connell (and there is no good reason not to think so), then Lowry's attraction to this story and his sending it to Brown as a draft of something he had written himself are further twists in the puzzling identification he clearly felt with the American. This Richard Connell business appears to be the first surviving evidence we have of Lowry's propensity for what he himself called 'hysterical identification.'

Editorial Notes:

a. This letter has been written in black ink on a single sheet of 16.5-by-25.5-cm school letterhead, which carries the name 'Leys School, Cambridge' and the school crest.
b. This story fragment is written in pencil on recto and verso of a single 20-by-26-cm sheet of paper. It is not clear now whether Lowry sent this item to Carol Brown separately or with one of his letters. I have included it here because it is this letter that focuses upon the Richard Connell connection. The postscript addendum appears in the lower right corner of the verso, and Lowry has printed 'I love You' in small letters beneath the last line.

10: To Carol Brown

P: Tulsa(ms)

> Leys [School,]
> no. 7,
> [Cambridge]
> [23 May 1926][a]

L'il gal,

I have been preserving what you would term a 'respectful silence.' As a matter of fact I've been suffering like anything. First of all I'm possessed of qualms of conscience that you must think I deceived you foully about Richard Connell – especially when I remember signing myself in one of my letters as Richard Connell.[1] Secondly – well I just love you so much that its jolly hard to preserve anything approaching a 'respectful silence.' Thirdly one of your photographs has gone to the wash. When I say that I mean that I keep

one in my pjama pocket and the other under my pillow. Sentimental no doubt – but there it is. Well one morning having to get up and dress with the accelerator fully trodden on – I left one, (the one where you're about 16 – I should think) in my pjama pocket. Well – I dashed up in the middle of the day sometime to transfer this same photograph to the jolly old gent's suiting – when I found that it had gone, been spirited away. What had happened was that it was washing day, and all the pyjamas had biffed off to the wash.
Consequently I need another snap. Beastly careless of me, but these things will happen – what.
By the way, you don't know anything like enough about me yet. For me to have told you about those snaps at all was a tactical error of the very deepest dye. One was given me – righteously. The other I stole. Why not? It didn't seem to belong to anybody very particularly, and I wanted it so badly. But I have been punished now. It has gone to the wash. If you think that I deserve one, just one more – please send it.
   I could not possibly take it for encouragement – because I have almost given up hope that you could ever love a misfit like me.
   I just wait – and hope I do still though Lord knows I have'n't any right to.
Every moment I live I love you more and more and realise what a hopelessly inadequate sort of person I am.

How can you think I should ever cool off. If I saw that I was deliberately inflicting myself on you, that you were thoroughly bored by me (which you may be – you've been kind enough not to show it), I should retire respectfully, but I should never cool off. I mean if ever you want my life, Carol, just walk along and take it.
– I'm writing a short letter to you for the simple reason that I'm desperately afraid of boring you. You see, here am I preaching about unselfishness – yet boring you. It seems that yours has been the real unselfishness. You wrote me pages and pages, wonderful it was, just – you said – to make me happy. For all I know it was a frightful strain to you to rattle off such an enormous lot to a mutt like me. But I did appreciate it so. I appreciated it so much that I can't describe my feelings – and it was so enjoyable – every word of it. And the drawings – superbes. Yes, I must introduce you to old Mac (& Nick – if he's knocking round.) Mac & I are spending Speech Day together.
   I should bury Richard Connell quietly in a corner of the garden. All the same if one of Carl's iniquitous letters is of any interest to you

– I enclose the thing. It is a great strain for me to write you a short letter – but I do it also because I don't want to be accused of using you as an outlet for romantic expression. I am trying (I shall never succeed) to make myself worthy of you.

Thine

Malcolm

[P.S.] Bury Connell & never mention his name again either to me or to anybody else. I feel rather ashamed of the blighter. But you have'nt told me yet whether you thought 'The D Box' a good story. Am looking forward tremendously to speech day.[2]

By the way I should hurry up & book a room at some pub or other if you have not already done so. They have a habit of filling up & especially about May Week.[3]

Annotations:

1 See Lowry's 27 April 1926 letter (4) to Brown, where, without hint of explanation, the name Richard Connell appears where a signature might be expected.

2 As Lowry points out in an earlier letter (3), Speech Day at the Leys was held on 18 June.

3 Cambridge University 'May Week' is the main social event of the university year. It comes at the end of the Easter term and lasts for ten days during the early part of June; it consists of college boat races on the River Cam, followed by college balls, concerts, plays and other entertainments. May Week usually brings many visitors and guests to the city.

Editorial Notes:

a. The envelope with this letter bears two postmarks and two addresses. It was first sent to Carol Brown at the City School of Art in Liverpool from Cambridge on 23 May 1926, but it was subsequently readdressed from Liverpool to Hillthorpe, Caldy, Cheshire, in another hand, and the Liverpool postmark is 25 May 1926. The letter has been written in black ink on a single sheet of paper approximately 23 by 18 centimetres. The postscript is written on a separate scrap of lined notepad paper, then folded and enclosed with the main letter. Because it seems intended as an addendum to the letter, I have included it here.

11: To Carol Brown

P: Tulsa(ms)

[Leys School,]
[Cambridge]
[May 1926]^a
End of *May* sometime

Dear Carol,

Thanks awfully for your letter. I received it during the midday browse of grilled cat. It helped me – digestively also. Good fun about the tennis – certainly red hot getting into the final. I must say I like the airy way you introduce me to Fred for the first time – as a matter of fact, he's a great friend of mine – introduced to me through you, of course – indirectly – but I've played golf with him lots of times, and even appeared at a ping-pong party he gave (you were there) in which, having no time to change, I appeared looking like the original of the Labourers Evening Hymn of Hate[1] – and forthwith climbed into one of Fred's suits, and appeared finally looking more like Wallace Beery[2] than ever . . You ask Fred if he does'nt remember it. When I say all this I mean roughly that I've known the child eighteen months longer than you thought, and that he's a nailing good chap – and when I say that, I mean that I'm very glad you are knocking out the Wirral District together – and hope sincerely that you walloped some poor humans pretty tough in the final – in fact, as Milton Hayes might say – you know what I mean.[3]

Mind you have won every tournament in the vicinity by the time I come back – what?

Concerning the jolly old speech what-not. It rests, as it were, with you. Only I know what I'd do in your place – I'd jolly well play in all the tournaments I could – and let old pie-face rot in Cambridge. As for old Coll [Colin Brown] – I don't suppose he wants to see you particularly – I know I never want to see any of my brothers, and my brothers simply abhor the sight of me – what? Except old Russ – jolly old bird – Russ. I do hope your mother won that golf tournament; we Browns always win everything – don't we? We do. Congratulations – then.   Well – well – let me know 1. about speech day . . 2. about your tournaments 3. The number of people who want to marry you – and by the way, if you're thinking of marrying old Fred – just let me know and I'll pop along a brace of Chinese vases for a wedding present – what?

Cheer frightfully ho –

Malcolm

Glockenspiel – Glôck-ēn-speel, a curious German musical instrument of the dulcimer family. Has a bell like tone.

Spelt Glockenspiel
Glockenspiel.

Faint heart, Oh Woman,
      never won fair lady
Will write to-morrow[4]

Annotations:

1 I have not been able to identify the 'Labourers Evening Hymn of Hate.' Lowry may well be parodying the title of an engraving or painting because the subject of the labourer's evening hymn was a popular one with Victorian artists, and prints of these works, such as the nineteenth-century French painter Jean-François Millet's *Angelus*, were often hung in pious, upper-middle-class homes like the Lowrys'.
2 Wallace Beery (1885/86-1949) was an American actor in Hollywood who moved successfully from silent to talking films. His elopement with Gloria Swanson in 1917 caused a sensation. His career began in 1914 with the role of a Swedish housemaid in slapstick comedy, and he prided himself on his 'ugly mug.'
3 Milton Hayes (1884-1940) was an English entertainer who wrote, composed, and performed many successful monologues and songs.
4 Lowry has scribbled these parting thoughts on a scrap of paper filed with the letter in the Lowry Collection at the McFarlin Library, Tulsa. His allusion is to the sixteenth-century proverb 'Faint harts faire ladies neuer win,' which has been frequently repeated over the centuries.

Editorial Notes:

a. This letter is written in black ink on a single page of 16.5-by-23-cm lined scribbler paper. There is no way of confirming an exact date.

12: To Carol Brown

P: Tulsa(ms)

[Leys School,]
[Cambridge]
[2 June 1926][a]
– Here and there
Then and now.

Pardon the typewriting

Madame – this to you:

Grats on your tennis effort: red–hot – I knew very well you'd win though. If you have the time and the energy a rough scenario of the game would be welcome.

Give my love to old Fred when you next see him. Talking about the cheery little subject of rooms. Old Coll [Colin Brown], like the sweetie in the song, would'nt tell me how why or when – you were or you were'nt – or you might be: or perhaps you might be coming down, and if so how many, and if not why if not why not. Therefore for the first month I have lain torpid as the Lethé weed, but it suddenly striking me amidships that some sort of something was necessary, I leapt up, as it were, like a rocketing pheasant – and swerved round to all the pubs in the neighbourhood, spending a pleasant quarter of an hours chat in each, with, in every case, a large and rotund female with crow's feet and teeth.

From these I gathered;

1. That June 18th – onwards was Mayweek.

2. That it was quite impossible to obtain rooms anywhere except in the coal hole (rent free) – as not only was it May Week, but also the beginning of the College Balls – also The Leys School speechday.

3. That it was Mayweek.

4. That I could not obtain any rooms – anywhere.

5. That I could not obtain any – er rooms – er anywhere. However we Lowry's are of the Bulldog Breed, and on receiving a letter signed yrs sincerely C. Brown – I felt that dash it – well, simply dash it must do something or bust. So I rallied round some – and eventually ran to earth a sort of Look-at-our-tennis-court-nice-bathroom place, with a thin manageress with positively no teeth at all: bearing the intriguing title of 'Shaftesbury House' in (what is not altogether unexpected) Shaftesbury Road – There are trees in Shaftesbury Road. Willow Trees? I am not sure. Anyhow trees. And a man in white painting gates green.

Well, at any rate, I popped into this place and saw the manageress and the tennis court and a bedroom and a room full of magazines.

And some washing spread over the tennis court to dry – which gave quite an expressionist effect.

They were'nt quite sure about the room, and, told me to come round to-day: and to-day they are sure – it is in fact, okay. There will be staying at the 'Shaftesbury' also quite a number of Leysian relations: including besides, of course, your noble selves – Mrs Tregoning, Mrs Garnett, Mrs Haller, and Mrs Morel. Does this interest you? It does'nt. However we may touch lightly upon the subject of Mrs Garnett: I have not the pleasure of knowing the lady, but I have the extreme displeasure of occasionaly having to walk through her son, who resembles in action and appearance no more and no less – a sweaty shiek in horn rimmed spectacles expelled from the Stamboul Borstal Institute.[1] You may therefore tell Mrs Garnett from me that –

All right don't.

Thanks for your letter. Yes – it is vastly intriguing to hear about your friends. My dear old bean – if these people must – they must. What?

I am greatly impressed by your six foot two actor[b] – but I am more impressed still to think what spiritual stimulus and exultant gusto it will afford both you and him, when you inform him that you are corresponding with a curious mud coloured kegeree faced individual of at least four foot two.

Well – well, old thing, a woman, as that great philosopher X once remarked is only a woman but – well, she is are'nt they, or don't you?

Bungho. I must hence. CCCCIV
IT   IS
[illegible]   I am.   (absent)

Far from being cheek I deem it the highest honour to be entrusted with the enterprise, and hope the rooms will, as the tailors say, suit.

Ripping, that tennis.

9.30 pm. I've just completed a one act play entitled 'Traffic.' It is nothing about material traffic at all – it refers to human traffic. The ceaseless roar of the material traffic may be heard (off) all through. It is not bad – but by no means good, as yet. This does'nt interest you. Yes? No? You once said you might pretend to love me. Will you? But perhaps this does'nt interest you either. But you tolerate my sloppy effusions. And I still hope. What? Oh Carol – dear

Thanks awfully for the snap, GloriabetogoodnessBebedaniels-Swanson.[2] I wish I could be a Thomas Meighan[3] to you. But unfortunately my hair is untidy. My shoes are nearly always dirty. My face is a Z15 model and above all – I am not Six Foot Two.

P.S. I cajoled the Shaftesbury woman into writing and telling you Dear how many eggs they gave one for breakfast – and all of that.

M

Annotations:

1 A Borstal institute is a prison-reformatory for criminals under the age of twenty-one, so called because the first was built in the town of Borstal in 1902. Stambul is the ancient quarter of the city of Istanbul (formerly Constantinople) in Turkey; thus, Lowry's joke is to describe his class-mate as a 'sweaty sheik' from a Turkish reformatory.
2 Lowry's joke, gloria-be-to-goodness, includes the names of two popu-lar film stars of the day: Gloria Swanson (1899-1983), the darling of Hollywood, and Bebe Daniels (1901-71), another American actress. Swanson and Daniels both appeared in Cecil B. De Mille's films *Male and Female* (1919) and *Why Change Your Wife* (1920).
3 Thomas Meighan (1879-1936) was a successful American actor of the silent screen. He appeared with Gloria Swanson and Bebe Daniels in *Male and Female* and *Why Change Your Wife*, playing the romantic male lead opposite Swanson in both films.

Editorial Notes:

a. 2 June 1926 is the postmark date on the envelope with this letter, which is addressed to Brown at Hillthorpe – Caldy, Near West Kirby, Cheshire. Lowry has written in black ink on four pages of 18-by-23-cm lined paper. The postscript has been written at the top of the recto of the first page of this four-page letter. On the verso of the last page Lowry has scrawled: 'This is the letter. Make no mistake about *it.*'
b. At this point, Lowry has written '(is he playing Falkland [sic] or Sir Anthony Absolute or Jack Beverly or who in She Stoops to Conquer?)' He has then drawn a line through this parenthetical remark and written above it: 'sorry – got mixed up.' Lowry is 'mixed up' in that Faulkland, Ensign Beverly and Sir Anthony Absolute are all characters in R.B. She-ridan's 1775 comedy *The Rivals*, not in Oliver Goldsmith's *She Stoops To Conquer* (1773).

13: To Carol Brown

P: Tulsa(ms)

[Leys School,]
[Cambridge]
[June 1926]
June Night – Fox Trot[a]

Dear old Carol,
    You have that inestimable treasure, a sense of humour. I hope that I, too, „   „   „   „   ,   „   „   „   „   .
        xxx
You, yourself, are an   „   „   ;   you silhouette excellently,

dance pricelessly, play tennis comme un cherubim: in fact you are everything, and no doubt can analyse everything in your own way, but strictly between you, me, and the O. Cedar mop,[1] you are entirely inaccurate on the psychology stunt.

If you knew, woman, how I read and reread your letters; how I'm thinking of you all the while; in short, how passionately fond I am of you; how this, and how that; you would see how hopelessly you fail to put your creed over the footlights. (Wait a mo, a cove has got the 'Fascinating Rythym' on the gramophone, and the record has just reached that piano solo part, and I can't keep still.). Where have I got to – oh – I see. Well – believe me. What I mean to say is this, without for a moment growing sentimental (because you hate me when I'm being sentimental), that in accordance with the Coué system of Arithmetical progression – I love you more & more.[2] And dash it – your letters are ripping, and I frenziedly (spelling very doubtful) look every gift postman in the mouth every time he does'nt bring one of your letters. I dart to and fro to the porter's lodge – every post, and come away with a grin or a groan, as the case mebbe. And if you really mean that ingenuous remark about my being a man in a hundred if I can still care for you, well, I raise my stetson to myself, I am a man in a hundred. What – ho!

Yes, and talking about laughing behind people's backs – we had an inspection to-day, you know, a sodden beribboned old field marshal with an eye glass swerved about and looked generally cynical, (have I made that remark before; I'm fond of nursing metaphors), and told us, after 4 pints of Bissekers Italian Vermouth,[3] that we were the world's best corps. West were fifth in the house competition, which is distinctly good considering there were, I believe at least five entries. However.

Your actor friends, your description, and your photographs (for which thanks very much: I can't bear to send back the one of you, but I suppose it's a point of honour, not that I have an honour or anything, but you know what I mean) are most interesting. I'd love to meet them; however conflicting circumstances conflict and all that. While in London on no account miss seeing a play called 'This Woman Business.' by Benn Levy, whom I wish I knew.[4]
After seeing this play (which is at the Haymarket) you will ask Canon who-is-it at the Parish Church to put up the banns immediately. Or don't we have banns? Never mind. What I was really going to say was this; Carol and her Band has given me a plot for a story. Thanks very much.

What on earth's a widow's peak, old girl?
It sounds a good title for a film.

	THE WIDOWS PEAK	
MARY	THE WIDOWS PEAK	MARY DUSTBIN.
IN		
DUSTBIN	THE WIDOWS PEAK	MARY DUSTBIN.
	IN	
	TO–NIGHT	
6.30.	to–NIGHT	8.45.
	TO–NIGHT	
AT	*THE* CINEMA.	

———

Sorry.

   Old Fred's a nailing good sort; one of the very best fellows; comparable only in admirability of character with one Thomas Boden-Hardy, who sits next to me in maths forms, and smiles cynically at the work I do.[5] He looks rather like Fred. Boden is my commission and typing agent at 5½ per cent; and is quite the best shot in the British army. However this is incongruous.

I hope that for the promotion of admirability of character, you will never either see or hear my play 'Traffic.' – which is a drunken soliloquy; which I am assured would run for years in the Fiji Islands as a curtain raiser, but here would not get within three feet of the Lord Chamberlain, who would have to use ink with a spray.[6] However it is quite sincere, but will, I'm afraid, have to be buried quietly, although it means well. Monsieur Emile Zola, and William Shakespear, confrères of mine – have had the same trouble. What?

My dearest old thing; it takes seven forwards all stamping on my neck in the scrum to hurt me, so don't be alarmed; and talking about Thomas Meighan – I can do that sort of thing.
                                        (herewith)
                                        (lover)
                                        Absolutely yours Malcolm
[P.S.][b]

         Did you
            mention
         he – men.
         Here's one!!
         I don't know how many per cent.
         Nor his name.

His wifes name, however, is very
Likely Wilhelmina Ermyntrude.

Annotations:

1 O'Cedar is the brand name of a popular line of household products.
2 Émile Coué (1857-1926), the founder of the healing system known as
   Autosuggestion, was very popular in England and the United States
   during the 1920s. In 1921 a Coué Institute was opened in London, and
   by 1922-23 his books were available in English translations. Coué popularized the saying 'Every day in every way, I get better and better'; hence
   Lowry's remark.
3 The Reverend Harry Bisseker (1878-1965) was the author of several
   books on religion and headmaster at the Leys from 1919 to 1934. If
   Lowry is to be trusted, Bisseker served Italian vermouth to distinguished visitors to the Leys.
4 Benn Levy (1900-73), who was educated at Repton and Oxford, became
   an active playwright after the success of his first play, *This Woman Business* (1925), which played at the Haymarket Theatre from 15 April to 25
   September 1926. The play was described in the *Times* of 16 April 1926 as
   a 'ludicrous exposure of misogyny' because the wife of the piece
   becomes a compliant angel in the house.
5 Thomas Boden-Hardy was a fellow student at the Leys.
6 The British Lord Chamberlain began his functions as play censor and
   licenser of theatres with the Licensing Act of 1737. His role as censor
   was not abolished until the Theatre Act of 1968.

Editorial Notes:

a. This letter is written in black ink on five pages of lined notepad paper
    approximately 16.5-by-18.5-cm.
b. This fragment may have been included with the letter as a comment on
    the reference to Thomas Meighan, but it is now impossible to confirm
    its status. It very likely accompanied a Lowry sketch of a 'he-man' that
    has not survived, and it has been written in black ink on lined 16.5-
    by-18.5-cm paper.

14: To Carol Brown

P: Tulsa(ms)

[Leys School,]
[Cambridge]
[7 June 1926]
Dates and things[a]

You're too sweet for words, Carol: you say, hope you're fit and happy – especially the last: yes, I'm as happy as anything thanks – that is if you are. I say, it's jolly good your winning all these tournaments and going in for them: poor girl – Aigburth's a rotten sort of hole to get to:[1] the last time I went there I went with Tom Pryce-Parry – (we were playing for Hoylake – v Liverpool II at rugger) – but there were baths and things to get into afterwards, and quite good browsing and sluicing: I remember one jolted there and back in a tram. Were you thinking of doing that? I like trams: it amuses me studying the expressions of the people strap-hanging. Good lord – woman, do you win everything, always. The fourth round, – it's perfectly ripping I think.

I say, I'm awfully sorry about that telegram. I'm afraid its my frightful fault of always trying to be funny: I mean, I wanted to be funny, and a telegram is such a poor medium for humour. I suppose you consider me several sorts of mess not being more explicit: however I'll write to your Mother telling Her exactly How – Why, and When. I've been endeavouring to write a love story for your delectation: not very successfully – either. Thanks awfully for the snap: I found the frog – you had kindly silhouetted him for me.

No, Carol you never once laughed at me. You've been kindness and unselfishness itself, all the time because its your nature, I know, and I don't care how conventional this phrase is, I'm not worthy to lick your shoes. And its me who's being selfish if I ever said I was unhappy, because I'm not. It's only a pose. I love you so much that it's you I want to see happy, and I feel afraid I'm annoying you and spoiling your peace of mind. Do tell me if I am.

If you suddenly took into your head to get engaged to your six foot actor friend or anybody, sudden-like – I'd say Hell or something probably, but I'd know you were happy – and I'd know you'd feel ill at ease because you thought *I* was unhappy. So I just would'nt be. I should hit old Russell on the back and say 'Hi, Russ. I'm the happiest man in the world': and go off & blub or something ridic, because that – I suppose – is what you'd like me to do under the circumstances.

I've been doing a certain amount of bathing lately up at a place called Byron's Pool – which is the world's worst place for bathing.

Reedy and foul, but it is better than the school baths which smell of peoples' feet. However it's not so bad, especially afterwards – it's quite nice to be in the sun being lazy and smoke Woodbines. Mac & Nick both rather disdain Byron's Pool – and I have'nt seen very much of them for some time – as I have craved solitude.

One can rarely find it up at Byron's Pool, though: [there're] so many trippers trying to find the idyllic spot of Byron's poem.[2] And between you and me – there's no idyllic spot at all. Several old syrup tins, a legging or two, an overturned Trespassers will be prosecuted notice among the nettles . . .

It's a wonderfully hot night and I'm writing this in prep. An aeroplane is making the deuce of a noise, and we've got a House Parade to-night: Officers Training Corps – bad institution: left right left right Carol-Carol – fix Carol
Bayonets – slope arms Carol Carol halt, stand easy a minute, Carol, Carol. Platoon. Properly at ease. Carol. A good slope. Slo-ap arms! Come on Lowry, keep in step – you're the world's worst soldier, left right, left right, Carol Carol Carol. Right. Halt. Form Two deep. Carol.

Sunday

Dear Carol: I mean far more than I may ever hope to put in words and all of that: but I've reached that state where I'm desperately afraid of feeding you up to the teeth with my sentiment.

You only like me, don't you – and I'm not anything like grateful enough for that.

Your pal always.

Malcolm

Annotations:

1 Aigburth is a suburban area of south Liverpool.
2 Byron's Pool is located at Grantchester, about two miles south-west of Cambridge, and it was a favourite spot for picnics and fishing in Lowry's day. Although Lord Byron (1788-1824) does describe the pleasures of swimming in the River Cam in 'Childish Recollections' from *Hours of Idleness*, the poem Lowry must be thinking of is the sonnet by Charles Edward Sayle (1864-1924) called 'Byron's Pool' from *Erotidia* (1889). See *A Book of Cambridge Verse*, ed. E.E. Kellett (Cambridge: Cambridge University Press, 1911), p. 337.

Editorial Notes:

a. The envelope with this letter is postmarked 7 June 1926, and the letter is written in blue ink on two pages of lined 16.5-by-23-cm scribbler paper with some deletions and additions in Lowry's usual black ink. 'Dates and things' has been added at the top right of the page in black ink. Lowry has also written 'Dear Carol' in the same ink but crossed it out.

15: To Carol Brown

P: Tulsa(ms)

[Leys School,]
[Cambridge]
[10 June 1926]ᵃ

Dear Carol

Excuse the typewriting, Never care! There's a good old thunder-storm rattling about outside: woops – a flash of lightening's just rocketed across the opposite window; one, two, three; brrrrr: a heavy one. A good accompaniment to writing a letter. What I really wish was happening now is that we were out in this jolly old thun-derstorm, and you were afraid of thunder or something, and I could protect you from it. As a matter of fact, you probably love thunder . . . . by Jove I swear I was struck by lightning then . . However, I'm still alive. To continue.

I'm writing an unpleasant story (inspired by Pirandello's 'Man with a Flower in his mouth'),[1] about a man with cancer of the lip, and almost at the end of his tether, who invites his old doctor down to spend the weekend. They pass the time away over the fireside by ex-changing yarns, and my man with cancer of the lip keeps forgetting that there's anything wrong with him.
Subsequently . . . . but that's as far as I've got, and I've committed the one fatal error in writing a short story, writing the beginning before the end. If you can think of any ending to the story – fire it along, and we'll go fifty-fifty. By the way, if you can think of any plots, send them along and we'll do a 'Malcolm Lowry and Carol Brown.'

A remark occurs;
'The doctors gaze narrowed, grew more intent; he did not exactly squint, but looked at me like a dog might when it knows its master is going to say Fetch-it.' That reminds me of one of Walter de la Mare's stories;[2] plagiarism is the form of theft least dangerous to society.ᵇ
Think of that when writing a poem on Spring.

Editors are taking to writing me letters. I had a letter from the editor of the New Magazine[3] – the other day, bearing the postmark Southend-on-Sea. The poor man was taking his holiday, and had had my story forwarded to him. Editors very rarely write letters. This laddie said that it took him two minutes hard brooding to understand the story. This, he said, would never do for the New. He welcomed fresh authors but . . . What about the Strand. Or Truth?[4] People in the train didn't want to think, or weep. They wanted to be amused. The New was essentially a magazine for the man in the corner seat: he would look out with great interest for a story by Malcolm Lowry elsewhere. It will take me all my ingenuity, and Thomas Boden Hardy's typewriting, placing, and power of licking stamps, to succeed.

Several days *later*

Carol, may I be sentimental?   I may.   Thanks.

It's rather a pity that boats are a couple of guineas a leak, sort of thing; it's May week, as you know, of course, of course. I've never watched the Mays yet: slack of me, but there it is, thousand of people stand on lawns in the rain, try and peer over peoples heads, and cheer a winning crew which they can't see.[5] Lot o' fun.

But the actual colleges themselves, as you know, are topping. Indubitably, so. Kings College Chapel is worth walking a hundred miles to see. I saw a good film the other day, at least it amused my little mind, about – what's that subtitle – where men are men, and women kiss straight from the shoulder: Buster Keaton in 'Go West.'[6] I must say that Brown Eyes, the cow, tickled me to death. Have you seen it? You have. Is it good? No – Sorry. Carol, my old girl; you must think I'm a dashed rotten sort of fellow; I've been most unstraightforward, I think; I told you I loved you, in a letter, I say almost everything by post like in the romance of Daddy Long Legs.[7] When can I tell you to your face, old dear? Will you cut the peculiarly boring swimming exhibition which follows the ghastly speeches and let me just talk to you, for four minutes, five minutes, a quarter of an hour, anything just to let me hear all about yourself. Oh, and tell me something about yourself – won't you: you say that your letters are egotistical – why, there not egotistical enough! Carol, my little darling – I love you. Oh, far more than all these three other people; they may have loved you, but they didn't LOVE you.

I'm writing this in no. 7 classroom, which is divided by a thin wall from the junior dormitory, where Mr W.H. Barrel-organi is reading 'The Monkeys Paw.' aloud. I reverently think that that is, next to Conrads 'Typhoon,' the best short story ever written.[8]

I can almost hear Coll [Colin Brown] shaking with fright.

Well, well; must get a drop o' sleep.

Good night, Carol, you old Bohemian—

—I love you.   Malcolm

P.S. You'll never know how much I love you. It's too much for words.

6,000,000

The *day after to-morrow*.

—Carols. v. dear. I;

　　　　　　I can't write anything very much because
this pre is regarded me very balefully: thus,

if you understand me:
most offensive. Can't
draw.　　However.
Awaiting yours.
　With fear,
　　　trembling
　　　and delight

Malcolm

Figure 4

Annotations:

1　Luigi Pirandello (1867-1936), the Italian playwright, novelist and short
　story writer, remained a favourite of Lowry's throughout his life. His
　most famous and influential work in the English-speaking world was his
　1921 play *Six Characters in Search of an Author*. *The Man with the Flower in
　His Mouth* (*L'Uomo dal fiore in bocca*) was written as a story in 1918, then
　as a play, and translated into English in *Dial* 75 (1923): 313-22. This
　grim little play about a man with a carcinoma of the lip who pours out
　his obsessions to a stranger is an intriguing choice of model for the
　seventeen-year-old Lowry.
2　Walter de la Mare (1873-1956) was a popular English poet and short
　story writer. Lowry is paraphrasing a passage from de la Mare's story
　'Missing,' which was first published in *The Connoisseur and Other Stories*
　(London: W. Collins Sons, 1926), pp. 47-97. Like so many of de la
　Mare's stories, 'Missing' contains two characters, but these two re-
　semble those in Pirandello's story; they are a man who listens to a tragic

story and a disturbed stranger who tells it. The plot of 'Missing' has little in common with the situation Lowry describes in his story, but at an early point de la Mare's narrator describes his loquacious companion in the words Lowry has chosen to borrow: 'He looked at me, his eyes seeming to draw together into an intenser focus. He was not exactly squinting, but I have noticed a similar effect in the eyes of a dog when its master is about to cry "Fetch it!"' (52) De la Mare's collection of stories first appeared in May of 1926 and was reprinted twice in June; therefore, Lowry must have been reading 'Missing' while he was working on his own story. In his following reference to plagiarism, Lowry is not plagiarising de la Mare but, whether he knows it or not, Voltaire, who described *le plagiat* in his *Dictionnaire philosophique* as 'assurément de tous les larcins le moins dangereux pour la societé.'

3 *New Magazine* published light fiction during the 1920s from its London address on Ludgate Hill.

4 Both *Strand Magazine* and *Truth* were London magazines that published short stories.

5 In 1926 the boat races took place from Thursday, 3 June to Saturday, 6 June. The races consist of many crews of 'eights' in one long line chasing the boat immediately in front and attempting to 'bump' it. The object of the race is to move up a total of four places in the line by bumping the preceding boat on each of four successive days. Spectators stand along the banks of the river and are able to see only what occurs at their observation point.

6 Buster Keaton's *Go West* was released by Metro-Goldwyn-Mayer in 1925. Keaton both directed the film and played the role of its hero, Friendless, who develops a true friendship with the cow Brown Eyes.

7 In Jean Webster's 1912 epistolary novel *Daddy-Long-Legs*, the orphaned heroine writes regularly to her anonymous benefactor. The novel ends with her discovery that 'Daddy-Long-Legs' is in fact the young man with whom she has already fallen in love.

8 W.W. Jacobs' story 'The Monkey's Paw' (1902) must have been a favourite at the school, or at least with Mr Balgarnie. In the following term, on 17 November 1926, the dramatized version of the story was performed before the Literary and Debating Society. Joseph Conrad's 'Typhoon' first appeared in 1902.

Editorial Notes:

a. The letter, written partly in pencil and partly in black ink on three pages of 16.5-by-23-cm lined paper, is undated, but the postmark on the envelope is 10 June 1926. Judging from Lowry's reference to the Mays, it must have been written during the first week in June. Lowry has written a number at the top of each page thus: 1, 2, 303, 4004, 500,005, and 6,000,000, and he has sketched a rather comical-looking prefect on the left side of the third page; see Figure 4.

b. Lowry has printed MAD in large letters in black ink across this pencil paragraph.

16: To Carol Brown

P: Tulsa(ms)

[Leys School,]
[Cambridge]
[June 1926]ᵃ
Avenue de Blazes –

Dear Carol; Thanks awfully for your letter.
Poor Carol! I didn't mean to worry you ever, I didn't know for certain that you liked me enough for that. And as for the intemperance question in the British Isles, don't confuse it with any sort of courage. I am capable of saying anything in my half ribbicked frog moods; when you really go out of your way to be uneccessarily nasty; and I'm perfectly certain, if I had not given up hope – that I should just cry hoot and drown my sorrow in seven pints of bitter a day for a week, which would make me tight for a fortnight. This would be repeated; and this is not a sign of courage at all, but of superlative weakness. But on reflection, I have come to this conclusion. There's considerable hope. In the first place you don't know your own mind, old bean. You write one thing; you say another; and you act altogether differently to both. No matter; I like it that you were once stung over 'This Man Business.'
That doesn't make me feel jealous, it only makes me want to have been able to put my hand on your shoulder and sympathise, when you must have experienced that horrible, empty, feeling, which told you that nothing would ever come right again. Poor dear little Carol!
Otherwise, for all your eighteen years, you're only a child. (I'm almost seventeen, and I know.) You don't know what you want, except a good time. Righty ho. Ça va bien. Have your good time. If I was ever engaged to you – all my good time would be just looking forward to when I was going to see you again. You, you say, would play the super-super-faithful woman. There was never anything so sweet; but one may be faithful, love, go to dances, and have a good time all at the same time. Reflect on that.
And besides one's only eighteen once (or seventeen), and remember the song; you will find it (by some irony of fate,) on the other side of 'Just a little drink' – on Columbia.[1]
– I should like to meet your actor friend; mind you, don't believe for

a moment he's in love with you, none of my business of course, but he isn't, he likes you to take him out in your Austin 7:[2] there's a difference, you know. Carol, I don't know however you got it into your head that I was a serious, responsible, cove – with principles. Although I've met quite enough women, none of them are worthy to lick your shoes, and the idea of 'mixing with other women' in the way you suggest sounds pretty grim to me. Dash it I'm not a misogynist or anything, and there're plenty women in Cambridge. Also if it wasn't for you, I'd hardly have a care in the world. Certainly before I met you I swear I was always lighthearted.

Mac and I have heard a joke at breakfast, laughed all through chapel, and through four morning periods, heard another joke at lunch, laughed all afternoon, laughed so much at our 3'oclock coffee at the Friar House that we were nearly chucked out – laughed into chapel at night, out of it again, into bed – laughed ourselves to sleep and woken up with a smile on our faces.

That, I admit, does sound serious.

When I met you, it struck me all of a sudden like that it was about time young Malcolm pulled himself together, and looked as though he meant something.

Do you know that beyond a certain perspicacity (spelling very doubtful) to write, and not much of one at that – I am the world's greatest 'don't care two hoots,' or try to be. What on earth is the good of worrying – of rotten little principles about life, and all of that – why not live while you've got breath and eyes?

I love you because I feel you're part of me; and hitherto I've felt rottenly shy and awkward in your presence: —— (re Description of a Demented Frog, Hudsons Book of Nature).[3]

Kind hearts, woman, are better than coronets;[4] there's no need to go about shouting the fact, but there it is. What you want, Carol, is to be thoroughly spanked with a slipper & by me, if it comes to that. You're too sweet for words, but you want to get rid of these notions about my being a staid old parson. Religion, I assert, is like a school tie tied round a pair of white flannels – if it is tight, it is uncomfortable; and if it is loose, you might as well have none at all.

You say, old thing, that you like 'em bad. I don't know what you mean exactly by bad, but the school rule is yet to be made which Mac and I haven't broken. I should think we've done most things short of sprinting off to London after chapel, and spending the night at Ivor Novello's Fifty-Fifty Club where evening dress, I understand used to be optional, before the club was struck off the register.[5] Sorry, I haven't done that for you, but there is yet hope.

Balgarnie used your very words to me the other day;
He said:

(cough) Lowry, we mustn't be so irregular, we must (cough) obey school rules more – (cough). I was thinking of reccommending – er – you for (cough), a sub-prefect next term, but I perceive we're going to be irregular gently (cough) – we mus'nt be so irregular – don't be such an *irresponsible fool!*

I don't claim to be your very own irresponsible fool at the moment, because you apparently next door to hate me. There is also nothing to be proud of in being one – but you appear to so like him!

Yes, you were very cruel to me during the Speech day weekend, your best remark being the one:

'Oh, of course – I've only been yielding lately. You see I had to go through the spring alone. I don't like you nearly enough . .'

That's good enough for a play. I like it. Wonderful. But don't think I'm particularly literary; I like reading good books, as I think you ought to, and I like writing, but that's only my whim, like your drawing.

Well, god bless you

The Barnacle

P.S. You will find 'The Ringer' at Wyndhams, a show of The 'Bat' calibre. Red Hot. See it. Wyndhams telephone no. is Regent 3028.[6]

P.S. I'm afraid I've never been vain enough to push along to those dear old blighters whose motto is smile and the world smiles with you, cry and the world smiles at you – you know what I mean – what d'you call 'ems – photographers, for the purpose of obtaining a facsimile of my face. Mac however took a photo of me the other day on an asbestos film (I hope) – if this same comes out, I will send it to you. If you don't want it, send it back again. As there was more or less the party of us, we all so to speak, took photographs of each other. I will send you photographs of each other. If you don't like them – send them back again. If you consult the back of your Magazine Programme at the Theatre – you will discover that it is impossible to buy an ice or a chocolate after 9:30. Don't forget that. Don't forget me either. And if you don't like this letter, send it back again.

Annotations:

1 The song on the other side of Columbia's 1925 recording of 'Just a Little Drink' is 'Dromedary.'
2 The Austin 7 was the first English compact car and marked the start of mass motorization in Great Britain. After its appearance in 1922 as a diminutive family car, two-seater coupes and sedans were designed for a sporty look.
3 In *The Book of a Naturalist* (London: J.M. Dent & Sons, 1924), W.H. Hudson describes the frog pursued by a snake as follows: 'After some futile efforts to escape, the creature collapses, and stretching out its forefeet like arms that implore mercy, emits a series of piteous, wailing screams' (134-35).
4 Lowry is echoing the words of the male speaker in Alfred Lord Tennyson's poem 'Lady Clara Vere de Vere' – 'kind hearts are more than coronets' (l. 55). See *The Poems of Tennyson*, ed. Christopher Ricks, vol. 2 (Harlow: Longmans, 1987), p. 64.
5 The Fifty-Fifty Club, run by Constance Collier and Ivor Novello, flourished in London's West End during the mid-1920s. With its relaxed atmosphere and orange and blue interior decorated with theatrical caricatures, it was intended primarily for theatre people. After the socialites discovered the place, however, the actors stopped coming and the club died. It was 'struck off the register' in April 1926 after a police raid on 27 February. Club members were arrested and fined for consuming liquor without food after hours, but the premises were closed for only six months; see the *Times* for 24 March and 14 April 1926.
6 *The Ringer* (1926), a detective drama by the popular English novelist and playwright Edgar Horatio Wallace (1875-1932), played at Wyndham's Theatre in London from 1 May 1926 until 23 April 1927. *The Bat*, by Mary Roberts Rinehart and Avery Hopwood, was one of the most popular mystery dramas on Broadway; it ran for 867 performances in 1920 and went on to become a favourite with stock and amateur theatres.

Editorial Notes:

a. This letter is written in black ink on both sides of three pages of lined paper of differing sizes. The postscript continues on the recto of the fourth page. Since Lowry describes Carol Brown below as having been 'very cruel' to him on Speech Day, this letter must have been written *after* 18 June.

17: To Carol Brown

P: Tulsa(ms)

[Leys School,]
[Cambridge]
[23 June 1926]ᵃ

Dear Carol,

– Do you know the story about Mʳ Stringfellow? You don't. This is it, in brief.

Mʳ Stringfellow was a little man, who did the same things at the same time, rotted in a little office, had never had any excitement, whose lanlady came of a class who would scratch and scrape through life for an expensive funeral after death, who delighted in horsehair sofas and stuffed parrots. Mʳ Stringfellow eat rusks. And then an aunt died in Colombes (near Paris) – leaving Mʳ Stringfellow £80 odd (11200 fr. 0 cent. circa); it was therefore necessary for purposes of executorship or something that he should go to Paris. Mʳ Stringfellow obtained permission from his office (Hoopdrivers Ltd.) and went – and had the very devil of a time in Paris, just for a week. And then he had to go back, back to rot in his little office, back to his lanlady who would scratch and scrape through a laborious insolvency in life – for an expensive funeral after death, who delighted in horsehair sofas and stuffed parrots – back to his rusks, (his memory of the only enjoyment he ever had in his life uppermost in his mind – yet never to be repeated,) and always in his ears the reccolection of the whoosh-whoosh of the boats at Boulogne . .

For the moment I am Mʳ Stringfellow. (modernized version). Cambridge (for 3 days) has been my Paris.

A promise is a promise, and I'm not talking about IT – but when you say, and this is a direct quotation from 'The Letters of Carol Brown' (Chatto & Windus[1] 7/6) – 'and if I can help it, you will not have another rival for many years to come,' and 'when you grow up I think you will be the finest man I have ever met' – and 'though I don't love you as yet, I think I may come round to your way of thinking in a year or two'; though I understand it now as being merely lines dashed off, as you would dash them off for anybody else, just for amusement's sake – You can understand, that being a more or less human sort of a fellow, I thought, and indeed – have, ever since I have known you – thought, and do still think, that you were and are the Only, Only One——FOX TROT.

SAVOY ORPHEANS (at the Savoy Hotel, London).[2]

This made me think that you liked me slightly, and after all, it is but natural that I should believe what you say, whatever time of the day or night you may have written. Admit that – you can't deny it. But, here, I'm a brute saying all this. Forget it, like I am trying to forget that your first, last, and middle name is amusement. I've been thinking hard, and come to the conclusion that I was, and am selfish. Not intentionally. I perceive that however low a type of human being I may be, you must take some sort of indefinite interest in me, for the simple reason that I love you. Parallel; a dog: qualities, faithfulness, devotion; only you don't like me nearly as much as that: however you experience some sort of feeling of proprietorship and responsibility that I shouldn't absolutely go to the devil. If I went by your letters, I'd say you were positively fond of me, but then I am learning not to do that. The net result of all this is that loving you as I do, I shall try to devote myself to trying to make you happy. The way I shall do this is presumably to write you less, and to act as mediator for any scrapes you might like to pass off on me. I will do anything for you – even if it is to affect a reconciliation between you and someone else.

And, though I love you, I'm inclined to think that there are drawbacks if ever in the dim future _we_ did get married. (God forbid, says Carol) No 1: – My eyes aren't exactly the world's best manufactured articles; therefore my dreams shattered and all of that – I prefer to stand as your Friend, which seems to me to be the only reasonable way out of the difficulty (– unless –)

Thine

LOBS

P.S. R.S.V.P. at The Vaudeville is a good revue.[3]

Annotations:

1 Chatto & Windus is the name of a London publishing company, founded in 1855 and later associated with the Hogarth Press and with the Bodley Head and Jonathan Cape group.

2 'The Only Only One (for Me)' was a romantic song of 1924, with words by Bud Green and music by James V. Monaco and Harry Warren. It may well have been played by the Savoy Orpheans, a very popular dance-band first directed by Debroy Somers, which began playing at the Savoy Hotel in London in 1923. The Orpheans made regular radio broadcasts and were one of the best-selling recording groups of the 1920s.

3 *R.S.V.P.*, by Archibald de Bear, Norman O'Neill and Greatrex Newman, played at the Vaudeville from 23 February to 6 November 1926.

Editorial Notes:

a. This date is from the postmark on the envelope with this letter, which
    was mailed from Cambridge to Carol Brown at Little Gables, Stanley
    Gardens, Wallington, Surrey. Lowry has written in black ink on five
    pages of 16.5-by-19-cm lined notepad paper.

18: To Carol Brown

P: Tulsa(ms)

Deep Elm.

[Summer 1926]ᵃ

Dear old Carol,

I'm sorry I've been so long in replying. It's not spite, or anything;
it's just that I felt so glad I didn't know what to say. And now I've
waited long enough in all conscience, I don't know what to say a bit,
either: except of course that I'm glad – not for myself of course – but
for you, really. I'm not posing. I suppose you mean you've fallen in
love with some priceless old bean – Eh? Or have you only won a
tennis championship. I suppose the happenings mean the former.
Well, old thing, accept my very heartiest congratulations in all directions; I always was a complete mug myself, and I couldn't possibly
hope that you could love me, despite my hideous rantings, and
arrogance; I mean that I'm exactly the same as ever, but of course a
jolly old friend and all of that. Dying to see you next hols.[1]

[unsigned]

Annotations:

1   If I am correct in suggesting that this is Lowry's last letter to Carol
    Brown in this sequence of letters, then the next school holiday would be
    the summer vacation, which ran from 28 July to 16 September 1926.

Editorial Notes:

a. This undated letter is written in black ink on the recto of a 16.5-
    by-19-cm page of lined notepad paper. The page is badly worn, torn in
    places, and appears to have been crumpled up and then smoothed out
    again. It has clearly been folded in half, as is characteristic of Lowry
    with this size of paper, but it is impossible to say when it was written
    or whether it is complete as it stands. I have put it last in this sequence
    of letters to Carol Brown because it seems to signal the end of Lowry's
    little romance.

19: To The Editor, the Leys *Fortnightly*

P: Leys
PP: *Fortnightly* 51, 892: 109-10

Leys School,
Cambridge
16 December 1926

Dear Sir,

I am not going to be arrogant here about Mr Gardner or Mr Raper, whom we know personally as admirable and capable higher brethren; rather do I mildly declare that it was not without a certain emotion that I read not long ago in your *L.F.*, chronicled in the account of the Old Leysian Debate, published by the admirable Mr Gardner and attributed to the capable Mr Raper the following statement, 'Public School men are better than self-made men,' classified boldly as one of 'three good points.'[1] Just like that. Now I did not attend the meeting and so was not privileged to hear Mr Raper's no doubt excellent speech, but I do affirm that if ever he did drive such a point home (and many unscrupulous things happen in our Lit.) it was most emphatically not a good point, and I consider that some degree of fault lies with Mr Gardner in not hushing it up immediately instead of pillorying it in the *Fortnightly* with the lurid remark the following Friday week. A mere bagatelle; yet I may say that less self-complacent remarks than this have caused journalists to make revolution in Fleet Street, outraged teetotalers to marry barmaids, and rusk-eating vegetarians to write testimonials for the Mustard Club. 'Public School men are better than self-made men.' Why on earth? Are we such extraordinary men? Surely something is lacking if a statement like that can be singled out by a level-headed prefect and labelled 'a good point.' Granted Mr Gardner wrote in a hurry, and Mr Raper spoke impromptu (for all I know); yet such an idea ought never to occur to us. So called Patriotism, backing up one's House and School in lieu of a country comes more or less naturally; if it doesn't, it is soon taught. But 'Public School men are *better* than self-made men' is not Patriotism – it is not even snobbery – it is, for lack of a better word, childish. It points to the fact that we have had more 'jelly-bellied flag-flapping' than is good for us. It is like a sick child flaunting a platinum-faced doll before one of those creatures on the back of Barnardo's[2] matchboxes and saying, 'I'm better than you. Look at my raggedy-ann.' The matter is apparently accepted more or less without discussion: we *are* better than self-made men, bless us. If it is someone's curious idea eventually to become 'better,' as it is vaguely called, then let him not cultivate the habit of making remarks like that before he has been started in the process. As I have said, I am attacking neither of the two individuals named, nor the Public School system, nor the Literary and Debating Society, nor the _Leys Fortnightly_, nor dolls, nor Barnardo's matchboxes: I am not altogether a Socialist, nor particularly any sort of fanatic; but I do say that the epigram sky-signed as a good point caused one of your sober and most law-abiding readers to feel as though he were being slowly beaten to death by a short-sighted spinster with Freudian leanings with a sack full of wet dough on a rainy February night in Wigan.

Yours, etc.,

Camel

Annotations:

1 Lowry is responding to J.B. Gardner's report in the _Fortnightly_ for 26 November 1926 of the Annual Old Leysian debate, held on 12 November. The resolution read 'That a public school education is not altogether an advantage,' and it was lost by a vote of twenty-four to sixty-one. G.F. Raper is reported to have made the 'best speech,' and this claim to superiority of public school boys over self-made men was one of his points. Lowry, who was a member of the Literary and Debating Society (as were Gardner and Raper), had been praised by Gardner as having given the best paper at the 14 October meeting of the society. He spoke on 'The Hockey Tour to Paris,' and apparently gave 'an amusing account of the Frenchman's characteristics illustrated with excerpts from his vocabulary' (45-46).
2 Dr Thomas John Barnardo, an English physician, social reformer and philanthropist, founded the Barnardo Homes in 1870. These homes took in destitute children, many of whom were sent out to countries like Canada to live and work.

Lowry could not have known it, but this letter marked the beginning of one of the most dramatic and important relationships in his life. Sometime between the summer of 1926 and the winter of 1928 he had discovered the poetry and fiction of the American writer Conrad Aiken, and so deeply was he moved by Aiken's language and subjects that he wrote to this complete stranger to pay homage. The act was bold, presumptuous, perhaps 'fated,' as he suggests, but it was also typically Lowryan. This reaching out through the written word to the absent, desired interlocutor was one of Lowry's most

characteristic gestures. And it usually worked. Aiken responded by allowing Lowry into his life, his home, and his imagination, only to watch his young protégé steadily out-drink and out-write him.

20: To Conrad Aiken

p: H(ms); UBC(phc)
pp: *SL* 3-4; *LAL* 6-7

> 5 Woodville Road,
> Blackheath,
> London SE3
> [Winter 1929][a]

I have lived only nineteen years and all of them more or less badly.[1] And yet the other day, when I sat in a Lyons (one of those grubby little places which poor Demarest[2] loved, and the grubbier the better, and so do I) I became suddenly and beautifully alive. I read . . . I lay in the warm sweet grass on a blue May morning, my chin in a dandelion, my hands in clover, and drowsed there like a bee . . . blue days behind me stretched like a chain of deep blue pools of magic, enchanted, silent, timeless . . . days before me murmured of blue sea mornings, noons of gold, green evenings streaked with lilac . . .[3]

I sat opposite the Bureau-de-change. The great grey tea urn perspired. But as I read, I became conscious only of a blur of faces: I let the tea that had mysteriously appeared grow clammy and milk starred, the half veal and ham pie remain in its crinkly paper; vaguely, as though she had been speaking upon another continent, I heard the girl opposite me order some more Dundee cake. My pipe went out.

> – I lay by the hot white sand-dunes . . .
> Small yellow flowers, sapless and squat and spiny,
> Stared at the sky. And silently there above us,
> Day after day, beyond our dreams and knowledge,
> Presences swept, and over us streamed their shadows,
> Swift and blue, or dark . . .[4]

I paid the bill and went out. I crossed the Strand and walked down Villiers street to the Embankment.[5] I looked up at the sea gulls, high in sunlight. The sunlight roared above me like a vast invisible sea. The crowd of faces wavered and broke and flowed.

Sometime when you come to London, Conrad Aiken, wilst hog it over the way somewhere with me? You will forgive my presumption, I think, in asking you this.

I am in fact hardly conscious myself of my own presumption. It seems quite fated that I should write this letter just like this on this warm bright day while outside a man shouts Rag-a-bone, Rag-a-bone. My letter may not even interest you. It may not be your intention' *ever* to come to London even to chivy up your publishers.

While on the subject of publishers I might as well say that I find a difficulty bordering upon impossibility in getting your Nocturne of Remembered Spring. Have you got a spare copy of this in Rye that you could sell me?[6] If you have, it would be a good excuse for you to write to tell me so. You could also tell me whether, if you are coming to London any time, you would have any time to see me. Charing X is only a quarter of an hour away from here. But perhaps this letter has infuriated you so much that you have not read thus far. te-thrum te-thrum;[7]

te-thrum te-thrum;

Malcolm Lowry

Annotations:

1 Conrad Potter Aiken (1889-1973), poet, novelist, and short story writer, was a contemporary of T.S. Eliot's at Harvard, but he never became as influential a force as Eliot in modern letters. His work is autobiographical and his prose style highly allusive and lyrical. Like Lowry, Aiken drank heavily, and his influence on Lowry – in this and on literary matters – was not always beneficial. Despite a savage disagreement with Aiken in Mexico in 1937, Lowry retained fondness and respect for the man and his art.

2 William Demarest is the chief protagonist in Conrad Aiken's *Blue Voyage* (London: Gerald Howe, 1927). Lowry goes on to echo Demarest's comment that he liked such places as Lyons tea-houses, 'and the grubbier the better' (342).

3 Lowry is quoting from Aiken's poem 'Palimpsest: A Deceitful Portrait,' *Coterie* 5 (Autumn 1920): 15, which was reprinted as part 4, sections 3 and 5 of *The House of Dust: A Symphony* (Boston: Four Seas, 1920). He paraphrases lines from *The House of Dust* passim.

4 See Aiken's 'Palimpsest: A Deceitful Portrait.'

5 The Strand is the theatre district of London on the north side of the River Thames near Waterloo Bridge. Villiers Street connects the Strand to the Victoria Embankment on the north bank of the river. Lowry may also be echoing lines 65-66 from part 1 of T.S. Eliot's *The Waste Land* (1922).

6 In 1924 Aiken bought 'Jeake's House' in Rye, Sussex. At the time of this

letter, however, he was living in Cambridge, Massachusetts, where he was a tutor of English at Harvard University. Aiken's *Nocturne of Remembered Spring and Other Poems* was first published in 1917.

7 'Te-thrum te-thrum,' the refrain running through Aiken's *Blue Voyage*, is meant to suggest the sound of a ship's engine.

Editorial Notes:

a. Breit and Margerie Lowry give 1928 as the date for this letter; Sugars suggests early 1929. Lowry, who would turn twenty on 28 July 1929, spent January to June 1929 in London being tutored for his Cambridge entrance exams by Jerry Kellett, a former master from the Leys. The Blackheath address was Mr Kellett's home, but how long Lowry stayed there, like so much about the period from late 1927 to early 1929, is not clear; see Lowry's 22 November 1940 letter (**156**) to Aiken.

21: To Conrad Aiken
P: H(ms); UBC(phc)
PP: *SL* 4-7; *LAL* 8-11

5 Woodville Road,
Blackheath
12 March 1929[a]

Tuesday Night.

Sir. (which is a cold but respectful exordium)

It has been said by no less a personage than Chamon Lall once general Editor of a quarterly of which you were an American Editor that – sorry I'm wrong. It has been said by no less a personage than *Russell Green*[1] (and I don't say that it is an original aphorism because one of his others 'Sentimentality is a name given to the emotions of others' is sheer Oscar Wilde) that the only criterion of love is the degree of impatience with which you wait for the postman.

Well, I am a boy and you (respectfully again) are a man old enough to be my father, and so I may not talk of love in the way that Russell Green intended, but all the same, I may here substitute love for – shall we say – *filial affection* and, to apply the aphorism, since I wrote to you my attitude towards postmen has completely changed. Once they were merely bourgeoisie beetles carrying their loads.[2] Now they are divine but hopeless messengers. The mirror opposite the foot of my bed reflects the window set between two mysterious green curtains to the right of the head of my bed and this window – I cheat myself that it (this) is good for my health – I keep open all night. In the mirror I can also see the road behind me when it is light. Early yesterday morning, it must have been about dawn, when I imagined that I could actually *see* in the mirror, I saw a long and never ending procession of postmen labouring along this road. The letters were delivered and among a great pile for other people was one for me from you.

I cannot now remember what you said.

You were pleased that I ended off my letter to you with *te-thrum te-thrum*; *te-thrum te-thrum*; but I can't remember anything else except your handwriting. Of course it was, as I realised bitterly when I woke up, merely a rose–festooned illusion. You had no intention of writing me. {You didn't like the way I asked if you would have time ever to see me in London when you might have *time* but hardly time enough to trouble about having a lunch on someone you'd never seen. I perhaps didn't make it clear enough that I'd go anywhere within my reach from Pimlico to the Isle of Dogs if only there was half a chance of seeing *you*.[3] And then it is possible I should have sent a postal order in anticipation for Nocturne of Remembered Spring because even if you hadn't got it I take it even though you would have found it a nuiseance (spelling mine) you would have sent the postal order back which would have meant at least a cautious letter of some sort ?}[b] But I'm wandering off the point.

The point is this.

I suppose there are few things you would hate more than to be invested with any academic authority:

Well, this I shall say. Next October I am going to Cambridge for three or four years to try and get an English Tripos[4] and a degree. Until October I am more or less of a free lance and a perpetual source of anxiety to a bewildered parent.

The bewildered parent in question would be willing to pay you 5 or 6 guineas a week (I should say six personally, but tacitly) if you would tolerate me for any period you like to name between now and then as a member of your household.

Let me hasten to say that I would efface myself and not get in the way of your inspiration when it comes toddling along, that my appetite is flexible and usually entirely satisfied by cheese, that although I can't play chess and know little of the intricacies of gladioli – I too have heard the sea sound in strange waters – *sh-sh-sh* like the hush in a conch shell, and I can wield a fair tennis racket.

All I want to know is why I catch my breath in a sort of agony when I read;

The lazy sea-waves crumble along the beach
With a whirring sound like wind in bells
He lies outstretched on the yellow wind-worn sands
Reaching his lazy hands
Among the golden grains and sea-white shells . . .[5]

And I want to be in Rye at twilight and lean *myself* by the wall of
the ancient town – *myself*, like ancient wall and dust and sky, and
the purple dusk, grown old, grown old in heart. Remember when
I write like this, remember that I am not a schoolboy writing a
gushing letter to Jeffrey Farnol[6] or somebody.
(Remember too that you must respect me a little for having such
an intense admiration for your poetry. I know you are a great man in
America and that you have your own school of followers, but to me
– in the dismal circle in which I move nobody had ever heard of you,
my most intellectual moments, such as they are, being spent entirely
alone, it was as though I had discovered you and I like to preserve
this absurd idea in my childish mind and give myself a great deal of
unearned credit for having done so.)
Well, to continue I won't weary you by eulogising what you know
yourself to be good (good is quite stupendously the wrong word but
I don't want to appear to gush, you understand.)
  I know almost before you reply – if you do reply – that you are
either away or that you would not have the slightest intention of acting for the shortest period of time as my guardian and/or tutor, but
at any rate do you mind reading this letter sympathetically because
you must have been pretty much the same as me in heart when you
were a kid? And I do want to learn from you and to read your earliest
and most inaccessible works and perhaps even your contributions to
the Dial.[7] I go back home (here is my address – Inglewood, Caldy,
Cheshire) next Monday. Nobody reads at home: the only paper we
take is The British Weekly; there are few books in the house more
exciting than Religions and Religion by James Hope Moulton[8]
(although a careful searcher might find in a somewhat inaccessible
region Donne, Chatterton, The Smell of Lebanon, Crabbe's Inebriety and Blue Voyage)[9] and although I have had a certain amount
of youthful success as a writer of slow and slippery blues[10] it is as
much as my life is worth to play anything in the house – that doesn't
worry me so much – but when they see me writing anything serious
they don't exactly discourage me but tell me that it should be sub-
ordinate to my real work. What my real work is, heaven only
knows, as the only other department that I have had any success in, is
in writing seriously and that success rarely meant acceptance but

quite often sincere encouragement from people whose opinion could hardly be taken to be humble.

But I don't want to worry you with anything I've written and indeed after reading this rackety incoherence you would probably be extremely averse to being worried in that way.

Look here you don't hate me already do you? (hate is too dignified a word.)

Now *if* you are in London any time between when you receive this letter and Sunday (inclus) could you let me know, because you see we have put things on somewhat of a business footing?

I could meet you anywhere in London. And anytime.

Between now and Montag. If not write to my address in the dismal swamp.

Klioklio.[11]

C.M. Lowry

Annotations:

1 During the winter of 1920–21, Russell Green succeeded Chaman Lall as editor of *Coterie, A Quarterly: Art, Prose, and Poetry*, a magazine that published seven issues in London between 1919 and 1921. Aiken was an American editor from 1919 to 1921. *Coterie* was followed by *New Coterie*, which published six issues between 1925 and 1927. Both little magazines were devoted to publishing the work of the avant-garde (including Eliot, Huxley, Aiken, H[ilda] D[oolittle]) and to establishing links with the continent and North America, and they included visual art by leading contemporary artists such as Augustus John, André Derain, and Archipenko. Aiken, Green, and Lall included their own work in the magazine.

2 It is possible that Lowry had read, or heard of, Franz Kafka's (1883–1924) story 'Metamorphosis' (first published in German in 1915 and translated in 1937), and that he is alluding to Kafka's anti-hero Gregor Samsa.

3 Pimlico is an underground station and a district in central London nine kilometres west of Blackheath, and the Isle of Dogs is an area two kilometres north of Blackheath. Shortly after writing this letter Lowry travelled from London to the United States to see Aiken; see annotation 4.

4 Lowry was accepted by St Catharine's College, Cambridge, in March 1929, but he spent the spring and summer with Aiken in Cambridge, Massachusetts, before entering college in October. He took three years to get his degree, a class 3 in the English Tripos, in 1932.

5 Lowry is quoting from 'The House of Dust,' which forms the third symphony in *The Divine Pilgrim*; see Conrad Aiken, *Collected Poems* (New York: Oxford University Press, 1970), p. 137.

6 John Jeffrey Farnol (1878-1952) was an English novelist, author of *The Broad Highway* (1910) and *The Amateur Gentleman* (1913), among other works.
7 *Dial* was an American literary magazine founded in 1880. Aiken was a contributing editor from 1917 to 1919, and he continued to publish poetry and reviews in *Dial* until its last issue in July 1929.
8 James Hope Moulton (1863-1917), a classical scholar educated at the Leys School and King's College, Cambridge, was the author of *Religions and Religion: A Study of the Science of Religion, Pure and Applied* (London: Charles H. Kelly, 1913).
9 Lowry's private library at this time contained a curious mix, including some of the work of the English poets John Donne (1572-1631) and Thomas Chatterton (1752-70); *The Smell of Lebanon: Twenty-four Syrian Folk Songs*, collected by S.H. Stephan, trans. E. Powys Mathers (Leipzig: Talybont Dyffryn Merioneth, 1928); George Crabbe's (1754-1832) poem *Inebriety* (1775); and Aiken's *Blue Voyage* (1927).
10 Lowry is referring to two songs by himself and Ronald Hill (a friend at the Leys School): 'Three Little Dog-Gone Mice: Just the Latest Charleston Fox-Trot Ever' (London: Worton David, 1927) and 'I've Said Good-Bye to Shanghai' (London: B. Feldman, 1927).
11 'Klio klio' is a refrain used by Aiken in *Blue Voyage* to suggest the cries of seagulls.

Editorial Notes:

a. This date is the first postmark on the envelope. Aiken, however, was still in the United States and not in Rye; therefore, the letter was forwarded to Plympton Street on 14 March 1929.
b. The preceding passage has been lightly crossed out, and Lowry wrote diagonally along the lines of the crossing-out: 'Can't express myself properly here sorry.'

22: To Conrad Aiken

P: H(ts)
PP: *LAL* 12-14; *CP* 40-42

[Inglewood,]
[Caldy, Cheshire]
[March/April 1929]

Comments about the poems:[1]
I have included only the poems which I thought would aid you in getting a better understanding of what type of person I am. That

does not mean that I'm a raving radical or some maladjusted fool trying to complain about my fortunes. As a matter of fact, I am quite
carefree and easy to get along with. I have only one word to say in
defense for my work and myself; we're both young and could stand a
goodly amount of polishing. Mr Aiken, I plead with you to give me
a frank criticism and a word of advice. I need it badly in the right
way. And that is: Do you think I have any individual style of my
own or am I unconsciously imitating someone's work. I have been
told by some that I have a tendency to rely upon Whitman.[2] I think
not. I feel that my work is going to be and is different both in text
and spirit. But do I show it. Please give me your frankest opinion.

In my prelude to the Iron and Steel series, I have placed myself
beside Whitman and Sandburg as a singer.[3] I feel that I have a right
to. I did not intend the eyes of mortal man to read a word of the iron
and steel group until I had established myself as a singer comparable
to both. Perhaps the day will never come, if it didn't I intended to
destroy every word, because I, only a nineteen year old youngster,
would be called a fool for attempting to even think myself a man
comparable in standing to Whitman and Sandburg. As you read the
Prelude please remember that I have lived everyword and that all I
need is a better medium of expression for clearer thoughts and
words. I hope that I will receive either your honest encouragement
or your frankest discouragement.

                              Please excuse _poor_ typing.

                              Spiderweb
          The moment hangs from Heaven like a webbed
          Bridge to that invisible wherein
          Necessity's dimensions sometimes win
          Harbors of air, from which the storm has ebbed.

          But we are spiders. And with waiting eyes
          We see sail by, beyond old reach and hope,
          Doomed wings of a distance, small as periscope,
          While dining on a diet of dead flies:

          The black and gold, the gross and gullible,
          We are those spiders who of themselves have spun
          Nets of sad time to sway against the sun –
          Broken by secrets time can never tell.

                              Alcoholic
                    I died so many times when drunk
                    That sober I became

Like water where a ship was sunk
That never knew its name.

Old barnacles upon my sides
Ringed round with pitch and toss
Were given me by mermaid brides,
Immaculate as moss.

Here now, with neither kin nor quest,
I am so full of sea
That whales may make of me a nest
And go to sleep in me.

(Those angels of the upper air
Who sip of the divine
May find a haven holier
but less goodbye than mine.)

Dark Path

By no specific dart of gold,
No single singing have I found
This path. It travels, dark and cold,
Through dead volcanoes underground.

Here flicker yet the sulphurous
charred ends of fires long since I knew.
Long since, I think, and thinking thus,
Ignite, daemonically; anew.

Yet, burning, burning, burning Lord,
Know how this path must likewise come
Through multitudinous discord
The awful and the long way home.

Sonnet

This ruin now, where moonlight walks alone
Uncovering the cobweb and the rose,
I have been here before; loved each dim stone;
If there were shadows I was one of those.
There listening, as in a shell, I heard
Through some invisible, unlettered whole
One true, if not at all eternal, word
Wrung from the weird mutations of the soul;
Palace or hovel, ruin will at last
Make peace of what is waste; take for a time

The hungry future and the bloody past
Into her night. Only the moon will climb
Up broken stairs to towerd might have been
And rest a little, like some poor, blind queen.

cheery ain't they? Spirit took the spider, don't know why – love l.

Annotations:

1 The four poems included here were enclosed with the letter. For
  annotations of the poems, see Scherf, 236.
2 The work of American poet Walt Whitman (1819–92) has little in common with Lowry's verse unless it is the stress upon self-expression.
3 No discrete series of poems called 'the Iron and Steel series' appears to
  have survived, nor is a 'prelude' poem to such a series extant. The
  American poet Carl Sandburg (1878-1967), who was influenced by
  Whitman, is known for his celebration of America and his collection of
  American folklore and ballads. Both poets are noted for the musical
  qualities of their verse. Sandburg published a collection of poetry, *Smoke
  and Steel* (1920), whose title poem attempts to find beauty in modern
  industrialism, and Lowry may have been using this poem as a model
  for his own.

23: To Dolly Lewis

P: unknown
PP: Day 108–09

[ss *Cedric*,]
[September 1929][a]

I ought to be having a good time.[1] A party of Americans & four
architectural students bound for Rome adopted me & unintellectual
whoopee has been made every night. Amazons of liquor flow. Uku-
leles are played, songs are sung. There are heaps of pretty girls on
board and I have kissed three so far. It is all only too easy. One is
even sure she loves me. That is ocean air and gin.

[. . .]

[. . .] that also maybe your mother (kind to me as she was and desperately grateful to her though I am) even now is telling you that she
dislikes me, that I am not enough of a he-man for her, or that she
thinks my hands, which God was not quite sure to make those of an
artist or a bricklayer, and decided on an unsuccessful compromise

between the two, are effeminate. She will undoubtedly tell you that I am bound to have an unsuccessful life and having enumerated the times I have stumblingly contradicted myself will show you just when and where, and how corrupt a liar I am.

[. . .]

I cannot kiss anybody else without wiping my mouth afterwards. There is only you, forever and forever you: in bars and out of bars, in fields and out of fields, in boats and out of boats [. . .] there is only love and tenderness of everything about you, our comings in and our goings forth, I would rather use your tooth brush than my own: I would wish, when with you on a boat, that you would be sick merely so that I could comfort you. Nor is there one ounce of criticism in this. I do not conceal in my heart the physical repulsion which, not admitted to oneself hardly, exists usually in the filthy male. I would love you the same if you had one ear, or one eye: if you were bald or dumb: if you had syphilis, I would be the same; it is the love that one stronger algebraic symbol in a bracket has for its multiple – or complement . . . it cannot live without the other.

[unsigned]

Annotations:

1 After spending the summer with Conrad Aiken in Boston, Lowry accompanied Aiken to South Yarmouth on Cape Cod, where he met Doris 'Dolly' Lewis, the stepdaughter of Charles D. Voorhis, who was a friend of Aiken's. Dolly was in her late teens, according to Day (107), and a competent painter and writer, and the two spent their time together talking about literature and going for long walks. Lowry sailed back to England in September 1929 on the ss *Cedric*, and on the voyage he wrote back frequently to Dolly. See also Bowker (89–90).

Editorial Notes:

a. This letter is described by Douglas Day as being twenty pages in length, but the original letter is not available for transcription. The reprinted fragments are quoted by Day.

24: To Conrad Aiken

P: H(ms)
PP: *LAL* 15-18

> St Catharine's College,
> Cambridge
> [October 1930]

My dear Conrad

Many thanks for your letter; and also for shading, annotating, and connotating the disbursements;[1] myself have had quite a smoothly smiling sort of letter from the old man, which presages well for the future . . . I've moved into new rooms (but the same address) and spent yesterday decorating them, and drank a bottle of whiskey in the process. Half my books seem to have been stolen, blast somebody's eyes. But to make it worse I can't remember precisely what I *did* have. My Sir Thomas Browne's gone, anyway, I'm sure of that: and a Thomas Heywood, in the mermaid edition, or did I lend that to somebody?: and 'Dubliners,' – why Dubliners? ——[2]
'Experiment' is out.[3] I'll send you one as soon as I can lay hands on a copy. Everybody thinks the first prelude's swell – but most everybody is mystified by the third. Who is this person who must be disembowelled, and shown in the *marktplatz*?[4] But I dare say they'll find out, soon enough. There's a large poster of 'Experiment,' with your name in large letters, and all the little suckers in small letters. Damp from the womb!
I played *hockey* for Cambridge town against Fenstanton last Saturday. I've decided on hockey as against rugger, because their team secretary called round (actually!) and said that I was *wanted*, because I hit the ball firmly and hard, and was really quite a person. I'm playing against Peterborough to-morrow, and Trinity Hall college on Saturday, and my own college the week after next sometime which really should be damned good fun. It pleases me immensely playing against my own college. Yet at school I should have hated to play against my own house . . . Still St Caths is different. It looks like a barracks generally. The dining room looks like a mortuary. The college that god forgot! Or a moloch which, sometimes, raises its stone hand to strike —— Nearly all the other colleges have something cloistral and Canterburyian about them, or have produced a Marlowe or a Milton. I'm having dinner to-night in Pembroke in Grays' old room. And both Crashaw & Christopher Smart lived in the same block! . . Canterbury Cathedral.[5]
Christ, that place has ceased to be a fact: I feel it, darkly, in my

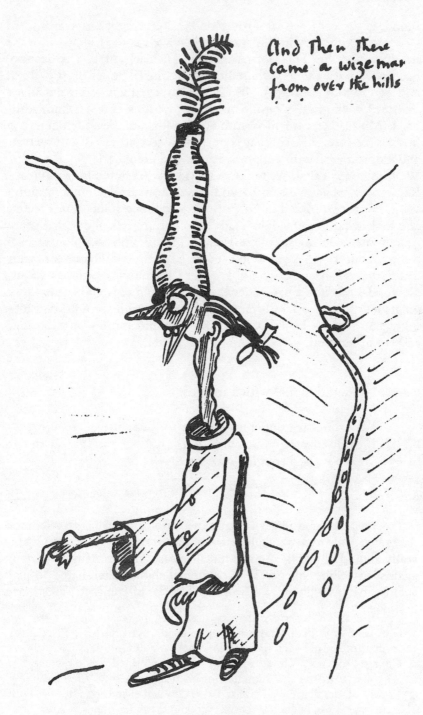

Figure 5: *Lowry enclosed this drawing with his letter.*

blood; in the very plasm of my blood, as one might say: transmuted
– by some kinship with the insentient as well as the living – into the
matrix of my life. The Norman tower. The dark entry. The bapistry
garden. Trinity chapel, where lie the canonized bones of St Wilfred
and St Odo! St Odo! . .[6] Or am I at Crecy, then, with the Black
Prince? I walk gravely beside him. My sword is in its leathern scab-
bard. My leathern shield is embossed with the lilies of France, the
flowers-de-luce. The surcoat is of quilted cotton, faced with velvet,
and embroidered with emblems in silk and gold . . .[7]
Well, my boy, I shall write you a long letter, dictated to my typist.[8]
Remember what I've said to you about drink and women. I don't
want you to get mixed up in any – er – drinking bouts. I never did,
and look what I am to-day. There's no need to talk about that other
little matter, self-abuse, of course not. I know you don't know anything about that. You won't even be tempted. None of your
brothers have been tempted. None of the Lowry-Lowries of In-
glewood-Inglewood have ever drunk, or been tempted in any way
whatsoever. And money – please give me a careful account of everything you spend – I think you spend too much money on shooting,
and repairing your gun –

As ever

Malcolm

I have a gramophone, with 2 records.

you don't mind waiting a little while for your 'Blue Voyage.'? . .
I'd like a game of ping-pong with you, my god! And a visit to Mr
Neeves.[9] Or a walk through Gods acre.

Annotations:

1 Lowry had been sending chapters of his novel, *Ultramarine*, to Aiken for
   corrections; it was not published until 12 June 1933 by Jonathan Cape.
2 Sir Thomas Browne (1605-82) was the English author of *Religio Medici*
   (1643); Thomas Heywood (ca 1574-1641) was an English Renaissance
   playwright; 'Dubliners' is the collection of stories called *Dubliners* (1914)
   by James Joyce (1882-1941).
3 *Experiment*, a Cambridge literary magazine, began in 1928 under the
   editorship of William Empson and produced seven numbers. The editors
   from 1929 to 1931 were Jacob Bronowski and Hugh Sykes Davies.
4 Conrad Aiken's 'Three Preludes' was published in *Experiment* 6
   (October 1930): 33-36, and later included in *Preludes for Memnon* (New
   York: Charles Scribner's Sons, 1931). Lowry is referring to the lines
   from 'xxv': 'God take his bowels out, and break his bones, / And show
   him in the market as he is.'

5 Milton resided in Christ's College from 1625 to 1632; Marlowe in Corpus Christi from 1581 to 1587; Thomas Gray in Peterhouse from 1734 to 1738 and 1744 to 1756; Richard Crashaw in Pembroke from 1631 to 1634 and Peterhouse from 1636 to 1638 (he became a Fellow of Peterhouse in 1637); and Christopher Smart was made a Fellow of Pembroke in 1745. St Catharine's claims James Shirley (1615-17), after whom it names its Shirley Society.

6 Saint Wilfrid, Bishop of York, and Saint Odo of Canterbury, Abbot of Battle, were both at one time supposed to be buried in Canterbury Cathedral.

7 The Black Prince was Edward of Woodstock (1330-76), the eldest son of Edward III of England. He became famous for his victory over the French at the battle of Crécy (1346) during the Hundred Years' War. Lowry, however, appears to be mimicking the voice of a literary character that I have not been able to identify.

8 What follows is Malcolm's parody of Lowry senior's voice.

9 Tom Neeves was the owner of the Ship Inn, Rye, where Lowry and Aiken drank together; see Lowry's April 1952 letter (**516**) to Neeves.

John Davenport – 'beloved old John' and 'dear old Davvy' – was one of Lowry's closest friends. The two met as undergraduates at Cambridge where Davenport introduced Lowry to a set of drinking and writing men. Although they lost touch when Lowry disappeared into his alcoholic abyss in Mexico in 1937 (see letters **73** *and* **78**)*, Davenport re-established contact after* Under the Volcano *was published, and the two enjoyed an appropriately bibulous reunion in Paris in December of 1947. They picked up their friendship again when Lowry returned to England in 1955, and Davenport was one of the last people to whom Lowry wrote before he died. The mixture of drunken word-spinning and literary exegesis in this earliest surviving letter to Davenport typifies both the men and their friendship.*

25: To John Davenport

P: Harvard(ms)
PP: *MLR* 29/30

27 October [1930]ᵃ

Caravan of silence[1]

The third – (Richard Ghormley Ebehart!),[2] unamazed in meditation, looked up from Persia – more likely sailing down the coast by Iloilo,

Zamboanga, Sabang,[3] anywhere, Ebehart Icarus at this time[4] – the tent being not a tent at all so much as the common sea-awning underneath which the crew sleep the deep sea sleep while the ship somnambulates under the Southern Cross: while the mast spears millions of stars: while the feet of Orion blaze: while Hydra, the water-snake, trails her candescent slime: while Alphard glows: and the meandering river of stars, Eridanus flows on in grains of bright translucent rice to bright Achernar: while Scorpio spits his silver venom, Sirius barks his white, hydrogenous bark . . . Alpha Crucis, apogee of the cross, Enunciates his triplexsplutter of helium blue.[5] Drunk. Spiralling wings beyond creation, beyond the mast, beyond the candle shadow, legal fiction, drunk und so weiter drunk. Besoffen![6] That's me.

The *first*,[7] beside him (a seaman sleeping on the hatch!) 'laid his elbow on sleep, on his donkeys-breakfast,[8] all this next part is plain, only the awning is projected into the desert, the seaman is perhaps a *Persian*, & the whole business is objectified on the desert, he had been a pilgrim from Jeddah to Mecca –[9] 'Camels & he like dunes would sleep till the gold ball came over, . . .' hunger & sleep & the *slight untroubling dreams* ununderstood, & never labouring the farsight of cities where no cities stood – not a dreamer not a dreamer, but leave him, pass![10]

The *second* looked upon himself with profound narcissistic compassion & desire, tortured, tired, twisted, betrayed, thirsty etc – a Persian too – he longed for the friendly lights against the night in his home-town Macassar or Basia[11] – in his *mind* he toed warm sand. 'There is a green land and water clear as the night is scarved, place where wait wife and daughter, & the opal unbornface (the child he was expecting when he got home, opal because a *persian*) – The wish is a loud silence & the hope is a star power that shake night with innocence (as the gushes of wind shake the topmast ladder) soft hour on dark hour etc. He took the stigmata of rapture. He drowned in misery & delight. The desire for crucifixion. Here are my hands, drive nails into them! Sharp blows! . . Sea. Sea. Sea. Sea. Sea. Sea.[12] The third – Ebehart himself again – lay awake under the tropical dew, becoming cold, into the third awareness, coming to understand in men's action mankinds desire and destiny[13] – 'the tent was not need for him nor destiny' – Things suddenly were what they really *are* – a Revolution from complex to simple. [Drunken cosmological behaviour] A sudden cosmological vision, as he lay cold & wet on the hatch under the awning, of the x and the y, of the 500 and the

3000, and of the 57 varieties.[14] He knew the oldness of sun & man. He knew 'Earths coldness & goldenness' – which considering [in the light] of the philosopher who turned the globed world *colder* & *goldener* – meant really not cold & gold, but by comparison, emerald and green. Earth is old etc [He lay awake till there was a light in the galley] —— By the philosopher he

> [Red petals in the dust] quite possibly means
> [under a tree the] 'Scientist', merely the man

who denies the existence of fairy rings (on Midsummer Common!)[15] & came to the conclusion that

> Red petals in the dust
> under a tree
> Even so small a thing
> beauty may be/[16] and so on

You mentioned the other night that you desired explication of Caravan of silence. The Caravan is, of course, the ship & the ship the world. This, drunkenly, on the night of October 27th,
    with the love and friendship of your
                      boozem companion
                                  Malcolm

This is clarety (as Bronowski says)[17]

Annotations:

1 This letter-cum-explication was composed for John Davenport (see Lowry's 31 August 1937 letter, **73**, to Davenport) about 'Caravan of Silence,' the title of a poem from *Reading the Spirit* (New York: Oxford University Press, 1937) by the American poet Richard Ghormley Eberhart (1904–). The poem first appeared in *Cambridge Poetry*, ed. Christopher Saltemarsh, John Davenport and Basil Wright (London: Hogarth Press, 1929), pp. 31-32, and was one of sixteen poems, from the thirty-one published in *Reading the Spirit*, to be included in his *Collected Poems, 1930-1960* and in *Collected Poems, 1930-1986*. The poem was dedicated to John Lennox Sweeney, a friend of Eberhart's and Aiken's. Lowry's 'explication,' as he calls it towards the end of this letter, is more a mixture of parody, pastiche, and meditation upon both 'Caravan of Silence' and Eberhart's *A Bravery of Earth* (London: Jonathan Cape, 1930). The two poems are thematically related, but Lowry has virtually conflated the two. In order to interpret the tent in 'Caravan of Silence' as a ship, he is reading the poem *through* the final shipboard section of *Bravery*. He is also, of course, 'drunk und so weiter' (drunk and so on).

2 'Richard Ghormley Eberhart' is a line in *A Bravery of Earth* (121), and Lowry has misspelt, if not parodied, the name throughout this letter.

3 Iloila and Zamboanga are coastal towns in the Philippines, and the Sabang in question is probably the coastal town in Sulawesi (formerly Celebes), Indonesia, on the Makassar Strait (names echoed by Lowry in *Ultramarine*). There is also an inland town called Sabang in Sulawesi and another Sabang Island off the northern tip of Sumatra. However, all these place-names recur in *A Bravery of Earth* (72, 101, and 120) to chart the exotic wanderings and experiences of the eponymous hero of the poem, and Lowry has lifted them from that context to insert them in his own conflation of Eberhart's poems.

4 Eberhart, who later came to know Conrad Aiken very well, had completed the Tripos in English at St John's College, Cambridge, in 1929, several months before Lowry went up to Cambridge. During 1928-29 he was working on *A Bravery of Earth* and studying under F.R. Leavis, I.A. Richards, and T.R. Henn. Friends and acquaintances included many of the people, such as William Empson and Kathleen Raine, who also knew Lowry, and both Eberhart and Lowry had work published in *Experiment* 7 (Spring 1931). The parallel between Lowry's and Eberhart's lives is striking, a fact that Lowry was aware of (see his 7 February 1940 letter, **125**, to Aiken). I have discussed the editing of this letter and Lowry's use of Eberhart in the *Malcolm Lowry Review* 29/30 (1991-92): 64-77. In Greek myth, Icarus, the son of Daedalus, does not listen to his father and flies too close to the sun, which melts his wings; as a consequence, he plunges to his death in the sea. The romantic image of the doomed artist (given a new profile by Joyce in *A Portrait of the Artist as a Young Man*, 1916) appealed to Lowry as well as Eberhart, so if Lowry is being ironic about Eberhart's self-image, he must also be aware of the relevance of the irony to himself.

5 This listing of constellations and stars is characteristic of Eberhart's *Bravery*, but Lowry has deliberately exaggerated the effect.

6 *Besoffen* is the German adjective meaning 'plastered' or 'roaring drunk.'

7 There is no 'first' in 'Caravan of Silence,' but there is a 'third' who is the wakeful philosopher/poet and two others – 'the one beside him' and 'the second' – each of whom sleeps, indifferent to the 'third.'

8 A 'donkey's breakfast' is a sailor's term for his straw mattress, and Lowry uses the expression in *Ultramarine* (43).

9 Jeddah (Jiddi) is a seaport on the Red Sea in the west Saudi Arabia province of Hejaz, and Mecca is the capital of Hejaz and the spiritual centre of Islam.

10 This entire paragraph (like the rest of the letter) is a mixture of direct quotation, which Lowry indicates with single quotation marks, incompletely marked quotations such as 'laid his elbow on sleep,' frequent unmarked quotation, and Lowryan asides and interjections. See 'Caravan of Silence' in *Collected Poems 1930-1986* (New York: Oxford University Press, 1988), pp. 5-6. Images of dreaming, dreams, and

dreamers are frequent in both 'Caravan of Silence' and *A Bravery of Earth*.

11 Makassar (now Ujung Pandang) is a coastal town in Sulawesi (Celebes), Indonesia. There are two Basias, one in India, the other in Sierra Leone. Neither place has any relevance to 'Caravan of Silence,' but Lowry is playing with the sounds of exotic names much as Eberhart does in *Bravery*, where, at least, the hero of the poem travels to the Orient and down the coast of Africa.

12 The phrases from 'Here are' through to 'Sea' are taken from Conrad Aiken's novel *Blue Voyage* (15, 190). Lowry has written 'drive nails into' for Aiken's 'drive nails through.'

13 Here Lowry is quoting from the coda to *A Bravery of Earth*:

> Into the third awareness coming
> To understand in men's action
> Mankind's desire and destiny,
> Youth lies buried and man stands up
> In a bravery of earth. (128)

14 '57 varieties' is a reference to the well-known phrase 'Heinz 57 Varieties,' adopted by the American business man H.J. Heinz in 1896 to advertise his products. The expression was originally inspired by a wide range of shoe styles, but it has now come to be used as a joking reference to something that is a hodgepodge of styles or breeds (as in dogs).

15 Midsummer Common borders the River Cam to the north of the colleges of Cambridge University and to the east of Jesus Green opposite the university's boat-houses.

16 Lowry is quoting Conrad Aiken's 'Red Petals,' an obscure poem first published in *Cartoons* magazine 16, 6 (1919): 919 and not included by Aiken in later collections of his poetry. That Lowry continued to like these lines is clear from his October 1945 letter (**205**) to Aiken, in which he suggests that Aiken reprint it.

17 Jacob Bronowski (1908–74) was a contemporary of Lowry's at Cambridge and a regular contributor to and editor of, along with Hugh Sykes Davies and William Empson, the magazine *Experiment*. Bronowski later became famous for his books on literature, evolution, and science, and for his work with the Salk Institute for Biological Studies in San Diego. The pun on 'clarety' (clarity/claret), which Lowry attributes here to Bronowski, was an allusion and a joke that he shared with John Davenport, who was certainly a 'boozem companion.' In his 12–13 April 1947 letter to Lowry (UBC 1:17), Davenport, who had been reading *Under the Volcano* and remembering his and Lowry's Cambridge days and friends, remarks that they 'should know one another well enough – having indeed shed blood "for clarety" – .'

Editorial Notes:

a. This transcription has been made from an unusual pencil holograph at the Houghton Library, Harvard. Lowry has written on both sides of a single page of approximately 20-by-28-cm heavy, grey-brown paper with the watermark The Fall, 22 Baker Street, W1. The holograph carries no inside address, no name of addressee, and an incomplete date, but it was almost certainly written to John Davenport during 1930-31. When the manuscript was first advertised for sale in the catalogue (item 381) of House of Books, New York (ca November 1965), the entry quoted 'a note sending' the explication to John Davenport (see Woolmer's *Malcolm Lowry: A Bibliography*, 134). Moreover, internal evidence suggests that Lowry was writing to Davenport (see annotations 1 and 3). Lowry could have read 'Caravan of Silence' as early as 1929, when it first appeared in *Cambridge Poetry*, but *A Bravery of Earth*, which Lowry also quotes and paraphrases, did not appear until 1930, thus making the earliest date for the letter 27 October 1930. All material shown in brackets has been lightly deleted by Lowry, but I have retained it in the text in order to suggest something of the impromptu nature of this letter.

26: To Conrad Aiken

P: H(ms)
PP: *LAL* 19-21

2 Bateman Street,
Cambridge
[December 1930]

My very dear old Conrad:

I am a hell of a god-awful correspondent as you know, but Christmas is coming, and Donner and Blitzen are having their manes combed, and anyway I owe you one. I am working hard here, mostly on the novel [*Ultramarine*]. Charlotte Haldane[1] (the wife of J.B.S.) has offered me her body if I finish the revision of it this term. This is all right but I told her that I would masturbate after finishing each chapter in that case with the result that I would run out of semen before *la moment critique*. I think this is very funny. She is very pretty. I don't think I have ever seen anybody so pretty. I read the first chapter, revised and intensified and polished; and she was a bit drunk and fell down on her knees and wept; so I didn't have the heart to tell her that if there was anything good about it it had been copied from you. Christ what a breeze!

Everybody in Cambridge now says Christ what a breeze; and one is not jeered at for an uncritical remark if one says such and such a thing is the 'bees knees' because I tell them you say it.[2] Everybody thought your poems were marvellous, and thinks you are a great man which you are, and a gentle man because you say Christ what a breeze, and bees knees.

I drank a lot of whiskey with Charlotte Haldane last night who is a don's wife and was nearly sick into her mouth when I was kissing her. She says she loves me. This is rather awkward, but very gratifying. She has just published a novel, Chatto and Windus, on monyzygotic twins. It is good and I have reviewed it favourably in an Oxford paper *Revolt*.[3] It is not overflowing with sensibility: and the architechtonics are all away to hell: it is nothing very much, you understand, only very exciting and quite amusingly bawdy. It is full of bloody awful cock, however, even worse than Ultramarine in that respect if you can believe it. Its amateurish, but exciting. She is a first-rate biologist and she wants to meet you. This is not a very good letter. It is sort of early Portrait of the Artist business, without cohesion, however, and a sprinkling of bad Hemingway. Never mind. There is a don's wife in Trinity who has Gonorrhea. Three of my friends have Gonorrhea and I go with them to Addenbrooks hospital and see them irrigated. As for me, I wish I had Gonorrhea, because that would mean I'd had a good fuck which I haven't for the hell of a time. I'm all inhibited in that direction, and have lost my jumbly girl,[4] and am having a bad time with masturbation. I think I am glad I have lost my jumbly girl. Thank god I won't have to buy her horrid little sister a Christmas present! It's damned good your having a radio: but I like a gramophone better sometimes, you get such awful programmes from 2LO, & occasionally even Königswusterhausen[5] lets you down. I know a man who makes the noises in broadcast plays from the B.B.C & we went down to London briefly on one occasion and I saw how it was done. I also know a man called Redgrave,[6] who reads poetry there. He read The Hollow men last week, and we all want him to broadcast you and he wants to and is going to if he can and I have lent him my Priapus and the Pool because you can't buy it in England. The man who makes the noises is a homosexual, but quite decent, and I know him because we are taking part in a film called Bank Holiday,[7] a sort of 'Last Moment' business, next March. Strange!

I have been elected the Editor of Cambridge Poetry – published by the Hogarth Press every year in Hogarth Living Poets series.[8] God – God knows why. Not only my poetic faculty but also my capacity for plagiarism has gone west. But this seems to be an honour. In fact it was the only ambition I had left up here. I must be the first Editor who doesn't know the difference between a trochee and a spondee: and hardly between a sonnet and a chant-royal.

However. My other ambition is to stop masturbating. Which is just bloody impossible. If there were a book on that there would be some sense in making me Editor! I love everything, from soap dishes to medicine bottles. This is damned awful, and all poisoning: as you remarked 'the most all poisoning of all illnesses. But we return to our vomit' . . .[9] Yet ah remain, niggah, and ahs so mighty dat de tornadoes and de hurricanes dey just follow me aroun like little pet dogs, yeah, just like little pet dogs, an ah spits lightning an ah breathes thunder and ah'm the DOOM of Israel . . . And ah'm the champion wirepuller in Tennessee –

I'd just love a copy of John Death, Conrad, it was sweet of you to suggest it.[10] And I'll buy a Selected poems off you – and by god I haven't got that copy of *Blue Voyage* yet, curse me and curse me. Well, I'll see you soon, and we'll break the bloody buskins of the town, and drown in the white winds of the real day.

Better to fall with Icarus than thrive with Smith.[11]

Malcolm

Annotations:

1 Charlotte Haldane (1894-1969) was a journalist and novelist who married the British biochemist and geneticist John Burdon Sanderson Haldane. During their years in Cambridge Charlotte Haldane hosted a literary circle at Roebuck House in Chesterton, into which Lowry was introduced by John Davenport in 1929. See photograph 9. In her third novel, *I Bring Not Peace* (London: Chatto & Windus, 1932), Haldane portrays Lowry as the romantic James Dowd, and she describes Lowry in her interview with Tristram Powell, in *Malcolm Lowry Remembered* (55-56).

2 Aiken uses these expressions in *Great Circle* (1933), the novel he was working on at this time, and Lowry may be mimicking his mentor. Both American expressions, however, were current in England and were used to describe anything especially attractive.

3 Lowry is referring to Haldane's novel *Brother to Bert* (London: Chatto & Windus, 1930); however, no review of this novel was published in *Revolt*, which appeared weekly from 13 October to 1 December 1930, or in *Cherwell*, which took over *Revolt*, during the early months of 1931.

4 By 'jumbly girl' Lowry meant the girl he had sexual relations with. The verb 'jumble,' to copulate, originated in the late sixteenth century and became standard English about 1650.

5 2LO was the frequency 'call sign' for an experimental radio station

established at Marconi House in London on 11 May 1922. Programs were more serious than those available on other stations such as 2MT, broadcast from Writtle. Königs Wusterhausen is the name of a small town located roughly twenty kilometres to the south-east of Berlin. This is where the German radio station Deutschlandsender began its broadcasts on 7 January 1926. It was especially noted for its evening arts programs.

6 Sir Michael Scudamore Redgrave (1908-85), the English stage and film actor, was educated at Clifton College and Magdalene College, Cambridge. Redgrave was a joint editor (with John Davenport and Hugh Sykes Davies) of *Cambridge Poetry, 1930*, Hogarth Living Poets 13 (London: Hogarth Press, 1930), in which Lowry's poem 'For Nordahl Grieg Ship's Fireman' appeared. In his autobiography, *In My Mind's Eye* (London: Weidenfeld & Nicolson, 1983), p. 73, Redgrave speaks of reading Eliot's *Waste Land* over the BBC, but not his 'Hollow Men.'

7 The film *Bank Holiday* (or *Three on a Weekend* in the United States), directed by Sir Carol Reed, was produced by Edward Black in 1938. Lowry's name does not appear in the credits, but Sugars suggests that the man Lowry mentions may be his friend from the Leys School and Cambridge, Michael Rennie (1909-71), who played the part of the guardsman in *Bank Holiday*.

8 The proposed issue of *Cambridge Poetry* to be edited by Lowry was never published.

9 See *Blue Voyage* (195).

10 Aiken's poem 'John Deth' was published in *John Deth: A Metaphysical Legend, and Other Poems* (New York: Scribner's, 1930).

11 Frank Smith is a character in *Blue Voyage*. See also Lowry's 8 September 1931 letter (**35**) to Nordahl Grieg.

27: To Conrad Aiken

P: H(ms)
PP: *LAL* 40

> 21 Woodland Gardens,
> Highgate,
> London N10
> c/o John Davenport
> [January 1931]

My dear Conrad:

I would have written you before this only I got beaten up in an Ulyssean brawl near Kleinfelds' in Charlotte street the first night of my arrival,[1] and have been nursing an injured chin and a twisted lip since then; not so hot. I can't achieve a venividivici look at all in the looking glass, but no doubt I shall get better ——

I shall descend on Rye sometime on Wednesday, I seem to remember there's a train gets in round about 4, but don't depend on that because I don't know whether it's still running; if you're out I'll put up at the Ship or the George or the Mermaid – [2]

As a matter of fact I did write at length four days ago, a dead letter 'that self-conscious, half-literary, hinting thing which I always achieve, – how disgusting!':[3] and I tore it up.

σιγα σιγα[4]

Malcolm

Annotations:

1 Lowry spent Christmas 1930 with his family at Inglewood, then travelled to London to stay with John Davenport over the New Year. According to Bowker (118), Davenport and Lowry were very drunk when they started a fight with a group of Welsh miners in the Fitzroy Tavern, a popular pub with writers and artists that was run by 'Pappa' Kleinfeld. The Ulyssean brawl may be a reference to the 'Nighttown' chapter of James Joyce's *Ulysses* (1922) or simply a description of the size of the fray.

2 These are the names of some of the inns in Rye.

3 Lowry is paraphrasing Aiken's *Blue Voyage*: 'The letters had been in his very worst vein – the sort of disingenuous, hinting thing, self-conscious and literary, which he always achieved (how revolting)' (107). *Blue Voyage* contains several 'unsent' letters in this vein.

4 The translation from the Greek is 'silence silence.'

28: To Conrad Aiken

P: H(ms)
PP: *LAL* 22-25

Globe Hotel,
Hills Road – Camb.
Wednesday
[11 March 1931][a]

Well, buddy, you know what a damned awful correspondent I am by now which is all the fault of my god-complex – is it? – anyway here I am again 'as large as life and twice as unnatural,' a little bit tight, or at any rate a pleasant jingle, which is informing my consciousness of how pleasant it will be to get down to Rye again and see you: that is not to say that my consciousness in this regard is any the less intense when I am coldly and despairingly sober. I don't know so much about the continued despair, in many respects it's just so much bloody nonsense, but in other respects my lack of indifference towards life being divided by this persistent 3, LXX/.333,[1] is deep rooted in an honest enough transmission. Royall Snow, Who would wish to be Royall Snow? or Mrs Untermeyer, the first?[2] or any of the ignoble army of unmartyrs Who are incapable of objectifying their own misery.

The influence that keeps me away from St Catharines really reveals to me how little to myself Death ever leaves me.[3] At all events the force of this revulsion has kept me away now for a whole term from my own college; I hate to connect the place with anything but the buttery[4] [where] you can buy sherry or to give a glimpse of the curiosity that has been on the point of moving me. Now however I am asking myself if I shall stay away for ever from the fear of this muddle about motives. An intricate tangle! . . Anyway, to hell with it. Are we no greater than the noise we make along life's blind atomic pilgrimage whereon by crass chance billeted we go because our brains and bones and cartilage will have it so? . . One mild, two bitters, one Gin. De Kuyper's old square face.[5]

> Our father which art in earth
> our mother which art inturd . . .
> as Martin Case[6] remarked

Thursday

. . . Well, for Christ sake, away with all this melancholy. To day has dawned like the first day, the blessed day of days, when god saw that it was good – – I have been down the road as far as the Varsity Express Motors Ltd to buy a ticket, March 14th, no x 18736, ref no 611, from Cambridge to London, pick up at Drummer St, Run. Time 1:30, for 1 adults at 5/-, no children at nothing, returning date nothing and time also nothing or less than nothing, which will land me in Regent St whence I shall get directly as I can to Rye. I don't know what time I shall arrive at Rye, so don't bother Jerry[7] to get me any supper, but if you could leave me a couple of hard-boiled hen-fruit in a cupboard somewhere that would be – the bees knees I was going to say ——

Yes, this latest Cambridge sausage was as clever a piece of work as ever you saw in a bleeding lifetime, a monster of more than calculation, as you would say, which has left me quite exhausted.[8]

How is the Austrian girl?[9] I believe you showed me her photograph on one occasion and it seemed to me then that she was definitely one of the guards. Am I right? . . A kind of Frau Fletcherchen. Or is she Fraülein? Anyway we shall see what we shall see what we shall see –

The preludes (which I did not acknowledge) – well! Just – er – well! If you won't jeer at me for an uncritical remark, as Cummings might have said, they are among the huge fragilities before which comment is disgusting. Darks edge remains my favourite among them.[10]

Which I did not acknowledge? And after all why should I? . . . is this mr demarest? not william demarest? not william demarest of *Yonkers*? . . yet, even so, what's his address?

Besides I wanted to wait developments which took the form of other contributions – otherwise the book would be a book of preludes published by the Hogarth press, your old friends,[11] & no more, which would be a far better book anyway than the postulated anthology, but scarcely according to the academic points of the compass. Actually the contributions have been so grim, either of the:

      '– the wind was soughing in the boughs –' type
or the   when death   came the critic
      death   came
       when   into
    when d e   the
      a t   roo
      h   m type –

and in the latter case being without any poetry separable and unidentifiable with the so-called strangeness to justify its existence on paper at all that the project has been postponed and with it inevitably our foul crime against truth tra-la . . .

Meantime, 'The dead man spoke to me & begged a penny' (which was not among the ones you sent me but which I learnt by heart some time ago,) is increasingly seeming to me to be one of the greatest poems ever written . . .

  'poor devil why he wants to close his eyes
  he wants a charity to close his eyes
  and follows me with outstretched palm, from world to
               world,
  and house to house & street to street
  under the street lamps & along dark alleys
. & sits beside me in my room, & sleeps
  Upright with eyes wide open by my bed . . .

&

      . . . & all the while
holds, in that void of an unfocussed stare,
My own poor footsteps, saying, I have read
Time in the rock & in the human heart
space in the bloodstream, & those lesser works
written by rose & windflower on the summer, sung
by water & snow, deciphered by the eye
translated by the slaves of memory,
& all that you be you & I be I
or all that, by imagination aping
God, the supreme poet of despair,
I may be you, you me, before our time
knowing the rank intolerable taste of death
& walking dead on the still living earth – [12]

. . . I always think of you being damned angry with me for coming
back late from Hastings —— as ever

                  Malcolm

Annotations:

1 LXX divided by .333 ('this persistent 3') yields a recurring decimal: 210.210210.

2 Royall Henderson Snow was the American critic who reviewed Aiken's *Priapus and the Pool* in 'Agonized Adoration,' *New Republic*, 21 June 1922, 113. 'Mrs Untermeyer, the first' was Jean Starr (1886-1970), an American poet and first wife of the American writer and editor Louis Untermeyer (1885-1977), author of a number of critical reviews of Aiken's poetry and editor of several anthologies of American and British poetry that included Aiken's work.

3 It is likely that Lowry is making oblique reference here to the November 1929 suicide of a fellow St Catharine's student and friend, Paul Launcelot Charles Fitte, which haunted Lowry all his life. For a discussion of the suicide, see Bradbrook (113-16). Between the time of Fitte's death and the writing of this letter, however, there had been a number of other tragic deaths. For example, during February and March of 1931, the Cambridge undergraduate paper *Varsity* featured reports of a student's death at Sidney Sussex College, and the local papers were blaming this tragedy, as well as an earlier suicide at Peterhouse and a double murder-suicide at Kings, on the university and its dons.

4 A 'buttery' is where basic staples such as ale and bread are stored in Cambridge colleges.

5 John de Kuyper & Sons, a distilling company founded in 1695, makes square-face gin and liqueurs.

6 Martin Case, a student of biochemistry at Cambridge and an assistant to
   J.B.S. Haldane, was a close friend; see Lowry's December 1937 letter
   (75) to Case. Lowry's punning couplet is an allusion to Aiken's poem
   'Changing Mind.'
7 'Jerry' was the nickname of Aiken's second wife, Clarissa M. Lorenz.
8 Lowry appears to be responding to a remark by Aiken in a preceding letter, which might explain the nature of 'this latest Cambridge sausage.'
   However, no such letter appears to have survived, and the slang expression 'sausage' could be used for anything from a sexual exploit (i.e.
   penis), a prank, or a misdemeanour to lack of money.
9 The Aikens had an Austrian *au pair* girl staying with them during March
   and April. See *Selected Letters of Conrad Aiken*, ed. Joseph Killorin (New
   Haven: Yale University Press, 1978), p. 174.
10 See Aiken's *Preludes for Memnon* (New York: Scribner's, 1931), p. 62:
   'At the dark's edge how great the darkness is.' In the preceding sentence
   Lowry is paraphrasing the American poet e.e. cummings (1894-1962).
11 Aiken's 'old friends' are Leonard and Virginia Woolf, who published
   Senlin: A Biography in 1925. The Hogarth Press also published *Cambridge
   Poetry*, and Lowry was hoping to include Aiken's 'preludes,' together
   with other contributions, in the next issue.
12 See Aiken's 'XLV,' *Preludes for Memnon* (79-80). Lowry is quoting
   correctly, except for variations in punctuation and capitalization.

Editorial Notes:

a. The postmark on the envelope with this letter is 12 March 1931, and
    Lowry began the letter on Wednesday, 11 March.

29: To Conrad Aiken

P: H(ms)
PP: *LAL* 26-29

                                              [St Catharine's College,]
                                                         [Cambridge]
                                                              Friday
                                                   [24 April 1931]ᵃ

      ' – for Jesus sake – '
      ' – for Jesus sake – '[1]
Well I've just had a motorcar turn over on me at fifty-five and I'm
pretty dopey anyhow; and moreover in several sorts of shite – from
the 'parrots paltry pigment' to 'bombs from the bison's bung'[2] and
any other sort of pickled noblemen you like to think of and I feel so
that every time I read a line I break a bloodvessel. But to be specific

and mostly matter of fact, & to answer the old man's gut-lifting questions.[3] (I) The subject is general English Literature, (II) the exam is on the 20th May although this is subject to slight alteration fore and aft (III) There is only one *Examination* but spread out three hours morning and afternoon for three days or three days and a half & there are no different *subjects* merely papers on different departments of English Literature, first, an original essay on a subject we don't know yet, any given subject; second, a paper on Chaucer & Langland and/or the Life & Thought of that period – you answer only six questions out of a whole gamut; third, the Elizabethans – Ben Jonson & his circle and/or Life & Thought of that period; four, Shakespeare by himself, contexts, folios, rhymes, rhythms danks & darks, imponderables & impalpables, the whole of him but with particular attention to Antony & Cleopatra & Hamlet & Measure for Measure; five – Restoration comedy, Wycherley & so forth and/or Life & Thought of that period; six – General criticism paper, Aristotle – Plato – Matthew Arnold – Coleridge und so weiter: seven, the Preraphaelites, even down to Mr Preraphael himself:[4] eight, the Victorians (and the Orig. Contribution) . . . This is not quite specific because there will be questions backwards and forwards on the whole range of Literature which is impossible to foresee.

(IV) – how well prepared is he in each subject? . . Come on po feet ah needs you now – remember when ah was a chile you promised to be kind to me —— [5]

What about: – in real 'old man' style —— something like this with modifications? He has a good and clear understanding of the trend of Literature and of the nature of the questions involved in the tripos, he is a little weak on Langland and on Restoration comedy & I have told him to work those up during the month left to him, and also to revise the 'criticism' & to do as much general revision as is reasonably possible. As far as I can judge from the papers of former years which Malcolm has – er – showed me they are often of a type which suggests that in preparation for them the student may well be blurred as to the real meaning, the sturm und drang of Literature, and hate it ever after; moreover the time is so limited, that for answering them one has to have a mind like a sort of machine gun, you have no time to think if you are to answer the necessary number of questions, and no time, except (with luck) in the essay to let yourself go on something you really love! Your answers have to be staccato and angry, and a brutal concision is demanded of the student. I think success in this strange examination depends a good deal on temperament. Malcolm is a slow writer, & an even slower thinker, an abnormally slow thinker, which although not itself a fault makes him a bad examinee. I have done everything in my power to correct this for his exam but it is one of those things I have found not only cannot be corrected but ought not to be – it might make him – *tee-hee*! – artificial and false in his reasoning in later life. The thought of failing him worries him on your account and he is quite capable of forgetting all he ever learnt in a flash. Shortly, I think he is the sort of person who can never be tested adequately in the impromptu manner demanded by the tripos. I know he will do his best – I don't think he will fail, heavens knows we have worked hard enough! tchtch joke over – but if he gets in one of his unreasoning panics – say over the Preraphaelites – he certainly will – It is impossible to be more specific than this because the whole thing is *one subject* & if you go down badly in one department it affects the whole thing. I think a pass is all one can expect for someone as temperamentally involved as Malcolm. And even a pass with honours could not add to the value of his degree when he gets it because he will have to take another subject next year, – only after that does he become eligible for the degree –

Experiment has come out, a noble looking paper. The London Mercury says a sketch written in a mixture of Negro Greek American and (occasionaly English – thats me – & a fragment from *Work in Progress* are the only things which live up to the Editorial which is full of post-war-group guff.[6] Heinemann publish it, by the way. They have taken no notice of my correction of the proofs, the dashes are all too long, its full of misprints, & the title is wrong. It makes me sick to look at it so I won't send it you till I pluck up courage.

I'm damned sorry about Pete's book[7] – it's sure to pick up though – & anyway it's of historical importance or bibliographical rather as being the only decent study of your work; that makes it of historical importance as well for future biographers will always have to refer to it & all this time anyway it will be selling splendidly as I guesse.

Burra must have been a trial for that long.[8] Lovely! Thank God Dolly's got a job.[9] I was thinking last night of her saying – I'm so excited you GNAW, I must always get a little bit aTIPSY you GNAW MRS CHERRY MRS CHERRY oh I'm so excited you GNAW. Jesus bloody christ I was nearly sick when I thought of her – I wonder why she knocked at my door the last night all the same ——

Don't tell the old man about the motor accident because he'll think all sorts of things which are probably true; anyway if things get really desperate I can always use it in three weeks. There were three of us in the car, Davenport myself & Forman,[10] & we were all pieeyed & decided to go to africa and just sat on the accelerator for about twenty miles till the thing just overturned from sheer vexation. None of us were killed, but personally I wish I had been.

We got off with bruised hips & banged heads. Not so hot. I'm sorry the old man should give you this trouble of questions blast him. However . .

> I should like to die said Willie
> if my poppa could die too –

wotthehell

> my love to Jerry

> Malc

don't tell him that all I know of the Life & Thought of any period is that people once wore tights.

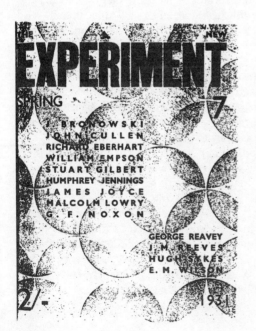

Figure 6

Annotations:

1 Lowry is quoting from his story 'Punctum Indifferens Skibet Gaar Videre,' *Experiment* 7 (Spring 1931): 64. This story was reprinted in revised
form as 'Seductio ad Absurdum,' and was later rewritten and incorporated into chapter 4 of *Ultramarine*.

2 See *Ultramarine*: 'And the parrot's household pigment strewn along the
deck . . .' ' (271) and 'Bombs from the bison's bung, eh?' (271)

3 Lowry's father had asked Aiken for details concerning the examinations
his son was about to write. As Lowry more or less explains, he is preparing for part 1 of the English Tripos, which was attempted at the end
of the student's second year. For the next several years Arthur Lowry
was obliged to seek news of his wayward son through others.

4 Lowry no doubt means Dante Gabriel Rossetti (1828-82), the English
poet and painter.

5 Lowry is echoing the speech of Brutus Jones in Eugene O'Neill's *The
Emperor Jones* (1920). He uses this type of speech and similar phrases for
the dialogue in chapter 6 of *Ultramarine* (259).

6 See Figure 6 for the cover and contents page of *Experiment* 7. The
London Mercury review of *Experiment* 7, with Lowry's story 'Punctum
Indifferens Skibet Gaar Videre,' reads: 'a sketch, which is certainly
not academical, written in a mixture of American, Negro, Greek, and
occasionally English. But with the exception of this sketch, and
an extraordinary fragment from Mr. James Joyce's Work in Progress,
the magazine does not appear to transcend the spirit of academicism'
(23, 138 [April 1931]: 522).

7 Houston Peterson's *The Melody of Chaos* (New York: Longmans,
Green, 1931) was the first critical study of Aiken's work.

8 Edward John Burra (1905-76) was a British surrealist painter and a
friend of Aiken's; see photograph 11. Lowry did not like Burra, who
ridiculed him publicly in Granada in 1933; see Day (176).

9 Doris 'Dolly' Lewis, the stepdaughter of Aiken's friend in South Yarmouth, Charles D. Voorhis, was the young woman with whom Lowry
fell in love in the summer of 1929 (Day, 107); see letter **23**.

10 Thomas Vivian Forman (1910-) was a Cambridge friend to whom,
along with Elizabeth Cheyne, Lowry dedicated *Ultramarine*. Forman
entered Trinity Hall College in 1929, and he earned a third on the Inter-
collegiate Examination in English in 1930, but the college records show
no further trace of him. Forman gave Lowry an MG Magna in 1933, but
Lowry 'disembowelled it on a great tombstone of a rock' (Day, 181).
See Lowry's September 1933 letter (**59**) to Jan Gabrial.

Editorial Notes:

a. According to Aiken's 25 April 1931 letter to Walter Piston (*Selected
Letters of Conrad Aiken*, 174), Malcolm had just returned to Cambridge

after five weeks in Rye. For Aiken to know about the car accident, he must have received this letter from Malcolm by 24 or 25 April. On the versos of the first two pages of the letter are typed passages, one with handwritten alterations, from drafts of *Ultramarine*; the third page is written on the verso of a March 1931 cover of the *St Catharine's College Magazine*, and the last two pages are written on notepaper.

30: To The Editor

P: Cambridge
PP: *Varsity*

[Cambridge, England]
9 May 1931

An Open Letter to 'Varsity': Police Court Reporting

Sir. – It seems to us both invidious and improvident that you (a University paper) should from time to time have given unnecessary publicity to the petty offences of undergraduates;[1] in fact we may go so far as to say that as undergraduates are largely responsible for the sales of your paper, such action on your part is tantamount to pointing out to a proctor a man without a square,[2] or to borrowing a man's shirt and then having him up for indecent exposure; on the other hand we see perfectly that to omit legitimate *news* would come as close to a destruction of your own *amour propre* as the publicity is in itself a destruction of ours; and we realise perfectly that the pewter Al Capone and the tinfoil Küerten,[3] or whoever makes the latest Cambridge sausage, is as necessary to your front page as the clover to the bee. But we are referring strictly to petty offences, or offences of a semi-nonproven nature.

We have remarked your practice for some time now and with increasing disgust, so that when the case of a friend of ours, a case which had already sufficient prominence in papers not definitely connected with the University, was put on your front page, we thought it time to take action.[4] (We need hardly say that your publicity has done irreparable damage to the friend in question). As for the case itself, if it can be called one, in Masefield's words 'the same might come to any one of us,'[5] even – dare we say it? – to the guileless editors of *Varsity*, although I can hardly see your news editor writing himself up for the front page! We write you this on behalf of our friend, and to give you fair warning that if your unpleasant policy continues your news editor may well find himself not only on the front page but also in the In Memoriam column.

We must add that it is a mystery to us that such a treacherous paper should have any circulation whatsoever among the people it betrays. Still, *de gustibus*,[6] as the farmer said when he kissed the pig.

Yours between the woodwind and the water music,

> (Signed) Malcolm Lowry
> John Davenport
> P.J. Macdonald
> Paul Marx
> Arthur Tillotson
> John Palmer
> John Green[7]

Annotations:

1 The *Varsity*, begun in January 1931, is a Cambridge University weekly paper published by the undergraduates. During the first months of its publication it regularly featured news about students who had been involved in various peccadilloes or charged with minor offences. This letter appeared on the second page of the 9 May 1931 issue of the paper, and the editor published a reply with an apology beside it.

2 In Lowry's day at Cambridge all undergraduates were required to wear full academic attire, both gown and mortarboard, when out of college after dark. To be 'without a square' is to be without a mortarboard, and the offender, if caught by a proctor, would be fined. For the *Varsity* to report such petty offences would be ridiculous, which is precisely the point of the comparison with the paper's 'police court reporting.'

3 Capone's rule of Chicago crime syndicates ended with his arrest in 1931, and German mass-murderer Peter Küerten was executed that year; thus 1931 saw some rather more serious and spectacular crimes than anything committed by Cambridge undergraduates.

4 On 2 May 1931 *Varsity* featured a report on its front page under the title 'Tripos and Intoxication.' An undergraduate called H. Rudyard of Selwyn College was charged with driving under the influence of alcohol after he knocked someone off a bicycle. His tutor gave evidence that Rudyard was under stress because he was preparing for his Tripos examinations. The *Varsity* stated that, despite a plea of not guilty, he was fined £2 plus costs and had his driver's licence suspended for twelve months. Three further articles on drinking and driving were published in this issue of the paper.

5 John Masefield (1878-1967), who succeeded Robert Bridges as the poet laureate of England in 1930, gained stature as a contributor to the Georgian movement of protest poetry during the first twenty years of this century. After the First World War his verse became sentimental and pastoral, but his earlier narratives and lyrics of the sea and common life, such as *Salt-Water Ballads* (1902), *The Everlasting Mercy* (1911), and

Dauber (1913) remained popular. This quotation is from the narrative poem "The Widow in the Bye Street" (1912), in which a young man about to be executed for accidentally killing the man who has replaced him in the affections of a "whore" is taken to his cell. We are told that his jailers were 'kind "for what the kid done . . . well / The same might come to any one of us."' See *The Collected Poems of John Masefield* (London: William Heinemann, 1923), p. 184.

6 *De gustibus* is a short form of the Latin expression *de gustibus non est disputandum*, which means: There is no disputing tastes.

7 Of the seven undergraduate signatories to this letter, only Davenport was a close friend of Lowry's (see letters **25** and **73**), and the letter reads as though it were composed by Lowry with Davenport's help.

31: To Kenneth Wright

P: UBC(ms phc)

[Bateman Street,]
[Cambridge]
[May 1931][a]

Dear Kenneth[1]

I have to go to the ADC tonight; a private show & I want to go to Festival tomorrow[2] – so what about Thursday? I'll have Troilus & Langland done by then – you have Keats & something else.

A short story of mine (which neither of us liked) has been selected by Edward J. O'Brien in his volume the 8 best stories of 1931.[3] I'm in the company of Tomlinson & Coppard.[4] W'ot ho she bumps. You can sell this letter!

Malcolm

Annotations:

1 Kenneth Wright (1909–) went up to St Catharine's College, Cambridge, in the same term as Lowry, Michaelmas 1929. Wright, who was perturbed by Lowry's close friendship with Paul Leonard Charles Fitte, who committed suicide on 15 November 1929, did not become friendly with Lowry until the winter of 1930, when they discovered that they lived close to each other on Bateman Street. In his recollections of their first evening together in Wright's room on 27 February 1930, Kenneth Wright describes Lowry talking about spiritualism and about the contact he had made with Fitte, whose spirit was afraid that his body was poisoning the earth because he had committed suicide by gas poisoning. The death of Fitte haunted Lowry all his life, and the character and story of Peter Cordwainer in *October Ferry to Gabriola* is based, in part, upon these events; see Bradbrook (113-16).

2 The Amateur Dramatic Club (ADC) and Terence Gray's Festival Theatre were popular Cambridge spots that produced challenging plays at a very high standard.

3 Edward Joseph Harrington O'Brien (1890-1941) was a well-known editor and anthologist who edited *Best Short Stories* (American and British) from 1915 to 1941. 'Seductio ad Absurdum,' later incorporated into chapter 4 of *Ultramarine*, was published by O'Brien in his *Best British Short Stories of 1931* (New York: Dodd, Mead, 1931), pp. 89-107. The story first appeared as 'Punctum Indifferens Skibet Gaar Videre' in the Cambridge literary magazine *Experiment* 7 (Spring 1931): 62-75.

4 A.E. Coppard (1878-1957) was an English writer who published several volumes of short stories during the 1920s. His style is characterized by its lyricism and simplicity. H.M. Tomlinson (1873-1958) was well known by 1931 as a novelist, essayist, and travel writer. Coppard's stories were occasionally chosen by O'Brien, and Coppard is regularly listed in O'Brien's editions as among the year's story writers of distinction. Tomlinson, however, is rarely listed; therefore, it is not clear why Lowry should boast of being in his company. Neither Coppard nor Tomlinson has a story in *The Best British Short Stories of 1931*.

Editorial Notes:

a. According to Sotheby's catalogue for their 18 December 1985 sale, where both letters (**31** and **32**) to Kenneth Wright were sold, this letter was written in pencil on the verso of part of an account for Kenneth Wright's lodgings. Internal references to Chaucer, Langland, Milton, and Keats in these letters suggest that Lowry and Wright were preparing for their examinations, which began on 20 May.

32: To Kenneth Wright

P: UBC(ms phc)

[Bateman Street,]
[Cambridge]
[May 1931]

Dear Kenneth –
    I've left it here after all – I expect its full of howlers – but it's the best I can do – you might get a hint from it on the Harddy – I don't know what it is not that I know what any of them are – [1]
    By George, these things demand patience of a wet May Sunday!
    Could you leave them in a conspicuous place somewhere so I can collect them morgens

Malc

I've borrowed Areopagitica, that famous poeme. I always thought it was a sequel to Paradise Regained[2]

Annotations:

1 Lowry and Wright often discussed their creative writing, and Lowry may be referring to an essay or to a part of *Ultramarine* that he had left for his friend to read. Wright has recalled that 'one afternoon he spent some time pulling to pieces the style in which I had attempted to write a short story. It was the most valuable English lesson I have ever had.'
2 Lowry's joking reference is to *Areopagitica* (1644), a prose pamphlet on the liberty of the press by the English poet John Milton (1608–74). It is not, as Lowry well knew, a sequel to Milton's *Paradise Regained* (1671).

33: To Conrad Aiken

P: H(ms)
PP: *SL* 7–10; *LAL* 30–35

8 Plympton Street,[a]
[St Catharine's College,]
[Cambridge]
[ca 14 June 1931]

My dear Conrad:
    It was very good of you to write me about the tripeos: as for that I can't tell as yet, but we did our best – we did our best. I wrote a fairly good essay on Truth & Poetry, quoting yourself liberally not to say literally, and Poe and the Melody of Chaos; I was all right on the criticism paper, and I think I bluffed my way through on literature from 1785 to the present day – I knew my Keats better than I thought I did, for instance; & on the whole I have nothing to complain about from the papers, (which I'll try & get together & send you), and if I have failed, and that's on the cards, I was more stupid at the time than I thought.[1]
    Meantime I have been leading a disordered and rather despairing existence, and you can probably guess at the reason why I was incapable of replying promptly: your telegram, however, brought me to my senses and made me feel rightly ashamed of myself.
    My d. & r.d.e[2] is due to a complexity of melancholy reasons none of which are either particularly complex, melancholy, or reasonable, and I have made up my mind about only one point in this business of living which is that I must, and as soon as possible, identify a finer scene. I must in other words give an imaginary scene identity through the immediate sensation of actual experience etc: This, you

say, I may have already done in some part, and is becoming with me a desire for retrogression, for escaping from the subtle and sophisticated: that it is not deep-rooted in honest transmission at all and has nothing to do with really wanting more experience and to rub off more prejudice, to use more hardship, load myself with finer mountains and strengthen more my reach, than would stopping home among books (even though I should reach Homer!) but is nothing more than wanting alternately to kill Liverpool and myself: that I am in *truth* – although occasionaly straining at particles of light in the midst of a great darkness – 'a small boy chased by the furies'[3] & you can sympathise with me as such. Well – if t'were so t'were a grievous fault —— [4]

I prefer to think sometimes that it is because I really want to be a man rather than a male, which at present I'm not, and that I want to get from somewhere a frank and fearless will which roughly speaking does not put more mud into the world than there is at present. Nonsense.

Then I must read, – I must read, – I must read! Dostoievsky & Dante: Donne, Dryden, Davenant and Dean Inge . . .[5] Again, nonsense; but then at the moment I despair of all literature anyway. If I could read Homer – however much he may have roared in the pines, I'm sure I should hate him: Donne means damn all to me now, Herrick is terrible, Milton I can't read & wouldn't if I could: all restoration comedy & most all Greek tragedy is a bore . . . Tolstoy? My god what a bloody awful old writer he was!

Well, there is Melville & Goethe, you say.

Well, there was the story of Hamlet, I said and fell into silence –

(By the bye Experiment was reviewed in the Times Lit Sup of a week or two back side by side with a review of Martin Armstrong's collected, – or are they selected? – unaffected, undetected and well-connected poems,[6] I can't remember whether the review was a favourable one or not, I rather fear not – of my own contribution it remarked that it was a kind of prose fugue, with recurring themes, consisting of the tough talk of sailors or something, 'effectively contrived' – I can't remember it in detail but I felt quite pleased. I haven't sent you a copy of it because the punctuation, length of dashes & so forth, was all wrongly done & I was sure it would give you a pain in the neck to look at: this is a rather selfish reason for as a matter of fact the rest of the paper in my opinion is well worth reading. So I might send you a copy after all!)

I am delighted to hear that a novel is under way: it is really quite intolerable that I should have been so long sending you the bone dream –[7]

Here it is however . . .[b]

It occurs to me also, & with some horror, that I have not paid you the £4 I owe you. This has not been because I could not afford to pay it but simply because I have wasted my substance in riotous living – I have just put it off, & off, & there is no doubt whatever but that you could do as well with the four pounds as I could do well without it, but as I write this it so happens I have only a farthing in my pocket: moreover I can never think of the peculiar circumstances under which the debt, or ¾ of it, was accrued, without terror, inchoate flashes of nightmare – and perhaps this procrastination is due in a very small part to the fact that to pay the debt means writing about the circumstances & therefore remembering them. No, I am not Mr Sludge the medium, nor was meant to be . . .[8] But I wish I knew where the hell that three pounds was all the same; the memory of Dolores von Hempel is like a miasmic stench from the docks.[9] A pock-marked, Eurasian, memory –

The reason why I have a farthing, and not a halfpenny or a penny or a half-crown in my pocket is a peculiar one. The other night I was walking outside a Fullers café, the windows looked something like Selfridges & not very different from any of the other modern buildings erected all over London or Cambridge, except perhaps in size, – all the windows were filled with chocolates or chocolate coloured cakes, – I was in despair, when suddenly I caught sight of myself in the shop window & saw myself murmuring: Can he warm his blue hands by holding them up to the grand northern lights? Would not Lazarus rather be in Sumatra than here? Would he not rather lay him down lengthwise along the line of the Equator? . .[10] When at that moment a small boy suddenly came up to me, a small & very grimy urchin, & said 'Would you like a farthing?' So I replied. 'Well why not keep it – it's good luck to have a farthing? Besides I haven't got a penny to give you for it.' And he said 'ho, I don't want it, I've given my good luck to you.' He then ran away. Strange!

7am

  I am King Elephant Bag
   King Elephant Bag
   From de rose pink mountains.[11]

I enclose you a letter from one Edward O'Brien,[12] all the more mysterious because he failed to take any notice of my reply . . . Moreover his letter miscarries to *me* – it pursued Noxon[13] half round Europe – I sent him hopefully my biography (in cameo), as it appears at the back of the letter – at the same time giving away that I was an

English writer, not an American. If you have any notion what O'Brien means, meant, or intends, if anything, could you let me know some time if your brain will function in that direction? . . I never submitted him any story, & the only story he can have read from Experiment is the one about the mickey, all of which improves the joke.[14]

I can assume only that he did mean to publish the thing in the 1931 volume, American & have already informed the old man on this score to counteract in part the effect of my (possible) failure in the exam which gawd forbid. O'Brien either ignored or didn't receive a couple of replies, so I sent him a wire asking him if he could give me some information 'as was going to Peru,' & received the answer. 'O'Brien in the Balkans – O'Brien,' which seems to me funny. Still, I would like your advice. It is a nice point.

And it's that story, you know, in all its pristine beauty, Conrad, full of 'stop its-he-muttered.' & 'they growled's' & they howled's & 'There are you better now's,' far away, yo hai,'s

long ago, yo ho.

Malc

Annotations:

1 For a description of the examinations in the English Tripos part 1, which Lowry wrote in May 1931, see his 24 April 1931 letter (**29**) to Aiken. He sat the English Tripos part 2 in June 1932 and received a class 3. When Lowry says he quoted Poe, Aiken, and from 'the Melody of Chaos,' he is referring to Houston Peterson's *The Melody of Chaos* (New York: Longmans, Green, 1931), the first critical monograph on Aiken's work.

2 'd. & r.d.e' is Lowry's short form for 'disordered and rather despairing existence' in the preceeding paragraph.

3 As so often in his letters, Lowry quotes words and phrases from his fiction. In this paragraph, for example, see *Ultramarine* (99 and 253).

4 Lowry is paraphrasing a line from Mark Antony's famous speech in *Julius Caesar* III.ii.85: 'If it were so, it was a grievous fault.'

5 Sir William Davenant (1606-68), English dramatist and poet laureate, and William Ralph Inge (1860-1954), Dean of St Paul's Cathedral (1911-34) and philosopher, are interesting, perhaps ironic additions to Lowry's alphabetical list of the greats.

6 The reviewer for the *Times Literary Supplement* of 4 June 1931 remarked that Lowry 'contributes a short story ["Punctum Indifferens Skibet Gaar Videre"] consisting almost entirely of the rough dialogue of a group of sailors playing cards; a kind of prose fugue with recurrent themes, effectively contrived' (450). The English poet Martin Armstrong (1882-1974)

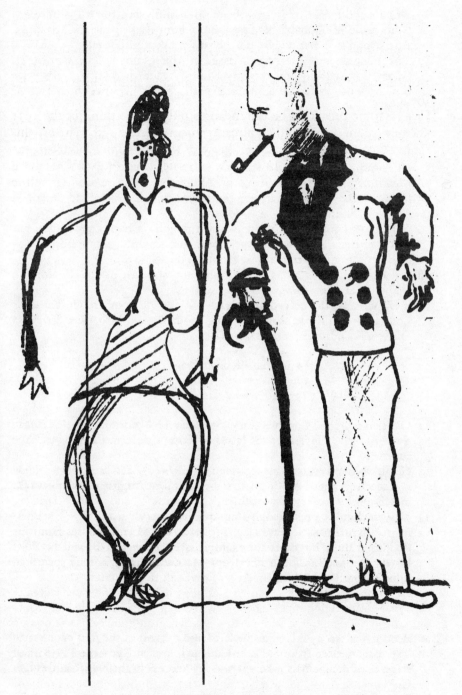

Figure 7: *Lowry's drawing appears on the verso of page three of this letter to Aiken.*

was a good friend of Aiken's from 1911 until the latter's 1929 divorce from Jessie McDonald, his first wife, whom Armstrong then married. Armstrong is rather cruelly portrayed by Aiken in *Ushant*.

7 The 'bone dream' refers to a passage in Aiken's novel *Great Circle* (84). Aiken was working on the novel in 1931 and discussing drafts with Lowry, who was more influenced, perhaps, by this novel than by *Blue Voyage*.

8 Lowry is echoing Prufrock's observation in T.S. Eliot's (1917) poem 'The Love Song of J. Alfred Prufrock': 'No! I am not Prince Hamlet, nor was meant to be.' Mr Sludge is the contemptible figure of the editor or biographer in Robert Browning's (1812-89) poem 'Mr Sludge, "The Medium"' (1864), and in his 22 November 1922 review of Robert Graves's *On English Poetry* for the *New Republic*, Aiken had described Graves's 'fatuous' efforts as 'sludgery.'

9 The context suggests that this woman may have been a prostitute, but whoever she was, Lowry evokes her memory with a phrase from *Ultramarine*: 'A miasmic stench rose from the docks' (118).

10 See Ishmael's reflections as he walks the streets of New Bedford in chapter 2 of *Moby-Dick*.

11 It is, perhaps, the preceding narrative about the poor urchin that leads Lowry to recall this snatch of song from Ronald Firbank's *Sorrow in Sunlight* (London: Brentano's, 1924), p. 30:

> I am King Elephant-bag,
> Ob de rose-pink Mountains!
> Tatou, tatouay, tatou.

12 O'Brien included Lowry's story 'Seductio ad Absurdum' in *Best British Short Stories of 1931*, but his letter to Lowry does not appear to have survived.

13 Gerald Noxon was a close friend of Lowry's at Cambridge. They renewed this friendship in 1940; see Lowry's 26 August 1940 letter (**148**) to Noxon.

14 The 'mickey' is a pet bird that drowns in Lowry's story 'Port Swettenham,' *Experiment* 5 (February 1930): 22-26. A revised version was published by Whit Burnett and Martha Foley as 'On Board the West Hardaway' in *Story* 3 (October 1933): 12-22, and Lowry later reworked it for chapter 5 of *Ultramarine*.

Editorial Notes:

a. A note written by Aiken in the left-hand margin of the first page reads: 'No date: written from St Cath. College to me, at Rye – the 8 Plympton street is of course M's joke – it was *my* address in the *other* Cambridge. C.A.'

b. Enclosed with this letter is a page transcribed in Lowry's hand from Aiken's 'bone dream' manuscript that differs in style, though not in imagery, from the published text. It bears an interpolation in the left margin that reads: 'C, like the story of the feller who dreamt he saw the results of – stop me if you've heard it – .' On the verso of this page Aiken has written: 'A fragment of Great Circle (or B. Voyage? I can't find it) which Malc proposed to incorporate in Ultramarine – I said No! The interpolation at left is Malc's I think. C.A.'

34: To Conrad Aiken

P: H(ms)
PP: *LAL* 36

> [St Catharine's College,]
> [Cambridge]
> [15 June 1931][a]

I thought Socrates might be in the novel so am sending you this. See page 471 of six plays.[1] It's not bad, but not really good. They're too many pipes of pan & fauns & females playing leaden flutes: & Aristophanes gets hiccups. Such rugs & jugs & candle lights: which reminds me that I saw the Antigone & the Lysistrata exceedingly well done here at the Festival[2] . . . Well, as I said before, its not good, but might suggest something to you, it is after all, Socrates speaking & he says something about a windflower, too . . . And talking about the Festival – when is Cambridge going to see you? Could you for instance invite yourself on her this week end, say the 18th-23rd, or are you too busy, & *rooted*? It would be swell to see you though.

> [unsigned]

Annotations:

1 See Clifford Bax, 'Socrates,' *Six Plays* (London: Victor Gollancz, 1931), pp. 461-578. The play begins on page 471. Exactly what Lowry is sending to Aiken is unclear, but the novel he refers to is Aiken's *Great Circle*.
2 Lowry is referring to Terence Gray's Festival Theatre on Newmarket Road, where, according to M.C. Bradbrook, students could enjoy 'one of the most advanced experimental theatres in Europe,' with plays by 'Pirandello, Elmer Rice, Eugene O'Neill, Goethe, Strindberg, Kaiser, Toller' and the classics; see 'I.A. Richards at Cambridge,' *I.A. Richards: Essays in His Honor*, ed. Reuben Brower, Helen Vendler, John Hollander (New York: Oxford University Press, 1973), p. 64. Gray founded the Festival Theatre in 1926 and, under the influence of Edward Gordon Craig, began experiments in staging, lighting, and choreography. His non-naturalistic style was especially effective with classical tragedy or expressionist plays, and his use of platform and steps recalled the work

of Leopold Jessner. Robert Donat, who was later to star in *Goodbye, Mr Chips*, performed at the Festival Theatre in 1929-30.

Editorial Notes:

a.   This informal note to Aiken is on a single 18-by-25-cm lined page torn from a notebook. There is no inside address or date, but the dates mentioned for Aiken's visit suggest mid-June for the letter; 18 to 23 June 1931 ran from Thursday through to the following Tuesday, thus covering the weekend.

The ghostly presence of the Norwegian writer Nordahl Grieg haunts much of Lowry's writing, as it did Lowry's life. Unfortunately, only two of his letters to Grieg appear to have survived, and letter 35 *is by far the most important of the two (see also letter* 85*). If Grieg ever replied, his letters to Lowry have disappeared. Although his influence on Lowry's fiction has been much discussed, what the collected letters reveal, through Lowry's frequent allusions to Grieg and to his novel* The Ship Sails On, *is the degree to which the Norwegian represented the heroic ideal of the artist as a man of action, a romantic* other *whom the contemplative, narcissistic Lowry could only admire.*

35: To Nordahl Grieg

P: Oslo(ms)
PP: *SM* 44-51

> Hotell Parkheimen
> Drammensveien 2
> [Oslo, Norway]
> 8 September 1931

Nordahl Grieg, I greet you![1]
Will you forgive me having to write, throughout, in English? – I was actually thinking out a letter to you when I met you in the Red Mill:[2] and now can't be altogether sure about the meeting; it might have been imagination. This is not the letter: but this *is* to say that I hope profoundly – provided I *did* meet you and you *are* in Oslo – that you will find time for us to talk again before your return to the mountains or to Bergen, or to both.
Still, in case you can't, in case the chief engineer burns me up for more speed, in case of thunderbolt or act of God which may make it impossible for us to meet in Cambridge, herewith the following

detail about Rupert Brooke which you may not find elsewhere. (I don't know whether his John Webster and Elizabethan drama is in print in England, or even procurable in Cambridge, & I have no copy.)[3]

The year before the war, in reviewing the new edition of Donne's poems, Rupert Brooke remarked that between 1595 and 1613 'English literature climbed and balanced briefly on the difficult pinnacle of sincerity.' 'Donne belonged to an age when men were not afraid to mate their intellects to their emotions. Hamlet with his bitter flashes, his humour, his metaphysical inquisitiveness and his passion, continually has the very accent of the secular Donne. To Ophelia he must have been Donne himself – '[4]

I mention this only because it shows, especially in the light of what follows in my letter, that Brooke also had within himself the germs of a metaphysical inquisitiveness which he had not time to develop, which the war finally killed – & him with it. Most biographers have overlooked this metaphysical side of Brooke, I think – the more terrible and bloody side – in a sense, if I may so put it, the 'skibet gaar videre' side of his nature – that which was, like Webster (in Eliot on Webster)

> . . . much possessed by death
> And saw the skull beneath the skin:
> And breastless creatures underground
> Leaned backward with a lipless grin.
>
> Daffodil bulbs instead of balls
> Stared from the sockets of the eyes!
> He knew that thought clings round dead limbs
> Tightening its lusts and luxuries.[5]

and have been content with him merely as The Great Lover, as the author of[a] such admirable poems indeed, but deceitful biographically as I shall attempt to show, as The Hill: and The Soldier: and The Fish (squamous, omnipotent & kind, but which please God may not get either of us!)[6]

Because, because, for one reason, it was Brooke astonishingly who appreciated more fully than anybody before or since the far reaching importance of John Marston, an Elizabethan misanthrope who revived the old Senecan tragedies of blood on a subtler plane, and with what complicated or triumphant issues God only knows: it was Brooke again who first expressed the historical fact, & with brilliant concision, that Marston more or less invented the *malcontent* character which led, by devious mists and poisons, to Hamlet, to Jacques or

to Flamineo: to the clerk in Georg Keiser's 'From Morn to Midnight'
I might add, and in a different art-form, to Daedalus & Demarest &
Swann, not to mention all the ruthless women who foreshadowed
Webster's flaming duchess 'The Duchess of Malfi': and exhibited a
clinical interest in satyriasis and nymphomania – by that I mean,
roughly speaking, in the dirt, mud, or blood, of sex, in its eternal
and ruthless power rather than in its subtleness and goodness – which
is like Strindberg and O'Neill.[7]
    It was left to Brooke to point out in his 'John Webster & Eliza-
bethan drama' that Marston was one of the most sinister, least
understood, figures in Elizabethan literature: that more than anyone
else he determined the channels in which the great flood of those ten
years (1600-1610) was to flow: that he is responsible for that peculiar
macabre taste, like the taste of copper, that is necessary to, if it is not
the cause, of their splendour.[8] While Webster, as Swinburne said,
took the last step into the darkness – Well![9] . . . I think you will agree
with me that this interest in, this trouble taken on behalf of old
bloody minded Marston is partially if not definitely indicative of
some sort of identity between the two, which Rupert Brooke somehow felt tremendously: in other words I think, to go a step further,
not only would Brooke's poetry have become harder, tenser, more
complex if he had lived but that it is even possible that later he might
have devoted himself, largely, to the drama (he did in fact write one
one act play, called, I guess, *Lithuania* which in England has been
produced only once and that if I am not mistaken at the Everyman
Theatre Hampstead, for a short run);[10] that briefly he was *approaching
a Keatsian predicament.*
Certainly, unlike Keats, he had not yet reached the brink of the
chasm, that canyon in his genius where he was going to wonder
whether or not his work was sufficiently according to an intellectual
formula: whether unless he devoted himself more to philosophy and
metaphysics his poetry would degenerate into mere sensibility un-
accompanied by thought: certainly not, not yet, and he never lived to
wonder *hard* at it but nevertheless in his most uneasy moments without having his temperature altered he was already trembling with the
symptoms of that most terrible of all fevers, spiritual ambivalence (I
mean split mind, divided mind –) or schizophrenia, – ηβηφρενε,[11] is
it?, – call it what you will.
Is it not at such times, sir, that one climbs, or attempts to climb
Mount Everest? It is at such times that one roller skates to Saigon or
Tastizond: or to the South Pole or Arcturus or Popacatapetl.[12] It is at
such times that one hops on one foot from Sofia to Jerusalem and
dies at the foot of the cross, the weeping cross.[13] At such times one

works for ninety-nine years in a Chinese ricefield, sleeping in the mud. Or one goes to sea, or commits suicide; or delicately combines the two . . .

In his case the war came along and that as you very justly pointed out in Bygdo, is a sort of artificial Katharsis, a mechanic purgation for such a state of mind: and my brother Stuart (who served in the war with some distinction) bears you out on that point, although he is not without a nostalgia for fighting any more than we can hope to be entirely without a nostalgia for the sea, however fiercely we hate it! To dream of both is to dream of comradeship, of danger: although perhaps underneath it all is the desire for crucifixion on the basis that misery is creation, and creation is love . . . A soldier once said to me that if he had been a war-poet he would have started a poem – 'Not all of us were heroes.' The war was better than 'pushing a pen in the guvnor's office,' he said!

So, was it not natural that he should have celebrated the war: that Brooke should have celebrated it poetically in this sense, that the glory and the pity war distilled was partly a magnificent substitute, – or a ghastly compensation!, – only dimly perceived by him, for the metaphysical danks and darks he would never absorb, *could* never absorb? sheerly in terms of mud and blood was it not going one better than Marston? or to put it all more brutally was not the red sweet wine of youth nobler than all the property red ink of all the Antonios and Mellidas and Malcontents and Insatiate Countessas, not to mention Sophonisbas, on the Elizabethan stage or off it?[14] Was it not better to fall with Icarus than thrive with Smith? fall I mean in that international, unscenical, Tragedy of blood which was the great War?

There seems to me no doubt, to give another parallel, that Keats saw in the death of Chatterton the consummation of his own poetic theory so that he was ready for and even delighted by the prospect of his own death;[15] he died *consciously*: so with Brooke the 'Dark Self that Wants to Die' (that's not a bad title for a book, by the way) was always present even when he himself was most happy and vigorous.[16]

It is possible that some of all this sounds unnecessarily portentous, possible also damn it all that you knew it all already or had dismissed it as beside the point, and I have wandered rather from the central fact which is simply that Marston should have had to wait for Rupert Brooke, whom one had thought to be sitting safely on the other side of the spectrum, so perfectly to apprehend him, that that in itself is a remarkable thing, and has seemed to me worthy of your notice if not of course, necessarily, in its ramifications, of your agreement.

In conclusion I must say that I can think of noone more qualified to write a book on Brooke than yourself: or of anyone who could surround his position more skilfully: or of anyone who is just such a literalist of his own imagination as to be able to do it.

Needless to say it is an extraordinary compliment to England and to English literature that you should have thought of doing such a thing. I speak at such length because I feel strongly that there are few people in Cambridge who will talk either sympathetically or knowledgeably about him except as a picture postcard, as a sort of present from Grantchester![17]

It is difficult to account, except vaguely (the counter influence of the grim realist, Sassoon,[18] for instance) for his extraordinary falling off in public favour. The best explanation I can give is your own. As with the *Mignon*, so with literature.[19] New men crawl up into the bunks of those that have left, and so on ad infinitum. They take their leavings, and the ship sails on. And so does the whirligig of taste, to yet another cultural cataclysm! –

Lastly, I have long been a friend of Benjamin Hall's, and I am delighted to have met the earthly author of his blood, and very grateful to that author for having been so hospitable to one who was a complete stranger. But when I remember how often Hall and I have tired the sun with talking and sent him down the sky I do not feel so much of a stranger.

By the way, Marston (whom we were discussing) wrote the line,

> Rich happiness that such a son is drowned.[20]

That is good, isn't it?

Well: I hope we may meet again before the worm pierce our winding sheet & before the spider makes a thin curtain for our epitaph.[21]

But most of all I shall never forget looking at the Viking Ship[22] and then suddenly we were speaking in whispers –

Yours affectionately:

Malcolm Lowry

Annotations:

1 Nordahl Grieg (1902-43) was a Norwegian poet, novelist, playwright, and journalist. He was a complex man, an adventurer and romantic, a patriot, communist, and pacifist, and when the Nazis invaded Norway he became active in the resistance and the military. He died during a bombing raid on Berlin. The influence of the man, but more particularly of his 1924 novel *Skibet Gaar Videre* (translated by A.G. Chater in 1927 as *The Ship Sails On*), on Lowry has been well documented by Day and Hallvard Dahlie (see annotation 2).

2 According to Hallvard Dahlie, the 'Red Mill was a popular night spot in Oslo's theatre district between the wars. It was torn down in the late 1930's, as was the Hotell Parkheimen.' For Dahlie's discussion of this letter and the Grieg/Lowry connection, see 'Lowry's Debt to Nordahl Grieg,' *Canadian Literature* 64 (1975): 41-51, and *Swinging the Maelstrom* (31-42). Lowry's description of his lost manuscript 'In Ballast to the White Sea,' in his 25 August 1951 letter (**467**) to David Markson, shows how profoundly he was influenced by Grieg. Moreover, the overlap in reference and event between this letter and the later one to Markson provides convincing evidence that the two men really met.

3 Rupert Brooke (1887-1915) was a British poet who had been an undergraduate at Cambridge and later a Fellow of King's College, Cambridge. After his untimely death, something of a myth grew up around him that stressed his romantic good looks, his youth, and his nobility. Lowry is attempting to convince Grieg, who was writing a book on Brooke when he and Lowry met in the autumn of 1931, that Brooke was a more complex and interesting writer and person than the popular idealization of him allowed. *John Webster & the Elizabethan Drama* was written in 1911-12 as Brooke's dissertation towards his fellowship at King's College, and it was first published in 1916. Brooke was in the vanguard of the twentieth century's rediscovery of Webster, and his study was well thought of. Clearly, Lowry knew the book well (see annotation 6) and was aware of T.S. Eliot's later attention to Webster (see annotation 4). Because these characteristics are typical of Lowry's work, it is worth remembering that Brooke praised the emotional power of Webster's language, stressed the vitality and darkness of his vision, and defended, at length, Webster's so-called plagiarism of his sources. Moreover, Lowry's admiration for the Elizabethans may well have been shaped and encouraged by Rupert Brooke.

4 Brooke reviewed H.J.C. Grierson's two-volume edition of *Donne's Poetical Works* (Oxford: Clarendon Press, 1913) twice: in 'John Donne, The Elizabethan,' *Nation* 12, 20 (1913): 825-26, and again in 'John Donne,' *Poetry and Drama* 1, 2 (1913): 185-88. Lowry is remembering the first review and is quoting almost verbatim from the fourth paragraph.

5 Lowry has quoted verbatim the first two stanzas of T.S. Eliot's 1920 poem 'Whispers of Immortality.' The first line begins 'Webster was.'

6 'The Fish,' 'The Hill,' 'The Great Lover,' and 'The Soldier' are poems written by Brooke, and all four were included in the 1931 Tauchnitz edition of the *Anthology of Modern English Poetry*, which Lowry was reading during this visit to Norway. See his comments about the Tauchnitz in his September 1931 (**36**) letter to Conrad Aiken. Furthermore, Aiken's protagonist, Demarest, in *Blue Voyage* (142) remembers discussing Brooke, and the line 'Squamous, omnipotent, and kind' appears as a fragment of thought without quotation marks.

7 John Marston (1575?-1634) is largely remembered for *The Malcontent*

(1604), *Antonio's Revenge* (1602), *The Insatiate Countess* (1613), and various collaborations. Following Brooke's argument, Lowry goes on to connect Marston's malcontents with Shakespeare's *Hamlet* and Jaques in *As You Like It* and with Flamineo in Webster's *The White Devil*. The addition of Georg Kaiser's bank clerk from his 1917 expressionist play *Von Morgens bis Mittermachts (From Morn to Midnight)* to the list of Marston filiations is Lowry's own idea, as are the connections with novels as different as Joyce's *Portrait of the Artist as a Young Man* (1916) for Daedalus, Aiken's *Blue Voyage* (1927) for Demarest, and Proust's *A la recherche du temps perdu* (1913-27) for Swann. The association of the destructive, sex-obsessed females in the plays of August Strindberg and Eugene O'Neill (who was deeply influenced by Strindberg) with John Webster's *The Duchess of Malfi* (1614) is, again, Lowry's idea, but it shows the extent and thoughtfulness of his reading by this stage in his life.

8 Despite his claim, in the second paragraph of this letter, that he has 'no copy' of Brooke's Webster study, he is quoting exact terms and phrases from the book; see *John Webster & the Elizabethan Drama* (New York: Russell & Russell, 1967), pp. 67-68.

9 Lowry is quoting Swinburne's remark – 'The last step into the darkness remained to be taken by "the most tragic" of all English poets' – from 'John Webster' in *The Age of Shakespeare* (1908); see *The Complete Works of Algernon Charles Swinburne*, vol. 11, ed. Sir Edmund Gosse and Thomas James Wise (London: William Heineman, 1926), p. 293.

10 Rupert Brooke's one act play *Lithuania* was first produced at the Chicago Little Theatre on 12 October 1915, and later at a special matinee at His Majesty's Theatre in London. It was first published in London by Sidgwick & Jackson in 1935, with a note by John Drinkwater, who had acted in the London production.

11 Lowry has written the Greek approximation for hebephrenia (hebe, ηβη; phren, φρην), which is a form of schizophrenia occurring in puberty and characterized by hallucinations and emotional disorders. He uses the term again in his first 'Prelude to Mammon' poem in his summer 1937 letter (71) to Aiken.

12 Lowry's list of exotic cities, famous mountains, and the star Arcturus also includes what appears to be an English transliteration of Tashi-Chho-Dzong, the name of the fortress and Buddhist headquarters at Thimphu, the capital of Bhutan.

13 Lowry is using phrases from *Blue Voyage* (139-40).

14 The characters that Lowry lists all appear in the Marston plays mentioned in annotation 5, with the exception of 'Sophonisba,' the title character in Marston's 1606 tragedy.

15 Thomas Chatterton (1752-70), sometimes described as a poetical genius, poisoned himself at the age of seventeen. Coleridge, Wordsworth, Shelley, and Keats saw Chatterton as a symbol of unfulfilled genius, and Lowry may be thinking here of Keats's 1815 sonnet 'To Chatterton.' John Keats (1795-1821), who also died young like Chatterton, was one

of the poets on whom Grieg was working at this time for his book *Die unge døde* (1932; *The Young Dead*).

16 Lowry is quoting a passage from Aiken's *Blue Voyage*: 'the Dark Self Who Wants To Die' (241). At this point Demarest is lost in a Freudian dream about his parents, who are closely based on Aiken's own mother and father, and he later identifies this idea of the 'Dark Self' with the character Mr Smith (247).

17 Brooke is still known today for his nostalgic poem 'The Old Vicarage, Grantchester (Café des Westens, Berlin, May 1912),' about the pastoral hamlet of Grantchester outside of Cambridge. Brooke lived in Grantchester at several points during his life.

18 Siegfried Sassoon (1886-1967), who was educated at Cambridge and fought in the First World War, was known for his realistic and satirical war poetry and memoirs.

19 The *Mignon* is the name of the ship on which Benjamin Hall is working in Grieg's novel *The Ship Sails On* (*Skibet Gaar Videre*).

20 Lowry is referring to John Marston's *Antonio's Revenge* V.iii.3; see the Regents Edition by G.K. Hunter (Lincoln: University of Nebraska Press, 1965), p. 78. The line is also used, without citation, by the character Mr Smith in *Blue Voyage* (257, 261). Lowry, however, quotes the line again in Sonnet v from 'The Cantinas' (*CP*, 58), where he cites Marston.

21 Lowry is paraphrasing the lines of Flamineo, that arch hypocrite and schemer, from John Webster's 1612 play *The White Devil* V.vi.153-57:

> O men
> That lie upon your death-beds, and are haunted
> With howling wives, ne'er trust them: they'll remarry
> Ere the worm pierce your winding-sheet; ere the spider
> Make a thin curtain for your epitaphs.

See *The Selected Plays of John Webster*, ed. Jonathan Dollimore and Alan Sinfield (Cambridge: Cambridge University Press, 1983), p. 126.

22 Lowry reconstructs this scene with Nordahl Grieg in chapter 2 of *Ultramarine*, where he has Dana Hilliot remember walking with his father (whom he models upon Grieg) 'after we had dined at Jacques Bagatelle in the Bydgö Allé, that day we saw the Viking Ship.' See also his 1933 letter (**48**) to Jan Gabrial.

Editorial Notes:

a. This four-page letter has been written quite neatly, albeit in Lowry's tiniest script and with sloping lines, and there are relatively few deletions and interlineations. One substantial deletion of about five and a half lines occurs at this point, but Lowry has repeated and developed these points concerning Brooke in the subsequent paragraph. The only marginalia to this letter are the roman numerals i through iv, placed in the left margin, which divide the text very roughly into four parts. On the versos of pages three and four there are three lines heavily crossed out that begin with 'My dear Nordahl' and suggest that Lowry had trouble starting this letter.

36: To Conrad Aiken

P: H(ms); UBC(phc)
PP: *LAL* 37-39

Hotell Parkheimen,
Drammensveien 2, Oslo
[September 1931]

Hi there, Colonel Aiken –
SS Fagervik[1] – of which, curiously, very many happy memories – has been laid up & I am here waiting a few days for another ship. It is a small place; but the smallest place in it, up in the mountains, is called Frognersæteren.[2] The language is quite fantastic & driven into myself, I do little else but read Tauchnitz editions;[3] and so doing I have discovered one first rate author, an American, Julian Green, who writes in French, which is translated back again into English.[4] So.

My writing has changed – my hair is going gray – I enclose you a poem about ducks which is in the Tauchnitz anthology of English poetry of English & American authors![5] Take it to the Ship Inn with you if you are in Rye, order a half quartern – & I beg of you to drink my health – & have a good laugh! And there's another one by Gerald Gould, too.[6]

Once I could play panjo fine –
Nobody speaks English here, & in the only conversation I have had about literature I was surprised to discover that the most famous English writer here was Gibson. As the conversation progressed I noticed that somehow they'd got his christian name wrong, Henry instead of Wilfrid.[7] I pointed this mistake out, & seeing my chance which I had been waiting for all this time, I told, stumblingly, your famous story about Frost & Gibson at the English fair. They were astonished at the irrelevance of this because, as I later discovered, they were talking all this while about Henrik Ibsen –[8]

Is that funny?
It is perfectly false – I have just made it up.[9]

Anyhow,
Heaps of
love.

Maltz

THE SHRIEK!

Figure 8: *Lowry's parody of Munch is with his letter to Aiken.*

Annotations:

1 Lowry sailed to Norway on the ss *Fagervik* in the hope of meeting Nordahl Grieg; see letter **35**.
2 Frognersaeteren is today a suburb of Oslo and a mere thirty minutes by tram from downtown. It is located on a hill overlooking the city.
3 Baron Christian Bernhard von Tauchnitz (1816–95) was the founder of a publishing house in Leipzig that began issuing an English-language collection of British and American authors in 1841.
4 Julien Hartridge Green (1900–), the Paris-born American writer, was christened 'Julian' but chose to use the French spelling of his name. Over a long and distinguished career he has published many novels and plays, nine volumes of his journals, and seven autobiographies, and he was the first foreigner elected to the French Academy. Lowry owned *The Dark Journey* (1929), which is mentioned in *Dark as the Grave Wherein my*

Friend Is Laid and referred to in early drafts of *Under the Volcano*, and he continued to be an admirer of Green's work.

5 Lowry is referring to F.W. Harvey's poem 'Ducks' in the *Anthology of Modern English Poetry*, selected by Levin L. Schücking (Leipzig: Bernhard Tauchnitz, 1931), vol. 5000, pp. 120-23. This light-hearted poem concludes with the line: 'And He's [God] probably laughing still at the sound that came out of its bill!' Lowry's copy of the poem is not extant with this letter.

6 Gerald Gould (1885-1936) was a British journalist, poet, and critic. He had two poems in the 1931 Tauchnitz anthology that Lowry was reading: 'Alien Enemies' (116-18) and 'Wander-Thirst' (119).

7 Wilfrid Wilson Gibson (1878-1962) was a British poet and playwright also represented in the 1931 Tauchnitz anthology. Aiken's 'famous story' concerns a trip made by Gibson and the American poet Robert Frost to an English fair in 1915. Gibson felt he had wasted his day because he found nothing to write about; see Sugars (39).

8 Henrik Ibsen (1828-1906), the Norwegian playwright, is often referred to by Lowry in subsequent letters.

9 Lowry's drawing of *The Shriek* after Edvard Munch's famous lithograph *Geschrei* (1895) is on the verso of the letter. The painting on which the lithograph is based was done in 1893, and the image began to be discussed and reproduced as early as 1896. See Figure 8.

37: To Unidentified

P: H(ms)

[London]
[ca September 1932][a]

Dear George[1]
Will be back in arf an hour. Joan is downstairs.
Name a pub near.

Malcolm & James

Annotations:

1 This note may have been intended for George Hepburn, a younger brother of James Hepburn. During the summer of 1932 Lowry met the poet Anna Wickham, and often went to her house on Parliament Hill in London, where he met her sons James, John, and George. It was George's pet rabbit that Lowry accidentally killed; see James Hepburn in *Malcolm Lowry Remembered* (61).

Editorial Notes:

a. This note, in Lowry's hand, has been scrawled on the verso of a 1 September 1932 letter to Lowry from Sidney Thurston, who worked at St Catharine's College, Cambridge. Lowry has signed both names.

*Lowry's biographers have speculated at length about his relationship with his parents, but the available letters to his mother and father provide few answers to the many questions that remain. Letter fragment **38** is the first extant evidence of the difficulty Lowry had in writing to his father. Between 1933 and 1940 their communications grew increasingly strained, with the father demanding filial respect and the son always insisting he was misunderstood. Despite their personal estrangement, however, father and son remained in touch, and the four letters collected in this volume (**38**, **76**, **129**, and **172**) represent only a small portion of their actual correspondence.*

38: To Arthur O. Lowry

P: H(ms)

[London]
[February 1933][a]

Dear Daddy – [1]
    I wired you on your birthday but sent you no present which I now proceed to do. I refrained from sending you the present from reasons entirely based upon logic & sentiment; I couldn't think of anything . . .

[breaks off unsigned]

Annotations:

1 Arthur Osborne Lowry (1870-1945) was a successful Liverpool business man. He was often absent on trips connected with his cotton business, and he seems to have been a stern, middle-class, Victorian father. He was keen on sports, especially swimming – an enthusiasm Lowry inherited – but he was not an intellectual. He wanted the best for his four sons, which meant he wanted them to enter the family business, as the three older brothers did. But that said, it must be remembered that Arthur Lowry tried to do what he thought was right for Malcolm; he sent him to sea and to university, and he sent him money regularly.

Editorial Notes:

a. This letter was begun on letterhead from the Astoria Hotel, 12 Greek

Street, London W1, where Lowry was staying during February and March. On 14 February 1933, Arthur Lowry wrote to his son from Liverpool as follows: 'My dear Malcolm, Many Thanks for your wire just received, and for booking me a room at the Astoria Hotel for Thursday night. Best love, Your affectionate, Dad.' Lowry's reference to a wire suggests a 12–13 February 1933 date for this letter fragment to his father.

39: To Unidentified

P: H(ms)

[London]
[February 1933][a]

In a reply to your letter from Allied Newspapers[1] I would like to say that while I agree with the correspondent of the Manchester Evening Chronicle when he says that few young people would get beyond the first page of my story 'Seductio ad Absurdum.'[2] But it is not irrelevant to mention that as I wrote it at nineteen I almost come into this category myself: moreover some of the characters are younger than that. Perhaps we ought to have known better. I do not consider my own defence to be as important or amusing as the issue raised by this withdrawal: but while concerned with the former it is worth while mentioning that in excuse of its apparent continuous battery of abuses, that the thing is the fourth chapter of a novel (Ultramarine [to be] published by Jonathan Cape in May),[3] & as such it is consequent upon Chapter 3 & anterior to Chapter 5: equally serious happenings serious happenings & the both of these chapters are lyrical, or what have you, contagning no dialogue or 'Censorious' material, – 4 is for lack of a better word, a contrast to these 2, being a kind of prose fugue, with recurring themes – Mr O'Brien has decided that it is a whole in itself, & I am no person to disagree with an expert who does such painstaking work as he, his idea being to put his finger on the pulse of living work wherever it can be found, of work, which pompously speaking, seems to him a criticism of life. He makes no claim that a criticism of life in 1931 is a criticism of it in 1933; & quite likely by now the word it my paltry story is out of date, & all the bad words fallen out of use – into 'innocuous desuetude' in Manchester as well as anywhere else.

conclusion

I do however agree that it should be removed from the children's section. But how in the name of Doodle Dandy & the public pool of shame did it ever get there?

Leave them to Tristram Shandy & Don Quixote & Gulliver & the other school books[4]

[breaks off unsigned]

Annotations:

1 Allied Newspapers was a syndicate of British newspaper properties owned by James Gomer Berry, First Viscount Kemsley, and renamed for Kemsley in 1943. The Kemsley empire was bought by Roy Thomson in 1959. It is not clear whose letter Lowry is replying to, and this response carries neither addressee's name nor address.

2 In an article called 'Library Chairman Calls in a Book,' *Manchester Evening Chronicle*, 8 February 1933, 5, it is announced that 'all copies in the Manchester Public Libraries of "The Best Short Stories of 1931," in which one of the stories is entitled "Seductio ad Absurdum," by Malcolm Lowry, were returned.' Apparently Lowry's language had so deeply offended city councillor Frank Farrington that he wrote a letter of protest to fellow councillor I.W. Maitland, chairman of the Manchester Libraries Committee. The *Chronicle* article, however, is a response to the 'round-up,' which took place that afternoon, and its unidentified author is clearly unhappy with this decision. He or she praises the story as 'brilliantly written,' 'a little classic in its own style,' and well beyond the skill or interest of the average reader. A brief item in the *Manchester Evening News*, 13 February 1933, announces that, after a meeting of the Book Selection subcommittee of the Manchester Libraries, the volume will be allowed to remain in circulation – whether or not in the children's section is unclear.

3 *Ultramarine* was published by Cape on 12 June 1933.

4 Lowry's self-deprecating list of classics such as Lawrence Sterne's *Tristram Shandy* (1760-67), Miguel Cervantes' *Don Quixote* (1605; 1615), and Jonathan Swift's *Gulliver's Travels* (1726) is surely an ironic reminder that his story shares with them both a criticism of life and some earthy language.

Editorial Notes:

a. This letter has been drafted on the verso and recto of a 14 February 1933 letter from Arthur Lowry to his son. A brief note (or telegram) to Aiken (40) is also drafted on the letter from Lowry senior.

40: To Conrad Aiken

P: H(ms)
PP: *LAL* 41

[London]
[February 1933]

Conrad Aiken Jeakes House Rye
Conrad may I come down and see you
today it is urgent but I ask with
a bowed mind   Malc[a]

Editorial Notes:

a. This 'letter' appears to be a draft for a telegram. It is written at the
    bottom of a 14 February 1933 letter to Lowry from his father, who was
    to arrive in London two days later, Thursday, 16 February. Although
    the reason for Malcolm's desire to see Aiken is not certain, this 'letter' is
    scrawled beneath the end of letter **39** concerning obscenities in 'Seductio
    ad Absurdum,' which had appeared in O'Brien's *Best Short Stories of
    1931*. Lowry may have needed advice about the book of stories or about
    his father – or both.

41: To Conrad Aiken

P: H(ms); UBC(phc)
PP: *LAL* 41-42

[London]
[1933]

Some more cracks.[a]

Hilliot is a man who admittedly lives in 'introverted comas'[1] &
that is part of his trouble, however typical it may be: his is a
vicariousness beyond a statement of vicariousness because it is un-
objectifiable, he is never sure that any emotion is his own, & he quite
genuinely is 'cuckoo', he *is* a poet who can't write & may never be
able to. And this is where I must try to find some mitigating factor in
its being parasitic on 'Blue Voyage'. First, I find it in Ultramarine
however much a cento[2] being written at all, it has given me for a
time, a dominant principle – & if Blue Voyage does that for 1/15000
of its public, what about the other 14999? Second, under the reign of
Bloom & Sweeney,[3] a greater freedom seems to be permitted, these

are being absorbed into the racial consciousness: Blue Voyage, apart from its being the best nonsecular statement of the plight of the creative artist with the courage to live in a modern world, has become part of my consciousness, & I cannot conceive of any other way in which Ultramarine might be written.

I am probably to blame for certain slavishnesses in Chapter III, because they're not good enough, (but I couldn't do it in any other way), – & also for sheltering my Protean nature behind a certain understanding of The Waste Land. Philosophers & tinkle tonkle etc could be hooked out if you want them yourself. (Shantih means a song & a brothel as well as the Peace that Passeth all understanding)[4] Nevertheless I have sat & read my blasted book with increasing misery: with a misery of such intensity that I believe myself sometimes to be dispossessed, a spectre of your own discarded ideas, whose only claim to dignity exists in those ideas. Never mind – the book knows its got a paper cover, – forgive the forgoing somewhat pompous cracks – someone said 'a seer & a pathfinder' –
Well: once more I am
asking you the way –

Malcolm

Annotations:

1 Dana Hilliot, Lowry's hero in *Ultramarine*, 'believed himself to live in inverted, or introverted, commas . . .' (19).
2 A cento is a piece of writing composed of quotations from other writers. Lowry is already acutely aware of what would be his lifelong fear of being called a plagiarist.
3 References to James Joyce's Leopold Bloom in *Ulysses* (1922) and T.S. Eliot's 'Sweeney' poems (1920, 1932) are used here as a shorthand for their authors. Eliot's *Sweeney Agonistes*, first published on 1 December 1932, was frequently performed as a one-act play between 1932 and 1954, so Lowry's reference to the 'reign' of Sweeney may well echo the view of Eliot at that time.
4 See the closing line of T.S. Eliot's *Waste Land*, 'shantih shantih shantih,' and *Ultramarine*, 'she shantih' (59). The influence of Eliot, among others, is pervasive in the 1933 edition of *Ultramarine*.

Editorial Notes:

a. Aiken has written at the top of the first page: '3 pages missing – C.A.' On the verso of the two extant pages are typed passages from *Ultramarine*, which Lowry was revising for publication.

42: To Tom Forman

P: H(ms)

[London]
[1933]ᵃ

Tom,[1] by airmale
delivered from denoted by (subtle) emempthisis, thrive

    Tom my old aerialmale posthumous
    Tom Tom, the snipers run
    mein leber vorster Freud,
    Emperor of evigkeit and center of the boyd
    Punchus pilot of Portmadoc more than navvygarter thou fore-
                         most fighting fell[2]
    Seal up seal up the ships boys eyes The bosuns arse as well
    In the name of the foreman and of the layman and
        of the holy toast   ahthen.
    Hear my bleeding massage from X Oberannacow[3]
    tom tomb the the snipers run mein leber vorster freud
    underlined for emempthisis thrive and scenter of the boyd
    thrive scenter of the rebelled buoyed so may your dorsey fin
    grey brush the chords of christ away & tie them up a gin
    7 pint to pointman horseman whorseman & the rest

    Seal up the womb seal up the tomb seal up the charing cross
                o jeers
    keep mongrels in their mangers and kenelms in their foss
    Seal up seal up the ship boy's eyes the bosun's arse as well,
                    agn
    Like Brunswick in the field foremost phairghting fell.

[unsigned]

Annotations:

1 Tom Forman, a close friend of Lowry's and John Davenport's during
their Cambridge years and the early thirties, owned his own plane,
which perhaps accounts for Lowry's sending this letter 'by airmale.'
Forman seems to have faded from Lowry's life when Lowry left London
for Paris at the end of 1933, but Jan Gabrial remembers a trip to Wales in
Tom's plane sometime during the fall of 1933, and she has described his
girl-friend, Elizabeth Cheyne, as possessing the 'hauteur' of the 'landed
gentry.' See Lowry's 24 April 1931 (**29**) letter to Aiken.
2 Lowry's parodic reference here and in the last line of this letter is to

Byron's poem *Childe Harold's Pilgrimage* III.23.207: 'He rush'd into the field, and, foremost fighting, fell.'

3 Lowry's joke involves a pun on the name of the Bavarian town Oberammergau, where passion-plays have been held every ten years since 1634.

Editorial Notes:

a. Lowry's poetic parody has been drafted on letterhead from the Astoria Hotel, 12 Greek Street, London W1, and at the top of the page he has written: 'scenter of the wash bôyd.' At two points in the last three lines, he has inserted interlinear phonemes that suggest puns.

In the spring of 1933 Lowry travelled to Granada, Spain, with Conrad Aiken and his second wife, Clarissa Lorenz. The trip was not a happy one, and Lowry, who was drinking heavily, made a spectacle of himself in the streets of the Spanish town. All this changed dramatically, however, when a beautiful young American woman arrived on the scene. Lowry fell immediately and passionately in love with Jan Gabrial, who had heard of his writing and was writing fiction herself, and their happy, intense romance flourished on the potent mixture of youth, literature, conversation, and cervesa. When Jan left Granada to continue her tour of Spain, Lowry was bereft and began to chase her around Europe with letters. Until now, very little has been known about this chapter in Lowry's life, but the following letters from the summer of 1933 to the summer of 1934 trace Malcolm and Jan's relationship from meeting and courtship to marriage and a period of separation when Jan returned to New York to see her mother in April 1934. These letters provide new information about Lowry's activities, his writing, and his troubled relations with the Aikens. They also cast some light on Lowry's precarious emotional and psychological balance at the time.

43: To Jan Gabrial

P: private(ms)

[Granada,]
[Spain]
[22 May 1933][a]
9:30 a.m.   Hollywood   Bar Granada[1]

Darling – darling – darling, said the Chinese nightingale[2] – Every now & then a streetcar passing obliterates the noise of your memory, so that memory itself becomes a terribly attenuated sound of singing iron – transformed into a thousand brazen bells, which keep time in my brain to a million more, one for every second, or hour, or aeon we spent together – but here I am off again on an evasion of my real feelings, which are bloody awful. To hell with these purple passages – but what's a fellow to do when language itself, purple or otherwise, is an evasion & despair, & one feels oneself to be on the threshold of this – Would this look less or more selfconscious if it were typed; even if silence is the only honesty; but writing to you brings me nearer to you. Once more you are here drinking cervesas, your shadow runs before you along the street, a man shouts something as we pass – but isn't that the meaning & object of life? – And then your nearness strikes into me like a red-hot operating needle, & a shapeless swarm of questions, anxieties, speculations, hurdle into my mind; in a kind of anaesthesia I wonder how far you've got in the last hour, whether your I'm sure admirable modest efficient tool of society, quiet upholder of the conventions Frenchman has proposed once more,[3] what a *word*, good god, *what* a word, whether he is disposed – to get off at Ronda or come to Sevilla – & indisposed which last I hope speaking generally – & why go to Sevilla via Ronda, – isn't it rather like going to New York via Greenland, but I hope you're happy, & oh hell, damn, blast & putrefaction anyway. When I was an editor, for a short time, of a Cambridge rag,[4] I loathed untidy m.ss, – they gave me a pain in the neck & I usually didn't take so much trouble with them, as with the typed & immaculate ones, the truth being that the untidy ones were so often the worst – however said editor's going to write a love letter in pencil & if necessary, sometimes painfully untidily if his lady will forgive him ————

Hullo, i've come into the cathedral, ssh – will you come with me, damned ugly I call it, a chap at the door asked me if I'd like to visit the royal tomb – Ferdinand & Isabella wasn't it,[5] & wasn't she the lady who didn't change her drawers for forty days and forty nights? – I replied no but had come in here to cry was that a compliment, – could I cry –

I have now cried, so I don't know what else to do save pray. Don't leave me, Jan, will you, I can't bear that you should go away, so I shall have to write my prayer out so that I can still be with you, but I can't think of anything to say except what the hell god, so I'm going to cry again & you in twenty four hours in Pilate's house or the Palace of Gold & I'm going to cry over again – I don't give a damn who sees me

                                        [breaks off unsigned]

Annotations:

1 Jan Gabrial was born Jennie Bermingham van der Heim in New York City on 11 June 1911; from the age of seventeen she has called herself Jan Gabrial after one of her father's ancestors. She was the only child of Lion van der Heim (1873-1924), a classical violinist, and Emily Betts (1874-1949), a public school teacher. Jan's father was born in Rotterdam, Holland, and studied music at the Brussels conservatory in Belgium. He emigrated to the United States, where he met his wife, and they settled in New York City.

2 Lowry is quoting Vachel Lindsay's 1917 poem 'The Chinese Nightingale'; see his 1939 letter (**88**) to Carol Phillips and his October 1956 letter (**675**) to Margerie Lowry.

3 According to her records, Jan left Granada on 22 May, 'only two days' after meeting Malcolm. She continued her tour of Spain by going on to Seville. The 'Frenchman' Lowry refers to was probably a Syrian whom Jan had met on her travels, but he and Jan were not lovers.

4 Lowry was actively involved with *Experiment* magazine between 1930 and 1932, but his name does not appear as an editor. At various times between 1928 and 1931 the editors are listed as William Empson, Jacob Bronowski, and Hugh Sykes. Gerald Noxon, a close friend of Lowry's, contributed regularly and is described as the magazine's publisher.

5 Ferdinand II (1452-1516) and Isabella I (1451-1504) were the monarchs who consolidated the Spanish state in 1492 and established the Spanish empire in North America.

Editorial Notes:

a. All Lowry's letters to Jan included in this edition are holograph; most are written in pencil, and all lack dates. This letter, however, appears to have been written immediately after her 22 May departure by train from Granada.

44: To Jan Gabrial

P: private(ms)

[Granada,]
[Spain]
[May 1933]

The next morning – I live only for your letter Jan, will you tell me about what story of your own you like best, what you are reading, what you plan to write, what you are thinking of, what you are not thinking of, what makes you happy, what makes you unhappy – no you can't possibly answer all these questions, but you could tell me what's nearest your heart so that I can carry it near mine, oh most of all, tell me that my girl, and also tell me about your childhood, – goldenrod & the arrowy-leaved ailanthus tree. And if you are writing a story can I possibly make any suggestions – Oh Jan if we got together there's nothing we couldn't do, the world is ours. If we could meet as we did, we could knock Lawrence & Moses for a row of milkbottles as prophets.[1] And talking about the former, couldn't you be perfectly frank with me about sex, affairs etc: if you think that by being reticent or evasive you would save hurting or angering me, – I do not flatter myself that you care about these particular two things but for the moment we shall assume that you do – then I would point out that evasion is precisely what does hurt: if you are merely bored at the idea of being frank about matters which would seem to concern only yourself may I point out that I love you, & that fate intends that you should love me, & if we didn't love each other, then the earth will start to go backwards once more when it has found out about until it has discovered its mistake, or what it dropped on the way, or who's fault it is, & all will be corrected, & that therefore it does concern me, – to the point of agony: and that furthermore if you fell down on the road & broke your nose – as by the way you very nearly did several times – I should be sorry for you first & jealous of the road afterwards.

I love you, Jan, & with a red heart, somebody said the voice of your eyes is deeper than all roses, & god I could cry when I think of you, nobody not even the rain has such small hands,[2] – could there be a more cruel word than 'affair', a more paltry, cruel, killing word than that – 'I'm not going to have an affair with you, Mr Lowry, if that's what you mean.' – But I suppose you were right. Not God almighty & all the principalities & powers & your namesake angel, could have known what Mr Lowry he did mean, yes perhaps old God knew, – well he must have done, it being his arrangement & winked his one eye, (the other one was looking the other way,) & adjusted his bispectrum spectacles, – & said 'God eternally damblasts the word affair, as used by Jan Gabrial [&] Lowry', & somebody said – or if your wish be to close me, I and my life will shut very beautifully suddenly, as when the heart of this flower imagines the snow carefully everywhere descending; nothing which we are to perceive in this world equals the power of your intense fragility whose texture compels me with the colour of its countries, rendering death and forever with each breathing . . . was it Edward Estlin Cummings who said that at ½ past God on an evening in Granada?[3]
Oh Jan, I could make you so happy and we could run the reading public and I shouldn't have taken a scrap of notice of what you said

on that morning should I? Oh Christ, we shall be so happy in one another and you didn't even leave me four words behind, – but you left me a lifetime, Jan, an eternity, & the idea of a world, & a task.

But time no longer rules me, as it has ruled me, or as it ruled Baudelaire[4] once – with his brutal dictatorship, or can drive me, like a beast, with his double goad: 'Pull on sweat slave, live & be damned.' I can dictate to time, & I give him three months to cleanse the Aegean stables[5] of my consciousness, with its fiendish cloaca of memories, fears, agonies, nightmares, rages, & panics – most of them imaginary, which had reduced me to a state of 'ceaseless nervous terror.'

Oh Jan Jan, love me, please – think, would you leave me and England or China to see a monastery in Turkey – could not we build it ourselves if we wanted one? I know that the man you met was a dead one, dead for lack of love – your love, who has had little enough to his credit except to make an incredible mess of other people's lives, – but he had sought you oh so long in the town & meadow & in the sky & now he has found you in a kind of no man's land between heaven & hell. I love you, Jan, I have always loved you, your voice has been the pity in the voice of the gale, in the compassion in the voice of the howled night storm, the tenderness & goodness in the voice of the terrible fire – I love you, & I cannot live without you, & if I cannot have you I shall die, as God surely would intend me to die, if I could not have you.

Couldn't we make of life one good, strong, faithful, thing – So that not even Mr Death could in any wise part us? – So, thinking of you the consciousness becomes a country fair, & I'm going down to the station to look at the bright railway line which saw you last.

As ever & ever without end

Malcolm

Annotations:

1 D.H. Lawrence (1885-1930), the English author of such novels as *Sons and Lovers* (1913) and *Lady Chatterley's Lover* (1928), also wrote a wide range of essays and poems on religious and prohetic subjects. Lawrence was important to Lowry at this time in his life; see his 1934 letter (**60**) to Jan.

2 Lowry is, in fact, quoting verbatim the last two lines of e.e. cummings' poem 'Somewhere I Have Never Travelled' (1931): 'The voice of your eyes is deeper than all roses / nobody, not even the rain, has such small hands.' Lowry continues to quote from this poem; see annotation 3.

3 e.e. cummings said precisely 'that'; see the third and fourth stanzas of 'Somewhere I Have Never Travelled' (1931).

4 Charles Baudelaire (1821-67) often characterizes time as an enemy

devouring his life in *Les Fleurs du Mal* (1857); see, for example, the poem
'L'Ennemi.'
5 Cleansing the stables of Augeas was the fifth of the twelve labours of
Hercules.

45: To Jan Gabrial

P: private(ms)

[Gibraltar]
[May–June 1933]

My own love – I'm leaving Gibralter on the Strathaird about five
minutes ago, so to speak – ;[1] Cook's is still sorting the mail but I shall
be too lucky if I get a letter so I'm trying not to expect one.
The solitude just drones on from everlasting to everlasting without
you, & the voyage – my god what a prospect!
The same cauliflower faced stewards, smells of degenerate soup,
horse racing & every conceivable self-conscious device to make passengers miserable. We would have fun though – I love you so, Jan,
my heart seems to be racing like a propeller all the time. And Jan, do
be happy, won't you, be as efficient & hasty as you please, but be
happy: & remember sometimes that I hear & speak only one name
which is yours & that I mean to earn you & my dear bury all the
things which cause you pain, as a man on the shore buries a poor
paper in the sand.

My love to you, my lady

Malcolm

P.S. I'll write you from the ship, & I'll be explicit then about
address.
I'll see what's happened to my blasted book, – see what I can
do about the play, & then down the little hell.[2] I shld probably
sail from Hamburg in which case. And then, & then, England
& you & all loveliness

Annotations:

1 According to Clarissa Lorenz's memories of this holiday in Spain, the
Aikens, with Malcolm in tow, must have set sail at the end of May
or beginning of June for the return trip to England; see *Lorelei Two:
My Life with Conrad Aiken* (Athens: University of Georgia Press, 1983),
pp. 153-59.
2 Lowry was looking forward to the publication of *Ultramarine*, which

appeared on 12 June 1933. The play he refers to is probably his adaptation of Nordahl Grieg's novel *The Ship Sails On* (*Skibet gaar videre*, 1924); see his September 1933 letter (**51**) to Jan.

46: To Jan Gabrial

P: private(ms)

ss *Strathaird*,
[June 1933][a]

– I've thought hard of something interesting to say, & god knows enough is going on round me: the blokes coming home on leave from India all seem sorry they ever started; encrusted out there I suppose, – & beginning to get melancholy, alot can happen for good & evil in 3 years, our last 3 have been swift & cataclysmic enough!

London bears the [brunt] of the war – Ultramarine – it's a small thing perhaps, – but cld it seem that I've written it for you? (which I have) or, if it has any success, wld you be pleased: – otherwise such success wld be merely bitter. I don't think it's a bad book, although they are very rotten things in it, but I expect it either to be dropped on from a great height, or just simply ignored: but if it isn't & it goes, – especially (if its by any chance accepted there –) in America – would you be pleased . . . just a small bit. Otherwise – to hell with it.
But I'll never write another book as disintegrated, psychically, as that: it might well have been, & very nearly was, a posthumous book . . . do you mind my talking about our blasted work – could we write alot of short stories together someday, – masterpieces, – its a limited form of art, dying? – but we could something new, cut a Suez Canal through the whole bloody business of living, – & even if some of the [blasters] didn't come off, oh how happy we could be in one another, {I've said that before}
—— [leap] the Vin gogh prison wall I hear so much about W the P that it wld seem that [illegible] I can't say anything but [this:] If I don't die of love: it has been done. Troilus did . . . Can't help being jealous of your Diomeds,[1] – but its certainly impossible for you to see a bullfight without one, – also to be happy, – 'be happy', – I meant to put that in my marconigram. I wld send you another one saying that & that alone now but I can't face the wireless operator again for a bit – last time he said 'Don't look so fearfully desperate:' Did you see a place in Spain called Ceba or Seba or Zeba – anyway pronounced Theba, obviously some corruption of Thebes:[2] twenty

or thirty miles from Ronda I imagine – I saw it from the train & I thought 'we must go there.' Its an unearthly place looking like Poe's Usher, or Kafka's Castle place I've ever seen.[3]

I didn't enjoy Ronda, although its good: I can't share a place anyway, as a rule, – a few college pals of mine perhaps, a few firemen I've known, but with the Aikens, no no no, & again **NO** It gives me great pleasure to write that – since faith is cured . . .

Oh Christ that my love were in my arms & I in my bed again[4]

I'm not in l. with an ideal – not nympholepsy – I don't close my eyes . . . {what is the life of a writer?} I think, objectively, – & ultimately: – that everything depends on faithfulness, – Baudelaire said of his lady love: you are more than my religion, you are my superstition – isn't 2 days a lifetime? [illegible], it is possible to reply of 2 days – but what of 2 months, of 22 months, of 22 years – 'the dance of hours, the dance of houses – The whirligig dance of people – the even decline cakewalk of imaginary genius, the long delayed recognition becoming undeserved before it arrives, another case of the crucifixion going backwards, the whirligig of taste, of fashion – oh, that chap, who's he? – not that anybody has read him: – And, ultimately, is there anything to say? . .

– So dedicate one's life to the truth? Jesus Christ . . . At any rate the burden is on me; When I met you I was going, quite merrily, to hell: dementia praecox was [rocking] in the luggage racket of my consciousness above me, another jolt, a sudden stop! a shock & I think it & all its frightful contents would have spilled about me: In spite of this . . . I had my life in control, –

I say to you with a black passion – or if you prefer it a black & white passion – that I do not mean this. I started life as a potential golf champion, – although that's hard to believe. But I never planted any nasturtiums or trees or nightscented stock, I never had that nearness to earth which I have now – I was wondering whether I've gone too far away from it, whether I've gone too far into the world of myself that there [illegible] myself there *is* no hope. Its all right I know differently now. For some unknown reason, life has been the dark, silent thing for me, & that's all there is to be said: god I'd like to work in a garden now, to see things grow, our plants, the rows of sweet peas, the hundred lilac trees planted in moonlight, all those things which are really good: – really to create with you, to see good things come up with you & to 'stand together' & wonder at it: God, the suspicion, – the meanness, the cruelty, & the utter imbecility in most forms of work & in most relationships – the besetting meanness

[breaks off unsigned]

Annotations:

1 In classical mythology Troilus is a son of Priam and he is killed by Achilles in the Trojan War. He is also the hero of Chaucer's poem *Troilus and Criseyde* (1385) and Shakespeare's tragedy *Troilus and Cressida* (ca 1601). In both of these works Cressida betrays Troilus with the Greek soldier Diomedes.

2 Teba is a small town to the north of Ronda on the railway line between Granada and Algeciras in Spain. Lowry retained vivid memories of this town; see his 1950-51 letter (**433**) to Viking Press.

3 Edgar Allan Poe (1809-49) creates a mysterious, decaying mansion in his story 'The Fall of the House of Usher' (1839), and Franz Kafka's castle is that strange, elusive place that K, the protagonist of *The Castle* (*Das Schloss*, 1926), has trouble reaching.

4 This line is from the anonymous Middle English lyric called 'Western Wind'; Lowry uses it again in his 22 August 1939 letter (**100**) to Margerie Bonner.

Editorial Notes:

a. This two-page holograph has been written on ship's stationary, but it is undated. There are numerous deletions and interlineations that make the writing illegible at several points.

47: To Jan Gabrial

P: private(ms)

[ss *Strathaird*,]
[June 1933]

– Just a short note to get the 12 o'clock post. Now our lives go along the parallel lines that meet.

I got your long letter by the 4 pm post. My poor darling: what the hell, its a poor bait etc most of us wriggle after, but no longer: I can't speak, but oh my poor sweet sweet darling, let me say just this – I'm sure all those who are really good have to be tried by fire, & every second that you suffered will be an hour of peace, I know that may sound alot of guff but it's true, & if any pain remains for god's sake give it to me, because you've had enough: the pain you suffered on that table will be bloody well avenged with a white hot slice bar in a furnace, every blow you received on your face will be returned with thanks to fate with a shovel until fate screams for mercy, but her hands we shall leave uncannily alive to sew up the wounds she has already begun to draw together.[1] Does that sound too drastic –

Jan, Jan, Jan, Jan, your name speaks to me all day & she went on to say that desire is whatever & etcetera, that satisfaction is unwhatever & unetcetera that love perhaps is possession & what is possession sans faith sans trust sans love.² I agree, damn all, but wld reply that all we know is that our love is the sum of all these otherwise idiot trifles & that noone of them exists wholly or hugely without what you & I know, & that the language is too exhausted to explain any of it anyhow: & its no good accounting for every emotion intellectually, it can of course be did but if the stimulus to acct for it be strong in a fellow bad cess to him – he doesn't know what I know.

I haven't left the next letter you wrote me out of my hand, oh my dear, I slept with it in my hand, & I bear it through the streets like some huge fragility which I am frightened to drop in case it should get hurt.

Thanks awfully for 'urgente'ing the second one, or I shouldn't have got it till to–day. I sail to-morrow on the s.s. Strathaird, but cld you write

c/o Astoria Hotel	{a queer little place in
Greek Street	Soho which has marvellous
London	Chianti}³

To be left till called for
(in the style of the 1830's) – for I doubt whether a letter wld get to the Strathaird in Tilbury in time.

By the way, I posted a letter in Gib.[raltar] with a Spanish stamp: I'm awfully sorry; you'll probably have to pay on it – but I'd been writing it in both Algeciras & Gib & on the ferry & I must have clean forgot what country I was in. I had to post it in a hurry too & what I was thinking of was whether the Spanish stamp wld stick on or not because it didn't seem to have enough glue. Stupid of me.

All my love to you, my Jan & then all over again

Malcolm

Annotations:

1 While she was visiting Majorca, Jan's hand became severely infected and she was obliged to return to a clinic in Barcelona for an operation that kept her hospitalized for ten days.

2 Lowry is rather inappropriately echoing the closing lines of Jaques' cynical summary of life in Shakespeare's *As You Like It* II.vii: 'Last scene of all, / That ends this strange eventful history, / Is second childishness and mere oblivion, / Sans teeth, sans eyes, sans taste, sans everything.'

3 Chianti is a dry red Italian wine. The Astoria is the hotel where Lowry stayed off and on during the late summer and fall of 1933.

48: To Jan Gabrial

P: private(ms)

Cottage Hospital,
Moretonhampstead,
Devon
[England]
[Summer 1933]

My Jan
– I'm bitterly sorry that you should have been without a letter in
Madrid, but I was so tied up with pain that I couldn't unravel anything to say:[1] I think of you all the time, & I love you – I don't think
you would want me to say more than that. But I'm so shot through
with injections that the passage of the arm to the table is an arc of a
hundred miles, the grasping of the pencil is an act of faith lasting 100
years, & the writing itself seems to be done by someone else. Where
I'm not burnt up with pain I'm burnt up with desire for you, & this is
a kind of noise as well, like the pneumatic drill which is tearing up
the road outside. Do you ever feel anything for me like that? –
The photos were, are, swell: one or two of them have got a bit
creased through having been under my pillow: & one, for the same
reason, has actually come in half, but its left you perfectly intact: I've
smoothed them all out, & stuck that one together again, so they're all
O.K, & considerately looked after, but they get so much looked at,
they have a tough time. But I don't really need a photograph at all to
remember you by –
Just one, on a fellow's desk to talk to – Hells delight – I hope this
gets you in Barcelona –
Scandinavia? Well, I know only Norway, which is a spiritual
home or something of your doppleganger & me & you & my doppleganger: if you go there queer things will happen, I promise you
that. In the first place it's as full of ghosts as Spain is empty of them &
they'll all try to help you at once because they'll recognize you. If
you go there do as I tell you, & you won't become confused.[2] I
should spend two or three days in Oslo, & if you do go to the Røde
Molle & drink sherry under the geraniums: go down the Holmerkol-
len, from there, which is the Oslo underground, just turn to the left
at the Nationaltheatret exit from the Røde Molle, that being an ugly
looking theatre with Ibsen, Bjornsen, & Hieberg outside it,[3] & walk
up the hill a bit: the entrance to the underground is on the middle of
the square behind the Nationaltheatre – go down the *right* entrance,

& when you see a tram come along with Frognarsaeteren on its fore-
head, take it, pay 90 øre I think it is, & go all the way; it will take you
up a mountain which is just the best thing in the world & there's a
restaurant up there where they speak German for you. If you *want* a
quiet & excellent restaurant in Oslo, Jacques Bagatelle in the Bygdø
Allé is marvellous as I remember it. And I should visit Bygdø itself,
& see the Viking ship & drink wine & look out on the fjord. By god,
I'll be there with you in spirit all right all right Jan. If you say you are
the wife of one of the best friends of Nordahl Grieg it might help: his
address used to be 68 Bygdø Allé & Skibet gaar videre is his book
from which my play is adapted.
Eine länger Brief kommt sofort, aber Liebe kommt hiermit[4] is the
nicest thing anyone ever said: & I say it back to you with an unending
ache of love in my heart

                                                                    Malcolm

[P.S.] You should of course try & see Bergen, also: & if you ever take
a train journey for god's sake do it in the daytime because the
country's marvellous

Annotations:

1 For a period during the summer of 1933 Lowry was in hospital in Devon
   followed by a rest in Torquay. His claims to have been suffering from
   dysentery and an infection have not been substantiated, and it is also
   possible that he was being treated for his alcoholism.
2 Lowry had visited Oslo in September 1931 and, as these instructions to
   Jan indicate, he had a precise recollection of places in and around the
   city. The Røde Molle (Red Mill), Bygdø Allé, Frognersaeteren, Jacques
   Bagatell and the Viking ship are all mentioned in his 8 September 1931
   letter (35) to Nordahl Grieg, and they retained special significance for
   him.
3 Statues of the three most distinguished Norwegian dramatists, Henrik
   Ibsen (1828-1906), Bjørnstjerne Bjørnsen (1832-1910), and Gunnar
   Heiberg (1857-1929), are located outside Oslo's National Theatre.
4 Jan's German greeting is: 'A longer letter is coming soon, but love
   comes with this one.'

49: To Jan Gabrial

P: private(ms)

Couldn't keep my promise about the letter before, for reasons below. This is it.

> Moretonhampstead,
> Cottage Hospital,
> Devon,
> England
> [Summer 1933]

Sweet Jan: damn it to hell, I thought I might take the count, & I have done; I've gone down for 9, & only just not 10, in which case I wouldn't have been at the boat to meet you at all. As it is I've been delirious for 4 days, during which time I think I've learnt a little of what pain you must have gone through on that blasted table: like a tree of pain, growing inside you, spreading its branches with broken bottles jangling on each one – was that the kind of thing? –

Dysentery it is, & I must have had it in a latent form, for a very long time, only its never been properly analysed; & behaving in the most tropical way so that I feel like a character in White Cargo now:[1] you saw various manifestations of it in me, do you remember mopping my brow for me once very kindly about 10 times in succession? And how all the rest of the time I was, & how I couldn't hold a drink steady . . . Well all that was the effect of the shock of loving you, which made my blood run like an ocean of fire, having angered this stupid sleeping little bug, angered him, because he had to wake up because it was too hot. The counter shock of leaving you so suddenly, – the shock of not being able to have you in my arms, which made my blood cool everywhere but in my heart, left me open to his attack.

Well thank god I can get rid of him, & all the bloody complexities & imaginary terrors he has evidently been responsible for all the while, in one, & be a fit man once more.

Whenever the pain was most unbearable & it was getting impossible to carry on I would just say – Are you there Jan – And you would reply – Yes, Mr Lowry, as distinctly as anything. And everything was O.K. Thanks for your last letter, it was topping. But to hell with being Lowry the Writer & Lowry the Man & all that, – I may be a failure at both those – I'd much rather you loved me if I was a bootblack or whatever sort of creeping Jesus I was.

I'd watch over you wherever you are just the same – send along as much of your story as you can – I love you zwanzig mal – & there ain't no pain at the moment & its peaceful here, no London papers so I don't know how Ultramarine's been received – only a good pine tree outside the window & a cow. I have a sudden desire to kiss you on your breast – do you mind that?

love

Malcolm

Annotations:

1 *White Cargo* (1930) was a turgid film adapted from an equally melodramatic 1925 play by Leon Gordon. Both the play and the film were based on Ida Simonton's novel *White Cargo* (1923) about a drunken doctor and a young Englishman who ruin themselves in a west coast African town.

50: To Jan Gabrial

P: private(ms)

[Sussex,]
[England]
[Summer 1933]

My girl:

I mailed a letter, 2 letters, to you yesterday: forgive me for leaving you for almost a week without a word, but for that week as I explained I was winning the horizontal championship with fever, so instead of writing to you I talked to you, my head on my beloved's breast. This is going to fly by airmail if there such a thing in this comic old country, so it may get you before the other two; that's why I repeat the explanation.

I'm still in Sussex, but tomorrow I go to the above address & get the letter which I pray you've written.[1] And even if you haven't – (– Fragment of conversation going on in this pub – 'Mark Antony had a fish shop back of the market, but he got run in – he was a communist! What do you make of that, Watson?')

Yes, tomorrow I go to London & start once more to live, or live as well as I can without you: I start to live for the time we meet again.

Even if you haven't? . . I was going to say that you won't find it possible to betray me with the flicker of an eyelid: obviously, if you must, you will have eyes for other men than me, & thoughts of others – I'd be a very poor sap if I flattered myself you hadn't – but you can't betray me, you can't be unfaithful to something which is strong & faithful itself, & my love for you is that, & if it lives in me it

must live in you too: & in the hour that you need more than me alive
I shall be dead because for you to have needed more than me alive
you must have needed me dead: & even then my love would still remain as strong & faithful as before. So there we are, aren't we.

do you ever think of our meeting: I want to hug you, all the beauty
of you, all the morning light, to sink into you as into sand: oh the
comfort of you, my god the comfort & peace & calm after the sea-
weariness & blood & sweat that will come & that has been.

I love you with all my heart, Jan.

This is from

Malcolm

Annotations:

1 This undated letter has been written on Astoria Hotel letterhead, the
London address that Lowry had given to Jan earlier in the summer, but
it is clear from the context that he is writing from a pub somewhere in
Sussex.

51: To Jan Gabrial

P: private(ms)

As from
Vernon Court Hotel
Torquay, [Devon][1]
[England]
[August 1933]

My dearest.

I just got your postcard – I've been in London racketing about
from theatre to theatre, & from producer to producer, with my
play:[2] I don't know yet whether I've struck oil.

Apart from this, no news; I live to see you again, a waiting world
you call it.

London was hellishly hot and dusty, but the thought of your loveliness made it bearable. Oh god, to touch you again, to see you, to
hear your voice. It will be like harbour after the tempest.

I haven't written for some weeks, there is something to be said for
being silent. A story of mine comes out in New York in October, in
Story.[3]

All my love

Malcolm

Annotations:

1 Torquay is a popular seaside resort in South Devon overlooking Tor
  Bay. Several of the following letters to Jan are written from here because
  Lowry was recuperating from an illness (or his bout with alcohol) that
  had troubled him during the trip to Spain. See Bowker (159-60).
2 Lowry's dramatization of Grieg's novel *The Ship Sails On* has not
  survived.
3 This is 'On Board the West Hardaway,' *Story* (October 1933): 12-22.

52: To Jan Gabrial

P: private(ms)

> Vernon Court Hotel,
> Torquay
> [August 1933]

My own Jan.
   I haven't written for five or six days. I've been in a black mood: I
would start a letter to you, and abandon it, start another, and abandon that. You also left me for some time without a letter – then you
sent me a lovely postcard: but the letter which followed it worries
me! There's no need for you to feel you've got to say you love me,
was what I said to myself – is that a good title for a song? –
   No – don't feel that, please. You must know that I know that you
know that we know that there's no need to say anything. God knows
its comforting to hear you say it, and I pray that you mean it, but if
its one hell of an effort I'd rather you didn't say anything. Perhaps it
was my fault in the first place for expecting the morning to come
before the dawn, which never can happen, perhaps just because I
foresaw that the morning was, and is, inevitable anyhow: I shall win
you, on far coasts: even now I tread the air beside you, sword in hand
to keep the wolves away. Oh, these bloody chaps of yours, I hate
them, because I always suspect the spoiler or destroyer in their
midst. As soon as people find out, they try to spoil. We must protect
our love from the world because the world will do its foul damnedest
to scratch it away from us: only the gods are on our side, and it is to
them that we have to look for sympathy & help, when we need it.
What the hell, you say, but it's true.
I can't say how tenderly I feel, Jan, it's a warm, queer melting feeling
in the heart.
   Its wonderful to know that soon I shall see you again. In about a
month now? . .

I hope that you are not lonely, and yet I hope also that you can be quite happy when you are alone: oh I am telling the truth when I say that I am there with you, I love you so.

In spite of what I said, I hope you do write me a love letter.

But don't forget that I said also I had to win you: time is a concertina, & gawd plays tunes backwards, so sometimes the prize is given before the game is won, but the game has to be played all the same.

My love to you

Malcolm

[P.S.] I hope you go to Naples. A very particular friend of ours once lived there, many many years ago. He was a wild Irishman and has since gone to his people, whoever they were, but I think you'd know what I mean if you went there – despite the pestiferous stinkadore.

53: To Jan Gabrial

P: private(ms)

Vernon Court Hotel,
Torquay
[August 1933]

Jan: no news from you, I do hope you're not ill or in pain or unhappy or restless or tired or blue. It's extraordinary how blindly one trusts a postman just because he's a government official: how do I know he won't take this letter & copy it out & send it to his sweetheart, although he couldn't love her as much as I love you. (By the way I'm getting much better now, & feel that I go out & knock down a few stonewalls before lunch.)

I think of you looking like a flower. And do you love me not, & is chaos come again, do you peer at all my faults through a telescope. And take a Chinese fireman out to lunch. Well it all comes back to me in the end, I've stolen your destiny & I've got it in a casket. Meantime beware the woman with the dark glasses, the humpbacked surgeons, & the scissors man. And remember – I've been watching you for hours, all this time, over the garden wall. I've got a very special sense of fun I have.

always, your

Malcolm

54: To Jan Gabrial

P: private(ms)

> Vernon Court Hotel,
> Torquay, Devon
> [August 1933]

My sweet sweetheart, gosh I'm sorry about your hand, – your shoulder, I hope it didn't hurt too much, – why couldn't I be with you.[1] But I am & was with you, but I can't bear your suffering. Oh Jan, I love you so much, so much, I carry you about with me like a father carries his child – I wish I could have taken all the pain from you. I would have come right over to your side, I'd have flown over – only that wld have killed me – I wouldn't be so much good to you dead, although my love is stronger than that. I love you, love you, love you, Jan – how's your hand now. I got to go to sleep now & will you say you love me – goodnight. I'm holding your hand now so that it won't hurt so much.

Will you be faithful to me – not that we could betray each other. My blood stirs for noone but you.

> Malcolm

[P.S.] I convalesce at above address – write there. My roving days are over for a bit. Sending you Ultramarine. It's had a very mixed reception in England but has aroused some enthusiasm.

In Scotland it's been misunderstood & attacked so savagely it's almost had to be withdrawn from publication.[2]

Fancy all this over one melancholy little book.

Annotations:

1 Lowry is referring to the operation that Jan had had in Barcelona for an infected hand; see letter **47**.
2 The Scottish attack appeared in the *Glasgow Herald* for 15 June 1933. In an anonymous article on four books called 'New Novels: Highbrow Sailormen,' the reviewer damned *Ultramarine* as boring and silly, with 'page after page of incoherent maunderings' in a language that is 'monotonously profane and obscene without being realistic' (4).

55: To Jan Gabrial

P: private(ms)

[Vernon Court Hotel,]
[Torquay]
[August 1933]

Write: Vernon Court Hotel, Torquay, England.

Jan: I set out to post a letter to you but when I got here I remembered I forgot to remember to bring it. The truth is I've been with you all the time & I suppose it must have struck me as queer to go post a letter to you when you were by my side: although I have written one to you when all of you was: remember? This is a funny, tawdry place, on the sea, like a pub picture of China gone crazy, only its got speedboats & plenty of sea & diving boards & this afternoon a cruiser, god knows where it came from. And we shall spend some blue sea mornings here. And today Ultramarine got a review which said it was great which it isn't but our life together will be is because I see it just so. Sez you. Sez me. And I don't care who knows it, & if you've read this far, postman, you'll know too won't you, & good luck to you. Yes, and you too. And you. And please god tell her to look after her hand & don't let it hurt her, & you too god please don't let half a tear drop from her eye because I love her & love her & love her again.

Mr Lowry has spo[ken]

56: To Jan Gabrial

P: private(ms)

Vernon Court Hotel,
Torquay, Devon,
England
[August 1933]

Dearest Jan –

Got your letter from Barcelona this morning: I think you'll find quite alot of mail between Biarritz and Marseilles: I do hope you got some of them in Barcelona.[1] I don't pretend to understand the intricacies of continental mail, but I don't see any reason for a letter bound for England to go via Alaska. The photograph you sent is swell: 2 photographs in one to be precise: they are swell. In a way, too good altogether because you look like a vision of the Ideal, – you are, of course, – but what I mean is its difficult to believe you exist from the photo. If I didn't know your swift, cool, & clear beauty I wouldn't believe it, I'd say nonsense, & have another pipe of opium, if I had an opium pipe, & some opium.

I told you Torquay was drab in daytime but at night like a picture postcard of China. Its a loveable & laughable kind of tawdriness though: the harbours full of immense toy battleships, quite cuckoo. I hope all the while your hand gets better & better. Life is empty without you. Don't write if it hurts: but if it doesn't do. A letter from you, & the universe (that's me) sings.

Could you say when you see England, to yourself, this is his land. That is to say ours.

Even an American crook film gives me a queer pang, & I went to see a dilapidated musical comedy called The Belle of New York just so as I could think about the title –

Well, my dearest, – the sun grins, soon we'll be together –
be happy

immer your

Malcolm

[P.S.] I've just discovered something so perfectly amazing about our destiny that I can't write it down. I'll tell you, though, when we meet. [It looks as though] our names are written together sure enough on God's old foolscap.

Annotations:

1 During June, July, and August, Jan continued her travels in Europe, and Lowry was sending letters for her to American Express in the cities along her way.

57: To Jan Gabrial

P: private(ms)

[London]
[September 1933][a]

As from Southill Pk. Hpstd.[1]
3 am
Jan, my dearest –
'Yours in the traffic's roar,'[2] in each bright window, in every doubt & hope. Oh gee, I shall win you so many times perhaps before you

see what we mean to each other: do *hope* that its me who wins, even though I do and shall win. Jan, hold me to your heart at this moment. Things are keen, aren't they though & you have been absolutely swell.

I'm not *in* love with you as if who should say . . How nice to be in such & such a place, Capri, Florence – with 'someone' you love – I love you for yourself, for being yourself: I'm so proud of being part of you, – and proud of us. Can you ever feel this about me, that you love me, rather than are in love with me – I hope that as well – I wld like to earn that feeling anyhow from you. I shall know if you ever do feel that, so you don't have to write it –

Hope either that you send me another address, or that the express is open Sat aftn. in Paris: or that they will deliver immediately from there

Christ let me bury my face in your breast

Malcolm

Annotations:

1 During the fall of 1933, and after his bout with dysentery, Lowry spent some time living in the Hampstead flat of his former tutor from Cambridge, Hugh Sykes Davies; see Davies' recollections of this time in *Malcolm Lowry Remembered* (67-69).
2 Lowry may be thinking of the popular Cole Porter song 'Night and Day' (1932): 'In the roaring traffic's boom, in the silence of my lonely room, I think of you, night and day.'

Editorial Notes:

a. This letter is written on letterhead from the Cranston's Kenilworth Hotel in London, but the letter has neither inside address nor date; see annotation 1.

58: To Jan Gabrial

P: private(ms)

[London]
[ca 11 September 1933]ᵃ

Sweethearts – I've written you about ten enormous letters, none of which expressed what I wanted to say, so I tore them up. Anyway they did in no wise move from the be-all end-all phrase 'I love'. So you know more or less what they were about.

To be more particular – I strongly advise you *not* Dieppe-Newhaven, not Calais-Dover, but Havre-Plymouth. Yes, Havre-Plymouth, – have you got that?[1] When you get there, things will solve themselves. It may cost a little more than one of the more conventional channel crossings, although I don't think: but its ultimate advantages to both of us in the sum are so many and various that I think Havre-Plymouth should be the by-word, the pass-word, the by-password and the pass right down the car word. A 'giant ocean liner' will take you. A boat goes the day after tomorrow, but that is probably too early for you. However, don't be misled by this, a boat also goes on Wednesday week, the 20th, with a dance floor of polished glass, a rifle range a midget golf course, carrying a cargo of bellbuoys and raw alcohol. The voyage takes about nine hours.

A tourist single ticket costs £2:0:0, or what used to be about $10. Cabin costs 10/- more – you may find that worth it, but whatever happens you could not find the First worth £1:5:0 more than that.

As it happens the ship you would take the *Paris* hasn't got a cabin class, so I should go tourist, unless you're feeling uncommonly affluent.

When you get to Plymouth a strange, or perhaps not so strange, man, will meet you on the dock, who will then play knight, to your nymph, errant. And whatever declarations you may make at the customs the one he makes outside them is going to be important to you.

So. Havre-Plymouth. s.s. Paris. Three funnels.

Will you have red wine or white, I replied both tonight. Sept 20th, I suggest, or this Wednesday, the Île de France goes. Don't go to New York by mistake yet. There is a Punch & Judy show I love.[2] I enclose partic

O saisons, o châteaux![3]

Malcolm

Annotations:

1 Of the routes from France to England that Lowry mentions, the Le Havre-Plymouth one is the longest, and Plymouth, which is at the south-west corner of Devon, is the farthest from London. It is, however, close to Torquay, where Lowry was staying during the summer and early fall. Although the other routes were faster, cheaper, and brought passengers closer to London, there was a certain glamour to the Le Havre-Plymouth route in the thirties because passengers could take a 'gigantic ocean liner' like the *Normandie*.

2 Punch and Judy are the characters in the popular English puppet show.

3 'O saisons, ô châteaux!' is the first, third and last line of a poem from
part 2, 'Délires,' in *Une Saison en Enfer* (1873) by Arthur Rimbaud (1854-
91).

Editorial Notes:

a. The holograph is undated, but judging from Lowry's suggestions in his
last paragraph, he would have been writing Jan at about this time.

59: To Jan Gabrial

P: private(ms)

[September 1933]^a

Sweethearts – I'm damned disappointed about Plymouth. I think
you were angry because Plymouth semed out of the way from
London & that I was acting without thinking of you. On the
contrary I would have motored you up from there to London but
our destinies are certainly bound together because I've had my truck
accident now: I smashed the car to blazes just after you're letter & we
were damned lucky not to go over a precipice. Its a blessing you
weren't in it, so thank god anyway.[1]
I'm not allowed to move from here, but I'm certainly going to make
a break to get to Victoria & meet you.[2]
   If I can't it will be only because its financially & physically impossible.
   If I'm not there – leave a message at Astoria Hotel for me, in Greek
Street. Take a taxi. You might do worse than to stay there. Its cheap,
& rather grubby, but the food's marvellous. Friday at 6 at Victoria.
And if I'm not there its only because I can't be & I'll be along as soon
as possible.
   Don't forget me.

love

Malcolm

Annotations:

1 Lowry's Cambridge friend Tom Forman (letter 42), had given Lowry
  an old MG Magna, which Lowry managed to destroy on a trip to south
  Devon; see Day's description (181).
2 Jan arrived in England on 22 September 1933 and went directly to
  London. Lowry did not meet her train at Victoria Station and did not
  put in an appearance until about four days later.

Editorial Notes:

a. This letter was written some time after 11 but before 22 September when Jan arrived in England.

60: To Jan Gabrial

P: private(ms)

7 rue Antoine-Chantin,
[Paris,]
[France]
[April 1934]
Tomorrow & tomorrow[1]

My little love Jan –

I love you so: I feel like a tiger who's had his cub taken away, my love for you ranges inside, I can feel it moving within you too, now.[2] If only that terrible sea were not flowing between us, and within us, only like the sea of our love in its restlessness and endlessness, not in its constancy; and if the sea why not also 'time,' but it is that which I would wish closed, wrinkled up like an old concertina.

I hope the ship is not being too grim, how I hate ships and how long they take to bring a letter to the girl I love, and from the girl I love! Oh, poor Jan, that smoking room and the people looked so *damp*, feverish almost; but although its tough having your only friend on board in another class, and although it may be a bit beastly, I think you might find it vivid, because you can be sure those people are really third class, not just second rate like those guilty ones hiding between the woodwind and the saxophone. But extremes are sometimes better; so next time I'll try and earn enough so that you can go first.

I wandered around Havre, & it was nice – although so sad without you; we would have had real fun there, there were so many nice little cafes down by the waterfront, something like the French West Indies, a real salt of the sea feeling it gave you: but I have never hated the sea so much. I ran after the Ile de France till it was out of sight, I had half a hope I might be able to stop it or make it come back – do you hear me you people, you've left me behind. Julian walked in yesterday – he brought good news of Davvy and Clem, for which I am very glad;[3] the wound seems to have closed a little, his own exhibition was a great success {although one critic said: We do not think Mr Trevelyan will float very far on his cork pictures!}, which is good, & he looked well & happy.

I feel lost, perdu, says the cleaning woman, without you; although I hope you think of me, I hope it doesn't hurt like this; physically its bad enough – the torture just smoulders on and on.

I love you really, dear dear Jan: look, I'm putting my hand on your heart now. I think we should be proud of what we have made; we escaped to 'somewhere' – not just to nowhere; in spite of the pain and anxiety you suffered. Now we've known happiness, we have to find peace; I know that we can do that together. I need your help now, tremendously, and your trust; for gods sake let me feel that you are encouraging me, & are with me. I think we ought to have the courage to do what [D.H.] Lawrence says,[4] often to act on his advice which seems so peculiarly for us, not simply to praise him, or pity him, or deride him, or admire the way he says it – we ought to have at least the courage to admit that he sometimes tells us something we might not have otherwise found out: I'm sure that what he says about the sun, easy to ridicule though it is, is right – right for us. Listen to this, from *Apocalypse*, its easy to ridicule, in a Wooster Wodehouse & Blair Eggleston manner, but all truths are, and this is just damned true, even if he hasn't got much of a sense of the ridiculous {you know I have}, & who cares about that anyway? 'Who says the sun cannot speak to me! The sun has a great blazing consciousness, & I have a little blazing consciousness. When I can strip myself of the trash of personal feelings and ideas & get down to my naked sun-self, then the sun and I can commune by the hour, the blazing interchange, & he gives me life, wild life, sun-life, and I send him a little new brightness from the world of the bright blood. The great sun, like an angry dragon, hater of the nervous and personal consciousness in us. As all these modern sunbathers must realize, for they become disintegrated by the very sun that bronzes them. But the sun, like a lion, loves the bright red blood of life, & can give it an infinite enrichment if we know how to receive it. But we don't. We have lost the sun. And he only falls on us & destroys us, decomposing something in us: the dragon of destruction instead of the life bringer.

And we have lost the moon, the cool, bright, ever-varying, moon. It is she who would caress our nerves, smooth them with the silky hand of her glowing, soothe them into serenity again with her cool presence . . . For the lovers who shoot themselves in the night, in the horrible suicide of love, they are driven mad by the poisoned arrows of Artemis; the moon is against them; the moon is fiercely against them . . . There is an eternal, vital, correspondence between our blood & the sun: there is an eternal vital correspondence between our nerves & the moon. If we get out of contact & harmony with the sun & moon, then both turn into great dragons of destruction against us. The sun is a great source of blood & vitality; it streams strength to us. But once we resist the sun, & say: It is a mere ball of gas! – then the very streaming vitality of sunshine turns into subtle disintegrative force in us, & undoes us. The same with the moon, the planets, the great stars. They are either our makers, or our unmakers. We can't get the sun in us by lying naked like pigs on a beach. We can only get the sun by a sort of worship; & the same with the moon. – I want to make it quite clear that the foregoing is a quotation from D.H. Lawrence, (not from E.E. Cummings, but that what follows is not: it is, I think really true & important for us that we should, as Lawrence says 'go forth to the sun': it sounds a bit absurd, cliquey and Nachtkult (in spite of his evasion of it,) perhaps smacks a little of therapeutics, is a little affected when put like that; but, in spite of this, I know you & I have recovered the sun, that within the last few months, within ourselves & through the fulfillment of ourselves in the body, we've discovered the sun once more to be kind, a 'life-giver,' and the moon too we discovered to be within us, a giver of light in the darkness, and some part of our love we discovered only to be visible in that light, that twilight, that darkness, to be visible only by the nocturnal light of the moon within us: and I think it was only when we denied these powers within us that we were ever unhappy. Further than this, I think our relationship is naturally, ought to be, like that of the sun and the moon, each sharing the power within the other, sharing our own sun and our own moon, we were both born practically equidistant from midsummer, you under Gemini, the twins, so that you are divided in your own nature between spring and summer, you have more of the moon in you, and a natural tide in you swayed by her: I, under Leo, the lion,[5] divided between the life-giving heat and light of summer, of the sun, and its complementary darkness disintegrative and deathly, of autumn: only complementary because we had made it so, by not understanding: our autumns should be mellow when we may think of the gifts and light of summer, & spring too is a mellow moon month, when we look forward, but I have never known such an autumn & in America you scarcely have a spring at all to know. So we have in each of us those opposite forces which the other needs: you need more sun but not the disintegrative sun, I more moon but not the angry murdering moon: my bright lifegiving sun will turn your angry murdering moon, your healing cool moon will in the law of night freeze to

death my disintegrative sun: so that we shall both have only the life-
giving sun, and the healing cool moon: and the rays of these forces
will flow between us for ever. Your life which is already more ful-
filed than anyone's I know will attain the real independence you have
always desired, – I think the better word is *inter*dependence – because
there is something more than being just casually *lustig*, as with any
Tom, Dick, or Harry Peg or Meg or Florence, between us, doing
what you like at the moment is not establishing any kind of independence within ones guts: by all means let us do what we like,
but let us sacrifice it when we see that it will make something which
we like better impossible in future: live on the moment, but not on a
moment of clock-time, rather on one of space-time. (For instance, at
this moment, I am lost without thee, I don't want to work, to learn
French, to go to the gym, to pay the cleaning woman, to see about
my car, to write to my Father, to wind the clock, to wash my face, to
make a parcel of laundry, but I see that if I do do these things as
honestly as in a dishonest world as possible, utterly trivial as they
appear, I shall in some way be preparing myself for you: it would
have been too bad if St Christopher had just sunk over his neck:[6] and
although the sun may have, as the poet says, 'innumerable coined
light', that isn't going to help to pay for your coming back from
America, or for me to go to it to get you, so that we can be in that
sun: Anderson comes this afternoon to type the rest of Bulls, I've
practically finished A goddamn funny ship: & have made a Synopsis
of So we live, as a novel: I'm praying that it will go as a novel:[7] but
I'm sure I can get enough short stories done to make a volume by
your return: I shall keep to one short story a week, too.)

To return to the powers & sources within us, the sun & moon, –
powerful individuals: I think you ought to get rid of your scepticism,
a tendency to be enclosed in what used to be known as 'cynicism,' a
tendency still to generalise from a disillusion you have already in
your own life, proved false, – the reality wasn't all beer & skittles,
but surely it was grander than any illusion could be, – be that as it
may, perhaps I too have gone to the other extreme of mumbo-jumbo
in your eyes, certainly the most trivial things are to me the most difficult & I never used to believe I was capable of doing difficult things,
& this attitude is vaguely analogous to believing many trivial accom-
plishments miracles – but miracles do exist! – but to return, I think as
we grow older we shall find that there is something more than just an
abandonment to the sex, the person of the other, of each other –
great as that has been alone: There must always *be* that abandonment,
to our *sex*, but also to the supernormal psychosexual forces within

the other, which our own fusion has aroused – we are part of the cosmos, we love: & as we must be repeating something like the first cause of all things, it is only natural that these forces should have been aroused. We ought, therefore, to respect them, & often to obey them: if we force them out, they will try to destroy us: does the moon try to *force* a total eclipse? Well, whatever the moon may be for purposes of argument, she is certainly not cold; Lowry added courteously . . . In this way we shall know peace, as well as happiness & love: & knowing peace will obviate the fearful pain, the despair & torture of love, which I feel now and pray you don't: because without you I feel ill, fevered, lost, uprooted – you must rest up & have some peace without me, you deserve it, you must have it, and not feel like this: I am anxious that you rest, don't draw too much on your reserves of energy, you've been through a terrible nervous strain, a cataclysm; in the last two years the world has been before you and it has been exciting and tremendous, a dream becoming less palpable, and in the last three months you have given your wanderings a unity, and you have signed it with blood & tears & laughter, with desire and hate and happiness, you've died and are alive again now: for god's sake now, Jan, rest in your mind now, oh my sweet sweet Jan, – I see your face before me all the time, hear your voice, I could have sworn I really did see you, about an hour ago, suddenly you were beside me, your face near mine, and you flung your arms round my neck in such a trusting way; oh my god, I wish and wish you were here, or that I was there, anywhere just to be with you, and that I could feel the coolness of your lttle cheek, and the warmth and sweetness of your body; what a swell person you are, Jan, there is nobody so nice as you, anywhere.

Oh Jan can you feel me kissing you, I think now of all the things I might have done that would have made you more happy; arguments and hurts I might have avoided for you if I had been more surely and strongly myself for you, with all the sweetness of my memories of you is mixed some remorse for the times I have been bitter when I should have been forbearing, weak when I should have been strong, things of which I am truly ashamed, but oh I love you and these last three months have been so sweet, you have been so lovely, that there never could be any bitterness, just some sadness which is part of my love is all that remains of our most violent dissension; we had to go through those things, we had to learn, and when all is said, we have so much really to be proud of, that will always be really ours; and although the gale has howled around us like hell, we have nearly lost the ship, we have been driven back out of our course, have lost a score of times our dignity, our bearings, our charter in the black storm, our harbour with quiet hills is there now, for the first time we can see it, with sun on its arms and foam on its breast.

Jan, oh pray for us, so that we shall quite exorcise from our relationship these devils of self-indulgence and self-pity, who sometimes crowd around us, gibbering with their manacles. Do I talk too much?

But I love only you, and I want to make you happy always, to be the good husband and companion and comrade you've dreamed of, really that is all I desire, that you and I shall be happy together in our love and our books and our work and our sun, and later in our children: and you will be happy, oh my dear. We have been happy, too, sometimes without knowing it: but it is peace within yourself, a security, a harbour there that I want to give you, to build there, within yourself, and it is that that I would kill myself to give you, if it killing myself would help, but it wouldn't help it would only set us back: we are destined for each other, and I am the man who is to *live* for you. Only you must have peace; we know it often together; but you must have the green pastures, the wind, shadows of trees, things which are kind and good in your soul: you must have that: you must not be harried, tormented, torn, lost by our love, driven along blindly by it: I feel at the moment that I have no heart, no guts, just a wound inside, that you have torn out my heart and carried it away with you: you must not feel like that, you must be happy: if you are lonely and want me and it is unbearable you must not give in, be happy in the fact that I love you, will be thinking of you, wanting to comfort you when you are lonely, if ever you feel a little unhappiness, don't give in to it, but come to me, it doesn't matter that I seem to be far away, I am with you, and if you must cry, cry on my shoulder, I love you, dear gentle Jan, and am thinking of you, and am planning for you, and getting on with my plans, its not all a dream, or a fairy tale, its all true and its better than a dream or a fairy tale, its not just romantic although it *is* romantic, in the real sense, its true, and we've endured just about all the worst phases of that truth, and we've known the best, and it is still true, and there's no marzipan or sugar much about it left, but its more lovely than any dream could be; I shall only feel down if you give in to any loneliness, I think you feel a bit melancholy at the moment, as I write, and so I have a bit of despair too – only lets rejoice together, shall we, instead: we've got alot to be thankful for. There, Jan, will you do your rabbit for me?

It must be grand to see your mother again after so long: & it will be very strange seeing U.S again, & your weeping willow tree, and your room, & your clothes. Your bag with its dear injured labels will look so strange and homeless, so expatriated, and you will not know whether to laugh or cry with joy: oh, I do know and can share with you that feeling of return, only I was not returning to anyone who really loved me, or to a home where I had been happy or understood or had achieved anything, I returned from a vacuum into a vacuum; but always in a homecoming ones emotions are polar, opposites are always involved, dichotomies (my spelling) must be reconciled, but you can always say to yourself that you left someone who loved you, for another someone who loved you, and you can count yourself lucky in that, and that you love your mother, and that it was there, in spite of the bad luck you had, that you made the very important decision to go to Europe, that you were happy in Europe where there is another home in a man's heart, but that now it's good to be home again once more with a mother you love.

Well, Jan dear, you must have peace I decide as well, and it is true what someone says about asking an angel to help you: So if you'll just be happy, and trust me, & remember that I love you, I'll move the rest of the stones away, if there are any: will you be my angel? It won't be long. My love to your mother.[8] I'm getting a photo taken. Bless you, sweet Jan. Your husband –

Malcolm

My angel.

Annotations:

1 'Tomorrow & tomorrow' is an echo of Macbeth's speech in *Macbeth* V.v: 'Tomorrow, and tomorrow, and tomorrow / Creeps in this petty pace from day to day, / To the last syllable of recorded time.'

2 Jan Gabrial returned to New York in early April 1934 to see her mother and to rest.

3 The English painter Julian Trevelyan (1910–88), a friend of Lowry's from Cambridge, stood up with Lowry at his 6 January 1934 wedding. He was also communicating with Arthur Lowry, who was sending support money to Paris for his son. In a 6 January 1934 letter to Trevelyan (with the Trevelyan papers at Trinity College, Cambridge), Arthur Lowry thanked Trevelyan for helping Malcolm in Paris but explained that he would not send further funds until his son wrote to him himself. Davvy and Clem are John Davenport and his first wife.

4 The long quotation that follows is from part 5 of Lawrence's extended essay on Revelations called *Apocalypse*. The text was first published in 1931, with a British edition in 1932.

5 Gemini is the zodiacal sign for the period 23 May to 21 June, and Jan's birthday is 11 June; Leo is the sign for the period 23 July to 22 August, and Lowry's birthday is 28 July.

6 According to legend, when St Christopher was carrying a child across a

river, the child became so heavy that he could barely continue. However, the child revealed himself to be Jesus Christ and explained to Christopher that he was carrying the weight of the whole world. Since then St Christopher has been known as the patron saint of wayfarers.

7 Lowry was working on his story 'Bulls of the Resurrection,' which was not published until 1965. The other stories do not appear to have survived, although Jan recalls that Lowry worked on 'A goddamn funny ship' in New York during 1935.

8 Lowry met Jan's mother later that year when he joined Jan in New York, and they were very fond of each other; see Jan Gabrial's recollections of these months in *Malcolm Lowry Remembered* (98).

61: To Jan Gabrial

P: private(ms)

7 rue Antoine–Chantin,
[Paris,]
[France]
[May 1934]

Darling Janl.
I am working like the devil at stories, really working; already are mailed Bulls of the Resurrection & Goddamn funny ship; [¼ lines??] a Hotel Room in Chartres is nearly finished, & I have written last night 3000 words of a story for you, it will be mailed by the end of the week, it is called 'In Le Havre' – you don't like my titles? – but you will like the story I think, it is your story, the tragic one we thought of going down in the train, 'I don't love you, I never have,' you remember he cries as the ship is going; I have put so much of what I feel for you {stupidly said – don't misinterpret it. It *is* your letter though.} into this story that I find it difficult to write to you, until I receive mail from you which I have not yet done & this will revive me; the story is as it were a letter to you; as I am working for you it *is* your letter.[1]

I am really working against time, because I want to get lots of things done, & accepted, then go & tell the old man, & then come over to U.S as quickly as possible.

I have a letter from you which says, oh I won't tell you what it says it is too beautiful to repeat.

I worked all last night. I desire you terribly. This separation is awful, I hope you don't feel it as much as I do – give your light to other people a bit if it gets you down too badly: its no longer a question of trust, that goes without saying, I am devoted to you, & I want you to have our children in the sun.

Now, even without you, I feel strong: I feel you with me. I'm coming for you soon. The idea of your coming back to Europe without me in 3 months is absurd. We were mad to think of that – your mother must think me crazy – I could like, admire, but love nobody else; it would only be a rag of a heart.

I see now how crazy I was about contraceptives etc – we won't have that trouble again. I hope to God that clot of blood spelt no further trouble, but you would have called.

My foolishness, but then in that important sense you were older than me then; you've no idea the agony it caused before I fully satisfied you – & we were fully satisfied: then oh god, oh god, how tender a mistress, & lovely a wife – oh your moistness.

I don't want anybody else. One thing I have learnt, that man doesn't know, love like ours can't die, everyone says love dies: but fools it is they themselves that die, the illusion dies in their souls & they with it: don't you see. Havelock Ellis can go hang: I know more.[2]

And as for the grave being a fine & private place but none I think do there embrace,[3] that's their lookout.

We would find a way: we would embrace.

love to your mother
love

Malcolm

Annotations:

1 Lowry sent 'In Le Havre' to his London agent, Innes Rose, who placed it with *Life and Letters* 10, 55 (1934): 642-66. The story consists of the dialogue of two men in a bar in the French port town of Le Havre. The younger of the two has just seen his American wife off on a ship bound for New York; because they have quarrelled, he fears that he has lost her. The older man becomes disgusted with the young man's self-pitying complaints and accuses him of loving only 'your own misery.' Although there are several parallels between the story and the Lowrys' lives (Jan had just sailed for New York from Le Havre, and she had had an operation shortly before that), it would be a mistake to press the analogy too closely. She and Malcolm had not had the bitter fight described in the story, and they fully intended to be reunited as soon as possible.

2 Havelock Ellis (1859-1939) was a British critic, writer, and editor known for his books on the psychology of sex, such as *Sex in Relation to Society* (1910), *Marriage Today and Tomorrow* (1929), and the seven-volume edition *Studies in the Psychology of Sex* (1897-1928).

3 Lowry is paraphrasing two lines from the poem 'To His Coy Mistress' by the English poet Andrew Marvell (1621-78): 'The grave's a fine and private place, / But none, I think, do there embrace.'

62: To Jan Gabrial

P: private(ms)

[Paris,]
[France]
[June 1934]

My god Jan.

I need you so. Your last letter was grand. This to you, as girl, as dearest of all. Believe me, beloved Jan, when I say that nothing will ever change my love for you. Nor can our third person now do anything but help us. This is the second truly proud moment of my life, when I can write you now, (and when I see you can say) that I have fought a losing battle with myself and won.

Not St George could feel more proud of having vanquished the dragon than myself at this moment of victory over my devil.

Now at last I can come to you and take you, unashamed, your man, certain and secure in victory.

You ask me what my devil is are there not many devils and do not all creative writers have devils and can't I have a devil mister Just spare me one wont you because yours sho is a devil-devil from what I've seen of him.

And how do you get over the paradox of OFlaherty whose devil was hankering after fame and the fruits of success and social respectability, and whose angel was a fornicator and a tavern set.[1] Are not you like that with the added curse that you are in love and constant. And was not constancy in the old days one of your devils, and your angel the potential fornicator you now are with your wife.

My answer to devils and angels is this: God rot all my work not done through the flesh of my wife. Devil take all my work not done through the spirit of my wife, which I have not approached through the flesh. The devil says: A writer like you must be a low-down fellow, creeping in the gutter, dirty and drunken, waiting to pounce on his victim like a weasel. If you had not been a low-down fellow, with sex transformed to a drunken intellect, how account for your hapless book Ultramarine? (Which even your wife has ceased to bother about.) A writer like you must account to noone, must wear his rags round his heart, must be as nothingness, must pawn his wife's rings for drink.

To which I reply: If that is genius, it is too easy. If you are stimulated to write only in proportion to the suffering you cause others & yourself by your improvidence then it is better not to be a writer: if your intellect is contained within such a nucleus better not have one at all. The one thing worth doing is to love your wife, and the only work worth doing is that which it is part of that love to do.
Start again, at the bottom. And instead of training your intellect, train your body.

When your body is perfect, see how your clear brain will reflect it.

And so I have been keeping fit, and writing only that which is part of my love for you.

I long for you, when our bodies and our minds will be together.
When you receive this Jan, stand in the sun a long time & swear that we will never betray each other that we shall be those seemingly impossible people who can always be happy in one another and always beautiful.

And lets die together with that oath on our lips.

I long to fuck you.

Malc

Annotations:

1 Lowry may be thinking of the Irish novelist Liam O'Flaherty (1896–1984), who dedicated his life to the pursuit of spirituality in and through the senses and cultivated the role of the artist as romantic outcast.

63: To Sylvia Beach

P: Princeton(ms)

Hotel du Pont St Prést,
Eure et Loire,
Near Chartres
[France]
[June 1934]

My dear Miss Beach,[1]

You're rather hard on me, but perhaps with good cause. I *did* despatch the letters to you, but by a not very trustworthy acquaintance, & I can assume only – as I also lent him some money – that he got drunk on the way & lost them. I don't know how a situation of such moral obliquity arose between us: I was trying to explain that I was under a complete misapprehension about the letters, that I had, wrongly, understood that they had been lent to me, that that anyway was an absurd thing to understand or rather to assume understood, and that although I was no good at mathematics I would indeed pay in addition to the formerly miscalculated total whatever was actually due, would in fact then have paid – indeed I offered to buy the book then and there, if you remember, but you would have had me blamed for the presumption I was already trying to correct at that time and would have none of me! However, enough of this. I also wrote to the firm that my subscriptions etc might be renewed, 600 francs or whatever it is, & there has been delay about this simply because they have a weeks holiday at Ascension & nobody was there. This will be shortly attended to. When you receive it charge me the price of the book + whatever etceteras are due on it: anyway the book's worth it.

I was writing you to apologise for my insensitivity the other day, & I now do so. You've been angelically kind to me & sharp words over a few francs does not seem a very courteous reciprocity. The truth of the matter is that I've been terribly worried about my wife, who really had been much more ill than I thought: that, & being away from her,[2] and not having slept for about ten days at that time, was responsible for it, & I do ask you to forgive me. You have been nothing but kindness itself to me.

But I never knew how much I really loved my wife until she went to America: I never should have let her go, & its been hell.

But everythings all right now – she's all right & we'll be together again in 3 weeks. I was just momentarily deranged.

So please forgive me really.

I shall be executive in this matter, & when it is done, don't lets refer to it again.

I don't think the world would let the Shakespeare bookshop die, I'm sure it won't, so don't you worry, although I realize if everybody was as erratic as I even the world would not be much help.

Yours very affectionately

Malcolm Lowry

Annotations:

1 Sylvia Beach (1887-1962), the American champion of modernist writing and publisher of Joyce's *Ulysses* (1922), opened her famous Paris bookshop, Shakespeare and Company, with Adrienne Monnier on 17

November 1919. It rapidly became a landmark and a gathering place for famous, or soon to be famous, contemporary writers.
2 Before returning to New York, Jan had had a minor operation. After a brief visit to England, Lowry joined her in August; see Bowker (181–83).

64: To Whit Burnett

P: Princeton(ms)

> 447 Commercial Street,
> Provincetown, Cape Cod,
> Massachusetts
> 31 August 1934

Dear Mr Burnett,[1]

It is swell of you to ask us to the party on the 24th & we shall be able to make it because we'll be in New York by the 17th. I'm sure your book will go well, & I hope 'Canal Third's in it if you haven't already used it elsewhere.[2] For ourselves we hunted the white whale all the way back to Nantucket via New Bedford but all they said there was 'What's all this stuff about Goby Dick?' I didn't know the whaling industry had died & Jan was decidedly disappointed by New Bedford after my reports of it. Meantime we're having a grand time here and the sea comes right up to our front door.[3]

I was very proud you accepted Hotel Room & that put a bloom on my arrival after Goby Dick had betrayed us a little.

I should like to enter Ultramarine for the contest, and I won't get another novel straight in time.[4] As Jan says you have a copy of the book, could you enter it for me?

If I had known it was eligible I would have pruned it a bit as there is a kind of 1910 pornography about certain parts which are perhaps neither good manners, good art, nor incidentally, good pornography. And I would have supplied a foreword explaining the symbolism of the Tarot Pack & the pigeon etc. Could you tell me whether there is time to do this, or if it is simply inadvisable in any case?

And have you any time before the 24th when we might have a word together.

My kindest regards to Martha Foley[5] & yourself, & from Jan.

> Yours cordially
> Malcolm Lowry

Annotations:

1 Whitney Ewing Burnett (1899-1973) was an American correspondent and short story writer who co-founded and co-edited *Story* magazine with Martha Foley in 1931. *Story* ceased publication in 1964 after three decades of discovering and supporting writers. After her return to New York in the summer of 1934, Jan had shown Burnett Lowry's story 'Hotel Room in Chartres,' which he accepted for publication in *Story* 5, 26 (1934): 53-58. He had already published 'On Board the West Harda-way' in *Story* 3, 15 (1933): 12-22.

2 Whit Burnett's story 'Canal Third' appeared in *Story* 1, 3 (1931): 5-29. It is a simple narrative about a ship sailing from California through the Panama Canal on its way to New York. The young men aboard get off in Havana to see the night-life, but little happens and the story lacks focus or motivation.

3 After Lowry's arrival in the United States, he and Jan had a happy reunion and set forth on a visit to New England.

4 Lowry is referring to the competition for the 'Best Novel written by an Author who has had a story published in' *Story*; the prize was $1,000, and the contest was co-sponsored by *Story* and Doubleday, Doran & Company. See Martha Foley's *The Story of STORY Magazine* (London and New York: W.W. Norton, 1980), p. 253.

5 Martha Foley (1897-1977), an American newspaper and fiction writer, was the co-founder and co-editor of *Story* magazine. In 1941 she left *Story* to edit *Best American Short Stories* at the behest of Edward J. O'Brien, who had been killed in the London blitz. As well as lecturing at Columbia University, Foley continued to edit *Best American Short Stories* and to write until her death. In *The Story of STORY Magazine* she re-members Lowry as the 'most heartbreaking writer to visit my office' (206): he was separated from Jan at the time (spring-summer of 1936); his work was being rejected, and he had been put in the psychiatric wing of New York's Bellevue Hospital, which, Foley comments, 'was a terrible thing to do to him' (246).

65: To Alfred Mendes

P: Harvard(ms)

[Hotel Somerset,]
[New York, N.Y.]
[Winter/Spring 1936]^a

Dear Alfred:[1]

I have been trememdously pressed for time to get a job of work done & I am only part way through 'Black Fauns'[2] unfortunately: I was hoping incidentally to read it this afternoon, when I am free, but would v. much like to see you.

I am lunching with Whit Burnett, so if I am not back by 3 or before this letter, tell me where you will be & I shall join you. I won't be later than 4 anyhow. Try to be in the vicinity, though, at some local pub: otherwise I may have difficulty in getting there.

Jan is working at the library & may join us later.[3]

Black Fauns is very swell so far & I can't see why it isn't published over here. The dialogue & character drawing are excellent, the unitys are subtly maintained, & I have no criticism at all, save of myself, for not having finished it yet.

What you say of Ultramarine I agree with.[4] It would be better sans hero & heroine.

Malcolm

Annotations:

1 Novelist and short story writer Alfred H. Mendes (1897-) was born in Trinidad and educated in England. After fighting in the First World War, he returned to Trinidad, where he later helped to form a literary group that published the avant-garde journal *Beacon*. His first novel, *Pitch Lake*, was published in 1934 by Duckworth in London which published his second novel, *Black Fauns*, the following year. In 1933 he moved to New York, where he established contact with many American writers and where he met Jan and Malcolm Lowry. Mendes worked as a reader for Whit Burnett's *Story* magazine and later for the Works Progress Administration (WPA) Federal Writers' Project before returning to Trinidad in 1940.

2 *Black Fauns* has been twice reprinted since 1935: by Kraus Reprints in 1970 and by New Beacon Books of London and Port of Spain in 1984 with an introduction by Rhonda Cobham. It is a novel of social realism about the lives of a group of poor 'barrack-yard' women in the capital of a Caribbean island. Mendes, as Lowry points out, has successfully captured the speech of these women in excellent dialogue.

3 Jan was conducting research for a book at the New York Public Library, and the two would often meet there.

4 Lowry had always been dissatisfied with *Ultramarine* and nervous about his borrowings from Aiken and others, and it was at about this time that he was charged with plagiarism by a New York writer; see his 19 May 1940 letter (**141**) to Burton Rascoe.

Editorial Notes:

a. According to Jan Gabrial's memories of their time in New York (*Malcolm Lowry Remembered*, 99-100), she and Lowry lived in the Hotel

Somerset for just over a year, from early 1935 to the spring of 1936.
Letters **65**, **66**, and **67** to Alfred Mendes appear to belong to this period.

66: To Alfred Mendes

p: Harvard(ms)

Hotel Somerset,
[New York, N.Y.]
[April 1936]

Dear Alfred:

Thanks very much for your letter and as we did not see you Saturday we must assume that you are more than living under a sign of
'amor threatening' – & the best of luck with whatever you decide to
do. About Thursday, we should very much like to come out then
only we are moving on Friday, the first of the next month & we have
so much packing to do we fear we shall be unable to.[1] But when we
get settled we must make a new plan for meeting.

Your friend the literary sleuth did not call for 'Black Fauns,'
though we expected him to come, so I shall either send you this or
leave it at your brother's apartment: I think the latter is the safer
course. Since we are both bad at making up parcels.

When I get down at a typewriter again I shall send you a detailed
account of my impressions of Black Fauns, but you must excuse me
from that now, for Jan has just called to say I must meet her in ¼ of
an hour: and I cannot assemble my feelings intelligently in a short
time. For the time let it suffice that I think it is a grand book, exciting
& colorful & juicy with life, birth, death, & with excellent dialogue,
& I cannot understand why a publisher has not taken it yet.[2] But
then, perhaps by the time you receive this one will have. I hope so
sincerely.

Thank you for interrupting our squabble . . . And the moral to
that is: Never imagine yourself not to be otherwise than what it
might appear to others than what you were or might have been was
not otherwise than what you would have been would have appeared
to them to be otherwise (said the Duchess) . . .

Will send you new address when I know it for certain, & congratulations again on the book – & best of luck in general.

Love from us both.

Doodoo[3]

Malcolm

Annotations:

1 The Lowrys moved out of the Somerset Hotel to rooms on Eighty-sixth
  Street on Friday, 1 May 1936, which means that this letter must have
  been written in late April.
2 Lowry means that an American publisher had not accepted the book. It
  was published in England in 1935, but has never appeared in the United
  States.
3 'Doodoo' is a term of endearment used by the barrack-yard women in
  Mendes's story 'Sweet Man,' *Story* 5, 27 (1934): 26-38, and in *Black
  Fauns.*

67: To Alfred Mendes

P: Harvard(telegram)

New York, N.Y.
17 May [1936]

Alfred Mendes
12 Davison Pl., Baldwin N.Y.

MUST SEE YOU SUNDAY AFTERNOON ANGELINAS RESTAURANT.[1]
TERRIFICALLY IMPORTANT. WHILE YOU WERE TURNING WATER INTO
WINE I WAS TURNING WINE INTO BLOOD.[2]

MALCOLM LOWRY

Annotations:

1 After leaving Jan at their Eighty-sixth Street rooms, Lowry went on a
  drinking binge with a homosexual friend, Tony, and stayed in his dingy
  room above Angelina's Restaurant in Greenwich Village for a while.
2 See William Demarest's reflection in Aiken's *Blue Voyage*: 'While
  Wetherall was turning wine into blood, I was turning blood into wine'
  (132).

68: To Innes Rose

P: H(ms)

PO Box 17: again:
[1936-37][a]

Dear Innes:[1]
    Thanks a hell of a lot for everything: the play: the arrangement by
Stuart: all. God bless your old good guts.

Love from Jan & me. This is an inadequate and lousy note But there is really nothing to say.

I can't pay back the Cape thing yet. Life goes by merrily and smoothly.

God bless us : you

Malcolm

Intolerable I haven't written before this:

I have a lot of damned difficult problems to settle. Or does one solve them? Or wake up with the solution on your chest, god damn it.

Or what.

– Here, a long letter –

(Please don't say 'I'm a shit' – meaning me For not writing more when you have dealt so kindly with me. It's just that my mind won't work. – when you read this. I am having alot to contend with right now.)

(Remaining happy)

Jan sends love.

Annotations:

1 Innes Rose (1909–84) was a contemporary of Lowry's from Cambridge and his London agent with John Farquharson's Literary Agents.

Editorial Notes:

a. There is neither date nor inside address on this holograph. Douglas Day (229) claims that Lowry wrote this note to Rose from the depths of alcoholic despair in the autumn of 1937 shortly before Jan left him in Mexico, but it is equally possible that the letter dates from the troubled spring and summer months of 1936 in New York.

In the autumn of 1936 Jan and Malcolm put the troubles of the spring and summer in New York behind them by travelling. They set out across the United States by bus in September, spent some time with John Davenport in Los Angeles, and arrived in Cuernavaca, Mexico, by the end of October. Very little detail is available as yet about the 1936-37 period, except through Lowry's fiction and the recollections of those who visited him in Mexico, but the two surviving letters to Jan included here (69 and 72) provide an image of life, as Lowry *saw it, in the summer of 1937. And this image is of a loving couple beset by hostile guests.*

69: To Jan Gabrial

P: private(ms)

[Calle] Humboldt,
[Cuernavaca,]
[Mexico]
[June 1937]

My dearest sweetheart:

I hope you are having a grand time, but don't go too fast & get yourself sick at the stomach.

You say you will come back a bigger & brighter rainbowpuss. Well now – don't come back bigger perhaps; that *is* a queer way to put it.

But the trip ought to do you good & I am thinking of you all the time. Where to write to god only knows. But I hope you have left some forwarding address at Patzcuaro.[1]

I am having a very dull time here without you. Conrad [Aiken] is really not a friend at all though he pretends hard he is.[2] He is, in fact, a born chiseller – of everything, of his friends & wives, & of verses. I am having to put up with alot one way & another. Mary is nice, but their constant wrong, hasty judgments, with occasional emasculated ejaculations from Ed [Burra], – on practically all matters of any importance, not excepting the aesthetic, make me feel even sicker than I actually am. I hope however to get him to talk about poetry one day. When the chiseller talks about his chiselling we may expect some sense. At least some about the process if not about the object chiselled. Meantime as a gift horse one has the sense of being not only looked in the mouth but chiselled out of all one's teeth as well.

I have never experienced such disillusionment about my friends as in this year. You may be right about expecting too much. Still one is always surprised to receive less than nothing. The best friends we have are the simple & farseeing ones.

The best friends also we have are each other.

For god's sake let's get close together again – as we were, & fundamentally are – & are –

The house goes well thanks to your prearrangements though it sadly misses you. As do I. I love you & long to travel with you again. I cannot tell you how much I long for you in this Timon's environment[3] of the distant & hostile – Mrs Lowry –

Though you may be far geographically you are nearer always than anyone else, my tinfant,

Your loving husband

Malc

[P.S.] This written in bed – hence typography.

Annotations:

1 Jan had left Lowry in Cuernavaca in order to do some sightseeing in Mexico. Pátzcuaro, a small town on a lake of the same name, is just west of Cuernavaca and south of Guadalajara.
2 Conrad Aiken arrived in Cuernavaca in late May 1937 to seek a divorce from his second wife, Clarissa Lorenz, and to marry Mary Hoover. Ed Burra, the English surrealist painter and a friend of Aiken's, was with him. Conrad and Mary stayed with the Lowrys until their marriage in July, but the visit was not a happy one.
3 Timon, in Shakespeare's late play *Timon of Athens* (1608), is betrayed by his friends and guests and suffers greatly as a result. Lowry frequently identified with Timon.

70: To Daily Herald

P: UBC(telegram)

Western Union
[Mexico City]
25 June [1937]

DAILY HERALD inteltube londres presse collect[1]

following yesterdays headcoming antisemitic campaign mex=press propetition see tee emma inexworkers confederation proexpulsion exmexico quote small jewish textile manufacturers unquote twas learned today perreliable source that german legation mexcity actively behind the campaign etstatement that legation gone length sending antisemitic propaganda mexdept interiorwards borne out

propamphlet possession local newspaperman stop pamphlet asserts
jews influence unfavourably any country they live etemphasises
quote their belief absolute power etthat they gain their ends without
conscience or consideration unquote stop

[unsigned]

Annotations:

1 This telegram (UBC, Templeton 1:2) appears to be a draft for an actual
  telegram sent to the London newspaper the *Daily Herald*. It is, of course,
  the telegram attributed to Hugh in chapter 4 and read by Geoffrey in
  chapter 12 of *Under the Volcano*. In the notes to chapter 4 that he sent to
  Albert Erskine with his 5 July 1946 letter (**229**), Lowry explained that he
  'sat in at the concoction' of the telegram, which was sent by a reporter
  who gave Lowry verbal permission to use it. My check of the *Daily
  Herald* from December 1936 through 1938 did not reveal either a publication of the telegram or an article based on its data. The *Daily Herald*
  was a very influential left-wing English newspaper supported by the
  Labour party and by the unions during the twenties and thirties, and in
  his 1940 letter 'To the Censor' (**143**) Lowry claimed that he had worked
  'for a time' as a 'correspondent on an English liberal paper.'

71: To Conrad Aiken

P: H(ms); UBC(phc)
PP: *LAL* 43-46; *CP* 60-64, 108-09

[Charlie's Bar,]
[Cuernavaca]
[July 1937][a]

Work for Conrad.[b]

Strictly impersonal exercises in excess.

(1)
Prelude to Mammon.[1]

Sir: drinking is a problem without doubt:
Whether or not we like it, whether or not
The goddamn thing will put you on the spot
With heebiejeebies hebephrene or gout:
Or lumbago will set you tapping out
On brass ferrule to stool, to rest, to rot.

Though rotting's a fine pastime for a sot
It seems when we excrete we should not shout;
While even when we rest it's more discreet
That we should unambiguously rest.
What others think is one torment of drink
But these have dung not dew upon their feet
Whose dry concern for us is manifest
In the ubiquity of the parched soul's stink.

– This was an iambic pentametre that was: gawd knows
what this is but call it

(2)
Prelude to another drink

This ticking is the most terrible of all
You hear this sound on ships, you hear it on trains
It is the death-watch beetle at the rotten timber of the world
And it is death to you too; for well you know
That the heart's tick is failing all the while
Always ubiquitous & still more slow.
In the cantina throbs the refrigerator
And against the street the gaunt station bums.
What can you say fairly of a fat man
With a bent hand behind him & a cigarette in it?
Yet death is in the room, there is death every-where:
That man carries it though I can't see his face:
The upturned spitoons mean it, it is in the glass,
The girl who refills it pours a glass of death
And if there's death in her there is in me.
On the calendar, set to the future, the two stags battle
To death: man paddles his coracle to the moon
Which, seen also in light, is as divisible as death.

(Oh
yeah.)

, the 2
stag
beetles
ttle to
death.
ill, we
take
rselves
ously.)

Gawd knows what that was & Christ knows what this is, (though
we are coming back to the iambic pentametre,) so suppose we call it,

(3)
Prelude to another drink.

Is this an airplane roaring in my room?
What is it then, an insect, god knows what:
God probably does know which is the point;
Or did know – leave it at that – some sort of hornet.

(daughter;
especially
when the
announcer
pro-
nounces
his r's like
w's.).

Airplane or aeroplane or just plain plane, –
Some hint of something more than this is here.
Insect, vision, or terrestrial visitor, –
(Some hint of something more than this is here.)
Some hint is here & what should it be but this?
To watch this quest, to see what it does.
It taxies like an Avro skidding through the flying field
Rises like a Sopwith, flits into a rage
Bangs against the light, settles on the printed page
Soars: then falls: then can't get up
When I try to help him his hands evade my help –
I myself seeing the only possible exit.
So God watches us with lids which move not.
But this is a repetition of an 'idea'
Before the terrible delirium of God.

Here we are, the old iambic again, just to show my old Conrad I've did my lessons, but God & mezcal help me I can't think of anything to call it but

(4)
Prelude to another drink.

Where are the finely drunk? the great drunkard?
This imponderable, small mystery
Perplexes me at midnight constantly
Where is he gone & taking whence his tankard?
Where are all gone my friends the great unanchored?
They drink no more: they go to bed at three
In afternoon yet dream more easily –
– (Livers at last of lives for which they hankered!) –
Of endless corridors of boots to lick,
Or at the end of them all the Pope's toe.
Where are your friends you fool you have but one
And that a friend who also makes you sick
But much less sick than they: & this I know
Since I am the last drunkard. And I drink alone.

Well: my host in Cuautla[2] went nuts. Had to be held down, taken to hospital. It was trying – for him, too, I guess, – & I'm glad Jan was spared the experience.

(It suddenly occurs to me how much I love you both. You old Mephistopheles. Be happy, you two. I kind of feel you will.)[3]

Come to Charlie's, where I am, soon: old Aggie's got the orrors somethink orful.

Malc

Annotations:

1 The title is a play on Aiken's *Preludes for Memnon*, the poems that had so impressed the undergraduate Lowry. These poems are parodies of the kind of poetic exercises Aiken would set for Lowry when he was his tutor. Their subject, treated with wit, pathos, bitterness, and irony, reflects Lowry's state in the summer of 1937, but also recalls the drinking sprees he had enjoyed with Aiken in the past. For annotations to the poems, see Scherf (249-50, 273-74).
2 Cuautla, Morelos, is a town twenty kilometres southwest of Cuernavaca in the Morelos valley; the identity of Lowry's 'host' is not known.
3 Lowry may have intended these poems as a kind of wedding present for Conrad, who was remarried on 7 July. Certainly, his feelings about both the Aikens were deeply ambivalent at this time, as his June 1937 letter (**69**) to Jan, who was away on a trip, makes clear.

Editorial Notes:

a. Aiken has written at the top of the first page: 'Sent to me by hand from Charlie's Bar in Cuernavaca, *1937*. C.A.' Aiken and his third wife, Mary Hoover, whom he married on 7 July 1937, arrived in Cuernavaca in May 1937; they stayed with the Lowrys until just after the wedding.
b. This letter and the poems are written on three pages of paper with the letterhead: 'VAUGHN-AIKEN / Publishers' Repesentative / Apartado 7162 / Mexico City, Mexico.' Lowry changed the 'Vaughn' on each page into 'Vaughan,' to play on the name of the English metaphysical poet Henry Vaughan (1622-95). On the first page he added 'Vaughan-Aiken – it's a Marvell!' – an allusion to the poet and satirist Andrew Marvell – and on the second page he added 'Vaughan-Aiken – *aherrick*! (pardon, just a little onomatopoeic!)' The reference here is to Robert Herrick (1591-1674), an English Cavalier poet. On the third page Lowry wrote 'Vaughan-Aiken – all Donneations please to Lowry/Charlies' to get a nice pun on the name of John Donne. Lowry's marginal comments on his poems have been reproduced as they appear in the holograph.

72: To Jan Gabrial

P: private(ms)

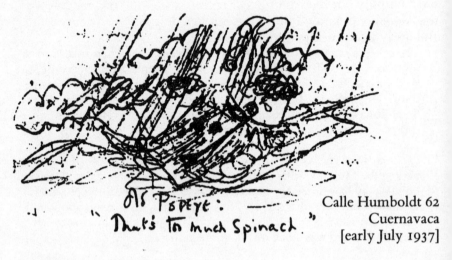

Calle Humboldt 62
Cuernavaca
[early July 1937]

Darling!

Bright days in the middle of the rainy season![1] But they're all gloomy without you.

Conrad says his wedding papers will take longer to get through than he thought & has suggested taking a room up town later. It is difficult to concur at this time without offence but I think it's a good idea just the same. I'll wait for you though.

I think he's an extraordinarily evil person, capable of the profoundest harm to everything more human or with a more progressive nature than a cat: (The tender connotations of our sacred animal don't enter here.) I mean the only thing he wouldn't harm is, literally, a cat.

He pretends to the deepest friendship for me, to admiration for my work, but secretly he is jealous, unreasoning, bitter, while the only real depth in our relationship is the extraordinary malicious extent of his hatred; but this is hatred for life too. It is wretchedness become evil –

I am still playing a 'part' of host but I can no longer bring myself to listen to the arid nonsense he talks.

Ed is at heart an <u>arid</u> & contemptible fellow too. To hell with these degenerate, stupid people. My old Grandad was right, whatever you may say! He knew. It is only our admiration for genius even in its darkest flights that keeps us harbouring such a person as Conrad under our roof. I set out to write of love & I have written, alas, of hate: but Jan, I love you, you are finer than all these people put together, you have more genius, more guts: only you must stick to one thing more, not disperse your fine talents. And you & I must at once simplify our lives & organize them – *alone* – do not misconstrue the 'alone'; you know I don't mean it in a destructive, *extreme* sense. But away from such evil friends as these.

All my love –

Malcolm

P.S. I hope from the bottom of my heart you are having a fine time. I wish to God I were with you. Do you remember Cholula with its two peluquerias the 'Toilet' & the 'Harem.'[2] I hope Lake Pazcuaro is nice, yet I feel that though you may well make it bright, it is dark, thievish, malicious & ugly – & dirty – as though Conrad, Mary & Ed had all bathed in it. No, mischievous was the word I wanted. All my love: & take notes, notes: sweet Mrs Lowry.

Annotations:

1 The above sketch depicts the shared joke of Malcolm's and Jan's that re-appears in chapter 3 of *Under the Volcano* when the Consul comments, 'Old Popeye ought to be coming out again pretty soon,' and Yvonne replies: 'He seems to be completely obliterated in spinach at the moment' (83).
2 The town of Cholula, east of Cuernavaca, is where the Great Pyramid, dedicated to the god Quetzalcóatl, is found; it is the largest ancient structure in the New World. A *peluqueria* is a hair-dressing salon.

73: To John Davenport

p: UBC(ts)
pp: *MLR* 21/22

Calle Humboldt 62,
Cuernavaca,
Mor[elos,] Mexico
31 August 1937

My dear John,[1]
I received your note on a back of a bill forwarded to me. Thanks. I expect you are busy. Conrad has now returned to Rye with his new wife, one hopes he won't be sued for bigamy.[2] He remained in a state

of trance while he was here, saw little of the country in the most unpleasant time of the year, and chose to take away with him, from all the fabulously lovely things that can be had here cheaply, four little wood-carvings of human excreta in various scrolled forms. Dirt cheap!

Talking of Conrad, however, of how one grows out of friends like old clothes or not, brings me to what I can scarcely speak of without bitterness, your own eloquent silence. I sometimes try to persuade myself you did not mean it to be eloquent at all, that it meant no more than one of my own silences, though I honestly think this can scarcely be the case. Not under the circumstances. What has hurt me most deeply about it is that it has been, to all appearances, and continues to be, a silence between house and house, rather than between you and me. The latter is only to be expected after all and for long periods: were this such a silence there would be no cause for this letter. So is the other kind of silence to be expected from time to time. Why not? There is no claim on either house obligating it to write letters. If such a claim existed it would be intolerable. But it did seem to me, does seem to me, that this situation definitely calls for some word from you, not to say explanation. I mentioned Conrad for two reasons: to make a point, and because he is the bearer of news. He stayed a long while, we helped him a good deal, to the best of our ability, we parted, it appeared, the best of friends. But, so far as I was concerned, we were not the best of friends at all. For a very sufficient reason that has no place here. I'm sure he still would claim to be a very good friend of mine indeed, but it is not the case. Well, to hell with the old Medusa! A dirty, destructive, and excessively amusing fellow. But to get to my point. Ratio autem alicujus fiende in mente actoris existens est quaedam prae-existentia rei fiendae in eo. The ground for doing a thing in the mind of the doer is the pre-existence of the thing done.[3] One might say, also, the ground for not doing a thing. Hence I believe whatever it was kept you silent you were well aware of before our parting just as I was well aware at parting I no longer thought of the pro-fascist Conrad as a friend. The immensely important difference is this, I can rack my brains without finding a ground for your silence, if ground there be. You know perfectly well that we, as a unit, wish you, as a unit, well: or don't you? If you don't let me hasten to assure you that we do. Do you imagine the only reason I write is because I want to get something out of you? Granted I would have liked, would like, to land some sort of a job in Hollywood: who wouldn't? But all that is quite extraneous. If you had been able to help in that way it would have been swell but since you couldn't, that was all right, that wasn't even what one wanted to hear, whether you could or not. I didn't even want the book so much as a signal that you wished us well, that there might be an opportunity of all of us getting together again. Believe me it was all as simple as that. You could not get down here? Understood! But can't you see that your silence was like a blow in the face from both of you? Our marriage got little ratification from any source. It would have been pleasant to think it had from you. Besides we might have had some other people down for Christmas, but put them off, expecting you till the last

[breaks off unsigned]

Annotations:

1 John Lancelot Davenport (1908-66), the English writer and editor, had been a close friend of Lowry's at Cambridge (see letter **25**) and helped him with *Ultramarine*. On their way to Mexico in the fall of 1936 the Lowrys stayed with Davenport and his first wife in Hollywood, where Davenport was trying to write for films. For Davenport's memories of Lowry, see *Malcolm Lowry Remembered*. The two men renewed their friendship in 1947. The note Lowry mentions has not survived, and the reason for the apparent distance between the two men to which Lowry refers is unclear.

2 Conrad Aiken failed to reach an agreement with his second wife, Clarissa Lorenz, about a divorce in May 1937; therefore Aiken arranged for a Mexican divorce. This divorce, however, was not legal in England. As he was living in England with Mary Hoover, whom he had just married in Mexico, Clarissa Lorenz could have sued him for bigamy. The divorce from Lorenz became legal in England in 1938.

3 Lowry's translation of the preceding sentence in Latin is correct.

74: To Alfred Miller

P: UBC(ms)
PP: *MLR* 21/22

[Hotel Francia,]
[Oaxaca]
[December 1937][a]

Dear Alfred.[1]

Have been impounded in a jail together with my mail not, as you will probably think, for being drunk but for a rash expression of genuine political opinion in what was a pro-Franco joint.

Had I got my papers with me they could get into a hell of a row for this but unfortunately I haven't so they are within their legal rights in holding me imprisoned. I would tell you more, & shall, when I get to Mexico City.

What they have no legal right to do is to steal your private letters as they stole two letters I was about to post to Jan in lieu of papers & the lack of which must leave her devilishly worried.

Their subsequent behaviour leaves absolutely no doubt as to the character of the head of the P.D. It is a fascist organization just going under cover of a photograph of Cardenas[2] & a bogus popular front.

I could tell you more but won't here. They gave me thorough-going third degree methods & I of course instantly renounced all knowledge of Harry[3] who is as reckless in the hotel dining room with his opinions, & the hotel is one of the centres too – though it is a good hotel & the hotel keeper bailed me out – as I had been else-where.

I felt so strongly that the situation was a truly dangerous one that I did not even ask to see Harry but by a coincidence the next day he found me there. Someone had told him I was.

He immediately started to talk about drink but the truth was I was arrested at 11 o'clock in the morning after one coffee, & it was not I, who only had a bit of a hangover, but those who arrested me who were drunk, that is the Inspector General of the town, a thorough-going fascist, & an obvious homosexual, of the brutal sort, into the bargain, & three marshals.

[unsigned]

Annotations:

1 Alfred and Marsha Miller were friends of the Lowrys in Mexico City, and they were holding Lowry's passport and papers for safe keeping. Alfred Miller sent Lowry his passport later in December.

2 Lázaro Cárdenas (1895-1970) was the leader of the National Revolution-ary party when he won the Mexican election of 1934. He provided money for rural education, nationalized the oil companies and created a more liberal environment in which the foundation of the Mexican femi-nist movement was possible.

3 Harry Mensch was an American friend of the Lowrys who had worked for labour organizations in the United States before going to Mexico for a rest. He accompanied Lowry on this trip to Oaxaca.

Editorial Notes:

a. This letter was written in black ink on both sides of one sheet of Hotel Francia letterhead and folded three times (as is typical of Lowry) for mailing. At a later date Lowry crossed out the salutation and wrote the following instructions in pencil at the top of the page: 'Note for Dark as the Grave' and 'Dialogue for Sigbjørn second part of Dark as the Grave.' At the end of the letter he wrote in pencil: 'Or for use in the Volcano.'

75: To Martin Case

P: UBC(ts)
PP: *CP* 55-56

[Oaxaca]
[December 1937][a]

LETTER FROM OAXACA TO NORTH AFRICA[1]

—— Martin[2] I cannot say to you, old friend,
Dearest of all my friends, that I can see
You softly borne over a wayward sea
To this alcoholic or sardonic end,
Or that colic shore . . . I wish I could find
Your image studded somewhere in the void,
Or under some shining, ocean-stormed waterproof,
Or shooting the greater horned whiffenpoof . . .
Selah. Is no 'gnus good gnus?' Not at all!
(– All this I find upon an obscene wall,
Inspecting an Oaxaquenian gaol,
Written by one, a spy, Vigil Forget,
And scrawled in blood and urine and his own sweat –
Some say his name was Peter Gynt or Gaunt,
He wrote these lines and then was promptly shot.)
– Are you in Spain, hell fire, Liberia gruesome?
Nyasaland with delirium tremens and stamp album giraffes?
Spain! But here I hold my obverse laughs,
Remembering other friends and sons of fiends,
And how much else which dark and goodness holds,
And hope which dies and yields, but never ends,
Or, when it does, its bleeding past defends . . .
– Well – what the hell – yes, what! – the giraffe has a long neck,
And too much longitude, by all Tehuantepec,
And infinite therapeutic and a technique,
Demanding reciprocal exactitude in love's arithmetic.
Ah, *you* must be the Nubian three-horned
To deal with one so forearmed! Be forewarned . . .
Sincerely, I suggest she is not toothsome,

Too much being asked to satiate her loathsome,
Her thoughts jump like beans when you say Timbuctoo,
Her body's striped like boys at bleak Harrow,
Or visions of the Aldershot tatoo.
Or, simply like another giraffe, in another zoo . . .
– Oaxaca? Si, Oaxaca, Oax., Mex!
Where is Oaxaca, Vigil, you ask, what annex,
Niche, pitch, is this? What age is it? What sex?
Mexico? Is it not the place of the lost?
Goal of all Americans who want to be divorced:
Of all Norsemen who want to be unnorsed:
Of all horsemen, already unhorsed:
Licences by Lawrence, by pouncing serpents endorsed.
– Chingarn chingarn chingarn chingarn chingarn,
In Oaxaca I strum my bawdy tune,
Which says, let there be happiness for you,
But delivery, my friend, from ancient heaven,
For God must know it is too badgery,
And retrospect with harps and harpies too,
All botched and bungled with celestial grind . . .
Hush hush I hear the sound of last no-trumps, –
(that strumpets bid before they go to bawd
Warmed by the blood-stream of Wasserman turnips? . . .)
Which are the military police.
– How long since I was last in hell, oh Lord?
Since the last heartbreak of a broken record?
The last memory of a lovely laughing face?
All lost in mistress time and virgin space.
Ah, ghouls are nursling to this bosom,
My heart a widowed spider trapping grief,
Its strings are wrung with agony of Ed Lang,
From floribundia to rose of gall and lung,
It knows the dungeon and must know the gun.
Ah, Martin, would I were in Birmingham,
With old complaints and duns upon my pen!
I love the sun yet I would trade the sun,
For 'In a Mist' by Beiderbecke's ghost,
A break from 'Singing the Blues', a phrase from Bach,
'Walking the Dog' in 1929; Liverpool;
Frankie Trumbauer's 'Imagination', and good Gogol;
For Birmingham-erratum-Edgbaston . . .
(Inverted have we been from Grantchester!
. . . Strange, I shall know death tomorrow, which siesta,

May turn out simply just one more fiesta. . .)
And the nighted storm glistening on the wet fruit,
And Ralph and Bob and Margaret to greet,
Quietly again, in rainy Gillot Street. . .

Annotations:

1 No trace of an actual letter to Martin Case has survived; therefore, it is
not possible to say whether Lowry ever wrote to Case from Mexico or,
if he did, whether he wrote his letter in the form of a poem. I have
decided to include this poem/letter here because it is a fine example of
Lowry's blurring of genres; however, the idea of writing a poem in an
epistolary style is not Lowry's invention, and one cannot rule out the
possibility that this document was always and only intended as a poem.
For a full description of the text, see Scherf (46-47, 55-56) and Ackerley's annotations to the poem (241-45).
2 Dr Edwin Martin Case (1905-78) met Lowry sometime during 1929-30
at one of Charlotte Haldane's gatherings for young men at Roebuck
House, Cambridge, and they became good friends. Case, a biochemist
who worked with J.B.S. Haldane, went to Kenya in 1934, where he
worked for the Coffee Board of Kenya. He is credited with having
rescued a complete draft of *Ultramarine* 'from waste paper baskets and
firegrates' after Ian Parsons of Chatto and Windus had the manuscript
stolen from his car; see Day (127-35, 147-52).

Editorial Notes:

a. This transcription of Lowry's poem/letter to Case has been made from
the photocopy of a three-page typescript (UBC 5:12) that carries one
correction in Lowry's hand and the instruction 'Dedication to Martin &
Margie.' Lowry's addition of a dedication suggests that he intended to
publish the text as a poem. Margerie has added the year 1936 to the title,
but internal evidence confirms that the poem could not have been
written (in its first form) much before December 1937, during Lowry's
dark night of the soul in Oaxaca.

76: To Arthur O. Lowry

P: UBC(ms)
PP: *MLR* 21/22

Hotel Francia,
Apartado Postal Num. 92,
Oaxaca, Oax., Mex.ª
[December 1937]

We've had a good deal of bother lately what with our house being robbed & leaving Mexico.[1]

So we decided each to get jobs, Jan going to Los Angeles for a bit, I on an assignment here of an innocent nature.

I thought it a good idea, on account of the frequency of robberies, to leave my papers behind, since to get here requires a 24 train journey during which it is necessary to sleep, if at all, on the floor.

You go through the Tierra Caliente[2] & it is an amazing experience.

But an even more amazing one awaited me here.

After expressing mildly a liberal opinion I was promptly clapped in the local chokey where, having no papers to prove who I was, I had to remain indefinitely, sleeping with no cover on a cold floor, with a bunch of criminals, who, were a great deal more courteous, I am thankful to say, than the municipality.

After a time there it struck even them that it was mildly absurd for me to be there, and I was let out into the outer world only to be shadowed everywhere by detectives wearing dark glasses.

I then assumed dark glasses myself but was promptly arrested again, this time as a spy.

What I was supposed to be spying on I might not have known, but for their consummate idiocy in arresting me which gave away something very interesting of a political nature.

Once more in the outer, or inner, shall we say, world since we now have a hotel, we continue to be shadowed. We are in no danger since we have the liberal govnt of Mexico behind us, & all that is awaited, are the papers, which inevitably must arrive from the capital sooner or later. The only thing that is not funny is that all my important letters to you & more important, to mother have been impounded, as well as a letter to Jan, who must be worried. If this gets you for Xmas well & good let it serve as wishing you & Mum all the best wishes in the world.

The situation would be irrestibly comic but for the fact that because of it all you will not be able to receive our Christmas presents & I fear you may be worried because of the sad tone of my last letter & heaven knows some of these detectives may be from Cook's Tours[3] or somewhere, but if so, for heaven's sake take them off me, since there are enough without them, and the limit to amusement is where it turns into a sense of persecution.

But there is no possible danger as I am backed up by the Mexican Government, & they assume I am much more important than I am & by the time you receive this letter I shall be out of Oaxaca, probably well out of Mexico with my visa & on the way to Los Angeles to join Jan, who is trying to have a writing assignment waiting for me there.

God bless you & a Merry Xmas to you both, & many happy returns to you, Mum – I am sorry about the other letters being impounded, but it just could not be helped, that's all –
This letter will

[breaks off unsigned]

Annotations:

1 For Jan's description of the robbery of their house, see her 1975 interview with Robert Duncan in *Malcolm Lowry Remembered* (121). She returned to Los Angeles to find work early in December 1937.
2 Tierra Caliente is Spanish for 'hot land' and describes the Mexican climatic zone from sea level to about three thousand feet.
3 The well-known British tourist and travel agency Thomas Cook & Son employed tour guides or 'leaders' who were 'tall men in dark blue uniforms with as much gold braid as naval officers' and, on occasion, British ex-Army officers. See Edmund Swinglehurst, *Cook's Tours: The Story of Popular Travel* (Poole, Dorset: Blandford Press, 1982), p. 169. As this allusion to Cook's Tours makes clear, even Lowry realized that the so-called spies and detectives about which he often complained may have been quite harmless. Nevertheless, there really was a private detective hired by Lowry's father's lawyers to report on his activities during these months in Mexico; see Bowker (237).

Editorial Notes:

a. One or more pages of this letter appear to be missing, so that it begins abruptly and breaks off in mid-sentence, unsigned. It is written on Hotel Francia letterhead. In the top right corner of the first page there are the following pencil addenda in Lowry's hand: '(Dec 1937),' '(to father),' and 'N.P.'

77: To Unidentified, possibly Juan Fernando Márquez

P: UBC(ms)

[Hotel Francia,]
[Oaxaca]
[December 1937][a]

Here, by the way, I am in another bloody fix.

I bought this morning a small bottle of mescal for 30 Centavos –
incidentally they promised to give it to me for 25 Centavos & they
overcharged me by 5 Cents. Then I obtained 2 drinks extra of
mezcal, for which I paid 20 Centavos. Yesterday I got a few drinks
here on what I imagined was credit – about 30c worth.

I was brought some Camarones[1] I did not know I was paying for
at all. Then some sort of oyster juice.

You must in short come over here & help me either by word or
deed immediately else Senõr Cervantes will put me in the Jug again.

Boss or not you must come;[2] because this was all perfectly in good
faith. They have taken my passport & a book of Shelley.

Immediamente   *Malcolm*

Annotations:

1 *Camarónes* is Spanish for 'shrimp.'
2 Lowry's reference here to his addressee's 'boss' suggests that he may
be writing to his Zapotecan friend Juan Fernando Márquez; see letters **80**
and **140**. Lowry calls him Juan Cerillo in *Under the Volcano*, Juan
Fernando Martínez in *Dark as the Grave*, and Fernando Atonalzin in his
essay 'Garden of Etla,' *United Nations World* (June 1950): 45–47. See
Day (240–44).

Editorial Notes:

a. This letter is written on Hotel Francia letterhead, but Lowry has crossed
out the heading and inserted to the left of it: 'That is, at your little cantina: c/o José Cervantes.' The letters 'N.P.' appear in the top right
corner of the page.

78: To John Davenport

p: UBC(ms)
pp: *SL* 11-13; Day 234-36

Hotel Francia,
Oaxaca de Oaxaca,
Mexico
[December 1937]

S.O.S.   Sinking fast by both bow and stern.
S.O.S.   Worse than both the Morro Castle
S.O.S.   And the Titanic – [1]
S.O.S.   No ship can think of anything else to do when it is in danger
S.O.S.   But to ask its closest friend for help.
C Q D.[2] Even if he cannot come.

John.
My first letter to you was impounded by the police here. It contained both congratulation for you & Clem[3] & commiseration for myself.

Better so, because it was a letter nobody should read. Commiseration = commisario de Policia.[4]

I have now destroyed this letter but with it also myself. This letter might be prettier too.

No words exist to describe the terrible condition I am in.

Jan is not responsible for this – but from what I have heard, and from what she has written, I deduce only too perfectly where she is.

This I cannot stand.

In short, I am politely invited to write my wife,
it
care/of/Friede.[5] Shadenfreude![6]

I have, since being here, been in prison three times.

No words exist either to describe this. Of course, this is the end of introversion. If you cannot be decent outside you might as well have a shot at being decent in.

ªHere I succeeded but what shots will be needed now even God would not care to know.

Everywhere I go I am pursued and even now, as I write, no less than five policemen are watching me.

This is the perfect Kafka situation but you will pardon me if I do not consider it any longer funny. In fact its horror is almost perfect & will be completely so if this letter does not reach you, as I expect it will not.

At any rate an absolutely fantastic tragedy is involved – so tragic & so fantastic that I could almost wish you to have a look at it. One of the most amusing features of the thing is that even an attempt to play Sidney Carton[7] has resulted in a farce. I thought he was a good man but now my last illusion is destroyed. It was not that he was not good so much as that he was not allowed to be. Excuse me if I speak in riddles but the eyes of the police are polyganous – is it polyganous? Perhaps polygamous. Finally – I cannot play second fiddle to Harpo Marx.[8] Ah, how the police will try to puzzle this out – they will think I mean Karl! For obvious & oblivious reasons I cannot write to my family: for reasons so obvious they are almost naked I may not write to my wife. I cannot believe all this is true; it is a nightmare almost beyond belief. I looked round in the black recesses of what used to be a mind & saw two friends – yourself & Arthur Calder-Marshall.[9] I also saw something else not so friendly: imminent insanity. I have no conceivable idea how you could help me; or anyone else, unless it is by sending money that will be inevitably ill-spent. I can only send greetings from death to birth and go to pray to what in Mexico they call 'the virgin for those who have nobody with.'

There is a church here for those who are solitary & the comfort you obtain from it is non-existent though I have wept many times there.

Another complication is that never in my whole life have I been to a place so fantastically beautiful as this, &, in spite of all, it would be difficult for me to leave. It is absolutely as fantastic as the afore-mentioned tragedy with which I am involved. The people are lovely and gentle, polite, passionate, profound and true. I hope the police-men who read this will believe it. Even they, with reservations, are the same. But – well; just but . . . .

Incidentally, I smell.

Nobody but the Oaxacquenianos will say a good word for me.

The Spanish detest me; the Americans despise me; and the English turn their backs on me.

If I were able, I would turn my back on myself.

Or wouldn't I?

I scent – (or might if I did not smell so badly myself) some integrity in all this.

Like Colombus I have torn through one reality & discovered another but like Colombus also I thought Cuba was on the mainland and it was not and like Colombus also it is possible I am leaving a heritage of destruction. I am not at all sure about this but in a Mexican prison you have to drink out of a pisspot sometimes. (Especially, when you have no passport.)

But, even without this, I am in horrible danger: & even with it.

Part of this, of course, is imaginary, as usual; but for once it is not as imaginary as usual. In fact danger, both to mind & body, threatens from all sides.

I am not sure that the danger is not ten times as bad as I make out.

This is not the cry of the boy who cries wolf. It is the wolf itself who cries for help. It is possible to say that this is less of a cry than a howl.

What is impossible is to eat, sleep, work: & I fear it may rapidly be becoming impossible also to live.

I cannot even remotely imagine that I am writing these terrible words, but here I am, & outside is the sun, & inside – god only knows & he has already refused.[b]

I cannot see Jan now. But for god's sake see she is all right. I foresaw my fate too deeply to involve her in it.

I would like to see you. Whether you would like to see me is up to you. At such a time it is probably impossible, & with such responsibilities as yours: but I fear the worst, & alas, my only friend is the virgin 'for those who have nobody with,' & she

is not much help, while I am on this last Tooloose – Lowry $\left.\begin{array}{c}\text{us}\\\\\end{array}\right\}$ trek.

Love: & to Clem: & to Natalie[10]: & to Malc.

P.S. To Arthur love and to Ira [Ara] too and alas to Jan.

Annotations:

1 The *Morro Castle* was the flagship of the Ward Line, which took American tourists to Cuba. On Wednesday 5 September 1934 the *Morro Castle* left Havana for New York, but on Friday the captain of the ship died under mysterious circumstances, and on Saturday a fire broke out on board that left 124 passengers dead. Some evidence later emerged to suggest that the same sailor who had murdered the captain was also responsible for the arson. The British luxury liner *Titanic* sank on 14 April 1912 in the Atlantic about 150 kilometres south of the Grand Banks of Newfoundland. The great ship, which was considered unsinkable, struck an iceberg and sank in two hours and forty minutes with a loss of over 1,500 passengers.

2 S.O.S. is a wireless code signal indicating extreme distress. It is not, in fact, an abbreviation, just an effective combination of letters. C.Q.D. is another wireless signal for distress or danger, but, like S.O.S. it is not an actual abbreviation. Popularly, however, S.O.S., is often taken to mean 'Save our souls' and C.Q.D. to mean 'Come quick! Danger.'

3 Clement Forbes-Robertson was Davenport's first wife.

4 In Spanish the word *comisario* means 'commissioner,' or here, 'chief of police.'

5 Donald Friede, co-owner of the Covici-Friede publishing firm and a close friend of Whit Burnett and Martha Foley, knew both the Lowrys while they were in New York in 1934-36. He was later a good friend to Jan in Los Angeles in 1938, hiring her as an editorial assistant and including her in social gatherings.

6 Lowry here refers to the German word *Schadenfreude*, meaning 'malicious joy about someone else's misfortune.' By dropping the 'c' – 'Shadenfreude' – he is better able to pun on 'shit.'

7 Sydney Carton is a character in Charles Dickens' *A Tale of Two Cities* (1859), who sacrifices himself for the happiness of his love.

8 Harpo was one of the three legendary 'Marx Brothers,' who made comical movies in the 1920s and 1930s. Harpo got his name from the fact that on occasion he would play the harp, whereupon everyone else would fade into supporting roles or 'play second fiddle' to him. 'Harpo Marx' was also Lowry's nickname for Donald Friede.

9 The English writer Arthur Calder-Marshall (1908-92) was introduced to Lowry in London in 1932 by John Davenport. He and his wife, Ara, had visited the Lowrys in Cuernavaca during the fall of 1937; see Day (224-230) for a description of this period.

10 Natalie was John Davenport's daughter.

Editorial Notes:

a. In the left margin Lowry has written 'c/o Arthur Calder Marshall, 91 Ocean Way, Santa Monica California.'

b. At this point Lowry has jotted the following sum in the left margin:

1 mescal
7 mescalito
10

79: To Jan Gabrial

P: UBC(ms)

[Oaxaca]
[December 1937][a]

not want to see you because if I did my suffering is such I should probably go into a fit which wld only land me in the prison again.[1]

Perhaps in 2 months. But perhaps not.

Arthur could not help though I love him too.[2]

No Theodore Watts-Dunton[3] can help me out of this fit.

I want to say though, at the last – that I loved him & Ara. That it was good to see them

That I loved you – alas!

But no work has been done by the big cat.

The cigarettes I smoke are called – Alas! too.

John L.D.[Lancelot Davenport] might fly down & he, alone, could help me.

He has responsibilities of his own, though. He is the only man cld help. I have turned into a good poet though cannot write my poems down much.

Like Toulouse-Lautrec[4] I write in brothels etc. Perhaps the poor devil meant to paint & perhaps this poor devil meant to write.

You must show this letter to John because I have made a joke about Toul. Lautrec which I think good.[5] Ref Ibid

Well; he may not ever receive the letter so I shall tell it you.

TOOLOOSE–LOUSY–TREK.

Well; I shall go into the mountains & work in a mine.

I have 1 friend here – a Mexican.

Maybe I shall work in worse than a mine.

But in any event:

(1) My soul is breaking in anguish with the sea.

(2) The serpent is shut out from Paradise / the wounded deer must seek the herb no more / In which its heart-cure lies / The widowed dove must cease to haunt a bower / Like that from which its mate with feigned signs / fled in the April hour. I too must seldom seek again / dear happy friends a mitigated pain. /[b]

Well: This is horribly true.

This page probably smells of oysters – Guaynex Ostiones al Natural[6] – just stood me by an old pal – a policeman, watching me.)[c]

TELL JOHN TO COME DOWN HERE

Tambien

The crane over seas & forests seeks her home
No bird so wild only has its quiet nest,
When it no more would roam;
The sleepless billows on the ocean's breast
Break like a bursting heart and die in foam.[7]

[unsigned]

Annotations:

1 Jan had returned to Los Angeles early in December 1937 to find work, but Lowry, who was drinking very heavily, was certain that she had abandoned him.

2 The autumn 1937 visit of Arthur Calder-Marshall and his wife Ara provoked Lowry to a drinking binge of extreme proportions, which, together with their lack of funds, convinced Jan that she should return to California for work early in December. For Calder-Marshall's lurid version of these events, see *Malcolm Lowry Remembered* (109-13).

3 Theodore Watts-Dunton (1832-1914) took care of the English poet Algernon Swinburne (1837-1909) during the last nine years of his life by weaning him from liquor. Some believe that Swinburne's poetic genius was stifled as his physical health returned; others argue that Watts-Dunton made it possible for the poet to complete much of his best work. Lowry has his Consul make a similar reference to Watts-Dunton in chapter 2 of *Under the Volcano*.

4 Henri Marie Raymond de Toulouse-Lautrec Monfa (1864-1901) was a French painter and lithographer. He became famous for his depictions of life in the brothels and revue theatres of Paris.

5 See Lowry's December 1937 letter (**78**) to Davenport. Lowry delighted in this particular double pun on his own and Toulouse-Lautrec's names.

6 This is probably a standard Mexican term for 'oysters in the natural state.' These words have been scribbled in the top left corner of the second page of the letter.

7 Scherf has included these five lines as a fragment in *Collected Poetry* (361).

Editorial Notes:

a. One or more pages of this pencil draft letter appear to be missing, and it may never have been posted to Jan, for whom it was intended, because some of Lowry's letters to her and his parents were seized by the authorities.

b. The following remark and drawing of a deer appear at the top of the second page: '(This is a deer for the sake of that barman who thinks I am Shelley.)'

c. The second page of this letter has been badly stained at this point.

80: To Juan Fernando Márquez

P: UBC(ms)
PP: *SL* 13-14

[Oaxaca]
[December 1937]

Juan: I am here because there is much hostility in my hotel.[1]

I am trying to do some work here but my life is so circumscribed by your detectives who walk up and down the street & stand at the street corner as though there were nothing better to do than to spy on a man who is unable to do anything anyway & never had any intention of doing anything but be gay and love and help [. . .] help was necessary that I am rapidly losing my mind. It is not drink that does this but Oaxaca.

Do you wish me to leave with the impression that Oaxaca, the most lovely town in the world & with some of the most lovely people in it, is a town consisting entirely of spies & dogs?

This is unfair to me but it is a hell of a sight unfairer to Oaxaca.

The English are sufficiently stupid but the stupidity & hypocrisy of your detectives and the motives which are behind their little eternal spying-Tom activities completely transcend any criminality and stupidity I have ever encountered anywhere in the world. Have these guys nothing better to do than to watch a man who merely wants to write poetry? As if I had not enough troubles on my mind!

I do profoundly think that the Oaxaquenans(?) are among the most courteous, sweetly gracious, & fundamentally decent people in the entire world! I think this too of your boss & of yourself & of this lovely town.

However, the whole damn thing is being raised to an insane state of suspicion.

People even camp outside my bloody door to see if I am drinking inside & of course I probably am because it is so difficult or becoming so difficult to drink outside.

If I do not drink now a certain amount there seems no possible doubt that I shall have a nervous breakdown. If I have that; equally I shall find myself in that goddamn jail to which I seem to be progressing almost geometrically & as you know, when one goes there sober, one comes out drunk.

It seems almost that I have a kind of fixation on the place because, like the novelist, Dostoievsky, I have practically a pathological sympathy for those who do (what others think is) wrong & get into the shit.

What I have absolutely no sympathy with is the legislator; the man who seeks, for his own profit, to exploit the weaknesses of those who are unable to help themselves & then to fasten some moral superscription upon it. This I loathe so much that I cannot conceivably explain how much it is.

Nor, – for that matter – has any man a right to legislate upon a person (who has paid through the nose as I have, who has his house robbed, his wife taken away, in short everything taken away, simply to be in Mexico) – for his own goddamned stupid political reactionary reasons when anyhow, it is only a country that he himself – I mean the legislator – has criminally stolen – you know what I mean, of course. Of course it is true, Monteczuma – not the beer – may not have been much better than Cortés or Alvarado.[2] However: this is another story.

[unsigned]

8 o'clock here – Fernando. . . .[a]

A story 'Oaxaca; Oax; Mex.' . . .
Begins with letter from Mother.
Dec. 1. to January 1.
Composed of letters, documents, etc,
accumulated here.

The slow breaking of his mind day
by day: a ruin; composed of these
notes. Mitla of Malcolm.[3]

Oaxaca is the town of those who
love their mother.
Those who love their mother love Oaxaca.
Progresses till Jan 1.
Letter from Jan, too.
Then ending: Felices Año nuevo.[4]
     – Sank you.
     – Sank you.[5]

– In 31 parts.

Annotations:

1 This unfinished letter is almost certainly intended for Márquez; see letter **140**.
2 Hernán Cortés (1485-1547) conquered Mexico between 1519 and 1521 by defeating the leader of the Aztecs, Moctezuma. Pedro Alvarado

(1485-1541), another conquistador, participated in Cortés's war on the Aztecs and conquered Guatemala in 1524, where he became governor.
3 Mitla was the thirteenth-century centre of Zapotec culture and the name means 'Place of the Dead.' The 'Mitla of Malcolm' is both the notes he speaks of here and the ruinous state he is in.
4 *Felices Año nuevo* is Spanish for 'Happy New Year.'
5 At the end of chapter 7 of *Under the Volcano* Señora Gregorio makes the same pronunciation mistake and is corrected by the Consul.

Editorial Notes:

a. This holograph letter has been scribbled on both sides of two worn pages torn from a ruled notebook; see UBC 1:76. A third page of identical paper contains the material that follows from this line, '8 o'clock here – Fernando,' which resembles an inside address and salutation. There is no way to be certain that Lowry intended these jottings to be a separate letter or part of this one, but I have included them because, in the context of this letter and of Lowry's working methods, they are of intrinsic interest.

81: To Antonio Cerillo

P: UBC(ms)
PP: *MRL* 21/22

On a horse in the mountains.[1]

=====

[Oaxaca]
[late December 1937]

Dear Antonio:[2]
You will be thinking I am dead by this time but I am very far from dead and from everything else too.

It was really much better for everyone concerned, especially me, that I left as and when I did.

I count you as my friend; but you know, really, these people or most of them who pretend to be thinking of a man's welfare are not thinking of it at all but of something quite different. Of course, they do not give a damn whether you live or die. The whole point is they have so little culture or intelligence that they have nothing else to talk about but a man who simply wishes to get to hell away from their company and all other company for that matter or nearly all.

There are, of course, some friends. You, are one: Mr Waterhouse;[3] another. And the people that I am now with are friends. In a very real sense, a very very real sense.

But my nerves cannot stand having people stamp round the town watching me. I appreciate your hotel; your food is as good as any anywhere and often better; but I cannot appreciate the constant misunderstanding, hypocrisy, and spying. And the laugh, of course, is on them!

You speak of mezcal as 'progresion al ratos,' but believe me, you do not need to drink mezcal in order to progress to the rats: I have only to go out into the street for ten minutes to discover one watching me with a drunken expression of heavy disapproval on its face; and there is one man or something that follows me whose resemblance to a rat is so perfectly astonishing that I move from where I happen to be at the moment simply to avoid getting bubonic plague from it.

However, it is not of these things, or of the justice, or of the magnificent hospitality meted out to me in your town that I wish to speak.

The point is; I am leaving it. I shall be back in a few days from where I am – (not, I may say, the place on the postmark of this letter) – & leave as immediately as possible, before anyone has time to serve me with my moral homilies.

What I wish you to do if you are a friend is to conserve carefully even down to the most crushed piece of newspaper everything in my room. You know, of course that I have left my passport etc, in my drawer. But I want everything in that drawer as well; it all may possibly have value to me.

And, if you can, make some reduction for my absence from the hotel and also from meals etc. That would be welcome because I shall need much money to send my wife whom I am going to rejoin &, also, to leave this country.

It is possible I may have to wait for next month's money. If not, I shall require you as a favour to forward my mail to Wells Fargo Ltd Avenida Madero Mexico City & also to make sure, when you visit the Banco Nacional de Mexico, that, as before, no money for me has got stuck there.

You need not inform anyone save Mr Waterhouse, whom I would like you to get to interpret this, of my expected return. They will only inform that Prince of Justice, the Inspector General. And you need not tell any friends of mine you think I have been drunk.

A little wine; a little beer: but no mezcal used to be the watchword –
Yours very sincerely
Malcolm Lowry

Annotations:

1 In his 'Garden of Etla' essay Lowry tells of accompanying Juan
Atonalzin, who carried money for the National Bank of Mexico into
outlying areas by horseback, on one of his journeys from Cuicuitlan to
Nochixtlan in December 1937.
2 Antonio Cerillo was the manager of the Hotel Francia in Oaxaca.
3 Mr Waterhouse, a friend of Lowry's in Mexico, has not yet been further
identified.

*Exactly how Lowry spent the months between December 1937 and April
1939 is unclear. This period was, without question, one of the darkest in his
life. He was in and out of Mexican jails and alcoholic crises; he was obliged
to leave Mexico penniless and go to Los Angeles where his marriage to Jan
collapsed around him. Understandably, his surviving correspondence from
these months is sparse, but he did continue to write: desperate cries for help to
Aiken, an incoherent promise of new work to Cape, a confession to Grieg,
and rambling, tortured letters to Jan that are not available for publication.*

82: To Conrad Aiken
P: UBC(ms)
PP: *SL* 15; *LAL* 47

[Oaxaca]
[January 1938][a]

Dear old bird.
Have now reached condition of amnesia, breakdown, heartbreak,
consumption, cholera, alcoholic poisoning, & God will not like to
know what else if he has to which is damned doubtful.
All change here, all change here, for Oakshot, Cockshot, Poxshot
& fuck the whole bloody lot! My only friend here a tertiary who pins
a medal of the Virgin of Guadalupe on my coat, follows me in the
street – (when I am not in prison, and he follows me there too several
times,) & who thinks I am Jesus Christ, which, as you know, I am
not yet, though I may be progressing towards thinking I am myself.
I have been imprisoned as a spy in a dungeon compared with

which the Chateau d'if – in a film – is a little cottage in the country overlooking the sea.[1]

I spend Christmas – New Years – Wedding Day there. All my mail is late. Where it does arrive it is all contradiction & yours is cut up into little holes.

Don't think I can go on. Where I am it is dark.

Lost. Happy New Year.

Malcolm

Annotations:

1 The Chateau d'If contains the dungeon in which Edmond Dantes is imprisoned in Alexandre Dumas's (1802-70) *Le Comte de Monte-Christo* (1844-45). There have been several film versions of this popular story, including three in English in 1913, 1922, and 1934, and Henri Fescourt's 1929 *Monte Cristo*.

Editorial Notes:

a. The note written by Margerie Lowry at the top of the page reads: 'to Conrad Aiken 1937,' but if Lowry spent his wedding anniversary, 6 January, 'there,' as he says, this letter must have been written shortly after that day. The letter is on Hotel Francia, Oaxaca, letterhead.

83: To Conrad Aiken

P: UBC(ms)
PP: *LAL* 48-50

[Oaxaca]
[early 1938][a]

A mi padre
My dear dear fellow: – at the end of my goddamn life, you are the only man I wish to write to.
– In my churlish way or not so churlish (churchish not richard)

ref. Richard Church.[1]
ref. Landscapes etc.
ref. memory.

way or as it ochurls to me bygosh not a churlish way at all: hell & a typhoon of strumpets: I meant – tucket within, & a flourish of strumpets: & let Plympton Street weep in the East wind: my life was a mignotorio of grief & an excu(ruci)*sado of hate, – Rewritten:

'excrucifiado of hate.' – Joke over.[2] (*Note: Excusado is Mexican for lavatory.) & you were a prophet. I have done you dirt once & a half twice but never seriously & always it was with Jealously – & _love_. Please believe in my sincere friendship & if I die, give me sanctuary.

> – is how to write a verse
> Whether or not you like it/whether or not
> (and petrarch will not save you from the curse.)[3]

Was shot, imprisoned, ruined, bitched, tortured, Castrated (not successfully); – here. Tolstoy says This does you good. – At any rate, I learnt the meaning of stool pigeon. Simply: he sat on the stool all day reported what we said. . . . If you ask me what I think he was it is this: a shit.

> But I suggest: put on your rough red pad.
> Take the Leviathan. Come & see Conrad.
> N.B.
> P.S. And what about a mutual crack at dad?

> μαλcολμ. = pobre Malcolm

P.S. I see some of Mary Hoover's (Mrs Aiken's) pictures.[4] They seem to me brilliant.

> And all love to her.
> and you.
> and Jane.   & John   & Joan[5]
> and rye & camberbeach & the tram[6]

Annotations:

1 Richard Church (1893-1972) was an English poet, novelist, critic, and advisory editor for J.M. Dent & Sons from 1933 to 1952. The reference to 'Landscapes etc.' is probably an allusion to Aiken's *Landscape West of Eden*, which was published by Dent in 1934.
2 *Mingitorio* is Spanish for 'urinal,' but Lowry is punning on 'ignore' and 'notorious,' and he carries on with the Spanish words *excusado*, 'washroom' or 'toilet,' and *crucificado*, 'crucified.'
3 Presumably a joking reference to poetry exercises set for him by Aiken in the past, these fragmentary lines would stay in Lowry's mind; see also his 1942 letter (**174**) to Mrs Bonner.
4 Aiken's third wife, Mary Hoover, is a painter.
5 Jane, John, and Joan are Aiken's three children with his first wife, Jessie MacDonald.

6 See Lowry's 26 August 1940 letter (**148**) to Noxon, in which he remembers their trips from Rye to Camber Beach, where they could swim in the English Channel. This last remark has been added beneath a small sketch of what looks like waves on a beach; see Figure 1.

Editorial Notes:

a. This transcription has been made from a very rough draft version of the letter on the verso of a typescript page for the story 'China' (UBC 8:2). It is undated and may not have been sent to Aiken in any form. Lowry's use of the page, however, is especially interesting (see Figure 1), and compares with his use of the page in his many letter-notes to Margerie.

84: To Jonathan Cape

P: UBC(ms)

Jonathan Cape Ltd,
30 Bedford Square,
Near British Museum,
London,
England

[Los Angeles]
[Spring 1939][a]

Dear Sir:
     Since your publication of my novel Ultramarine, I have fallen on stony ground.
     Much of my work has been stolen or mutilated in the recent [three words illegible]
     However, I have three novels & a play on the shelf.[1]
     Meantime, I thought I would send you this.
     None of these poems have been published either in U.S. or England.
     I send it direct to you because my agent – Farquahson,[2] 8 Halsey House Red Lion Square – do not handle poetry.
     In the event, however, of your accepting this book, or being interested, I would be obliged if you would get in touch with Innes Rose, of Farquarhson's, who handles my work.
     If there is any percentage I would like them (Farquahson) to have

it; also Rose himself happens to be a true poet whose judgment I re-spect & I would like to give him carte blanche so far as any corrections or errors are concerned.

I am too far from home obviously to attend to such matter & life threatens to send me even further

Yours sincerely

Malcolm Lowry

Annotations:

1 What Lowry calls his 'novels' are probably no more than the manuscript drafts of *Under the Volcano*, 'In Ballast to the White Sea,' and what would become *Lunar Caustic*. He also had plans to write a dramatization of Nordahl Grieg's *The Ship Sails On*; see his 1933 letter (**45**) to Jan Gabriel and his 1939 letter (**85**) to Grieg.
2 John Farquharson and Company were Lowry's London literary agents for several years, beginning with *Ultramarine* in the early 1930s. Their pre-war files were lost during the Second World War.

Editorial Notes:

a. There are two marginal addenda to this letter concerning Lowry's address (not Cape's). At the top right of the first page he has written 'V. important. If there is a change of address, please forward,' and on the verso at the bottom left corner of the page 'Try to find me at this address however.' The letter has been drafted on a piece of lined paper torn from a notebook, and the final copy, if there was one, does not appear to have survived with Jonathan Cape's papers. There are no poems extant with the draft of this letter, but Lowry may be referring to the poems he was working on for 'The Lighthouse Invites the Storm.'

85: To Nordahl Grieg

P: UBC(ms)
PP: *SL* 15–16

[Los Angeles][a]
[Spring 1939]

Dear Nordahl:

– Thanks for your letter, of 7 years ago, almost to the day.[1] I read it by the Atlantic, – Atlanterhavet –[2] sitting on a rock in the sun.

Although I have not written to you my consciousness has never been far away from you: nor has my friendship.

I did not write because I felt myself too deeply lost in a dark purgatory blind.[3]

Ah, the world must still be very young![4]

How did your book on Rupert Brooke[5] go?

I wish I could tell you all the extraordinary coincidences which led up to our meeting. One day I shall. My identity with Benjamin[6] eventually led me into mental trouble. Much of U. [*Ultramarine*] is paraphrase, plagiarism, or pastiche, from you.

I have been married, lost my wife, importuned & been importuned by fascists had a terrible sojourn in Mexico. I am but a skeleton – thank God – of my former self.

I read with delight your words on Ossietsky:[7] but, while myself disgusted with Hamsun,[8] I cannot refrain to repeat as coming from myself, that your words *storm in me* day & *night*.

I am sitting here alone & pretty ill trying to finish 2 short novels by May 1. If you would write me a letter it would cheer me up more than I can say. Wish me at least, God speed. Else, like Hermann Bang,[9] I shall die of grief, sitting bolt upright in a Pullman car, in Utah: without a country. I have written a book of poems. 'The Lighthouse invites the storm.' I will send it you if I can light on a copy. I think you would approve

I could not get The Ship Sails on in Eng. as I promised you because it was out of print. It is a great book

I hope Edward Thomson is allright.[10]

I have always looked on you as the greatest of living poets.

Tell me where you are, where you will be.

Remember me. (

Perhaps because I have difficulty in remembering myself.)

I am the age you were when I met you then but

The world must still be very young!

Is the Lighthouse invites the storm [illegible]

    I am now the age you were then but

        ah, the world must still be very young!

                Yours.

                      Malcolm Lowry

[P.S.] I have finished The ship sails on & I have been faithful to it, I think. I think U.S. stage would be interested in this. It would be terrific but I need your formal permission here to go ahead. I wish I could see you & we could collaborate on this. I am not thinking of the financial angle of this. It has been my dream to see it on the stage here.

– apart from other version all these things I must tell you about. Where are you now visible?

Annotations:

1 The only letter from Grieg to Lowry that appears to have survived is a brief note dated 17 September in which Grieg explains that he is too busy to 'accept your kind invitation.' The note was very likely written in 1931, when Lowry was in Oslo, and it is now with the Conrad Aiken papers at the Huntington Library.

2 *Atlanterhavet* (1932) is the name of the play that Grieg was working on when Lowry met him in Oslo in September 1931. A translation called *The Atlantic* was published in 1935.

3 Lowry is echoing line 80 from John Keats's poem-letter 'To J.H. Reynolds, Esq.':

> Or is it that Imagination brought
> Beyond its proper bound, yet still confined, –
> Lost in a sort of Purgatory blind,
> Cannot refer to any standard law
> Of either earth or heaven?   (78-82)

See *The Poetical Works of John Keats*, ed. H.W. Garrod (Oxford: Clarendon Press, 1958), p. 486.

4 'The world must still be very young' is the translation of the title of Grieg's novel *Ung Må Verden Enne Vaere* (1938), a title that Grieg had borrowed from a poem by Henrik Wergeland (1808-45).

5 In a study of English poetry called 'The Young Dead' (*De unge døde*, 1932), Grieg wrote about and translated some of the poetry of Rupert Brooke, Wilfrid Owen, and Charles Hamilton Sorley, who died in the First World War, as well as Keats, Shelley, and Byron, who all died prematurely. Lowry discussed Brooke at length in his 8 September 1931 letter (35) to Grieg, and the two writers may also have talked about Brooke when they met because Grieg was working on this book at the time.

6 Benjamin Hall, a young man on his first sea voyage, is the protagonist of Grieg's *The Ship Sails On*. Dana Hilliot, Lowry's protagonist in *Ultramarine*, bears some resemblance to Hall.

7 Carl von Ossietzky (1889-1938) was a German writer and editor of such left-wing, pacifist periodicals as *Die Weltbühne*. As a result of his experiences in the First World War, he had become a pacifist, and he was arrested twice for his criticism of the military. After Hitler came to power in 1933 he was arrested again and sent to a concentration camp. Ossietzky, who was awarded the Nobel Peace Prize for 1935 was not allowed to accept it, and he died two years later in a Berlin hospital under police supervision. Beginning with an article, 'Svar, Ossietzky!' in *Dagbladet*, 22 November 1935, Grieg wrote about Ossietzky several

times in Norwegian; I have not been able to trace an article in English or a translation.

8 The Norwegian writer Knut Hamsun (1859-1952), who won the Nobel Prize for literature in 1920, first gained attention among English readers with the translation of his novel *Hunger* in 1899. In most of his fiction he celebrated the life of the peasant and the soil, and his work became especially popular among members of the right-wing 'Heimat' movement in Germany. Hamsun was strongly attracted by National Socialism, and after Norway was liberated in 1945 he was tried for treason. Lowry must be referring to Hamsun's political sympathies.

9 Herman Bang (1857-1912) was a Danish novelist, poet, and critic who was popular in Germany and of particular significance to the Decadent movement of the 1890s. While on a reading tour in the United States, Bang allegedly poisoned himself on a Canadian train and died in Odgen, Utah. Lowry's comment 'in Utah: without a country' is a reference to Bang's *De Uden Faedreland* (1905), which was translated as *Denied a Country* (1927).

10 I have not been able to trace an Edward Thomson with any connection to Grieg. Lowry, however, *may* be thinking of the well-known First World War English hero, poet, novelist, playwright, translator, and expert on India, Edward John Thompson (1886-1946). Thompson, who had liberal and non-conformist views, was a popular Oxford don from 1922 until his death, a Fellow of Oriel College, and Spalding Senior Research Fellow at Oxford University from 1936 to 1946. Grieg may well have known Thompson during his time at Wadham College, Oxford, between 1923 and 1924.

Editorial Notes:

a. In *Selected Letters* this letter is dated 1938 from Los Angeles, which, judging from the contents and what we now know of Lowry's health, seems early. My transcription follows the manuscript (UBC 1:76) closely, but the draft is very rough, so that it is not clear where Lowry intended the marginalia to appear. There is one important difference between this version and the one in *Selected Letters*: on the verso of the letter Lowry has scribbled an entire second part that follows his signature on the recto; the editors of *Selected Letters* cut and re-ordered this material. By retaining the original order of the draft I hope to preserve something of Lowry's frame of mind at the time of writing. The postscript material has been scribbled above the salutation.

*Five 1939 letters to Carol Phillips (*86, 87, 88, 94, 117*) are, with one ex-*
ception, all that survive from Lowry's close friendship with the young
woman who typed a version of 'The Last Address' and an early draft of
Under the Volcano. *Lowry and Phillips met in Los Angeles in April*
1939, not long after he had begun to work seriously again on his manuscripts,
and she, an aspiring writer herself, was so impressed with his charm and
knowledge that she agreed to help him. When Lowry was whisked off to
Canada by the attorney Benjamin Parks at the end of July, neither he nor
Parks had paid Phillips for her work on Volcano, *which Lowry left with*
her to complete. After Under the Volcano *was published, Phillips wrote to*
him to ask for her share in the book – the 25 per cent of royalties he had
promised – but she never received a reply. Only a draft of his unfinished 1948
*letter (*342*) to her has survived.*

86: To Carol Phillips

P: UBC(ms)

[Normandie Hotel,]
[Los Angeles]
[April 1939]ª

Carol¹ I wanted to phone you but thought it more expedient
to write:–
What I said to you I more than meant! –
Thanking you from the bottom of my heart.
Whether or not you like it, for better or worse,
This is certainly not the way to write a verse.
But in the vase still is yesterdays undisdained bouquet:²
& the Last Address, in the hat.³
Siempriemente.⁴   Malcolm

– or should I add in case I seem to brag,
that thanks to *you we've* got it in the bag!   M

Annotations:

1 Carol Betty Phillips (1915–) prepared typescripts of 'The Last Address'
and *Under the Volcano*, and Lowry helped her with her poetry and
stories. When she married in 1942, she dropped her first name to
become Betty Atwater, and she went on to lead an interesting personal
and professional life as a well-known psychic and author of *The Curse of
the Soñador* (1981). She and Lowry worked together during April, May,
and June 1939, first on the story, then on the novel. Sometime towards

the end of 1939 or early in 1940 she gave the manuscript of *Under the Volcano* to Benjamin Parks to send to Vancouver, where Lowry was anxiously awaiting it. She remembers her relationship with Lowry as 'close, stimulating, [and] terminated by circumstances beyond our control.'

2 See the line deleted by Lowry from the Phillips poem in letter **88**.

3 Phillips' first typing job for Lowry was to prepare a clean copy of 'The Last Address,' to be sent, very likely, to Whit Burnett in New York. Benjamin Parks paid Phillips twelve dollars for her week's work. 'The Last Address' was never published (see Day, 197, and Woolmer, 62), but Carol Phillips recalls Lowry showing her a letter from a publisher who asked to see the manuscript; she believes that this letter may have been from Burnett. A second version of this novella about a man's visit to Bellevue Hospital in New York City, called 'Swinging the Maelstrom,' was translated into French by Clarisse Francillon and Michele d'Astorg for publication in *Esprit* 1956. The novella now known as *Lunar Caustic* represents an amalgamation of the two versions of this story.

4 'Siempriemente' is not correct Spanish, but Lowry is presumably trying to say 'As always' or 'As ever.'

Editorial Notes:

a. During most of his year in Los Angeles, from July 1938 to July 1939, Lowry lived in a residential hotel called the Normandie on Normandie Avenue in Hollywood. It was a respectable, comfortable establishment with its own dining facilities.

87: To Carol Phillips

P: UBC(ts)
PP: *CP* 365-66

> [Normandie Hotel,]
> [Los Angeles]
> [May 1939][a]

– the asperin tree[1] outside told me to say
her leaves were trembling for your good beauty
but the pingpong bird and the scissors man were in the vicinity
as they have trembled since it wore the the cross
you didn't know Christ was crucified on an asperin tree but so he was
she since has trembled both in gale and calm
[But] for me I am unable to reply
too boiling with malaria am I[2]

besides which I am too goddamned hungry
for you and far too parenthetical too –
we are simple lovers who love the rain
but a poem no I did not mean it
for christ and all deciduous things we love the sun –
and as for you you love what is sane in man
and I I too what is sane in woman.
– perhaps perhaps perhaps we love the sea?
that rose you wore in the sargasso sea?
well damn it that was another thing again
which brings us to the ubiquitous insane
that nauseous trap where love and hate are two
or are they one? and yeah, what about Thomas Chatterton[3]
and who made grey days grey and St. Louis blue? –
but all I wished to say was I love you
not only at sunset: and this is no sonnet.
malcolm.

Annotations:

1 The 'asperin tree' was the aspen outside Lowry's second floor window at
the Normandie Hotel. As Betty Atwater has explained, Lowry christened it with this name and endowed it with a beneficent personality. In
the poem, however, Lowry makes it an ambivalent sign of suffering,
perhaps because the aspen, a type of poplar (*populus tremula*) known for
its leaves that quiver in the wind, is supposed to have provided the wood
from which Christ's cross was made. See Lowry's poem 'And, when
you go –' (*CP*, 102).
2 Lowry often claimed that he had been seriously ill while in Mexico, and
Atwater remembers him as having delicate health in some unspecified
way. He never spoke to her of malaria.
3 The English poet Thomas Chatterton (1752-70) was one of those who,
in Nordahl Grieg's words, 'died young,' by committing suicide at the
age of seventeen.

Editorial Notes:

a. This poem/letter for Phillips is transcribed from a typescript that carries
some holograph corrections of typographical errors and the insertion of
the word 'But' in line seven. The poem/letter is unsigned; Lowry's
name is typed.

88: To Carol Phillips

P: UBC(ms)

[Los Angeles]
[May/June 1939]
ss {Normandie} Titanic[a]

[I] can see you from here leaning on your bicycle which puts my heart with you in the Austrian Tyrol – if it still exists.[1] (That goes for the heart too.)

I try from time to time to get some records but there seem to be conflicting opinions upon the – er – existence of these.

Wasn't there something about a submarine in Under the Volcano? There is a play by W. Shakespeare called Timon of Athens.[2] My soul has been standing still for a week – or is it a year or a thousand? – without you.[3]

Darling, darling, darling, said the Chinese nightingale.[4]

The tree outside is sad. It will die, I think.

From one whose altitude at one time, was not so.

M.

[P.S.] Why don't you send 'A Matter of Mountains' to the *WEEK*?[5]

[A poem by Carol Phillips as revised by Lowry.]

> Betrayed! Betrayed!
> We are the betrayers
> Seeking out each new love
> To fulfill an unfolding personification;
> But what would you have
> Who bleat like lost lambs
> In the darkness of your undoing:
> Romance – coming to heel like a dog
> And glamour hanging in your closet
> Like a glittering sequined shawl
> {Have done!
> It is a new day, a new love,
> Even – – grows old in love [?]
> And frantically paws the ash heap
> For yesterdays disdained bouquet.}[6]

Annotations:

1 Phillips had given Lowry a photograph of herself standing beside a

bicycle against a backdrop of mountains at Palm Springs, California – hence Lowry's reference to the Austrian Tyrol.

2 *Timon of Athens* is a Lowry favorite, but Phillips did not know it. The figure of Timon is tragic in so far as he loses all his wealth through generosity to a host of would-be friends who refuse to help him when he is in debt. Timon dies an outcast and a misanthrope.

3 Towards the end of May, Phillips had begun to suffer from a recurrence of tuberculosis contracted in infancy, and this forced her to stop her trips into Los Angeles in early June. During much of June and July she and Lowry did not see each other, and she did not tell him about her illness. Because she did not have a telephone, Lowry could only reach her through a sister, who by this time was displeased with Lowry for not paying Carol and thus discouraged him. According to Margerie Bonner, she and Lowry met on 7 June 1939 and fell instantly in love; Lowry's continued letters to Phillips, however, cast doubt upon Margerie's version of events.

4 See Lowry's May 1933 letter (**43**) to Jan Gabrial.

5 'A Matter of Mountains' was a short story by Phillips, and the *Week* was a local magazine that published short fiction.

6 Lowry deleted these five lines from Phillips' poem; otherwise, he simply rewrote her lines, with minor changes in punctuation.

Editorial Notes:

a. This letter fragment appears to be missing its first page(s), and there is neither a proper inside address with an addressee's name nor an inside date. The words 'ss {Normandie} Titanic' have been written, with lines through 'Normandie,' at the top right of the page, and this suggests that Lowry was writing from the Normandie Hotel. His reference, of course, is to two famous ships – the huge French ocean liner called the *Normandie*, launched on 29 October 1932, and the equally splendid luxury liner *Titanic*, which sank in the North Atlantic off Newfoundland in 1912. It is not clear whether the poem was enclosed with a letter and if so which letter, but it belongs in sequence with his letters to Carol Phillips from this period.

Sometime during June 1939, Malcolm Lowry met the petite, pretty, and dramatic ex-starlet Margerie Bonner. The rest, as it were, is history, except that for Malcolm and Margerie it would also always be fiction. This is the first extant letter to Margerie; it was written on his trip north to Vancouver, British Columbia, a day after he was forced to leave her behind in Los Angeles. Over the next two months he wrote to her twice a week, first about his plans to join her in Los Angeles and then with pleas that she join him in Vancouver. She did. And in the years that followed, he wrote her daily, *either in tiny love notes (see Appendix 1, Volume II), or on the pages of his manuscripts.*

89: To Margerie Bonner Lowry

P: UBC(ms)

> Hotel Georgia,
> Vancouver, B.C.[a]
> 30 July 1939

Margie darling –[1]

We got here in 2½ days at an average speed of approximately 63 mph.[2] Once we hit 97. The first night we spent in a place called Weed. Weed! I don't seem to be going so good on this letter so far: it is so long since I wrote one I have almost forgotten how. The second night we spent in a place called – Grizzly![3] There were birds in both these places: doves. Oregon I thought the most beautiful place I have ever seen & I have seen some. One day we shall go to Crater Lake & be so happy in one another.

I have quit drinking but Señor Barleycorn still shakes my hand either as though he were perpetually glad to see me still alive or were persistently taking leave.

I think of you all the time & your photograph is beside my bed. She talks to me.

I wish I could put all the words of tenderness & love in the world into this letter. But the one simple humble vocable 'love' does as well.

I will move the Himalayas to see you again soon: somehow.

But we can never be far away from one another. Look after Jack:[4] give him my love: I shall write. I will try & send some money when I have got rid of Parks. I hope Omar & Princess are well.[5] Think of me & we will sleep in each other's arms just as before & it will be as though we are not away from each other. Nor are we.

I love you. May God keep you safe.

> Your
>
> Malcolm

Annotations:

1 Margerie Bonner (1905–88), Lowry's second wife, had been an actress in Hollywood. At the time they met, sometime in June, she was working for actress Penny Singleton and writing mystery stories. She married Lowry on 2 December 1940 in Vancouver.

2 Benjamin Parks, the Los Angeles attorney in charge of Lowry's finances and affairs, drove Lowry to Vancouver, where they arrived on 30 July.

3 Weed is a town in northern California, situated on the interstate highway approximately fifty kilometres from the Oregon border. Grizzly, which is ten kilometres off Highway 97 in Oregon, is a small town approximately two hundred kilometres from the California border.

4 Jack Garnet Wolsley King was an Englishman living at the Normandie Hotel, where Lowry stayed during his year in Los Angeles. Lowry and King became friends, and through him Lowry met Margerie Bonner.

5 Omar and Princess were Margerie's pets.

Editorial Notes:

a. This letter is written on Hotel Georgia letterhead, but the letterhead has not been crossed out or replaced with an inside address as was Lowry's practice when using a hotel's stationery. Parks and Lowry stayed at the hotel when they first arrived in Vancouver.

90: To Margerie Bonner Lowry

P: UBC(ms)

2825 S.W. Marine Drive,[1]
Vancouver, B.C.
[early August 1939]

I've been spending a week looking forward to news from you & having a honeymoon all to myself. Ever since I've been away from you I've felt as though I were being torn apart by wolves, like Grandmother's grey goat.

I can't say how marvellous it felt getting your composite letter this morning.

The place where I spent my single honeymoon was an island named Bowen:[2] it is isolated & full of tall firs & horses & completely surrounded (as you may have assumed!) by water. There was everything good about it, only you weren't there. I never spoke to a soul the whole time I was there except the tennis instructor at the local pub with whom I played a few foetid desultory games. I signed my name in the register – Mr Brink, which scared them. (– see movie, 'On Borrowed Time.')[3]

– But you would have loved the horses.

(continued)

Please write again soon[a]

[unsigned]

Annotations:

1 This is the address of Archibald B. Carey, the Vancouver business man whom Parks placed in charge of Lowry's affairs. Lowry lived with Carey and his family until early September, when he moved to the house rented by Maurice Carey (no relation to A.B. Carey) on Nineteenth Avenue in Vancouver. The large, gracious house at 2825 S.W. Marine Drive still stands on a large treed lot. Though not on the scale of Inglewood, Lowry's home in Caldy, it must have reminded him of the parental home, just as Carey reminded Lowry of his father.

2 Bowen Island is a small island in the Strait of Georgia at the entrance to Lion's Bay.

3 *On Borrowed Time* (1939) was the name of an American movie, directed by Sidney Franklin, about an old man called Mr Brink who refuses to die, and chases Death up the apple tree. The movie opened in Vancouver on 28 July 1939.

Editorial Notes:

a. The word '(continued)' has been added in pencil near the top of the page, but no continuation follows, and Lowry has written this last sentence in pencil above the image of the Hotel Georgia at the top of the page.

91: To Margerie Bonner Lowry

P: UBC(ms)

[Vancouver, B.C.][a]
[early August 1939]

Margie my little love, my darling, – what can I say to make you happy? What I can do is another thing: I think I am doing it.
– I think war will be postponed for the time being: England seems to be pulling herself together.

I have become terribly sober & fit & am working, of all things, for the British Columbian Government. My job: to help other people get jobs. In short I am on the unemployment board.[1] It is exciting. Vancouver seethes & the other day some labour agitators captured the post office for twenty-four hours.[2]

I have quite got rid of the jitters but sorry if you have had them, my darling. I have also gotten rid of Parks, but have to wait a bit for money.[3]

My god, I love you, Margie – what happened to us? I don't know how I can smile till I see you again, or exist without your love &

nearness & compassion: the sensation of underground bleeding, of being torn up by the roots like a tree by a big wind – do you feel that? God, I do! With all ones tendrils & everything that joined one to life & nourishment & earth upturned & smashed & freezing. Gurr. You have spoiled me for ever for any other relationship & you have spoiled all women for ever for me & I'm glad of it. Tell me all about yourself & send some white birds of love flying through the red forest of the post. Thank you for your last letter – please please write again! My god let's make it soon when we can be happy again on a tousled bed and at peace in spite of the pain. Forgive this dead letter & the I I, my my, refrain: tell me all your troubles & let me share them & god bless you sweet lady, woman; child.

Malcolm

– P.S. I think of your saying: 'Now I'll just put on a face –

Annotations:

1 Here, and in subsequent letters, Lowry describes himself as working with or for the British Columbia Ministry of Labour; however, extensive inquiries into provincial government personnel records have revealed no sign of Lowry's holding such a job. In his 22 August 1939 letter (**100**) to Margerie he describes this work as unpaid and 'purely nominal,' in which case it is highly likely that Lowry was simply working for A.B. Carey, who was the chairman of an organization called the Citizens' Recreational Council, formed in 1938 to assist unemployed single men. Carey, a member of the ultra-conservative, short-lived Reconstruction party and a candidate in the 1935 federal election, had been involved in this type of philanthropic work since at least 1935, when he chaired both the Central Clothing Committee and the Single Homeless Men's Committee of the party.

2 Serious labour agitation had occurred in Vancouver in the spring of 1935 and again in the summer of 1938 when the Vancouver Art Gallery and the Post Office were occupied for several weeks before the demonstrators were violently suppressed. By the summer of 1939 the worst effects of the Depression were behind Vancouver, but there were still close to ten thousand men out of work and on relief.

3 Before he returned to Los Angeles in early August, Benjamin Parks had handed Lowry's finances over to A.B. Carey, who was now in charge of Lowry's remittances from England.

Editorial Notes:

a. This letter is written on Hotel Georgia stationery with the letterhead crossed out.

92: To Margerie Bonner Lowry

P: UBC(telegram)

Western Union,
Gr Vancouver, B.C.
10 August 1939

MARGERIE BONNER
     6213½ GLEN AIRY HOLLYWOOD CALIF
HAVE WRITTEN I AM WITH YOU ALL THE TIME SO DO NOT BE LONELY BE
HAPPY PUT ON A FACE AND I WILL CHEER STOP A FEW STATES AND A
COUNTRY DO NOT SEPARATE US SWEETHEART LOVE JACK [KING] OMAR
PRINCESS AND CONTRAPTION.

MALCOLM

93: To Benjamin Parks

P: Liverpool(ms)

c/o A.B. Carey Esq.,
2825 S.W. Marine Drive,
Vancouver, B.C.,
Canada
[August 1939][a]

– Dear Mr Parks:[1]
   I think you will now be back in the Van Nuys Building, so I am
writing the promised letter.
   I went as per arrangement to stay with the Careys & later I came
with them to their summer home at Granthams landing.[2] The
weather has been very fine and I have spent most of my time swimming, climbing, and playing Badminton. Yesterday I swam 4 miles
to Keats Island, & the day before rowed eight.[3] I am very fit and
more or less black with the sun. I have not found any necessity to
drink at all – it seems that this problem is 'liquidated' – but the inner,
mental, weather is pretty over-clouded and threatens to remain so.
The fact that no pressure is put upon me one way or another, and
that I have a sense of freedom of action, is an important contributory
factor, however, in my remaining on an even keel at this particular
juncture and I think you may rest assured in your mind that your
arrangements have had the best results.
   I am sending you, – it will catch the airmail Monday, – a letter that

I would like you to get to Jan after reading it, if you think this expedient. I am not sure of her address, but it will surely be possible to get it from her telephone no: (Cr 13598, I think it is). If possible, also, – it being ethically feasible with her consent, – I would like you to *see* her: our circumstance having, so far, lacked any successful mediation.

I cannot obviously live here indefinitely with the Careys' and I really believe that my happiness and any satisfaction that my father can get out of my life depends on my reentry into the States & as much freedom over a specified period with specified results so far as my work is concerned as is compatible with reason, I would be obliged if you could send me the box full of my oddments etc & if you can see any letters from Jan therein I would like you to take them. Please try & move mountains in this business: I do not wish any further pain for the family, ill as their understanding is of the causes of this débàcle, they do deserve at least the peace of their hands from me.

I am glad we parted on such a happy note, and am grateful for the very interesting & beautiful journey.

Yours very truly:

Malcolm

P.S. I had a little more trouble with my teeth – a pulp stone in the bottom row left – & I am getting this seen to by a good dentist here.

Annotations:

1 Benjamin Stanley Parks (1897-1969), the Los Angeles attorney hired by Lowry's father to look after Lowry's finances and affairs, wanted to prevent Lowry from slipping into another marital disaster and to keep him away from Los Angeles until the divorce from Jan was settled. Vancouver, British Columbia, in Canada seemed a safe distance; thus Parks drove Lowry to Vancouver to make sure he would arrive without incident. The Van Nuys Building was the office block in the Van Nuys area of Los Angeles where Parks had his office. Two of the three letters from Lowry to Parks in this volume were found with the Lowry company files in the Liverpool Library, which indicates that Parks sent them to Lowry's father as evidence of his son's good behaviour. No other letters from Lowry to Parks appear to have survived, and in his 8 August 1961 letter to Earle Birney, Basil Stuart-Stubbs, who was then head of Special Collections at UBC and actively collecting Lowry material for the archive, confirms that he had contacted Parks and that Parks's files from the thirties and forties were destroyed to increase office space.

2 A.B. Carey had three children, David, Elizabeth, and Patricia. When

Lowry arrived in the Carey home, David was already at Oxford on a Rhodes scholarship, and Mr Carey was active in a number of philanthropic enterprises. Over the next few months Lowry complained to Margerie and Conrad Aiken about the severe moralism of his host, whose Christian, fundamentalist tone and views were pronounced publicly when he ran (unsuccessfully) for federal office with the conservative Reconstruction party in 1935. Lowry describes this trip in more detail in his 22 August 1939 letter (**100**) to Margerie.

3 Keats Island lies off the west coast of Bowen Island in Howe Sound just to the north-west of the city of Vancouver.

Editorial Notes:

a.   This holograph letter is undated, and there is now no way of confirming how long Parks stayed in Vancouver or when he returned to Los Angeles. References in this letter, however, such as to Lowry's trip to Granthams Landing, his being fit, and so on, are very similar to the comments he makes in his 22 August 1939 letter (**100**) to Margerie.

94: To Carol Phillips

P: UBC(ms)

> c/o A.B. Carey Esq.,
> 2825 S.W. Marine Drive,
> Vancouver,
> British Columbia,
> Canada
> [11 August 1939][a]

My dear: –

I left you without a word of farewell & your ring burns on my finger.[1]

If I behaved loutishly, forgive me: try & remember something good about me, if there is anything. Don't forget me, or us, & throw all we knew away like a poor newspaper: please don't do that. What is true is true forever, I don't care what people say.

What is the status of Under the Volcano? of course you can have your 25% – if they're any royalties – but I thought it more immediately constructive to leave your present address c/o Parks: he, or secretary, will, if the situation is as it was when I left, pay you for work so far – probably not enough, but it might be useful.[2] Whereas the other is a little bit ephemeral, until it's been published: but you shall have that & any mention in any form you may desire. (I lost your document somewhere.)[3]

I should be interested to know how it's going on. Please don't abandon it. I'd like to leave some record of myself in the U.S. Have you got the 1st chapter or have I?

I have quit drinking & am working, between seas, for the Columbian Ministry of Labour. It is interesting.

I am terribly lonesome without you but I know we shall meet again soon.

I think always of that tree & you standing there. You were so kind and sweet to me & compassionate. You're the grandest person I've ever known. You saved my life & I hope I can prove it was worth saving.

Try & do alot of reading: Thomas Mann's *The Magic Mountain*, & his collected stories: Gogol's *Dead Souls*: Conrad's *Youth, Typhoon, Heart of Darkness*: Kafka's The *Castle*, & the *Great Wall of China*: Hermann Broch, *The Sleepwalkers*. And as much modern poetry, [Stephen] Spender, [W.H.] Auden, Wallace Stevens etc as you can digest.[4] I'll go into more detail later.

Please, please write to me. I'll never forget you till my dying day & not even then but I'll have to stop now because I can hear you saying outside the door. 'Me.' & it's more than I can stand.

– Malcolm

P.S. I love you very dearly.

Annotations:

1 Lowry and Phillips had exchanged friendship rings during their brief relationship. At their last meeting, on or about 27 July 1939, in his room at the Normandie Hotel, he had been very stiff and formal. Margerie Bonner was in the room, and Lowry, who was already involved with Margerie, must have felt awkward. He gave Phillips the complete manuscript of *Under the Volcano* with instructions to continue her work on it; they exchanged a few general comments, and she kissed him goodbye. They never saw each other again.

2 Benjamin Parks had neglected to pay Phillips for typing *Volcano* – hence, Lowry's promise to reimburse her; see his 1948 draft letter (**342**) to her.

3 According to Betty Atwater, this 'document' was a letter, signed by Lowry, promising to pay Carol Phillips 25 per cent of royalties on *Volcano*. Lowry kept the only copy of this letter.

4 This list of suggested titles of modern fiction and contemporary poets is interesting for its inclusion of lesser-known works in translation – notably Franz Kafka's story 'The Great Wall of China' (translated by Edwin and Willa Muir in 1933) and Hermann Broch's *The Sleepwalkers* (translated by the Muirs in 1932).

Editorial Notes:

a. The envelope, addressed to Phillips in Long Beach, California, is post-
    marked 11 August.

95: To Margerie Bonner Lowry
P: UBC(ms)

> c/o A.B. Carey,
> 2825 S.W. Marine Drive,
> Vancouver,
> British Columbia,
> Canada
> [mid-August 1939]

My darling Marjorie:[a]

Two letters from you, both at once, which take me all the way
from petunias to the Pliades,[1] and from Jupiter to Jaguars. Yes, I love
circuses, or are they circi? I went to a Norwegian one long ago –
SPRINGBOARTOGTUMPLINAKT, is a word I remember. I remember also
the sort of fairy ring that the circus left after they'd packed up, on
Midsummer common in Cambridge: that was very sad. And the lion
that wept too, in a cage, in New Brighton, Cheshire, Eng, where I
was born. And two lion-faced ladies who wept, twice nightly, in another cage in the same place. They had come all the way from the
hinterland or somewhere. You observe astutely, 'sometimes I can't
read my writing myself when it's cold,' to which my only possible
reply could be 'and sometimes I feel I oughtn't to read it when it's
hot . . .' I've been suffering slightly from the jealousies, just slightly,
since your description of the circus: I'm not any longer though, I'm
just glad you had a good time. However, it's just the sort of light-
hearted gaiety we could enjoy together. I'm still waiting for the
news, and the tension is getting unbearable: and I have a passion to
share the things with you that make you laugh and gladden your
heart. Your mention of your birthplace[2] in a letter the other day
made me want to go there and be near the soil and the green graces
which shaped you. And somehow the very difference in our sex
moves me deeply when I think of it, a sort of compassion gets mixed
up with my desire, and I really do feel that I'm carrying you about in
my heart; Lord knows where these feelings come from, it's just love,
I guess. If the permission doesn't come I'm going to get down to you
somehow, money or no money. I think I have enough contacts still

to be able to raise some in California, & if not, I can sell some stories. It might be better, at that, to cut entirely loose from my income since, in spite of its advantages, it binds me & us cripplingly, as things stand. How long the visa will last depends upon what they say at the border: and also, on my news from England: but if the news is favourable this time, and I have played my cards wisely, I think we should have longer than we counted on having.

Please wait and be true to me, & us: the bottom has dropped out of the world of my generation: you and a love of the principle of beauty in all things are all that connects me to life: my god, what portentous rot that sounds! But it's true. Be with me to-night. I shall be with you.

Always, my beloved,

Malcolm

P.S. I'm sending you a poem written in a bleak moment. In a gay one, I'll write one about you, send it you to-morrow.

Annotations:

1 Lowry means the Pleiades, a cluster of seven stars in the constellation Taurus, of which six are visible.
2 Margerie Bonner was born in Adrian, Michigan, on 18 July 1905, the younger of two daughters of John Stuart Bonner and Anna Mabelle Clayton.

Editorial Notes:

a. During their first year together Lowry occasionally misspelt Margerie's first name. The poem mentioned in his postscript is not extant with the letter.

96: To Margerie Bonner Lowry

P: UBC(ms)

[Vancouver, B.C.]
[mid-August 1939]^a

Sweetheart.

I'm just sending this hurling through the post to get you on the weekend – there's been a slight misunderstanding with England which may mean a fortnight delay but only that at most – am writing & will explain fully – unavoidable – please go on loving me, I love you always & always & always, breaks my heart to disappoint you, but it will be all the sweeter when we do meet, which still will be soon. All love your Malcolm.

Editorial Notes:

a. This 'letter' was written in pencil on the front of an unused airmail envelope.

97: To Margerie Bonner Lowry

P: UBC(ms)

[Vancouver, B.C.]
[mid-August 1939]

My woman:
When you rang me up yesterday I hadn't received your letter telling me you were sick, & I didn't deduce it from your voice. I'm frightfully anxious and I ought to be with you and I feel desperate that I am unable to be. The reason for the delay is purely a matter of misunderstanding so far as England is concerned: it must be clear to you that in order to visit the U.S.A. at this time one must be able to produce a pretty good reason and somehow or another, New York got mixed up with L.A. – they thought I was going to the former. I have my visa, and also the money, but with the certainty in my mind that England could raise no possible objection to such a visit, I gave my word that I wouldn't use it for the purpose of getting back without that particular sanction: if I do, I face the possibility of getting my income cut off at the other end, which only concerns me in so far that what I can touch of it we shall need together: moreover, in spite of the delay, I feel that it would be quixotic in view of the fact that I feel certain that the sanction _will_ be given, since two individuals in very high office, one a Colonel in the secret service, the other in the Ministry of Labour, have undertaken to press my point: if the next cable comes back as swiftly as your friend's[a] did from London, & it is favourable, then we have shall have to wait no time at all. If it is unfavourable, I shall have to hitch hike, that's all: as for my word my scrupolosity deserves no praise, there being very little I would not do to get to your side at such a time: but the fact is that it is banked with the aforesaid Minister, who, belonging to the Oxford Group, suffers unnegotiable torments of conscience about giving it to me without the above sanction: the Colonel would do it like a shot, but he is on

secret service and hidden in a canal somewhere.[1] I know noone, either, to borrow it from: my belief is that there is no money in Canada at all. Or if there is, that is hidden, too. I'll tell you other details about my connections with the war in the course of time. As you may have gathered, you may be certain that I am not profiteering from it! When I received the news I felt just about ready to die that a misunderstanding should have arisen at such a period: the weather broke too into gloom, rain, murk although it was still hot: everything seemed to be sticking together in the unpleasant sense, clothes, hands, envelopes, and all the hothead factions of the mind, (which could not even stampede.) . . . I walked three times past the same letter box, each time thinking I'd posted a letter to you. Please please take good care of yourself & don't sink into depression too.

Don't throw desks about – sorry, decks, – the cards will doubtless prove quite right, after all.

Would you try, by just thinking of me & not getting exasperated, to bring us even closer together than we are at this time? And please don't be impatient, I'm doing everything I can in the world, – do believe me. It breaks my heart to disappoint you, but I have reason to think we may have very good news –– very soon: even better than we thought: so try & hang on till I get it. Oh Margie darling, I love you so much & I want so much to be near you & comfort you and put my hands on your lovely breasts which sort of talk to me, and feel your feet seek mine for comfort. Margie, please love me too. I adore the ground you walk on. And I even think about & love your little shadow, running before you along the street, I don't know why.

Good night, my darling. Do come to me tonight.

Your

Malcolm

Annotations:

1 The man in the 'Ministry of Labour' who, according to Lowry, belongs to the Oxford Group is A.B. Carey. Douglas Day calls Carey an attorney, perhaps confusing his profession with that of Benjamin Parks. It is clear from surviving records and Vancouver newspaper clippings from 1935 to 1948 that Archibald B. Carey had been connected with the rubber-plantation business in British Malaya from the time of the First World War until 1931, when he moved to British Columbia, and that he had become a well-respected business man and politically active citizen. The 'Colonel on secret service' was Victor MacLean (1896-1940), another Vancouver business man and philanthropist who organized a home for returned soldiers after the First World War and was killed

while conducting black-out tours of Canadian army camps in England on 1 November 1940. For further information on these men, see Cynthia Sugars's 'Lowry's Keepers' in the *Malcolm Lowry Review* 28 (1991): 34-39.

Editorial Notes:

a. Lowry wrote the following note, marked with an asterisk, at the top of the page to explain this point: 'I thought at first you wrote "she does something, I believe *e*xecution, at Columbia," not el**o**cution, (yes, it's spelt with an 'o,') & I've been visualizing your drinking cocktails with a female hangwoman ever since!'

98: To Margerie Bonner Lowry

P: UBC(ms)

[Vancouver, B.C.]
[mid–August 1939]

Darling sweetheart.
    I think of you as wife sister mother mistress friend.
Please please take care of yourself until I can get to you. I'm so dreadfully anxious about & worried about you I can't sleep or think.
    Damn & blast this cockeyed world not of our own making.
    I'm going nuts waiting for news; & you there ill & needing me.
    I can't find anybody going to Los Angeles as yet or I'd come news or no news & trust that I could clear up things with my attorney at the other end.
    Meantime I think he is deliberately stalling, or England is stalling, with the idea that I shall enlist in this benighted country, which naturally I have no intention of doing now, since that is an irrevocable step & would knock things on the head so far as we are concerned.
    Please look after yourself, darling, I shall be thinking of you all the time & praying that you are well & happy. Your

Malcolm

99: To Margerie Bonner Lowry
P: UBC(ms)

[Vancouver, B.C.]
[ca 21 August 1939]ᵃ

My darling darling Margie –
Thanks frightfully for your letter. I desire & love you more & more
as each day and intolerable night goes by. I never knew it was possible to be so happy as I was with you nor to want anybody as much
as I want you. I have been taking pleasure in working & keeping fit
because I feel that you would want me that way more. The Dantzig
show has made things more difficult to predict, so far as we are concerned; & Jan makes it more difficult still. With the future I have to
offer you as ephemeral (and if we let it slide) as indefinitely postponed
as it is – how can I say anything that is as concrete as you wish? One
thing is certain, that we could not be married for a year, and that that
year is going to produce changes within whatever security I do enjoy
if affairs in Europe continue as they threaten to do.
We run a danger, if we do not act, of wearing ourselves old & grey
behind a barrier of time.
I have no right to jeopardise your own security, such as it is, with
the offer of something less secure. On the other hand I love you, you
me.
The idea has struck me that I [breaks off]

> [frosted]
> Snow-freaked rocks the eagle alone questions
> on the spirit, or wandering freighter!
> Sometimes the writing [. . .] art, to get away.
> It is as though the trees marched down to water
> From the perennial headache of snow.
> They could not shake loose that hangover of the fog
> Blest when it gathers the lost to his (lost) brother.
> Blest when [breaks off]

[unsigned]

Editorial Notes:

a. This letter fragment is a pencil draft, on yellowed notepaper, of the first
page of the *first* 22 August 1939 letter (**100**) to Margerie. I have included
it as a separate item because of its interesting differences from the *second*
22 August letter (**102**) and because it is likely one of the 'anguished fumbles' described by Lowry in that letter.

100: To Margerie Bonner Lowry

P: UBC(ms)

> c/o A.B. Carey Esq.,
> 2825 S.W. Marine Drive,
> Vancouver,
> British Columbia,
> Canada
> [22 August 1939]ᵃ

– Darling Margerie:

I got into one of my paralysed moods, my emotions were exceeding all possible expression, so I sent you a telegram: I had already written but I hoped it would get you for the week-end. I enclose a couple of anguished fumbles: left unfinished like Liverpool Cathedral, with the crane on top. The above address will get me.

Although the hearing was originally set for the sixth the divorce proceedings actually open fire on the thirtieth: Jan is being as murderous as possible, so far, & if she gets away with her charges she will make it neatly impossible for me to return to the United States at all. I am suitably impressed with her extreme sportsmanship.

Nevertheless, I shall find a way: what we created between ourselves will help: and, moreover, it's unlikely she will get away with it. What will in all likelihood happen: she will change her charge, get her divorce by default, & I'll pay her lawyer. It all seems incredibly dirty seen from any angle.

Meantime, desire for you is gnawing me to pieces but you wouldn't notice it. I am getting myself very fit and don't recognize my reflection at all. I am also working (at the moment, practically without pay) for the Columbian Ministry of Labor.[1] I am housed with a delegate. This evening the ministry is going off on a fishing trip – me too: it is camping in a place called Grantham's Landing & I shall write you from there.[2] The country is heavenly, & god how I wish you were coming along. I loathe fish personally, but there are woods & horses & mountains and friendly people, the weather is grand, & it is cheap.

Parks has departed long since – he was not very popular here. He may come in useful in L.A. however. I quit drinking: I've had only about 3 beers since I've been in Canada. Although no feeling of guilt pertains to it I thought I might as well show us both I could do it. I am surprised my abstention was not succeeded by complete collapse: but no, to the contrary. I shall undoubtedly get tight again from time to time in my life, & I do like to drink & with you, but after my late bounce I think you'll find alc has been put in its place. I hope. If I saved up some money, do you really mean you would come & see me, if it proves impossible for me to come to you. This letter goes on.

I love you & want you, god how much – M

(continued)

Annotations:

1 Inquiries with the Ministry of Labour and the records branch of the government of British Columbia show no evidence of Malcolm Lowry's ever having worked for any branch of the provincial government. This is probably another reference to his volunteer work for A.B. Carey's committee to help unemployed single men; see also letter **91** to Margerie.

2 Grantham's Landing is a pretty town, founded by Frederick Charles Grantham (1871-1954) in 1909, located on the Sechelt Peninsula and facing Howe Sound just to the north-west of Vancouver. See the map of the Vancouver area, photograph 23.

Editorial Notes:

a. The telegram of 22 August 1939, addressed from Grantham's Landing, B.C., suggests that this letter was written on 22 August prior to his departure on the fishing trip mentioned in the letter. No enclosures are attached to this letter, and no continuation appears to have survived.

101: To Margerie Bonner Lowry

P: UBC(telegram)

Western Union,
Granthams Landing, B.C.
22 August 1939

MARGERIE BONNER
6213½ GLEN AIRY HOLLYWOOD CALIF
WROTE YOU LONG LETTER AIR MAIL TODAY[1] DELAY WAS
GEOGRAPHICALLY UNAVOIDABLE SUBSTANCE OF LETTER WAS COULD
YOU COME UP HERE IF I SENT MONEY WOULD HAVE A HUNDRED AND
FIFTY A MONTH WITHOUT INTERFERENCE SEE NO OTHER WAY AS PERIOD
IN HISTORY DIFFICULT BUT DONT WORRY ALL THE LOVE IN THE WORLD

MALCOLM

Annotations:

1 See Lowry's 22 August 1939 letter (**102**). This telegram was recorded on 22 August and received on 23 August 1939.

102: To Margerie Bonner Lowry
P: UBC(ms)

c/o Carey,
2825 S.W. Marine Drive,
Vancouver, B.C.,
Canada
[22 August 1939][a]

My darling one:
Thanks frightfully for your letter which stormed in me day & night. I desire and love you more & more as each day and bereaved night goes by. I never knew it was possible to be so happy as I was with you nor to want anybody as much as I want you. In all your lineaments is gratified desire.[1] If I could only hear you cry out again! But I need you so much, your warmth and friendship and comradeship: I hope only your need is equal. Darling darling Margie I can feel your warmth and your heart beat under my hand as I write. I have been working & keeping fit – I swam four miles yesterday, against a current – and there is pleasure in this inner and outer health, because I feel I am doing what you want. I have been long over writing this letter because I have wanted to say something definite and with the world & one's affairs tangled & in a state of utter tentativeness it is difficult, but not impossible. Dantzig has made matters more [un]-predictable:[2] Jan, but for the certainty of my love for you, would have rendered them untenable. The solution is inherent in the power of this certainty which burns & purges, intoxicates & torments, like a fever. But we run a danger of letting the future be indefinitely postponed. We cannot be married for a year and it is a year which will produce, possibly, undreamt of chaos. Unless we act, we shall wear ourselves old & grey behind a barrier of time. I have no right to jeopardise your own security, such as it is, with the prospect of something ephemeral: but, on the other hand, if ever there was a time to tear one's passions through the grates of life, like a lion, this is it. But, if it comes to that, you *are* life. I need you, & you need me. True, others have needed you too, and probably still do: & you, upon others, have a certain dependence; and you have to weigh risks

against advantages in the consideration of anything I may say. So far as I can gather, I shall be the recipient of $150 a month, here, exclusive of what I earn, and as I am geographically removed from all trusteeship, I am my own master of this. On the other hand, were I to return to Los Angeles, the money would automatically, come under trusteeship again to a certain extent, but worse than that, I would also have the uncomfortable feeling of Parks around. I am working with the Ministry of Labour here, but it is a purely nominal position, and not one which, as yet, yields – or would be allowed to yield, under Canadian law, strangely enough – any return, until I have been here much longer. (But writing I can earn as much as I like.) I am, and I think will be, permanently, an exile from my family, and the firm, where the money is, will continue to exercise remote control, and – because of my past intransigeance – will have no difficulty in doing this or even in proving, that, since I am neither this income's factor by virtue of any drawn agreement nor have I shown myself – witness Mexico, a disastrous marriage etc etc – in the past capable of using it in a constructive manner, the money is not mine at all but dependent on their behest. This, of course, works both ways: for instance, Parks would have no trouble proving even that, legally, _I_ had no money at all _yet_; which is protection from someone who as good as blackmails me, such as Jan. The possession of this amount of money, or shall we say, the relative possession, is at once a curse and an incredible advantage: which also goes for the way in which it is administered: for it would seem that so long as my course is rumoured to be a constructive one no humiliation pertains to it, but the moment anything is heard, to the contrary I become smothered in legal drapery. I have not the slightest doubt that I am not believed, (with & without reason) and I have come to look upon this source with hostility, since it has more than once denied me the right to work, nor have I any doubt either that news of my assumption once more of the responsibility of marriage after one disastar would have equally hostile repercussions, because here the argument is cleverly used on the other side i.e: 'This money is for Malcolm, & he has no right to use it for anyone else.' Well, they need not know: & the thing to do therefore, is to work towards some irrefragable position: to use the money as a constructive means to an independency of it for _us_, which independency, however, far from resulting in the funds' cessation, would possibly result in its increase: (yet, you see, that I am in a paradoxical position: because, eventually, if I am to re-succeed as a writer in the way I have planned, I shall have to return to the States, a (something which even now Jan may be rendering impossible.))[3]

Now out of all this complexity – this *long dissertation*, this *horsing about* – emerges, like the knowledge of God from ignorance, the simple fact of human need. Could you – supposing I send you $100 or so – take a 'holiday,' – & still leave your job open, if you wish on your return. It would cost you about 50$ (?) to get up here by train; I could save up beforehand for six or seven weeks, – then we would still have the $150 a month to live on: and whatever I made. Of course I would check and countercheck and make triply sure there was no hitch to all this before expecting you to leave. Anyhow: even looking at it as a business proposition; – I could pay you more than Penny [Singleton]⁴ pays you now, for 4 or 5 months for sure, – if you would do some typing for me: you needn't do it, of course; but if you did, it would be helping me, & building towards our future, which, judging by the news to-day, is Under the Volcano, indeed. We could not live grandly, but we could be together: it is a marvellous place: we could hire bicycles & go to zoos & pick flowers off mountains and go to movies when it rains & be happy & good & simple in a cottage or an apartment in Victoria or somewhere. *And we would be together*. It would seem to me, the Gods willing, a practical thing: & noone would interfere with us. Anything I do from now on is not likely to have my family's ratification anyhow but they need not know about us yet and I'm sure you do not care a whoop about that end of it. If you cannot come without making a clean break, of course that's up to you. What's mine is yours & I'll stand by you through thick & thin. But the facts & question before the house are these. (1) it is mad to wait a year without each other. (2) I may not be able to come to America. (3) It would be good for you to change your environment. (4) We love we. (5) That love will find a way etc is truer than you think: if we trusted to that, it would help us alot. (6) What can you lose, if I stand-by you? (7) If you want to marry me still you get both English & American citizenship. (8) I am going crazy without you. (9) War?

– Margie darling, mother, wife, child, the thought of you flows full-billowed through my veins; I want you so much, to sink into you, to possess you, to comfort you & be comforted, & to feel you near, I can't express myself: please try & make some sense of my poor words. This very wanting of you is a pain and it is a physical entity that will haunt the world & your little house and your soul forever for its uneaten bread unless we placate it. Margie, I simply can't stand this desolation without you.

Please write immediately, & you think too, hard, what is best to do. Please think of me, & oh god Margie, I know it's your business, but don't give yourself to anyone else. I won't either. It's torture to think of your doing that. I don't want anybody else: I only want you, & with agony: & I want you so to want me too, my precious.

Christ that my love were in my arms & I in my bed again![5]

Malcolm

Annotations:

1 Lowry is paraphrasing William Blake's 'question answered':

> What is it men in women do require? –
> The lineaments of gratified desire.
> What is it women do in men require? –
> The lineaments of gratified desire.

See *The Poems of William Blake*, ed. W.H. Stevenson, text David V. Erdman (London: Longman Group, 1971), p. 167.

2 The crisis over the Baltic port and free city of Danzig, with its large German population, was used by Hitler to start the Second World War. On 10 August the *Vancouver Sun* reported on a meeting of the Danzig Nazi leader Albert Forster with Hitler in his summer residence in Berchtesgaden. Forster declared after that meeting that, despite threats from Poland, Danzig would belong to Germany. Following fruitless attempts by the League of Nations to meet Hitler's demands for a political reunification of Danzig with the Reich, Germany attacked Poland and took Danzig on 1 September. Chamberlain gave Hitler an ultimatum that if Germany did not pull out of Poland within twenty-four hours, Britain would declare war. On 3 September Britain declared war on Germany; after a week's delay, which allowed time for Parliament to decide Canada's action, Canada formally entered the war on 10 September.

3 The divorce from Jan could not have caused Lowry to be denied entry to the United States.

4 When Margerie Bonner met Malcolm Lowry in Los Angeles in the summer of 1939, she was working for the actress Penny Singleton and writing mystery stories.

5 Here, as in his 1933 letter (46) to Jan Gabrial, Lowry's reference is to the anonymous Middle English lyric 'Western Wind':

> Western wind, when will thou blow,
> The small rain down can rain?
> Christ, if my love were in my arms
> And I in my bed again.

Editorial Notes:

a. In the 22 August 1939 telegram Lowry refers to this lengthy letter with his suggestion that he send her the money to join him in Vancouver.

103: To Margerie Bonner Lowry

P: UBC(ms)

c/o A.B. Carey,
2825 S.W. Marine Drive,
Vancouver, B.C.,
Canada
[ca 25 August 1939]

Darling Margie:

I got your telegram, & hastened to reply to it. You will have got a long letter succeeding that. I don't suppose the letter was very clear. I have always managed to muddle what is perfectly simple by long explanations. Actually, the situation is such. In order to come & see me you will have to make a temporary sacrifice of what ties you to life at the moment. I can send you enough money for that & we will have enough money here. We cannot live grandly but we can be happy. So far as I can see at present, I will not be able to return to the States anyhow for several months. In these several months the world may turn the other way up. It may not. I may not be able to & return to the states. Anyhow, we can have as long together as the world would let us, & it will not interfere as much as you think, if at all. You are not happy without me: nor I, without you. As for the future, conditions at the present make it a gamble. There may not be any. But there is an immediate future & I don't see why we should lose that. I am hurt not to hear from you in reply. Don't worry about the war: Forget the possibility exists: consider it as a vexation. I sense a smooth smiling persuasive enemy in the background. He has a bad temper. I do not like the man – may the devil break the hasp of his back! I want you. Malcolm.

– Enclosed – pome one a penny.[1]

Annotations:

1 Lowry's allusion here is probably to James Joyce's chapbook *Pomes Penyeach*, a collection of thirteen poems first published by Shakespeare and Company in 1927. Lowry occasionally uses the word 'pome' in his letters to Aiken; see his 4 December 1940 letter (**158**). Unfortunately, no 'pome' is extant with this letter.

104: To Margerie Bonner Lowry

P: UBC(ms)

c/o A.B. Carey,
2825 S.W. Marine Drive,
Vancouver, B.C.
[late August 1939]

Cher être:

I am sitting on a log – or an outpost of empire – writing this. The world is at my feet, in the shape of river with waves bright as you can be, all hastening to the sun, (image borrowed), one seagull with a nice face, the only seagull I know that has a nice face; a few Chinamen with cymbal shaped hats working in fields, & a few aeroplanes flapping about: as a matter of fact there are no planes; that was just put in. I'm damned annoyed about their being rude to you at the Normandie:[1] will you tell Jack off for me, & tell him to tell them off?: I certainly won't go there again, but I don't like to think of you & Jack losing touch over something nasty but remediable like that: you can tell Jack from me that unless those people bloody well apologise a curse is on their lousy pub from now on, they will go bankrupt, & the place fall around their ears in a year.

I am trying to write you every day now; since I have more time, where I can be alone with the sweet thought of you but I am still waiting for a cable from England: it should come to day. I wired you to pray that it was a favourable one, but I can't explain the danks & darks of it till I see you. If you love me as you say you do you ought to be perfectly frank with Bob[2] & make it clear to him that the one thing that has stood between you being frank both now & in the past, is his own jealousy. He must be a poor sort of human being if he imagines he can buy a human soul with a few pieces of silver: but, as for the security part of it, it might, of course, since you value that commodity so much, be better if you did marry him eventually, & I am not jealous of you: but loving you passionately, I _am_ vulnerable. As for what security I can offer you must know perfectly well that I am caught by forces utterly beyond my control, & you ought to make allowances for this. And again to revert to Bob – much as you like him, love him etc, is a man who pulls a gun every time his ego is afflicted, likely to make you happy? The same, of course, goes for a man who, every time he feels low, or frightened, jumps into the vino or what have you: In this connection I would like humbly to point out that during this period of having had the very best opportunity & excuse I have ever had both to feel low & frightened – & with my ways & finances unhampered also – I have not so much as looked at a drop. (I do not feel self-righteous, however.)

Since we love each other my desire to talk over your future is – he remarked pontifically – a very natural one, so don't make any rash decisions before discussing them with the now collocated Lowry.

As a matter of fact, you are never likely to suffer from lack of security: you could marry any one you liked & sometime it wouldn't be a bad idea if you (& I too) puzzled your (in your case pretty) head about precisely in what true pride & freedom inheres. The negroes, for instance, merely exchanged one form of slavery for another: but that is by the way.

Now, for God's sake let us think of one thing at a time, in their due order of importance, & the first thing is, I must see you again. So pray for that.

Then we will come to the second thing.

I love you. Please Love me, & want me, too. Please forgive any apparent bedevillment in this letter.

> All I know is that I love you.
> And Samson said if yo' shave ma hair
> Jus' as clean as ma *hade*
> Ma strength – a will become – a like a *natcherl* man[3]
> For gawd's – a g'wine t'move all de troubles away
> For gawd's – a gwine t'move all de troubles away . . .

Malcolm

x x x x x x x x x x x x x x x x x x
These crosses are noughty kisses.

Annotations:

1 Lowry is referring to the Normandie Hotel in Los Angeles, where he had stayed between July 1938 and July 1939 and where his and Margerie's mutual friend, Jack Garnet Wolsley King, was still staying.

2 Robert Ragsdale, the son of a colonel in the American army, had known Margerie for several years and had asked her to marry him. Priscilla Woolfan, Margerie's older sister, remembers him as pleasant, courteous, and a close friend.

3 The preceding three lines are a paraphrase of the fourth verse of the gospel song 'Samson,' but the refrain is 'An' if I had-'n my way, I'd tear the buildin' down.' See Jerry Silverman, *Folk Song Encyclopedia* (New York: Chappell Music Company, 1975), vol. 2, p. 106. Lowry's refrain is familiar from 'Negro spirituals,' and he uses both the verse and the refrain at the end of chapter 4 of *Ultramarine*.

105: To Margerie Bonner Lowry

p: UBC(ms)
pp: *CP* 367–68

[Vancouver, B.C.]
[late August 1939]

The Slough of Despond:[1]
or The House of Hope.

My dearest sweet tender Margie:
I hate the dogs, the cats, the road, the weather, the shadows, everything that seems to be conspiring to keep me from you.
I know what you must be feeling, my precious, but since love is the only thing that can mount in this cockeyed world, we will win out & we will be together soon, I know, somehow.
I am still waiting for further news from England.
The only thing that keeps me alive are your letters.
Oh my dearest sweet tender darling, I know this waiting is hell for you.
But with a fair wind, you won't have to wait much longer: I will find a way, in any event, and take any risk.
For the present still try & be patient. Do things you've put off doing, & all that sort of bunkum.
Please be true & to the thought of me. It is still the reasonable thing to do to wait; I shall be bound to hear before the week is out, & if there is an unfavourable reply, I'm just going to figure out the means of getting to you anyhow, as I said. I am deliberately curing myself in our future interest from rash, independent, action, so far.

I'm trying to work desperately at stories so that I can make enough to be with you independent of this bloody control: the war has knocked most everything else on the head in the Labor Depnt. The trouble is, I'm so anxious to be with you, our personal problems keep intruding, my work won't sit down & be objective.[2]

I love everything about you, every hair & bone of your body, including those I either cut off or broke.

Your

Malc

Annotations:

1 In John Bunyan's (1628–88) *Pilgrim's Progress* (1678), Christian leaves the City of Destruction but must pass through the Slough of Despond and the Valley of Humiliation before reaching the Celestial City. Allusions to Bunyan's work are important in *Under the Volcano*.

2 In *Collected Poetry* (367–68) Scherf reproduces the text with regular line breaks, and she concludes at this point.

106: To Margerie Bonner Lowry
P: UBC(telegram)

Western Union,
Vancouver, B.C.
1 September 1939

MARGERIE BONNER
     6213½ GLEN AIRY HD
WILL SEE YOU FIRST WHATEVER HAPPENS ALL MY LOVE

MALCOLM

107: To Margerie Bonner Lowry
P: UBC(ms)

[Vancouver, B.C.]
[early September 1939]

From me.

Like the snail, who has fivehundred teeth, which is why he always looks as though he's going to the dentist. I am, (that is, going to the dentist) & have just stopped for a Denver sandwich on the way. Outside, the Irish Fusiliers are playing recruiting songs by the recruiting office. A child of six is waving a baton at a bunch of bulgy pluguglies. Yeah; ugly is the word; ugly, ugly, ugly. The face of the war is an ugly one. I'm still waiting for news from England damn it, and am pouncing about like three cats on four hot bricks with the anticipation of seeing you. I'm worried sick by the delay in the news, I know you are too: but it's getting to the point where one actually feels glad, not sorry that other people (not you!) are also suffering delay, disappointment, and on errands of life are proceeding to death:[1] as the English stationmaster said – all change here for Allshot, Ballshot, Cockshot, Halfshot, & —— the whole bloody lot. These (with the exception of the dash) are all the names of bonafide English towns so there is no need to pardon my French. But death + hell + destruction just the same. If the absolute unforeseeable immedicable worst comes to the more than damnable desolate worst I shall have to enlist here: in that case we'll just have to figure out some other way of seeing each other.[a] Anything more perfectly scarlet in colour than joining the fifteenth removed British Columbian Irish less than Fusiliers four times removed I can't imagine: the only consolation would lie in such an action being utterly abstract. But bear up: cables are taking a week or more to get from England now, even allowing for that, I should hear to-morrow morning at the outside latest, & the chances are 8-2 the news will be favourable. Continue to pray that it will be, however. Good bye Mr Chips, is about my school.[2] The real school, the Leys, Cambridge. (This is apart from college, I was at St Catharines, Cambridge.) The schoolboys in the picture are from Repton, another English school. The author is James Hilton, who burnt my first chair at the Normandie (the second was burnt by Jack.)[3] He was a friend of my brothers at school during the war, and Mr Chips' real name was, & is, Balgarnie,[4] who was their house-master, & ten years later was mine. Hilton edited the school magazine The Leys' Fortnightly which is the – er – best magazine of any school in England: (I edited it ten years afterwards.)[5] For the magazine, Balgarnie, (his nickname was the Hooley not Mr Chips) was sponsor, treasurer & editor-in-chief. When Balgarnie retired he went to live opposite in a place called Brookside. In the movie the school is called Springfield. 'Leys' means 'field.' James Hilton first sold the story of Mr Chips through his agents J. Farquharson, 8 Halsey House, Red Lion Square, London Eng, who are also my agents in London, & that is also my London address. There are more coincidences too if I could think of them. Lowrys have been at the Leys as long as I can remember, & one has just left, my nephew, aged 19, to join up, & another nephew, aged 14, has just gone there.[6] Hilton was going to get me back in movies but we both got plastered & then we forgot about it. He wrote his first book, Catherine Herself,[7] when he was at school. Much of the story is true to life & must be a source of some embarrassment to the old Hooley who cannot be so doddering as all that. I saw him from time to time when I was at college after, & we have always been the best of friends. We must toddle over there when war is over & have a look at him.

I am so glad you are seeing Jack. I do not think incidentally that I would have lived after that bar without the fortification of B^1. But I fought the horror, & I know that I could fight it again & win now, if necessary. I am not going to drink anything whatsoever until I see you, & then it will be in its place as it ought to be, a mutual pleasure, & not a ghastly, delirious, necessity. I have not had a drink now in over a month, nearly two months. The nervousness is caused by malnutrition almost entirely & lack of the aforementioned vitamin: it is the convulsions that can cause worse. Mentally, I found the experience profitable but I do not think many would. Physically, it has not made the slightest difference. My life has been certified A 1 if you can believe it! I can't think of a moral to this.

I think I understand about Bob allright, & am only glad you have such a secure, faithful friend: Jack I am sure is another real friend. I shall always think of him as a true one.

> The only thing that Jack had
> lacked
> in life
> – besides an understanding wife –
> was tact.

I like your 'series of cold showers' as a panacea – for what? Jack used to put his feet in cold water. I have tried hopping on one fast about the room, and reading with my feet on the mantelpiece, so that the blood will go to my head. The former is quite inefficacious: as for the latter, you always have to get up eventually, & then the blood just comes down again. Too bad.

Well, old darling, we just have to hang on for the present: I feel in my bones that the news will be good. So don't worry, I am with you spiritually anyhow, & I know I shall be, in the flesh, soon. They also serve who only stand & wait.[8] (Yeah.)

To thee, as from between the mantelpiece & the next installment of a cold bath. How sweet that name is: Margie.

– I've just got your new letter here which is grand: & it was so swell, too, to get a letter on Sunday, special delivery, – as well as one yesterday. I'm so glad to hear Jack is going good & hope he gets his new job. God, you are a grand person, & I'm tickled to death you've got over the gruesomeness. And Jack too, his different sort of gruesomes. No such thing as special deliveries from these Limey countries, it seems, unless it's a matter of obstetrics. No news yet, but am on tiptoe for it, any moment. Pray.

Love.

Malcolm

The numerology is German in case you didn't know.[9]

Annotations:

1 Herman Melville's story 'Bartleby, the Scrivener' closes with the lines: 'On errands of life, these letters speed to death. Ah, Bartleby! Ah, humanity!'
2 Lowry is referring to the 1939 film version of James Hilton's 1934 novel

Goodbye, Mr Chips, which opened in Vancouver on 3 August with a very lively promotion. The film was so popular with Vancouver audiences that it was held over twice and played for three weeks. See the 24 December 1939 letter (**122**) to Aiken for a discussion of Lowry's response to the film.

3 English writer James Hilton (1900-54) is best known for his novels *Lost Horizon* (1933) and *Goodbye, Mr Chips* (1934), both of which have been adapted into films. In 1935 Hilton moved to Hollywood and wrote a number of screenplays. I have not been able to confirm that Hilton visited Lowry at the Normandie Hotel in Los Angeles. Jack is Lowry's English friend Jack Garnet Wolsley King.

4 W.H. Balgarnie was one of the young Lowry's favourites at school; see letter **8** and photograph 6. Lowry published a commentary, 'The Real Mr Chips,' on the 1939 film version of Hilton's novel; see letter **122**.

5 Although Lowry wrote regularly for the Leys *Fortnightly* from 1925 to 1928, he did not edit the paper.

6 These nephews were the sons of Lowry's eldest brother Stuart.

7 *Catherine Herself* was published by T.F. Unwin in 1920.

8 Lowry is quoting the concluding line from Milton's famous Sonnet XIX, 'When I consider how my light is spent.'

9 Lowry has written 'Heinz,' 'Fie,' 'Dry,' 'Fear,' for *eins, zwei, drei, vier,* at the top of each of the four pages of this letter.

Editorial Notes:

a. There is a dark stain on the blue airmail paper at this point, and Lowry has written 'shoo fly don' bother me' before drawing a circle around the spot.

108: To Margerie Bonner Lowry

P: UBC(telegram)

Western Union,
Vancouver, B.C.
8 September 1939

MARGERIE BONNER
6213½ GLEN AIRY HOLLYWOOD CALIF
UNAVOIDABLY DELAYED WRITING BUT LETTERS ON WAY HAVE TO AWAIT CABLE FROM ENGLAND BEFORE DEFINITE NEWS BUT SHOULD BE WITH YOU THURSDAY AT LATEST KEEP THE HOME FIRES BURNING[1] DONT WORRY BUT PRAY I GET FAVORABLE REPLY BE HAPPY ALL MY LOVE ALWAYS
MALCOLM

Annotations:

1 'Keep the home fires burning' is the opening line of the famous First
  World War song first published as *'Til the Boys Come Home* in 1914. The
  music was composed by Ivor Novello (David Ivor Davies, 1893-1951),
  with lyrics by Lena Guilbert Ford. The song was an instant success and
  quickly passed into popular culture and myth. Vera Lynn (1917-)
  revived the song during the Second World War.

109: To Margerie Bonner Lowry

P: UBC(ms)

> 2825 S.W. Marine Drive,
> Vancouver,
> British Columbia,
> Canada
> [9 September 1939][a]

Beloved.
　　You have been always in my thoughts but my energies have been
devoted to trying, – a practically impossible task, – to get a visa back
to the States so that I can see you again, since it seemed inexpedient
for you to come to me. I have succeeded but I will have to await a
cable from England, so I may be about a week. Please be brave &
love me & be close to me until I come because it will give me
strength: and we both need it. I thought that the best thing I could do
for us both was to get this visa somehow. There is no question of
sheep or being *drawn* in to this war, but I am sick of the subject & if
we must talk about it, we must do so as dispassionately as we can.
We love each other, and our passion belongs to this. War is being
declared to-morrow here so perhaps you can understand that I have
been working under difficulties, but difficulties negligible compared
with what others have to go through. If you feel like breaking, think
of all the other dreams unfulfilled, the children unseen, the books un-
written, the work never to be done, the last nights together, the
countless acres of anguish and the darkened haunted cities: consider
the pity war distils & ourselves as creatures of luck, compared with
the others who can gain no last moments more. I implore you, for
our sakes, be brave, & thank God that at least we have a reprieve.
Long for me as I for you, forgetting, what will be inevitable, the
long black aftermath of pain. There is nothing more I can say at present, but I shall write you a note every day now that I have done

what must be done. If you truly love me as I love you greet me as one come back from a long journey & who must go again, as I must. If you want me enough I will come back a third time as whole as I depart: if you do not, you will not see me but I shall look on & help. I love you. Love me: *& be calm.*

I will see you soon.

Your Malcolm

P.S. I am at a loss to account for this, but it cannot be lipstick, unless it is teleportedly yours: perhaps you were putting on a face, as I wrote. Please wait for me so that you will be all mine. I haven't thought of anybody else since leaving you. The sheer pain of wanting you, of desire for your loveliness, for the smoothness of your body & your breasts, is unbearable: if you must suffer, please suffer with this pain as I do, which we can soon assuage. Oh God, my darling, want me as I want you, want me to take you.

Editorial Notes:

a. As Lowry points out in this letter, Canada entered the war on 10 September 1939; therefore, he is writing to Margerie on the 9th. Although the letter is written in pencil, the postscript is in ink. Lowry has drawn two arrows to some pink traces on the paper that he cannot explain.

110: To Margerie Bonner Lowry
P: UBC(ms)

[Vancouver, B.C.]
[10 September 1939]

Darling, I'm sitting on an old wharf by the Frazer River and there's alot of sun and wind & blue sky. War was declared here to-day & you can hear the recruits sloping arms & they're quite a few planes about. To-day I think I sent you off a letter, either with nothing in it, or with the wrong letter in it: if the latter, just send it back. What happened was that the envelope, which was already addressed to you, must have got gummed up by the sun: I didn't find out my mistake until I found the real letter in my inside pocket all of which being so it's likely it has nothing in it at all: I am wiring you when I get back so that you won't be disappointed. I couldn't write you yesterday & I can't say anything absolutely definite now about my coming to Los Angeles: however I should know before the week is out, when a cable will have arrived from England, & the chances are that this time next week, thank God, we'll be in each others arms again. All news from England is heavily censored, & what news there is black; & for all I know half my family may have been wiped out already. Do try to realise that I am an Englishman, that there are no heroics about whatever I maybe called upon to do; but that my allegiance is to my country, grimy little island though it is. As part of me, as one with my blood in you, try & realise this: & stand by. I will stand by you. Don't attempt, at a time like this, to look too far forward into the future, your predictions will probably prove inaccurate if you base them on logic & appearances in a time of utter chaos. I have been delayed writing – this is wartime – but I would have been unavoidably hindered from it anyhow, while I thought hard, after your letter about Bob. I was in half a mind to join up here, & never see you again, for fear of making the situation too unbearable for you. But you & I are too seriously involved. We are too interwoven and intertwined in our very guts, for such a sacrifice to have any meaning at all: and so I have moved mountains and even the law to come & see you, which is something only an unfavourable cable from the old country can hinder now, & perhaps not even that. Please be my woman & help me to be brave by your thoughts, let us make the most of what time God has given us now, & the chances are you will have your reward in the future. Nothing can be worse than what we have already imagined. I have died a thousand times in your thoughts & you been lost a thousand in mine. But we are still here, & there *is* still the future, after all. Just postpone looking at it & it will roll in ecstasy at your feet. I love you.

Malcolm

111: To Margerie Bonner Lowry

p: UBC(ms)

[Vancouver, B.C.]
[mid–September 1939]

Margie – darling, can I sleep with my head in your bosom?
I'm still waiting, thinking it better to put off the hitchhike which probably won't be necessary.
– I got your letter this morning; oh, bless you my dear. Why, this is hell, nor are we out of it.[1] It breaks me up to keep asking you to be brave; I don't feel so brave myself. The one good thing is that our

love is being forged into stronger metal the more fire it has to take. But what a hell of a metallurgy it is! Poets have been saying, for thousands of years, that the sweetest of all love is that which is snatched under the shadow of the sword – (I expected to have news this morning: but still none.) – & we have to clutch at whatever straws of happiness we can, even when we are separated like this. God knows it can't be much comfort to you. But also, God knows it can't be long, before I get word again. Do try & hold out. I'm moved more than I can say by your letter saying you would come here if you could, but I feel certain it won't be necessary. The ironic thing is, had you replied in a positive way to my *first* proposal that you come here – papa spank at this point, you didn't acknowledge my telegram! – I could have sent you the money, we could have been here now, and I would have had control of it. Your objection was, that Bob would not allow you to do something which would damage your reputation, and would not hear of your doing such a thing unless you were going to get married. Since we don't want a little bigamist in the family – by the bye, the divorce has gone through without a hitch, so far as I know, – & we couldn't get married immediately, obviously, the Canadian law in this case not pertaining, – I therefore concentrated my efforts upon returning to Los Angeles, to you, a process which war interrupted, since in spite of the visa, the question had to be put to the B. Govnt, whether or not my duty was in England, or Canada, & in either event, whether it was lawful to me to have transit to a foreign country before returning to the one or the other, both being in a state of war. Obviously, since I have the visa, the American Govnt has no objection; on the other hand, without sanction from England, I would face both the possibility of having my income cut off for ever at the American end, and of not being able to obtain a job, since I would have only the status of a transient. Therefore, it is wiser to wait a little while to see if the sanction arrives, and there is no good reason why it shouldn't. A month or two ago the weather was marvellous here, it was cheap, & there were a thousand places we could go. Now the weather is a little bit dubious, economically too, till I hear from England: not in fact, but simply in fact of control. You are not perhaps acquainted with the law governing people leaving their dominions in wartime: the British border comes first. Now just wait a little longer, & we'll know what to do. For better or worse, we will be together soon.

That much I do know. Let us try & be patient & wise. I love you & love you & want you more each moment.

Malcolm

Annotations:

1 Lowry is echoing Mephistopheles' line from Christopher Marlowe's
1593 play *Doctor Faustus* 3.79: 'Why this is hell, nor am I out of it.' Allusions to Marlowe's play are common in *Under the Volcano*.

112: To Margerie Bonner Lowry

P: UBC(ms)

Care Carey,
2825 S.W. Marine Dr.,
Vancouver, B.C.

Sometime in September 1939.

Sweetheart:

Am still waiting for an answer to the cable: it may be longer coming than I thought: there is strict censorship in England, widespread
delay etc. By now you should have quite a lot of angry snarls from
me; forgive me, these are black times, and my vexation conceals only
tenderness I can't express. Your last letter did me good, & it gladdens
me to find you in a good mood. I like your 'sheer surprise,' as a concomitant of frustration: I know the feeling. But you seem to
overlook the hard facts of English conscription. Still, I am in a
favourable position compared with some poor fish. I quite agree 'the
contemplation of other peoples' grief has never helped in the slightest' etc –: it is true, with pity is involved self-pity, & so on.
However, what the devil are you to do? It is just about as efficacious
as whipping the sea to give way to one's own grief, – with a profound narcissistic compassion, (yeah). And we still have real ponds
with real ducks in them, so what the hell. It's the devil of a mess, &
don't think I don't know that the first casualty in war is the truth: and
don't make the mistake of thinking that we want to go: the prevalent
feeling is here that we're going to hang on to our guns when we get
back. I have seen a number of bad films, the worst of which was a
cartoon called Playful Polar Bears which keeps turning up in every
movie I go to. This is positively ghoulish. I thought Wuthering
Heights was perfectly lousy too: a marvellous story directed by a
charwoman.[1] I did not see why it was necessary to select a vacant lot
off Vine St with a few bedraggled goldenrod to typify the Yorkshire
moors, nor why high piled thunder clouds coming up against the
wind should be a photograph of a still life of a blancmange painted
on a backdrop, nor why Lawrence Olivier should do his damnedest

throughout to impersonate Paul Muni.[2] I also saw 'The Hound of the Baskervilles,' which is altogether too deep for me[3] A poor devil keeps losing his left hunting boot for no very valid reason, and there is a harmless looking pooch that lives in a grave. The criminal I think turns out to be one of the hunting boots. The sets had apparently been designed for Wuthering Heights. The needle, my dear Watson! A sound performance is turned in by a relative of suspiciously adjacent nomenclature: Morton Lowry Well, I shall be hearing soon from England which must be one hell of a dreary place if it's still there. I told my father in July 1934 that there would be war in the autumn of 1939, – & he replied: 'What kind of a son are you to tell his father & mother that the world is hurling to disastar?' I continued to warn my family but they took no damn notice. Result: they'll probably not only lose all their money, but be killed: When they might have been living in Jerusalem or somewhere. Well, my darling, it won't be long now, before you'll be in my arms again, but I'm not going to give way to these thoughts, I want to have them all at once, when you really are. Please be true to me. And want me as I want you. I am carrying you about inside my heart, we go for walks everywhere. All my love.

Malcolm

P.S. – i now do take up my pen to rite over the otter untin wot is saw of witch i think is a armles little hanimel wot is unted by sportymen to be killed for sport. it his unbearabal that hoeing to pounds spent or waisted on hedicashun an civverlisashun that their is such peeple wot dont no eny better than they dose. if they must ave sport there is better wot i could teash them than hotter untin the otter and i culd rite notes about it two in yore valuabel book for them for their in-struckshun of a decent mind, as for myself I cud-not arm a bug reely. And if you want ritters i am pleased to forwood eny letter you would like me too send on eny subjeck of interrest at the presant moment without a lot of money. i must be sorrie i cannot send yew the fotoes of wot i red over the hotter unt of wot i meen, i ave lent em to my nayberrer to see for erself to see if you kair to see for yoreself you can see in them such kreweltie wot is disgustin to edducated peepal but thank goodness i am not crewelty, but a well brort up lady wot is atetie fore yeers of aged and will be atetie six next July thank goodness.

Annotations:

1 Lowry had seen the 1939 United Artists' film version of *Wuthering*

Heights, directed by William Tyler and starring Merle Oberon, Laurence Olivier, and David Niven, which, according to the *Vancouver Sun*, opened in Vancouver as early as 7 August.

2   Paul Muni (1895-1967) was a Hollywood stage and film actor best known for *Scarface* (1932), *The Story of Louis Pasteur* (1936), and *The Good Earth* (1937).

3   *The Hound of the Baskervilles* was a 1939 Twentieth Century Fox production, directed by Sidney Lanfield, with Basil Rathbone as Holmes and Nigel Bruce as Watson. According to the *Vancouver Sun*, it opened in Vancouver on 28 August 1939. In the description that follows Lowry has misquoted one of Sherlock Holmes's most famous lines, 'Watson, the needle!' but he was correct about an actor called Morton Lowry, who played the role of John Stapleton in the movie.

113: To Margerie Bonner Lowry

P: UBC(ms)

c/o Carey,
2825 S.W. Marine Dr.,
Vancouver, B.C.,
Canada
[ca 14 September 1939]

My darling sweet mopsy mopey Margerie – cheer up.
I'm sitting on the steps of the house here in the sun after afternoon tea. Yes, I've come to that. It's a very English day; & an English garden, chrysanthemums – or are they chrysanthemi? – (& who was it used to call them Christian anthems?), – roses, brambles, pansies, stocks, rubbish heaps, parsnips & what have you. And big cedar trees on the lawn with dead vertebrae of hollyhocks under them. There is a nice white cat prowling round that I suspect of being you, who has been trying to deliver me a message for some time, and an ancient sterterous Scotty, who smells like Chicago, asleep in the sun. Apparently *no* envelope with nothing in it was sent to the post, & no wrong letter: I had sent one, instead of two, that was all, the one being to my lawyer.[1] As you know, I won't be free for 11 months & a bit, & the law is the same here: but Jan's action won't affect my coming to the States to see you. Please don't look on the tough side of things only: it would be as if I saw only the dead hollyhocks in this good garden, & smelt only the dog. Do try & be a bit cheerful, I know it's rotten for you, & my heart breaks for you, but I'll be seeing you soon & then I can kiss your hurts & anxieties better.
There's still plenty of sunlight and rapid rivers and rain and fresh

grass & as for growing old – really. You never will! Just because there's a war that's no reason why we can't make plans: you talk as though I were dead already & you a toothless old hag or as if both of us were sort of gibbering human husks.

Me – I never felt stronger or better, war or no war: I'm just looking forward & counting the days till I see you again & not letting myself think of anything else. Won't you do the same, my sweetheart.

Brace up & be my woman.   and/or -ity⎱
Stand by: & no more of this pusillanimousness⎰ about the sere & yellow.[2] All my love.

Your

Malcolm

Annotations:

1 In his 10 September 1939 letter (**110**) to Margerie, Lowry explains what he thought was his mistake.
2 Lowry is alluding to Macbeth's speech in *Macbeth* V.iii: 'I have lived long enough. My way of life / Is fall'n into the sear, the yellow leaf.'

114: To Margerie Bonner Lowry

P: UBC(ms)

[Vancouver, B.C.]
[ca 18 September 1939][a]

Margie sweetest:
– Without afternoon tea this time, and very miserable, my only friend the large white cat, – I'm sure the cat is you, it jumped straight out of your story but it brings me comforting messages and remembrance of things past, & hope of things to be, when it is not walking through the wild wet woods waving its wild tail by its wild lone. This time last week I was sure I'd be with you by now, but we had a tough break – we're not: let's hope it will be this time next week: you see, if we assume that there's nothing but hope & disappointment, nothing between, which is absurd, we're bound to be pleasantly surprised: quod erat demonstrandum; reductio ad absurdum.[1] Which reminds me that you can find a short story of mine called *seductio ad absurdum*, in the Los Angeles Public library. It is in a volume called The Best Short Stories of 1931, (English), edited by Edward J. O'Brien. It is quite incomprehensible; and it's all about

a bridge game between a bunch of sailors, played all wrong. It really has (or has it?) quite profound meaning. There is also a book called 'Lawrence and his friends' – this pertains to Lawrence of Arabia – which contains a mention of *Ultramarine*, my first novel – as listed in his library: he threw out all the books that didn't mean anything to him, & apparently his edition of Ultramarine is worth a very large sum of money.[2] I haven't even got one of my own, let alone his. But you can also get the book 'Lawrence & his friends' out of the LA Public library; & look up, in the book, his own private library list. Never heard anything about this until my ex-mother in law wrote & told me. Lawrence of Arabia was England's war hero no 1, so this is something of an honour. I'm beginning to think that I'll have to hitchike to see you & pretty damn quick. The latest news is, Russia is going into the war, against England, has already invaded Poland.[3] What precisely the fight will be for then, I don't know. And what I do know I either cannot, or won't, admit. But keep your chin up; I'm going to see you again soon, come hell and highwater. I love you more than life.

Your

Malcolm

Annotations:

1 *Quod erat demonstrandum* is the Latin phrase often used in philosophical or mathematical treatises to signal a point that has been demonstrated. *Reductio ad absurdum* is Latin for 'reduction to the absurd.'
2 Thomas Edward Lawrence (1888-1935), who was famous as 'Lawrence of Arabia,' published the story of his service with the Arabs against the Turks during the First World War in *Seven Pillars of Wisdom* (1926). Lowry is referring to *T.E. Lawrence by His Friends*, ed. A.W. Lawrence (London: Jonathan Cape, 1937), p. 496, and to a list of several hundred books in Lawrence's library, 'Books at Clouds Hill,' which did contain a copy of *Ultramarine*.
3 The *Vancouver Sun* headline on 18 September 1939 announced Russia's invasion of Poland on 17 September. Russia did not declare war on England, but Lowry may be thinking of the non-aggression treaty signed by Germany and Russia on 23 August 1939.

Editorial Notes:

a. The headline in the *Vancouver Sun* for 18 September 1939 was: 'Russia seizes Eastern Poland; Pre-Arranged Plan with German Government.' Just before the end of this letter, Lowry refers to this news, which suggests that he is writing to Margerie on or shortly after the eighteenth.

115: To Margerie Bonner Lowry

P: UBC(telegram)

Western Union,
Vancouver, B.C.
23 September 1939

MARGERIE BONNER

6213½ GLEN AIRY HD

THANKS ON MY WAY BUS TERMINAL HOLLYWOOD ELEVEN MONDAY LOVE

MALCOLM[a]

Editorial Notes:

a. At the bottom of the telegram Lowry has jotted down part of the Vancouver-Seattle bus schedule.

116: To Margerie Bonner Lowry

P: UBC(telegram)

Canadian Pacific,
Vancouver, B.C.
26 September 1939

MARGERIE BONNER

6213½ GLEN AIRY HOLLYWOOD CALIF

REFUSED AT BORDER[1] MILITARY REASONS VERY TEMPORARY ADDRESS
DUNSMUIR HOTEL VANCOUVER BC FINANCIAL AFFAIRS I GUARANTEE
VERY DISPONDENT ASSISTANCE IMPERATIVE CONDITIONS UNBEARABLE
COME UP AT ONCE ADJUST MY SITUATION OTHERWISE ALL INTENTIONS
USELESS WIRE ME YOUR INTENTIONS

MALCOLM

Annotations:

1 Previous biographers, following Douglas Day (xii and 254), have maintained that Lowry made his drunken attempt to cross the border into the United States in *August* 1939 and that Margerie joined him in Vancouver before the end of the month. This telegram and his 23 September one (**113**) make clear that the event that led to his poem 'The Canadian Turned Back at the Border' must have occurred on 23 or 24 September. Margerie's response to this telegram was to give up her job and travel

north to join Malcolm in Vancouver. For a colourful description of
Margerie's arrival, see Maurice J. Carey's 'Life with Malcolm Lowry' in
Malcolm Lowry: The Man and His Work.

117: To Carol Phillips

P: UBC(ms)

c/o Major Carey,
595 W. 19th Avenue,
Vancouver, B.C.,
Canada
[September 1939]

Dear Carol:

This is by way of being a double S.O.S.

Will you please, for Pete's sake, send me Under the Volcano, the
whole of it, what you have typed, what you haven't typed, what I
typed myself, what notes there were, what notes you made yourself,
so that I can get it ready for the publisher before I go I don't know
precisely where? Whether you have finished it or not.[1]

And if Parks has written you about it, as he says, it is unwise to
neglect his letters, because you may be able to touch him for some
dough: it was more than I ever could.

Conrad Aiken & some others are trying to get all my work
published as it were en bloc. There is little chance, but some, of my
coming back to the States. I shall not forget my promise nor your
share in the thing, but now that I have an opportunity to work on it,
and the publishers are getting hot, please let me have it whether you
have done anything with it or not.

Or get in touch with Parks and let him have it, which will save
you postage etc. Anyhow I must have it immediately, whatever
shape it is in: and I know you will not fail me in this.

How are the kids? and remember me to the literary society?[2]

The thing is, Carol, I may not have another opportunity for a long
time to work as I have now for the coming weeks.

I'm going to confine this letter, then, simply to this request –
please note the change in my address[3] – Park's address is Benj. Parks
735 Van Nuys Building Los Angeles,

love,

Malcolm

Annotations:

1 It is not clear exactly when Carol Phillips turned the manuscript of
Under the Volcano over to Parks or when Parks sent it to Lowry, but in
his 27 January 1940 letter (**124**) Lowry tells Conrad Aiken that he and
Margerie are working on it together.
2 Carol Phillips was supporting two young children from her first marriage.
3 Lowry moved in with Maurice J. Carey (1897–1977) and his family at
595 West Nineteenth Avenue shortly after his failed attempt to return to
Los Angeles on 26 September. Maurice Carey, who had been a Com-
manding Sergeant-Major during the First World War, was not related to
A.B. Carey, and he claimed to have met Lowry in a Vancouver 'cocktail
lounge' (UBC 43:4). Lowry describes his life with this family in lurid
detail in a 1939 letter (**119**) to Conrad Aiken.

118: To Mrs Anna Mabelle [John Stuart] Bonner
P: UBC(ts)
PP: *SL* 17-18

> 595 W. 19th Ave.,
> Vancouver, B.C.,
> Canada
> 19 October 1939[a]

Dear Mrs Bonner:[1]

Since I am the cause of your daughter's present stay in Canada I
thought I had better write to you, as this country is at war, and I am
British, you must be feeling anxiety on her account. First, I want you
to set your mind at rest as to her safety. There is no likelihood of this
country becoming a battlefield for many years, and no possibility of
its being bombed so long as the Monroe Doctrine[2] exists. As for the
war itself, although it exists, in spite of its reality, as more or less of a
smoky rumour here, it is entirely responsible for any vagueness or
complexity about the situation in which Margerie and I find ourselves. As for myself, any definitive future which I myself might
have been able otherwise to predict or promise, is alike shrouded in
obscurity. I simply do not know, nor does anyone else what is going
to happen. All of which being so, it becomes doubly necessary for
oneself to take a firm stand, as though the war, which is a shifting
principle that can take any form whatsoever and so effectively block
any purpose, if you leave it out of account. The only stand I can take

is that I do truly love Margerie, and in spite of whatever adverse circumstances, I feel I can make her happy: the stand which she takes, likewise. We therefore wish to be married as soon as we can. From her point of view, due as I say, to the utter tentativeness of any given situation during wartime, there is almost every conceivable argument against doing any such thing and, objectively, I have tried to persuade her against it; on the other hand, I love her so deeply that I feel my persuasions are painfully half-hearted, in addition to which I am certain that her own happiness is bound up with being with me, and it is very difficult to persuade a person even objectively to give up their own happiness, whatever material compensations there may be.

All I can say is, that I shall postpone enlistment to the last possible moment which should give her less cause for worry. Had I been able to come to America a few weeks ago, the chances are I would have sailed for England before now, and be already fighting. But though I volunteered for this, I was refused, and the result is I am here.[3] What the future holds, I don't know. Nor do I know now whether, as I write, she may change her mind and return to Hollywood. But this much is certain, that while she is with me she is with someone she loves and who loves her truly, and who has her happiness at heart. Whether that happiness is worth the risk of the kind of grief which war distils, if you are unlucky, is a debatable point; but perhaps a similar risk is always taken anyhow.

I was very sorry not to have had the opportunity of meeting you in Hollywood, and I hope I shall soon. Margerie will be always in touch with you. Meantime, at all events, please be at rest in your mind, for she is happy and well; and we are working together on a book.[4]

Yours very truly,

Malcolm Lowry

Annotations:

1 Anna Mabelle Bonner (1865-1956) was Margerie's mother.
2 The United States government's policy of opposition to outside interference in the Americas had been in effect since the foreign-policy statement made by President Monroe in 1823.
3 Canadian government documents show no record of Lowry's having tried to enlist, and his own comments about enlisting are ambiguous; see his 8 November 1939 letter (120) to Benjamin Parks and his March 1940 letter (129) to his father.
4 The 'book' is the manuscript for *Under the Volcano*, which Lowry did not receive from Los Angeles until some time in late January 1940.

Editorial Notes:

a. The two-page typescript of this letter (UBC 1:77) bears small correc-
    tions, deletions, and additions in both black and green ink. The full
    signature, in green ink, suggests that this is not a draft but the copy that
    was sent to Mrs Bonner.

119: To Conrad Aiken

P: UBC(ms)
PP: *SL* 18-25; *LAL* 56-69

> c/o Sergeant Major
> Maurice Carey,
> 595 W. 19th [Ave.,]
> Vancouver, B.C.,
> Canada
> [mid-October to November 1939][a]

– Mein lieber alter Senlin Forslin Malcolmn Coffin Aiken:[1]
   Since my last bagful of news the situation has become so bloody
complicado that if we do not receive some help, and at that immediately, I shall lose what remains of my reason, not to say, life. It
is all, (like everything else), such a complexity of melancholy opposites, that, although I expect you to understand it all, I'm not going
to attempt to explain it: I shall just hang the more succulent looking
hams of misfortune in the window hoping to entice you in to where
the whole pig, that would be cut down, is hanging. When I returned
to Los Angeles (from Mexico) to Jan, whom I knew was living with
someone else, this journey being at the old man's request, – I
travelled by the Great Circle too, the railroad being built by a British
concession, paid by the kilometre so it naturally went the most roun-
dabout way, but the train did not hurry and it is rather farther as you
know than from New York to Boston, – I practically went to pieces,
this being due partly to illness, partly to Jan, who, wishing to ratify
her infidelity perhaps had written the old man that I was incapable
and should be certified incompetent or words to that effect, for
which information she received, per old man, a largeish sum of
money to look after me, which she pocketed later, I afterwards discovered and went promptly to Santa Barbara with her boyfriend,
leaving me, a sort of Lear of the Sierras, dying by the glass in the
Brown Derby in Hollywood: I don't, of course, blame her, – better
off in the Brown Derby, but no matter. My income was then put

into the hands of an attorney named [Benjamin] Parks, a crooked but amiable fellow with hay fever and some kind of legal rapport with the old man's London solicitors, who paid my bills but gave me no money. After a year alone, close to Jan's affair but seeing her only twice – I suffered horribly but was taken out of the Brown Derby & despair by a grand gal named Margerie Bonner but no sooner had this to happen than I was taken suddenly by Parks to Canada – I was taken suddenly to Canada, by Parks on the understanding that this jaunt here was simply in order to obtain a visa back to the U.S. Here he placed my money in the hands of *two* men whom he scarcely knew; one of whom, [Victor] Maclean, I believe to be honest enough, but who, being constantly away on secret service, was & is unapproachable: the other, A.B. Carey – don't forget the A.B. oh best beloved[2] – who was & is simply a dung cart except for the straw which is in his feet, but also the most upright citizen of Vancouver, & a member of the Oxford Group.[3] For him, no more dancing on hell's bright sabbath green, the uprightness having departed to his soul, which stinks equally if possible. Parks then vanished. After two months going quietly insane care of the Oxford group, war was also declared. All might have been well had not this Oxford Grouper discovered that I was in love with Margerie whom I hope to god you meet & love as you do me who had stuck by me through thick & thin mostly thin, sharing conditions with me which make Gorki's Lower Depths look like a drawing room comedy.[4] When A.B. Carey discovered that I was married, as a matter of fact my interlocutory decree had just been granted, & proposed to return to another girl, he sat on my money, abused my confidence, said that I was committing a mortal sin in loving another woman than my wife, read my letters, & actually interfered with my mail. Then war was declared, & here was I left on the wrong side of the border. Now I had the visa, to get back but A.B. Carey would give me no money. So I wired Margerie for enough money to make the trip back to Los Angeles, which she did, & was turned back at the border, A.B. Carey having already presumably informed the authorities that I would be unable to support myself on the other side.

In trying to get out of the hands of these bastardos by which I mean also the entire Oxford Group as well by any means and back to Los Angeles, where lived Marjorie, who was and is to me like those old Nicean barks of yore, and who dwelt among the trees that haven't had a headache as long as I have, and from whom I had also borrowed the money for the journey, and failing in the latter attempt because I had no convincing proof of income to show at the border – this part is very complicated, so I'll come back to it later – A.B.

Carey & Parks had guessed all that – I now found myself then in the hands of one Maurice (and don't forget the Maurice, oh best beloved) Carey, with whom I, that is to say we (I shall explain later) are at present staying. At this point I should state more clearly that I left Marjorie in Hollywood fully expecting my return, that I lived only for that return, but that a series of other circumstances I won't inflict upon you following on the previous difficulties in Los Angeles owing to the murderous bitchiness of Jan about divorce and culminating in my unsuccessful attempt to return to Marjorie, further complicated by the fact that Jan & she lived in the same town, and by Parks frustrating me on one side, A.B. Carey on the other, and the family solicitors on both, had brought me to the verge of a real breakdown, one of the kind with cast iron whistles whiskers on it. There was not only Marjorie, you see, but all my work, in the United States in one part port or another. There was the war, too, so I didn't expect to finish all the work, but did expect to see you, and appoint you, if you were to be found, a literary executor, and I *had* accomplished much. No excuse would wash with the family, though I *had* volunteered to fight for England in England, & even possessed a return ticket via the Berengaria,[5] which although long since broken up as a firetrap, is still a ship if only in the memory, and a return ticket is still a return ticket even if left behind in Mexico & turned in at Cooks in the Avenida de Madera. So, Conrad, to make a *long* short story longer, turned back and at the dock's dark's edge, knowing how cold the water was, I wired Margerie (with what was left of her fare) to come immediately to Vancouver, a distance rather farther than that from London to Warsaw, as I needed her, which she did. When she arrived she found me in such a state of despair that she wrote back & resigned her job at home to take care of me. Now the set up is this. Maurice Carey collects the pittance left by the other two, who sit on the money, – allowing me $2 a week for myself & Marjorie, in return for which we get a bed & one meal a day if we're lucky. And secrecy, from A.B. Carey & Maclean. There is a family of six, including a loud speaker, a howling wind which rages through the house all day, twins and a nurse, who sleeps with the youngest boy, aged 14. Mrs Carey, who thinks we are married, says that this isn't right. Nor do I. Nor would you, think so, we think. I forgot the dog, the canary, & a Hindoo timber merchant, educated at Corpus Christi, Oxford – you can't get away from Oxford – who sleeps in the woodpile in the basement, hoping, with his fine Oriental calm, that one day he'll be paid for the wood.

We are, therefore, as you might guess, more or less bedridden, not because we are more ill than usual – we have stoutish hearts too even if a trifle cracked – but because bed is the only place in Vancouver where we have found either pleasure or protection, protection because once it is known by A.B. Carey – A.B. for disabled semen[6] – that Margie is here, she will be deported, since she is by now in Canada illegally, to parts unknown, & ourselves separated. It is not that the bed linen is stamped with the lineaments of last weeks love & the muddy boots of the week before, not that one day the fear that the more detestable of the twins may be found – there was something appealing in its upturned face as we lifted it tenderly out of the toilet – mysteriously drowned, – not that the oversexed Hindoo has an axe downstairs & that we know he intends to use it nor that the sound of the radio is like the voices of the damned howling for help, or that Maurice Carey, who is an ex-sergeant major with a disability, and how, has a habit of drilling an imaginary platoon up & down the stairs at three o'clock in the morning, not that Vancouver is like the Portobello Road magnified several thousand times[7] – not misery hath Demarest – and is the most hopeless of all cities of the lost, not all the bells and clashes of the night, which appal us: it is the thought rather of the absolute injustice of all this, of the misunderstanding, of the hopelessness of communication, and the thought also that a sentence which is beginning (with of course the above reservations) to be fair, may at any moment be finished with a blot: that will stamp our lives out. But, from brass bedsteads to brass tacks. For by now you can see by now that we cannot remain here much longer or God knows what will happen.

Now, as to the line, the hook line & sinker, to use with the old man, if you see fit to take one. Before you take any though, perhaps it is best to know that my relationship with M. Carey is further complicated by the fact that he has written to my father asking to be made trustee for my money here, with the understanding that he would then turn it over to me for a certain cut each month. Being so desperate to be with Margie I agreed to this as at the time he seemed sympathetic – to do him justice, he is sort of, – but what with the twins & the Hindoo & all we all have our bloody troubles & have to use certain methods to solve them not sometimes the real right thing, – but he has since proved difficult, for instance, he pawned my typewriter one day without my knowledge, which I didn't exactly like, – *this* one is borrowed, & should he get control of the money, we might not get enough to live on, & anyhow there is always the terrible fear that Margie may be deported: so you must not say anything about this to the family because, if it is impossible for you to help us (& try & realise that your help is not just help, only, I must see *you* & also owe a duty to you), & we are forced to remain here, we shall have to depend on him. Margie is American helpless, & utterly without money, & were she deported it would be to Hollywood, she would have nothing to live on, & moreover, she would be, for many reasons in an untenable position & also she could not stand being without me. Anyhow I am very near a mental & nervous collapse, though cheerfulness is always breaking in[8] & I know that if Margie (whom you & Mary would adore) & I were separated, unless I could feel she were going to you, or a friend of yours, or somewhere where she could be near at least the hope of seeing me again, or near some encouragement of that hope or assuagement of its loss, which she would not have in Hollywood, she would break up because – but why go on? We would both break. As to jobs here I would take any one, but I cannot because of my status here: nor are they taking any more recruits. I have frequently wanted to go to New York or Boston where I would be in touch with friends of yours and get a job but have been foiled always by Parks who would never trust me with the money – & I never seemed to be able to earn any at the right moment – then there was Jan & I was feeling a bit knocked oop about that, & so on ad finitum: and the family idea, of course, always was, at a distance, having the most sinister and mostly (but not always) fanciful idea of my goings on, that I would be horsing around, 'free lancing,' as they put it, 'not under proper supervision,' – etc

It is queer, when all I wish is to be independent, that I should now be placed forcibly in a position where it is virtually impossible, although all this is quite consistent with the pattern of my father's general attitude.

Now you could suggest to my father, if the plan doesn't work by cable, (a little long perhaps) which would be better, among other things which may occur to you, that:

(1) You would be the trustee of my income & my guardian, but that your position would be to try & help *me* find a position in which I can be independent, in short you know you can find a job for me, subject of course to the limitations of my status, & time.

(2) You certainly would be more likely to expend it, that is my income, if any, for my benefit than an utter stranger, with whom I'm unsympathetic & who cares nothing for me.

(3) My letter suggests to you that I am desperately unhappy, absolutely alone & without friends in an abominable climate, but particularly unhappy because of the unfairness of not only

being rendered unable to finish all my work, but unable to convince Parks or England that it exists, or is important, or that the definite understanding was that I should be allowed to go back to America.

(4) They objected to my going East on my own hook before to see publishers because they would not trust me: therefore you must make it plain that I will be under proper supervision: viz, in your home & in your constant care: also that I *have got* publishers who are influential people who are interested in my work.

(5) That I have made every attempt to enlist here, apparently, but have been turned down either because of health or status, you don't know which, & now they are taking no more recruits. However, if two birds must be killed with one stone, your own home is only a short journey from Eastern Canada, & later, when my work is in the right hands, & they are again taking recruits, I could have another shot from the East. (I may agree with you eventually, Conrad, that there are better institutions than the army but it probably would not be tactful to say this to people who may be being bombed, even as you write.)

(6) Can you make it plain to my father that what he has heard of me has been mostly through other people, and that I am anxious to state my case, through you, who know me better than anybody.

(7) That I feel that my father is being exploited in the present situation, which is intolerable & hopeless, but that as my word is obviously discredited, I feel it useless to make any statement of my own side of the case, which is a matter of constant torment to me, & that you could act as mediator between myself, & you, who know and respect both parties

(8) That injustice is being done to me, that my presence in Canada was none of my own seeking & was not, in the first place, necessary, since my visa would have been extended: & that I am very unhappy about the estrangement & I am appealing to you, desperately, to help me personally adjust the misunderstanding. Which goes as between myself & my mother too. (In spite of the fact that misunderstanding will always be as complete as ever, of course.)

(9) That above all I [am] among strangers who neither understand me, & if I am to go to the war, you would like me at least to have his friendship.

(10) That I am still perfectly willing to go & enlist in England, as I stated to them when war broke out, but since they will not pay the fare over, I could earn it with you, & anyhow Boston is the most sensible port to sail from in this hemisphere.

(11) You can say further, that if they are anxious about *drink,* that if there is still anxiety in that regard any longer on their side from what you can gather from my letter it is unfounded: but that'll *you'll keep a strict eye on me in that regard.* (Here's looking at you.)

(12) If their idea is to cut me off without a penny fairly soon, why not give me enough to live on for some months in Boston anyhow, which you would administer, so that at least I would have a fair chance, having none in Vancouver.

Now the family as you probably have gathered, are not likely to take kindly to the idea of my marrying again so soon after one marital disastar, (though in this connection it should be mentioned that I can't anyhow, having only an interlocutory decree I can't be married for a year.) – so besides everything else we must keep Margie a secret for the time being & you must not mention her in your letter. It might, however, be as well to state that with you I would be at least thousands of miles away from Jan, of whom you thoroughly disapproved & against whom you had warned me again and again, that she had been the source of a kind of antagonism that had sprung up between us at one time, and that the only thing that ever went wrong with our own relationship was that you knew I was fundamentally unhappy with her, that I knew that you knew, that I resented that knowledge, and therefore took it out upon you practically to the point of betraying our friendship, for my self-conceit, which is the truth as it happens, because I know now that all you really desired was my happiness: so, no Jan. Nevertheless, my plans for the future must include Margie, as you can well understand; for our devotion to each other is the only thing holding me to life & sanity. We are perfectly adjusted to each other, & perfectly happy: And she is just the kind of a gal you always wanted me to have: and you always said I'd be all right if I had the right gal: & I do have the right gal, & I'm all right as anybody can be who feels he's just waking from a nightmare; & were it not for this God awful environment of rain and fear, for although we fear no longer fear itself is about us, and the war with its smell of dead truth, its first casualty, in our nostrils, we'd both be all right.

Of course eventually I shall probably have to join up to fight for the forces of-er-reason but at the moment I am more concerned with preserving my own which I consider no less valuable & certainly as remarkable as Hitlers. Meantime we want to be together as long as possible & grab what little happiness we can & definitely be together until we can be married before I go. This will probably be impossible in Canada because conscription will come before the year is out but do not suggest to the old folks that I consider it also impossible in America because of my nationality thereby implying that I might wish to change a blue passport for a brown one

Upon reading this over I fear that you will come to the conclusion that I have already lost my mind but despite cheerfulness always breaking in you can see that we really are in a desperate situation. If my suggestion does not seem to you to be practicable can you think of anything else to do & for God's sake whatever you do do it quick before we sink for the last time.

I have some other ideas about approach to the family: one, seriously, if it could be afforded, by cable, one, which would suggest that you had heard I was stranded in Vancouver & that Canada was taking no more recruits, that you had seen my publishers who wanted me on the spot, and could I come, because something important had developed for me, & that I could then stay with you: or perhaps put a publisher, or Bernice, or Linscott,[9] or someone wholly imaginary, up to sending a cable saying that I was wanted in America for some work, & could it be made possible: or something like that. Any of these things might work. As for the financial end of it, my God, Conrad you know as well as I that you are far more my father than my own father & that once I was on the *spot in Boston* with you, everything could be engineered from there; financially it has been done before: as for ourselves, it would save our lives: as for myself, personally, it would be the perfect reconciliation, either to a happy death, or to a new life: for I never felt more like working in spite of all this misery, & never more sure of myself: this would be, in reality, a great circle.

But to get back to Margie. We cannot be married for a year so we shall have to steer close to the wind during that time, & I do want for her sake to stay out of the army long enough to marry her, & if I stayed in the states that would give me time to do God knows how much work, & who knows, the bloody war might end? I've

volunteered in both England & Canada & been refused in both places
& I can't do more than that. If England still wants me, I think it only
logical that I should see you before I go. But to avoid the possibility
of the deportation angle, would it be too much of a trespass upon
your compassion for me to suggest, that if [I] can lay my hands on a
few hundred bucks I, as it were, *Send* Margie, who can cross the
border whereas I at present cannot, on first to you as a sort of ambassador of the whole situation, while you meantime work like hell on
the old man. If I can then come on afterwards, everything will be
marvellous: but if I tragically cannot, I could by that time possibly
have amassed enough money to get sufficiently far East in Canada,
to be not more than a nights journey from Margie, Mary & yourself,
– I am presuming of course you could find somewhere for Margie to
stay in the meanwhile, – & from that point of vantage, being once
there & *near*, & one might start arguing with the old man all over
again? If this isn't too much of a presumption on Mary & yourself.
You can point out, if you like, by the way, quite bluntly, that you
feel definitely from my letter, that now it has turned impossible to
join the army in Canada, that if I am thwarted in my desire to see you
& finish my work in the states, the results will be immediate &
tragic.

Well, now for the work angle. I have written Whit Burnett to send
you a book of poems called The Lighthouse Invites the Storm;[10] have
written Ann Watkins[11] to send In Ballast to Bernice: have written to
Los Angeles for Under the Volcano & a play:[12] & am sending you,
by the beginning of the next week, the copy of a thing called The
Last Address,[13] the original of which I am sending to Bernice. As this
is, among other things, about a man's hysterical identification with
Melville, I think it might interest Harry Murry,[14] & would be grateful if you would pass it on, if you too think so.

So, Conrad, old fellow, please help. So deeply do I feel that yours
is the only star we can guide our bark on now I sense that my heart
had made provision for so turning to you in the end by its first
journey years ago to Boston & the Cape. You can save two good
lives, I think, & lives worth saving, & lives you will be glad you have
saved. Now, thank you from the bottom of my heart for the suggestions you have already made:

My very best love to Mary, I have seen some of her Spanish
pictures, Man with concertina etc, lately, reproduced, which are
marvellous, & do you send me news of you both and news too of the
voyage that never ends.[15]

Margie sends love.

Malcolm

P.S. Is the new novel 'Reading a book'?

P.S. Since finishing this letter last night things have become suddenly even worse and if something doesn't happen pretty damn quick the situation will become like the postulated end of Kafka's The Castle, in which K. was dying, surrounded by the villagers, worn out with the struggle, which Kafka himself was too worn out to write. he was too worn out to write. we are staying in bed to try and keep warm, though we haven't enough blankets and we've put what's left of our clothes over us we're still freezing. There is an icy rain which hasn't stopped for days and the room is damp, we have both caught severe colds and Margie has a bad cough. We actually haven't had enough to eat and now we think Maurice, due to his injuries from the last war, has really gone a little crazy. He has told us that we must get out of here on Tuesday, which is the day he collects money for my board from the other Carey, and if that happens we will actually be penniless, in a strange & believe me damned hostile & ugly country with no place to go and no friends. The situation is too complex to explain just why this will be so, but if Maurice turns us out he will have to lie about me to save himself (one more black eye to the family) and if I tell the truth about him, it looks even worse that I should have been staying with, and endorsing to the family, a man of his character. I assure you, I simply had no choice in this matter, knowing no one here and having no status nor any money I was forced to trust him and hope for the best – well, it has turned as you see. I actually fear – as for, different reasons, I feared A.B. Carey – trusting him with my mail so when you reply perhaps you'd better address me at the Hotel Georgia where I shall *not* be staying but shall make arrangements to receive mail, and better send another letter here, just in case. Another idea: an appeal to Davenport, whose address I don't know, might help. We had an understanding about this. Or what about an advance on a novel on this situation by both of us, or all of us, to be called Night Journey Across the Sea? Or can you say that something has turned up for me, that you must see me somehow, & get funds from the old man that way: or could you get him somehow to finance your expedition here, since it is so serious, I mean it, Conrad, it is damned serious: & for once I am not to blame for most of it. But whatever you do, Conrad, for God's sake do it quickly before we sink for the last time into this more than sea, this Sargasso sea of despair.

We huddle in bed like gaboons in the jungle to keep warm, no blankets or one, and pinchbeck overcoats: we freeze: the icy rain which hasn't stopped for days doesn't even bring melancholy any longer: the room is damp, muscles contract with rheumatiz, noses run, we cough like sheep, I fear Margie may become really ill. We haven't had enough to eat, one plate of beans a day, we no longer dare make tea because Maurice, (because of a 'war' injury caused by falling off a streetcar) is having one of his 'crazy fits,' insults Margie, calls us 'fictitious people,' etc. Now – although he is entirely dependent on us – So you see, as well as snow there is fog.

Annotations:

1 The names added to the familiar German greeting, 'Mein lieber alter . . .' are from Aiken's works and, together with Lowry's play on his own name, create an amusing, rhythmic effect. Lowry had used the expression 'Mein lieber alter Freund' for his German sailor, Popplereuter, in chapter 3 of *Ultramarine* (144).

2 The phrase 'oh best beloved,' used twice in this letter and in other letters, is borrowed from Rudyard Kipling's *Just So Stories* (1902), where Kipling's narrator regularly addresses the reader/listener as 'O Best Beloved.'

3 The Oxford Group (not to be confused with the Oxford Movement) was the name given, in 1929, to the British members of the Moral Rearmament movement, founded by the American minister Frank N.D. Buckman in 1921. With influential support at Oxford University, the Oxford Group was incorporated under that name in 1939; its aims were to 'change lives' through the power of Christ and to evangelize. Moral Rearmament, as it is more generally known, is a conservative and primarily Protestant organization.

4 The Russian writer Maxim Gorky wrote his most famous play in 1902; it was translated as *The Lower Depths* in 1910.

5 The *Berengaria* was a ship named for the daughter of the Portuguese king Sancho I (1154-1211). The Canadian government has no record of Lowry's formal attempt to enlist or volunteer *in Canada*, and there now seems no way to confirm his claim. He may simply be referring to comments made to his father and brothers in letters to them that are no longer extant; see his tenth point to Aiken.

6 Lowry is playing on the nautical term 'A.B.,' meaning 'Able Bodied Seaman,' a joke he also makes in *Ultramarine*.

7 In Lowry's London days Portobello Road, now famous among tourists for its 'antiques,' was not especially salubrious. In *The Face of London* (London: Simpkin Marshall, 1932), Harold Clunn describes it thus: 'Situated on both sides of Notting Hill High Street and centred round Church Street on the south and Portobello Road on the north is Kensington's other squalid hamlet, comprising a rookery of mean streets and small houses' (p. 351). This 'slum' was nearly adjacent to the mansions of Kensington Park Road.

8 When under stress, Lowry frequently used the phrase 'cheerfulness is

always breaking in,' which is attributed to Oliver Edwards in *Boswell's Life of Johnson*, ed. George Birkbeck Hill (Oxford: Clarendon Press, 1934), vol. 3, p. 305. Edwards, who had known Johnson at Pembroke College, Cambridge, is reported by Boswell as saying: 'You are a philosopher, Dr Johnson. I have tried too in my time to be a philosopher; but I don't know how, cheerfulness was always breaking in.'

9 Bernice Baumgarten was Aiken's New York agent with Brandt and Brandt, and Robert Linscott (1886-1964), an editor with Houghton Mifflin between 1904 and 1944 and Random House between 1944 and 1957, was a close friend of Aiken's. See Lowry's 5 November 1947 letter (330) to 'Bob'.

10 Since his acquaintance with Burnett in New York between 1934 and 1936, Lowry had continued to send him manuscripts. 'The Lighthouse Invites the Storm' was Lowry's title for a collection of poems; see Scherf (46-99).

11 Ann Watkins was Lowry's literary agent between 1934 and 1936, while he was living in New York.

12 The play was a dramatization of Nordahl Grieg's novel *The Ship Sails On* (1927), which he was working on as early as 1933 and in Los Angeles in 1938-39; see Lowry's 1933 letter (51) to Jan Gabrial and 1939 letter (85) to Grieg.

13 'The Last Address' was Lowry's title for a story begun in New York in 1936; it portrays his experiences in the psychiatric wing of Bellevue Hospital in June of that year. Lowry submitted the story to Burnett (see Lowry's 6 July 1941 letter [165] to Burnett and Foley), who accepted it, but Lowry withdrew it and continued to work with the material until his death. The version he refers to here is the novella-length one prepared in Los Angeles in 1939. A later version, called 'Swinging the Maelstrom,' was published serially in a French translation by Clarisse Francillon in *L'Esprit* (1956), and the two versions were spliced together by Margerie Lowry and Earle Birney for the posthumous publication of *Lunar Caustic* (1968). See Day (196-212).

14 Henry Alexander Murray (1893-1988), an American psychologist, educator, and writer, was director of the Harvard Psychological Clinic. He was a close friend of Aiken's, whom he met in late 1926, and, like Aiken, was deeply interested in Freud, Jung, and Melville – hence Lowry's suggestion here.

15 This phrase, 'the voyage that never ends,' became Lowry's title for his projected sequence of novels. For a discussion of the project plans, see Grace, *Voyage That Never Ends* (6-19).

Editorial Notes:

a. This letter appears to exist only in a draft holograph (UBC 1:77). For this reason the sequence of paragraphs cannot be determined with absolute certainty. *Selected Letters* contains many omissions and errors;

the version in the Sugars edition appears to be accurate. Lowry drafted this letter on several pages that contain fragments of other typed or holograph materials; therefore, I have made one substantial change from the Sugars version. The following poem fragment has not been included after the first postscript because it is not, in my view, an integral part of the letter.

iambic pentametre.　　10 feet.　　mystery　　blizzard
　　　　　　　　　　　　　　　　　mastery　　hazard.

A　The thing to know is how to write a verse
B　Whether or not you like it, whether or not,
B　The goddam thing will put you on the spot
A　And Petrarch will not save you from the curse.
A　You may be circumambient or terse
B　　　　　　　　　　　　　　　　　　　　?
A　　　　　　　　　,for better or worse
B　A thousand lines without a single blot.
C　Christ the great psalmist cannot save us here
E　He lisped in Numbers but no numbers came
D
C
D　Eliot and Pound were prosing all the time
E　And Whitman (Walt), alas, did much the same.

120: To Benjamin Parks

P: Liverpool(ms)

c/o Maurice Carey,
595 W19 Ave.,
Vancouver, B.C.,
Canada
8 November 1939

Dear Mr Parks:

Thank you for the reply: naturally I am interested to know what the instructions are from England and would appreciate it if you would let me know as soon as they arrive. I am grateful for all your efforts on my behalf, and if I must remain in Vancouver I certainly hope I shall be free of Carey (1).[1] Of course I understand that the divorce is not final for a year but am relieved to know the interlocutory decree has gone through with the least amount of trouble possible under the circumstances. With respect to my enlisting, I was at a loss to answer immediately because of the strange situation here which has developed. I was working towards my actually doing so – doing everything I could in that regard without actually doing so – but suddenly they stopped taking recruits altogether. So that's that, it's an impossibility; what it means, I don't know. At least I think I do know, but do not like to admit that I do know. Anyhow, I had decided to make every effort before to finish my work before actual enlistment and the sensible course seems to be to carry on with this until we see what's what, if we ever do. I am now completing one story and have already sent three manuscripts off to my publishers. I am particularly anxious to have 'Under the Volcano,' and am writing Carol Phillips to that effect but would deeply appreciate it if you would go to Long Beach and get the damned thing if that seems necessary: on cool second thinkings, please do go and get it because I've written my publishers about it, & they want to see it. When I thought I was going to buzz off to England any moment I was rash enough to accede to her request to give her 25% of the profits if she got it done quickly: this wasn't so noble as you may think because probably there won't be much, but nevertheless you might tell the good gal that unless she gives it you or me pronto there won't be any 25%, any profits, or any book. And, it's a good book. However, that, and the stuff you got from the Normandie² which contains valuable and irreplaceable notes on two other books, (not to mention a great deal of valueless but unfortunately inextricable material and a pair of Mexican boots which I contemplated bestowing upon Carey Jr (II!!)³ for Xmas), still do not complete the manuscripts and unfinished business which I wished to complete in the U.S.

I realize that if you are awaiting instructions from England you can do nothing about my return to the States until they arrive but since this is of paramount importance to me please write immediately you receive them. My status here does render my position a peculiarly useless one, if I must stay here, in this rectum of the world.

And naturally, since there is no earthly point in remaining in this cultureless rainy friendly place indefinitely it would be a damned good idea, now that I am in control of the drink situation, have got over Jan, & really want to work in a decent environment, (& certainly the most sensible idea,) to return to the States. Since there is some doubt in your mind as to whether I have any work to do, I enclose this letter sent voluntarily from New York by one of your largest publishing concerns. (*which please send back*).

The pipe goes fine & best love to you.

Malcolm

Annotations:

1 Presumably 'Carey (1)' means A.B. Carey, who was still in control of
   Lowry's English money from his father.
2 When Parks took Lowry from his room in the Normandie Hotel in Los
   Angeles for the drive to Canada, Lowry had to pack in a hurry and was
   obliged to leave many of his belongings behind.
3 According to the memoir of his experiences with Lowry (UBC 43:4),
   Maurice Carey and his wife had an elder son called Maurice Albert
   Carey and younger twins, Carol and Gordon. By Carey Jr (II), therefore, Lowry is probably referring to *Maurice* Carey's elder son, and since
   he was staying with Maurice Carey's family at this time, the boots
   would be a present for the boy.

121: To Conrad Aiken

P: H(ts)
PP: *LAL* 72-75

> 595 W. 19th Ave.,
> Vancouver, B.C.,
> Canada
> [December 1939]

Dear old Conrad: –
   A thousand thanks! I too received a cable from the O.M.,[1] more or
less identical, which is a seven league boot step forward. It certainly
does look as though you're letter had the necessary mollifying effect.
The end, though, as you say, is not yet.
   If worst come to the worst, or in preparation for the worst coming
to the worst, would it be too much to ask you to sow the seeds of the
idea in the O.M.'s mind that it would be advisable for me *anyhow* to
proceed east where I could be under your Eye? Then, if it is impossible to cross the border at least a change could be made for the
better without undue delay. But more of this later when I have more
to go on. One snag is that if permission went through meantime, it is
possible I would have to return here to cross the border. I think
though if you could see your way to dropping a note to Parks, saying
that you had heard from the O.M., it might help matters because
Parks is so dilatory and cynical that he may well hesitate to do anything at all until it is too late. At this point I want to say that I realize
that you are busy and simply may not have time to do these things,
but ask you also to realize that since I am engaged in the perhaps not
very useful occupation of saving my own existence I must ask them!

Were you to do nothing else at all upon my behalf you have still gone very far towards bringing matters to a solution for me and I cannot adequately express my gratitude. A lousy correspondent, and in some ways in the past not always the most dependable of friends, it grieves me to think that you may think I am only writing to you because I am in a jam. But such is not the case: at heart I am always your friend: and, jam or no jam, at such a period as this I would feel it of vital importance to see you or to contact you and would move heaven and earth to be able to do so. All of which brings me to the point that I am about to ask a few more favors.

Since I may have only a short time left, and so do not want to embark upon a new book, I think it wiser to complete what I have begun, especially as it represents several years work, and also as 'In Ballast', even in its incomplete and unsatisfactory version was practically accepted by Harpers, 'Under the Volcano' conscientiously awaited by Ann Watkins, 'The Last Address' by Whit Burnett. To return to 'In Ballast' – the copy which you have is the one which you read three years ago and said then that you liked very much – with the reservations you repeated in your last letter and with which I myself agree. Working along these lines I had rewritten it but that copy was lost in Mexico, so I now wish to rewrite it again. Since the version which has been lost was not open to the criticism you have made of the version you have, perhaps it would be better if you sent it on to me without bothering further about it and I'll get down to the job. But I do feel that it is worth redoing since it had much praise from many people (including – er – yourself.) Now about 'The Last Address' – I know that that too is worth doing and doing as nearly perfectly as is possible. Since you do not like the one long chapter, have you any *constructive* suggestions to offer as to what I should do with it? And also as to the parts at the beginning and end you did not altogether approve of. All this applies very much more to 'The Lighthouse' as well.[2] Could you not, in the Shitehouse, reread the Lighthouse? And now about 'Under the Volcano' – I left that in Los Angeles to be typed and sent on to me to finish here, and for five months I've been vainly trying to convince Parks that he must get it from the typist and send it to me – which he blandly ignores. If you write him could you say that it is imperative that I have the manuscript and finish it as you have definite commitments for it? Perhaps that will spur him to some action. I feel that you would approve of Under the Volcano: it takes the same things to town which you take in your general criticism of me and is the most mature thing I have done. And, finally, would you try and realize the difficulties of working, or trying to, in what amounts to a vacuum? However merited your criticism, and however much I agree with it I cannot, in the present situation, apply what is purely destructive. By which I mean that *since my object is to get something out quickly* I have to make the best of what material I *have* so that what I am asking you is more 'what can I do *without* scrapping the whole bloody lot?,' assuming, for my sake, that it is best *not* to scrap the whole bloody lot and that some of it, at least, can be published? I value your opinion more highly than anyone's and all that you have said will carry its own weight and value. On the other hand I have always found your opinion the most fructifying – for instance, a simple conversation with you about poetry produced, for better or worse, a whole book, The Lighthouse – and it is for that reason I would be grateful for anything I can apply constructively to the imperfections I shall be saddled with anyhow, – in short for a prelude to some plastic surgery. I rather gather from your letters that you feel there is too much of your influence all around, that I should be able to break away from it by now and paddle my own literary canoe. This may be all very well in its way, but, I presume, I am still permitted to ask the old maestro, who is invariably right, for technical advice, even if it is given in a 'Now this is what I think, go and do something quite different on your own hook' spirit. Telling me to throw away the whole boiling is, I submit, more moral, than technical advice. Ah, the whirligig of taste! But I should think what I have got, worked up into a more acceptable form, would constitute a pretty good restart.

I'm not sure I agree about the Moonlight and Roses, although your suggestions may very well lead to my showering you at a later date with a *diarrhea scribendi* of romantic poems – and I might suggest that even you might find it a little hard to write about the primrose at the old river's brim if you were living in fear of your life at the bottom of a stinking well in Vancouver! Then again, conversely, you might not.

And as for Ed,[3] I don't remember much moonlight and roses about his work a few *years* ago, which is the period you are really dealing with in my case. I would be interested to see his later pictures. Like yourself, though, I feel that he has always gone his own way, uncursed by trends. History has already made much of what I admired or pretended to admire during the last half decade quite senseless but since I *did* pursue a more or less middle course I think there is quite a lot I can restore, from the ruin in which I find myself, that would be by no means worthless with a slightly less arrogant facade.

So, for Gawd's sake, Conrad, if you can drop a pamphlet on me instead of a bomb, do so!

I would like to go on record as predicting, by the way, that your own work, past and present, will receive, during the next few years, the more general acclaim it has long so highly deserved.

There is something wrong with the style of this letter: reason, I have lately turned journalist, in the Vancouver Daily Province.[4] I hesitate, however, to send you any of my stuff in case you tell me that it is the best I have ever done!

Well: Gawd be with you, and the happiest of Christmases to Mary and you and love from us both.

As ever

Malcolm

P.S. Parks' address is:
> Benjamin S. Parks,
> 735 Van Nuys Building,
> 210 West Seventh Street,
> Los Angeles,
> Calif.

P.P.S. That there 'Itler, 'e's no King, 'e's no President, 'e's just wot you might call one of them there Dicktasters!

Annotations:

1 In his letters to Aiken Lowry always referred to his father as 'the Old Man,' or O.M. for short.

2 'The Lighthouse' refers to the sequence of poems that Lowry had been working on called 'The Lighthouse Invites the Storm'; see Scherf (46–99). Although he welcomes Aiken's advice on his fiction, Lowry is always more anxious for advice on his poetry.

3 Ed Burra, who visited the Aikens in Cuernavaca in 1937 when they were staying with Malcolm and Jan, was not a favourite of Lowry's. Lowry's reference to moonlight and roses, here and in the preceding paragraph, is in response to Aiken's suggestion (Sugars, 72) that Lowry give up the cerebral and ironic in his verse for more of the joyful and romantic.

4 Lowry wrote two articles and one poem for the *Vancouver Daily Province*: 'Hollywood and the War,' 12 December 1939, 4; 'The Real Mr Chips,' 13 December 1939, 4; 'Where did that One go to, 'Erbert?' 29 December 1939, 4 (poem).

122: To Conrad Aiken

P: H(ts)
PP: *LAL* 77–82

595 W. 19th Ave.,
Vancouver, B.C.,
Canada
[24 December 1939]

Dear Conrad,

I have your letter and please let me instantly reiterate my thanks, both to you and Mary. It is very gallant and sporting of you both to take on what you have. After repeated readings, Conrad, of your letter, I find myself more grateful than ever before, if possible, for your kindness, (and subtlety); I am glad, though, to be in a position to remove some of your very justifiable fears. I think that you intended, that for a time at any rate, until I had fully digested your words in all the ambiguously functioning organs of response, that a small, plangent Et tu Brute should sound among my Hosannas. Just as well, because, it was while chewing this part of the cud, bitter at first, that I was able to extract the more subtle juices of meaning from your letter, which I might otherwise have missed. In my sober mood it was a little difficult to realize at first that of course you probably expected me to arrive with a giraffe on either arm, to come howling and spewing into South Dennis and collapse in the Congregational Church. Then, later, the one shoe in the bathtub, the surreptitious vomit under the piano, the ukelele and the fractured skull.[1] It would be, on second thinkings, knowing me, very remarkable indeed if you did not wish to put yourself on guard against something of this sort. But please let me set your minds immediately at rest on this score! There will be nothing of the kind, it is a genuine striving for a Better Thing, and please assure Mary of it.[2]

Now, for the other problems. I do feel, Conrad, that although you are quite right to bring your perfectly naturel apprehensions on the subject out into the open, – on the principle that permanently to alleviate anxiety it is first necessary to dart a few added pangs, – I do feel, I am glad to say with all respect, that the whole responsibility will turn out to be rather less titanic than you suggest. I could not feel right about coming if I felt it would really result in any serious or protracted sacrificing of both your independences and privicies: but that you were willing to *risk* this however, in accepting Parks suggestion is something which moves me more than I can say. I do not, of course, know what Parks said, or what you deduced from it. I imagine something pretty juicy. Fortunately, it doesn't matter very much, as I hope to convince you when I have the opportunity of speaking to you personally. On the other hand, you have had no way of knowing for *certain* just precisely what the situation is, except from my own statements, which must have seemed to you fantastic as Parks seems reasonable. It means simply that I have all the more to thank you for.

Now what I had suggested, and thought by your earlier letters you understood and agreed with me about, was that you would do me the favour, since I was virtually non communicado with the family, of collecting my 'income' and turning over to us, less, of course, what might be compatible with your own time and trouble in the matter. This would enable us to live – quote, unquotes, and quotes – 'in a corner to ourselves where you could keep a Benevolent Eye glowing on us from a distance???'[3] I surmise, however, that your telegram may have inclined you to the belief that there is more to it than merely that. It is not an income at all, you may have been or will be told, because I have no money, a fact of which I have to be continually reminded, it is a sum of money put at your disposal to dispose of for me or not at all, as you think fit, it is something I ought not to have, that I ought to be ashamed of taking, something, in short, to my acceptance of which, especially in time of War, is attached the maximum amount of humiliation. On the other hand, if you take Park's place – as a matter of fact I upped and suggested as much to the O.M. in a moment of suddenly conquered phobia – you would get an additional fee, and if Parks is any touchstone, far from there being any responsibility attached to it, you would get this fee simply for putting me as far away as possible from you in some God forsaken place where I could not possibly be any nuisance to you whatever, where I would be unable either to obtain work or prosecute a normal life, and be driven slowly to the brink of suicide, which, as you had conscientiously put me first in the hands of the Oxford Movement, could not be possibly construed as your fault, or even anything to do with you in the least, nor, since the Oxford Group is notoriously prohibitionist, anything to do with anything save the Demon Rum, which, in spite of having no money at all I was still obviously able to obtain and consume in Pantagruelian Quantities. Your independence and privacy would be unimpaired because, in spite of any provisos, you had, after all, the final power of attorney, and if you chose not to sacrifice it, there would not be the slightest reason to do so. However, Conrad, you are not Parks, you are my friend, and I, believe it or not, am yours. Surely, this being so, it will be possible to hit upon some compromise, which

will not embarrass you or interfere with your work but which will
enable us to be free of this present tyranny, to be by ourselves, and to
work, but nevertheless near enough to you to see you from time to
time, which God knows, as I have pointed out before, would be only
what I would want to do, and which I hope would be what you
would want me to do, were the circumstances normal, under conditions in the world at present. I do not want to die off stage, like
Mercutio;[4] and you have perhaps reckoned without my purely filial
feeling for you, which is a genuine and true one. I would beg ex-
cusion for the monstrous and ungrateful accusations I made of you in
the past on the grounds that they were all in the general Oedipeian
pattern, but I know you understand this already. Such things will not
occur again, I assure you. This time a recreated Priam has to deal
with an Oedipus in his post-Jocasta period, but whose affliction does
not mean that he has lost his vision, or hope.[5]

Now I also see how your letter, – and I have to thank you also, for
this, – since it is one that I could scarcely show anyone who didn't
love me, gave me an 'out' with Margie, (behind which thought do
not think I do not also detect the hand of loving-kindness –) were
Margie some grasping female – you don't *know* after all! – whom I
had got into trouble, gave me a neat little pair of scissors to snip off a
relationship I might subconsciously wished myself rid of. Margie's
reaction as it should be was simply one of deep gratitude: she asks me
to say that of course she would be only too happy to help Mary and
you in any way she could while and if we stay with you: she is a good
cook, a good typist, quite capable of taking over any part of the
housekeeping which would be the most helpful. But as for the allowance – what can I say, Conrad? What I get will have to do us both,
since I can't bring Margie out into the open now, with either Parks
or the O.M. As things stand here, we don't get any of the allowance,
just three dollars a week that's all: it was three-fifty, sometimes its
only two. I make a few dollars writing articles about Mr Chips and
such beloney (Mr Chips happened to be my housemaster by the
way)[6] and what is not even the rest of the allowance goes to Maurice
Carey and his whole family live on it. The rest is being either misused or simply hoarded by Carey and Co., so there's damn little left
for us. To the best of my knowledge I have about $150 a month:
whatever Parks receives is outside of that. So if you receive what is
now Park's fee, what income I have, even if it is very much less than
the $150, under the new arrangement should enable us to live quietly
somewhere without in any way sponging on *you*. I expect the
amount will be left up to your own discretion. If there turns out to be
no additional fee to what was once my income, and your part of it

has to come out of that, I'm sure something satisfactory to you could be arranged, we don't need much: simply a break. But it is unfortunately just precisely that kind of a break which it is well nigh impossible to arrange at a distance. But at this point I do want to say I'm absolutely on the level, on the level about Margie, on the level about working, on the level about you, on the level about the situation here, and finally on the level about there being no problem about your having nothing to fear from my drinking or irresponsibility (does this letter or have my other letters *sounded* irresponsible?)

I forgot to say that there ought to be quite a bit accumulated here unless these Oxford Group bastards have grabbed it or sent it back to the O.M.: I don't know and they won't tell me.

We would be only too delighted to get out of this hell-hole immediately, but what to do about my permission to reenter U.S.A? I understand an appeal can be made through Blaine (where I was refused on the grounds of not being able to prove income, you remember) but Parks hasn't done a damn thing about my papers that I know of. He hasn't written me at all, and he has the proof. The appeal may have to go through Washington, presumably, would take time. Parks may be arranging for an immigration visa, however which would account for your being asked to take *full* responsibility. In that case it is a purely nominal thing and just a legal necessity of some kind, but Jesus, if that's what you took, or whatever you took – it's bloody decent of you – I miss my cue here, will content myself with saying lamely, but meaning it, that, by Shakespeare, I won't let you down.

At the moment it would seem that the most sensible thing to do would be to proceed to Montreal, where I would be within hailing distance, first having ascertained whether, in the event of my receiving permission to go to the States, it is possible to cross at whatever border town is nearest there, without having to come back here, to Blaine.

In any event we shall not be able to get our feet upon terra firma until you assume the power of attorney: as things stand, the broth is foul, the cooks corrupt, and it's all too insanely complicated.

There remains the problem of transportation, both for Margie and myself: the problem of the Careys: the problem of Under the Volcano, still in Los Angeles: the problem of hating to cause you trouble but unfailingly causing you more and more; the problem of feeling that if my presence in U.S.A. is going to cause you and Mary all the embarrassment you suggest it will I ought, as a point of honour, not to come at all; the problem of persisting just the same, and wondering whether I am right in feeling that, if all goes well, it ought not to be so terrible for you: the problem of the war, of possible death, of marriage, and so on –

But at least we come to Christmas – this Christmas Eve it is snowy – with hope.

In any event, I do not know how I am adequately going to repay you for having so triumphantly helped us even so far, but I do think there is a way and I shall try and prove it.

Now, again, all our thanks to you again and equally to Mary, for *her* self-abnegation in the matter, – God bless you both and a very Merry Christmas to you; and to Jane.[7]

As ever

Malc

P.S. I sent a question to the radio hour, 'Information Please,' the other day, for which I shortly expect to be receiving the Encyclopedia Britannica or some such. Since it is rather Jane's cup of tea, you might try it on her over Christmas. She may know, but I bet they're damned few people who do.

Question: What is the name of the book by an internationally famous American poet and novelist, which, having the Mississippi River as background and a Mississippi river boat preserving its unity of place throughout, has been compared, by an internationally famous American critic, not entirely to its discredit, with the great English satires of the eighteenth century, such as Gulliver's Travels?

Answer: The Confidence Man. The author: Herman Melville. The critic: Lewis Mumford.[8]

Annotations:

1 Lowry is recalling events from their past friendship, such as his arrival in Boston in 1929 carrying only a broken suitcase and a ukelele (CBC interview with Aiken, 1961). In 'The Father Surrogate and Literary Mentor,' *Malcolm Lowry Remembered* (40), Aiken tells the story of wrestling with Malcolm over 'the lid of the w.c. tank'; Aiken got the lid from Lowry but fell backwards and fractured his skull in the struggle.

2 In his 17 December 1939 reply to Lowry's desperate plea for help, Aiken said that he and Mary would welcome him in their home *if* 'you'll give me your word before coming that you're really going to make a damned fine and convincing effort to *behave well.*' For his stern, 'plain speaking,' yet affectionate letter, see Sugars (76-77).

3 The quotation is from Aiken's 15 November 1939 letter to Lowry; see Sugars (70).

4 See Shakespeare's *Romeo and Juliet* III.i.

5 These classical allusions to the separate stories of Priam, last king of Troy, and of Oedipus are used by Lowry to adorn his Freudian interpretation of the hostility between himself and Aiken in Granada in 1933 and again in Cuernavaca in 1937. See Lowry's summer 1937 letters (**69** and **72**) to Jan Gabrial, and see Day (174-80, 219-24) and Clarissa Lorenz, 'Call It Misadventure,' *Malcolm Lowry Remembered* (87-88).

6 Lowry's commentary, 'The Real Mr Chips,' *Vancouver Daily Province*, 13 December 1939, is his personal response to the 1939 Metro-Goldwyn-Mayer film *Goodbye, Mr Chips,* which was adapted from James Hilton's 1934 novel *Goodbye, Mr Chips*. The film was directed by Sam Wood and starred British actor Robert Donat (1905-58). Lowry recalls his days at the Leys School, Cambridge, with warmth and affection, and he describes W.H. Balgarnie, a master who was the model for Mr Chips, as 'something of an actor himself,' 'a crack fives player, an energetic tennis player [and] a vigorous walker.' Among Lowry and his peers, this man of 'brilliant incisive wit' was affectionately called 'the Hooley.' See photographs 5 and 6.

7 Jane is Aiken's daughter.

8 Lewis Mumford (1895-1990) was an American writer and critic. Lowry is referring to Mumford's *Herman Melville* (New York: Harcourt, Brace, 1929), p. 253, where Melville's *Confidence Man* is described as 'a companion volume to Gulliver's Travels.'

Beginning Again: 1940 to 1946

Blue mountains with snow and blue cold rough water –
A wild sky full of stars at rising
And Venus and the gibbous moon at sunrise.
Gulls following a motor boat against the wind,
Trees with branches rooted in air;
Sitting in the sun at noon
With the furiously smoking shadow of the shack chimney,
Eagles drive downwind in one,
Terns blow backward
A new kind of tobacco at eleven,
And my love returning on the four o'clock bus –
My God, why have you given this to us?

'Happiness' ca 1940-47

T HE YEAR 1939-40 is particularly interesting and rich for the
correspondence. In addition to the letters to Carol Phillips and
three surviving letters to the much-reviled Los Angeles attorney
Benjamin Parks, there is the series of twenty-six increasingly desperate love letters and telegrams, spanning August and September,
sent from Vancouver to Margerie, who was still in Los Angeles.
These letters, written against the background of the outbreak of the
Second World War, with the spectre of enlistment ever present, are,
nevertheless, closely focused upon Lowry's personal affairs – his
desire to be with Margerie, his determination not to drink, and
anxiety about his work.

After Margerie's arrival in Vancouver at the end of September,
Lowry's life took a sharp turn for the better. Despite their gruesome
living conditions and lack of money, they soon began revising the
manuscript of *Under the Volcano*, so that it was ready to send to Whit
Burnett and Harold Matson, Lowry's literary agent in New York, in
the summer of 1940. In addition to re-establishing contact with
Matson, Lowry also renewed contact at this time with a very good
friend from his Cambridge days, the Canadian Gerald Noxon, who
was living near Toronto, and with the Irish writer James Stern, who

was then in New York. By August 1940 Malcolm and Margerie had moved out of the city to a fisherman's shack on the foreshore of Burrard Inlet at Dollarton for a summer holiday, and that holiday turned into a fourteen-year interlude in what he thought of as his earthly paradise. Dollarton was the only place that the adult Lowry ever thought of as 'home.' The happy congruence of love, work, renewed friendships, and natural beauty in Lowry's life during the summer of 1940 signalled the beginning of a spiritual and aesthetic separation from Conrad Aiken, who had been in many ways a negative influence on him, and a new stage in Lowry's voyage.

But calm was never to last long in his life. The news, in September 1941, that the manuscript of *Under the Volcano* had been rejected caused only a temporary slump in his spirits before he settled down to revise it into the novel we know. The period from 1942 to 1944 – at least until June of that year – proceeded quietly and happily. Lowry swam regularly, lived simply, and wrote daily. His letters from this period to friends, particularly to Noxon, reveal his enthusiastic ability to discuss literature, writing (his own and that of others), and ideas. The 7 June 1944 fire that destroyed the shack, his papers (including his manuscript of 'In Ballast to the White Sea'), and most of their possessions brought an abrupt end to this idyllic period on the beach, and the shocked, grieving couple fled east, where they stayed with or near Gerald and Betty Noxon until February 1945.

Although Margerie was instrumental in bringing Lowry through this dark period and in preparing *Under the Volcano* for resubmission to Matson in June 1945, Gerald Noxon's friendship, practical support, and literary advice were also important to him during the fall and winter months of 1944-45. Noxon played the role in Lowry's life that Albert Erskine would do later: each of these men was his 'brother' and literary sounding-board. Lowry's need for this kind of fraternity was intense, demanding, almost as consuming in its dependency as his more complex attachment to Aiken.

After his return with Margerie to Dollarton in February 1945, Lowry put the finishing touches (in so far as one can say that Lowry ever felt he had finished) to *Under the Volcano* and sent it back to Matson on 1 June. Arthur Lowry had died on 11 February, but Lowry makes little comment about this in his surviving letters (or manuscripts, for that matter). He had not seen 'the old man' for almost fifteen years, and the two had never really reached a state of mutual understanding and forgiveness. Lowry was, however, corresponding regularly during the forties with his mother, Evelyn Boden Lowry, as one surviving letter (**249**) from 1946 makes clear. Sadly, almost all his letters to her have been lost.

He and Margerie spent the summer and fall rebuilding their home before they set off on a trip to Mexico, via Los Angeles, at the end of November. Again Lowry seems to have been preoccupied by his personal and literary affairs. The end of the war receives scant attention from him in the letters from these years. He was waiting for news of *Volcano*. When it came, reaching him in Cuernavaca, Mexico, it precipitated one of the most extraordinary literary letters ever written, certainly in this century. Lowry's 2 January 1946 letter (**210**) to Jonathan Cape is a *tour de force*, an apologia and explication of great eloquence and depth. Whether or not one believes that it is dangerous to take an author's comments about his or her own work too seriously, this Lowry letter commands attention – and respect.

However, 1946 was only beginning, and it was to prove a traumatic and momentous year for both the Lowrys. The trip to Mexico was rapidly turning into a nightmare that rivalled Lowry's *grand guignol* experience of 1937. In June, safely back in Dollarton, he sat down to write another exceedingly long letter (**224**), this time to the Los Angeles attorney and family friend Ronald Button. Lowry recounted, in painstaking detail, all the outrages he and Margerie had suffered in Mexico. What he expected Button to do for him is unclear, and nothing resulted from this letter. The Mexican experience was not wasted, however, because, as the 1946 letters to Matson and others show, Lowry set to work immediately on what would become *Dark as the Grave Wherein my Friend Is Laid*.

But 1946 was not all bad. It saw the acceptance of *Under the Volcano* in both the United States and England, and it brought a major new player into Lowry's life: his editor, Albert Erskine. To watch this friendship with Erskine grow in letters that span a decade, from July 1946 to December 1956, is one of the special rewards of the *Collected Letters*. Both sides of this correspondence, especially during the editing of the *Volcano* for its February 1947 New York publication, document a developing trust, respect, and friendship between two men who were deeply immersed in the abysses and swift currents of a literary masterpiece.

123: To Conrad Aiken

P: H(ts)
PP: *LAL* 84–88

595 W. 19th Ave.,
Vancouver, B.C.
[January 1940]

Dear old fellow:

Many, many thanks for everything, including the telegram,[1] please convey this immediate expression of my gratitude to Mary and Jane. Now, by god, it does look as though, as Ibsen says, the miracle of miracles has happened.[2] I cannot tell you how absolutely overjoyed we are. Yours is the genius which brought it all about but there is a special beauty about seeing the machinery of the whole thing begin to turn over. Even Parks has, at last, begun to cooperate! Yes, and how! He has been in touch with the immigration authorities and all I have to do now is to sign a few letters. He also has 'Under the Volcano' (in a state of eruption, I imagine, in its present form). However, as you would say, the end is not yet: it is in sight, we are already peering at Cape Cod, counting the windmills, (and promising not to tilt at any) and dreaming quohaugs and swordfish. But it is now, at this very moment of apparent perfection in the order of things that a sad possibility – as I hinted it might before – intrudes itself. With all the papers in the world to swear now that I will not be a public charge there is only a 60/40 chance of getting through. Earl (Epistomologer) Russell has been turned down lately, on account of the war: and others.[3] But even if I do get permission it will be an unusual bloody miracle if it arrives for two or three months. There was some mistake made at the border in the matter of my visa which may further complicate matters and also the business of my divorce. Meantime we are virtually dying here: if you have never yourself been in the clutches of the Oxford Group as I have you will think, (as I believe you could not help thinking before!) that I was just acting dramatic or talking tight. It is not so. Versed though you may be in the moral obliquities and vagaries of mankind I do not think that you can begin to know anything about hypocrisy until you have fallen foul of one of those bastardos. They have everything. Well, I feel so braced by the general outlook that I can almost feel a sort of tenderness for *them*, but the fact remains that so long as I am under their auspices, I am virtually a prisoner, and so is Margie: work, also, correspondingly suffers: and the future is drawing in like the winter nights. In two months, or three, – if permission is denied, – we should still be here, and rather worse off than before, because by that time it is likely that real hell will be popping in Europe. My duty in this regard is another thing again, it is not yet clear to me what form it will take. I refuse, however, while the possibility of other, clearer, cuties – strange typographical error! – remain to me, to be caught *off balance* by this war if I can possibly avoid it: that others have been is too bad for them: but since it seems I am, for the time being, a creature of luck, I am determined to finish what work I can, and to do my utmost to get the freedom to do it, before I cease to be so. That, I think, is a clear enough duty to the O.M., to yourself, and to myself. It is part, too, of my duty to Margie. For the rest, as with her, I can only strive to place her in as cheerful and constructive environment as I can, forgetting the end of Festus[4] (Faustus too) and that war exists. Margie is now in Canada legally, she has been to the immigration authorities here, and can remain in Canada indefinitely so far as they are concerned, but there is the constant danger, so long as we remain in Vancouver, of A.B. Carey and His Hot Gospel Groupers finding out that she is here, which might result in our separation and utterly destroy everything we are trying to sincerely to build up: you may laugh and say this is not so, but believe me these Oxford Groupers are worse than the Gestapo, they are all one's persecution complexes rolled into one stinking whole.

Now, Conrad, what I am driving at is this. In two, three months anything may happen. If the permission is refused, the spot we shall be on will be grisly indeed, and the trouble you have gone to all for nothing. For not only may by that time circumstances necessitate my joining up immediately here, but I shall be as far away from you, my nexus to redivivus[5] and the real world, for however short a period, as ever. Parks, Carey and Co., fundamentally indifferent, will still be in charge. A clause in Park's letter suggests that my family wish me to enter through Blaine, but that obviously, is Parks-inspired. The O.M. obviously doesn't give a hoot how I get into the States so long as I do so legally. Now I have ascertained through immigration here that so long as my application is made *through* Blaine, it doesn't matter through which port of entry I go. The most reasonable plan, therefore, would be that somehow or other we proceed to Montreal quam celerrime,[6] or some place in Canada, near Boston and near the border, in which I could be under your Eye, at a distance so to speak, as I am under Park's now. This, you have previously concurred with as a possibly good idea. Once there I could await the news from Washington and, if I do *not* get permission finally, at least I am not thousands of miles away from you, and perhaps we could figure some way out of seeing each other before The Deluge etc. Moreover being in touch with you about work and things would not mean that matters would be so absolutely hopeless even if I were refused. The difficulties seem to be these. Parks, Carey and Co. will object to my being in Montreal unless under proper supervision. If you therefore could wangle my coming to Montreal, it would have to be on the understanding probably that either you would meet me there, or that you could arrange for some friends of yours to be trustees for me in Montreal just as Parks did here in Vancouver. But whatever you said, as soon as I was in Montreal I would be out of Parks and Careys clutches, not, as you justly may have suspected, to feel free to go on an interminable bender, but merely free to what work I have to, and give Margie what happiness I can in whatever time may be allotted to us. That is the truth: and I assure you again that I am absolutely ready to cooperate in every way. I could send you receipts for everything, if necessary, we need little enough to live on, and would concur in anything you said or advised. I appreciate what you said about the O.M., and here, strange as it may seem, I too feel a responsibility, and also feel most strongly that the only way to go about discharging it is the exact one that has been chosen. I think that nothing in the world would give the O.M. and the mater a bigger bang than to have me have a few books accepted in the States in the coming year and to feel that you had been instrumental by your encouragement in bringing it about after such a downfall – and admit it Lowry, it was a kind of downfall – as I have had. And if I fail, what the hell, boys, we've done our best. The attempt may be worth more than one knows.

I am not saying anything about Montreal to Parks but am leaving the whole thing up to you. A cable to the O.M. would do the trick, I feel. I have eight dollars, saved somewhat forlornly, as against Margie's journey, product of the lampoon I send you.[7] If you think that a cable is the thing, I would be only too delighted to forward the amount. Parks, I know, would only fool about, postpone things, write a noncommital letter, which would go down in some Greek tramp steamer, and we'd all be where we were before. By the time you have received this I will already have made application to Washington. I am writing too to Seattle for further confirmation that it is possible for me to await news of the success of my appeal to Washington in Montreal or wherever. What I am suggesting is, however, that you obtain permission for me to come to Montreal anyhow, if there is no immigrational objection, immediately, and, if there is, to Montreal instead of Boston should my appeal be refused. This would dispense with fatal delay later. But I do believe this to be very important. Could you not suggest to the Parks that Be then that, in the spring you will be much more busy, but that now you have some time to put at my disposal, that you might be able to make a trip to Montreal, but that, anyhow, you have friends there, and so forth, all this, with the absolute understanding from myself, of course that I am absolutely sincere in this whole matter, which I hope by now you believe. I do feel that now we have got so far that you will agree that it might as well be successfully concluded and I shall not feel safe until I am under your aegis. I cannot adequately express my thanks, Conrad, to Mary and yourself for being so absolutely swell, so understanding and so sporting in this whole matter. I know full well what a bloody intrusion on your time I'm being and cannot say how much I appreciate your forbearingness and patience. As for the financial (and more superficial) end of it, for, as you see, it was not money so much as understanding that was needed in this case, – I am sure you will find that the O.M. will not be too difficult in the matter, and I also know he will be very glad, finally, that you were good enough to make the agreement with him.

Please give Mary our best love, and of course to yourself, and Jane, should she still be with you.

Malc

Annotations:

1 The telegram does not appear to be extant.
2 At the end of Ibsen's play *A Doll's House* (1879), Nora speaks to her husband of 'the greatest miracle of all,' a mutual personal transformation that would allow their union to be a true marriage of equals.
3 Bertrand Arthur William Russell (1872-1970), British mathematician and philosopher, was the Third Earl Russell and Fellow of Trinity College, Cambridge, until 1916, when he was dismissed for his pacifist beliefs and opposition to the First World War.
4 Lowry is alluding to Aiken's *Pilgrimage of Festus* (New York: Alfred A. Knopf, 1923), where, by the end of the poem, Festus realizes that his pilgrimage has been a failure.
5 The correct Latin expression is *nexus redivivus*, which means 'revived connection.' Aiken is Lowry's 'nexus to redivivus' because Lowry sees him as his connection with revival or rebirth.
6 *Quam celerrime* is Latin for 'as fast as possible.' Lowry has adopted the phrase from Aiken, and he uses it frequently in his letters.
7 No 'lampoon' or other enclosure exists with this letter, but Lowry may be referring to the poem 'Where did that One go to 'Erbert?' first published in the *Vancouver Daily Province*, 29 December 1939; see Scherf (223-24).

124: To Conrad Aiken

P: H(ts)
PP: *LAL* 90–102

595 W. 19th Ave.,
Vancouver, B.C.
27 January 1940

My dear Conrad ———

I was at first so bewildered and hurt by your letter that I was at a loss to reply but since there is, of course, a logical reason for everything you've said, I am no longer bewildered and hurt and am taking the bull by the horns and boldly doing so, answering your letter as fully as I can and begging you the favor of absorbing every word.[1]

I have thought long and carefully about your suggestion of my writing the O.M. telling him about Margerie and asking whether he would have any objection to my bringing her east as it were for your official inspection. On the face of it there would be no reasonable objection to this had I only the O.M. to contend with. But the fact is that the O.M. would then put this matter up to Parks who might then make inquiries which would lead to his discovery that Margie is in Canada. There is of course no reason now, since her position is above board with the immigration authorities, why Margie should not be in Canada. Even were it discovered that she were staying here, she is ostensibly at any rate properly chaperoned. But this discovery would lead to a referring of the ratification of Margie's trip east to A.B. Carey who, as I have told you before, is a man who believes that any passionate relationship between a man and a woman is an evil thing and who would be sure, however honest our own motives, to put a dishonest light upon the whole thing. Moreover there would now be an excuse for it, and the fact that he had already shed such a light when there was *no* excuse for it and that he drove us thereby to the decision we made, would have no bearing on the matter. Parks is trusted by the O.M., and he cannot very well admit, since he landed me here with A.B. Carey, that the latter is not only a man utterly unsuitable for the so called duty conferred upon him but a pervert in the bargain. I myself would have no difficulty in the long run in proving these allegations and worse, namely that Carey's affiliation with the Oxford Group dates from his contraction, due to whoreing, or boys, I am not clear which, of a very serious venereal disease contracted when married and with children. His vices do not interest me, but when I am forced to submit Margie's destiny to the final arbitration of a man who is himself dishonest and whom I regard with contempt (and pity) it is another matter. I cannot do this; I do not think, if you believe me, as you must, you would want or expect me to do it.

My own stock, as I warned you at the outset, and of which you now doubtless have abundent proof both from the O.M. and Parks, is zero. Although, ironically enough, there is plenty of inalienable proof that Parks also has not dealt honestly with the O.M. unfortunately the O.M., up to the present victimized by the various contending forces, would have, for the sake of his own amour propre at least, to pretend to others if he did not to himself that he had been dealt with fairly. At this point I ought to say, which is important, that my continual protestations that those entrusted with my affairs have been dishonest with the O.M. even though you may accept them, probably only has the effect of confirming you in your determination to be absolutely above board with him: I am inclined to think that you feel that in this way you are saving yourself in advance from any possible allegations which I, with my degenerated character (or because you have submitted to tirades in the past you may expect something of the same sort in the future) might make about *you*. Deeply sympathized with, fellow, but surely such things aren't so goddawful complicated between us as this. I have grown up you know, sort of, so let it be fully understood in advance there will be no nonsense of this sort, whatever you do or don't. Besides I deeply feel that what I am suggesting is the *honestest reasonable* course. Unfortunately, right here, there is also proof, for which I freely admit that I am suffering, that I did not deal formerly, as he might say, squarely with Parks, but here I have the very hefty excuse which you may take or leave, that in spite of his good points and in spite of the fact that he genuinely believed that drinking was my only trouble and did much, although he went about it in the wrong way, to prevent me from drinking, that I never looked upon him as a friend but simply as a crook who was to be outwitted. I do not overlook his merits as a lawyer, and think it unlikely, for his own sake should you have any dealings with him that he would dare to be dishonest with you. But fundamentally dishonest he is of which I also have abundent proof and I would be on your guard. Hence you will see, old fellow, that our attempts to achieve the 'truth' would be surrounded on all sides by loud gregarious lies which we would not have the allotted time to clear away in order to achieve our point. I would say further, that the only trouble I have encountered, so far as they are concerned, was when, partly in an effort to get away from this odiousness once and for all I told the truth to A.B. Carey with the bitter results you know. and I can only say it serves me right for trusting a licentious sentimentalist and a political cheat. I do not think it helps my point to condemn the other fellow, in fact his vices may be the only human part of him, but since the condemnation is just and all these people have done their damndest to make me feel abased in my own eyes I harp on it just to try and show you how thoroughly hypocritical the whole set up is and to try and convince you that *before* we can do anything a complete break must be made by both of us from it. It is the hour of the knife, the major operation.

Another thing is that such a course as you suggest might, even if successful in the final analysis, result in placing Maurice Carey in the red, which would not be exactly the sporting thing to risk for although he has not failed to extort certain things from us, even practically to blackmail us on the basis that blackmail in Vancouver, just as it was in the eighteenth century in England, is merely part of the mechanics of a business transaction, at least we are grateful to him for our being together at all during the last months, and moreover when, with much trepidation, it must be admitted, but by way of laying the ground work for a later and complete honesty all round, informed him that we were endeavoring to get away from him and had been striving to do so solidly for the last months, reacted in a manner which was far more than surprising, (a manner which reminded one of the fantastic Christian acts which Dostoievsky attributes to some of his darkest characters) which seemed to us almost sublime! Not only did he seem genuinely pleased for our sakes that we would have the possibility of living in a normal fashion, but said that he would write a 'cracking letter' to you about it, of which we have heard some queer excerpts and gather, although we have not heard definitely, that he was some time ago with much creaking of syntax and tortured recollections of the paradigms of such complicated verbs as to be, and also because he asked us no less than three times how to spell blackguard, was actually improving it, and by now may well have posted it. We can only guess at the nature of the completed masterwork which you have received, or will receive – we were hard put to it not to laugh, which would have hurt his feelings, at what parts we heard, but here again I should be on your guard because it may well be that here an erring is made in another direction, and we feel uneasy, especially if he has seen to regard you as a sort of 'conspirator' which we know that you will not like. On the other hand, whatever it says, it scarcely can fail to convince you, if there are any facts in it at all, that there is something definitely wrong on the other side of the case, and since this man is the trusted appointee of A.B. Carey and hence of Parks, that unnegotiably paradoxes exist in the present set up and that if Maurice Carey is not all

that should be desired as an ambassador of verity, then neither are
A.B. Carey or Parks. That you will not wish to be associated with
this kind of thing goes without saying, and I now want to say flatly
that the appeal to yourself was very largely made in order that we
could be delivered once and for all from this nightmare of confused
wills and directions, dishonest and otherwise, in our lot. In this respect we have appealed to you so to speak as the Truth and if the
Truth finds itself to be on the spot a little it is no wonder, but I think
that we may have done something so far in this letter to remove certain superficial doubts in your mind as to our integrity with you
which *is*, which has been, and will continue to be and must be for all
our sakes, complete.

Now before discussing some of the other matters brought up in
your letter, I wish, if possible, to account briefly and as best I may,
for I myself am not yet acquainted with the whole painful story, for
the reason *for* all this and *why* any allegations have been made at all by
Parks and the O.M. of such a serious nature that they have obviously
caused you, in spite of the fact that I said before hand that they would
be of such a nature, apparently to change your mind regarding helping *us*. Do you remember [Alfred] Miller, the little communist in
Mexico?[2] My troubles seem to date from my association, of a purely
friendly and non political nature, with him. I will not go into detail
but I strongly suspect here the hand of blackmail that a certain person
or persons have volunteered information of a defamatory character
to the O.M. with the view of extorting money based upon my
purely superficial relationship with him and with some of his confrères. In spite of the fact that I was not even then of their persuasions
and only the mildest kind of pink and in spite of the fact that these
allegations were monstrously untrue they were nevertheless undoubtedly made, with whatever motive, and the fact that I had been
associated with these people in any way whatsoever has served to
blacken my name and to act as a working hypothesis for investing
me not only with DISEASES but CRIME as well. I have heard the most
incredible stories about myself which I know have got back to the
O.M. and in only one of which is there a grain of truth. Unfortunately this one was by all odds the most damaging of all. A female to
whom Parks had been introduced and with whose 'set' I had been
consorting soon after the interogatory state of affairs with Jan, had
one hell of a brawl for herself when tight and with her husband in my
room where they had come, whiskey bottle in hand, seeking me.
Although I was not even there at the time and only arrived later,
when the hotel clerk and I tried to get them out, the damage had
already been done. The female had apparently got it into her head

that she wanted to commit suicide, hysteria and usquebaugh was all over the place, she had a black eye and a cracked rib (her husband had cracked this for her three months previously, though) but I was on the carpet. It did little good for the female some days afterward to spring to my rescue or even the hotel staff to affirm that it was not my fault, the onus was entirely on me. Fortunately it was only a localized row, no police, or anything like that, and Parks, I think, to do him justice, would not have reported this matter had not we violently quarreled at this point and I called him a crook. In despair as to how this affair would sound in the Wesleyan hush of my father's house I sent a telegram to Stuart,[3] telling him that Parks was a crook and asking him simply for enough money to get me by the next couple of months and then to inform the O.M. that I was absolutely through with any money from that source from then on, which should enable me to go to New York, – I had not met Margie at this time, – and try and make a fresh start on my own hook. Parks intercepted the telegram at the desk and sent it to my *father*, having told them that he would simply get it sent for me. (This for your delectation is a criminal offence. But what, under the circumstances, could I do?) It was then I got wind of the general idea that the O.M. had formed from these reports of me, which was to have me declared incompetent and have me shut up in a sanitarium where I could be of no further harm to anybody.[4] Tears of rage might well stream down the old countenance at this, and also at the effect of what must have been a ghastly report of something, which however might have happened to anybody, upon the aunts and prostitutes at home, it did not alter the fact that from that time on my goose was cooked. You speak of my O.M. coming to the rescue, but in point of fact, although this is what the poor old fellow thought he was doing no such coming to the rescue has taken place at all, nor was any rescue needed in the sense you suggest, the only person who came to any rescue was Margie, yes, financially too, because you must remember I never saw a fraction of the money sent out for me! And indeed the only time I appealed to the O.M. for help was lately when in despair at convincing him that both he and I had been caught in a web of falsehood I wrote him an absolutely despairing letter in which I begged, much as I dislike to *beg*, to be able to see you whom of all people I felt alone able to trust to make an absolutely impartial collocation of the news with regard to myself without, I felt, any due favor to me. I included the latter because when you did not write me – I mean you, personally, didn't: not Mary. – after leaving Mexico I was left with the conclusion that something, I do not know precisely what, was rankling. With this in mind I was not as astonished as I might otherwise have been at the tone of your recent letters. I want to assure you again now that I intend, have intended, intend in the future, and have done in relation to Margerie to tell you the absolute truth and nothing but the truth. I deeply value your friendship and at such a time as this I wish profoundly that if there are any worms in either of our bosoms they should be removed. There is not one fact that I have wittingly distorted to you. In order to make my story more plausible to you I wish that I could paint A.B. Carey less black, Parks less cynical, myself less exploited, than I have done but the fact remains that although I do not wish to make a song about it I have been more bloodily misused than any five people you can think of, if we except the Czechoslovakians and the Finns, and if you love me as a friend as I believe and can only conclude from what you have done for me already that you do, I feel that you will do something about it.

As to drink rotting one's honesty, alas, that is true. At one time I felt indeed that more than rotting my honesty it was destroying my identity as well. Many of my troubles, but also many of my wisest decisions, are due to it but I am not, as Parks has suggested, allergic, whatever that means, to it. I have at last gotten wise to it, ceased to tell myself polite little lies about it, forced myself to realize what allowances are made for one when tight, and hence how much one deceives one's self, and have at last put this bogy where it should be, as simply a concomitant of social intercourse. In short, I still like as much as almost anyone you can trust to have a few drinks, or even on occasion, more than a few, but on the other hand it is the first time in my life I might almost say I can take a drink if the occasion seems to demand it or I can leave it alone altogether. I am capable of probably more self dicipline than you imagine and I think you will be relieved to hear this and that no exhortations are any longer necessary on this subject. With wine and other bootleg liquor as cheap as it is and with Maurice almost constantly barracho[5] it would be quite possible for me to keep quite plastered here week in and week out even on the amount of money that I have should I wish to do so, so temptation could not possibly be any worse in Boston than it is here. The bogy may raise its head again but not if I say so while you are the arbitrator and even if it does both Margie and myself are well equipped to deal with it. Principally I have been forced to this attitude by the realization that it did actually rot one's honesty and by the deteriorating and vaporous effect it had both with my work and in my relationship with Margerie who, able to stand it and never complaining about it, is the only person who has ever convinced me that it was worth while regularizing. But if drinking rots the honesty it is a curious thing to say I have yet to meet the teetotaler whom I can wholly trust. However. So much then, for alc.

You refer to my 'obliquity' in Mexico and I think you will agree that I am justifiably hurt that you refer and have referred to that and nothing else in connection with your visit. I did my very level best to accomodate you and to make you and Mary happy while you were there. I took you all as well as I could to my rheumatic bosom, a more reasonable divorce lawyer was procured than you might have otherwise been able to obtain, and although you are under no obligation to me whatsoever about this, I like to feel I played my poor part, in spite of the manifest relief I do not blame you in the least for feeling when you went, in sending you and Mary upon your destiny. You must remember that I was probably more seriously ill than you knew, my illness having since been diagnosed as a (non-infectious) sort of *atrophy*, approaching infantile paralysis, which sometimes is the accompaniment of rheumatic fever in them parts.[6] The report, through what channels I do not know, got back to the O.M. that I was suffering from both epilepsy and WORSE and I was incidentally abandoned by Jan still much in the same condition, which did not add to my pleasures. All of which together with the fact that whatever I may have said I really felt myself to be walking on the edge of a precipice with Jan, may go far to account for what obliquity the alcohol may not account for.

Regarding the epilepsy and WORSE: you may say that people do not do these things, and of course I have only Parks' word that they were said, but your own reaction to my father's letter would seem to justify the existance of such reports. It was upon the basis of these lies that Parks formed his first opinion of me and I mention this as a touchstone of the probable accuracy of most of the reports you have received about me. I need scarcely say that these things are ridiculous but not the best things in the world to feel that someone far away is charging against you. I must add that so far as the company I kept is concerned I have been afforded a rich lesson by my experiences which I will not forget in a hurry. The majority of the reports that went home apart from those from some mysterious source in Mexico, probably an individual by the name of Mensch[7] whom I got out of a frightful jam at my own expense, have emanated from Jan and later Parks. Since Parks discredited Jan's word to England and Jan, Parks', and myself, now, both of their words, and as I am telling you the absolute unvarnished truth, you can make up your mind for yourself how much credence to give to what you have heard. I do not expect you to make any final judgement until we have the opportunity of speaking together but I am asking you at least to suspend

judgement upon accusations which I could not answer. Nevertheless
I can see that Parks and the O.M. have quite naturelly had their influence upon you and it is the purpose of this letter to give as much
light as I can upon past events which I hope will result in your feeling
less uneasy about Margerie and myself should we be able to come.
(Another thing I have heard about myself. That I had got into
trouble with the Police, due to drink. I never have. Except once,
years ago, at college. It is a bloody lie. And it can be proved.)

I see the difficulty you are placed in with regard to Margie with
your conscience. You may like me but on the other hand you do not
want to be in any way the instrument of attaching me to somebody
who might prove such a headache to the O.M. as Jan. The situation
is entirely different. My wish is to support Margie by my own
efforts as soon as possible and it has always been my wish. If it so be
that some money continues to be forthcoming so much the better for
us, but so far is the situation unlike anything which occurred with
Jan that Margerie had expressed herself as perfectly willing and even
eager to support *me*, until such time as I got on my feet, and had she
not given up her job with Penny Singleton would have been abun-
dently able to do so. You do see however the position in which both
war and circumstances have placed us and if we forget the former for
a moment America is clearly enough the solution. On the other hand
although I think you might have put it more cheerily I can see your
position as one having the power to have me cut off without a penny
and do freely *absolve you in advance* should you consider this to be the
wisest course and since I know that you would not advocate this unless I let you down I want it to be understood here and now and
hereafter that this makes absolutely no difference to my feeling of
friendship with you. Perhaps it might turn out even to be a good
thing and we would all be happier if we are living contiguously at
such a time if the monetary element did not complicate our natural
generosities towards each other. But, as I have said before and for
reasons totally unallied to the conditions of the transaction, I have *no*
intention of letting you down. Another aspect of the situation has
occurred to me. You may feel that by harboring Margerie you are
running the risk of having her family rising in indignant protest
about it. Margie has had to tell some of her friends that she is married
simply in order to avert gossip. Her mother, however, knows that
there are obstacles to our marriage and that we have to wait until
such time as they are removed. She is satisfied that we are staying
with a married couple and is also pleased with the idea of her going
to Boston where she would be living under the same, but better,
conditions, which would be, if you demand it, the conditions which

she believes exist. Here again the extenuating circumstances of the
war have combined to persuade her to waive any objection to the apparent unconventionality of our status and I ask you most earnestly
also to take into account in regard to my not writing the O.M. at this
time these self-same extenuating circumstances. It might be all right
but I dare not risk our possible separation. I suggest to you as one
who is enlightened that this respect of the conventions with regard to
the O.M. might do more harm than good and I am loathe to tell a
sort of half lie as suggested by you, i.e.: that I've just now informed
you of the situation and that you have agreed in advance to Margie's
coming along later for a visit. It is true that if it worked it would put
things on a securer footing but if it did not work it would mean disaster and I think after you have digested the above you will agree
with me that I would have no choice but to decline to go to America
at all, hang on here on some excuse or another as best I could, join
the army, and then, until we are able to be married decree Margie my
common law wife and support her on $35 a month. Did this promise
me any future it might be a valuable experience but on the whole it is
a course which you would not wish me to have to take. I have to say
right here and now, putting my foot down as hard as I can without
bringing down all that has been so skillfully engineered upon our
heads that I would definitely renounce any personal gain that might
accrue to me by going to America alone and stay here. We can be
married next October and even if I have to go shortly after, at least
Margerie would have the satisfaction of awaiting my return as my
wife. I think that as the circumstances of war will continue to be
more extenuating as time goes on that if you feel that our actions justify your raising your voice on our behalf that perhaps there would
be not such a grave parental objection either But if the O.M. knew
that we had lived together before our marriage, which were I to be
completely honest with him I would have to admit that we had, he
would be opposed to it. Surely, Conrad, you can see that *this* is a
matter more of convention than of honesty. I can even go further and
say that even if the O.M. suspected that we had lived together before
our marriage he would rather not know about it, put his telescope
to his blind eye, so that he would not be forced by the rigidity
of his Wesleyan spirit to object, and this brings me down to the
subtle difference between honesty and what I think Ibsen called the
'disease of integrity.'

Margie and I have striven with all our souls to make our relationship as fine a thing and as honest a thing as we could under the
circumstances and it seems a pity that all we have built up should be
smeared by a convention which in this case, having regard to the war

and the fact that it will probably last a very long time indeed, would be a sort of sin in itself to respect, and having regard to that war, once more, Conrad, have you thought about it sufficiently with all its little implications in regard to us? Has it occurred to you, to put it as cruelly as possible, that it may very well not make any difference whether the O.M. cuts me off without a penny or not?

Then there is the matter of work in which Margie has become essential. In drawing together, work has become a communal thing between us. Margie is now as much interested in Under the Volcano as I am. We work together on it day and night.[8] I feel that it is the first real book I've written. The certainty of war has let loose a hell of a lot of pent up energy and all played against the background of the false idealisms and abstractions of peace that we wasted our time with when we should have been thinking about living, of which we are bitterly reminded when perhaps there is not much time any longer. All this is making for a real drama, something possibly first rate, within its limits. I'm more than glad I never got a chance to finish it without her because we too seem to be playing our parts within the drama. I don't see how the hell I can finish the book without her anyhow now that we've got started on an absolutely new and important character in it which is her idea.[9] This again is an important point: it is something about which you will want to be shown, I admit, but I can't show it to you without being on the spot, and I can't, moreover, hope to explain it to the old man without getting the whole thing hopelessly misconstrued, even were there time, which there may not be.

Another thing I would like you to take into account is the old man's peculiarities in certain respects. He did his best to queer Stuart's marriage, which turned out well, because he did not make quite the right tactical approach. (He was sporting about mine but need not have been drawn into its failure, had he only let me alone.) And I am not the first son to have had spies put on his tail.[10] Stuart, when in France, had the same thing done to him. What the O.M. needs is *assurance* of some sort that all is now as well as it can be, and though I might wish that assurance to be made anyhow for his own sake I certainly do not wish it for my ends; and since we have already understood that you will not make any assurance unless you feel that the situation deserves it, you will perhaps see that I am doubly anxious that you should be convinced.

I think that the wiser course and the juster would be as I have said before that you suspend judgement upon whether you can ratify our relationship as a good thing, if such ratification is needed, until you have the evidence of your own eyes. There is nothing to prevent at least my getting engaged without my father's knowledge and my first marriage having proved an embarrassment (to *him* through no fault of my own) and a failure, he is not likely to look upon any attachment I may form at the present time with favor until you are convinced that it is otherwise. Why do you not consider our relationship to be a necessary experiment? I cannot see that my father can expect me entirely to dispense with female company. If Margie did not exist you would probably suggest, even if I kept a pair of scissors handy as you say, that I take upon some female relationship which reason itself would not demand you to tell my father about and of which he would not expect to know. The pair of scissors so far as you're concerned is in your own hands and I have said beforehand that if you do not approve our relationship eventually and if, by the way, any continuation of it implies a letting of you down tantamount to the drunken horrors you expect to cope with, then as I say, it is all right by me and you are still all right by me and I will just have to figure a way out of our difficulties without your assistance and approval but with, I hope, in that case your unexpressed blessing. Parks' remedy for my troubles was the saying, At night all cats are grey, and it seems to me it would be a tragic thing and a contradictory one that while a passing relationship with a harlot might be condoned by Parks et al one which is in itself a simple, honest and good thing is not. The risks we are taking we take with our eyes open.

I had hoped that in this letter I had managed to clear up some of the suspicions which I feel you have come to hold since receiving the letters from the O.M. and Parks and I hope also that after you have absorbed every word of this letter that you will be convinced that the only first step towards a securer footing and finally a secure footing is for you to see and be shown by yourself. Otherwise I think I should inevitably become the victim of some such justice as befell my friend William Empson when his fellowship at Cambridge was taken away, himself sent down and his career ruined, because he had been abnormal enough to have some contraceptives in his room, and normal enough to inform the dons that they were not ornaments and that he used them.[11]

For the rest, for the hope you extend about Montreal should the American idea blow up, my deepest thanks and also reiterated thanks for everything you have both done for us. Very finally I want to say again that so far as we are concerned there will be no dishonestness round corners, no drunken sailors smuggled in from the Navy Yard at night and above all no communistic talk under the banana trees. My only hope is that after all our ups and downs our relationship and relationships as you once prophesied the last time I left Rye, could and would be pure Sierra Nevada and so, as Chaucer said, go litel book, which I am afraid this has become, go litel myne tragadie,[12] and bear in mind that whatever it may not be written with it is written with love

As ever,
with Both our Loves

Malc

P.S. I enclose an old self-explanatory, unposted, p.c.[a]

Annotations:

1 On 19 January 1940 Aiken had written Lowry his toughest letter yet. He urged Malcolm to be honest with his father about Margerie, told Malcolm that in a recent letter from Arthur Lowry the 'old man' had threatened to cut his wayward son off completely, and emphasized that he felt himself to be in a false position: 'I feel we *must* be honest,' he insisted. But perhaps what most hurt Lowry was Aiken's suggestion that his drinking had damaged his ability to be honest; see Sugars (88-90).

2 Little is known about Lowry's actual relations with Alfred Miller, but one 1937 letter (**74**) to him has survived.

3 Stuart Lowry (1895-1969) was Lowry's eldest brother.

4 According to Jan Gabrial in *Malcolm Lowry Remembered* (124), Benjamin Parks was responsible for putting Lowry in 'a drying-out place' that resembled New York's Bellevue Hospital, where Lowry had spent ten terrible days in June 1936.

5 Lowry has misspelt the Spanish word for 'drunk': *borracho*.

6 Lowry had suffered from malaria and lumbago during his months in Mexico with Jan.

7 Lowry mentions an American friend called Harry Mensch in his letter (**74**) to Alfred Miller. Jan Gabrial remembers Mensch as having left-wing interests and sympathies.

8 Benjamin Parks, who had received the manuscript of *Under the Volcano* from Carol Phillips sometime during December 1939 or early January 1940, had finally forwarded it to Lowry.

9 During the winter of 1939-40 Malcolm began revising *Under the Volcano* with Margerie's help. It seems most likely that, at this early stage in the revising process, Lowry is referring to the character of Lacretelle/Laruelle, who, as a movie director, may have been suggested by Margerie. Later changes to the relationships of Geoffrey and Yvonne or Geoffrey and Hugh were not made until after 1941.

10 Lowry knew that his father had hired a detective to follow his movements in Mexico; his brother Russell Lowry confirms that their parents did not make it easy for the sons to marry.

11 William Empson (1906-84) was the well-known British critic and poet

who studied at Winchester College, 1920-25, and Magdalene College, Cambridge, 1929 (see photograph 9). He was a student of mathematics and English who, under the tutorship of I.A. Richards, came first in the English Tripos in 1929, and he was editor of the Cambridge literary magazine *Experiment* in 1928. In his autobiography Michael Redgrave also tells of Empson's being 'sent down, or "rusticated"' because he had contraceptives in his room; see Michael Redgrave, *In My Mind's Eye* (63).

12 See Chaucer's *Troilus and Criseyde* V.1786: 'Go, litel bok, go litel myn tragedye.'

Editorial Notes:

a.   There is no postcard extant with this letter.

125: To Conrad Aiken

P: H(ts)
PP: *LAL* 104-05

> 595 W. 19th Ave.,
> Vancouver, B.C.
> 7 February 1940

My very dear Conrad:
    I am overjoyed by your letter. Thank you for your thoughtfulness in trying to make it possible for us to have a nook to ourselves, and, with such sanctuary, I trust we may prove a stimulation to work rather than a hindrance.
    We are working night and day on Under the Volcano and am sure at last have got something. It has blood, guts, rapine, murder, teeth, and, for your entertainment, even some moonlight and roses.[1] And a couple of horses.
    Dick Eberhart[2] was at Cambridge a little before my time: he was a friend of J.D.'s [John Davenport]. I had many strange döppelganger[3] like remote contacts with him. He was a sailor, wrote a goodish first book of poems, 'Bravery of Earth.' Since, he does, as you say, seem to have gone mad as a hatter. He is now devoted to another form of what you call 'indoor Marxmanship.' I believe he is a brilliant fellow, but he seems to me to be tone deaf, poetically. Once, when accused in the Cambridge Review by I.A. ('Granada') Richards, of 'sucking his poetic thumb,' he confronted him personally with said thumb, made a rude gesture, asked, 'How do you like this?'[4]

I hope to hear news soon from Washington. Please tell Mary I am writing her personally to thank her for all she has done on our behalf. Tell me something funny.

As ever, love from us both,

Malc

Annotations:

1 Lowry is referring to Aiken's 15 December 1939 letter, in which Aiken criticizes *In Ballast to the White Sea* for being derivative of himself and others. He urges Lowry to try instead for 'something with a little more gusto . . . sunsets and sunrises, moons, stars, roses'; see Sugars (71-72).
2 Richard Eberhart (1904–) was an American poet studying at St John's College, Cambridge, who received his B.A. in 1929 and M.A. in 1933. *A Bravery of Earth* was published by Jonathan Cape in 1930. See Lowry's parodic explication of Eberhart's 'Caravan of Silence' in his 27 October 1930 letter (25) to John Davenport.
3 The German word *Doppelgänger* means 'double.'
4 Ivor Armstrong Richards (1893-1979), the British literary critic and poet, was at Magdalene College, Cambridge, during Lowry's Cambridge years; he left Cambridge in 1939. His influence on Cambridge and English studies, especially after the 1925 publication of *Principles of Literary Criticism* and the 1929 publication of *Practical Criticism*, was profound. Richards, who had shown interest in Eberhart's early poetry during his years at Cambridge, 1927 to 1929, accused the young American of the habit of 'suck[ing] his poetic thumb' in a university magazine, *Granta*, but for a very different description of Eberhart's reaction from the one Lowry gives here, see Joel Roache, *Richard Eberhart: The Progress of an American Poet* (New York: Oxford University Press, 1971), pp. 59-60.

126: To Conrad Aiken

P: H(ts)
PP: *LAL* 108-10

595 W. 19th Ave.,
23 February 1940

Dear Conrad:

The axe has fallen, as I thought it would. I am refused – and cannot go back to the States. I have been assured by the Immigration here that the refusal is a technicality – in other words that it is not etiquette for one department of Immigration to overrule another. This makes it impossible for me to apply before September 23. This is A.B.

Carey's and Park's fault, I told them both that this would happen and they still persisted in saying it was for my benefit. Surely this is proof that they are not able to handle my affairs. By September 23 anything may have happened. The sitzkrieg become a blitzkrieg,[1] so on and so forth. Unless the war has stopped I may not be able to enter the United States again. Meantime I have work to finish, and now, when everything seems lost, it seems all the more important to finish it.

[At this point, Lowry's letter is interrupted by the following letter from Margerie. Phyllis was Maurice Carey's wife.]

Dear Conrad and Mary:

Malcolm had started this letter to you but I am going to finish it, I will make it as brief as possible but it is a really desperate appeal for the axe has fallen doubly. You are the only people we have in the world to appeal to or who can help us and I cannot put it too strongly how urgent our situation is. Maurice is on the most ghastly drunken rampage you can imagine and things have become so intolerable that Phyllis says we must leave as soon as possible. She is afraid of what may happen. Last night Maurice suddenly went for me and knocked me half way across the kitchen, then turned on Malcolm, who although wild with fury because Maurice had struck me, behaved with the most marvelous self-restraint and only tried to defend himself – you see, he didn't dare hit Maurice because Maurice has a very bad heart and his intestines, stomach, etc., were so badly shot to pieces, he is such a sick man that one good blow might very easily kill him. I can not tell you how crazy he is – even when sober he behaves in such an irrational manner that he is dangerous and when drunk he is a mad man. We have had to stand aside and see him beat Phyllis and his three children, smash the house up, and fight with anybody who was around and he has gone for days without speaking to us except to threaten us, but now this – he didn't hurt me very much but Malcolm has one eye completely closed, a badly cut mouth and injured hand, and Maurice is still drunk and crazy. Phyllis fears that he will have another breakdown and be sent to the hospital any moment, or that his heart will give out in one of these frenzies. But in any case, if another row like last night were to happen, which it very well may at any moment despite anything we can do, we have no lock on our door and he come raging in at all hours, and if he were to die from sheer excitement or some slight chance blow from Malcolm merely trying to defend himself, or even me if Malcolm

were not at home, I need not tell you what a catastrophe that would
be. We must get out of here and quickly. Here, of course, we have
no place to go. We do not know what to suggest as we do not know
what would be best for you or what you would rather do but this
much we will say: If you could meet us in Montreal or Quebec or
whatever point in Canada is nearest for you – if, after talking to us
and seeing us, you are not absolutely convinced that we are right,
completely honest with you about everything, and with Malcolm's
word (and mine too, of course) never to let you down, if you are not
convinced that we are trying with all our minds and souls to simply
make a decent life for ourselves, then you can simply wash your
hands of the whole thing, write Malcolm's father whatever you
think and abandon us to our fate. Malcolm *has* been the victim of
bitter and tragic circumstances and has been badly treated and even
A.B. Carey has admitted to him that they were wrong. Malcolm
saw him the other day and A.B. Carey said so, said that Malcolm
was absolutely O.K. and that he had been in the wrong and wound
up by saying that he thought Malcolm should try and help Maurice!
My God, what irony!

Meantime we have been working like mad on Under the Volcano,
which Malcolm is completely re-writing and which is now about
half done. It is unlike anything he has written before and, I think,
will be truly a great book when it is finished – *and it must be finished*.
Malcolm is a genius and if you could see the work he is doing now,
under circumstances and conditions that would appear impossible to
one less determined and, yes, less inspired to write, you would agree
with me.

He is sick with disappointment over the news from America, I
can't tell you how he was looking forward to spending some time
with you – he talked of it constantly. Besides he will not be able to
write or type for awhile because it was his right hand that was hurt so
that's why I am writing for us. I'm sorry if this letter seems rather incoherent but I am writing against time so that this will catch the air
mail out today – also I am a little dazed myself today, but you should
get this by Monday and could you let us know soon – if we just have
some assurance from you we can hang on by our teeth and toenails
somehow for a little bit longer.

And now again, our deepest, undying gratitude to you both for all
you have done for us and our absolute assurance that all we ask is just
enough to live on and a chance to work and be together and to prove
to you, and Malcolm's family, that we mean what we say.

Our love to you both,

Margerie

Dear Mary:

I was writing you personally to thank you for your sweet help on our behalf when Maurice's fist fell along with the axe. I have read Margie's letter and although it doesn't sound sort of likely you may feel, about me, it is all true so help us. That is, all save the genius stuff; but the new book *is* going well. We are at our wit's end and I can barely see to write or hold a pen what Margie will transcribe, and ask you to accept this note in the meantime as expression of my gratitude. Could not Conrad, perhaps, take *carte-blanche* under these circumstances? Any expenditures would be fully repaid. I hate to put him to any trouble just when his book is coming out, but we are really harmless good folk and please do not be alarmed by the fact that our fate is in your hands. Please help us.

Malcolm

Annotations:

1 A typical Lowry word-play in German: the sitting war becomes a lightning war.

126-a: To Benjamin Parks

P: Liverpool(ts)

595 W. 19th Ave.,
Vancouver, B.C.
27 February 1940

Dear Mr Parks:

I have received a brief, polite note of refusal from Mother Goddam saying I cannot reapply before September 23.[1]

This is only to be expected; the Immigration Authorities having beforehand informed me that one department does not, as a matter of etiquette, overrule another save in a very exceptional case, and I can assume only that my case does not appear to be sufficiently exceptional.

It was hinted to me by the same source that perhaps my appeal as one of the 'intelligentsia' was against me; perhaps, they thought, as in the case of Earl Russell, also refused, that I intended or was liable to disseminate propaganda in the Allied cause or some such.[2] Be that as it may, there is nothing to be done about it – their machinations being confidential – and although I feel bitter that I was not allowed to apply, by A.B. Carey, sooner after getting my visa, according to the Consul's instructions, it is futile now to do anything about that either. Nor do I blame you for leaving me in the clutches of this man, for the simple reason that A.B. Carey, as Time this week says of your Mr Dewey, – is a man whom it is impossible to dislike until you know him well.[3] And you did not so know him. That I am not alone in this feeling was publically demonstrated here recently upon his retirement as Varsity rugby coach but then, come to that, I cannot very actively dislike any man who is making an effort to be honest with himself. Maclean has dropped out of the picture long ago: I only saw him once after you left. He was, on the whole a pretty good egg, I thought, and I am sorry I saw no more of him.[4] Perhaps by September the war will be over and everything will then be simple.

Meanwhile, to offset the bad news, I am glad to report that I have excellent and hopeful news of my work from Aiken's publisher, and a very cheery letter from my mother, to whom, I am pleased to say, a Christmas present I sent wound is convoyed way safely.[5]

For the rest, I owe it to my Father to work as hard as possible in whatever time is left and it is not at all outside the bounds of possibility that in a month or two I shall manage to land a contract. My contact with Aiken is all-important here and as I gather from my Mother that she is as anxious as I am for me to make that contact as close as possible, as he can assist me with my work, I have written him in this regard.[6] In this regard too I would also consider it senseless, in this interrogative stage of things, to enlist {Anyhow, it is still impossible.} until I have absolutely accomplished all I can. There will doubtless be time enough for battle later: or, perhaps, as I have said, the foolishness will end. Anyhow I think that, come what may, we have scored a sort of triumph. At least there seems no reason still to be treated as a minor and a half-wit. I had certain things to get over, as you know, and it seems I have got over them. Perhaps not sufficient allowance has been made for this????? I do not any longer drink, nor, so long as I am not subjected to exhortations on the subject, do I ever feel any inclination to. This is something, as you know, upon which one has to make up one's mind oneself. I do not suppose I've had three glasses of beer in as many months, though there is plenty opportunity, much more, it turns out, than in L.A. It is not, therefore, for its dryness that I loathe Vancouver. I think you would loathe it too. It is more the stultifyingness, the boringness, the Oxford Group, the women, whom I shall never forget your referring to as looking as though they had sore feet, the fact that I have been working hard – 45,000 words since January – and that both I, and the book, badly need a change of scenery – that puts Vancouver in the dog house with me.

Finally, I do want to express my very real appreciation of what you personally have done, executively, to assist me to return to America, (and in other ways), and, while I do not feel that it is my fault in this case that at the moment it is impossible to do so, let it be perfectly understood that I certainly do not consider it yours, and that I feel only gratitude towards you and a sense of personal friendship.

Yours cordially,

Malcolm

Annotations:

1 This 'polite note' from the American immigration authorities refusing Lowry's appeal to be allowed to return to the United States has not survived. See Lowry's description of his rejection in his 23 February 1940 letter (**126**) to Conrad Aiken.

2 Bertrand Russell was teaching at the University of California, Berkeley at this time, but he found the intellectual atmosphere there repressive and the American authorities had refused to extend his alien visitor's permit beyond the end of December 1939; see Lowry's January 1940 letter (**123**) to Conrad Aiken. When the College of the City of New York publicized their decision to offer him a position as Professor of Philosophy, they were immediately denounced by conservative clerics, one of whom described Russell as a 'propagandist' against morality. The debate erupted in the press on 26 February 1940 and led to a court case that resulted in a withdrawal of the offer.

3 Thomas E. Dewey (1902-71), a Republican politician and crime investigator in New York City, served three terms as the Governor of New York State. In *Time* magazine, 26 February 1940: 15-18, there is an article on his campaign for the Republican presidential nomination in which he is described as a man whom 'it's almost impossible to dislike . . . until you know him well' (17).

4 Lowry's view of A.B. Carey is consistently negative, but he appears to have liked Victor MacLean. From Benjamin Parks's long 16 August 1939 letter to Arthur Lowry's lawyers, held in the Ayerton and Alderson Smith file in the Liverpool library, however, it is clear that Parks thought very highly of Carey and believed, or wished Arthur Lowry to believe, that Malcolm also liked Carey. His report to the lawyers includes the following observation: 'Mr Carey handled Malcolm in a very marvellous way; in fact, it was one of the finest exhibitions of tact and psychology that I have ever seen.'

5 Unfortunately, neither of these letters has survived.

6 Lowry had, of course, written to Aiken several times about his plight, but see his February 1940 letter (**127**), which was written at about the time of this letter to Parks.

Editorial Notes:

a. This typescript letter, held with the Ayerton and Alderson Smith papers at the Browne, Pictou, and Hornby Libraries in Liverpool carries a few minor cancellations and insertions. See Appendix 3 for what appears to be Lowry's only surviving letter to this legal firm.

127: To Conrad and Mary Aiken
P: H(ts)
PP: *LAL* 111-16

> 595 W. 19th Ave.,
> Vancouver, B.C.
> [late February 1940]

Dear Conrad and Mary: (Apologies in advance, Mary, for this self-conscious 'Waile of a letter' which contains much I have no right to bore you with – only I wanted it to be to you *both*)

I am sending another note hotfooting it after you through the crashing snowflakes in the hope of suggesting a possible redistribution of the solutions of our current problems which is not too much at variance with *your* various plans outlined in your exceedingly welcome, cheery and good letter which gladdened our souls. Reason for this legal prose, this 'rummy' style, I am dictating the letter, my hand being wounded. There is the same infinite misery here as before upon which we will not expatiate save that my enormous black eye seems to be simply glaring demoniacally through the whitewash with which we have lavishly painted ourselves to you and continue, in spite of the black eye, to paint ourselves with *truthfully*. We are not only writing Under the Volcano, we are living smack down in it. We cannot help kidding about it but nevertheless our position is bloody desperate.

I've just received a very cheery letter from my mother, not cheery because she has given up all hope of coping with the world at all and is now counting on the unseen, but in which she says that she has heard that I'm going to stay with you and that in any event she is anxious that I should in some way contact you because she feels, she cannot know how rightly, however intensely she feels, that you would be a help to me. From this I deduce that, since anything that

makes the mater happy makes the O.M. happy too, that even were I
to proceed to Montreal or elsewhere to be under your auspices, it
would be the real right thing from her point of view and hence from
the O.M.'s. All of which makes me think how simple all that could
be if I could only explain it to the O.M. personally and not have my
explanations sidetracked by the blasted Oxford Groupers and
lawyers. All that being so, the only practical suggestion I can make
now is this: if you could take just a few days off and come to Montreal or wherever to meet us, as we said in our last letter, if we do not
convince you, then you can simply quit the whole thing and still
have our blessing for trying. If you are convinced of our honesty,
which you must be by now, then perhaps we could do this: go to
some small town near the border, on the Gaspé Peninsula maybe,
where living would be very cheap and the surroundings beautiful,
and settle down for the summer to work.

Meantime the O.M. could be gradually broken in to the idea that
Margie was coming to visit me. We – if it came to that – would
gladly give you half of what I think I have – i.e. half $150 – or if war
has reduced that to $100, say 25% of it, which might help, in addi-
tion, of course, to Parks' fee which you would be getting. I hope you
will not think my motive for suggesting this invidious: it is simply
that in Canada we could live on $75 a month, we have fewer re-
sponsibilities than you, and you, on our behalf, more than may seem
to be taken care of by the fee, although I would do my utmost to
make these as few as possible for you. Moreover, we are anxious to
impress you with the fact that all we need is enough to live on and
work. Because the whole problem seems to be a matter of money
when it is canalized as it is through the present sources the socalled
'immorality' seems to be that I should use part of the money for
Margie. This is much of an obliquity because in the first place if we
could get somewhere where she could cook and keep house we could
both live for what it would cost me to board or live at a hotel alone. I
cannot get my work done without Margie, I realize my fault is,
roughly speaking, too much loquacity and not enough action, and
hams in the window, and there she helps me immeasureably by her
censorship and suggestions. Besides which if I did not have her I'd
have to pay a typist. Apart from the fact that I love Margie she has
become an inextricable part of my work. (I do not mean in the Ludwig Lewisohn[1] sense.) Objectively speaking I think that such a
dependence might not be a good thing in many cases but in *our* case it
definitely works and even though one may be working in the dark
and against time to the fate of some kind of obscure posthumously
second order Gogol, nevertheless what work we are accomplishing,

for better or worse, does have just that very quality of intensity which work in the dark against time etc. has given the Gogols and the Kafkas: we may not be so good so far but I feel parts of Under the Volcano bear this sort of comparison and we have been given encouragement through this to feel that if only we had the time and could stick together we could produce not just one book but a large body of work stamped at last with an individual imprint. But how the hell to get all this over to the O.M. in the light of my dismal failures in the past I simply don't know: and I am forced to the conclusion that the only thing to do is to prove the practicability of the arrangement first, which in all its aspects, its unconventional complexion at the moment renders impossible, and get it over afterwards when I have something concrete to show. Meantime since Margie has renounced all claims on me and hence all possible claims etc on the O.M., Margie remains my responsibility, one which, if even much less provision is made for me than has hitherto been made, I am capable of holding. But not only this – it is abundantly clear to me that only through Margie can I reach the stage of independence from responsibility etc. which is generally desired, taking with me only just that necessary part of my psychic turmoils which are, to put it bluntly, saleable; and if Under the Volcano is no Anna Karenina,[2] and was not meant to be, at least, unless I am very sadly deceiving myself, it is 'publishable at a profit.'

Were I not very well aware of the many matters relative to Mary's work and your own unities & health such as the Summer School, your book, the impending dental misery which we hope will not turn out too painful, etc., I might have been able to suggest, perhaps without forwardness, that our Lady of the Snows,[3] (in the not remote Montreal regions which I understand are very beautiful,) might have held some possibility of attraction for yourselves in Summer. As it is, realizing that such a thing is impossible but at the same time not allowing myself utterly to despair of the fact of the possibility of our not being able to see one another once more – and this would be a very real despair should I give way to it, since what truer father have I than you, and as Thomas Wolfe[4] says, are we not all looking for our fathers – I can only place once more our problems before you, less complicated as they are now by having fewer solutions, and entreat you once again to try and help us, I having already given you my word as an artist, a man and a friend not to let you down. As your own method of dealing with the O.M. seems to have been much more successful than anything I could hope to suggest I hesitate to make any suggestions but I feel that if at this period you could give the O.M. to realize how desperately in earnest I am about accomplishing my work in whatever time may be alloted to me, of how proximity to yourself, even if in Montreal, would benefit me in that regard and how already certain encouragement has been given me by, for instance, [Robert] Linscott, which makes for some promise of definiteness in all this, that I have certain matters to talk over with you and certain problems – I won't go on, you know all the circumstances here, use your own good judgement about what you say, but could you ask for carte blanche to do what you think is best for me? Since our situation is so urgent, could you not send a cable (for which you'd be reimbursed) or if not, a letter by the Clipper, otherwise it may take too long. The letter from my mother was written just after Christmas and she spoke of other letters she had written me which I never received. My Mother says in her letter how much *she* wants me to succeed in my work and now I *know* that I am really on the verge of doing something about it if I can only finish the Volcano and re-write In Ballast as I see it now. But, Conrad, we cannot stay here for the situation is really dangerous and growing increasingly more so, at any moment something may happen which we cannot avert which will destroy everything we have tried so desperately and worked so hard these last months to build up. It would be particularly bitter now, since the encouraging letter from Linscott (I feel certain the Volcano will be a better bet with him) and your own encouragement about the Lighthouse – I can't begin to tell you how much that meant to me.

Should you receive carte-blanche from the O.M. I fully realize the difficulties involved in doing what is best for me and still retaining your own integrity and honesty with the O.M. To that end I can only say that if after seeing us and talking to us you feel that I am to be trusted and that I do mean what I say, perhaps you'd be justified in giving us a chance in these next few months to prove to you, and the family, that we are sincere in trying to make a new life for ourselves. This might entail telling a few white lies to the O.M. but we know in the long run he'll be grateful to you for giving us that chance and for rescuing us from this horror here in Vancouver. If you do not feel you can do this we can effect some sort of compromise whereby we could find someone wherever we were staying to simply pay our bills – perhaps the bank – and give us an allowance of whatever you think – all not to exceed an agreed sum. There I would be under your aegis as I am under Parks' here – via an intermediary – but would be free of the bungaling hypocracy of Ibsenish A.B., Dostoievskish M., Carey, and possibly you could come up for a day or two now and then and see for yourself what we are doing. If this won't do, perhaps we could find some couple who would let us stay with them so that we were properly chaperoned and who would board us as we are here but in a more decent and wholesome atmosphere. There is so much work I want to do in these next few months if I can only have the chance to do it – finish the Volcano, re-write In Ballast, re-write the Lighthouse with your suggestions and The Last Address with ditto, several short stories and a new novel, Night Journey Across the Sea,[5] in the offing. And nobody seems to realize that these next few months may be all I'll have to do my work in, or to be with Margie, for I may have to go to war immediately after we are married, or even before, for that matter since I shall be in Canada. If you only knew what we wouldn't give just to have a chance to live, to breathe, to have a little freedom to work and peace of mind as well. Not to mention a hot bath now and then, we get one between us, lukewarm, about once every three weeks. The Finns get one once a week, by the way – and a decent meal, we haven't had a square meal since Christmas, and even that was sort of triangular – we had to depend upon the tail end of it until damn nearly the end of January – We've had *no fresh milk, butter, eggs, fruit or vegetables* in *five months* and live on a diet of bread, soggy potatoes and watery stew. Very well, you say, go out and earn it, but this is only precisely what we are asking for a chance to do!

The house sounds swell but I am sad I shan't see it: perhaps in September. Haven't heard from J.D. [John Davenport] for three years when he phoned me at Cuernavaca. His umbrages are incident but soon forgotten. Thank you very much for writing him on my behalf. *And*, a thousand thanks for interesting Linscott: the Volcano might do for him. And for your remarks about the poems I am likewise very grateful: I was kind of hoping against hope there would be a few you'd like: particularly one about the Harkness light, and another about Crusoe's footprints or some such.[6] Well, I'm immensely beholden to you for all you've done for me, for us, and do hope you will still be able to help me with the Lighthouse. Talking about Lapland: Nordahl Grieg is there on military service, sent there as a punishment for defending Russia in the Arbeiderbladet:[7] serve him right, perhaps; but what an ending to In Ballast to the White Sea!

Well: here goes another Decline and Fall of the Roman Empire – And our very best love and good wishes to Mary and yourself, *'powerful' to help these guilty lives* –

yours very west of Eden[8]

Malc & Margie

Annotations:

1 The novels of Ludwig Lewisohn (1883-1955), American editor, critic, translator, and novelist, often deal with marital problems.
2 *Anna Karenina* (1875-76) is the tragic Russian novel of love and death by Leo Tolstoy (Count Lev Nikolayevich Tolstoi, 1828-1910).
3 Rudyard Kipling (1865-1936) visited Canada on at least four occasions, in 1889, 1892, 1907, and 1930. Kipling saw in Canada the place where his dream of Anglo-Saxon empire could be maintained, and in 1897 he wrote the poem to which Lowry refers in praise of Canada's decision to grant England a preferential tariff. The poem concludes: 'I am first in the battle / Said Our Lady of the Snows,' but Canadians were not flattered by his image of Canada as a loyal, snow-bound extension of empire.
4 Lowry may be referring to *The Web and the Rock* (1939) by American novelist Thomas Wolfe (1900-38), in which the rock symbolizes the father.
5 Lowry's reference here is to an *idea* for a novel that he mentioned in his long November 1939 letter (**97**) to Aiken. No 'new novel' with this name was ever written or begun.
6 Lowry is referring to 'Quartermaster at the Wheel' and number XX (also called 'On Reading R.L.S.' in a 1936 version). The latter poem went through eight revisions to be called 'Old Freighter in an old Port' in 1947; see Scherf (88, 97, 115).
7 The *Arbeiderbladet*, founded in 1884 by Holtermann Knudsen, was the official mouthpiece of the Norwegian Labour party. It was shut down during the Second World War when the Germans occupied Norway, and was started up again after the war. Hallvard Dahlie confirms that Grieg was sent to Lapland, but he doubts the reason given here by Lowry. See 'A Norwegian at Heart: Lowry and the Grieg Connection,' *Swinging the Maelstrom* (36).
8 This is an allusion to Aiken's *Landscape West of Eden* (London: J.M. Dent, 1934), and to Lowry's distance from Aiken.

128: To Conrad Aiken

P: H(ts)
PP: *LAL* 117-19

595 W. 19th Ave.,
Vancouver, B.C.
3 March 1940

– We thank you both from the bottom of our hearts, and want you to know immediately that, whether the O.M.'s reply is favorable or not we are eternally grateful to you both even for trusting us and helping us and that if ever there is a thorn in the Hoover-Aiken[1] claws we will go through hell and high water to pull it out. Spring comes, sunlight begins to again 'roar like a vast invisible sea'[2] – this is the first spring I have really been aware of since I used to read fragments of the House of Dust in old Coteries on Hayes Common twelve years ago.

Meantime, in the maritime world, all is not so good. There are few ships I have written about that have not met their fate in a sticky manner. Ariadne N Pandelis and Herzogin Cecile in In Ballast went to the bottom a few weeks after I had written about them. Athenia leaves the same port, sinks in the same place with Norse boat to the rescue, as Arcturian in In Ballast! But that is nothing to what has just happened, by way of coincidence, to two ships, real and imaginary, in my first early plagiaristic paen to puberty, Ultramarine. Do you remember a German wireless operator in the book? He is mentioned as coming from a German ship, the Wolfsburg (which I had seen in the Suez Canal)[3] The Wolfsburg was torpedoed a fortnight ago by an English submarine, half the crew rescued. The Nawab in Ultramarine was really the Pyrrhus (the ship I was actually on). The Pyrrhus was torpedoed by a German submarine off the West coast of England the day before yesterday, a total loss and half the firemen killed. Strange: The Acushnet, the real Pequod – in Moby, met similar fate to Pequod, after he had written the book.[4] Nothing in it my dear fellows, but these here correspondences of the subnormal world with the abnormally suspicious are damned queer, if you like to think so. Joyce says that nearly all the characters mentioned in the funeral scene in Ulysses, or people with the same names, have met a strange fate. One mentioned, not accounted for: Lowry.[5] That Telemachus is a sister ship to the Pyrrhus cannot apparently have anything to do with the subject![6] I have the strange feeling that the disaster to my old ship, coming on top of everything else this last week, was intended, by some queer subaqueous *force majeure*, finally to polish *me* off. If so it certainly did not succeed! On the contrary perhaps that was just all my past life with its false bulkheads, firemen, funnels and windlasses sinking below the waves! Somehow we fooled 'em.

Margie, who is an expert, has inveigled me into reading astronomy. (*Not* to be confused with *astrology*, Margie begs me to insist, doubtless pained to think this should be associated with the other mumbo jumbos in my letter.) I still do not know which stars are coming or going, but the enclosed poem emerging from the following metaphysic makes me think that, with practice, I might develop into an Eliza Cook yet.[7] 'That when Venus is nearest to the earth she appears as a thin crescent, almost invisible, as the distance increases, more of the bright disc becomes visible, the increasing distance tends to make the planet appear less bright, but the change in phase acts in a contrary direction; the result of the two effects is that the brightness continues to increase for about 36 days from the time Venus is at her nearest. Thereafter the effect of the increasing phase is more than counterbalanced by the greater distance. When at her brightest, Venus is much brighter than any star or any other planet and can be seen without difficulty by the naked eye in broad daylight. I have on more than one occasion seen it without looking for it and without realizing at first that I was actually looking at Venus.' Here is something else too, which would seem to be fructifying, if applied to mankind. 'The light reaching us from Venus can be compared with the light which we receive directly from the sun. In neither case is the light pure sunlight. The light which we receive from the sun directly has some wave lengths weakened or missing because of absorption in the atmosphere of the earth.' Or perhaps you have already expressed this somewhere. Or thought it not worth expressing.

I gather from *Life* that England is none too popular in American quarters. I am very sad I shall not be able to see Mary's pictures for some time.

There is a photograph of former Hoover subject, 'Man with Concertina' Elliot Paul, in Time this week, playing boogie-woogie in the temple.[8]

Once I could play boogie-woogie fine . . .

All thanks and love again to both from both.

Malc & Margie

P.S. A mysterious photograph of a sailing ship, very much the worse for wear, called the Lawhill has appeared in our local drugstore. Lawhill is the name of the ship in The Last Address. The Lawhill has also been – er – recently sunk. But what the hell boys and girls. Hoppla! Wir leben![9]

The Volcano is rapidly reaching its last belch.

Annotations:

1 Hoover is Mary Aiken's maiden name.
2 Lowry is quoting Aiken's 'Movements from a Symphony: Overtones,' *Coterie* 3 (December 1919): 53.
3 Hans Popplereuter is the name of the German wireless operator from the *Wölfsburg* with whom Dana Hilliot talks and drinks in chapter 3 of *Ultramarine*.

4 The *Pequod* is the name of Ahab's ship in Melville's *Moby-Dick*. Lowry was familiar with Lewis Mumford's *Herman Melville* (New York: Harcourt, Brace, 1929), and Mumford notes that the 'crew of the Acushnet was an ill-fated one . . . the ship itself foundered in the very year [Melville] wrote Moby Dick' (p. 44). The *Achushnet* was wrecked on 16 August 1851, the year *Moby-Dick* was published.

5 See *Ulysses* (London: The Bodley Head, 1960), p. 113: 'Mr Bloom's glance travelled down the edge of the paper, scanning the deaths. Callan, Coleman, Dignam, Fawcett, Lowry.' The names Bloom reads were purely fictitious, but Joyce was superstitious about naming living people. In his 25 August 1951 letter (**467**) to David Markson, Lowry again mentions Joyce's superstition 'about the name Lowry, which occurs in his funeral scene. No sooner had he given them these . . . than one after the other these names acquired living, or rather dead, counterparts, all of which . . . were found to have come to grotesque and tragic ends! I never checked up to see if a stand-in called L. has already let me out.' The Lowry listed in Bloom's *Freeman's Journal* may have been Dan Lowry, who owned a Dublin music-hall; see R.M. Adams, *Surface and Symbol: The Consistency of James Joyce's Ulysses* (New York: Oxford University Press, 1962), p. 107.

6 The first part of *Ulysses*, which covers the early morning hours, begins with 'Telemachus' – hence Lowry's association of the ship's name with the *Pyrrhus* and with *Ulysses*. The funeral of Paddy Dignam occurs in the 'Hades' episode of the second part of Joyce's novel.

7 Eliza Cook (1818-89) was an English poet and a regular contributor to the *Weekly Despatch*. From 1849 to 1854 she published *Eliza Cook's Journal*, and in 1860 she brought out *Jottings from My Journal*, a collection of her essays and sketches that represent her simple, unpretentious, if somewhat moralistic prose style. The passages quoted by Lowry, following his reference to Cook, have not been identified, and there is no poem extant with this letter.

8 Lowry is referring to a painting by Mary (Hoover) Aiken of Elliot Harold Paul (1891-1958), the American novelist and jazz pianist who was founder and co-editor with Eugene Jolas of the literary magazine *transition*. An article on Elliot Paul, 'Bach and Boogie-Woogie,' appeared in *Time*, 4 March 1940: 48.

9 *Hoppla! Wir leben!* is the title of the 1927 play by Ernst Toller (1893-1939), who, with Georg Kaiser, is the best known of German expressionist dramatists in the English-speaking world. *Hoppla!* presents a satirical critique of a corrupt Weimar Republic through the efforts of Toller's ex-revolutionary hero to survive in the 'madhouse' of his world. Its stunning première, 3 September 1927, established its director, Erwin Piscator, as the leader of Germany's 'political theatre.' Lowry knew the play and was deeply moved to learn of Toller's suicide in New York on 22 May 1939; see his poem 'To Herr Toller, Who Hanged Himself' (Scherf, 106) and Lowry's 7 June 1947 letter (**305**) to Robert Pick.

129: To Arthur O. Lowry

P: UBC(ts,ms)

> 595 W. 19th Ave.,
> Vancouver, B.C.
> [March 1940]ª

My dear Dad:

There is a side of the moon always turned away from the earth, and this is like an attempt to get in touch from that quarter.

It is impossible by letter to cover all the territory I would like, and I shall not attempt to. An important letter for both of us, I shall try and confine myself to immediate essentials. First, let me say immediately re my proposed visit to the East, that I appreciate your position, your own attitude. To you, suffering the real dangers, the real privations of war, it must seem a trivial matter as to whether I am in Vancouver or Montreal or anywhere else. Briefly, without going into all its ramifications, you will consider (rightly) that I am lucky to be safe in Canada, to be provided for by your generosity. You have already been generous, even though it was too late, in giving me permission at all to return to the States to wind up my affairs. For this gesture I am truly grateful. Meanwhile, I perfectly see the objections to my going East on the grounds that later I might have to return, go East again, if and when I enter the States for a short period next September. On the face of it, this would seem an added, unnecessary expense. And finally, since I seem to be doing so well here, even though it is impossible to enlist, why shouldn't I stay here? It is with no intention of minimizing the validity of these reasons that I make my appeal. Very briefly the appeal is based on the fact, (and I give you my solemn oath upon this and upon all that follows) that my situation is not what it seems to be.[1] The people who are my guardians are not what they seem to be. One faction among them is violently pacifist. Another, Oxford Group. Another has another ism up his sleeve. Each think I should be working for them. I am no pacifist, I have no intention of ducking out of the war by any back door, for years I have been very anti-Hitler, and I have now grown to detest the Oxford Group. This Oxford Group faction denies it receives any profit from watching my so-called welfare. Another guardian (by going over accounts behind the other's back) discovers inalienable proof of such profit. One tells me something about himself which in my eyes disqualifies him for ever, not only as fit to be my guardian, but fit to be a man, which I must, being a gentleman, keep dark. Were Mr Parks (who, in good faith be it said, left me with people whom he had never met before in his life) [the arrangment is now four times removed from what it was originally i.e. Mr Parks was recommended to someone else who then recommended someonelse who ratified some else who finally had to deal with yet *someone else*]^b to come here, I would be bound, for instance, to defend both the person I am living with (because he has children and needs the money he is getting) and the other, the real villain of the piece, because, being dependent upon their administration of your funds for my bread and butter, I have to maintain some balance between the two, sometimes the three or four! Meantime my initiative and my self repect and, I fear, your respect for me, is being crushed by these people, all semblance of a normal self-respecting life with normal emotions is being destroyed by these humiliations. One guardian tells *me* actually to help another guardian, to bring him to God. The former's own son is a pacifist and a bum. Is there not a paradox here? It is not Mr Park's fault I admit, but it is not mine. I know now for certain that many of the reports you have had of me were false or misleading, but I have felt too bewildered to try and combat them since I did not know what they were till too late. Consequently I felt myself to be abandoned, allowed myself to sink into a state of despair. But even admitting my own foolishness I know in my heart that if you knew the truth you would not wish me placed in the position I am in. If I have won good reports here both from friends and enemies it is because I am sticking to my guns. But these guns are stuck to not because of, but in spite of my environment. I have never in my whole life lived in such noise and confusion, in such discordant undesirable confusion of every kind, nor was there ever more opportunity or excuse to drink. Please believe me when I say drink is a thing of the past. I have kept my head, shut my door, not drunk, worked like the very devil himself. I have to do it, for my own peace of mind, and because I have only one underlying principle in my mind: to make the very most of what months are left to me and prove myself to yourself and Mother. Apologies, explanations, are futile: tangible accomplishment is the only hope. In spite of losses, disappointments, follies, all these years I have been writing simultaneously on several books which I have partly described to Mother. It may be that I shall have now only a few months in which to bring to fruition the work of these years and now, that everything seems lost, it is doubly important to do so. But only a limited time in which to do it! If I could be near enough to Conrad so that he could come occasionally to see me and talk things over I could accomplish in weeks what it will take months to do here. I could be only a few hours distant and still in Canada. Mr Parks is 3 days distant from me.

And Conrad, being a real friend of many years, would be far more concerned about my welfare than these strangers. I need to do research work for the book I am dedicating to yourself – there is no library here worth mentioning.[c] There is a branch of my English publishers in Toronto with whom I am in communication.[2] It is important too to contact them personally. As to the extra fare; Conrad is in touch with people in Washington and may bring influence to bear so that I shall not have to return here to make my entry *if* I ever do, *if* there is no conscription, *if* the war stops. *You see, I may only have these six months and possibly less*! I would write, keep you both informed of my doings, and we could, even though at a distance, somehow, if we can bury the past, reestablish all our relationships on the sincere, decent happy plane on which they should be and which I have brought low through my inexperience and folly & through the slanders of other people. And this would make Mother happy! Which I want, yes, sincerely, above all! I am yelling at you over a thousand miles of mine-infested Atlantic and 4 thousand miles of land. *I am cooperating with you. Will you help? Drink, follies, are a thing of the past. (This is the last chance.)*

> With deep affection and respect,
> my Congratulations on your birthday

> [unsigned]

P.S. There is no threat here. I shall stick to my guns anyhow. The question is: will they stick to me? There is little chance of accomplishing what *you* desire unless things are changed. As for the fare, if I had to come back I shall probably be able to *make* it by that time, if Conrad keeps up his interest. He has made it perfectly clear to me what a responsibility I have to him. To show I have not been entirely idle, the enclosed.[3] You might send the verse to Punch, missing out the 'bleeding.' The article to Liverpool Echo. They are feeble but caused widespread approval and syndication, but I could not work regularly for the paper for the same reason I cannot take any employment here, I have no status. Besides, I have more serious work to do which will net more money in the long run. But they did make me – some months ago – $30. You might sell them in England, put it against my fare, should you give me permission or if not keep it to go east. I write this in the sincere belief that by compelling me to stay in Vancouver as I am you are defeating your ends and mine, and in the hope that the coherence and sanity of this letter, which I hope is proof of my state of mind, in spite of my disappointments, will cause you to see the whole thing in a clearer light and reverse your decision, without which reversal there is little hope, however much I try – and still I shall try – of keeping the near promises I have already made to Mother. I have committed much folly through youth, indiscretion, impetuousness, but all that is a thing of the past. Having gone so far to help me, when I did not deserve it, would you withdraw such help at the very moment when there is a chance for me to succeed and vindicate myself to you and myself.

Must I,[d] simply because I am not trusted myself, and am hence virtually incommunicado with you be forced, as I was at the beginning to live in the house of a man, one whose admission to me was that when married & with children, in the far east he had visited numerous brothels & had contracted Gonorrhea. I hate to have to tell you this & I do not want to tell you or anyone again about it but it must strike you as absurd that this is the type of man who should be appointed legislator of my conduct, my emotional complications, & my very soul itself, even if such a man has 'come to God since.' Although this is I hear the report you have had about me I am willing to swear in a court of law that this is as *true* of him as it is untrue of me. Concerning A.B. Carey, who is this man, I want to be fair to him & say, I do not, as another guardian has asserted believe him to be dishonest with money or knowingly, in any other way, as the above admission on his part is proof. But I do believe him to be self-deluded, & his conduct & attitude has shown time & again that he is pathetically depending on *my* help, not I on him, save in a superficial sense. This help, the reports of which doubtless reach you in the guise of 'my cooperation' for my 'rehabilitation' or some such absurdity, I freely gave but since one of his 'messages from God' has been to discourage me in my 'present work,' I have to call a halt.

Not all manifestations of the supernatural or of God in man are the result of paranoia, as I know myself, but in him that is probably what it is & his excursions in the East only too tragically would account for it. Like most such people he is superficially charming, & it reflects no discredit on Parks that he should have been fooled. I was too. Nor has my relationship with him been wholly bad since the outrageousness of the position he has placed me in has given me the guts to speak up to you about the whole matter. And here I want to state flatly that should anything go wrong with our future communications & for your own comfort, that the whole situation reflects very much less discredit in me than you think: if you can bring yourself to forgive what was only due to folly and hunger of life in the end, whcn you have understood the true nature of what I have kept back, and why, I feel that you must say 'Damn it all, he *was* my son after all.' But I do not want to make my explanation through my present sources or with the concomitant adulterations or perversions of my point of view that that might entail. Later. The enclosed letter speaks for itself.[4] The Governor General here was John Buchan the writer who had heard of me through Colonel Lawrence who admired my work before the latter died. Verification of this is in the list of Lawrence's library books in a book called 'Lawrence by his friends' which you can get anywhere.[5] He [Lord Tweedsmuir] was aware of much that I shall tell you in due course, & was going to help me when he died. I wish you would return the letter to whatever address I am at for I value it. If a man who was second only to the King could treat me lately as a personal friend encouraged me & admired my writing, (unknown of course to my 'guardians') would you countenance reports which still doubtless brand me as an incompetent, fit only for a drunkard's home & not to be trusted? It doesn't make sense. The connections Lord Tweedsmuir made for me out East still stand, of course, should I go there & have sufficient freedom to utilize them.[6]

Many congratulations sir, on your seventyeth, if you had not already received them from me.[7] How I regret sometimes not having more absorbed the wealth of great material that a closer friendship with you would have brought.

But perhaps it is not too late.

Your affectionate son

Malcolm

Annotations:

1 Lowry also described his situation during the fall of 1939 and the winter of 1940 in his 27 January 1940 letter (**124**) to Conrad Aiken.

2 The Canadian agent for Jonathan Cape between 1938 and 1942 was Nelson of Toronto, but they have no surviving record of any contact with Malcolm Lowry.

3 It is not clear which items Lowry sent to his father, but the following articles and poem had already been published in the *Vancouver Daily Province*: 'Hollywood and the War,' 12 December 1939, 4; 'The Real Mr Chips,' 13 December 1939, 4; 'Where did that One go to, 'Erbert?' 29 December 1939, 4 (poem).

4 John Buchan, first Baron Tweedsmuir (1875-1940), author, lawyer, politician, and governor general of Canada (1935-40), wrote Lowry a supportive letter late in 1939. According to Day (255-56), this was a letter of introduction to the managing editor of the *Vancouver Daily*

Province, and it included a cheque for fifty dollars, but unfortunately both Lowry's letter to Buchan and the reply described by Day have disappeared. However, see Appendix 2 for a letter to Lowry from Buchan that has survived. Lowry valued this letter, which he sent to Whit Burnett with the manuscript of *Under the Volcano* as a sort of reference letter (see letters **143** and **144**), but it was never returned to him, and he believed it to be lost.

5 See Lowry's 18 September 1939 letter (**114**) to Margerie Bonner.
6 In his 5 April 1940 reply (UBC 1:38) Arthur Lowry rejected Lowry's appeals and warned him against blaming others for his own mistakes. He did, however, offer some encouragement and support: 'I was very interested to read your articles and will endeavour to do as you request about getting them published here, also the nice letter from Lord Tweedsmuir, which I return and of which you should be proud, as indeed I am, they all confirm my view that if you will only keep on sticking to your guns all will be well.'
7 Lowry had already sent a greeting card.

Editorial Notes:

a. This date is in pencil in Margerie Lowry's writing, and the contents of the letter and the address confirm a late March date. In his 5 April 1940 reply to Lowry (UBC 1:38), his father answers him on several points, quoting Lowry's phrases, and this further confirms a March date. Day's 22 April 1940 date (274) is incorrect. The draft of this letter (UBC 1:79) consists of one sheet of single-spaced typescript on both sides with several marginal additions and insertions in pencil, plus a manuscript page, a fragment in Margerie's hand, and a half-page of typescript. Without the final copytext it is impossible to know what order Lowry intended to use for the various sections or even if all were to be included. I have followed the general structure of the text as typed, inserting material where indicated. Editorial intervention is explained as necessary.
b. The material in square brackets has been written by Lowry in the left margin and marked for insertion at this point. He had written 'Mr Parks was recommended to MacLean,' but he then crossed out the name and inserted '*someone else*' in superscript.
c. For insertion at this point Margerie has written in the margin: 'which book I feel would be a service to the Empire and the Allied cause.'
d. From this point to the complimentary close, I have had to reconstruct the letter from holograph, marginalia, and typed fragments.

130: To Conrad Aiken

P: H(ts)
PP: *LAL* 122

> 595 W. 19th Ave.,
> Vancouver, B.C.
> [March 1940]ᵃ

Dear old fellow:

Not melancholy Lowrys are we, but overjoyed at the sweetness of your letter, which has mitigated our bitter disappointment.

If all blows up, including the world, I shall cherish as long as I live that wise sensitiveness which informed what you said at this bad time. It means more than I can say and more than I have said. We continue also to be unable to express our appreciation of what you and Mary have done and are doing on our behalf![1]

Lately I wrote a pretty good letter to my mater who seems pro my going to be under your Eye, and this, coupled with your letter, may still do the trick, change the O.M.'s mind. Also I wrote the O.M., sanely, sobersidedly, emphasising the practical importance of going east anyhow.

Meantime, we work with renewed vigor upon the Volcano. Elsewhere, also, are volcanoes.

Am looking forward tremendously to reading the Conversation.[2]

Paris change, mais rien de ma mélancholie, s'a bougé . . .[3] Very pretty, but not true, in our case. The ship sails on.

> Love zu haus zu haus.[4]
>
> Malc

Annotations:

1 In his 7 March 1940 letter, beginning 'My dear defrauded longsuffering Malc,' Aiken describes his efforts with Arthur Lowry and Benjamin Parks, and Mary's, through her mother, to extricate Lowry from his Vancouver volcanoes.

2 Aiken's *Conversation: Or Pilgrim's Progress* was published in 1940.

3 Lowry is quoting from Charles Baudelaire's 'Le Cygne,' in 'Les Tableaux parisiens,' *Les Fleurs du mal*: 'Paris change! mais rien dans ma mélancolie / N'a bougé!' (Paris changes . . . But in sadness like mine / nothing stirs –). *Les Fleurs du mal*, trans. Richard Howard (Boston: David R. Godine, 1982), p. 269.

4 *Zu Hause* in German means 'at home,' but presumably Lowry intends to send love from 'house to house.'

1 Malcolm Lowry seated at a small writing table in the back garden of Inglewood, ca 1914.

2 Malcolm with his father, Arthur Lowry, on vacation at the Isle of Man, summer 1920.

3 Malcolm on holiday with his family in Guernsey, 1923.

4 Malcolm Lowry (back row, centre) as Percy in *Tilly of Bloomsbury* at the Leys, March 1926.

5 *(below left)* The Leys School, Cambridge, 1925. 'West House' is in the south-east corner of Back quad.

6 *(below right)* W. H. Balgarnie, master at the Leys from 1900 to 1930, was the model for Mr Chips in James Hilton's novel *Goodbye Mr Chips* (1934).

7 Lowry's family home, Inglewood, at Caldy, Cheshire, on the Wirral Peninsula.

8 Malcolm playing his 'taropatch' in the garden at Inglewood, 1932.

9 Malcolm Lowry with fellow
students on the lawn behind
Charlotte and J. B. S. Haldane's
home, Roebuck House,
Cambridge, 1932. From left
to right: William Empson,
J. L. Cowan, Lowry, Ronald
Burghes (Charlotte's son),
unknown, Charlotte Haldane,
Robert Lazarus.

10 St Catharine's College,
Cambridge, from the front gate.

11 Ed Burra, Clarissa Lorenz, Malcolm Lowry, and Conrad Aiken at breakfast in the Pension Carmona, Granada, Spain, ca May 1933.

12 Conrad Aiken and Malcolm Lowry in the Generalife Gardens at the Alhambra, Granada, Spain, ca May 1933.

13 Malcolm Lowry and Jan Gabrial Lowry in Cuernavaca, Mexico, early July 1937.

14 Nordahl Grieg, ca 1940–42 *(left)*.

15 James Stern, ca 1950 *(below left)*.

16 John Davenport, ca 1950 *(below)*.

17-20 Carol Phillips, Los Angeles 1939 *(top left)*; Malcolm Lowry, Los Angeles, spring 1939 *(top right)*; Margerie Bonner, ca 1939 *(bottom left)*; Jan Gabrial, ca 1946 *(bottom right)*.

21 A.B. Carey, ca 1935.

22 Malcolm Lowry and
Margerie Bonner,
Vancouver, October 1939.

Editorial Notes:

a. On the typescript of this letter in the Aiken collection at the Huntington, someone has inserted a date – [April] 1940 – at the top left corner. Internal references suggest, however, an earlier date, probably mid-March; see annotation 1.

131: To Conrad Aiken

P: H(ts)
PP: *LAL* 123

> 595 W. 19th Ave.,
> Vancouver, B.C.
> 20 March 1940

Just a mumbling word sending you both the best of our loves and the very best of luck with *The Conversation*!

May it have as triumphant a voyage as the Queen Elizabeth, dodging all torpedoes from submarines of mean reviewers on both sides of the Atlantic and coming to rest gloriously in the Pier 16 of the best seller list! May it be *un*like the Queen Elizabeth only in passing unnoticed (and of course in being unfinished. This Queen Elizabeth analogy is getting us into trouble but it means well!) and may it receive a symphony of acclaim from friends and enemies alike! Which we know it will deserve!

In short: THE VERY BEST OF LUCK!

(Here:

> Ott flies to Dimaggio,
> Rippla pops to Dimaggio,
> Mcmathy flies to Dimaggio, –
> No runs, no hits, no errors.)[1]

Malc & Margie

Annotations:

1 Lowry's little jingle uses the names of real baseball players: Joe Dimaggio played for the New York Yankees (1936-51) and Melvin Ott for the New York Giants (1926-47). 'Rippla' may be a reference to Jimmy Ripple who played for several National and American League teams, but 'Mcmathy' remains a mystery.

132: To Mary Aiken

P: H(pcard)
PP: *LAL* 124

[Vancouver, B.C.]
[23 March 1940]ᵃ

> Portrait of Atlantis!
> Or some new patterns for one's
> Spring suiting!
>   God bless you.

Malcolm

Editorial Notes:

a. This postcard, postmarked 23 March 1940, shows a black and white photograph, taken at a distance, of the long masonry halls of one of the palace-like structures at Mitla, which is about forty kilometres southwest of Oaxaca in Mexico. Mitla, constructed during the thirteenth century, was a centre of Zapotec culture and worship, and its name means 'Place of the Dead.' The halls, as well as many walls, are covered with geometric stonework mosaics that create intricate arabesques based on the step and fret motif, set into red stucco.

133: To Conrad Aiken

P: H(ts)
PP: *LAL* 125-29

595 W. 19th Ave.,
Vancouver, B.C.
9 April 1940

Dear old bird:
  – awful sorry to hear of your reverses – yours and Mary's – so here is a letter, & a funny pome out of another existence, to cheer you up.
  It seems to me that these oaves of reviewers must have some grudge agin you. As though you had wounded some of these little men on their amour propres in bygone years. Else why is it you so often get stupid reviews, but what has been unfavorably reviewed never fails to get mentioned in the same paper a couple of years later by someone younger as a masterpiece? Which it proves to be.
  Anyhow, I think that you're one of the five living greatest writers

and most other people do too, to whom literature is not merchandise, and that's the kind of opinion that matters in the long run, though I sez it myself. Not always, damn it, to the purse, though probably, in the long run, to that too.

I read a more or less favourable but somewhat petty review in *Time*.[1]

By the way, might I very humbly and penitently ask if I may borrow a copy of *The Conversation*? We don't have enough money to buy it at the moment; libraries sometimes take 3 months to get a book from U.S. But I really *mean* borrow. Would return it definitely in a few weeks (if you can begin to believe me in these days). Later, when have enough money will buy it. I do not want to put you on the spot of feeling either after I have asked that you cannot very well refuse, etc. (And here may I go on record as apologising for not, those years back, acknowledged the Preludes and Osiris. The impertinence of this makes me now want to go and drown myself slowly in the nearest pool. But it was not maliciousness or anything else. I was merely tight, Conrad, just tight.)

I am on the last chapter of Volcano – a strange book and I think it makes an odd but splendid din. It is the first book of mine that is not in one way or another parasitic on your work. (This time it is parasitic however on some of your wisecracks in Mexico, & upon your political opinions! Poor Malc.)

If you remember at the time you said you didn't mind about this: in fact we both decided that it would be good fun for both of us to do a book about Mexico and see what came of it.[2] But apart from the wisecracks, the 'character' is not yourself. Nevertheless, I thought I would ask to be absolved in advance for any 'coincidences.'[3] The trouble is, you see, that this particular character gets – er – pushed over a ravine. (There is a horrendous real coincidence in connection with this for the day after I'd written that scene for the first time in Mexico, a man was shot and pushed over a ravine in exactly the same way, by name, William Erickson. My character was at that time named William Erickson, the same name as the guy in In Ballast.) Strange psychological goings on, here, I admit, but I do want to come to my own rescue by denying that while making pretty speeches to you with one hand I was at the same time engaged in shoving you down the ravine with the other. No, Conrad, the truth is the guy who goes down the ravine, disguised in dark glasses and a false beard, is partly myself, partly the little ghost of what was once bad between us, bad about me. There is also a bit of Margie's father, a bit of the guy who introduced Margie and I,[4] and a bit of you, to account for the good parts. And of course the wise cracks the opinions (and how right most of them were!) an incident with my cat (I made him love cats for a dramatic reason) I had to make the ghost an amusing fellow after all. But in a state of reconciliation with the burden of the mystery greater than I have ever reached I just wished to while reiterating my deep love for you – and I want you to know that I *mean* it – to ask you sincerely to regard any apparent similarities or NUANCES with the fatherly twinkle, and for the rest, with a detached psychological amusement. I could hardly write this letter were it not all right with me. Also for the rest, damn it, there *are* some similarities I can't help. The conflicts of divorce, conflicts of soul torn between England and America, the setting of Mexico itself, all these things are mine too; my anguishes and such, while again, my ancient doppelganger, I am, deep down in my psyche – if you will not be offended at my saying so – damned like you. My consciousness has not the intensity of yours and it has been a long laborious process teaching it to be tractable and work at all, but I'm surprised at the amount that is really there, waiting to be mined. Poetry, I believe too: some gold, less tin than I thought. But some of the processes of metallurgy are startlingly and *naturally* like yours: and this I can't help, and would not if I could.

But what I can and could do was to write a book which put down my own reflection of the moon in my own real broken bottle. And I think I have done.

This book is also as it were a gesture on the part of a grateful pupil to his master.

I have not written a single scene without first of all submitting it, as it were, to the Aiken microscope. That microscope has detected some faults, which will still probably be in when I send you the book, but not so many as usual. And finally, as I approach the end, it was with a sense of triumph – many things contribute to this. I feel, for instance, that it is the sort of book you would want me to write, that, in a sense also, it is a completion of the Bridge which Hart Crane did not finish.[5] And moreover it has been written under I think as horrible conditions as any book that has ever been written, and I do not except books written in prison, reformatories, cork lined rooms, ships or front line trenches. The mixture of physical discomfort, noise and gnawing anxiety that at one moment one would have to stop, or that we would be separated, produced something unique in abhorrent conditions. And out of all this effort, together with the letters we tossed to and fro, much, it seems has bloomed. Margie and I have really discovered something so real, that although we have not left our one attic room at all in the last months, that we feel we can laugh at everybody. And although you and I haven't gotten anywhere with the O.M., at least not yet, I feel much has been resolved between us which is purely good, in that grand effort you made on our behalf, in my endeavor to show you too, that at heart I was a loyal and sincere friend, with all of which the completion of the book in its present form, the pattern of our own lives, has something mysteriously to do. Excuse this portentousness, but I feel it to be so.

Margie has also written a detective novel (she scrapped an earlier version the plot of which was snaffled by Ben Ames Williams)[6] which, when cut a bit, will be damned good. It really does hold your interest and speculation to the very end and, in my opinion, it should sell. Anyhow, it's a definite professional and good piece of work in its own genre: and excellently constructed. Do you know anybody who might be interested?

And by the way, some time ago before you interested Lindscott [Robert Linscott] in it, I promised Whit Burnett, who now has the Story Press amalgamated with Lippincott, to submit the Volcano to him. What would you advise me to do? Anyhow, I shall send you a copy first before I do anything. But you might advise me meantime as to the ethics of this matter.

Please convey our sympathies again to Mary, to whom a letter goes on same post and here's hoping you'll be on your feet again soon, and that the reviews will pick up. The very last of my book offers stubborn resistance. Truly, as someone said, 'our books detest us.'[7]

Both our loves

Malc

You said you were staying at Commonwealth Av. till 8th. This is 9th, so we send it to S. Dennis.

[poem enclosed with letter (Scherf, 63)]

> The doom of each, said Doctor Usquebaugh,
> Quite clearly bids our loutish bones to stare.
> True, drink's unfruitful on a larger scale;
> Its music is an equinoctial gale:
> Still, unembarrassing: and, profounder,
> Outwinds the range of Cupid's organ grinder.
> If worms are sabattical in a drunkard's dream
> No fouler's this than love's nocturnal game,
> Since dream of love it is, love of the pit
> For its own sake, the virginity of the present,
> Whose abyss is a womb shall not deny

A wintry plunge to nescient ecstasy,
Unsheathed entrance to the spirit's Tarquin,
But featherless and free from overt din,
Extending a plattered Lucrece with ferment,
Yet deeper than she, and rich with moist consent.
So well might we inquire, content to rot,
What do you offer, love, which drink does not?

Annotations:

1 'Books,' *Time*, 25 March 1940: 97.
2 By the time of Lowry's letter, Aiken had written a novel loosely based on his 1937 trip to Mexico: *A Heart for the Gods of Mexico* (London: Martin Secker, 1939).
3 According to Margerie Lowry, the Consul was based largely upon Aiken (*Malcolm Lowry Remembered*, 133), and Lowry had put some of his arguments with Aiken, during their time together in Cuernavaca in 1937, into chapter 10 of *Volcano*.
4 This was Jack Garnet Wolsley King, Lowry's English friend who was staying at the Normandie Hotel in Hollywood in the spring of 1939.
5 Hart Crane (1899-1932) published *The Bridge* in 1930. While critics like Ivor Winters described it as lacking in integration, Crane compared it to Eliot's *Waste Land* in structure and unity; see *The Letters of Hart Crane, 1916-1932*, ed. Brom Weber (Berkeley: University of California Press, 1952), p. 350.
6 Ben Ames Williams (1889-1953), American journalist and novelist, was the author of a number of detective stories. Margerie was working on *The Last Twist of the Knife*, which appeared in 1946.
7 In his 5 July 1946 letter (**229**) to Albert Erskine, Lowry attributes this remark to Jean Cocteau. However, his source for Cocteau's comment is almost certainly Julien Green in his *Personal Record: 1928-1939*, trans. Jocelyn Godefroi (New York: Harper, 1939), a book Lowry knew well. Reflecting upon the uneasy feeling his current novel caused him, Green writes: 'This has reminded me of a curious remark which was made by Cocteau in my presence some time ago: "Our books detest us"' (297).

Lowry had other literary agents during his life (Innes Rose in London, Ann Watkins in New York), but Harold Matson was his chief agent and a friend. Although they first met in New York as early as 1935, no letters from the thirties appear to have survived. Judging from the tone of this 16 April 1940 letter, however, Lowry is picking up a correspondence and a relationship from where he had left them on some previous occasion. Relations with

Matson were not always smooth. Lowry doubted that Matson ever cared much for Under the Volcano, *and by the fifties Matson was leaving most of the firm's correspondence with the Lowrys to his assistant. But letters between the two men are always cordial, and Lowry was grateful for Matson's financial and professional support.*

134: To Harold Matson

P: Matson(ts); UBC(phc)

> Dollarton P.O.,
> Dollarton, B.C.,
> Canada
> 16 April 1940

Dear Hal:[1]

Herewith a story I hope you will like and I hope it has a market.[2]

I thought Esquire or Decision or somebody might take it. I worked very hard on it – thought perhaps it was even firstrateish??

Margerie Bonner has finished her new mystery for you and is trying it out on a friend before sending it.[3] Meantime, she is redoing the parts of the Last Twist of the Knife Virginia Stong kindly suggested might benefit by recasting.[4]

So I, we, are still here. But this is by the way. You'll get Margerie Bonner's mystery then, and a revised Under the Volcano, soon. Mexico, I see, couldn't wait for its publication before erupting.[5]

> Yours ever,
>
> Malcolm

Annotations:

1 Harold Matson (1898-1988) was Lowry's literary agent and friend from the mid-thirties until Lowry's death, and the Harold Matson Agency represented Lowry's work until 1979, when Harold Matson's nephew, Peter Matson, left the agency, taking Lowry's file with him to Sterling Lord Literistic. Harold Matson, who had been in the literary agency business in New York since 1932, opened his own business in 1938, and during his long career he represented such writers as Evelyn Waugh, Arthur Koestler, William Saroyan, and Herman Wouk. According to Jan Gabrial (*Malcolm Lowry Remembered*, 99), Lowry acquired Matson as his agent during 1935, when they were living in New York. His first agent in the United States had been Ann Watkins, but for reasons that are not entirely clear Lowry preferred Matson. When Margerie Bonner Lowry needed an agent to handle her fiction in early 1940, Lowry encouraged her to use Matson.

2 It is not clear which story Lowry enclosed with this letter. 'The Last Address' and 'June 30th, 1934!' were not ready for submission until later in the year.

3 Lowry may be referring to *The Shapes That Creep*, which was published by Scribner's in 1946, the same year as *The Last Twist of the Knife*.

4 Virginia Swain Stong (1899–1968) was an American novelist, editor, and reporter. See Lowry's 30 November 1940 letter (**157**) to Aiken for Stong's reaction to the revised novel.

5 Lowry must be thinking of the labour unrest in the Mexican petroleum industry, which increased in the early months of 1940. After President Cárdenas moved to nationalize the Mexican oil industry in 1938, and as a result of declining exports during the early years of the war, the industry required reorganization, which necessitated restrictions on labour. This led to costly strikes, political unrest, and the importation of stocks of munitions during the months leading up to the 7 July 1940 presidential election.

135: To Mrs. Anna Mabelle [John Stuart] Bonner

P: UBC(ts)
PP: *SL* 26–27

595 W. 19th Ave.,
Vancouver, B.C.
16 April 1940

My dear Mrs Bonner:

A line to thank you for the very interesting cuttings! Since receiving them, however, Denmark and Norway have been invaded,[1] even now some other crisis is brewing, so that since many of the political speculations in the cuttings are now fact, I will not discuss them.

As for those which deal with enlarging the frontiers of the mind, with immortality – these are subjects that have always interested me. I have always believed that that which impedes the motion of thought is false and that we probably do not use in daily life more than a fraction of our true capabilities. Have you read any of Dunne – 'An Experiment With Time' is a rewarding book if you have not.[2] And Ouspensky. 'A New Model of the Universe' which aims, among other things, to base eternal recurrence upon scientific fact is a terifically exciting book, even if you do not agree with it. Also his 'Tertium Organum.'[3] (He generally appears on the library cards under 'U', i.e., Uspensky.)

And a neglected, but exciting American writer, whose specialty is the analysis of peculiar coincidences for which there exists no scientific explanation, is Charles Fort, particularly for the three books, 'Lo!' 'The Book of the Damned' and 'Wild Talents'. I look upon the day I first hit upon 'Lo!' in a public library as a red letter day in my life. I know of no writer who has made the inexplicable seem more dramatic than Charles Fort.[4]

I try to learn about astronomy from Margie and I am getting along slowly. But the little I have absorbed so far has very much enriched my work.

As for the mysterious heads from Tabasco[5] – yes, here is something else which fascinates and torments me. I have before me as I write a folder of the Compania Mexicana de Aviacion which informs me that it is possible to fly from Mexico City to Yucatan and back for 331 pesos and 8 centavos. With the peso at 5 for a dollar this makes it only about $60. I sit here with this folder peering, as it were with a telescope, at Mayan ruins, at wonderful names such as Chichén Itzá, Tekax, Izamal, Sayi [Sayil], and when I walk about I walk on the white hot plough shares of lost opportunities, for when I was in Mexico I did not, for some obscure reason, visit, Itza, Tekax and so on. (I did however, live in Oaxaca for a time, among the ruins of Monte Alban and Mitla, which you find mentioned in Donnely's book on Atlantis.[6] My friends the Oaxaquēnian students would occasionally promote private excavation parties, which they called 'scratching the land.' One day while 'scratching the land' we came across a man, petrified in lava. How old he was I don't know but he certainly was not an ancient image or idol. When we tried to pick him up his head fell off. The rest had become so inextricably a part of the rock that we had to leave it. I shall never forget going back to Oaxaca at sunset, the natives triumphantly carrying the head before us. I told this to Jack[7] and he wouldn't believe me, and now, I must admit, I scarcely believe it myself.)

Margie and I are just finishing a long novel of mine about Mexico, 1/10 of a million words we have written since January. Put like that, it sounds a lot.

After this we are going to revise one of Margie's detective stories 'Dark Rendezvous'[8] which I feel is excellent and certainly saleable, if I think, directed to the right quarter.

Margie is well and happy.

Thank you again for sending me the cuttings which I always look forward to.

Yours sincerely,

Malcolm

Annotations:

1 The Nazis invaded Denmark and Norway on 9 April 1940.
2 J.W. Dunne's *An Experiment with Time* (London: Faber and Faber, 1927) was an important book for Lowry, despite his disclaimers to Matson about Martha Foley's criticism of the early 'Under the Volcano'; see his 12 October 1940 letter (**153**) to Matson.
3 P.D. Ouspensky first published *A New Model of the Universe* in English translation in 1931 and *Tertium Organum: A Key to the Enigmas of the World* in 1920.
4 Margerie gave Lowry a copy of *The Books of Charles Fort* (New York: Henry Holt, 1941) for their wedding anniversary on 2 December 1953.
5 Mrs Bonner's letter to Lowry has not survived, so it is impossible to confirm this reference to 'mysterious heads from Tabasco.' It is likely, however, that Lowry is thinking of the colossal Olmec sculptures of heads in the Tabasco Museum and the Archaeological Park.
6 Ignatius Donnelly's *Atlantis: The Antediluvian World* (New York: Harper Brothers, 1882) was an important study of the lost civilization of Atlantis. The book (and its author) play a significant, if minor role in *Under the Volcano*.
7 Lowry probably means Jack Garnet Wolsley King.
8 'Dark Rendezvous' was an early title for Margerie's novel *The Last Twist of the Knife*; see her 12 October 1940 letter to Harold Matson (Margerie Lowry Papers, UBC 51:2).

⌒

'He may be a little bit drunk but he's not disorderly.' This is how James Stern described Lowry, whom he discovered in the winter of 1933-34 lying on the floor of a Paris bistro in rue Daguerre with a guitar slung across his chest. The two men became instant friends and drinking companions, but the friendship was based on mutual respect and a shared love of writing, which provided the main subject of their intermittent correspondence over the coming years. Stern (see photograph 15) was one of the first of Lowry's old friends to congratulate him on Under the Volcano, *and he was one of the few friends whom Lowry wanted to see during the difficult period at The White Cottage, 1956-57. In his last extant letter (**653**) to Stern, Lowry urges him to visit and warns him not to be put off – 'as my other friends seem to be' – by the 'rumour' that there is nothing to drink in the Lowry house but Cydrax!*

136: To James Stern

P: Texas(ts)

> 595 W. 19th Ave.,
> Vancouver, B.C.,
> Canada
> 24 April 1940[a]

Dear Jimmy:[1]

What the hell? So you are in New York. The other day I was taking a stroll up Little Mountain here, and noticing a boy climbing down a quarry I thought of your excellent story called, I think, 'A Sunday Morning,' where the boy climbs down the cliff instead of going with 'them girrrls,' and then can't get back again. Two days later, in a dentist's waiting room, I read again 'The Man Who Was Loved,' in Esquire, and even took the copy away with me to read it yet again, when I learned that you were in America. Well, and how are you? Damn it all, it's really good to hear news of you. I would give much to see your face again. I heard you were married, happily I hope. For myself, I have been happily divorced. A long, gay story. And hope to be married again next October.

I haven't the slightest idea what I'm doing in Vancouver – at the moment it is impossible to enlist. My passion for rushing headlong into the field, like Byron's Duke of Brunswick, and foremost fighting falling,[2] has somewhat cooled during this difficult period of waiting for the recruiting offices to open. One lives too in poverty, and worst of all, that part of my finances which is still flowing has got into the hands of the Oxford Group.

We do not know what we shall do in the future (that is, myself and Margerie, who steer close to the wind here) *but I have written what I believe to be a really good novel during these last few months – there are three others too, as yet unsold –* and it may be that next September I shall apply to enter the States for a while and wind up my affairs – I cannot apply before next September – at which time I very much hope to see you.

By the by, (and just to put a stop to the idea that this is one of those rare letters in which the writer is not trying to get something out of one,) I have one very long short story, called *The Last Address*, which is the best thing I've yet written, except parts of this last novel. I have to do a bit of rewriting on it, but I was wondering if I sent it to you, when this was done, if you could possibly send it along to *Esquire*, with a recommendation of some sort, which might charm them, as it were, into taking it?

Every short story I have written – there are not very many, but still – has either made O'Brien or his honour list, and this together with what you say – that is, if you like it – might influence them to take it. It would be a great help to me if they would because I very much want to move east, which this might enable me to do.

All the very best, for the 'sake of new times,' as you once inscribed in 'The Heartless Land' to me.[3]

Malcolm Lowry

P.S. I sent these few poems as an afterthought, wondering if I could beg the favour of your sending these to Esquire for me too first, if you think they stand any chance. This might expedite their publishing the story later. I would, of course, pay you an agent's percentage. It seems to me that an unsolicited manuscript stands damned little chance of being even looked at coming from this neck of the woods, & that is why I ask you this kind favour. Moreover these may be the last months of freedom etc I shall have & I should not like to leave without leaving some mark & so on & forth.

Annotations:

1 James Stern (1904-93), was an Anglo-Irish short story writer, translator, and author of the short story collection *The Heartless Land* (1932). For Stern's reminiscences of Lowry, see *Malcolm Lowry Remembered* and his essay 'Malcolm Lowry: A First Impression,' *Encounter* 29, 3 (1967): 58-68.
2 Lowry is referring to canto 3, stanza 23 of Byron's *Childe Harold's Pilgrimage*. See also his joking reference to Byron's Duke in a 1933 letter (**42**) to Tom Forman.
3 Lowry's original copy of Stern's *The Heartless Land* does not appear to have survived. In New York, on 19 February 1947, publication day for *Under the Volcano*, Stern inscribed another copy of his story collection for his friend as follows: 'The last copy, for my oldest & best friend Malcolm Lowry on the day of his Great Birth, & to Margie for the sake of Human Imagination & the Newest Times.'

Editorial Notes:

a. The original typescript has been signed in black ink but carries an addendum to the postscript, underlining in the third paragraph, and a few typographical corrections, all in pencil. The poems mentioned in the postscript are no longer extant with this letter.

137: To Conrad Aiken

P: H(ts)
PP: *LAL* 130-32

> 595 W. 19th Ave.,
> Vancouver, B.C.
> 24 April 1940

Dear Conrad:

I hope that by now Mary convalesces happily, that all is well with yourself too, with both yourselves.

For *ourselves*, we are well and still holding our oasis in the desert of nightmares. *Under the Volcano* only needs two or three weeks more polishing and then will be finished. Apart from that, extraordinary, and possibly marvelous news! Marie Proctor, the Head of the Immigration Board at Seattle, Washington, through whom my application had to go to Washington D.C., has written to me to say that I do *not* have to come back to Vancouver if I go east – I can make my application anywhere in Canada, only *she* will forward the papers of the case to whatever port is convenient to me thirty days before next September 23, which will expedite my entry.

This would seem to indicate, since Parks had told me and the old man that my application had to be made through Blaine, – near Vancouver – that he has manipulated all this so that I would be kept here for his own ends. Even A.B. Carey was amazed at this and said he thought you and my father should be immediately informed!

What I have done, however, is to send the original of the letter, by clipper, to my father, and a copy to Parks, which gives him the sporting chance to save his face by cabling the old man and so getting his news in first, now that he sees he is on the spot. Otherwise, my fear is that my father and he – for the sake of preserving the unimpeachableness of authority – will cook up something like the form master and the uncle did in Thoma's story . . .[1] (Both the form master and the boy's uncle had it in for the boy who had come to the school with a 'bad character.' One day the boy asked the uncle to do a sum for him. To save his face and with much grumbling the uncle did the sum. When the boy got the sum back from the form master it was covered with red ink. 'Only a donkey would do it like that,' said the form master, and gave him detention. 'But I only copied it from my uncle,' said the boy. 'You're a liar,' said the form master. For this detention the boy then got a hiding from the uncle. 'But' he protested to the uncle, 'It was your fault for not doing it right.' The form master said: 'Only a donkey would do it the way you did it.'

'You're a liar,' said the uncle and gave him another hiding. Later the uncle and the form master were seen talking together. The next day the form master sent for the boy and said: 'I have had another look at your sum and it is quite right, only it is done an old fashioned way, a way we don't use nowadays. But you thoroughly deserve to be kept in just the same, for your insubordination. Anyway, you did not even copy the sum correctly from your uncle.' But the boy had exactly copied the sum. Later the uncle wrote to the boy's mother to say that he should not be expected to receive any more help from him since he could not even copy things down correctly and that this put him in a false position . . .)

Anyhow, there it is, Conrad. There is nothing for the world now to prevent my coming east, if the old man will only see eye to eye on the subject.

So, it may be that the O.M. will cable you – probably making all sorts of untenable provisos.

I know full well that you can't and do not expect you to do anything about us while Mary is sick and yourself seedy and I am anxious about that for your own sake, not for ours. You may take the philosophical viewpoint about an operation, but they are beastly things nevertheless and our sympathies are deeply with you.

I feel in the face of this a heel for even mentioning our problems. But I suppose I better had. It appears that June 1 is our approximate deadline. The Maurice Carey's plan to let this house at that time anyhow and a reshuffle of some sort then is inevitable. If we cannot go east by then it will of course be tough on us. Nothing else seems to have changed, save for the better.

I received, a week ago, a very kindly letter from the O.M., in which he demurred from my going east purely on the grounds that it would cost too much (presumably for me to go east, come back here, proceed east once more). So I have presented him with the new evidence, and once more one must wait. I assured him, and I meant what I said, that I wanted to give him some satisfaction in me at last about my work, that I was nearing proof of this, but that some closer contact with you was essential. As for Margie – if this were simply a frivolous love affair, or even just a love affair – or even if it were solely 'love' – I think I might hesitate to ask you still to count us 'als einer'[2] without first obtaining ratification from the O.M., etc. But Margie, apart from anything else, is now so absolutely inextricable from my work that I can't get along without her from this point of view alone, and were I to be separated from her I could not keep the promises about my work I have made both to the O.M. and to you! Meantime we have written something which I feel might compare not unfavourably with Kafka's 'The Trial'. It costs no more for us both to live than one alone, we are uncomplicated by expecting any children, we are not even married, yet, – so what?

Could you not lend me 'The Conversation' – blast ye – if I return it? I shall buy it when I can.

All our very best loves to you both.

Malcolm

Annotations:

1 Ludwig Thoma (1867-1921) was a German novelist, short story writer, dramatist, and essayist. Lowry is closely paraphrasing, at times quoting, from the story 'Uncle Franz,' translated by Basil Creighton in W. Somerset Maugham's collection of stories *Tellers of Tales: 100 Short Stories from the United States, England, France, Russia and Germany* (New York: Doubleday, Doran, 1939), pp. 509-11. 'Uncle Franz' was first published in Thoma's *Lausbubengeschichten* (1905).
2 *Als einer* is German for 'as one.'

138: To James Stern
p: Texas(ts)
pp: *SL* 27-31

595 W. 19th Ave.,
Vancouver, B.C.
7 May 1940

Dear Jimmy:

Jeeze, it was certainly good to hear from you and to think you've been in this hemisphere a year without my knowing it! I really caracoled on receiving your letter and am truly glad you made a happy marriage. You are one of the very best short story writers we have so I know you will never stop writing so long as you have a pen. I sympathise with you about novel writing though. There is no, as it were, satisfactory design-governing posture for a true short story writer, and I can understand how, difficult to please as to form, you kick at the amorphousness of the thing. So the short story writer (like Tchechov) wanders around graveyards thinking it is no go. It is probably not that you can't write a good novel but that no novel suggests to you that you want to go and do likewise. Nevertheless it seems to me that a writer like you would produce the best kind of novel, that is the shortish one perfect in itself, and without being full of inventories (like Joyce) or poems (like Faulkner) or conjunctions (like Hemingway) or quotations from quotations from other novels (like me, 7 years ago). It is possible to compose a satisfactory work of art by the simple process of writing a series of good short stories, complete in themselves, with the same characters, interrelated, correlated, good if held up to the light, watertight if held upside down, but full of effects and dissonances that are impossible in a short story, but nevertheless having its purity of form, a purity that can only be achieved by the born short story writer. Well, all that is as may be. (And I don't mean the kind of novel, written by not quite true poets, such as The Hospital, by Kenneth Fearing, or the Seven Who Fled by Prokosch,[1] in which the preoccupation with form vitiates the substance: that is by a writer whose inability to find a satisfactory form for his poems drives him to find an outlet for it in a novel where the underlying disorder of his mind can have fuller play. No. The thing that I mean can only be done by a good short story writer, who is generally the better kind of poet, the one who only does not write poetry because life does not frame itself kindly for him in iambic pentameters and to whom disjunct experimental forms are abhorrent; such a man probably will end up anyhow by being a poet, in the manner of the later Yeats, but meantime, my thesis is that he is capable of writing the best kind of novel, something that is bald and winnowed like Sibelius, and that makes an odd but splendid din, like Bix Beiderbecke.[2] But that is all by the way and my God what brackish bilge is this on a cold posthumous Monday anyhow!)

Yeah, I know David Reeves.[3] I found him sitting on my doorstep the day I was married and he seemed to know his way around my apartment better than I did. Nice fellow though; good on the flute too. Also experienced: had been a Volga boatman and had hopped on one foot from Sofia to Jerusalem, to die at the foot of the weeping cross.[4] That sort of thing. His brother, poet J.M., loathed me at Cambridge for three years.[5] I remember Peggy Lippe, Brock – where is Brock? – et al, with varying nostalgias. Poor Rollo in Gibraltar – well, God somehow bless them.[6] As for me, my life since last seeing you has been a sort of mixture of Manon Lescaut and Crime and Punishment.[7] I was thrown for a time, in Mexico, as a spy, into durance vile, by some fascistas in Oaxaca – (by mistake, they were after another guy. How it arose was; – he was a friend of mine, very sober and a communist, and they could not believe, because he was sober, that he was an agitator, and therefore thought he must be me, who was not sober, but, nevertheless, not an agitator, not a communist.) – I subsequently found it difficult to explain why I absolutely had to be drawing a map of the Sierra Madre in tequila on the bar counter sole reason was, I liked the shape of them. Jan had left me some months before so I had no alibis and the other guy quit the town. On Christmas day they let out all the prisoners except me. Myself, I had the Oaxaquenian third degree for turkey. Hissed they (as Time would say): 'you say you a wrider but we read all your wridings and dey don't make sense. You no a wrider, you an espider and we shoota de espiders in Mejico.' But it was an improving experience. For instance I learned the true derivation of the word stool pigeon. A stool pigeon is one who sits at stool all day in prison and inveigles political prisoners into conversation, then conveys messages about them. If he's lucky, he gets a bit of buggery thrown in on the side. So simple, but to think that I might have lived my life without knowing to what heights humanity could rise. They tried to castrate me too, one fine night, unsuccessfully, I regret (sometimes) to report. It ended up with a sort of Toulouse-Lautrec scene, myself, gaolers and all, simply walking, roaring with mescal, out into the night. They are looking for me yet.

We are living the most god awful existence here compared with which my dungeon in Mexico (compared with which in turn I may say the Chateau 'd'if's are simply as sunny rooms in a cottage by the sea,) is a mere picnic. Some people in the Oxford Group have been made trustees for my money after my numerous mishaps in one part of the globe and another, and they don't let me have any of it for myself. Margie is not supposed to be here at all and our landlord blackmails me about her so if I could sell a few things it might well save our lives. At any rate, we have been working like hell, Margie has turned out very much to be the right gal, and being both partially screwy of course, we should be sunk without each other. To make matters worse, what driblets of money there are for our blackmailer's rent threatens to be cut off. I already had some contact with [Bernice] Baumgarten through Conrad Aiken but she found what I had too cerebral and unsaleable. But the work I have been doing and am continuing to do is different. So, Jimmy, the odd honeyed word, the diplomatic smile on your part, to some George Davis[8] here, some editor of Esquire there, might be our salvations, which with a more or less objective look at the novel about to be finished, would be worth while.

If we got enough dough we would plan to go east: Toronto – Montreal, and get away from all these crooks. I would dearly love to go to New York in the fall, before which I cannot apply, but I have not much hope. If we went east, near New York but in Canada, would there be any chance of your dropping up to Canada to see us? If we are independent by that time, our house is thine. It is, incidentally extremely cheap living in Canada, but I daresay, your obligations as a prospective citizen would keep you in the States anyhow. Only, this may be the last summer I shall have for perhaps next summer I shall have to be sufficiently proficient in arson and murder to take part in the 'Crusade,' against the dicktasters. A dim outlook. One waits to see curiously what Mussolini (whom Haile Salassie once called 'My Enema the Douche') will do.[9] As for the pomes: Esquire *does* publish pomes, sort of pomes we might be expected to write, sort of pomes I sent you, *wiv picshurs too*! And in that very number with your story in it! Esquire is the obvious place. So maybe you could still charm them????? I'd be immensely beholden to you if you would put in the odd word.

Love zu haus zu haus and to your better half,

Malcolm

P.S. What do I look like? Somewhat less foul. I seem to be getting younger: probably second childhood. Where is Macalmon[10] if at all? Is he the last man at the Dome?[11] He was a kind sort of man. I should be glad to hear of it if somebody has anything good to say about me: so would you, if you lived in a freezing, bison-smelling attic in Vancouver not knowing when there will be a knock on the door, with blackmailers duns and Englishmen who think God an Englishman eight feet high upon your pen. (Not Cape though I fear, who recently refused me an advance; no good words from him.) By the way, is 20 E 68 half in Park Avenue, half in Yorkville, near the Metropolitan?[12] It seems to me I once lived there or thereabouts so it may well be that you will observe my little doppleganger poltergeist soul hoisting a drink in a bar in them parts. . .

P.P.S.[a] Have just, at the moment received the endearing news from England that the Government won't let _any_ funds out at the moment. Yes sir, all this right at this moment by cable. _So_, would you, for God's sake, please send those poems off immediately to *Esquire*, because there are the kind of poems they print (wiv picksurs as I said before.) Since we are obviously right down the spout in a country where we have no status and no right to get a job, let alone go on relief, you will agree with me that the time has come for action. The poems may not seem to represent action but the $50 odd they would pay would keep us for a month and moreover they might become interested in other work which would net us enough for several months. I have a *very* Esquirish story called June 30th 1934! that I could get ready in about a week. Could you tell me the name of the Editor – is it Arnold Gringrich or who[13] – & I would send it him direct to him if you would do me the favour of just paving the way a little meantime with some guff about O'Brien or something. The story is about their length, no great shakes, but is Esquirish as I say & potentially O'Brienish & wouldn't let you down. So please rally round, my dear old egg, will you. We are faced with the buttons off the chairs in the station waiting room for our next meal. We progress from Manon Lescaut to Crime & Punishment to – possibly, shall we say? – 'Two years as a Scab Lavatory attendant in Saskatchewan.'

Cheers

Malcolm

Annotations:

1 Kenneth Fearing (1902-61), the American poet and novelist, published his novel *The Hospital* in 1939. Frederic Prokosch (1908-89), also an American writer, published *The Seven Who Fled*, a novel about Russian exiles, in 1937.

2 Jean Julius Sibelius (1865-1957), the Finnish composer, is best known for his symphonic tone-poem *Finlandia* (1905), and Bix Beiderbecke (1903-31), the American jazz cornetist, was one of Lowry's favorites.

3 David Louis Reeves (1913-), an English painter and author, had been at Cambridge and was an acquaintance of Lowry's in Paris in 1934. Apparently he was in New York in the spring of 1940, when he had been talking with Stern about Lowry.

4 This line from *Blue Voyage* (139-40) is one of Lowry's favourites; see also his 8 September 1931 letter (**35**) to Grieg.

5 John Morris Reeves (1909-78), who wrote poetry for *Experiment* during the same years as Lowry, later became a prolific poet, playwright, fiction writer, and editor. He published under the name of James Reeves.

6 In his 1 May 1940 letter to Lowry (with the William Templeton papers in the UBC Lowry collection), Stern tells Lowry that two people have been talking about him: Jonathan Cape, there on a business trip from London, and a friend from the Paris days in 1934, 'Peggy Lippe of the rue Daguerre.' He then goes on to ask Lowry if he remembers 'the night Brock burnt his hands' and tells him that 'Rollo Hayes is censoring in Gibraltar.' According to Jan Gabrial in her interview with Robert Duncan, Brock was an English artist and an acquaintance of Julian Trevelyan's, and both were witnesses at her marriage to Lowry on 6 January 1934; see *Malcolm Lowry Remembered* (96). According to Trevelyan, the 'burnt hands' were caused by Lowry, who was seeking revenge against an Englishman called Brockenshaw, who had stolen Trevelyan's girl-friend; see 'And the Truth of the World Became Apparent,' Trevelyan's interview with Gordon Bowker in *Apparently Incongruous Parts* (6).

7 *Histoire du Chevalier des Grieux et de Manon Lescaut* (1731) is a novel by Abbé (Antoine François) Prévost (1697-1763); Giacomo Puccini's opera *Manon Lescaut* (1893) is based on the novel. *Crime and Punishment* (1866), one of Dostoevsky's best-known novels, is a favourite of Lowry's. See Lowry's repetiton of this witticism at the end of the letter.

8 George Davis was a fiction editor with *Harper's Bazaar*.

9 Lowry's pun turns on the fact that in 1935-36 Benito Mussolini (1883-1945), Italy's fascist leader, or Duce, had invaded Ethiopia, which was ruled at the time by Emperor Haile Selassie 1 (1892-1975). When the capital of Ethiopia, Addis Ababa, fell to the Italians on 5 May 1936, the emperor fled and Italy annexed Ethiopia to Eritrea and Somaliland.

10 Robert McAlmon (1895-1956) was an expatriate American writer and publisher who lived primarily in Paris between the wars. He was married to Winifred Ellerman (Bryher) and famous for his bohemian parties and for his friendships with the famous writers and artists of the day.

11 The Café Brasserie du Dôme was a popular Paris spot among the literati and Anglo-American expatriates who frequented the Latin Quarter during the 1920s and early 1930s.

12 Stern was living at this address.

13 In his 27 May 1940 letter to Lowry (UBC 1:64) Stern explains that he sent the poems to *Esquire* but they were rejected by the editor, Arnold Gingrich (1903-76).

Editorial Notes:

a. This postscript is written in pencil on the verso of page two of the typescript. Three other holograph additions to the letter are brief, and their points for insertion are clearly marked.

139: To Conrad Aiken

P: H(ts)
PP: *LAL* 134-35

1236 W. 11th Ave.,
Vancouver, B.C.
15 May 1940

Dear old Phaller:

Thanks a lot for your letter and I'm very relieved Mary's operation turned out O.K. That's really splendid news and I wish I had as good to match it from this end.

I would love to see your eighteenth century ruin but I have to admit, alas, that the only ruin that we are like to see is a twentieth century one, and that not in America.

Hellzappopin in Europe now and it doesn't prophet this prophet (more exact than most) a damn thing that he was a prophet.

Conscription may come at any moment and at our back we almost hear Time's 'phibian tanks a'changing gear, not to say, the first 'goosestep' of God . . .[1]

Meantime – bad news from England, which has tightened up, all of a sudden, on the money.

We swung a fast and lucky one on A.B. by getting out of Maurice's clutches into another room for $15 a month, and we now have $10 a week in addition to do *everything* else on.[2] But our peril is increased thereby and the only thing that I can say is: that we are right, and that some God of some sort of good, (probably you in disguise) seems to be helping us to finish our work.

For the rest: stark, staring tragedy may face us, and it is a good thing if so that one can face it calmly and fearlessly and soberly and even without anger, and I can assume only that we are able to do this because we have already bled our souls as white as bone.

I am trying desperately to sell some stuff to Esquire in the hope that then, still, we may be able to go east and spend what few months we have left in peace.

Judging by the muddle-headed vindictiveness I receive from time to time from Parks, – via presumably the old man, who has, however, written one pleasant but rather confused letter – one can expect little understanding from that quarter. But I still think I may give the OM some happiness in me.

The Volcano is on its last typing – re which I have, by the way, received an enthusiastic letter from Whit Burnett (Story Press and Lipincott, any good?) and what with that, and even better, your letter from Linscott, we have hopes of selling it. I have not much doubt but that it is a good book.

I do not see how you can assist us any further save by letting your genius storm into our spirits from time to time in these strange hours, but by helping us thus far in our struggle as I have said, far more has been achieved than meets the eye for good and good alone between us all.

All the best to Mary from us both.

As Haarlem burns and Joe Venuti[3] swings,

yours,

Malc

Annotations:

1 Lowry is echoing T.S. Eliot's familiar parody of Andrew Marvell: 'But at my back in a cold blast I hear / The rattle of the bones, and

chuckle spread from ear to ear' (*The Waste Land*, 185-86). The original lines are from Marvell's 'To His Coy Mistress': 'But at my back I always hear / Time's winged chariot hurrying near.'

2 The Lowrys left Maurice Carey's home in mid-May 1940 and moved into more congenial quarters in the home of a Vancouver building contractor, J.D. Smith, at 1236 West Eleventh Avenue, where they stayed happily until they moved out to Dollarton in August. See Salloum (11, 44, 131).

3 Guiseppe (Joe) Venuti (1898-1978) was an American jazz violinist who led the jazz group 'Blue Four,' and was one of Lowry's long-time favourites. John Davenport recalls Venuti and Eddie Lang records being played in Lowry's rooms at Cambridge (*Malcolm Lowry Remembered*, 48), and in chapter 6 of *Under the Volcano* Hugh remembers his own enjoyment of Venuti, Lang, and others. 'Haarlem burns' refers to the German attack on Holland 10-14 May 1940; the Dutch surrendered to the Nazis on 14 May.

140: To Juan Fernando Márquez

P: UBC(ts)

> 1236 W. 11th Ave.,
> Vancouver, B.C.,
> Canada
> 15 May 1940[a]

Dear Juan Fernando:[1]

You will be glad to know that I gave up drinking to the point only of the necessary drink, that I am well and strong and have thrown away that part of my mind that should be thrown away.[2]

I do not know how soon I may have to be fighting, but in any case, I would take this opportunity of swearing to you my undying friendship. Perhaps had I not been so stupidly drunk all the while in Oaxaca we might have had an even more magnificent time than we did but in any case I shall never forget it and it was magnificent enough.

I could not give back your coat because it was stolen in the train and I did not replace your friend's jacket because sickness in my body and soul was too great to permit me the courtesies which I would have normally shown. But I do not forget these kindnesses and one day I shall make restitution for them.

If ever you are in any trouble, I want you to know that my home, even if it is only a shadow, is yours and that, whether I am in New Orleans or not, a plate of beans is always at your disposal.

From you, and your friends, I had an example of courage and true courtesy and chivalry which it should be any man's ambition to live up to, and among all my friends I shall always count you as one of the dearest.

Please remember me to your friends and to Coco and Senor Cervantes and the boy whom I called Don Quixote and remember, and if necessary pray, for one who is always your true friend.

Malcolm Lowry

Annotations:

1 The presence in the Lowry collection of the original typescript of this letter, showing Lowry's characteristic fold creases for mailing, together with its envelope bearing three official stamps from Oaxaca (for May, June, and July) and the return-to-sender instructions, confirm that this letter was never delivered. His friend Juan Fernando Márquez had been killed in Mexico in December 1939, but Lowry did not learn of this death until his 1946 trip to Mexico; see Day (353-54). In 'Garden of Etla,' *United Nations World* 4, 6 (1950): 44-47, Lowry describes the beauty of the landscape around Oaxaca and celebrates his Zapotecan friend. See Lowry's December 1937 letter (**80**) to Juan.

2 The references to throwing away his mind in the first paragraph and to sickness of the soul here are allusions to Dr Vigil's warnings in *Under the Volcano*; since Dr Vigil was loosely modelled upon Márquez, presumably they echo Juan's own remarks to Lowry.

Editorial Notes:

a. This date is taken from a clear Vancouver postmark on the envelope, which bears Lowry's name and new address on the back.

141: To Burton Rascoe

P: Pennsylvania(ts); UBC(tsc)

1236 W. 11th Ave.,
Vancouver, B.C.,
Canada
19 May 1940

Dear Burton Rascoe:[1]

As life closes in one remembers its kindnesses and forbearances, and I think of yours towards me about the matter of the Latin Quotations,[2] which, I assure you again, was not deliberate plagiarism on my part, but it might as well have been for indeed that whole book was hopelessly derivative. You could, however, had you chosen, have been ruinously witty at my expense and that you did not so choose gives me at this moment a pause for gratitude and a belief that this anguishing life is not so bad after all, when such things can happen.

I am working hard on a book for Whit Burnett which I hope to complete before I am called up and I like to think you are wishing me luck.

I reread the other day, and with delight and profit, 'Titans.' Milton absolved me a little.[3]

Yours sincerely,

Malcolm Lowry

Annotations:

1 Burton Rascoe (1892-1957) was an American editor and author of several works of fiction and non-fiction. He was also a drama and literary critic for various New York magazines. The Burton Rascoe papers, including the original of this letter, are held in Special Collections at the Van Pelt Library, University of Pennsylvania.

2 On 22 November 1954 Burton Rascoe added the following note to Lowry's letter at this point: 'This is a curious letter, showing at once a deliberate attempt to put into writing a falsehood and an evasion regarding a deliberate and conscious plagiarism, freely confessed when I faced him with the texts of his *Ultramarine* (Jonathan Cape: London, 1933) and of my *What Is Love?* from a novel in progress, published in *American Caravan* (an anthology edited by Alfred Kreymborg, Lewis Mumford and Paul Rosenfeld: Macmillan, 1928) when he threw himself upon my mercy and I assured him I would not expose him or disclose the theft to anybody if he would protect *me* against any possibility of anyone's *accusing me of plagiarizing from him* when, and if, I completed my novel in progress, and it embodied the matter he had plagiarized and padded out and called a novel. He deposited a confession with Ann Watkins, his literary agent, witnessed by Harold Matson, employed by the Watkins agency in summer, 1935. Lowry not merely lifted *Latin quotations* from my text, but whole paragraphs.' Rascoe goes on to say that he 'did not want to read his highly praised novel' *Under the Volcano* because he feared it was plagiarized, and he explains his discovery of *Ultramarine* as 'the fateful accident of Matson's sending me a copy.' A careful examination of Rascoe's story confirms that the charge of plagiarism against Lowry is preposterous, and in her 29 June 1991 letter to me Jan Gabrial recalls the fuss made by Rascoe but does not believe there ever was a signed 'confession.' I have not been able to trace such a document.

3 Milton, of course, is well known for his use of Latin, and he was another great writer accused of plagiarism. In his idiosyncratic collection of essays called *Titans of Literature: From Homer to the Present* (New York: G.P. Putnam's Sons, 1932), which Lowry has just praised, Rascoe writes that '*Paradise Lost* is one of the boldest plagiarisms in the history of literature . . . a pastiche or a mosaic of pilferings' for which 'Milton had stolen the whole scheme . . . from a little known Italian contemporary' (p. 281).

142: To Conrad Aiken

p: H(ts)
pp: *LAL* 137-39

> 1236 W. 11th Ave.,
> Vancouver, B.C.
> 10 June 1940

Dear old Conrad:

I haven't written because we've been slaving away madly at the end of the Volcano, which protruded some unexpected peaks.

I'm awfully sorry the Conversation is dead in America: but maybe it is by no means dead here. Enclose review of it in local paper;[1] I enclose the McCarthy review with it simply as an illustration of one of these material occasions when essences recur or something or other, for I seem to remember your saying that McCarthy was one of the few people who spoke up in England for what seems to me now as well as at 18½ that work of satanic and marvelous genius: Blue Voyage.[2] – (I am trying to get the Province to let me review Conversation.)

Meantime, your letter made us laugh heartily amid the chaos.

Yes, it was hard to change our address, under the noses of the Careys, in fact, practically impossible, but we did it, without mishap, but do not think we have any more money for that or that it is any the less tough. We now live on $55 a month, which has to take care of *everything*, and we are faced with less.

But we have had one good break. Parks has been fired, and my old man's trust seems restored in me and he is going to deal with me personally. We shall be lucky if we get anything under the circumstances under which the O.M. is placed and I've told him it doesn't matter I'll make out somehow myself, but the main thing is in my eye that he and the mater should get some happiness out of me – perhaps one bright spot on a disastrous horizon.

I feel myself on the way up, definitely, and that some money will have accrued from the Volcano and elsewhere even before he manages to send me any funds and that, henceforward, I shall be able to fend on my own.

The whole European situation is such that I have been told to abandon America altogether but I had already done so, so that is no surprise.

Nuy fo noy yhink hoerbrt yhsy er – this is such a good typographical error I'm not going to erase it. – But do not think however that were we now in the States we would have been a charge on you at this time: Margie could have got a job and there are still a few hundred dollars over and moreover, as I say, I am on the way up. Up where?

Whether our efforts will be truncated by conscription I don't know, but hope not. If we make enough money we will still go east, if we can, where we could be, more or less in hailing distance of you at least.

Although the reasons for Parks' demise are largely financial I have reason to believe from my father's letter that I have succeeded in demonstrating the fact that he was an out and out crook. For his own sake the O.M. is well shot of a man who made such a fine thing of his exploitation of human souls, because he merely exploited the O.M.'s anxiety about me, trusting implicitly that I was too far gone as an idiot and a drunkard to ever refute him.

I received also a letter from Jan which, paradoxically enough, puts me in the clear too. She too, says that Parks has shown himself to be a crook thus corroborating now, somewhat too late, in other ways, the truth of my contribution to the Lowry Legend.

So do not take too seriously what you heard from Parks [–] And do not, worse, think that I've turned into a pious teetotaler [–] which at one time I thought perhaps you did: and remember too, that what the O.M. heard about me was from Parks too.

No – I asked your *advice* about sending Under the Volcano to Whit [Burnett] first, rather than to [Robert] Linscott because while, or before, we were tossing letters to and fro, and *before* Linscott's letter arrived – I had already more or less promised to send it to Whit. I do not know quite what to do: I don't know anything about the new Story Press, but I feel that I owe a certain loyalty to Whit since he trusted me for a long time. What would say offhand like? I feel that if I did send it to Whit first I am sort of letting you down. But on the other hand if I sent it to Linscott first I am sort of breaking my promise to Whit. So I'm in a bit of a dither. Perhaps you could make a suggestion. I hope to have it completed and ready to mail off by the end of this week or the first of next, so if you want to give me any advice about this, please do it now.[3]

I told my mother I would dedicate The Lighthouse Invites the Storm to her, so, if the Volc gets accepted, I am going to try to get that published after.

Could you help, do you think, a bit here? I would like to keep that somewhat rash promise to the old lady, if only because it would make her feel good. I think it could be a good book.

With all the best love to you and Mary from both of us,

Malcolm

P.S. I see I have written, in another, unposted letter to you: – re your bad reviews: 'Once upon a time, Conrad, you hurt the feelings of MEDIOCRITY so badly she will never forgive you.'

Annotations:

1 Victor Fellowes's review 'Aiken Adopts Effective Style' appeared in the *Vancouver Sun*, 25 May 1940, 7, but a copy does not survive with the letter.
2 See Desmond McCarthy's review of *Blue Voyage* in the *New Statesman*, 25 June 1927, 344.
3 Lowry sent one copy of the manuscript to Burnett in June 1940 and another copy to his New York agent, Harold Matson, in July; see letters **144** and **146**.

143: To Censor

P: Matson(ts)

[1236 W. 11th Street,]
[Vancouver, B.C.]
[June 1940]

TO THE CENSOR[1]

Sir:

The writer of the following book, an Englishman, has made his home in the United States for the past six years. At the outbreak of the war, he volunteered for service in the United Kingdom but was ordered to remain here in Canada, where he was on a visit and where at that time he found it impossible to enlist. Having leisure therefore on his hands but never, of course knowing when it would be ended, after consulting with his friend, John Buchan, Baron Tweedsmuir,

Commander in Chief of the Canadian Armies and Governor General of Canada, he decided that the most useful way to occupy this time was to continue with his work, the writing of this book, the notes for which had been gathered on a visit to Mexico in 1936-37, where for a time he was correspondent on an English liberal paper.[2] The book, intended simply and solely as a work of art, is, although non-political, by implication a denunciation of the Nazi system and Nazi methods.

The characters argue and suffer and have different opinions or it would not be a novel, but it is in no way 'subversively tainted' or pacifist. The principal character of the novel is a young American who comes to realize his own country may be in danger only when the kind of philosophy which informs a bitter personal attack upon him and his country is made clear. The book was discussed with Lord Tweedsmuir, who gave the author his assistance to continue his work on it, and if for no other reason than this, the author hopes you will send his book on its way with your blessing, as he regards the completion and publication of it as partly the fulfillment of a trust to the late Governor General of Canada. (Letter appended).[3] The Mactavish mentioned in this letter is the editor of the Vancouver Daily Province, for whom the author has done some articles upon the American attitude to the war, etc.[4]

Malcolm Lowry

Annotations:

1 This letter accompanied the manuscript of *Under the Volcano* when Lowry sent it to Whit Burnett in June 1940. With the outbreak of the Second World War, censorship in both the United States and Canada had been increased. Laws like the 1940 Smith Act in the United States were aimed at controlling Communist activity, but their effect was to heighten a general sense of suspicion and caution, and articles on censorship were a regular feature in the Vancouver newspapers during 1939-40. It is not clear why Lowry particularly felt a need to write this letter or what he feared would be so objectionable as to cause the Canadian or American customs officials to open, read, and confiscate his manuscript, but Lowry was extremely suspicious of all authority and always felt persecuted by officialdom. As a result he has concocted here a rather misleading, indeed laundered description of himself and his book.

2 According to Jan Gabrial, Lowry did not work for any newspapers while in Mexico. In the notes accompanying his 5 July 1946 letter (**229**) to Albert Erskine, Lowry claims to have known a correspondent for the *Daily Herald* when he was in Mexico and to have helped him to write the

telegram attributed to Hugh in chapter 4 of *Under the Volcano*; see the 25 June 1937 telegram (**70**) to the *Daily Herald*. Inquiries to the head librarian of the Mirror Group newspaper chain, the archivist of the newspaper library at the British Library, and others confirm that the files and records of the *Daily Herald* have not survived; thus it no longer seems possible to confirm whether or not Lowry had any connection with the paper.

3 This letter is a brief and friendly note to Lowry from John Buchan (see Appendix 2), found in the Matson Company Lowry file. It was originally sent to Whit Burnett with this letter to the censor and the manuscript of *Under the Volcano* in June 1940, and then passed on to Matson when Burnett rejected the novel. Lowry treasured Buchan's letter – see his March 1940 letter (**129**) to his father – and in his 22 June 1940 letter (**144**) to Burnett he asks to have it returned to him. More than a year later, in a postscript to his 6 July 1941 letter (**165**) to Burnett and Foley, Lowry again asks for the Tweedsmuir letter.

4 W.L. MacTavish (1892–1951) was the well-known and respected editor of the *Vancouver Daily Province* at this time. Lowry published 'Hollywood and the War' in the *Province* for 12 December 1939, 4, and an article called 'The Real Mr Chips' and a poem, neither of which concerned the war, later in the month.

144: To Whit Burnett

P: Princeton(ts)

1236 W. 11th Ave.,
Vancouver, B.C.,
Canada
22 June 1940

Dear Whit:

My novel is now on its way to you.[1]

Please do not let any of the gentlemanly words outside prejudice you as to its contents: it was necessary to make them, that's all. But I wonder if you would be good enough to return in due course the letter from Baron Tweedsmuir [John Buchan] which I rather value.[2]

I have made this book as good as I possibly could. The epigraph from Henry James[3] at the beginning explains the rest: you will see how it is both a comment on the bridge between the treacherous years and the years themselves, the past and the present, and upon the Atlantis theme, and how it illumines the whole book like a revolving light. The book, of course, begins in the present, and then, without any break greater than a chapter demarcation, proceeds in the past. I have been at pains to give the illusion – and indeed the consistency is perhaps not an illusion – of continuity. But for the general reader it is as well to assume that any new conception of time strikes him as an affectation: hence the sense of timelessness in Mexico is stressed, the clocks striking wrong hours, the same things on at the movies, as happens in real life, three years later. I would beg of you not to be put off by the beginning with its protracted nightmare. You will see, as you go on, that it is intended simply as a musical statement, in which all the many themes, which I later try to tear to pieces, are stated. In places the book's style could certainly stand being more stripped, harder, and more winnowed: I think this, however, is a minor defect, and I am relying on your eye to see faults where mine, by repeated rewritings, as many in places as 19 or 20 – has become hypnotized. I would also like to disarm at the outset, if possible an opinion that the whole book would be better were it set in the present. I do not think I stand in such a ruin of my beliefs as many other writers: nine tenths of what I was writing about has come true – what is imagination anyhow? – so that (I believe) you may gain a certain feeling of the sense of time being in this book what I have never discovered who said it was – an inhibition to prevent everything happening at once.[4]

It is my hope that the book may not unfavourably compare with such books as Kafka's Trial: but well do I know that such books as Kafka's Trial can rarely be sold at a profit. In fact it would seem that the primary condition of their sale at all is the author's persecution and death. So that it is also my hope that this book manages somehow to be more *entertaining*: and that, although it lacks a spiritual solidity, lacks the – as it were – stratification of genius, the economy and restraint of the writer firmly rooted, philosophically and religiously, in some such belief, say, as Kafka's, that the supernatural demand for righteousness in all things is absolute, or that all human effort, even at its highest, is in the wrong – it does manage, by choice of a dime novel theme, (in which however the historical, economic, and even esoteric position of all the characters is plotted, in relation to a world which is a sort of villainous extention every which way, of a dime novel plot,) and by a certain universality I have given it – to have a much wider potential appeal. But I have also tried to invest it with a certain quality which 'The Castle' possessed: 'Inexhaustibility.' I hope this doesn't sound too pretentious! What I mean or am venturing to say is that you could read it many times and still get something new out of it: that you might come to look on it as upon, say, a good swing record – or in parts even better – which you could play over and over again in certain places without getting fed up and then throw the needle back and play the whole thing again for that effect too.

The musical interrelation and interdependence implicit in this has resulted in places in what is held to be a grave fault, namely the overlapping in diction and consciousness on the part of certain characters which may make you think the effect striven for is that of a melancholy *cauchemar* of ghosts and voices: but to counteract this tendency I have been at pains to try and develop 'character' along strictly 'conventional' lines, indeed on lines which belong to a different cheaper sort of novel altogether, so that I feel Bruce the butcher's boy could read it and get something out of it. I admit he might have to skip the first chapter though here again I have let the reader slowly down into imponderables by using a sort of ' "Hell," said the Great Lawyer, sipping his whiskey and leaning forward earnestly,' technique.

Care, however, in all of it has not prevented me from putting such a phrase as 'another spiral had wound its way upward,'[5] for instance, into several differing sensibilities, and since I came to detect some of these errors too late perhaps, if you accept this book, you would glow upon them with a glittering eye yourself and pluck them out.

If the book is accepted it may be that I shall have time to finish another: but at any rate hang on to it, if you do not. If you do take it – or do not take it and still think it may be sold – I feel that I owe it to Hal Matson, if he would be willing, to handle it. But I do not want to saddle him with just so much useless waste on postage stamps. I feel however, that I have eliminated much of the longwindedness and vapourousness which made my previous work inacceptable.

And I feel something more, that I have perhaps been writing this book, as it were out of Europe's 'unconscious.' Muzzle a dog and he will bark out of the other end. As the last scream of anguish of the consciousness of a dying continent, an owl of Minerva[6] flying at evening, the last book of its kind, written by someone whose type and species is dead, even as a final contribution to English literature itself, the final flaring up and howling, for all I know – and other things pretentious – this book, written against death and in an atmosphere of total bankruptcy of spirit, might have some significance beyond the ordinary.

At all events it is written: which is something: it protruded a few unsuspecting peaks which is why I couldn't send it earlier. And if you take it it may be that will enable me to live a little longer in this world where everybody cheats, and to produce more.

Would you let me know as quickly as you can, even, perhaps, by telegram, when you have decided, because life is full of venoms and uncertainties and scorpion moves, and one does not know, from day to day, what one must do, or whether a continent will stand between Wednesday and Friday? I grant you it is a strange time to embark upon a career.

All the best to Martha [Foley] and yourself,

Malcolm

Annotations:

1 Lowry sent a copy of the 'third' draft of *Under the Volcano*, which he and Margerie had been working on since January of 1940, to Burnett under separate cover. This is the version of the novel that was rejected by thirteen publishers during 1940-41 and that Martha Foley criticized for its handling of time. See Lowry's 4 March 1941 letter (**163**) to Harold Matson.

2 See Appendix 2 and Lowry's March 1940 letter (**129**) to his father; Lowry greatly prized this letter and Tweedsmuir's support.

3 Lowry had two epigraphs for this version of *Under the Volcano*. The first was from Henry James's 4 August 1914 letter to Howard Sturgis; the second was from Matthew Arnold's poem 'Dover Beach' (1867). The sentence from James's letter that Lowry chose is one of James's many laments over the outbreak of the First World War; it begins, 'The plunge of civilization into this abyss of blood and darkness,' and ends, 'is too tragic for any words.' See Percy Lubbock's edition of *The Letters of Henry James*, vol. 2 (New York: Charles Scribner's Sons, 1920), p. 384. Arnold's poem seems prophetic of twentieth-century wars and tragedies, which is no doubt why Lowry chose it for *Volcano*.

4 In his 6 March 1950 letter to Derek Pethick, Lowry comments on 'the Bergsonian idea that the sense of time is merely an inhibition to prevent everything happening at once,' and in his essay 'Garden of Etla,' *United Nations World* 4 (June 1950): 47, he explains that this remark, 'or so claimed the source I mentally borrowed it from, is Bergson's.' I have not been able to locate this comment in Bergson, but Lowry's 'source' is I.A. Richards. In *Practical Criticism: A Study of Literary Judgment* (New York: Harcourt, Brace, 1939), Richards writes: 'It was Bergson, I think, who once described Time as resistance – the resistance namely against everything happening at once! Without inhibition everything in the mind *would* happen at once, which is tantamount to saying that nothing would happen or that chaos would return. All order and proportion is the result of inhibition; we cannot indulge our mental activity without inhibiting others.' *Practical Criticism* was first published in 1929, with a second impression in 1930 during Lowry's first academic year at Cambridge, where Richards was teaching, and Lowry was well aware of the significance of Richards' work. If, as is likely, he read the book at that time, it is perhaps not surprising that by 1940 he had forgotten the source of this remark about time.

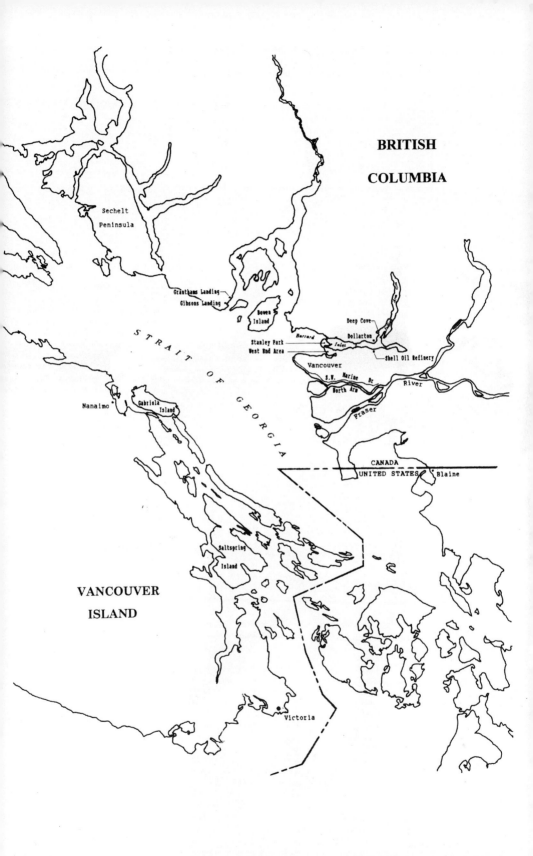

24 Harold Matson,
ca 1985 *(above)*.

25 Norman Matson,
ca 1950 *(left)*.

26 The Lowrys' second shack at Dollarton, British Columbia, ca 1942.

27 The Lowrys' third shack at Dollarton, British Columbia, ca 1945.

28 *(above)* James and Elizabeth Craige in Vancouver, April 1949.

29 *(top right)* 'Jimmy' – James Craige in front of the Lowry's shack, ca 1945.

30 *(far right)* Priscilla Bonner Woolfan and Dr E. B. Woolfan, Lowry's
sister-in-law and her husband, ca 1945.

31 Gerald Noxon and Malcolm Lowry in Niagara-on-the-Lake, Ontario, ca February 1947.

32 Jonathan Cape, ca 1930 *(below left)*.

33 Malcolm Lowry in Cuernavaca, Mexico, ca February 1946.

34 Malcolm Lowry on the Beach at
Dollarton, ca 1946.

35 Albert Erskine in his office at Random
House, ca 1952.

36 Margerie Bonner Lowry, 1946; 37 Malcolm Lowry, 1946.

38 Malcolm and Margerie Lowry on board the *Donald S. Wright* en route to Haiti, December 1946.

5 Lowry is thinking of Grieg's *The Ship Sails On*: 'a new spiral had wound its way upward' (167).
6 Minerva, an ancient Italian goddess of the dawn, is best known as the Roman goddess of wisdom and the patroness of the arts. Her sacred creatures are the owl and the serpent. Lowry, however, may be alluding to a comment about the owl of Minerva made by the German philosopher Georg Wilhelm Friedrich Hegel (1770-1831) in his preface to *Philosophie des Rechts* (1821).

145: To Conrad Aiken

P: H(ts)
PP: *LAL* 142-43

1236 W. 11th Ave.,
[Vancouver, B.C.]
19 July 1940

My dear Conrad:
I finished the Volcano and sent one copy to Whit Burnett, haven't heard from him yet. I had your copy all ready to send, but meantime – two days later, to be precise, by the time it took me to tie up the parcel anyhow, a collossal censorship descended on the land – magazines banned from the States, including, alas, Time, and everything and everybody suspected, the dark ages on us. The book is really anti-Nazi, as you know, but people in it have different opinions and state them frankly, and I am dubious about getting another copy through the mails. At least until such time as I get back the more or less censor-excluding letter about it from the late Governor General, which I sent with Whit's copy. This may be unnecessary persecutions on my part, but I don't want to take any chances at making explanations with unsympathetic people and being tied up with red tape. And besides, we are now living on $45 per month, which leaves us practically no money for anything except food and a place to live. Our only diversion is going swimming every day, fortunately we are within walking distance of a beach – where we find ourselves surrounded more or less by negroes, Chinese and Indians, since we live in that part of town. Still, it is a beach, and we are keeping fit: (for what?)
I am meantime helping Margie on her detective story [*The Last Twist of the Knife*] and we shall have it finished before long.
I would to God I could see you. I feel I could be a good poet if I knew what sort of discipline to subject myself to. I can read scarcely

any living poets save yourself and Wallace Stevens and the modern dead ones, who fructify me, like Rilke, wrote in languages I can't readily understand.[1] If I were more, or less, of a poet I suppose this desire for a design governing posture of some sort wouldn't worry me. I think even now, poems as good as the Spender-Auden-Rukeyser run of the mill suggest themselves to me and I won't let myself write them. Another thing: once a poem is written, I hate it, seem to lose it deliberately, do not want to send it anywhere. Of course you can advise me against this. But I think I must really want to be squelched, to be a posthumous rather than a living poet. The Keats and Chatterton idea you once suggested.[2] A 'orrid thought. Well, you can advise me against this too. But give me some advice, I generally follow yours as one hypnotized.

I had thought to dedicate the Volcano to Margie and you and Mary: but if you feel the Mexican scene is too mutually affective or whatever, I'll dedicate another one to yez. Anyhow, for better or woise, it's written to you, or at you.[3]

I am more or less persona grata with the O.M. now, probably thanks to you . . . I much value that letter you wrote us . . . Did you get the review I sent you on Conversation? . . . Margie and I seem to have discovered a Better Thing via our honeymoon in chaos . . . Yes, Conrad, by God, love certainly is something, in fact, everything . . . Please glow on us with some of it even if at a distance . . . There is conscription here on August 19: don't know yet whether it applies, or should, if it doesn't, to me.

And love: *tons* of it, to you and Mary
from us both.

Malc

P.S. – N.B. Would you be kind enough – if it ain't too expensivish, or maybe send them collect – to send along the Lighthouse and Last Address so that I can immediately start working them over as I have no time to waste (remembering possible conscription). If you have any suggestions for either, *do* please send them. (The same thing applies perhaps to In Ballast as to the Volc, for the present anyhow??)

Annotations:

1 Wallace Stevens (1879-1955) was an important modern American poet, and Rainer Maria Rilke (1875-1926), the German poet and author of *The Duino Elegies* and *The Notebook of Malte Laurids Brigge*, fascinated Lowry, who worked passages from Rilke's writing into his story 'Through the Panama' in *Hear us O Lord* (81-2).

2 Keats and Chatterton both 'died young,' a fact Lowry had discussed with Nordahl Grieg; see Lowry's 8 September 1931 letter (35) to Grieg.
3 *Under the Volcano* was finally dedicated to 'Margerie, my wife.'

146: To Harold Matson

P: Matson(ts); UBC(phc)
PP: *SL* 31-34

> 1236 W. 11th Ave.,
> Vancouver, B.C.,
> Canada
> 27 July 1940

Dear Hal:

I read in Life this week that the knowledge a man is to be hanged concentrates the mind mightily.[1]

What with the sunset of the Western World, of the Boyg,[2] conscription imminent here, and a reprieve, in spite of volunteering, from enlistment which has been prolonged God knows why until now, and may go on long enough to complete more work, such a concentration has been operating here.

Some seven or eight months ago I wrote you about a former novel of mine, In Ballast to the White Sea, which Anne Watkins had.[3] Then my motive was to raise some money through a source which seemed hopeful. It did not work, but I have managed to get the work I hoped to do done just the same without the money or with a modicum from elsewhere.

Having completed some important part of it, my feeling was to see where my loyalty and obligation lay in case it should succeed.

It very definitely lay, in my conscience, with Whit Burnett and yourself (I am in a bit of an obliquity about Anne Watkins, not because I still owe her that $20) but whether or not what I might have accomplished was in the nature of an Indian gift to either of you I wasn't so sure.

Anyhow, I have written a book that I really feel might be important, Under the Volcano, and the honestest thing I could think to do with it was to send it to Whit and ask him to let you, if you wished or would, (for I am somewhat of a prodigal son) arrange the details of it, that is, either in case he took it, or really considered, if he didn't, that it stood a good chance elsewhere and would not so much waste – drain on a petty cash department as in the past.[4] I have not yet heard from Whit about this and naturally do not like to chatter about it to him while he has it. I would be, of course, tickled to death if he would publish it: but I am beginning to feel perhaps that I have over-estimated it, that he won't take it, or that, if he personally likes it, others in the firm do not. I am a bit hangdog about all this at such a time, but there it is. If it does not hit for him, Robert Linscott of Houghton Mifflin, Boston, has, through Conrad Aiken, professed an enthusiastic desire to see it, which might be borne – if it be not un-ethical – in mind. Anyhow, in the position I am placed, I do not want it tossed to and fro across the border, so, as time closes in again, I am asking if you would do me the favour on Whit's advice when it comes, of taking charge and having a friendly look into it. It is 'original:' if you fear for past Websterian, not to say Miltonian minor lack of ethics on my part,[5] nor is it drunkenly translated with a hand-pump out of the original Latvian. It is as much my own as I know of.

Under the Volcano might, I feel, be a *really* good book: might be, I threaten it. Some parts of it the war has undone. There are a few abstractions and meaninglessnesses which a state of peace would have written out of the thing, and which, even, now, a friendly eye would freeze out, and its worth be enhanced.

So much for that: there are others to follow, if given time: but that is a start, or a restart. It is for you to judge or say no.

Meantime I have a quite different kettle of fish a'boiling. I am ex-pecting (as well as to be hanged) to be married again, as soon as maybe, which one has been hoping is not too late. My collaborator in this venture, one Margerie Bonner, has just completed a 'mystery novel' by name 'The Last Twist of the Knife.' She is here in Canada under the same compulsions as I. If I seem too much of a Jonah[6] alto-gether from any point of view I would be immensely beholden to you if you would read this book and calculate its chances and act for them, if you think they are good. I can promise, as I cannot for myself at present, many from this same pen.

The book, hers, has a swiftly moving, excellently told, dramatic and logically worked out story: it is not full of the same kind of per-mutations and combinations as mine: and I believe there is a ready market for this and what might follow it up. It has the commercial virtues (I believe) and it is intelligently and sensitively written. And it is a good *narrative*.

Anyhow, may I send the book along, and quite apart from what you may decide to do about me, or should I say my other me, (either, in this case being to some extent the other's neither,) may I ask you to consider it? I would deem that a favour: and I do not think you would regret it. Her potentialities are steadier and more easily to be gauged than mine. We ourselves are a firm with a divided nature but a shared purpose. The success of one prolongs the other's life, all things being (as they sadly are not) equal.

Yours faithfully,

Malcolm Lowry

P.S. Re Linscott, of Houghton Mifflin. I am more or less committed through Aiken to give him the first refusal of the Volcano if it fails with Whit. I mention this to you because it might be that Whit has already given you the book and has not, to save my feelings, wanted to say anything about it to me until some verdict has been reached between you to its saleability. It may very well be that you will not want to handle it at all because of the fact that my work was already out of your hands. But in this regard I made no commitments elsewhere. At the time I last wrote you I was desperately in need of money and Conrad Aiken had suggested that perhaps his agent, Bernice Baumgarten, might give me a price on the whole bolus, as it were through Aiken, as at that time I thought I would be called up any minute. It was a very vague idea which politely came to naught: Conrad Aiken now has most of my work. If the Volcano is taken, there are at least three books, already written, to follow that up. My motive, however, in writing you now is not primarily financial or a business one at all. I felt I had written a good book which justified the trust you and Whit had put in me. If Whit takes it I want you to have the commission on it and handle my work, which has now been brought to practical fruition, in future. If not, and I seem still to have potentialities, I would have the satisfaction of knowing that I had acknowledged as well as I could my great feelings of obligation to you both. I had meant this to be a sort of surprise, pleasant, I hoped, to you, coming through Whit. The uncertainty of events and the near completion of Miss Bonner's book, impels me to write to you now. If you feel it unorthodox to handle my work, I would at least like Miss Bonner to have as good an agent as yourself. Anyhow, please let me know what you feel and whether you will read, at least, which of course commits you to nothing, her book. In that case it would arrive in about two weeks.

M.

Annotations:

1 Lowry's source in *Life* magazine must have been paraphrasing James Boswell's *Life of Samuel Johnson* (1791). Boswell records a discussion with Johnson on 19 September 1771 in which the doctor remarked:

'Depend upon it, sir, when a man knows he is to be hanged in a fortnight, it concentrates his mind wonderfully' (Aetat. 68).

2 Peer encounters the 'Great Boyg' in Henrik Ibsen's *Peer Gynt* II.vii. The
Bojgen or Boyg is a troll from Norwegian fairy-tales who appears in
Ibsen's 1867 play as a terrible, mysterious 'Voice' and presence that
attempts to envelop and annihilate the wandering hero. Peer describes
the Boyg as 'Slime; gray air, / Not even a form,' and as such he is a for-
midable enemy. Peer is saved from the Boyg by a woman's love, but the
symbolic threat and power of the monster has elicited many interpre-
tations. Here Lowry is associating its deadly menace with the war.

3 Ann Watkins (1886-1967) was a well-known New York literary agent
from 1910 to 1957, but whether she ever formally represented Lowry's
work or not is unclear. In her 31 January 1938 letter to Lowry (UBC
1:71) she praises parts of *Under the Volcano* that he has sent her from
Mexico and asks to be his agent. Since he was working on 'In Ballast to
the White Sea' (the manuscript intended as the 'paradiso' in his trilogy,
but destroyed in his 7 June 1944 fire) during 1935 in New York, it is possible that she also had a copy of this work-in-progress.

4 In June 1940 (see letter **144** to Whit Burnett), Lowry had sent a copy of
the *Volcano* manuscript to Burnett in New York with the hope that he
and Martha Foley would like it. As it turned out, of course, Burnett and
Foley were not able to take the manuscript. Here Lowry is asking Matson to represent him as his literary agent; see Appendix 2 for Matson's 7
October 1940 letter regarding the fate of the manuscript between July
and October of that year.

5 Lowry is alluding to John Webster's and John Milton's literary borrowings, which have often been described as plagiarism.

6 Jonah is the unwilling prophet in the book of Jonah from the Old Testament. Jonah is swallowed by a whale when he tries to evade his
commission from Yahweh, and then he becomes angry when his predictions do not come to pass. Lowry is thinking of Jonah here with
reference to the apparent failure of his manuscript in which he has had
such high hopes.

147: To Harold Matson

P: Matson(ts); UBC(phc)

1236 W. 11th Ave.,
Vancouver, B.C.
9 August 1940

Dear Hal;

Thanks a lot for your letter. Miss Bonner's mystery story will be
finished Sunday, will go off to you Monday or Tuesday.[1]

My own novel, Under the Volcano, I *sent* to Whit at Story Press in June.[2] No reply as yet, simply an acknowledgement. He has had it since June 27th. If Whit doesn't take it, Linscott of Houghton Mifflin is interested.

Of course, I'd like Whit to take it. I wrote to Whit that if he did, or thought it was saleable, to get in touch with you. I thought the book was so good when I finished it that he would take it probably. Perhaps as time is really closing in, it would be better if you found out what he is thinking of doing.

It may really be that the book is unsaleable and not worth your time: I honestly don't think that, but you and Whit ought to know, if anybody.

Anyhow, that's all about the books. And thanks again for offering to have a look at them.

Cheerio,

Malcolm

Annotations:

1 Margerie Bonner's first novel, *The Last Twist of the Knife*, was not published by Charles Scribner's Sons until 1946, when it appeared without its final chapter; see Lowry's 20 September and 30 September 1946 letters (**247** and **250**) to Maxwell Perkins.
2 See Lowry's 22 June 1940 letter (**144**) to Whit Burnett.

August 1940 was a most propitious month for Lowry. On the fifteenth he and Margerie had moved from downtown Vancouver to a fisherman's shack on the beach at Dollarton where they could relax, swim, and enjoy the beauty of unspoiled natural surroundings. To these blessings was added the further joy of rediscovering a special friend from his Cambridge days. Gerald Noxon (see photograph 31), who was working for the Canadian Broadcasting Company in Toronto at this time, was himself a writer, but he recognized genius in Lowry and was prepared to support him in many ways. Noxon read and commented upon drafts of the Volcano, *sent Lowry money and Margerie script-writing jobs, and finally gave the Lowrys shelter when fire destroyed their home in June 1944. In 1952, after Noxon had moved to the United States, the two men lost touch, but Lowry's last surviving letters (**501** and **523**) to 'beloved Gerald' confirm his lasting affection for his friend.*

148: To Gerald Noxon

P: Texas(ts)
PP: *LLN* 27–28

> Dollarton P.O.,
> Dollarton, B.C.
> 26 August 1940

My very dear old Gerald Noxon, by God[1]

Throw that highly important letter you are writing straight out of the window and drop me a line instantly.

I heard from Conrad, who seems in marvelous form, that you were in Toronto, where we'd been planning, this summer, to go, incidentally, though we were frustrated. Wonderful news. How are you, man? For heaven's sake tell me quick? I haven't seen a human face it seems in a decade, have snarled at no human beast in a year. And how are John Davenport, Julian Trevelyan, Hugh Sykes, Michael Redgrave? Do you know, and if you do, how are Tom Harrison, Tom Forman, Arthur Calder-Marshall?[2] Who is dead, or imprisoned, or interned and what kind of hope do any of them or us hold out if any of anything?

I came here to Canada from U.S. just before the war, couldn't get back to the States when it broke out, probably, now, can never go back. My mss etc were all on the other side of the border, not to say money, and a wife, who has since divorced me. I volunteered, however, to go to England and enlist and was told to stay here, which I did, that is, stay: as for enlisting, I shall probably hear from the Canadian navy circa 1960, just in time to help blockade the Donkhobors.[3] Meantime, I have been and am on, as someone said, the horns of a Domelia. Perhaps you can make matters a bit clearer to me, the Domelia less uncomfortable: the war, that is! I can't hew my way through the sanctifications into any kind of daylight. I do not care, I tell myself at present, to live in a world where everyone cheats, so do not live in it, but rather, like Timon of Athens, on the edge of it: a shack on the sea in a deserted village. Once this was a place where they built ships (Dollar liners):[4] only evidence of this now are the slipways overgrown with meadowsweet and black-berries and the forest. It is a fine wet ruin of a forest full of snakes and snails and terrific trees blasted with hail and fire. We dive from our front porch into a wild sea troughing with whales and seals. We have a boat, now diving at anchor. Everywhere there is a good smell of sea and timber and life and death and crabs.

'We' are Margerie Bonner, the ex movie (child, silent) star and I. We plan to marry in October. If this looks like cradle snatching I ought to point out that the said child film star is now of age. Since November '39 I've written two novels: there is a book of pomes: am hoping Lippencott and Story Press will take the whole bolus of my work – approx. 5 tomes in all, excluding early plagarations, beginning with 'Under the Volcano', a novel about Mexico. (Where I spent a vexing Christmas cooling my heels in a fascist dungeon, expecting to be shot.) So that you see, or if you don't see, I should point out, that with me, in spite of the Timonesque surroundings, it is going well. But one cannot live forever in peace of mind without knowing what is happening to those one loves and respects in the ex-world.

Do you recollect that you are my first editor? Ten years ago we took a Camber train, walked Camber beach: Hugh Sykes was going to be married.[5] We drank much beer, and smoked Balkan (it's like eatin') Sobranie. You told me then about the economic situation in Canada in terms I now comprehend somewhat better. Now, will you please tell me the truth about this bleeding war and what you imagine is going to happen? It may be, if one is really needed in England, I should [go] there on my own hook: should I? Noone can say but myself, who has just discovered it's really very good to be alive. But you can tell me, so far as you are able, what I cannot read, and may not wholly deduce, the truth: the truth, at least, as you see it. So, let's have it, please, unvarnished, and unsurrounded by loud gregarious lies as it must be. For one thing, how long do you think it (the war) is going to go on, at least in its present *outward* form?

Conrad tells me you may go to the States. I don't think I *can*, but still hope. But I do look forward to some opportunity of seeing you. If you are broke though, or in need of sanctuary, or somewhere to invite the soul where you will be insulated from the current pandemonium in everything but intellect, or all of these things, or none, why not come here? We have about enough money, if all our projects fail, to last till December: I have this Volcano book boiling: Margie is on the point of selling a detective novel. We pay $10 a month (!) for our shack: there are lots of other shacks, creaking 'live here' in the southwest wind. It would be swell to see you. It is a magnificent place to live, work, or commit suicide. Julian (Midnight) Green may make a dark journey here. Count on us, if you need to count: and bear us, you and your wife, to whom all the best, in mind, anyhow.

The baked oysters are calling! *And every night the supper wine*; not forgetting, either, the Balkan (it's like eatin'), Sobranie.

In reply to yours of July, 1930, inst. etc., I am

Very respectfully yours etc.,
Malcolm Lowry

Annotations:

1 Gerald Noxon (1910-90) renewed his friendship with Lowry during the early forties after he returned to Canada to work on films and radio. At Cambridge Noxon was publishing editor of *Experiment*, a writer, and an avid film buff, publishing reviews in the Cambridge papers and in international journals such as *transition* and *Close Up*. He contributed a short story, 'Bordeaux,' to the second issue of *Story* in 1931. For further biographical information see 'Gerald Noxon 1910-1990,' *Malcolm Lowry Review* 27 (1990): 12-14, and for both sides of the Lowry/Noxon correspondence, see Paul Tiessen's *Letters of Malcolm Lowry and Gerald Noxon, 1940-1952*.

2 Julian Trevelyan (1910-88), the English painter, knew Lowry at Cambridge and in Paris during 1933, when he acted as Lowry's 'guardian'; see Day (173-74). Tom Harrisson (1911-76), a friend of Lowry's at Cambridge, later became an eminent ethnologist, professor, and writer; see Day (133).

3 The Doukhobors, a sect of Russian Orthodox dissenters, emigrated to Canada in 1898 after continued persecution in Russia. In 1908 a group of Doukhobors settled on farms in southern British Columbia, and many years of trouble, disputes with the provincial government over education, and protests followed. In 1939 the community lost their farms through foreclosure, and Doukhobor affairs were much in the news at the time. Activism and unrest persisted through the fifties and sixties.

4 Dollarton took its name from Robert Dollar, who owned and operated a sawmill on Burrard Inlet from 1916 to 1929 and from 1932 to 1943. The Dollar Mill did not build ships, but Robert Dollar operated four vessels, each of which bore the dollar insignia on its chimney stack. Lowry frequently compares himself to Shakespeare's lonely hero in *Timon of Athens*.

5 Hugh Sykes Davies (1904-84), Fellow of St John's College, Cambridge, and the poet Kathleen Raine (1908-) were married for a short time in the early 1930s. Both were friends of Lowry's at Cambridge and both wrote for *Experiment*. Davies, an editor of the magazine, also served as Lowry's unofficial 'tutor.' See their memories of Lowry in *Malcolm Lowry Remembered* (41-46, 52-55).

149: To Harold Matson

P: Matson(ts); UBC(phc)

Dollarton P.O.,
Dollarton, B.C.
6 September 1940

Dear Hal:

A new address in the backwoods!¹

Would you do me the favour of forwarding the enclosed letter to the publishers of my friend, Julian Green, the novelist, who is now in America, a refugee from France?² That is, unless you yourself know Green's address. Harper's published his early work: but I'm not sure who put out 'Personal Record,'³ his last book, and I have no way of finding out here in the backwoods.

I'd be awfully grateful if you would do this for me.

More work is nearing completion for you. If I hadn't felt practically certain that this time we really had something I wouldn't have bothered you.

Yours truly,

Malcolm Lowry

Annotations:

1 Their new address is the fisherman's shack on the foreshore of Burrard Inlet at Dollarton. Instead of being just a place for a month's holiday, Dollarton was where the Lowrys decided to live. After fire destroyed their second shack, the Lowrys returned and rebuilt their home; see photographs 26 and 27.

2 No letter to Julien Green has survived with this letter to Matson. Green had long been a Lowry favourite; see his September 1931 letter (**36**) to Aiken.

3 *Personal Record, 1928-1939*, translated from the French by Jocelyn Godefroi, was published by Harper & Brothers in 1939. It represents a portion of a journal that Green had been keeping in his effort to achieve 'a clearer realization of my inner world,' and in it Green frequently discusses his current work-in-progress and his other novels. Given his comments upon his personal and literary life ('I am *all* the characters') and about current politics, it is not difficult to see why Lowry would be interested in Green and his work.

150: To Conrad Aiken

P: H(ts)
PP: *LAL* 145-46

> Dollarton P.O.,
> Dollarton, B.C.
> 6 September 1940

Dear old Conrad:

Note new address! We live in a shack on the sea. Dollarton is an old shipbuilding town, Dollar liners – now dead: slipways covered with brambles, enormous blasted oaks in a fine, deep forest. Outside the window, a vast white calm where sea is confused with sky, and the Rockies. We have a boat: and one day, out for a row, a whale came up beside us! I think it was Herman Melville in disguise. Anyhow it is a weird and wonderful place and we love it, the more so since it is costing us only $10 a month rent to live in it, and after October, will cost even less, if we are still here. A Maltese cat with golden eyes has adopted us while she has her kittens: we call her Ping because she does not purr. We are delighted with everything and with ourselves: for we have outwitted the Careys, and cooked Park's goose – he has turned the remaining money over to me – and, incidentally, made the O.M. and the mater as pleased as they can be about anything at this period. I haven't yet told him about Margie, but it looks as though I shall be absolutely on my own hook. We have enough money to hold out till December: the authorities have told me, being a visitor, I don't have to, or rather can't, register. I don't know, at that rate, whether I shall be called up at all. Maybe the war will soon be over. I suppose I must hope not. Anyhow here we are and a bloody miracle I calls it. So that now we have a sporting chance. I still have not heard from Whit about the Volcano, but if he doesn't take it, it is going to Linscott, and it maybe even now on its way. Don't know how to send you a copy yet. Margie's detective novel – 'The Last Twist of the Knife' – is off, too. Is the Bob Morse you speak of Robert Ely Morse who wrote a poem ending 'This swan upon the icy waters of my heart glides ever on,' in the Dial, 1926?[1] Anyhow, poor devil, I am sorry for him. Thanks for Gerald's address: I wrote him, no answer as yet. I've told Julian Green to go and see you: you are both from Savannah. Much of his early work I thought, was superb: but his genius seems to have run slightly aground. Perhaps you will set him afloat again.

We would come east like a shot if we could afford it: but perhaps we shall soon be able to. We read your article in the Atlantic[2] and caracoled: I have a lot to say about it which I'm reserving for another letter. Margie really thought you'd expressed everything she wanted to say but couldn't: yo, tambien. I read some new sonnets of yours in Harpers[3] which I thought contained two of about the best poems I'd ever read by anyone, anywhere . . .

Yes: please do send the Last Address, *quam celerime:*[4] I plan to re-write it, cutting the dialogue Great Circle passage – but have no copy, and we want to start working full blast again right away. God bless and much love to Mary and you from us both.

Malc

Annotations:

1 In his 18 August 1940 letter to Lowry (Sugars, 144), Aiken says he is ex-pecting a visit from a friend called Bob Morss, who has pulmonary cancer. Lowry, however, is referring to Richard Ely Morse's poem en-titled 'This Swan' in the *Dial* (September 1927): 222.
2 Aiken's 'Back to Poetry' appeared in *Atlantic Monthly* 166, 2 (1940): 217-23.
3 Aiken's 'Five Sonnets' were first published in *Harper's* 181 (August 1940): 268-69, and were later included in *And in the Human Heart* (1940).
4 The correct Latin is *quam celerrime*: 'as fast as possible.'

151: To Gerald Noxon

P: Texas(ts)
PP: *LLN* 30-33

Dollarton P.O.,
Dollarton, B.C.
21 September 1940

Dear Gerald:

Yours was most welcome and omnivorously read: many thanks. News here is as infrequent as on shipboard: when it does arrive one often feels his correspondent may be dead. Strange you should have been at Conrad's. All things return, the eternal return as Conrad, who writes nowadays with such gusto he must make many of the poets of our generation feel they have one foot in the grave, might say. It is refreshing to compare his later work with Eliot's later, the Family Reunion, etc., which is as necrophilic as ever.[1] I believe that Conrad's early work sent one even further down the drain than Eliot's, if possible. The trouble even with Eliot's kind of drain is that it reeks of sanctity, whereas Conrad's honestly and majestically stank. I see no reason why one should not be lead down the drain: I believe it an important experience if the drain is fulsome enough. The long and short of it is: Conrad is a poet, in the sense that Shakespeare and Keats were poets. There is the same love of good and evil, that fierce glare which sent Eliot on all fours away from it into the church to keep his inhibitions warm, and Tolstoy gibbering into a station waiting room at three o'clock in the morning at the age of eighty or thereabouts, howling and spewing, and still certain, though it can have been but cold comfort to him, that Uncle Tom's Cabin (he was perhaps more unconsciously influenced by Eliza's escape over the ice cakes than by Lear's biding the pelting of the pitiless storm) was greater than King Lear.[2] It must be admitted that Conrad doesn't give much of a damn about certain things. For my part (to oversimplify) I find him, as a poet, a more and better influence than he was to me at twenty. Much of his work has been heretofore shockingly underrated or fallen upon by pimps and rogues. This is very unfair, but all this will change. I think he has made a very fine marriage. I much admire both Mary and her work: that I should have, even in a very small degree, have assisted at this gives me much pleasure.[3]

Now, about going east. This is precisely what we strove to be able to do for many months. We found ourselves in a hateful position here, I won't go into details now, but later, if I see you, I perhaps will, for much, though it seemed tragic then seems amusing enough now: suffice it that, had not the possibility of going Conradwards burned like a beacon before our eyes, there would have been plenty in our lot difficult to bear. While passing over many of these things that would have been difficult to bear I might mention this apprehension as the most personal & because it still exists: that one should proceed headlong into this war without first at least having taken one's bearings with one's friends. Since one is not in the first line of defense one ought to try to create the opportunity, and among British Israelites and Oxford Groupers here – I do not speak of those of course who have already gone, only of those who remain – this is difficult. Is it possible to be a pacifist and at the same time fundamentally bloodthirsty and hypocritical? That is how certain people here strike me. Rather more important than this is the fear that were I called up at present no provision would be made for Margerie, whom by this time you are aware of: not only no provision, but she would have no status. We cannot marry until October 15: even then there is no guarantee that, should I leave, she would be provided for. Every day I see in the paper some complaint from a woman whose husband is in the army: he has left her an allotment, but she has not received any money yet, even though he joined up on May 15th. It is true that Margie could get a job: but is it true? Margie would then be the wife of an Englishman, hence English and American, and an Englishman, that is a visitor, (or American) has no status, at least so far as a job is concerned. For instance I have not been allowed to register. When I applied to join up, noone even bothered to take my name. That is, as a soldier. Actually, my application to the Navy came to the same thing.

At the moment our situation is such. We have, not counting potentialities, about two hundred dollars. That sounds little: on the contrary, it is a fortune. Our rent costs us practically nothing: we hew our logs, draw our water: oil lamps and candles; and so forth. We cook, on a wood stove, such meals as remind us of Dijon. We have a boat, and so travel by water. Last Sunday I rowed fifty miles: why, I don't know, we have not looked at the boat for a week after that. Anyhow, there it is. With this money in hand, we were therefore able even to ask you down, without this being in the least a Mexican invitation. For it is possible to live as well as a king on next to nothing, a great deal better, in fact, than many kings I could think of. In addition to this there is a hope based upon a solid foundation that soon advances, or at least an advance, will be forthcoming on books. But my permission to remain in Canada expires October 31: Margie's on November 15, these permits having in the past already been renewed. Probably all that is needed to renew them is, as it was before, an appearance of opulence which can be simulated for ten minutes or so. Were I in Toronto it might be easier it is true. For my presence in Toronto at all would indicate that I had had at least enough money to get there from Vancouver and hence probably enough to remain. The question also arises: where, if I do not remain in Canada, should I go? Certainly not to the States. I do not expect there will be any difficulty, however, about remaining. Although I have been toiling with the prospect in view of existing quite apart from any funds I might get from England (for it looks as though these must be written off entirely in the future) when I read your suggestion that there was a possibility of work in Toronto, and at that upon films, and at that, possibly, with yourself, I rubbed my eyes. It is, of course, probably some kind of a joke – too good to be true. However, in case it is not a joke it has occurred to me that I might really be able to lend some useful assistance. I can only guess at the kind of work you have chosen or which has chosen you and I am assuming that, if that work is upon documentary films, that you have to struggle against the form but at the same time accept it much as a poet no fool for iambic pentametres but committed to them has to struggle with them and against them: I have seen a great film about a duck, about an African lung fish, about Latter Day Saints in Utah. As for propaganda, good propaganda, I take it, is good art. (e.g. The River.)[4] I have not seen the Hemingway film about Spain, but I did see one in Mexico called Espana in Llames,[5] which made me go straight out and land in gaol. That similar results were expected from such films as Storm over Asia[6] – I will never forget how you made the gramophone play, in the silver fox scene, Joe Venuti's bamboozling the bassoon – is presumably why they were not more widely distributed. Knowing nothing even though I had been a fireman at sea and through a Chinese Revolution at the time I first saw the End of St Petersburg,[7] I did not recognize it as propaganda at all. I merely thought, responding to it emotionally, that it was marvellous, the best I had ever seen (etc.) up to that point: the opening sequence of windmills on the steppes made me weep, as it were, 'from the sheer beauty of it.' In the same way, I was moved – or misled – by Alexander Room's The Ghost that never returns,[8] of which I can, though I saw it only once and that eleven years ago, remember every detail. Anyhow, good propaganda, for whatever cause, is good art. The Lion has Wings[9] would have done, I should have thought, damage to any cause, however noble. How many times and in how many English films do I have to see that bloody toy Spanish Armada, shot in a bathtub? There are a thousand things on this subject I would like to discuss with you: Paul Strand's Redes, Dovjenkho's Frontier.[10] I will keep them for another letter or occasion. What I am trying to say is such great films have stormed in me day and night! One day I would like to assist you make one. Meantime, if you are not pulling my leg, may I suggest to you that even if there is some possibility of helping in some such meek capacity as writing the least important part of the dialogue for a film about icebreakers, that I feel you would not regret providing that opportunity? As for films about regiments, the best one I ever did see was a French one about the Foreign Legion – not by Renoir, Duvivier, or Feyder, the director had some triple-barrelled name which I have forgotten. The music was by Eisler, and it was called simply, in Mexican, Una Aventura en Moroc.[11] An Adventure in Morocco. Have you ever seen such a film, and if so, who made it?

Our problem in any case would be to *get* to Toronto. Assuming the worst from our books, what money we have is nothing when one takes such things as fares into account, though a lot otherwise as I have tried to show. Perhaps you have some advice. *Our* invitation is still open, you know, but that sounds imposs. We might hitchhike.

At all events, it is not all impossible, if we ever get there, that

you might find, in me, a Pudovkin in the Outhouse. Here's a health
to your Thunder over Canada[12] whatever form it may take, then:
Margie joins me in sending our love to you and Mrs. Noxon –

Que viva – life!

Malcolm Lowry

Annotations:

1 T.S. Eliot's poetic drama *The Family Reunion* (1939) is a savage analysis
of family relations.

2 Tolstoy had read Harriet Beecher Stowe's novel *Uncle Tom's Cabin*
(1852) as early as 1854. He was deeply impressed by the book, which he
felt had been instrumental to the abolition of slavery in the United
States, and in the 1890s he thought of writing a new *Uncle Tom's Cabin*
to address the problem of land ownership in Russia. Eliza is a mulatto
slave who escapes across the frozen Ohio River with her child. Lowry's
comparison is with the third act of Shakespeare's *King Lear*.

3 Conrad Aiken and Mary Hoover stayed with Malcolm and Jan Lowry in
Cuernavaca, Mexico, prior to their marriage in July 1936.

4 *The River* (1937) is an American documentary film by Pare Lorentz
about the history and ecology of the Mississippi River basin.

5 *España in Llames* (1937) is a documentary film (and powerful propaganda) about the Spanish Civil War. The film, which was made by the
Spanish republican government with Soviet cameramen, was in two
parts: 'The Fight For Freedom' and 'No Pasaran' (They Shall Not Pass).

6 *Storm over Asia* (1928), by the Russian director Vsevolod Pudovkin
(1893-1953), was a propaganda film against oppression. For a discussion
of Noxon's activities as a film critic in Cambridge and of the films playing there between 1929 and 1932, see Paul Tiessen's 'A Canadian Film
Critic in Malcolm Lowry's Cambridge,' *Malcolm Lowry Review* 19/20
(1986-87): 27-42. *Storm over Asia* is one of several films remembered here
by Lowry that Noxon had screened for the Cambridge University Film
Society's 1929-30 program.

7 *The End of St Petersburg* (1927), also directed by Pudovkin, portrayed the
events of the Russian Revolution.

8 Abram Room (1894-1976) was a Russian film and theatre director and a
journalist. *The Ghost That Never Returns* (1929), about a South American
worker on a day's leave from prison, is an example of Communist propaganda.

9 *The Lion Has Wings* (1939), a British documentary about events leading
to the outbreak of the Second World War, is typical of the fairly crude
war propaganda of the day.

10 Paul Strand's *Redes (The Wave)* (1936) was a beautifully photographed,
moving documentary about a fisherman filmed in Mexico. Alexander
Dovjenkho (1894-1956) was a leading Russian film director and, with
Eisenstein and Pudovkin, one of the great masters of early Russian

cinema. Lowry is referring to his 1935 film *Aerograd (Air City, Frontier)*.
11 Lowry must be conflating two films concerning the Foreign Legion,
    Josef von Sternberg's *Morocco* (1930) and Jacques Feyder's *Le Grand Jeu*
    (1934). Von Sternberg has the triple-barrelled name, but Hanns Eisler
    (1898-1962), a German composer and socialist who worked with
    Brecht, composed the music for Feyder's film.
12 Lowry's allusion is to *Thunder over Mexico* (1933) by the famous Russian
    film director Sergei Eisenstein (1898-1948). In his complimentary close
    Lowry refers to Eisenstein's unfinished masterpiece, *Que viva Mexico*, of
    which *Thunder over Mexico* is only a part.

152: To Harold Matson

P: Matson(ts); UBC(phc)

Dollarton P.O.,
Dollarton, B.C.
4 October 1940

Dear Hal:
Skoal!¹ We'd be awful grateful if you'd send us some news –
always bearing in mind that you probably have not heretofore
because it was bad, but no matter – of our posthumous works? If
Whit still has the Volcano by now, it must be growing somewhat
extinct: and how twists the Last Twist of the Knife?
We have more work going along for you – and good, we feel – but
the anonymity (than which there is none more perfect) of silence
from the U.S., together with the hangdog news from the old homestead – not to say *our* old homesteads – and this and that, makes us
feel that we are struggling in a kind of void. . .
No matter what, let us know: we meant, mean, well anyhow.
As ever,
Malcolm

Annotations:

1 The Scandinavian expression 'skoal' is used in a toast to drink someone's
   health. Contemporary Danish is *skaal* and Norwegian is *skål*, but the
   term comes from the Old Norse, *skāl*, for bowl.

153: To Harold Matson

P: Matson(ts); UBC(phc)

> Dollarton P.O.,
> Dollarton, B.C.,
> Canada
> 12 October 1940
> remember it is Canada![1]

Dear Hal:

Thanks for your letter, after which I believe in my book, rather more, if anything, because I do not think these individuals can have read it carefully: I am somewhat hurt about Whit, who has said not a word to me all this while. As for the Dunn theory of time I just vaguely know what it is but have never read Dunn and so cannot be preoccupied with it: perhaps they meant Ouspensky:[2] anyhow, the book has nothing to do with such a thing: Martha's [Martha Foley] remarks prove that she has seen fit to know as little about my poor book as I about Dunn,[3] that's all; which is unfortunate, but not I hope, fatal. Perhaps it was they who were experimenting with the Dunn theory of time by keeping it for so many months without a word when I had told them that I was working against, no theory, but time itself. But thank *you*, personally, a lot: – what about Linscott, however, of Houghton Mifflin? I don't think you can have got my letter about him: so here goes because it is important.

So, N.B.: etc. Bob Linscott, of, I think, 2 Park Street, Boston, anyhow of Houghton Mifflin, was sent some things of mine by Conrad Aiken – when I was trying, unsuccessfully, to raise some money – and expressed himself very interested, wanted to see Under the Volcano. It was as encouraging a thing as I'd heard in a long while and so help me God it was entirely because I felt I had an obligation to Whit that I sent the latter the damn book in the first place. I told Aiken to tell Linscott that the book was not 'free' at the moment, but that he should see it, with your permission as soon as it was. Might I suggest then, that Linscott – of Houghton Mifflin – would be a good bet? Particularly since he is holding a book of poems and a rough draft of In Ballast to the White Sea until he sees Under the Volcano.

I am such a hopelessly long way away (and threatening at any moment to be even further away) that the ethics of a thing have got a bit muddled, I know, but may I ask you humbly not to let these suggestions & counter suggestions try your patience: I owed Linscott a note so have already told him that you have the book: and he will, I hope, be looking for it.

I do not think I have deceived myself about its merits; what do you privately think? News on the other side of the family is more encouraging. There – strangely enough – Linscott also plays or may play a part, he having seen a first version of Margerie's 'Last Twist of the Knife' some time ago, I now discover, and having encouraged her with it, and asked her to let him see it again should it be rewritten, which it was, under my dubious and obscure auspices.

Well, thank you for everything, Hal. I am determined that one day you will not be sorry you have borne with me so long.

Yours Sincerely

Malcolm

Annotations:

1 Matson had sent his letter with just the town and province; therefore, Lowry is reminding him to include the country in the address because Dollarton, B.C. was scarcely well known.
2 It is clear from Lowry's 16 April 1940 letter (**135**) to his mother-in-law, Anna Mabelle Bonner, that he had read and enjoyed Dunne's *An Experiment with Time*, as well as Ouspensky's work, and in his 6 July 1941 letter (**165**) to Burnett and Foley he agrees that the novel is 'confused by Dunne stuff.'
3 See Appendix 2 for Matson's 7 October 1940 letter to Lowry with Martha Foley's criticisms.

154: To Harold Matson

P: Matson(ts); UBC(phc)

Dollarton P.O.,
Dollarton, B.C.,
Canada
17 October 1940

Dear Hal:

I feel that this story – which we tried to sell under the title of Metal years ago, ought to have a market now.[1]

I have only made negligible alterations: surely *some* magazine would be able to see that it has a certain power and grim irony. Or you could persuade them.

I sent it out last spring myself to Esquire and the Atlantic, both of whom refused it.

Every story – they are not many – that I have ever had published has either made O'Brien or his honours list: I don't see why this should be an exception. But if *Story* is the only possibility I would rather you tore it up, on bitter thinkings.

Yours sincerely,

Malcolm

P.S. Did you ever get, by the way, a letter I sent you to forward to Julian Green?[2]

P.P.S. 'This story' has had to be sent under separate cover, may not arrive by the same mail.

Annotations:

1 The story to which Lowry is referring is 'June 30th, 1934,' which was published for the first time in *Malcolm Lowry: Psalms and Songs* (36-48). Metal is of key thematic and symbolic importance in the story. Matson, who was unable to sell it, returned the manuscript to Lowry in May 1941.
2 No letter to Julien Green appears to have survived, but see Lowry's letter to a 'Mr Green' in Appendix 3. Green spent the years of the Second World War in the United States, returning to France in 1945, and in his 6 September 1940 letter (**150**) to Conrad Aiken, Lowry mentions having suggested, in a letter he sent to Green care of Harold Matson (**149**), that Green contact Aiken.

155: To Gerald Noxon

P: Texas(ts)
PP: *LLN* 33-34

Dollarton P.O.,
Dollarton, B.C.,
Canada
2 November 1940

Dear Gerald:

I was very glad to hear from you – and very much hope you do come here rather than go to British Guiana. Dollarton is fine, the Rockies are very fine, Vancouver itself is a lousy place that stinks to high heaven with hypocrisy; as does much of everything and everyone else. Our case is now somewhat 'improved' in that, for some obscure reason, money has started to come from England: whether it hails from a forgiving old man, an elder brother suddenly heir to a forgotten investment of mine that thawed when noone was looking, or merely from some amiable eccentric, we have no way of knowing: it hails, however, from the Westminster Bank of Liverpool, which one had thought bombed out of existence long since, and is in the shape of 25 English pounds or $110 a month, to be continued until further notice. This now puts us in the position of being able to arrive in Toronto without feeling that we were imposing some kind of moral blackmail upon you by informing you we were there, and conversely, puts you in the position, should you arrive here, of being able to visit the Cabinet of Dr Caliglowry[1] without any unpleasant sense of grinding the face of the poor.

Thanks for mentioning me to Grierson. It seems a long time since I saw Drifters . . .[2]

Is Len Lye[3] over on this side, by the way?

Did you ever hear tell of one Karl Grune – a German Jew who years and years ago in Germany made The Street, and a few years back made Abdul the Damned in England, with Nils Asther?[4] Neither of those films are good looked at as a whole: both had genius, I thought.

Well: let us know what you are doing – here, as elsewhere, our morale is 'indescribable' – authoritative sources state, – nowhere do you find people more keenly aware of the war than in Vancouver – two million bayonets stand between us and the last quarter of an hour, and even the very lamposts stand ready to protect their 'honor.' We are very sincerely hoping to see you soon, whether we come east or you come west. Love to you and your wife,

Malcolm

Annotations:

1 Robert Wiene's expressionist film classic *The Cabinet of Dr Caligari* (1919) was one of Lowry's favourites, and he used it as an important allusion in *Under the Volcano*.
2 The Scottish filmmaker John Grierson (1898-1972) was the father of documentary cinema, a founder of the National Film Board of Canada and government film commissioner in Canada from 1939 to 1945. In the fall of 1940 Noxon was working with Grierson at the NFB. *Drifters* is a 1929 film documentary on the herring fishery in the North Sea.
3 Len Lye (1901-80) was a New Zealander who went to England in 1926 to work in the theatre and on films. An experimental filmmaker and a friend of Noxon's, he worked with Grierson in England during the 1930s and on wartime propaganda films between 1940 and 1944.
4 Karl Grune (1890-1962) was a German filmmaker whose best-known film, *The Street* (1923), was a good example of late expressionist cinema. *Abdul the Damned* (1935) starred the romantic Swedish actor Nils Asther (1897-1981).

156: To Conrad Aiken

P: H(ts)
PP: *LAL* 146-49

Dollarton P.O.,
Dollarton, B.C.,
Canada
22 November 1940

Dear old Conrad:

I think, dream, poetry all the time these days, struggling with the only form I know, the one you taught me. With a sort of a monad, gulped down into my consciousness like a stone in my adolescence, still stuck in my throat I wonder if I can ever achieve more than a half choked expression of myself and can hang myself one day on some sort of hall of fame, however obscure. We live Thoreau-like[1] here, in the deserted village where grey Panamanian freighters sometimes visit us. I keep remembering how I used to go on to Hayes Common and read the House of Dust[2] and pray one day I might meet you, which seemed to be impossible, because I could not see how you could be alive and at the same time reach such beauty, and all the time Jane was at school close by with the Kellett child, who was indeed my geographical excuse for being on Hayes Common at all.[3] How I appreciate now the colossal advantage of having known you and would that I had been better and honester and more *conscious* when I did! I sometimes think I am like a man who remembers having known Bill Shakespeare in his youth – but what a pity, he couldn't appreciate anything the fellow said, he was blind and dumb at the time.

Our cat has had kittens – four of them – for which we have found homes for two, alas and alas, at the bottom of the sea: now, from what we can hear of her peckerdilloes she is well on the way to having some more. I have not much of a way with cats, but Margie has and I improve. There are killer-whales in the bay – we encountered one while rowing, thought it was a porpoise with a poipose – and we have been viciously attacked by a goat – a symbol? No more tragedies . . .[4] Yeah. We still look forward with all our hopes to the prospect of seeing you again soon: immobilisation is difficult though. I can never thank you enough for lots of things. How could we have survived without the hope you gave us? And I know that, thanks to you, whatever the old man has to suffer will be much mitigated. . . . I hope Mary is well, give her our very special best and most special love. An article of yours I discovered in a yellowed New

Republic in the Vancouver Library,[5] inspired this, in which there ought not be more than ninetyfour plagiarisms. (Matter of fact, I don't think there are any unless 'derricks of the soul' recalls – without however benefiting by the comparison – 'who watches here, oh mariners and surgeons' & could be counted as such. It is not necessarily improved by this deficiency of having none & now I see another: 'muted.' B.V? [*Blue Voyage*])

> This wrestling, as of seamen with a storm
> Which flies to leeward, while they
> United in that chaos, turn, sea-weary
> Each on his bunk, to dream of fields at home
> Or shake with visions Dante never knew,
> The poet himself feels, struggling with the form
> Of his quiet work. What derricks of the soul
> Plunge in that muted room, adrift, menacing?
> When truant heart can hear the sailors sing
> He'd break his pen to sail an easting down.
> And yet some mariner's ferment in his blood
> Sustains him to subdue or be subdued.
> In sleep all night he grapples with a sail!
> But words beyond the life of ships dream on.[6]

Meantime nature poems, mature poems, hate poems, fate poems, – all, but great poems – pour out. At the moment I am toying with this pleasing Rabelaisian whimsy. People down from the direction of the saw mill, hearing suspicious blood curdling noises at night from this direction, come to investigate, (It has happened.) with lanterns, even a 'lifeboat.' It ends –

> Never in a comedian's life have I laughed till then!
> . . . Wherefore the legend grew that there were ghosts
> Somewhere between Dead Tree and Merry Island,
> And from our love revived an Indian slaughter.
> Oh you who something something something land
> May you too be blessed by such enormous laughter
> As even God and whales might not approve.[7]

But I haven't got the beginning yet: or, it might be said, the end either. Anyhow, Conrad, thus one's time is spent or mispent, waiting for a man from Porlock, who may never come.[8] I hope not. Meantime, the Volc is at Linscotts. I should have taken your advice and sent it him first. But I was duty bound to send it to Burnett, who, it turned out, didn't even read it.[9]

Can you tell me some mags where one might send pomes with hope of small payments?

Please write and tell us if you still love us as we indeed love you
from both

Malc

Annotations:

1 Henry David Thoreau (1817-62), the American transcendentalist philosopher and author, lived in a simple self-made hut near Walden Pond in Massachusetts from 1845 to 1847. It was there that he wrote his best-known book, *Walden* (1854), which celebrates life lived in simplicity, independence, and close to nature.

2 Hayes Common was near 5 Woodville Road in the Blackheath area of London, where Lowry stayed for a period during 1928-29 when he was studying for his entrance to Cambridge with an ex-Leys master, Jerry Kellett. Woodville Road no longer exists; it succumbed to urban development at the site of the present interchange overpass of Shooters Hill Road and Rochester Way. Hayes Common does not appear on maps from 1940 and may have been a local name. Lowry's first letters to Aiken in 1928-29 (**20** and **21**) were written from Woodville Road. Aiken's volume of poetry *House of Dust* was published in 1920.

3 Jane, Aiken's daughter, and Joan Kellett attended a school close to Hayes Common, and on Saturdays Lowry would take Joan out for tea.

4 Throughout *Under the Volcano* Lowry links goats with tragedy (from the Latin *trăgoedĭa*, meaning 'the song of the goat') and with cuckolds (from the Spanish *cabron*, meaning 'goat,' the horns suggesting cuckolding). Thus, the goat is a symbol of the Consul, especially in chapter 4 when it charges Hugh and Yvonne; moreover, as Dr Vigil knows, the Consul spends his life in 'continuous tragedies.'

5 According to Cynthia Sugars, Lowry may be referring to Aiken's 'Gigantic Dreams,' *New Republic*, 27 June 1928: 146-47.

6 The lines quoted here for Aiken appear in an altered form as the poem 'Joseph Conrad,' in *Selected Poems of Malcolm Lowry* (74); see Scherf (117-18).

7 These seven lines, without 'beginning' and 'end,' are published as a short untitled poem in Scherf (197).

8 The 'man from Porlock' is a reference to Coleridge's introduction to 'Kubla Khan' (1798), in which he explains that, while writing down the lines that he recalled from a dream, he was interrupted 'by a person on business' from the nearby town of Porlock, and as a result was never able to recollect the two or three hundred lines he had composed during his dream. Given Lowry's concern over plagiarism from Aiken in this letter, it is interesting that he should link himself with Coleridge, who of all infamous English plagiarists most resembles Lowry.

9 In his 7 October 1940 letter to Lowry, Harold Matson acknowledges receipt of the *Volcano* manuscript from Whit Burnett and reports Martha Foley's negative response. See Appendix 2.

157: To Conrad Aiken

P: H(ts)
PP: *LAL* 149-50

Dollarton P.O.,
Dollarton, B.C.,
Canada
30 November 1940

Dear old fellow:

Down the abyss crasheth the tabid world . . . Have you news – my God! – of John [Davenport]? Ed [Burra]? May they be safe. I have some news from my mater, who sounds pretty mad though her bloodthirstyness is directed at most everything. I have to admit, sceptical though I sometimes be about reports of indescribable morale, that she never sounded in such good form. God knows how or why, what with the hellish shellacking they've been giving Liverpool. But this letter was written before the worst . . . Our gardener is dead, a good egg and I have written this epitaph to be put on his grave.[1] Maybe they won't because they'd have to build a Grant's tomb to accomodate it. 'Would you like to see our son's poems? Then we'll all go off to the graveyard after tea . . .'

Linscott wrote me a very encouraging letter about the Volc. He was for it, others were agin.[2] I'm not distressed though – he thinks somebody will take it eventually. I'm not caring. We have enough just to scrape through for a month or two. Who could be luckier than we? Virginia Strong [Stong][3] has sent in a cracking good report on Margie's detective novel, so that's fine news.

But principally I don't care about the Volc because I'm writing poetry all the time now. I send you four poems, and wondered, if you liked them, or thought they were suitable or whatever, I could ask you the favour of sending them to the Atlantic Monthly with a benign word. I hate to give you trouble: but as your old – and present, more than ever, pupil I feel you would be pleased I was writing poetry, if it was good, or even if I were trying. I feel that they have something, a certain simplicity and strength, – a universality, maybe – that they may have an unusual dramatic quality. You told me once to send some poems I had written along and you will forgive me if

I have been taking you at your word ever since. I may be fooling myself about these particular poems and if I am I know you will tell me so, but please answer me this: may I keep on firing them at you until you think you see one which might be published in that there Atlantic for it seems to me a fine and traditional place to start? I can't tell you what a kick that would give the old creative instinct.

Divorce papers have not arrived till now and we are going to be married by a fine carrot-juice swigging Unitarian minister on Monday[4] – shades of your ancestors – We know you are wishing us luck – God bless you, & Mary, – love from both –

Malc

P.S. I have appended bloody little titles to the poems, after the Atlantic custom. I am no Wallace Stevens, unfortunately. And, of course, Gawd with a capital H. And good god, why not?

Annotations:

1 See Lowry's 'Epitaph on our gardener, dead near Liverpool,' Scherf (174-75). No poems are extant with this letter.
2 In his 19 November 1940 letter to Lowry, Robert Linscott quotes from an adverse report on *Volcano* and informs Lowry that he is returning the manuscript to Harold Matson. If this is indeed the letter to which Lowry is referring here, then it is difficult to see how he could call it 'very encouraging.'
3 In a 16 October 1940 letter to Lowry, Matson notes Lowry's misspelling of Stong's name. Stong had made suggestions for revisions to *The Last Twist of the Knife*.
4 The Lowrys were married on 2 December 1940.

158: To Conrad Aiken

P: H(ts)
PP: *LAL* 151

Dollarton P.O.,
Dollarton, B.C.
4 December 1940

Hi William! Herman! Conrad! Nathaniel![1] Help!
Between the blank verse and the cordite – Here is another version of pome I sent you. Lines 8 to 10 are different. In the version I sent you it looks as though Lycidas and not the sea stank so badly it would make whoever it was weep.

So I have rewritten the pome so that it merely looks as though it is the poem that stinks and not Lycidas.[2]

Herewith. It may be the fulfillment of a lifelong ambition to haunt a graveyard, anyhow.

We were married without a hitch, which is a paradox, and very fine too.

God bless you, my dear old bird, and Mary.

I much admire the poet jones, very.[3]

Love from both –

Malc

Annotations:

1 Lowry is placing Aiken in the company of major American writers: William Carlos Williams, Herman Melville, and Nathaniel Hawthorne, unless 'William' is a reference to the protagonist of Aiken's *Blue Voyage*, William Demarest.

2 Lowry is referring to 'Epitaph on our gardener, dead near Liverpool.' No copy of the poem is extant with the letter.

3 Lowry is rhyming on the name of the New England transcendentalist poet Jones Very (1813–80).

159: To Conrad Aiken

P: H(ts)
PP: *LAL* 152

Dollarton P.O.,
Dollarton, B.C.
11 December 1940

Dear Conrad:

I will promise not to send you another pome – save for Christmas, maybe – but am venturing to send you this, wondering if you had not already sent any of the other pomes to the Atlantic, if you would enclose it, if you were going to send any, that is, and please do not send any if you don't think it right, because it won't hurt me, I can't stop writing them anyhow – and anyway why don't I send them myself. The last is rather easily answered: nobody seems willing to take them nor agent handle them unless you are a 'name' or the pomes are solicited, or good, or something. '*Poetry*' may be an exception but I don't know the address. Maybe you could give me some suggestions . . .[1]

Once in Rye you wrote me a letter mentioning the strange noises my uke made.

With the aid of an introverted sensibility I have now turned this round a bit.

If a uke why not a guitar or a harp or a viol made out of a woman's breastbone or even the heritage poets leave behind for later singers?

Love from both to both

Malc

P.S.   My explanation of the poem is just balls, as usual: pay no attention.

Annotations:

1 In his 15 December 1940 letter, Aiken explained that due to an argument with Edward Augustus Weeks (1898-1989), then associate editor of *Atlantic Monthly*, he could not send Lowry's poems there. He praised 'Epitaph on our gardener' for being 'formally more complete,' but warned: 'do try to keep your numbers and quantities straight – ! Freedom comes *after* mastery not before –' (Sugars, 154). It is not clear which poem Lowry was asking Aiken to place for him because no poem is extant with this letter.

160: To Conrad Aiken

P: H(ts)
PP: *LAL* 154-55

Dollarton P.O.,
Dollarton, B.C.
20 December 1940

– I didn't send you a pome for Christmas, my dear old phalla, but here's an appropriate yeastsy thought for the New Year. (Not for the Atlantic *Monthly*.)

> BYZANTIUM: or Where the Great Life Begins
> (or Getting a bit knocked oop now.)
> – Don't come any of that Byzantium stuff
> On me, me swell young toff! Just plain Stamboul
> Is good enough fer me and Lamps and Bill.
> Constantibloodynople's right enough –
> Used to be, eh? Eh? Don't give me that guff

Like that wot you said a bout the ideal –
In a blind eye socket! But a girl's a girl
And bobhead tigers here will treat you rough
And give you, 'ideal!' *Farewell, smoke is real –*
And ukeleles mourn a ululu:
And engine stampedes: more fool you fool you:
And aeriel says: oh whither where away:
And sea: each one-eared dog will have its day:
And stars wink: Venus first, then Mercury.[1]

God enormously bless you both and give you Merry Christmas. We find life marvellous here, sea and snow – God goes by with white footfall – no men with black footfall from Porlock[2] – and a wild duck washed up on the shore.

Malc

N.B. Here's another called 'Deserter', also not for publication.

. . . 'Dead, in a refrigerator van at Empress.'
Then, lying on bare boards, in a small room
His father came from Coquitlam to see.
'There wasn't even a sheet over him.'
Brought his body down from Medicine Hat
That had been placed in Category C.
Military papers in his army greatcoat
– 'Should have been in England? Came home for Christmas?
– And did he have to bum his way back home?' –
Thus pass, from old Westminster to New!
Here is a tale that clangs an iron door shut
Against the heart, freezing sense: for pity
Cannot follow to the accusing root
Of this tragedy beyond tragedy.[3]

Annotations:

1 The thought is 'yeastsy' because the poem is an ironic reference to W.B. Yeats's poem 'Sailing to Byzantium.' Lowry's poem was published in slightly altered form as 'Byzantium' in *Selected Poems*; see Scherf (161–62).
2 For Lowry's previous use of this Coleridge allusion, see his 22 November 1940 letter (**156**) to Aiken.
3 See Scherf (139–40).

161: To Conrad Aiken

P: H(ts)
PP: *LAL* 156

> Dollarton P.O.,
> Dollarton, B.C.
> 3 January 1941

Dear Conrad –

Just received yesterday And in the Human Heart[1] for which a thousand thanks. It is deeply appreciated by both. Have not had time to digest as yet but can only say so far it was not so much like opening a book on words, but on a lightning, a sunlight. It was as though a coiled bright soul sprung out at us. Will elaborate later: what I have seen is great, and my feeling comes just after an attempt to do some hefty reading right through English Literature, Shakespeare, Jonson, Milton, etc. I feel there are in your book some of the highest touchstones of excellence in *all* literature. Will write at greater length later.

Margie says she's paralyzed by book – both send thanks to both and love –

> Malc

P.S. Feel a bit ashamed – as who wouldn't, after your book? – of myself, sending you *my* unpolished mumblings: but I am working very hard at trying to get the mastery you have indicated and which I agree is so necessary: so far am encouraged with results so I may bore you with some more.[a]

Annotations:

1 Lowry's copy of *And in the Human Heart* (New York: Duell, Sloan and Pearce, 1940) is with his library at UBC; it carries an inscription with Christmas greetings for both the Lowrys.

Editorial Notes:

a. There are no poems extant with this letter.

162: To Gerald Noxon

P: Texas(ts)
PP: *LLN* 35-36

Dollarton P.O.,
Dollarton, B.C.
15 January 1941

Dear Gerald:
    Very many thanks indeed for so promptly getting me out of the Jeacle.[1] And your aid was entirely effective for I have just received my passport all O.K. and countersigned by his henchman at Ottawa, one Mr Skelton. Sir Sparrowe has drawn a timid line through the Union of Socialist Republics of Soviet Russia, otherwise it still seems valid everywhere from Penguin Island to baboon-occupied Dahomey. Thanks a million! All luck with the novel:[2] I note what you said about bus traveling and agree it is good fun, though my last experience was gruesome. Though armed with a perfectly good visa and the right papers and all when I set off in September 1939 to see Margie in the U.S. – to say, as I thought, good-bye before going to England – I was turned back at the American border as without proof that I would not be a public charge. The law had changed between the time I got the visa and the time I set forth. That happened at a place named Blaine, well named indeed. It's happened to lots of people, including Canadians at that place. They pick upon bus travelers particularly because they assume they ought to be able to afford to travel by train if they can go to the U.S. A hell of a note. And if you don't appeal within 48 hours you can't go in for a year. Of course this was at the weekend, and with my G.H.Q.[3] in the States, I couldn't get the necessary dope in time. It was hellish. Do you remember Alexander [Abram] Room's 'ghost that never returns.' It was like that only different and worse. It probably saved my life as a matter of fact because I'd been fixing to go to England: but I didn't think of that at the time. So Margie came up here: and here we've stayed so far. I am thinking of a poem at the moment, called The Englishman Turned Back at the Border, beginning:

> A singing smell of tar, of the highway,
> Fills the grey Vancouver Bus Terminal,
> Crowned by dreaming names, New Orleans,
> Spokane, Chicago – and Los Angeles!
> City of the Angels and my luck,
> Where artists labor to insult mankind

With genius coeval to the age,
And city of my love come next Sunday.
Out of a flag-hung shop a sleeked puppet
Hands me my ticket and my destiny.

The blue exhaust speeds parting's litany.
Then, with pneumatic bounds, we herd the street.
The lights, symbolic, nictitate in day.
Cautious, but with mechanic persiflage
– Rolando's horn could no more strangely wind –
Past Chinatown and names like Kwong Lee Duck,
Our bus treads asphalt with the noise of bees,
By taverns mumbling of skidroad scenes,
Then double declutched my heart through neutral
And sang it into high for U.S.A.[4]

It goes on, of course: or rather, comes back. . . It struck me as a bit of a brainwave to put the rhymes or assonances in reverse so that you got the effect of the streets and the past slipping away from you but at the same time being intermeshed and interwoven with the present. When the bus comes back the rhymes are the other way around. . . The bus that brought me back was full of cheer, and I, most unrelievedly, of beer. . . So much for buses. My God, what brackish bilge is this. Thought it might make a good Venuti tune, Esquirish, however.

Our plans are vague but for the present we are staying here. We still hope to see you and Conrad sometime soon though don't know how it can be managed. Do let me know where you are. If you are in New York and have time why not look up my old pal Jimmy (Best Short Stories 32, 33, 34, 35, ad lib) Stern, whose address is 20 E. 68th St., New York City, who is a hell of a fine guy and who I know would enjoy meeting you.

Well, thank you again Gerald, the best of luck with the book again, too, and all the best to Mrs Noxon.

Malcolm

P.S. Sorry your film job folded, & [John] Grierson resigned as Film Commissioner. I heard him and Morley Callaghan[5] speak the other day. I thought they were good! But it gave me a glimpse too of the kind of goings on you probably had to wrestle with . . .

Annotations:

1 In his December 1939 or January 1940 letter to Lowry, Noxon writes:

'Have sent off your passport to the mean sounding Jeacle'; see *Letters of Malcolm Lowry and Gerald Noxon* (34). Noxon, who was staying in Virginia at the time, had served as a guarantor on Lowry's passport application form, but it is not clear why Lowry needed to renew his passport at this time or what kind of bureaucratic trouble he might have been in with the Canadian government.

2 Noxon was working on a novel, for which he hoped to find a New York publisher; see *Letters of Malcolm Lowry and Gerald Noxon* (4, 34).

3 G.H.Q. is an abbreviation for the military term 'general headquarters,' and it is Lowry's way of referring to the Los Angeles attorney Benjamin Parks.

4 This poem, called 'Turned Back at the Border,' first appeared in *Arena* 2 (1949): 58-60; see also Scherf (147-51).

5 By 1941 Morley Callaghan (1903-90), the prolific Canadian novelist and short story writer, was known for his stories in *Atlantic Monthly* and the *New Yorker* and for novels such as *They Shall Inherit the Earth* (1935) and *More Joy in Heaven* (1937).

163: To Harold Matson

P: Matson(ts); UBC(phc)
PP: *SL* 39-40

> Dollarton P.O.,
> Dollarton, B.C.,
> Canada
> 4 March 1941

Dear Hal:

I'm sorry I've only given you further disappointments with Under the Volcano, so far, and it may be that the adverse conditions under which the book was finally written influenced me to think it was an artistic triumph when it was only a sort of moral one.

I think on rereading that Martha Foley's judgement[1] is maybe a just one in part; there *is* too much preoccupation with time, and the pattern does not emerge properly.

So I am rewriting it. I think it foolish to embark on an absolutely new project at this time. And, in order to show you the kind of thing I am doing, I am sending you part of it as a short story,[2] which I feel you can sell, where you could not sell June 30, 1934, for instance, or even the book itself. I have cut and cut and cut and of the story as I send it to you I am extremely proud and would very much like to know what you think about it as soon as it is convenient for you.

I had three magazines in mind: Harper's Bazaar, Esquire, and Decision. I may be quite wrong. Anyhow, I leave it to you what to do with it, but please tell me what you decide because I do not think the feeling is wish-fulfillment this time, that I have rung the bell. What I had in mind was: that publication of the 'story' would be a good start, and would help the novel with the publishers. I do not know if Decision is any good: I heard it was influential, and perhaps you would tell me about this.[3] If you send it to Harper's Bazaar, (Ed. George Davis) perhaps you could mention James Stern's name, who has highly praised my short stories and who is a frequent contributor. He said I could suggest this, but maybe it wouldn't do any good. Might it be worth while – for the sake of getting it into print *quickly*, to try Decision, first, which sounds like a likely bet to me? And if you send it to Esquire, perhaps send it to Arnold Gingrich, whom I know slightly, through Jimmy Stern and by correspondence – well, use your own judgement.

I am under the impression that you do not handle poetry, Hal, isn't that right? Unable to help myself now in this respect – and the fact that I have not been a poet hitherto having been the psychological cause of most of my troubles, and yours with me – I have been writing a lot of poetry, and sending it here and there, without any success yet. If I am wrong about your handling poetry tell me. Would it be too much to ask you to send me the address of Decision, which I can't get here, so that I could send them some poetry? If I get a cheque for any of my poems I will send it straight to you without cashing it for I cannot otherwise send money out of the country; mean amount though it would doubtless be, it would be a symbol.

Oh, and Hal – do you have the hapless and ambulatory In Ballast to the White Sea – and the Lighthouse Invites the Storm: I thought I would put these in shape.[4] You will see the ruthless cutting in the excerpt from the Volcano I send you and that is how I would treat them.

Now – re Margerie Bonner. She is now finishing a new and better murder tentatively called 'Cloudburst in Deep Cove.'[5] I am helping on this and the plan is to have the final copy done by the end of the month, (sooner, she says) let it simmer for a fortnight, and during this fortnight to revise the earlier one 'The Last Twist of the Knife' bearing Virginia Stong's suggestions in mind, then send you both together.

Is this O.K. with you? We feel that the second one would implement the promise of the first. Please tell me about these things as soon as you may; I am absolutely determined you are not going to have had all this trouble for nothing and that one day your trust will be repaid.

Yours sincerely,

Malcolm

Annotations:

1 See Appendix 2.
2 The short story 'Under the Volcano' was not published until 1964 in *Prairie Schooner* 37, 4 (1963-64): 284-300. Based on the events depicted in chapter 8 of *Under the Volcano*, the story has been thought to pre-date the novel and serve as a kind of original germ for the major work; see Day (216). However, this letter confirms Victor Doyen's claim that in fact the story was excerpted from this early version of the manuscript; see Doyen, 'Fighting the Albatross of Self' (73, 294).
3 In his 6 March 1941 letter to Lowry, Matson dismisses *Decision* as a magazine of little importance. Lowry did, however, send poetry to *Decision* sometime during 1941-42, as an undated letter to him from the founding editor, Klaus Mann, makes clear. Unfortunately, nothing of Lowry's appeared in the magazine, which, after two years of publication, ceased operations in 1942, and the Decision Magazine archive at Yale University Library contains no Lowry correspondence. During its brief life *Decision* had such distinguished writers as Sherwood Anderson, W.H. Auden, Thomas Mann, and, a Lowry favourite, Julien Green on its editorial board.
4 In his 6 March 1941 reply to Lowry, Matson said he did not have these manuscripts but that they might be with Ann Watkins.
5 This may be an early title for *The Shapes That Creep*.

164: To Conrad Aiken
P: H(ts)
PP: *LAL* 158-60

Dollarton P.O.,
Dollarton, B.C.,
Canada
9 May 1941

Very Querido[1] Conrad – Mary –
    Thanks for the news (a wee bit contradictory, but all turned out fine) and sorry to have given you all the bother of my bloody Mss. anyway.
    But I do very much appreciate what you did for me and I want to

say to you too – what I have just finished saying to Bob Linscott – that so far as I was concerned the bother was not wasted. Your interest and kindness got me over a hell of a difficult period where I might have let down: as things stand I have been able to reorganize my life to a point where I am now really able to cope with that, and other, work. As your pupil this makes me feel good because I feel I am now justifying your faith in me: you wait. My life was always the most difficult part of my work, largely because it was too easy.

As for the old man, God knows what horrors are breaking over his poor head, but whatever they are, he and the mater now feel happy about me which is to them one major sorrow the less, for which I am eternally thankful. And the ghastly psychotic dance we led each other has come to an end. And you must take credit for this too.

As for ourselves, we did not succeed in coming to Montreal, and America is as far off as ever, but the hope engendered worked constructively. Stroke after stroke of good fortune has come our way and we have now *bought* a supershack on the sea – all paid for, no rent, no tax, but lovely, surrounded with dogwood and cherry and pines, isolated, and a swell place for work. It's no Forty-one Doors[2] but we love it just the same and it suits us fine.

Margie has written two mystery novels,[3] one plumb first rate from any point of view, and the agent's hopes of selling it are sanguine – and I three long short stories (including a pouncing horror) which have also called forth the warmest sanguinities from the hardboiled. I have been working hard at the pomes too, bearing your words well in mind, and I feel I've done something very worthy here too – about sixty new ones – may I inflict some on you sometime if you would say the word? The Atlantic [Monthly] has held on to one for nearly three months, having sent all the others back, which might be a good sign.[4] However, apart from one in England, I have met with no material success here yet, not even from Poetry.[5] But I don't care because I feel I am really getting somewhere.

In addition – all the Mss. from Linscott arrived on May Day! –

All of them are perfectly unreadable as they stand, which makes me grateful for your patience all over again, but as I say I am now able to cope with them, and it was a kind of good omen their arriving when they did, just as we had moved into our new 'house' which is really beautiful, by the way.

So – thank you Mary and Conrad! – and for your letters. And now, all the luck in the world to 41 Doors and your project.[6] How lucky, how lucky, and again lucky your pupils are, and what a God-sent opportunity they have. I suppose it's inevitable such opportunities should be very rare but what hope or help a European creative fellow could get out of Cambridge and its bloody triposes seemed to me to depend too much on luck and – but I won't get going on the 'system' now.

Well all the very best of luck to you, and your pupils, though they already have it, being such.

Blessings.

Malc & Margie

Annotations:

1 *Querido* is Spanish for 'dear,' and Lowry often addressed the Aikens in these terms of affection.
2 Conrad and Mary Aiken moved to Brewster, Massachusetts, in 1940. They called their renovated home 'Forty-one Doors.'
3 These are *The Last Twist of the Knife* (New York: Charles Scribner's Sons, 1946) and *The Shapes That Creep* (New York: Charles Scribner's Sons, 1946).
4 *Atlantic Monthly* did publish the poem they were holding; see Lowry's 13 August 1941 letter (**168**) to Aiken.
5 Lowry may be referring to Harriet Munroe's magazine *Poetry* in Chicago or to *Canadian Poetry Magazine*, which was edited in Toronto by E.J. Pratt in 1941. Lowry's first poem published in *Canadian Poetry Magazine* was 'Sestina in a Cantina' in XI. 1 (1947): 24-27, by which time Earle Birney was editor.
6 The Aikens had opened a summer school at Rye in which Mary taught painting and Conrad writing. They continued the school in Brewster until 1943.

165: To Whit Burnett and Martha Foley

P: Princeton(ts)

Dollarton P.O.,
Dollarton, B.C.,
Canada
6 July 1941

Dear Whit and Martha:

I was disappointed you didn't like the Volcano principally because I wrote it under such incommunicably vile conditions that I fooled myself into thinking it must be as enormous as the effort involved in writing it. But I find now that your words about it are quite right and just: the issue *is* confused by Dunne stuff, by my own situation while writing it, and it isn't spherical and whole as a work of art should be. My mind and life was in a sad mess, it must be admitted, as it was when I met you. Well, I am rewriting it, now I can see the thing clearly, and am no longer in a mess. It seems that most of the work I loaded on you at one time or another was really notation for the hard work of a later time: but that you believed in it then still gives me a lot of encouragement.

I recently got the Last Address into what I felt was the kind of form it deserved and have sent it off to Matson. I want to thank you for your help with this.

As nearly as I can remember I owe you about $45, and ironically enough, now that I am able to pay it, I am unable to send any money out of Canada. So I am sending you a story:[1] if you accept it, would you apply your current price for such a story against my debt? Do *not* forget and pay me, because I do not think I can send even a cheque back through the mail. Later I will send you another story. Please do not think this a sort of moral blackmail – you have rejected too many stories of mine in the past! But if you don't like it perhaps I could send some other on the same basis. It is not a great story or anything: but I think it is original – the odd way in which the sinister chords at the beginning are resolved – I feel it is perhaps a multum in parvo[2] – anyway, deserving of publication.

I am working hard now on a revised version of In Ballast too – very revised! – I live, pioneer fashion, in a forest by the sea, somewhat out of touch: nor have I yet been called up.

Thanking you again for your help, and sorry to have been of trouble in my time of eclipse.

Faithfully,

Malcolm

P.S. By the way, when I sent you Under the Volcano I enclosed a note for the censor, and clipped to it, as a sort of charm, the last letter I had from our late Gov. Gen. Lord Tweedsmuir. Maybe the censors or customs kept it as a souvenir, but he was a swell old boy and I should very much like to have the letter back if it did reach you, which I doubt.[3]

Annotations:

1 The story Lowry sent is 'Enter One in Sumptuous Armour'; Burnett's response to the story is not on record, but see Lowry's 30 January 1942 letter (**171**) to Matson.
2 The Latin expression *multum in parvo* means 'much in little' or 'a great deal in a small space.'
3 Before sending it to Burnett, Lowry had sent the letter to his father in an

effort to boost Arthur Lowry's confidence in his son; see his March 1940 letter (**129**) to his father, and Appendix 2.

166: To Gerald Noxon

P: Texas(ts)
PP: *LLN* 40

> Dollarton P.O.
> Dollarton, B.C.
> Tuesday [Summer 1941]

Dear Gerald:
   Please don't forget and Margie emphasises it to come to see us if you can when you return from good old surrealist Victoria[1] – make sure you see the delirious rosebushes, the angry totems, and Aristotle peeling among the lobelias, not to say the gangrened statue of the Queen herself, looking rather constipated and decidedly bed-raggled – when we were there we stayed at the Hotel Windermere and sang, nobody had ever sung in the Hotel Windermere before, it was almost a calamity: it was very fine to see you,[2] and if we can put on some sun, that would be good, one feels, as would a picnic on some such fine island as say, Jug or Dog or Pug or even Scug Island.[3] I could see you were tired, (though in splendid form) and I am afraid I did not make you any the less so by reading vastly from my book, but I may be forgiven, I hope, when I remind you again you were my first editor[4] and hence I look to you very earnestly for criticism, which was given and has already been most useful. I would not have troubled you had I not felt there was something very strange there, if slightly monstrous, and, if I may say so, though it didn't look like it at first, finally perhaps even your cup of tea. For the thing was partly conceived as a sort of preposterous five dimensional movie, a sort of Noxon Nightmare – believe it or not. . . But it is not to read you my bloody book of course, I, we, ask you to come, though I may trouble you in this regard sometime for the same honest reason, but because it is a pleasure to see you and because after making record-ings you will I hope find some pleasure in inviting the soul here.[5] So come any time you like and stay as long as you like, come un-announced, drunk, sober, or even leading a giraffe. Or even 'the little fellow behind you.' Who was he, by the bye? The man couldn't have meant you, who must be about six feet and so two or three inches taller than I, and he couldn't have meant me, who am not exactly little either, for it was me whom he addressed – and I know

the fellow quite well because I'm always chasing would-be thieves off his balcony. 'They're waiting,' he said, 'up there. Not for you, but for the little fellow behind you.' What if he saw someone else, affable I am sure, but invisible, and for whom perhaps something else was waiting, up there? Or perhaps he has gigantism. . .

Margie sends love,

Malcolm

Annotations:

1 Victoria, the capital city of the province of British Columbia, is situated on Vancouver Island, a short ferry ride from the mainland and from the large metropolis of Vancouver. Then, as now, Victoria was known as a retirement haven and a tourist attraction, and there are many reminders of the British queen in the city – though none quite matches Lowry's satiric description.
2 Noxon remembers visiting the Lowrys for the first time in the summer of 1941; see *Letters of Malcolm Lowry and Gerald Noxon* (39).
3 Jug Island is a tiny island in Burrard Inlet across from Deep Cove, which is just to the north-east of Dollarton. Dog Island, also tiny, is in the Queen Charlotte Islands off the north coast of Lyell Island. Pug and Scug are not shown on topographical maps of the area and are probably Lowry's alliterative inventions.
4 Noxon was a founding editor of the Cambridge magazine *Experiment*, in which Lowry published two early stories, 'Port Swettenham' and 'Punctum Indifferens Skibet Gaar Videre,' in 1930 and 1931. It was through the magazine that Lowry and Noxon first met.
5 Noxon, who was working with the Canadian Broadcasting Corporation (CBC) during the forties, made recording and research trips to western Canada, and these allowed him to visit the Lowrys in 1941, 1942, and 1943.

167: To Harold Matson
P: Matson(ts); UBC(phc)

Dollarton P.O.,
Dollarton, B.C.,
Canada
4 August 1941

Dear Hal:

– Sorry my damn stories won't sell – so far.

Meantime, here is the news: The Atlantic has taken a poem for their September number.[1] As a poem I think it might be of interest to you. I did not ask money for it, you will see why if you read it. I asked the Editor, with whom I had a correspondence, to give the money to Norwegian relief. But that does not alter the fact that it is a poem I have sold, so please deduct whatever is proper from what you may sell in the future of mine. They pay a dollar a line and there are fourteen lines.

My correspondence was interesting because it resulted in the Atlantic being held up till I sent them a telegram telling them they could print it in the Contributors Club.[2] It gave me a peculiar feeling of disporportionate importance for perhaps five minutes. It may be nothing: or it may be a wedge.

For the rest, I – we – are working day and night on revised versions of both Under the Volcano and In Ballast to the White Sea, and have very nearly completed first drafts of both. I am cutting mercilessly, while re-creating, and hewing above all to the pattern, the form, the meaning – while at the same time trying to make them exciting as stories qua stories – to try and achieve the spherical, single and whole: thus profiting from the criticism you sent me. In regard to this I want to say how much I appreciate your patience.

Linscott, of Houghton Mifflin, has sent me a letter in which he encloses a form for their fellowship.[3] The terms of this are as follows:

'I agree, if I receive an award, that in consideration of the payment to me of $1500 ($1000 outright, $500 advance against royalties) Houghton Mifflin Company are to have the right to publish my book written in whole or in part by me during the period of my Fellowship – (September 15, 1941- September 15, 1942) on royalty terms as follows: 15% of the receipts to 2500 copies of the book, 20% from 2500 to 5000, and 25% on all subsequent sales (royalty payments to be figured on the list price of the book less the average trade discount of 42%) with all advance payment on the day of publication based on the accrued royalties on that date over and above the $500 already paid. I further agree, in consideration of the above payments, that all rights in the work are to be assigned to Houghton Mifflin Company, but with the understanding that I shall receive 85% of the net proceeds of the sale, if any, of first serial, British, translation, dramatic, motion picture or radio rights; and 50% of the net proceeds of the sale of second serial rights, or of the sale of the work to a book club or similar organization.

In the event that an applicant has an agreement with a literary agent for handling the work in question, Houghton Mifflin Company will waive their interest in the first serial, British, translation, dramatic, motion picture, and radio rights, but will expect to receive 5% of the net proceeds of the sale of such rights.

I further agree that Houghton Mifflin Company shall have an option on the next two books that I write on terms which are mutually satisfactory.'

I had thought, with your permission, to send them the new version of In Ballast 'in progress.'[4]

I do not know whether to do this or no, but, in order to make allowances for delays, censorship, etc., I must dispatch the m.s. by September 1, so may I ask you to let me know what you think as soon as possible so that I may amass the necessary data in time, and I shall abide by your decision?

At the same time could you let us know what is the status of Margerie Bonner's work? She has another mystery plotted out, but does not want to start working on it until she hears whether the Last Twist of the Knife and The Shapes That Creep are potentially acceptable as they are or whether they require further alteration. She altered the Last Twist of the Knife in accordance with Miss Stong's suggestions: we felt that the new version stood a much better chance. She would greatly appreciate it if you would let us know what you think. She has an indefinite number of mysteries simmering, as a matter of fact, but she needs to derive some guidance as to future culinary tactics from your opinion of the two recently sent.

Yours faithfully,

Malcolm

Annotations:

1 Matson had returned both 'June 30th, 1934' and 'Enter One in Sumptuous Armour' after they had been refused by several magazines, including the *Atlantic Monthly*. 'In Memoriam: Ingvald Bjorndal' first appeared in the *Atlantic Monthly* 168 (October 1941): 501. A revised version of the poem was included, with the title 'In Memoriam: Ingvald Bjorndal and His Comrade,' in A.J.M. Smith's *The Book of Canadian Poetry*, rev. ed. (Chicago: University of Chicago Press, 1948), p. 372. In an introductory note Lowry explains that his poem is a recasting in poetic form of a letter originally written in Norwegian (presumably by the sailor Ingvald Bjorndal) and found in a corked bottle at sea in the North Atlantic. Interestingly, Lowry signed his first version of the poem 'Malcolm Boden Lowry,' thus emphasizing what he liked to think of as his own seafaring past on his mother's side; see Day (58–59) and Scherf (186).

2 This correspondence and telegram do not appear to have survived in either the files and archives of the *Atlantic Monthly* or Edward Weeks's papers for these years with the magazine, in the Harry Ransom Humanities Center at the University of Texas at Austin.

3 That Lowry did enter the competition for this fellowship is confirmed by his 6 January 1942 letter (**170**) to Matson, but my inquiry to Houghton Mifflin in 1989 showed that the company archives no longer hold any record of Lowry's entry or any correspondence.

4 Lowry did submit something from 'In Ballast to the White Sea,' but his manuscript was not chosen; see the 6 January 1942 letter (**170**) to Matson from Margerie Bonner and Malcolm Lowry.

168: To Conrad Aiken

P: H(ts)
PP: *LAL* 160–62

> Dollarton P.O.,
> Dollarton, B.C,
> Canada
> 13 August 1941

Muy querido Mary and Conrad:

Salud y peseta.[1] How goes the summer school? We are still sitting in our cottage on the sea – which we own, the cottage that is, and damn it, the sea too, why not? – until such time as Vancouver Aldermen investigate the squatter's problem, which will probably be never since we're not on city land – tax free, with getting on five hundred dollars in the bank which will probably be broke before the year is out, though it has a provident sound and it would probably have rotted if we buried it in the ground, striving for what you call a Better Thing, and gawd blimey how we have struv, and with diffident, remote, or occasional unillustriously local success as to things taken and sold, but two wows of mysteries by Margie called The Last Twist of the Knife and the Shapes that Creep that will come out sometime and one long short story utterly rewritten recast and deplagiarized and reborn by me, that Last Address which I think might live when I am dead and damned or something and a pome in the September Atlantic – about the only one of innumerable to click anywhere – called In Memoriam for someone,[2] not the gardener this time, probably buried away somewhere in the depths, not too bad, I hope you think, certainly it is muy correcto, only we wrote some music for that better (for the uke) only it's so depressing one cannot sing it without that self conscious tear drop glistening in the eye, and we had a slight altercation with Weeks[3] too, just to be in the family, in fact we held up the Atlantic which was more than Joshua could do or the Children of Israel and actually had to send it a telegram finally.[4]

For the last two months and for the next two we have been and are busying ourself exclusively with that Under the Volcano book and In Ballast to the White Sea, which have had to be thoroughly deloused and given two new handles and two new blades, otherwise its the same old cricket bat. However we decided that all the characters could not be equally dead and have all quite the same look – they had to be distributed in different postures throughout the morgue anyway – and this has presented some nice problems, most of them neatly solved, we feel. I think they may both end up first rate, which would be a miracle, but not impossible.

The current problem (damn it, can I ever get through a letter to you without asking you a favour) is re Houghton Mifflin's fellowship, the application blank for which Linscott has sent us, that is, in this case, me.

I have among other things to send in letters from *two* responsible persons – they may refer either to applicants character or literary qualifications or both. Do you think as an old pupil I could ask you humbly to send such a brief letter – that is, two brief letters, one from you and one from Mary, briefly passing over the fact that I might have neither: address them to Houghton Mifflin of course but please send them to me to enclose with the other things because I have not yet received permission to enter for the fellowship from my agent. I can guarantee the work in question deplagiarized and that it will be done, even if it has to be finished with a bayonet. And I'd be most grateful if you would do this for me.

But I must send off the letters, mss. etc. from here to Houghton Mifflin by *September 1* to allow for delays, censors, acts of God, etc.[5]

I hope all is very well with you both and well with your friends abroad. John [Davenport]? Ed [Burra]?

I haven't heard a mumblin word from Liverpool – well, just one slight ambiguous mumble – since before the bad airraids there. No word from anyone else. The world seems to have reeled away from one altogether into a bloodshot pall of horror and hypocrisy, a chaos without melody.

If you can spare more words of advice as well for one who wants honestly still to discipline himself to be a poet I'd be awfully grateful. I haven't sent anything along yet because not quite satisfied with anything.

We remain disgustingly well and happy: I unrecognizably fit, not a pouch, not an ounce, not a funeral bloat.

God bless.   Malc

Annotations:

1 *Salud y pesetas* is a Spanish toast meaning 'health and wealth.' Lowry uses it in *Under the Volcano*.
2 The poem is 'In Memoriam: Ingvald Bjorndal'; see Lowry's 4 August 1941 letter (**167**) to Harold Matson, annotation 1.
3 Aiken had had a falling out with Edward Weeks, the editor of *Atlantic Monthly* from 1938 to 1966; see Lowry's 11 December 1940 letter (**159**) to Aiken.
4 It was Joshua who led the Israelites across the River Jordan, whose waters parted to give them safe passage; see Joshua 3 and 4 in the Old Testament.
5 The archives at Houghton Mifflin contain no correspondence with Lowry, and no record of Lowry's application is extant.

169: To Harold Matson

P: Matson(telegram)

Western Union,
Dollarton, B.C.
2 September 1941

PLEASE WIRE COLLECT ANSWER LETTER RE FELLOWSHIP[1] MUST POST
TODAY

MALCOLM LOWRY

Annotations:

1 See Lowry's 4 August 1941 letter (**167**) to Harold Matson. There is a gap in the incoming correspondence from Matson at UBC from 5 September 1941 to 22 June 1945, but a copy of Matson's 2 September 1941 reply to this telegram with the Matson papers confirms his agreement to support Lowry's application.

170: To Harold Matson

P: Matson(ts); UBC(phc)
PP: *SL* 37-38

Dollarton P.O.,
Dollarton, B.C.,
Canada
6 January 1942[a]

Dear Hal Matson:
I am sure you will feel the same sense of relief at receiving this letter as we do at having finally made up our minds to write it. But first of

all let us say this, unequivocally and sincerely: we appreciate the difficulties involved and we are deeply grateful for all your trouble on our behalf and the fact that we have not succeeded is certainly not your fault. Perhaps it is partly due to our geographical distance and the difficulty of communication, partly to the almost prohibitive anxiety of the times, partly to just plain bad luck, and partly, let us be humble, to our *own* lack of proper material. Anyhow, it seems that we have become merely a liability to you and not the asset we hoped to be and therefore we feel that it is unfair to you to have us any further on your conscience.

On the other hand, we are not proposing to quit: far from it, we propose to redouble our efforts. Malcolm was determined, and still is, God willing and if time allows, to complete the work which he started and which represents so many years thought and effort. He has nearly finished his new version of *In Ballast* (which he sent in synopsis to the Houghton Mifflin Fellowship Contest and which was eliminated and we didn't want to write this letter until it was settled) and he is at present working hard on a completely new and, we are sure, better version of the *Volcano*. We realized ourselves, upon re-reading it some time ago, that it was unfair not only to you but to him to try and market it in the version which was sent to you. At that time he wrote you, asking you to withdraw it,[1] you will remember, and a new version has been growing in the interim which will eliminate most of its obvious defects, clarify and strengthen the narrative, etc. In thinking the book was so good when we sent it to you, perhaps we confused a spiritual victory with an aesthetic one, since it is impossible to convey to you the difficulties under which it was completed – which is, of course, no substitute for actual merit. But we know that within its matrix there *is* a novel which is not only truly good but saleable, and we only feel a relief and a sort of gratitude that by some fluke it was not sold in its present form. As for *In Ballast*, stripped of its former obscurity and lengthiness, it too has emerged, we feel, into its proper form and in the next few months we shall have something solid to go on.

As for me, well of course my work is in an entirely different category and all I can say is that while I am very naturally disappointed, I am not discouraged and I intend to keep on trying until something clicks, since I feel that mine is perhaps more merely a matter of luck – and of better writing on my part too, which will come I am sure with more work, maybe on the sort of trial and error method. Anyhow, I am struggling with the skeleton of a new one and I know that once I got started I could produce two books a year.

But all this determination and optimism on our part does not change the present situation for you: which appears to be practically a dead end. So we feel that the only fair thing to do is to release you from any further effort on our behalf, so just bundle all our stuff up and ship it back to us collect. We'll probably send it out ourselves from here and if we should sell anything we'd be delighted if you'd handle the business for us.

We hope you will understand how we feel, as we have tried to understand how *you* must feel by now. We believe that you will understand that we are deeply appreciative of our debt to you and are only trying to do what seems best. So once more let us thank you for all you've done and assure you of our sincere friendship and gratitude and wish you a full measure of whatever happiness and prosperity there can be in these anxious times.

Faithfully,

Margerie Bonner
Malcolm Lowry

P.S. Malcolm says don't waste money sending the *Volcano*, he has a copy here so just chuck it in the furnace. Specifically, just send my two books and Malcolm's *The Last Address*; I think that's all.

Annotations:

1 In his 4 March 1941 letter (**163**) to Matson, Lowry states that he is 're-writing' *Under the Volcano*; he does not clearly ask Matson to withdraw it from circulation to prospective publishers. On 5 September 1941 Matson wrote to tell him that the manuscript of *Under the Volcano* had been rejected by thirteen publishers.

Editorial Notes:

a. In *Selected Letters* this letter has been dated 1941, but the typescript is clearly stamped by the Matson company as received in January 1942. Lowry did not learn about the rejection of his work until September 1941; see annotation 1. This letter was typed by Margerie and signed by her for both of them. I have included it in the collection, however, because there can be no doubt that she is in large part conveying Malcolm's wishes, perhaps even typing what he has dictated.

171: To Harold Matson

P: Matson(ts); UBC(phc)

> Dollarton P.O.,
> Dollarton, B.C.,
> Canada
> 30 January 1942

Dear Hal:

The manuscripts arrived safely for which many thanks.

Re the letter you enclosed from Whit Burnett: there seems a slight misunderstanding. It is true I owe him forty five dollars (which was partly a personal loan) but I cannot now send money out of Canada owing to war restrictions and I had hoped to pay him in kind and you too. And there seems some confusion over the Last Address. In 1936 I understood him, rightly or wrongly, to have taken it and for two and a half years I looked at every number of Story expecting to see it. At the end of this time I finally asked him for it back in order to enter it for a competition, and he sent it, saying that if it didn't hit to let him, when I had got it 'in the fine form it deserved', see it again. This was puzzling, but I eventually did rewrite it and you sent it to him with this result. I only mention all this because last July, still worrying over the debt, I sent him Sumptuous Armor, after it had been returned by you when it was, so to speak, free.[1] That was a story you hadn't sent him, or at least your secretary didn't list it. Anyway, I told him I hoped to send him others eventually if that didn't click, but he made no reply and simply sent it back. Now it might look to Burnett as though I were trying to palm stories off on him only when everyone else had refused them. It might look to you (whom I had asked at one time, being mad over not hearing a mumbling word from Burnett about Volcano, not to send anything to Story anyway)[2] as though this request had been made on the assumption that my stories would be refused by every magazine but Story, and being returned by you could then be sent to Story in order to salve my conscience and my debt. It certainly wasn't meant that way and though I admit I hadn't worked out in my mind how a commission could be paid to you on a repaid debt I hadn't a doubt but that it could be solved some way. Well, it has not been solved. Only I ask you to believe it was more naïve than hypocritical. The moral to it all is I should not have tried to mix up the personal debts and the stories. It is inexcusable both that I did not pay the debt to Whit and the one to you as of Anne Watkins when I was able or even not able quite apart from my work. I have done a lot of things in my life up to the age of thirty which I find inexcusable and this was not helped by complete psychic disintegration. The way back over the acres of remorse is difficult.

But go back I shall (– and pay those debts, only major from a moral standpoint, too). It seems to me now I cannot have been yet in my right mind even when I wrote that revised version of the Volcano I handed myself so many encomiums for; it seems chock full of the worst kind of wormwood.

Nevertheless things are shaping up: the Volcano is almost rewritten again and is perhaps really this time first rate. The Last Address is being written again. And In Ballast only awaits its final draft. These three things make, strangely enough, one book, complementary in theme, an inferno, a purgatorio, and a paradiso, an honest Baedeker, I believe, for he who would travel[a] in hell. I am not asking you to handle it, for it is too much to ask you after all the disappointments and it is not finished anyway.

But if I manage to do anything with it – yours is the credit and the choice if you will take it. I feel myself in the kind of debt to you unrepayable by mere specie and I would like to think your faith had not been misplaced. I know you're busy, Hal, so don't bother to reply. Best of luck!

(Good God! on reading this over it sounds like nothing so much as 'Alice' –

> . . . . . .I gave him one, they gave him two,
> You gave us three or more;
> They all returned from him to you,
> Though they were mine before.
>
> If I or he should chance to be
> Involved in this affair,
> He trusts to you to set them free,
> Exactly as we were.
>
> My notion was that I had been
> (before he had this fit)
> An obstacle that came between
> Him, and ourselves, and it. . . . . . .)[3]

Malcolm

Annotations:

1 The short story 'Enter One in Sumptuous Armor' was not published until Margerie Lowry included it in *Psalms and Songs* (228-49). It is a well-written story based on Lowry's experiences at the Leys, and it is,

perhaps, Lowry's most *English* story. Matson returned it to Lowry on 24 June 1941 after it had been rejected by five magazines, and Robert Linscott sent it back to Lowry in July, claiming that he was 'allergic to stories of school life.' See Lowry's 6 July 1941 letter (**165**) to Whit Burnett and Martha Foley.
2 See Lowry's 17 October 1940 letter (**154**) to Matson.
3 With a few slight modifications, such as 'him' for 'her' in the first line, Lowry has quoted verbatim three verses from Lewis Carroll's (Charles Lutwidge Dodgson, 1832-98) 'Evidence Read at the Trial of the Knave of Hearts'; see *The Collected Verse of Lewis Carroll* (London: Macmillan, 1932), p. 69.

Editorial Notes:

a. Lowry has cancelled the words 'of the sojourn of a soul' and written below the line 'for he who would travel.'

172: To Arthur O. Lowry
P: UBC(ms)

[Dollarton P.O.,]
[Dollarton, B.C.]
[26 May 1942][a]

My dearest Father:
I have just received your letter to-day telling me of Mother's accident and am most awfully sorry about this but am mightily relieved she is recovering and that it was no worse and that you were O.K. I was beginning to worry at not having heard from her or you in so long so enclose her letter as per your suggestion.[1]
Father, as to my repentance, I want to say without any qualification whatever that I am dreadfully and passionately sorry for the suffering I caused you and Mother, and especially, if there may be an extra degree of sorrow, Mother. I state it and I mean it, and I am often filled with loathing and despair with myself for having caused it, and when I say that I mean to atone, so far as possible, and that no such suffering will ever be wittingly caused again, or is likely to be, I mean that too.
I would leave it at that; I do not like people as a rule who try to justify themselves when they have done wrong; I do not like the priggish sound some of my letters have still in my ears; however, as you know, lorries do tend to come along in life with their loads of cheese and sideswipe one, even if one was on the correct side of the

road, even if that road was slippery, and be one going never so slowly and carefully. I grant you there were an unusual number of lorries in my case to explain away (I am not suggesting that you had anything to explain away, only that you gave me a good symbol) and that I was not infrequently on the wrong side of the road, and that, though given every opportunity to state my case, I found myself mentally unable to do so logically; but even taking all these things into consideration, there still remain two sides more to every question of this kind, there may very well indeed remain both an unknown and an incommunicable element.

I do not know, of course, precisely what I have to refute: if half the things were true I heard vaguely had been reported of me I would not be worth forgiving. But to simplify as far as possible a situation in which you must at least admit, I dare suggest again, the possibility of some impalpables, what I would ask your forgiveness for – before I come to anything else – is for having stupidly caused the suffering, no matter how it was caused or why. That is to say that I indeed do and in no uncertain terms express my sorrow for the heart-breaking agony I caused you both. I indeed, repeating myself, give you full assurance that I have turned, as you put it, my back upon those dark happenings, in so far as they were dark, and in so far as they were happenings within my control. I do not crawl to ask, this for a number of reasons, nor did you suggest I should, but I ask it, sincerely and humbly, nevertheless. But as to what precisely I did and did not do and why and where they were dark – and there may be shades of darkness – ah, as to that, that is another thing again. If I have from time to time given the impression hypocritically of seeming to justify myself probably for the wrong reasons, I am ashamed of that too. And you must agree that at this time and distance it is impossible to retrace in detail the events and actions that led one to that absolute, black, horrible, lonely midnight of an upside down emotional Gethsemane:[2] a Gethsemane I am aware I invited as if against my will you both awfully to enter too. Nevertheless, part of the trouble has been that I have not been myself sufficiently for the last few years to be able to stand up for myself, to see my own lot clearly coldly and honestly; I had lost the will to try to explain and, almost, towards life. I had come to be, almost, prepared to believe that it was *only* selfishness and weakness and drunkeness that had placed me in that position and yet, this particular brand of organic cowardice was not logical, for me, not like me, even to my perhaps illogical self. And that, I feel, is rather important.

And here let me say that no one could have been more incredibly generous in meeting all my faults, illnesses and phobias half way than yourself. This, out of the deepest and most complicatedly sorrowful and remorseful emotions, I appreciate now with a sincere gratitude I will not try to express. If, in spite of all my promises – all of them apparently willfully broken even to an impartial and wise eye – if, in spite of all, illness were at the bottom of it, of my behaviour, of my state, – why then, you said, no expence shall be spared, nor trouble in getting to the bottom of *that*. So neurologists buzzed, doctors hovered, all of them as good as could be found anywhere, dentists drilled at me like expensive furies, half unwilling and ungrateful as I was – and I could not explain this monstrous half unwillingness and ungratefulness even to myself at the time, nor the sense that increased of an equally monstrous injustice being perpetrated upon me when all the time I was being treated apparently with an enlightened mercy I did not deserve.

Now I must say something that sounds utterly paradoxical: there really *was* a monstrous injustice done, it turns out (there were, by the way, two other injustices done – even worse, but of an ethical, and at the moment incommunicable nature, which I won't go into now, for though they redound obscurely as it were to my credit, and were fundamental in causing what followed, of which you could not have had any accurate knowledge without my at that time rightly discredited evidence, here again, I was to blame in inviting them to be committed) and this injustice was largely, as sailors say, my own bloody fault, with the sole reservation that what made it my fault then was partly what makes it now an injustice. As you know what was decided was that nothing was wrong with me more or less save liqour and self neglect. There was a dental problem, munificently taken care of. There was a morbid psychological problem too – there still is – but it is one that I am largely solving myself, and too much emphasis – my fault again – was damagingly laid on that. After a certain point, psychological problems are a matter of guts. However, that there was a serious medical problem beyond that of mere weak will everyone seemed predisposed to deny, including eventually myself, because the disposal to accept the medical solution seemed part of the morbid state I was half heartedly trying, and being encouraged to shake off. Moreover, medical examination didn't disclose any organic wrong. One doctor, to whom you must have paid an amount I shiver and grind my teeth to think of – as I do at the whole torturing expensive business for *you* at this juncture – did go so far as saying that the illness, which was severe & extremely painful, I'd had in Mexico – (on top of everything else my so called 'rheumatic fever' at that time had been complicated by malaria-paludismo and Jaundice –) was probably really poliomyelitis, or, in a modified form that *didn't cripple* one, infantile paralysis.[3] This was an ugly enough thought indeed, but for some reason it was forgotten in the general chaos. To get on – it was decided that I was simply drinking because I couldn't make up my mind to stop – and there is a great element of truth in this – and that that was the cause and effect of my ills. And I suppose some extraordinarily self-deceptive pride in me, since underneath all this I had been trying to turn myself into a sort of absurd Atlas, muscularly, – this will appear less absurd as we gather momentum – would not allow me to think, when up against the brick wall, I was other than essentially strong and fit, in spite of my morbid obsessions. There is a great element of truth I repeat, for in Canada here I did stop drinking, though I do not have any moral ideas on this subject, and while I welcomed the possibility of one day taking an occasional moderate glass like a normal Englishman and without having any stupid giant shadow of disaster or backsliding hanging over me, I did, both as a matter of discipline and out of what I had calculated by that time to be fairness to you, stop in the sense that I did not, and for that matter do not, have even that occasional glass. I continued nevertheless to be racked by despair and depressions and mental anguish – I had plenty of cause for so it didn't strike me as abnormal for me. I 'took it', as the saying goes, along with periodic wracking pains too, particularly a kind of vicious almost spastic cramp that troubled me from time to time, and went on with my work. I had gone on a voyage, I told myself, and true my ship had been virtually lost under me, most of the crew were gone and the cargo damaged if not beyond repair, but I was still on it, the thing was still afloat after all – why shouldn't I sail it triumphantly into port in spite of everything? What a pleasant surprise that would give the owner, who had after all made such a large and generous investment. Wasn't I English? So I argued, and continued to proceed, now at three knots, now at five, but with steerage way, and at least one was no longer awash. However to get back to dry, in the strictest sense of the term, land and a different metaphorical base, and passing over much, I now ran headlong into what approximates to the 'justification' I am confining myself to, and before I get down to it, I must tell you that nothing would have dragged it out of me at the expense of another Gethsemane for you had it threatened to have a sorry ending. For a while there was such a period when one didn't 'know.' In short, I should not have made this point or, even after your letter, attempted this justification, if justification it be, if it were to be only at the price of any even more complicated anxiety on your part than you have already had to suffer. However, since far from worrying you it may even afford you a wry kind of general relief, and a real relief in especial, I am going, after some thought, ahead.

I told you I had had what seemed to be trouble with my circulation, caused by perhaps the breaking of a small bone in the foot, and aggravated by varicose veins. That was true: but at this distance I reserved the right not to go any further than that since I was able to take care of it financially myself and did not want to worry you anyway. What happened was that I had been stacking a large load of lumber and had afterwards collapsed, not immediately afterwards, but the next day. What had happened did not seem plain enough though, even to the doctor in Vancouver who was located, one of the best diagnosticians in Canada, and a military doctor, as it happened, and to whom I was driven. In fact, it seemed rather unique. I had acquired, all of a sudden, an occupational disease, dread indeed and almost unknown to anyone save divers and those who work in tunnels, known as the 'Bends' or, I believe, technically, as Grayson's disease, or something similar.[4] All the salt having been sweated out of my system, a state had been artificially induced, so far as I can understand it, analogous to that pertaining sometimes in men who work in intolerable conditions of compressed air. That the circulation had been affected, that a small bone was broken in one's foot, that one had – who hasn't? – varicose veins, were incidental to this interesting fact which made, for the doctor, a rare if not unique case, to which partly at any rate I owe both the thoroughness of the investigation and the extremely reasonable terms imposed upon me by one of the highest medical authorities in Canada. That sounds like a novel, but it is the truth. There was not, so to speak, any 'danger' exactly, it seemed, but wait, was there not? That somewhat depended upon my history, so I gave the doctor my history, sparing nothing. He in turn spared nothing, blood tests, urinalysis, x-rays, all were made, and it seemed to boil down to this: that if I had had infantile paralysis, which was, possibly, before *our* 'trouble' there would be, or ought to be now under the circumstances which had come about, some destruction of the spine. If that were the case, then even the precious and sinister 'Bends' were incidental to the glum fact that I might as well make up my mind to being a kind of semi invalid if not quite a cripple for life. (Cheer up at this point, for our story has a happy conclusion.) Yet it was under these cheery conditions that I have written since Christmas, most of my letters home, a condition not improved by my having, as usual, even more sinister, however ill founded, suspicions. But I still had to keep that miserable ship afloat, fed up slightly though I sometimes was with it, so I threw a few more of the crew overboard, tightened my belt and settled down in the chartroom to wait and to work more or less as

usual. After a while strange portents appeared on the horizon. But
back to dry land again. First it turned out I could not have had poliomyelitis, or if I had, of such a 'mild' character, I say 'mild'
comparatively, (as had been apparently decided by Park's doctor in
Los Angeles) it had not produced any 'destruction'. Secondly I had
not (nor have had) any venereal disease, nor any liver trouble nor any
lasting 'result' of alcoholism in the past, however alcoholic I might
have been. Third, I *did* have, what might be worse than all these if
not taken in hand immediately, namely a largely *streptococcic* multiple
glandular infection, and this I had had not one, not two, not five, but
possibly for as long as *ten* years, during part of which time it must
have lain dormant. In short I have been, without knowing it, toxic,
living in a state of being slowly poisoned and undermined physically
and mentally, for the best part of the last decade. As I have said drink
cannot cause this, though naturally it aggravates it. As a matter of
fact none quite knows the cause. It is more mysterious than a lorryful
of cheese. And like cheese so has been my system all these long years.
I have looked at the horrors under a microscope so I know. Well, I
reacted to treatment like a house on fire and with this continued reaction has gone by now much of the anguish and all of the pains.
That is all but how much! *It can and is being completely cured*, though I
shan't be out of the wood for six months or more, during which
period I shall be out of the more obvious battleline too, unless one is
bombed here, when I have a responsibility. I do not ask you to draw
obvious conclusions from this or to make the obvious excuses for
me. Nor am I by any implication casting any *blame*, as I have said, on
anyone but myself, but surely, the blame is changed slightly in
degree, for that reason; and I feel the horrible anxiety you have had
over me, though nothing can take away its having *been*, might be
retrospectively canalized into something even approaching a queer
sort of triumph, for indeed the triumph inheres in the constitution
with which you seem to have provided me. The doctor assures me
he has seen many cases of great hulking loggers and longshoremen
who with this infection (though not necessarily similarly induced,
nor, through having got the 'Bends', discovered) become mere
skeletons, and utterly collapse. They give up their jobs, they become
a prey to such mental depressions they think they're going crazy.
They take to drinking and wind up derelicts of men. I stopped work
for ten days, that was all. Now I am almost cured, I know of course
now that my 'fitness' was merely my life illusion, that I have never
for as long as I remember until almost now, been or felt *really* fit –
but at the same time it was, in a way, this striving after fitness that
has saved my life. Perhaps, you can say, that was Stuart.[5]

Well, so much for that. I don't tell it you in any attempt to completely exonerate myself or justify myself but only because I have a right to feel that it must have had something to do with my otherwise illogical and inexplicable behaviour, and also because I am well enough now – the doctor's prize patient in fact – you need not be concerned about it, and finally I could hardly answer some of your questions without mentioning it. I am not suggesting it accounts for everything; there were so many complicating misfortunes and mistakes one would not be naive enough to explain them all away by that.

Now for your questions, the first I have answered.[6] Second, the divorce is now absolute, & that means what it says. Under what conditions am I living? I bought – or God gave me – a house on the sea and by the forest, for $100, where I live like a pioneer. I have a pier I built myself going from my front porch from which I can dive into ten feet of cold salt water. I have a well on the porch, with fresh mountain water, and chop wood for my stove. I also have a boat. There is a store fairly near, and rather pretty town. It is magnificently beautiful, the Canadian Rockies tower across the fjord. It is primitive but clean and healthy. Many townspeople of good families live in such houses for the summer, but I live here all year round. I don't like the city anyhow, but go there, twice a month now, formerly it was three times a week, to see my doctor. My only luxuries are a radio and a gramaphone. But I am by no means isolated from humanity. I have a few friends, both influential and simple, and am deputy A.R.P. warden for my stretch of beach.[7] I live in short as many writers would like to live when working, life reduced to its bare essentials, and with plenty of books, I like it.

What am I earning? At this very moment, I'm sorry to say, nothing. Since my illness incapacitates me for any sustained work except of the most sedentary kind and that at short intervals I have been unable to take a job of any kind. It is only the last months that I have been allowed any excercise whatever – fortunately I had enough wood chopped to last – even walking, more than was absolutely necessary; now I am told that I can begin to take some exercise again a little at a time, such as swimming and some rowing, so long as I do not become tired; it will be, the doctors estimate, approximately six months more before I am *entirely* well again, but my resistance against the streptococcus is 100%, so that it will probably be less. But meantime I haven't neglected that angle: I have had some articles accepted which have helped some and giving thought to the future I have made contact with a man here who is head of the second largest broadcasting company in Canada.[8] So that if stranded here, I shall get on all right anyhow, though it may eventually require a slight change of status, which by the way is all arranged with the authorities to remain as it is indefinitely. I like Canada anyway. Who knows but that I might not become a Canadian Ibsen or Dostoievsky? They certainly need one. They haven't got any writers, at all: they all become Americans if they do well. And that brings me to your last question re daily occupation. Well, it is the old story, with by this time a slight difference. I am working on a book, with two very interested American publishers in mind, but when I say working I mean regularly, eight hours a day, and when I say a book I mean a big book, in fact it is a trilogy, three long novels in one, to be called The Voyage That Never Ends, and composed of what I have been in spite of myself hacking away at and failing to sell, then selling bits of and not liking and cutting out for the last six years, but really, as an organic whole, it has only just begun to take shape so that in a way my illness has had this good compensation. When I say that I am not exactly aiming low, in fact that it aims to be a classic, I do not expect to be more than humored: just the same, it might be, it might be. In my heart I feel something of the sort and also that keeps jogging my elbow to spare no effort in getting it done. I have Mother's book, too, on the stocks, I have not forgotten, indeed no: but you must understand that being in Canada, much as I have come to like that, and writing for a prospective American market, and with the war on top of everything, makes things that much more complicated and harder. A year ago, hoping to have something to show you and myself, I entered a part of it with fairly sanguine hope for a fellowship contest.[9] I did not succeed in this, though I was one of the last to be eliminated – I was probably about sixth out of some hundred entrants – and doubtless have more failures ahead. But the same publishers wrote me a promising letter the other day, inquiring how it was getting on, etc., there are other favourable factors, and anyhow, nothing is going to stop me finishing it I feel. I ought to say that even when I was feeling my worst I worked as long as I was able every day, It is obvious that, previous to that, when perfectly 'sober' I mean, & quite lately, I was often deluded by illness in my writing, I am confronted with pages upon pages I do not understand myself now and have to cut. I shouldn't let Mother know about the streptococci; it would bother her, since she has been ill herself, it has an ugly sound and anyhow why bother her when I am practically recovered? But it might be a good thing to let Stuart know. Yes, I think I would like him to know, now it's O.K.

But everything is paid for – I have saved money, as I have said, and save, and with what I'd earned I've *really* got something in the bank above and to spare. So please don't think that I'm *asking* for anything.

Don't go to the other extreme now and pity me though. I don't deserve that. I'm very lucky. If you wish I'd be very glad to give you a letter from the doctor re my illness, but you have my word on the subject and I would be vaguely reluctant to do so on purely psychological grounds for some time anyhow since it is unwise, as I see it, to create even by implication any longer the situation so often foolishly produced by myself – where another person becomes surrogate or vicariously responsible for my welfare. Of course I fully appreciate that I left you no choice before. And concerning that: the guardian Mr Parks appointed for me here is dead of a not dissimilar illness.[10] I am sorry. Bear me witness that I did not say anything about the other fellow. Bear me witness that I did not say: the man recovered from the bite, the dog it was that died.

Yours very gratefully and with deep affection.

Your affectionate son,

Malcolm

P.S. And, I hope I have made it clear, don't blame yourself. You did more than all you could. So did Parks, *really*, & the doctors in Los Angeles. They didn't have anything to go on, not even a trustworthy report from myself, & did all they could too. And if you hadn't made it possible for me to have my teeth fixed so well I would be that much worse now.

Annotations:

1 In his 22 April 1942 letter to his son (UBC 1:38) Arthur Lowry describes a car accident he and his wife had had at Christmas. Mrs Lowry received cuts to her head and was hospitalized for ten days. He also asks that, when he writes, Lowry send '*separate* letters to Mum' so that she will be spared any disturbing news. This Lowry did, but the enclosed letter does not appear to have survived.

2 Jesus Christ was betrayed and arrested in the Garden of Gethsemane where he went to pray after the Last Supper.

3 The pathological term for malaria is *paludism* (from *paludous* meaning 'inhabiting marshes'), hence, 'Malaria-paludismo.' Malaria is a febrile disease transmitted by mosquito bite. See Lowry's description of his illness in Mexico in his 27 January 1940 letter (**124**) to Aiken.

4 Aeroembolism, commonly called the 'bends,' is the obstruction of the circulatory system caused by air. It may occur during surgery or as a result of a rapid, substantial decrease in atmospheric pressure experienced in high-altitude flying or deep-sea diving.

5 Stuart Lowry was Malcolm's eldest brother, but the point of Lowry's allusion is unclear.

6 In his 22 April 1942 letter Arthur Lowry asks for 'simple plain facts' in answer to five requests, the first of which is for assurance that Lowry has mended his ways and turned to his parents for forgiveness. Arthur Lowry proffers this forgiveness in his 25 November 1942 letter.

7 A.R.P. stands for Air Raid Precautions, a branch of civilian defence during wartime. The British A.R.P. came into effect in September 1938, so Lowry can assume his father's understanding of the acronym.

8 Lowry must be referring to someone (possibly Andrew Allan, who joined the CBC in Vancouver in 1942) he had contacted through his renewed friendship with Gerald Noxon.

9 Lowry discusses his application to the Houghton Mifflin contest in his 13 August 1941 letter (**168**) to Conrad Aiken; see also his 4 August 1941 letter (**167**) to Harold Matson.

10 Lowry is referring to A.B. Carey, but I have not been able to confirm a date or cause of death.

Editorial Notes:

a. My transcription of this letter has been made from a complete typescript draft that bears several pencil interlineations, marginalia, deletions, and corrections. A date, 'May 26, 42,' has been written at the top right in what appears to be Margerie's hand, but this date is confirmed by Arthur Lowry's 25 November 1942 reply to his son (UBC 1:38), in which he writes: 'But I have now regained [confidence], and what has brought this about is the paragraph in your letter of 26 May'; he then quotes at length from this letter. Unfortunately, the copy Lowry sent to his father is not available. Lowry has marked his holograph postscript, which is written as a 'P.S.,' for insertion in the last paragraph of the letter, but I have included it as a postscript because it disrupts the sense of the paragraph.

173: To Harold Matson

P: Matson(ts); UBC(phc)
PP: *SL* 40–41

> Dollarton P.O.,
> Dollarton, B.C.,
> Canada
> 25 June 1942

Dear Hal:
     Flecker's Magic indeed[1] – Permit me if I rather more than

vicariously triumph too. You make us a happy shack and shapes like justifications begin to float down the river. As for those beneath, it looks as though some of them have been brought ashore and found saleable timber and were only masquerading as derelicts. Let me add my deep gratitude to Margie's! But as she will tell you something of how the news affects *her*, a vague word of myself.[2]

I have been down these last months with a somewhat rare and comic affliction known as 'the Bends.' During treatment for this it was discovered that I had had a streptococcic glandular infection for about a dozen years.[3] This looks like unpleasing news but I see it good because, since treatment for this, eagles and mountains have dropped away from my mind. I am now nearly better. Doctors here didn't understand how I lived at all though. The toxicity thus, indisputably often at its maximum during your great and strained patience with me, might, if it would explain death, explain indeed some too apparent oddnesses & unratified irreliabilities on my part in the past, as well as the almost total fog in the Volcano as *was*, we have the doctor's word. (As it might to Whit.) I seem to see your face, around corners, looking at me less rebukingly now, *since we held on.*

But I shan't trouble you again until I have reduced the risk of being a strain on the petty cash department to a minimum. I promise you this: something really *good is* on the wing *this* time, sans self-deceptions, from this side. You will probably hear oftener from the more promising other, since, as I point out to Margie, *now* her work begins.

All thanks again and best wishes.

Malcolm

Annotations:

1 *Flecker's Magic* (1926) is a novel by Norman Matson (1893–1965), Harold Matson's brother, whom Lowry had met in New York in 1934 and would meet again in Paris in the winter of 1948–49; see Lowry's 23 February 1949 letter (**359**) to Harold Matson. *Flecker's Magic* is about a young man who meets a witch, and E.M. Forster discusses the story at length and in detail in his 1927 Clark Lectures, published as *Aspects of the Novel*, as an example of fantasy. Lowry's apparently casual exclamation here resonates in several ways. It is essentially a private joke between himself and Harold Matson, an allusion that links Lowry with both brothers and that relies upon a shared knowledge of Norman Matson's story for its full effect. In *Flecker's Magic*, with its echoes of *Faust* and Wagner's *Das Rheingold*, a young man named Flecker is given a magic ring and told that with the ring's help he can have or be anything he

wants. He is tempted to ask for money, power, or happiness. Lowry, of
course, is happy because Harold Matson has placed Margerie's novel
with Scribner's and this may bring in some money. What no one
realized at this early stage in Margerie's dealings with her publisher was
that this bit of 'magic' (rather like Flecker's) was going to bring the torments of her experience with Scribner's.

2 Harold Matson's letter to the Lowrys, informing them that Scribner's
had accepted Margerie Bonner's *The Shapes That Creep* (and possibly
alluding to *Flecker's Magic*), does not appear to have survived. Douglas
Day's statement (289) that the book was accepted in June 1941, however, is not correct.

3 The exact nature of Lowry's ailment remains unclear, but see Day (297-
98) and Lowry's 26 May 1942 letter (**172**) to Arthur O. Lowry.

174: To Mrs Anna Mabelle [John Stuart] Bonner

P: UBC(ts)
PP: *SL* 41-44

[Dollarton, B.C.]
Tuesday – [1942]ᵃ

Dear Mrs Bonner –

I have read Awaiting Palomar¹ with great pleasure and my feeling
about it could lead me into a disquisition on how all the arts in
general overlap only I want to be concise and relatively prompt for
Margie's reply.

I realise you wrote it hurriedly, but that was quite as it should be
for our, or my suggestion was made with the aim perhaps of finding
out what form was choosing you, rather than vice versa, which,
speaking from experience, I think is the major problem to cope with
when you are possessed with an unstaunchable impulse to create
order out of chaos.

That order was, recently with us, a pier:² and I assert that the pier
is a poem too: for argument's sake, let us assume that everything
which is good and has order and inner cohesion is a sort of poem;
definitely, and for the moment let's not go too far afield. I think that
all first rate short stories are first rate because they are essentially
'poems', they are bound together by an integrity which is essentially
poetic. *But* this does not mean that 'poetic prose' i.e. 'flowery', has
anything to do with poetry: it has less to do perhaps with it than
prosaic poetry has to do with poetry: let me not quibble however.

Roughly speaking, stark, bald and simple prose has more in common with poetry perhaps than elaborate and overweighted verse. So you might try your 'Ghost Star'[3] as a short story and send it us, though write it, if you like, as a poem, (and it still would *be* a poem) in stanzas: let the rhyme etc. go hang for the time being.

A poem, (or such a short story) is, I think, an entity apart from its author: but it may have to find out what it is from people apart from its author and be helped by various people to exist.

As an example of what I mean by a poem that is a short story, here is one of Rabindrinath Tagore's:[4] it is a poem, though it belongs to no fixed form and is more likly a question merely. You might experiment along this line as a sort of design governing posture (that's a good phrase) for the Ghost Star.

Day After Day

Day after day, O Lord of my life, shall I stand
before thee face to face? With folded hands, O Lord
of all worlds, shall I stand before thee face to face?

Under thy great sky in solitude and silence, with
humble heart shall I stand before thee face to face?

In this laborious world of thine, tumultuous with
toil and with struggle, among hurrying crowds shall I
stand before thee face to face?

And when my work shall be done in this world, O
King of kings, alone and speechless shall I stand
before thee face to face?

Back to Awaiting Palomar, of course it has, as you say, enough and indeed to spare, good material to encourage us to see what we can do with it; it has an ennobling theme indeed: on the other hand opinions differ, – different artists might treat it different ways, what we might do with it would not be what you could do with it: so it is to be hoped what one may have said will serve to encourage *you* further to work on it, which I think ought to give you more satisfaction than were we to say, which one might easily, 'By Jove that's marvellous material that, we must use that and buy that motor boat we've had our eye on with the proceeds.' – though, alas, the proceeds from poetry, even of the highest calibre, tend to provide a somewhat leaky potential boat: we would, of course, give you the proceeds: but poetry must never be approached from a financial angle to begin with *or* one will certainly never make any money out of it. To get back to Palomar. I personally prefer the idea of calling it simply The Milky Way. I would simplify, where possible, notice how in this example the discipline of poetry has clarified and rendered the prose excellent 'poetry' – if you strip it down a little further – quite without rhyme. viz. The beginning of an excellent story in the purest, the most excellent, the most ancient tradition of all – that of the fable, but in this case a modern fable, which could also be a poem.

> The Milky Way
> In the beginning, when man first lifted his eyes
> to the heavens, he saw a silver band of light trailing
> across the distances of space.
> He wondered at its beauty and pondered on its light.
> Since then, the ancients of every race, of every
> climate, have left to us the legends and myths of this
> marvel of the skies.

Do you see? I think avoid, in this prose or poetry, or both, in this 'order', 'poetical' words and cliches such as clime, etc. (Never mind your synonyms – you don't need 'em: the humble simple vocables are best) But this was intended – this and Tagore – as a pointer, for a way to do the Ghost Star possibly.

I thought perhaps that, while touching on the Eye of Palomar[5] if you like, you should not use it as the whole basis for your climax: though we do not of course know what the new telescope will disclose, it can hardly be anything more miraculous than the miracle of our own existence. Thus while you might have a sound cause for asking, will it do all this, the Eye of Palomar? the answer to 'can it do *less*?' is definitely yes, it can – even while you acknowledge all the genius and wonder of the thing. But whatever the real power of the real 280 inch telescope, you weaken the poetical power of your poetical telescope by attributing at once too much and too little power to it, and too much of an irrelevant kind of power, by making it into a kind of cure-all and Santa Claus as well.

So that it would seem to me a better idea if, while you bring in the Palomar telescope as the resolution of the Galileo[6] theme, as it were, and of the wisdom of mankind, you close your poem as you have begun it, more on the theme of the Milky Way itself. I most heartily approve of your theme. As Emerson says: 'Something is wanting to science until it has been humanized. The table of logarithms is one thing, and its vital play in botany, music, optics, and architecture, another. There are advancements to numbers, anatomy, architecture, astronomy, little suspected at first, when, by union with intellect and will, they ascend into the life, and reappear in conversation, character, and politics.

'But this comes later. We speak now only of our acquaintance with them in their own sphere, and the way in which they seem to fascinate and draw to them some genius who occupies himself with one thing all his life long. The possibility of interpretation lies in the identity of the observer with the observed. Each material thing has its celestial side; has its translation, through humanity, into the spiritual and necessary sphere, where it plays a part as indestructible as any other.'[7]

To go back to the more technical side of verse: you might try a few sonnets just for practice. The form is this: 14 lines, 5 beats – generally ten syllables – to a line and the rhyme scheme is abba abba cde cde, or ab ab cd cd ef ef gg. For instance:

a   The thing to know is how to write a verse
b   Whether or not you like it, whether or not
b   The goshdarned thing will put you on the spot
a   And Petrarch will not save you from the curse[8]

And so on for ten lines more. The iambic pentametre (above) is the real metric base of English poetry, also of blank verse: though I have tried to show how poetry and prose are, at their best, though in a literal sense opposites, somewhat mixed up.

Well, I hope this has been some help and you might have another go at it along these lines. And we are awaiting the Ghost Star with interest.

Much love
from

Malcolm

Annotations:

1   Margerie's mother often helped her with her mystery novels, and in return the Lowrys advised Mrs Bonner on her compositions. No trace of the poem 'Awaiting Palomar' appears to have survived.
2   The Lowrys bought their new shack (the second one at Dollarton) on 1 April 1941, and they spent the spring repairing and painting it. After moving in on 1 May, Lowry began to build his beloved pier with the help of Sam Miller and Jimmy Craige; see Bowker (307-09).
3   ''Ghost Star' may have been another name for 'Awaiting Palomar.'
4   Rabindranath Tagore (1861-1941) was a popular Indian poet, dramatist, essayist, and philosopher. The prose poem that Lowry quotes is song LXXVI from *Gitanjali*, a collection of translations from the Bengali by Tagore, first published, with an introduction by W.B. Yeats, in 1913. The volume was extremely popular, and Tagore won the Nobel Prize for literature that year and was knighted in 1914.
5   The 'Eye of Palomar' is a reflector telescope, known as a Hale telescope,

on Mount Palomar in California. The site for the telescope was chosen
in 1934, but the building to house it was not completed until after the
war.

6 Galileo Gallilei (1564-1642), the Italian physicist, mathematician, and
   astronomer, supported the Copernican theory that the earth rotated
   around the sun in a heliocentric system, and he was brought before the
   Inquisition for heresy in 1632. He was held under house arrest and his
   books were proscribed.

7 Lowry has quoted verbatim from part 1 of Ralph Waldo Emerson's
   essays on *Representative Men* called 'Uses of Great Men,' *Works of Ralph
   Waldo Emerson* (London: George Routledge and Sons, 1905), p. 147.

8 Lowry uses three of these lines in his desperate letter (**83**) written to
   Conrad Aiken from Oaxaca in early 1938. Francesco Petrarch (1304-74),
   the Italian Renaissance poet, developed the Petrarchan sonnet form.

Editorial Notes:

a. There is no inside address or date with this letter, but Margerie has
    assigned it to 1942 in *Selected Letters* and there seems to be no evidence to
    the contrary. Lowry's reference to the pier (see annotation 2) would
    confirm a date sometime later than the summer of 1941. After Lowry's
    signature, Margerie has added a brief note of her own.

175: To Gerald Noxon

P: Texas(ts)
PP: *LLN* 42

Dollarton P.O.,
Dollarton, B.C.
28 July 1942

Dear brother:

Thou leavest a gap in the woods, in the sea, at bus time and in our
hearts. Thank you for your very fine letter – the dahlias came out
when we read it.[1] This being more of a dispatch to remind how
delighted we would be if you get an opportunity to come hither
again soon.

We have planted more dahlias over a bad patch, our boat has a new
fine anchor – an axe – and a new rope and now dances at its moorings
clear of munching barnacles.

We have made one of our rare trips to town, this time to see Eisenstein's Alexander (Prospect) Nevsky[2] – miles and miles and miles
away I persuaded Margie to go to the Pug Island Palindrome or

somewhere which wasn't improved by a small boy with St Vitus Dance[3] in the next seat, about the only other member of the audience, and the fact that Private Snuffy Smith[4] on the same program got somehow transposed into the middle of it and we couldn't tell the difference for a time. Orangeman – as that organ of male prostitution in journalism Time would say – Prokovieff[5] made a very fine din and bell noises and there was twenty-five minutes of the most thrilling movie we ever saw but even making allowances for it being cut to hell it was a bit of a diappointment. Even taking dialectics and a new synthesis of contradictions and the fact that he always admired D.W. Griffith[6] (us too) into account it was pretty sad. We simply couldn't get the intention, or if we did, the yards and reels of Laurel and Hardy, Marie Dressler and even Captain Flagg and Sergeant Squirt seemed to belie it, and it seemed mostly like a horrible regression, and we would be glad of your opinion.[7] It took us twelve chocolate sodas, a carrot juice and the subsequent appalling hangover to drown ours.

Have been working very hard – both of us – since you left, and have wrought 100% improvements thanks to you, in the early pachydermatous prose of the Volcano. If ever you are in need of any of our ars est celowry artem[8] it is of course proudly at your disposal from this end if any use.

I am sawing the succubus on the shore, but. . . Nature is the most beautiful thing I ever saw in my life. Our best loves to you and Betty,[9]

Malcolm & Margie

Annotations:

1 Noxon's letter, written from the town of Trail, British Columbia, on 19 July, is indeed 'very fine' and highly supportive; see *Letters of Malcolm Lowry and Gerald Noxon* (47).
2 Sergei Eisenstein's 1938 film *Alexander Nevsky* was a costume epic about the famous Russian prince who defended his country against a Teutonic invasion in the thirteenth century. The film was intended to inspire the Russian people in the event of conflict with the Germans during the Second World War. '(Prospect)' is Lowry's reference to the famous avenue in St Petersburg (formerly Leningrad) called Alexander Nevsky Prospect.
3 Saint Vitus (?-ca 303) was a Christian martyr who was appealed to throughout Europe in the Middle Ages for help against epilepsy and similar disorders; sufferers were described as having Saint Vitus' Dance. The expression is more commonly used today to refer to extreme activity or restlessness.

4 Private Snuffy Smith, perhaps a character from a children's short or a war propaganda short, has not been identified.

5 The Russian composer Sergei Prokofiev (1891-1953) wrote the music for Eisenstein's film. His compositions in a wide range of musical forms are characterized by bold harmonic clashes, and *The Love of Three Oranges* (1922) is his best-known opera. This work may have inspired Lowry's epithet 'Orangeman . . . Prokovieff.'

6 David Wark Griffith (1874-1948) was the first American filmmaker of major status. Among his most famous films are *The Birth of a Nation* (1915) and one of Lowry's favourites, *Isn't Life Wonderful* (1925). Eisenstein knew Griffith's work very well, and he discusses his influence on Soviet filmmakers and his contribution to film form (notably the development of montage) in his *Film Form: Essays in Film Theory*, edited and translated into English by Jay Leyda (New York: Harcourt Brace Jovanovich, 1949), pp. 195-255.

7 Stan Laurel (1890-1965) and Oliver Hardy (1892-1957) were a popular American comedy team on stage and in films between 1926 and 1956. Marie Dressler (1869-1934) was a film actress known for her roles in silent romantic comedies; she made her debut in *Tillie's Punctured Romance* (1914) with Charlie Chaplin. Captain Flagg and Sergeant Squirt are the boisterous rivals in love from the First World War film *What Price Glory* (1917).

8 'Ars est celowry artem' is a nice Lowryan play on the Latin phrase *ars est celare artem* (It is art to hide artifice). This in turn is an aphoristic rephrasing of Ovid's 'Si latet ars, prodest' (If the art is hidden, it succeeds), from *The Art of Love*.

9 Gerald Noxon married the American painter Betty Lane in London in 1933. After their return to Canada in 1940 the Noxons lived chiefly in Oakville, Ontario, near Toronto, until 1944.

176: To Priscilla Woolfan and Mrs Anna Mabelle
        [John Stuart] Bonner

P: UBC(ts)

> Dollarton P.O.,
> Dollarton, B.C.,
> Canada
> 7 August 1942

Dear Priscilla and Margie's Mother:[1]

It was very sweet of you indeed to send me such charming things for my birthday, a date which, but for Margie, I had almost forgotten I possessed.[2] So the morning glory, the sweet peas and the nasturtium are all set now and it is going to be Jack and the beanstalk all over again to watch them flourish.[3] When I shall probably feel like a djinn. Spelt djinn. Only I hope there doesn't turn out to be a Jap or a giant living on top of one of them though for that matter we're well armed with machetes, brush hooks, rakes, trowels, nails, hammer, saws – everything to take care of the giant, if not Japs, and I doubt not Japs too. Margie does not seem to think they are playing mumbledy-peg, as she puts it, on the Aleutians, by the way – nor do I.[4] I didn't know the laundry bag was for me at first but now I do, and I'm most admiring and grateful. It is as useful as it is beautiful only I feel I do not deserve you should go to so much work for me. And ah, the cards that multiplied into so many other cards within cards that I nearly died of curiosity wondering who they were from – I expected to discover at the end that the philosopher's stone or a bomb or truth itself lay at the bottom – thank you for those too, deeply. Now I know what good old Ezekial felt when he saw those wheels within wheels.[5]

No news from here with the enormous exception of course of Margie's great success with Scribner's, which you know all about. I think she'll be getting the proofs any time now and we're terrifically excited of course. At the moment she is ¾ of the way through getting the first book you helped her with so much in a final order again and we hope that's going to make Scribner's too. Only a few minor things in it prevented publication, I think: chiefly a tendency to write down, as it were, to a less hardboiled public than exists for mysteries, or if it exists, is a magazine public and not the one she was aiming at. Also the principal character had to be changed from the first person to the third – and so on. Though the book I'm anxious for her to get on with is the one about Daisy which is however fomenting away merrily, thanks to ever new ingredients from yourself. There is terrific material there, don't you think – a real Wuthering Heights.[6] I like to plague her with titles: I tried to sell her on The Reel of Raisin River or Raisin River Reel, for a time, but she wanted something about Pegasus, so I thought of Horse in the Sky. That seemed so good we thought we must have heard it before somewhere, but apparently not. So far as can be discovered there is no other Horse in the Sky. So Horse in the Sky it is for the moment.

I am writing a trilogy called The Voyage That Never Ends – of enormous length and horrendous content. I feel I shall probably sell the first third of it, a novel in itself, this year. When you read it you will probably decide that Margie has married a lycanthrope. My talent for serious writing, after producing an initial success [*Ultramarine*] at 21, went fairly badly aground for years, but was refloated with thanks to Margie. Which was probably a good thing all round, since I am able to nag her pleasantly and usefully on the subject 'Now your work merely begins, etc.' But Margie has really got over the bump, and is already following up, as you can see, which was what I neglected to do and where perhaps my experience comes in.

As for her agents in Hollywood and the East, etc., that is a bit of a problem. I foisted my New York one on her and he turned up trumps with Scribner's. He is a reputable and excellent agent – Saroyan's,[7] etc., but possibly not so good as the one you know for Hollywood in Margie's particular case, but we've taken the whole matter up with him; contact is difficult at this distance and we haven't had a reply yet, there we are – doubtless it'll all clear itself up to everyone's satisfaction.

With much love and many thanks all over again,

Malcolm

Annotations:

1 Priscilla Bonner Woolfan (1899–) is Margerie's sister, and Lowry is writing to her and his mother-in-law.

2 Lowry's birthday was 28 July.

3 'Jack and the Beanstalk' is a famous nursery tale based on world-wide mythology about the beanstalk. In the tale Jack climbs an enormous beanstalk up into a strange land where he robs a giant (who has killed his father) of many precious things. When the giant pursues him, Jack kills him by chopping down the beanstalk.

4 Japan invaded the Aleutian Islands on 7 June 1942 and held them until July 1943. As a result, Canadian fear of a Japanese invasion on their west coast increased rapidly, and this led to persecution of Japanese Canadians living in Vancouver. These Canadians were being systematically rounded up and moved to detention camps in the interior of British Columbia during the summer and autumn of 1942.

5 For the prophet's vision of the wheels, see the Book of Ezekiel 1:15-21 in the Old Testament.

6 Emily Brontë's classic novel *Wuthering Heights* (1847) epitomizes the gothic treatment of class conflict, violent love, and tragic death. Margerie's *Horse in the Sky* (1947), with its story of the ill-fated union between an aristocratic Englishwoman and an Irish groom, has something of the gloom and fatalism of Brontë's novel, but the story may also owe something to August Strindberg's play *Miss Julie* (1888) and D.H. Lawrence's novel *Lady Chatterley's Lover* (1929).

7 Harold Matson was the agent for William Saroyan (1908-81), a well-known American short story writer and playwright whose works include *My Heart's in the Highlands* (1939) – the name the Lowrys gave to their beloved row-boat at Dollarton – and *The Time of Your Life* (1939).

177: To Gerald Noxon

P: Texas(pcard)
PP: *LLN* 43

> M. Lowry,
> Dollarton P.O.,
> Dollarton, B.C.
> 15 September 1942[a]

Dear Gerald:

Just a note to say you leave a gap. Forest, boats, islands etc – even cats – miss you. We look out for your radio programme, what time the battery fades. Meantime work progresses apace; Margie's proofs should be here any moment; you must come here sometime in September, not a soul, the tide is always in, and there seem to be three full moons – All the best to you & Betty

> from
> Malcolm & Margerie

Editorial Notes:

a. This is the postmark date on the card; there is no picture. Lowry has signed for them both, as he often did when writing to the Noxons.

178: To Gerald Noxon

P: Texas(ts)
PP: *LLN* 43-49

> Dollarton P.O.,
> Dollarton, B.C.
> 29 October 1942

Dear Gerald –

I – we – thank you very much for sending the poems which are very powerful, original and dramatic and should, if they are a touchstone of the whole, make an excellent book.[1] In fact better than I have said. Above all, it is refreshing to listen to a poet who speaks in his own voice and not through a dictograph borrowed from Hopkins-Spender-Auden et al[2] and who does not find it necessary to write in braille. (I may say in passing that I am not one of those who have objections to 'obscurity' etc. in case my praise should seem to have a curse in it. But a semanticist within me is more comfortable if

I can feel in the same room with the writer, or, if he happens to be Rimbaud, at least lying on the same pavement.[3] In this case the reader does feel himself on the same blasted heath, in the same ruin) We spent some exciting evenings reading and discussing them and I am sending you what emerges therefrom that might be useful, or constructive. Our opinions differed occasionally as to intention and meaning, but in the main we agreed, though I may start a few hobby horses of my own rocking a little later. First, though, I take it one is right in assuming that the 'one day in the middle of my life' of the opening strikes the Dantesque note for a kind of Inferno.[4] I think it is a very effective and deceptively simple opening. I think perhaps one would get along better if I took them separately, thus:

I   One's feeling was that the writer was going to play Virgil to the reader's Dante, and that there were not going to be any leopards, but right away a sun of some import setting.[5] Since the sun never sets in the advertisement in the London magazine programmes on the domain in question one has the sun placed and I take it that the poem is a sort of prelude and statement of the whole. The sense of helplessness in that case is as well conveyed as is that in the Prufrock poem by the etherized patient.[6] I like the imagery, which again is deceptively simple: that the apparent fire caused by the sunset is analogous to the actual fire seems an obvious enough thought at first but the more you think about it in this context the less obvious it becomes. (One does not miss either that since the fire is cupped in the people's hand that the fire is something more and also something more than mere firebombs.) Again: / I heard the sight of heavy things, / Falling in the night / seems at first merely an adroit way of conveying precisely that, but the more you think about it the more sinister it sounds. Actually the lines carry with them a sorrowful and dreadful weight, which explodes at just the right point in the reader's mind. I do not know either how you manage to make what is virtually an onamatopeia visual, but that is the effect. In short: this opening is a good deal more than merely 'right.'

IV   Some of the sidestreets can be counted on not to be sure of this poem at first, which is the way I like to feel. I do not like the delayed action bomb of the meaning to delay too long however, any more than I like to be blown to smithereens immediately. First of all I couldn't see any nexus between the opening lines and the rest of it but meantime there was a certain irony and bitter satire glancing off one and ricocheting here and there. Then we saw the dead man a'glowerin' at us and began to read it in different ways, each as good as the other; and each possibly wrong (or both possibly right) though I was very satisfied with my version. The poet asks the dead man wryly and bitterly and humourously the questions of line 3 4 and 5. And the dead man, in sepulchral monotone (as it were) gives his reply in the rest. Both questions and answers are dramatically pregnant with associations (cf. significance of fires with the fires in I) Margie had the poet as it were straightening up, after 'any old bones' and declaiming the rest himself. At this point one only didn't feel stupid for not seeing the whole thing immediately because of the suspicion that one was supposed to see three whole things simultaneously. Anyhow, it has a very sinister, almost Chinese effect and it was not lost upon us that the 'sidestreets' meant both more and less than sidestreets, and both less and more than 'people'. You felt that there were chords here that would be resolved later and one was certainly not disappointed even in the scope of your selection. One felt too a curious satisfaction too in the poem as a separate entity, though I had pleasurable difficulty with the word 'spent', which insists rebelliously on being attached to fires and in making an oblique and profound meaning out of the attachment too of a contrary nature, even when it more obviously applies to 'pots' etc.

V   The double exposure here too may leave some of your sidestreets cold but for our part this is a beautiful poem that makes a fine and mournful music. Neither the significance of the man with the band of gold nor what the dope-fed streets were, nor the peoples' face was, nor that the woods again were more than woods (possibly even the jungle) were lost on us. I think the chiasmas – is it chiasmas? – at the end is especially effective, and though I am at a loss for terminology just at the moment to approve your method, it seems again, more than merely 'right'. Somehow you make it possible for the reader to hold beautifully in his hand at the same time both the real city and the city in the pool. . .

VI   Here again was a deceptive simplicity. The things that are left after the bombardment, in the rooms exposed in the torn buildings, a bed, a stove, etc., have become as it were altars that mark where the people were sacrificed. Lares and penates.[7] This makes 'essential miracles' the more meaningful. (For another thing, in wartime 'miracles' are essential in other respects too, both homely miracles of freak bombardments for the papers and other kinds.) The five and ten is Woolworths[8] in England and since the woman hadn't a flag to hide her thighs, the scene of the looting might be taken to be an international one. Enter the sanctifying pimp – who might be taken

as any governmental caucus of cranks and cravens – with his exploitation of the ferverishness and thieving. The 'woods' seem to link
poem 5 to 6 here (jungle?) There is a suggestion of a new government in 'proper respectable house', but since the hot winds are
blowing in the oldest grange it is obvious the war is still on. If your
intention was not merely to tell a simple story, it still makes a powerful and gruesome cartoon. But clearly its full meaning will only
appear in relation to the other poems.

XIX   It is pleasant to see you really keelhauling a fat hypocrisy
alongside your poetic vessel, and I hope you send some more over-
side. I feel that an objection might be raised to your use of the word
aseptic, which does not – doubtless on purpose, and it achieves the
right evocations – precisely mean sterile, but I don't see any way
round it. Margie liked the honest anger in this one, and so did I,
though it is about the only place where I seem to hear a voice not
quite your own, the other voice doesn't come through clearly, but
you do half sense a little Daylewis Auden poltergeist spendering
around somewhere in the isherwoods, though perhaps this is only an
illusion.[9] I like its directness and intensity: though I was at first upset
by the aldermen even being able to find the rubble of their lives in
my conception of your woods.

XXX   We've read this so many times now it's become quite an old
friend and we admired this poem of the falling plane very much indeed. Bound to the crushing spiral / of the sky's intent are terrific
lines as are the ones preceeding – / And then I saw an unremembered
star / Falling to the wolves of centuries old / White to the black panes
/ of widowed night / a cross came Falling. The form substance
rhythm imagery are all finely spun together. The only criticism is
one of ourselves. Though its meaning sinuated and unfolded simply
and beautifully as a stalk with an opening flower on the end of it, we
were so on the look out for possible gliding mysterious paratropes
and floating parambiguities by this time that all of a sudden we became possessed of the notion that he hadn't, after all, landed safely
(and all that that implied) and that the plane's supremacy in the
tangled aftermath suggested the supremacy of death and rest for the
pilot, and a crash instead of his plausibly having pulled out of the
spin or at least pancaked magnificently or made a successful crash
landing. (I hear groans from the stage at this point of Go out) Of
course what actually happened to the pilot is beside the poetical
point, but what certainly led us off the track was our ignorance.
How could he pull out of a spin with his ignition gone? we asked.

Perhaps he could. But if not, you would know about it – so in that case perhaps the man bailed out, but no, that couldn't be, and so on, half the night we argued irrelevantly, until we came back to the original meaning again and did a two point landing into bed ourselves.

XXXIV – Noxon in Wordsworth (1805) mood[10] – This hit, as the saying is, with a terrific impact. Titanic cannot tell how deep / The chasms and the caves of night, has the same sombre reverberating ὃπουδαηπς[11] as some of the other lines I have mentioned (though there will always be some fool who thinks that Titanic is some sort of god or an image of a doomed ship thinking about an iceberg) Margie was carried away and had no difficulty it seems, but I had some about the 'consummate masters of the briefest sea,' since your use of 'waves' and 'wind' was so suggestive: for instance I couldn't be satisfied that the masters were the wind and sea only, for their personification is strangely carried out, and for 'waves' and 'wind' I had already substituted – detacheably and interchangeably – in my mind, sea-forces, air-forces, so that what I saw holding past proud heads in shame were the men themselves, possibly on both sides, and possibly you intend that some such inchoate emotions should blow up from your theme to your reader standing on his cliff like spray from thundering surf below and then occasionally that he would be blinded as with salt. 'On insurrection shore no new thing grows' bothered me for analogous reasons, since insurrection suggests an immediate rising up against civil or political authority so that I kept thinking still of waves, only this time differing somewhat emblematically, rising up against cliffs. I get your point, however; I feel, though, I could stand enlightening on some others. The incantatory remainder of Noxon's poem conveys with nervous power the sense of stunned gloom that (as the Times Literary Supplement might say) – The sarcastic ending is odd, and I guess, true, and probably right. Margie liked the first and last poems the best.

Generally speaking, though naturally I realise that difficulties one might have with the item may disappear with the mass and everything is qualified by this, I feel, if I may say so, that in a few cases the ambiguities seem to spring less from the necessity to express several layers of meaning (though there is this too, of course sine qua non)[12] than from some infectious necessity caught from the contemporary climate merely to be 'ambiguous'. It is true it wouldn't need to be contemporary, one might have caught it from Rimbaud or Hardy[13] or the Holy Bible, but the point is the bug I am thinking of is more a critical bug than a poetical one. A poet like Herrick, let us say, achieves certain unconscious ambiguities here and there and say, Richard's Bill points them out.[14] It isn't that Richards Bill isn't a poet too in his way so much as that the person that passes the bug on has caught it from R.B.'s criticism and not from Herrick and that the bug thereupon nips you in the critical apparatus when you come to write your poem with the result that sometimes you find yourself writing the poem less for the poet-critic in yourself than to satisfy some kind of (at the moment) ideal critic outside. I went on at length about this, dragging in everyone from Stefan Georg[15] to Jesus Christ, and came back to the subject. I feel that when you personally are most 'apparently' simple you are most effective, and also there is more 'thickness' of meaning, 'ambiguity,' if you like, in the best sense of that exhausted word, that is what you say seems *truer* on more levels. When you are being more overtly and consciously ambiguous, on the other hand, the conflicting meanings some times produce a kind of 'dislocation of affects' that weakens the poem. It is as though you had deliberately plunged a perfectly good line at heart in alizarin – or is it anthraquinone?[16] – and died it a different hue. Having said this I can't immediately find a good example, but I am going to let the criticism stand, perhaps because it sounds good, or perhaps because I feel that though it may be invalid in the case of these poems there is here and there, a *threat* of your doing something of the kind. I don't say it mightn't sometimes be cunningly done, of course. Anyhow, I'm all in favour of one who gives up all attempts to hijack the sadistic but essentially pantywaisted zeitgeist[17] and who leaves all the pansy boys (doubtless engaged now in some 'poetry of clarification' though its the same old absomphe,[18] you may be sure) to their solidarity and – incunabula was coming into the next sentence, so I'll quit: but in short, starts something of his own. Which is, I believe, in the main very much what you are doing, from what you have sent us: so all power to your arm! If the idea hasn't occurred to you already, might I venture to suggest that you include in the Branches three or four perfectly strict (not that yours are not strict according to their own special strictness) formal poems, the old abbaabba, a sonnet or two, even trotting out the barrel organ, if necessary – I seriously think the contrast would be very effective and might serve to buckle tighter the surcingle wherewith you bind your theme. Even a sestina might be a brainwave – (I was thinking of Dante's in the Vita Nuova)[19] a brainwave because so it seemed to me, you could then make magnificent play with 6 of your most symbolic words – say: sun, fires, woods, streets, night, cliffs, since not rhyme but repetition of end words characterizes the form, the end words of the first line being repeated in an order which lets the last end word of each stanza be the first end word of the next, the sequence being 123456, 615234, 364125, 532614, 451362, 246531, there is a three line envoy which has three of the terminal words at the ends, the others earlier in the lines (just in case you haven't been slap through your thesis on the sestina very lately) – well, it was just a notion, perhaps not so silly as it sounds.

Thank you very much for the photos which were delightful with some entrancing pictures of Betty and Nick. . . We look out for your programme on the radio. . . Shall we send the poems back, or are they in the nature of a copy it might be insurance to let us keep, for the duration anyway apart from our liking to have them? . . . We had them all ready to send back, then decided to wait your word. We would also very much like to see some more.

The weather is radiant with mill wheel reflections of the sun on water turning and sliding down the house, in which Nunki, our cat, has lately seen a ghost. I'm pretty sure it was a ghost and it was sitting in your chair. We saw Nunki behaving oddly about the chair and we put her in it three times and each time it was as if she'd had an electric shock and she shot straight up about four feet into the air. We decided it was a good ghost that was helping but who didn't like cats, and since its departure we've rather missed it.

It's too bad about Betty's citizenship, but I have a hunch that it will straighten itself out shortly all right. We sincerely hope so. There was a case here of an American who'd enlisted in the Canadian army and had been discharged as medically unfit and who not only lost his American citizenship but was unable to get back across the border; but I heard that had been straightened out.

We've been presented with a wreck: or rather it wasn't a wreck. We woke up one morning to find a boat full of water trying to moor itself to our pier – about a twenty footer, ironbound, absolutely covered with seaweed and polyps – and with only one small hole in it, it's impossible to find out the owner, and we're thinking of salvaging it, putting a motor and a sail in it and who knows – one far off day – sailing to the Happy Isles therein.

We had an airmail postcard – delightful medium! – from Conrad [Aiken], who seems in good form but busy – and by the way, did you get our snapshots? There's no other news with us: we're both working hard, Margie has started a new novel and I'm finishing the Volcano. Do write when you have time – we look forward to your letters. Best of love to yourself and Betty and Nick.[20]

Malcolm & Margie

Annotations:

1 Seven parts of 'Branches of the Night' by Gerald Noxon have been published, with an end-note by Paul Tiessen, in the *Malcolm Lowry Review* 19/20 (1986-87): 13-18.

2 Gerard Manley Hopkins (1844-89), Stephen Spender (1909-), and W.H. Auden (1907-73) are English poets of established reputation, and hence often imitated by other writers.

3 Arthur Rimbaud (1854-91) was a visionary French poet who led a bohemian and self-destructive life. His most famous poems are *Le Bateau ivre* (1871) and *Une Saison en Enfer* (1873).

4 Dante Alighieri (1265-1321) began his *Inferno*, the first book of *The Divine Comedy*, with the lines: 'Nel mezzo del cammin di nostra vita / mi ritrovai per una selva oscura' ('When I had journeyed half of our life's way, / I found myself within a dark forest'). Lowry uses these lines as an important motif, associated with Hugh, in *Under the Volcano*; see the beginning of chapter 6.

5 The voyager-narrator (Dante) of the *Inferno* meets the classical poet Virgil in the first canto, and Virgil offers to guide the visitor through Hell. The leopard is the first of three beasts that try to block his way.

6 The 'etherized patient' is the striking image used by T.S. Eliot in the opening lines of 'The Love Song of J. Alfred Prufrock' (1917): 'Let us go then, you and I, / When the evening is spread out against the sky / Like a patient etherised upon a table.'

7 Lares and penates were beneficent Roman gods who watched over a household. The phrase 'lares and penates' can also be used to refer to cherished household possessions.

8 Woolworth's is a chain of low-cost dry-goods and variety stores founded in 1879 by the American merchant F.W. Woolworth (1852-1919). Woolworth developed the idea of a 'five cent' counter, which grew into the concept of the 'five-and-ten-cent store.' The first Woolworth's store in Canada was opened in Toronto in 1897; the first in England was opened in Liverpool on 6 November 1909.

9 A 'little Daylewis Auden poltergeist spendering around in the isherwoods' is Lowry's playful reference to a false or derivative note he hears in Noxon's poem. His allusions are to the English writers C. Day-Lewis (1909-72), Auden and Spender, and Christopher Isherwood (1904-86).

10 In part 34 of 'Branches of the Night,' Noxon describes the current war-torn scene in Europe, and Lowry may be thinking of the dark elegiac tone of one of William Wordsworth's (1770-1850) poems such as 'Elegiac Stanzas' (1805-07).

11 Lowry's approximation of a Greek word, inserted in pencil, is not clear. He seems to have written ϭπϭυδαηπϛ, meaning roughly 'spondait(us),' perhaps with reference to a spondaic beat in Noxon's lines.

12 *Sine qua non* is Latin for 'without which not' and is used to signify something essential.

13 Thomas Hardy (1840-1928) is a major English novelist and poet.

14 'Richard's Bill' is Lowry's somewhat sarcastic label for a Cambridge acquaintance, William Empson, who was a protégé of I.A. Richards at Cambridge University and the author of *Seven Types of Ambiguity* (London: Chatto and Windus, 1930). In this study Empson devotes very little space (pp. 204-5) to the seventeenth century lyric poet Robert Herrick (1591-1674) because Shakespeare, Chaucer, Donne, and Shelley, among others, are of more use to him. There can be little doubt, however, that this study of ambiguity had a lasting, if dispersed, effect on Lowry's own writing. See Muriel Bradbrook's *Malcolm Lowry* (124, 131-32) for her observations on the Lowry/Empson link. To these I would add the following: Empson (16-17) likens the synaesthetic hallucinations of 'mescal-eaters' to the effects of 'pure Poetry' – an idea shared by Lowry; Empson (99-100) quotes and discusses T.S. Eliot's 'Whispers of Immortality,' a poem also singled out by Lowry in his 8 September 1931 letter (35) to Nordahl Grieg; Empson (197-202) comments upon Eliot's claim that he could not understand a stanza from Shelley's 'To a Skylark,' and Lowry returns to this point, via Edmund Wilson's *Axel's Castle*, in his February 1944 letter (186) to Gerald Noxon. My point is not so much that Lowry adopted these ideas directly or solely from William Empson as that Empson's book was an important part of a formative intellectual and artistic milieu for Lowry.

15 Stefan George (1868-1933) is a German poet and translator known for his meticulous use of language, his mystical, romantic images of youth, and his resistance to materialism and naturalism.

16 Alizarin is a chemical appearing in its solid form as reddish–orange crystals; it was one of the earliest-known dyes, originally obtained from madder but now derived from anthraquinone. Anthraquinone is a yellow, water-soluble, crystalline powder derived from anthracene and used in the manufacturing of dyes.

17 *Zeitgeist* is German for 'the spirit of the time' and refers to the predominant characteristics of a particular historical period.

18 'Absomphe' is Lowry's pejorative reference to absinthe, a strong, bitter, greenish liqueur with a licorice flavour made from wormwood and herbs. It was the fashionable drink of artists and intellectuals who frequented Paris bistros in the nineteenth and early twentieth centuries. In *Under the Volcano* Jacques Laruelle drinks anís (which is also licorice-flavoured) because it reminds him of absinthe; see the opening scene of chapter one.

19 Dante's *La Vita Nuova* (*The New Life*, ca 1293) is a collection of early poems on earthly and divine love.

20 Nick is the Noxons' young son.

179: To Charles Stansfeld-Jones

P: Texas(ms)

Dollarton, [B.C.]
[n.d. 1941-44]^a

Dear Stan[1]
Thanks awfully for your very excellent letter & the new papers. First
– no need to apologise for the length of your stay nor to submit us
for that matter to the penalty of not seeing you for some time or anything: we are always more than delighted to have you. Let's leave it
at an as it were Stan ding invitation to come whenever the mood
takes you or you feel like inviting the soul: formal invitations of any
kind freeze one to the marrow – but preferably, I think, or ought to
say against my will, for there is nothing I would like better than to
go on talking regardlesss of time, if any – the *best* time is tea time
anyday and say, that I may not have also to impose the penalty on
myself too often of working till some forsaken hour, any day from
3.15-5.30 up to & inclusive etc, d.v at which time unless we are abso-
luely swept away upstream by some current, I ought to get to work
again, reluctantly though I be to do so, especially when one feels it
may be more to the common weal precisely to go on talking. Were
that work going easily, it would be different: but the book I am trying to write is a collossus of calculation (though some of it looks
Lilliputian enough), too heavy for me altogether, & I don't know
how it is to be done quite nor when it is ever done should quite know
how – like the stone monoliths on Easter Island[2] – it has been done.
      Secondly: on the contrary, the last set of papers impresses & in-
trigues both of us & moreover with none of the faults of presentation
one imagined one saw in the earlier ones. They seemed lucid, evocative, philosophically and psychologically sound: from the latter point
of view the 'challenge' is especially good. Yes, one says to oneself,

[end of page one; page two missing]

Re the Chalice – I was enchanted by that, Margie too: that is, by its
learning, its revelation, its meaning.[3] The only criticisms I have are
irrelevant so far as the immediate impact of the book by which we
were delighted is concerned: they will keep.
      They concern literature in general. You make me aware of that
poetry perhaps *is* at bottom, & essentially a form of magic, as words
themselves once were. (and still are.) You therefore incline to be in a

too powerful position to see perhaps, what is right under your nose. Granted you are concerned with something greater & vaster.

Let me make myself really obscure.

– If a fish were to become capable of conscious observation possible the last thing it would be aware of would be the element, the medium in which it swam, namely the water. This would do better as an economic analogy. We do not understand money. But what about words?

All right, you do not want to be an analytical chemist. Neither do I. However, it seems to me that there isn't anything like that involved in literature at all. The range is frightfully small. The number of truly great books likewise small. The requisite knowledge – & far more – you already have. You have many kindred spirits you don't know. It of course flatters me to talk on these things to a man who has undoubtedly forgotten more than I have ever learned.

(to be continued however.)

Do not look for logic or even commonsense or anything of that nature in this letter: Margerie is preserving blackberries, I write in a Faustian atmosphere & I think I am the Hairy Ape – [4]

Yours ever sincerely

Malcolm

Annotations:

1 Charles Robert Stansfeld-Jones (1886-1950) was born and educated in England, where, according to Day (294), he had been associated with Aleister Crowley, the infamous black magician. Around 1908 he married Prudence Wratten (1887-1981), and by 1913 they were living in North America, dividing their time between Chicago and Vancouver. The Stansfeld-Joneses were a handsome and eccentric couple. He had a degree in philosophy, was an amateur water-colourist, and published several monographs with the Collegium Ad Spiritum Sanctum in Chicago under the name Frater Achad. She was a great reader who shared some of her husband's interest in the occult, but less of his enthusiasm for Malcolm Lowry; see Kilgallin (51-52). They adopted two children (actually taken into their home as foster children): Deirdre (1912-69) and Anthony (1934-). By 1934 they had moved permanently to Deep Cove, the little hamlet next to Dollarton, where Stansfeld-Jones probably called on the Lowrys as a census-taker on 2 June 1941. Day (293-95) claims that they met in the summer of 1942, but records show that the census was taken in June 1941; see also Lowry's 7 September 1943 postcard (**183**) to Gerald Noxon.

2 There are over six hundred gigantic stone statues on the small volcanic island in the South Pacific known as Easter Island. European discovery of the island occurred in 1722, but serious archaeological study of the

statues did not take place until 1914, 1934, and 1955. At the time of Lowry's letter very little was known about the creation, purpose, or transportation of the statues, which could weigh well over one hundred tons and stand over thirty-seven feet tall.

3 Stansfeld-Jones published *The Chalice of Ecstasy, being The Inmost Secrets of PARZIVAL by a Companion of the Holy Grail, a Magical and Qabalistic Interpretation of the Drama of Parzival* in 1923. It is one of seven monographs written by Frater Achad between 1922 and 1925 and published by small Chicago presses specializing in literature of the occult. Four of these monographs have survived in Lowry's library as well as the typescript of a fifth, but *The Chalice* is not among them.

4 The 'Hairy Ape' is the inarticulate hero, Yank, in Eugene O'Neill's early play *The Hairy Ape* (1921). Yank's great problem is that he is born human and therefore is condemned to 'make a bluff at talkin' and tinkin'.'

Editorial Notes:

a. This transcription has been made from an interesting incomplete draft of the letter to Stansfeld-Jones found on the versos of the manuscript of *Under the Volcano* that Lowry gave to Gerald and Betty Noxon in December 1944. Pages 1 and 3 of this three-page letter were written in pencil on what now appear as the versos of pages 32a and 32 of the typescript version of chapter II when it was foliated with a mixture of typescript and manuscript material to form a complete draft version of the novel. The second page of the letter has not been recycled with this manuscript and appears to have been lost. According to the inscription, in Lowry's writing, on the cover page with the manuscript, now in the Lowry collection at the Harry Ransom Humanities Research Centre at the University of Texas at Austin, this text was presented to the Noxons 'by Malcolm Lowry [. . .] in sincere gratitude and friendship by the author Christmas 1944.'

There is no way now of dating this letter precisely, but since Lowry met Stansfeld-Jones on 2 June 1941 (the day the federal census was taken for the fall election that year) and took the manuscript with him when he went to stay with the Noxons in Ontario after the 7 June 1944 fire at Dollarton, it must have been written sometime after June 1941 and before June 1944. As is common with Lowry's drafts, he has signed this letter. He has also added a postscript, which is cancelled and illegible.

180: To Gerald and Betty Noxon

P: Texas(ts)
PP: *LLN* 50-51

Dollarton P.O.,
Dollarton, B.C.
15 January 1943

Dear Noxons:

My name is Inarticulacy: –

You should not have – but since you did – herewith an expression of inadequate gratitude, the fear that it could not but be inadequate being the cause of my, our, having delayed till now to make it.

The picture, Betty, is marvellous,[1] and stormes in our room day and night, and we are very proud indeed to own it. One seems to see somehow in the driftwood a calamitous battle of marine monsters or of creation divided against itself. At the same time one seems to hear an inhuman cackling of scales and spines as of cactus in the plains of Yucatan.[2] Since I understand that even so it is but a detail perhaps I may presume to judge, as from a synecdoche, the greatness of the whole. (Nor does the Melvillean whiteness of the frame escape one).[3] And the picture gets better, if possible, all the time as one lives with it.

I wish you could see, Gerald, how much the room is improved by its prescence, but I won't go into that, since this must be short.

I wish you could both be here for we seem to see potential pictures for Betty everywhere and moreover we are putting on some magnificent freezing blue weather with the sun raining diamonds in Burrard Inlet and seagulls and the washing frozen on the line and a two hundred foot alder plunging above the house like the mast of a ship on a rough day in the Indian Ocean. Whenever we have a day of this kind we always say: 'It's a pity Gerald couldn't be here to see this.' If we have another kind of good day: 'This is rather like that day Gerald was here,' rather as if we were Indians and time were measured from the day the WHITE MAN came. 'Now when the WHITE MAN was here um – '

I hope you didn't suffer much damage in the storm that hit your part of the world. One heard grisly reports of hens frozen in their tracks and lines down and power cut off and God knows what and one was alarmed lest you might be affected.

Please tell me whether or not to send your poems back. What was said of Betty's picture as to 'storming in one' applies here likewise. On subsequent rereading I felt some of my remarks were probably a little stupid. But they were meant to be constructive as to the work in progress. One certainly looks forward to an excellent book.

Our radio irreparably and disappointingly gave out on the fourth installment of 'Joe'[4] so I have no very useful comments here since one cannot do justice and also since I have no touchstone to guide me in criticism in that line. What I heard often moved me but I am not quite sure if for the right reasons and am not sure either whether a certain personal loyalty doesn't interfere in this case with one's objectivity, the case not being primarily, so to speak, one of aesthetics. Perhaps the most useful thing I could say is that everyone I have spoken to about it seemed enthusiastic.

We work very hard here. No word from Conrad at all in months. Hope he's all right.

And here's to the next visit of the WHITE MAN – and may he upon that occasion, if possible, bring the WHITE WOMAN (to whom renewed thanks) too.

love

Malcolm & Margie

Annotations:

1 Betty Noxon had sent the Lowrys one of her paintings as a Christmas present. It was destroyed when the cabin burned down on 7 June 1944.
2 Yucatán is the name of the peninsula comprising parts of south-east Mexico, north Guatemala, and Belize, and of the south-east Mexican state in the peninsula.
3 'Melvillean whiteness' is a reference to the great white whale in Melville's *Moby-Dick*, but also to the sinister associations of white in the novel.
4 'Joe' was the teen-aged boy in Noxon's weekly CBC radio drama series called 'Our Canada,' which was broadcast from November 1942 to January 1943.

181: To Gerald Noxon

P: Texas(card)
PP: *LLN* 53

[Dollarton P.O.,]
[Dollarton B.C.]
3 May 1943

Trumpets sounding for you from the Wicket Gate –[1]
luck with Teresina – luck with Branches (let us see more)

May you have fair winds, strange and rich landfalls, and a good time. You will. All the best to Betty and Nick
– Bello, bello, il mare! A riverderci!²

Malcolm and Margie

Annotations:

1 Gerald Noxon was born on 3 May 1910, and this birthday card is from both the Lowrys. Lowry has underlined the threes in the date, May 3rd 1943, to emphasize the numerical coincidence with Noxon's age.
2 *Bello, bello, il mare* is Italian for 'the beautiful, beautiful sea,' and *arrive-derci* in Italian means 'goodbye'; Lowry, however, appears to be parodying the English pronunciation of the word.

182: To Gerald Noxon

P: Texas(ts)
PP: *LLN* 54-56

Dollarton P.O.,
Dollarton, B.C.
15 June 1943

Dear Gerald –
Many thanks for yours – did you get our birthday card by the way? – with the Sable Island thing.¹ Blimey, what a romantic story. It's the most exciting thing I've heard of – I suppose Sable Island is *the* original Isle of Lost Ships of legend. We counted 83 ships piled up to port and 112 to starboard, 195 all told. Yes: 'Bob Logic' and 'Hard Times' and 'Blooming Youth' and the cryptically 'lost' 'Ocean Traveller' are about the most tantalizing, as you say: but what about 'Reeves' (1876)?² And 'Inglewood' (1894) strikes near home.³ Then way up at the north end, on the left, you have the 'Worchester' (1899); while far down on the left, you have the '*Hattie* C. Worchester' (1890). Then on the right 'Echo' (1827) and on the left, as if responding to it nineteen years later the '*Lady* Echo' (1846) And what about the Rabelaisian brigantine, 'Farto' (1875)?

> – Oh, we are the lads of the Farto
> And we just don't give a bloody farto
> So we never become disconsolato
> Oh, the Farto's lads are we!

One would like to live on Sable Island for a few months after the war and write a book containing 195 chapters, one for each ship.

We look forward exceedingly to seeing more of Teresina Maria and hope you will send some chapters soon. It is going to be a very grand book. But you must put in Musso's tennis game[4] and a dark (or bright) transitional bit in mid-Atlantic. You are undoubtedly right, that it should end in tragedy, yet in that case don't you think Roberto should grapple a little more, kick against the pricks so to speak, toward the end. Granted that Teresina is your protagonist – all the same I feel Roberto has some nobility in him. I think you want to feel, when he comes to the U.S., that he has a choice, that he doesn't *have* to end in the gutter, and that he is aware of that too; on the other hand you know perfectly well all the while that he's going to. It isn't perhaps so much nobility as a sort of physical instinctive thing about him. But I believe you want to get a certain feeling of *waste* about his death, not just that Teresina's well rid of him, though of course I see her love for him is more the point. I think the contrast between Rome and Detroit or wherever will be terrific. But perhaps you'll be doing well if the chapters we see get as far as the picture or the seduction incident. What about Branches?[5] May we see some more? I don't think you'll have the slightest difficulty in publishing them, when you want to. What about New Directions?[6] But perhaps you don't relish being the Poet of the Month and that kind of thing? Perhaps the wisest course is to let them simmer till you've finished Maria and then get Schuster[7] or whoever takes that to put them out next. Meantime you can add a few more to round it off. We suddenly got Horse in the Sky off in a great hurry and burst of glory[a] – we're vastly pleased with it; took nearly all your suggestions and it seemed just right, so we got on the horse and bang. The Volcano smoulders to a finish in reverse, first chapter last, and will inflict it on you eventually with your permission. Am looking forward to getting down to the so-called Paradiso part – am full of ideas for it.[8] Well, it's very beautiful here – a little more spring like than when you were here last year, though we've never had a day as perfect as the one when we all walked to Deep Cove. You go to the store through a triumphal arch of salmonberries. While the other evening there was a grey ship with yellow riding lights lying at the oil wharf and behind it the grey smoke of a train and the grey-green hills and silver grey cylinders of the oil refinery and up above a moon in a blue sky with Venus alone burning hard in daylight, and then the smoke of the train going eastward to meet the smoke of the shingle mill, the grey smoke of the shingle mill hanging in the air mingled with the smoke of the train, and reflected, white, in the water; then afterwards the swift wash of another ship, like a great wheel, the vast spokes of the wheel whirling across the bay. And all these things with ourselves look forward to the next visit of the WHITE MAN.

I have a lot more to say, but Margie has gone to town for the day and there is major disorganization here: half a hard boiled egg in the sink, a shoe on the window sill, I have just dropped my cigarette case down the john,[9] and I have been attacked by a piliated woodpecker –

With best love to Betty, whose picture we admire without end, Nick and yourself – from us both

Malcolm

Annotations:

1 The 'Sable Island thing' is a map that Noxon found in Halifax and sent to Lowry with his 6 June 1943 letter; the map does not appear to have survived. Sable Island, infamous as 'the graveyard of the Atlantic,' lies 288 km east of Halifax. It is the visible part of a sandbank about 120 km long and 16 km wide, and the wrecks scattered amidst its shoals are marked on maps of the area.

2 The writer James M. Reeves (1909–78) was at Cambridge University and published in *Experiment* at the same time as Lowry and Noxon.

3 Inglewood was the name of the Lowry family home in Caldy, Cheshire, where Malcolm grew up.

4 Mussolini's tennis game in the grounds of the Villa Torlonia was included in Noxon's novel *Teresina Maria* when it was published in draft form (Waterloo, Ont.: Malcolm Lowry Review, 1986 [59–62]); see Lowry's 24 April 1944 letter (**189**) to Noxon about the novel.

5 Gerald Noxon's long poem 'Branches of the Night' has never been published *in toto*; see *Malcolm Lowry Review* 19/20 (1986–87): 13–18 for selected passages.

6 New Directions, the New York publishing house run by James Laughlin, was particularly known for publishing poetry and *belles-lettres*.

7 Simon and Schuster is another New York publisher dealing with biography and a wide range of fiction.

8 The 'paradiso' part of Lowry's trilogy at this date was 'In Ballast to the White Sea.'

9 The 'john' is a colloquialism for the toilet. The Lowrys' cabin did not having running water and plumbing. Instead they had a primitive 'outhouse' toilet behind their cabin, as was customary with such summer or country places.

Editorial Notes:

a. A single page of holograph draft for this letter, from this point to the end and including a signature, has survived with the William Templeton papers (UBC 1:2), but a complete draft of the letter does not appear to have survived. The draft page is interesting for the evidence it provides of Lowry's extensive revisions to a letter; see Figure 10.

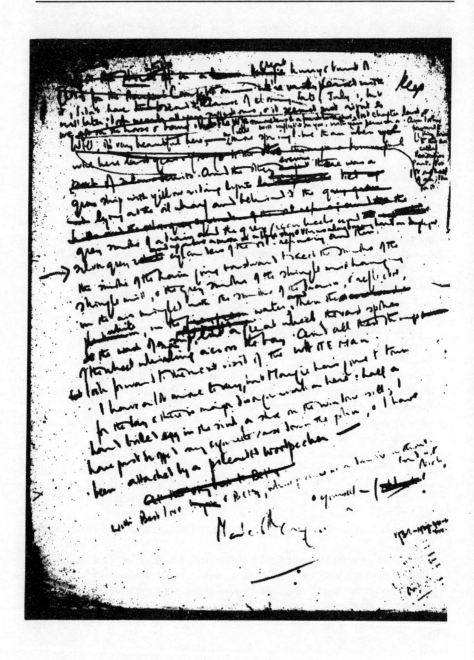

Figure 10: *This crumbling draft page shows Lowry's numerous cancellations, interlineations, and marginalia, and Lowry's habit of signing for himself and Margerie.*

183: To Gerald Noxon

P: Texas(pcard)
PP: *LLN* 56

[Dollarton P.O.,]
[Dollarton, B.C.]
7 September 1943

Dear Gerald:

We've been meaning to write 'The White Man' for a long time have in our heads many compendious letters – many thanks for yours of 25th July – but minor baffling harassments have put us off so far: no proofs of the Shapes, stupid reports on the Horse: we have made the acquaintance of a magician[1] ('the only thing for which there seems no rational explanation is sprites') – we listen to your voice on the radio Monday's with enjoyment – it comes out from under the bed you slept on now: we don't use it, scarcely turn it on at all save for you, & anyway its broken – yes, Mussolini being down the drain[2] ought to help Teresina which haunts tremendously – we had been looking forward to some more mss. before writing?? Don't shrink the Branches too much – first thoughts often best. Am still ill apparently but getting better. We are going on a picnic to-day as it were with you. Love to Betty & Nick.

God bless. (Writing)

Malcolm & Margie

Annotations:

1 The Lowrys probably met Charles Stansfeld-Jones, a local census-taker and cabbalist, in June 1941. They had come to know Stansfeld-Jones and his wife quite well and spent evenings at their home, where Lowry was able to use his friend's extensive library on the occult. They also dabbled in magic and experiments with the occult; see letter **179** to Stansfeld-Jones.

2 Mussolini was overthrown and arrested by Italian generals and politicians on 25 July 1943, when it looked as if Allied forces were about to invade Italy. He was exiled but shortly afterwards rescued by the Germans, and was then able to reconstitute his Fascist party. Italy was not free of the dictator until his public execution in Milan on 28 April 1945.

184: To Gerald Noxon

P: Texas(ts)
PP: *LLN* 57-60

[Dollarton P.O.,]
Dollarton, B.C.
28 September 1943

Muy querido hombre blanco y noble:[1]

Is your aunt in the garden with her strong stout stick? Escruch is an old man. He lives in England in a big house.[2] Old (viejo). Big (grande). The house (casa) – I give up; but the Latins must go through it too. . . Many thanks for your letter from the Yukon and feel guilty at so scanty a correspondence from this end. You have not been far from our thoughts, however. After a foul summer, and with everyone gone home, we have had a sublime Indian summer, like spring, all of a sudden; endless days of sunlight. We revisited the float where we ate lunch that day and like a signal the siren went off again, just as before. We have discovered other bays and crannies you must visit with us, notably a sunny cove on the dark side of the inlet. There are some queer isolated houses built on this side that get no sun in summer till five o'clock in the afternoon, and then only for an hour or so, though it is bright down by the water and we climbed up the cliff and found in the forest a tall lonely ruined house of four stories with a great wrecked fireplace and on the topmost floor, a square grand piano. You can imagine the strange chords that wind and rain must play there in the winter storms.

> Here him play
> That sinister melody
> That's what the people say
> When they hear those wierd chords
> The mice run out of the worn out boards
> To hear him play
> That sinister melody. . .

Your Donneish poem is very amusing: but Donne's new pseudo popularity via Hemingway[3] is as you say food for thought, suggesting some such as the following:

> *Donne he's regular*
> Once more thou art the rage oh good John Donne
> Once more Oh Donne hast thou set sail for Spain
> Once more thy fame as at the Cheshire Cheese

But now a greater cheese has called thy praise
Ah little thought'st thou, among the Anabaptist Germans
That plump shadow boxers would quote thy sermons
Puffing down the Boulevard Saint Germain saying 'son of a
    bitch' . . .

We have had some other long picnics when we wished you were
with us, and on one we found a beautiful sunken blue canoe called
Intermezzo. Life has thus been very fine on the paradisal side – but a
bit daunting on the work side. Scribners seems to have postponed
Margie's Shapes again and the first reactions on the Horse were
superficially so discouraging that I feel convinced that the book must
be even better than one had thought it. From the agent we have had
no reaction at all but one publisher thought it was 'handled with
facility but not significant enough for present time,' someone else
thought it was not improved by the 'trick ending,' (there is no 'trick
ending') but might have been a better book if part of the second half
was not so dull as the first, while Margie's mother, which is the un-
kindest cut of all, apparently thought that it was not only a bad book
but was very nearly the worst book she had ever read and went off
into a nervous decline about it all summer and (since she had felt she
ought to be the heroine) refused finally to write Margie at all and has
only just come round to doing that again: no one, so far, has judged
it by its intention, or its form. . . As a consequence your kind remarks, which I feel are true, were taken to our bosom. It will make
the grade in the end though, as you say; I am sure of that; but I am
filled with misgivings meantime that there is far less independence of
judgement on this side of the water than one would think; they have
to wait for some ratification or other to be imported by boat still.
    There are queer and unique difficulties that ever beset the trans-
planted too – which somewhat upsets this argument (and to get
somewhat off the subject and in a bracket) – why should not Conrad,
for instance, have made more of a mark in England?[4] He had as much
to say to us of value as Eliot, I should have thought, if not more.
Again why should Melville have been always more or less popular
in England and neglected in America? On the subject of Melville:
Margie gave me a collected Romances and I read, for the first time,
Redburn, the chronicle of Melville's first voyage on a ship called the
Highlander that sailed from New York to Liverpool.[5] It is all about
Liverpool in 1840 and there is one obscure statue in an obscure square
he noticed and chronicled (though in 1940 he suggests it will be no
longer there) that was always a favorite place of assignation near my
father's office of my brother's and myself, and I also described what

it looked like in 1940 in In Ballast. The actual ship that Melville sailed in *was* called the Highlander it is known and about this time you kindly sent me the graveyard of the Atlantic thing about Sable Island which I have been poring over with excitement ever since. Could it be – impossible! – but it was: Three quarters way up Sable Island on the right I found Pegasus (1830) Crofton Hall (1900) Hope (1828) Highlander! (1874) The Highlander was new when Melville sailed on her and his return voyage took him into those waters which she apparently plied fairly regularly: forty years is no great age for a sailing ship, so this might be a bit of a discovery. To continue in this Believe it or Not[6] vein, somewhat prior to this Margie had asked me to produce some rather foolish sounding American town in Montana or wherever for the Horse and I was looking through the Atlas, always in hope of finding too, for reasons I shall explain, where Pope County was. The reason was this, that I had one New Years Day in Vancouver here been accosted by a drunken man who informed me: 'I'm from the County of Pope. What do you think? Mozart was the man what writ the bible. You're here to the *off*, down here. Man here, on the earth, shall be equal. And let there be tranquillity. Tranquillity means Peace. Peace, on earth, of all man – '

And so I wondered vaguely where Pope County was, for I had popped this man and his miraculous (at least to me) dialogue into the last chapter of the Volcano.[7] But I had never found out where Pope County was. However this time looking through the atlas for Margie I turned to Minnesota. The first town that struck my eye was, in the County of Koochiching, a *town* named 'Margie.' Then my eye fell on another town, south of the Lake of the Woods but with no towns between it and 'Margie', named 'Malcolm.' It was at this point I discovered also, far southwest, the County of Pope, and in it, two towns fairly contiguous, the one named Starbuck, the other: Lowry! Starbuck is one of the chief characters in Moby Dick. Verily there are more things in heaven and earth, Horatio![8] But I think it is that there are intelligences in the void that sometimes like to amuse themselves at our expense, and feed our delusions of grandeur.

Which might bring me to our magician friend I told you about but perhaps I will tell you about him in our next. But meantime you might try your imagination on a conversation going on between Whitey[9] and the magician (*not* a stage magician but a real one, right out of the 12th century, the greatest living cabalist, no less) in our shack, something on these lines:

– Aw it's a crummy set-up, it's the bloody set-up.
– and I said to this wizard friend of mine, oh of course he was

strictly on the up and up, lived on the plane of Jupiter: I had invoked sulpher, you know, and banished earth –

– the bloody set-up, yis, that's it –

– on the plane of Mars, I think I was, by that time, let me see, and I said to this wizard, now about these elementals that have been bothering me lately –

I see, alas, that I shall have to catch the post. Let us see T.M. [*Teresina Maria*] when you have it. We're dying to see it. Sorry you're having trouble getting T.M. typed. Margie would have offered to do same for you save that it seemed impractical at this distance, but let us know if you get stuck and she'll rally round, she says to say, did before, but bafflements inhibited my writing.

How are the Branches coming? They should make a great mark if you let them. If you find the prospect of sending them round too grim why do you not send them to us when you have them in shape, being careful to keep copies, etc., and let us bear the burden of the few inevitable stupidities on our souls. We would be glad to. Permanently to alleviate suffering, first dart a few added pangs! say I.

Well do try and come here – since you're so near and yet so far in Edmonton – is there a merry devil there?[10]

We look forward to seeing you sometime again anyhow.

Best love to Betty and Nick.

God bless

Malcolm & Margerie

P.S. I bought Nick a birthday card, as from Leo,[11] but didn't send it because I got the idea then he might feel under some obligation burdensome to him to reply. Methinks I think too much.   M.

Annotations:

1 Lowry's Spanish translates as 'My dear white and noble man'; the Lowrys began referring to Noxon as 'the White Man' in their 15 January 1943 letter (**180**) to him.

2 In chapter 7 of *Under the Volcano* the Consul reads a version of these sentences in a child's exercise book as he sits on a bench collecting himself after his terrible ride on the Máquina Infernal.

3 The American novelist Ernest Hemingway (1899-1961) published *For Whom the Bell Tolls* in 1940. His title and epigraph are taken from John Donne's 'Meditation XVII': 'never send to know for whom the bell tolls; it tolls for thee.' As Lowry notes in the satiric lines that follow, Hemingway's novel is set largely in Spain, but Hemingway was already well known for his boxing matches and his experiences as an expatriate writer in Paris during the twenties.

4 Lowry could be thinking either of Joseph Conrad (1857-1924) or of Conrad Aiken, but his reference to the difficulties of the 'transplanted' suggests he has the Polish expatriate in mind.

5 This volume is not extant in Lowry's library, but it may have been *Romances of Herman Melville* (New York: Pickwick Publishers, 1928), which contains *Redburn* (1849), or the 1931 edition published by Tudor Publishing. In chapter 31 Redburn walks through Liverpool with his guidebook remarking that many buildings and monuments have changed or vanished since the book was written. He stops in the quadrangle of the Merchant's Exchange, where he admires a bronze statue, which he describes in detail, of Lord Nelson dying in the arms of Victory.

6 Robert Le Roy Ripley (1893-1949) was an American cartoonist, columnist, radioman, and writer. 'Believe It or Not' began as a sports cartoon and was first published in book form in 1928. *Believe It or Not* is still in print; it documents obscure and unusual facts and information.

7 Lowry gives this small speech to 'a man of uncertain nationality' at the bar in chapter twelve of *Under the Volcano.*

8 In *Hamlet* I.v.166-67, the prince of Denmark assures his friend, who doubts the intentions of the ghost of Hamlet's father, that 'There are more things in heaven and earth, Horatio, / Than are dreamt of in your philosophy.'

9 Whitey (Miles Went) was a Danish fisherman who lived at Dollarton and, together with Sam Miller, one of the Lowrys' few friends on the beach. It was Whitey who took them into his tiny place in the spring of 1945 when they returned to Dollarton and then, with Sam and Jimmy Craige, helped them to build a new cottage. Whitey is called Kristbjorg in 'The Forest Path to the Spring.'

10 The Canadian city of Edmonton is in the province of Alberta, and the name reminds Lowry of an anonymous Elizabethan comedy called *The Merry Devil of Edmonton* (1599-1604). The 'merry devil' in the play is a Cambridge scholar and magician who has signed a pact with the devil.

11 Lowry's birthday on 28 July means he was born under the sign of the Lion (Leo) in the zodiac, which extends from 23 July to 22 August.

185: To Gerald Noxon

P: Texas(ts)
PP: *LLN* 60-62

[Dollarton P.O.,]
Dollarton, B.C.
14 November 1943

Salutations to the White Man:

This is not in the general line (sic)[1] of correspondence but is one pro

Margie re Horse In The Sky, this long-suffering and admirable animal having now suffered more we feel undeserved punishment than the one in Raskolnikov's dream;[2] she wondered if she might ship it to you in the form of a carbon with a view to your looking it over and seeing if its points appeared as sound to you as when we read and collaborated on it all together last spring and if anyhow you might have some advice on the subject. This we meant to do as soon as she had it completed but I had the bad idea it might win the Harper's Prize so it went off there and the carbon to Hollywood, the other fairly complete copy being already ripening for damnation in the hands of Margie's mother.

Since then the comments upon it have been of such a peculiarly bloodstained nature and Margie's relations with the publishing world suffered such Kafka like permutations, that lesser victims might well have reached the end of their wit. Had Margie's agent not given up writing to her long ago in spite of impassioned appeals save vicariously in the form of moronic rejection slips I might be able to give you a more complete report. But what seems to have happened is that (1) Scribner's, after five promises that she was to have the proofs in a fortnight, seems to have postponed the publication of The Shapes That Creep indefinitely. (2) that Margie's other mystery The Last Twist of the Knife has not even been shown by her agent to Scribner's in spite of many appeals and has been making the rounds (several times) under the imprint of one mysterious Bonner Lowry, because her agent feels it would not be a good idea for two mysteries to come out in the same season, presumably 1967, under the same byline and for the same reason it has seemed better also to let it be known that this Bonner Lowry is a sort of man. (3) that Horse in the Sky, though not quite by this same Bonner Lowry, has been submitted, not to Scribners whom one might have thought interested in the versatility and productiveness of Margerie Bonner, as the first novel of a kind of Englishwoman, a namesake and also thus coincidentally by name Margerie Bonner, whose mysterious ambition it is to write short stories under the influence of Phil Stong about the Middle West.[3]

Of course we have put our foot down, but then one might as well put it down in the middle of the Atlantic ocean at this distance; well, the mysteries will doubtless look after themselves in due course but the comments upon Horse in the Sky, which has so far been rejected by Harpers, Houghton Mifflin, Doubleday Doran and William Morrow,[4] have been of the following nature:

(A) It is written with facility but it is not significant enough for publication at the present time.

(B) The background is interesting but the story seems to us a little too melodramatic to be convincing.

(C) It would be a better book if the last half were as good as the first. She uses many adjectives.

(D) I think this book is sketched rather than written. I don't believe any revision could help but I wouldn't be surprised to see it emerge in another form in another book some day. The ending of Thurles and Dungarvon is really quite funny, when it is meant to be tragic. She is one Englishwoman who can write about America (I don't believe I would have known her to be English but 'swine' at the fair stopped me.)

(E) The sales manager, myself, and the advertising manager, and the manager of one of the good Womrath bookstores all agreed it was unfinished and incomplete. Maybe it is an unfortunate sense of humour, but everyone here thinks the ending is funny, but not intentionally.

(F) The ending is magnificent, the descriptive passages are fine, but there are many gaps in the manuscript. We do not see our way to publishing it as it stands. However, we are very interested, and if she's ever around and hungry you tell her I'll take her to lunch with much pleasure.

(G) It has a trick ending – etc. etc. –

My own opinion, which I consider hard-boiled and objective is that it is a kind of classic and would establish itself as such if published. Its facade is deceptively innocent and perhaps not enough precaution is taken against the wrong reaction of the reader but it succeeds in its intention and is a formally beautiful and complete work of art. I feel objectively I would say something like that if I were a publisher's reader and had never heard of its author from Adam's off ox. But if we send it along to you, could you read it some evening when you aren't too busy and let us have your final opinion of it as a finished product? And if you still think it is as good as you did last spring, perhaps you'd give us some advice on it???? And if you don't think so, will you please say so?

And now the mail is going so in haste – What about the poems and Teresina? Let us have Teresina. Do not forget my offer about poems. Your radio broadcasts are listened to with enthusiasm. Hope you got back safe from the Yukon and that you received our telegram and letter sent to you at the Edmonton address. We still remember that you *might* be out this way this winter and hope for news of that too.

Best love from us both to you and Betty and Nick –

Malcolm & Margie

Annotations:

1 *The General Line* (1929) is a film by the Russian director Sergei Eisenstein about mechanization coming to a rural area.
2 In part 1, chapter 5 of Dostoevsky's *Crime and Punishment* (1866), shortly before he murders the old lady, Raskolnikov dreams his 'terrible dream' about his childhood memory of a group of drunken peasants who beat a horse until it was nearly dead and then killed it with a crowbar. This vivid, symbolic dream-scene is truly disturbing and memorable.
3 Philip Stong (1899-1957), an American writer who published many novels and stories about Iowa, was married to Virginia Stong, who had read and commented upon Margerie's manuscripts.
4 This is a list of American publishers. Lowry regularly sent his own material to Harpers or Houghton Mifflin. Doubleday, Doran & Co. and William Morrow & Co. are both New York general trade publishers.

186: To Gerald Noxon

p: Texas(ms)
pp: *LLN* 70-72

Dollarton etc.,
February etc.[1944][a]

– Dear old Gerald:
   Margie just went to town for a hair-do; I sit drinking coffee looking into a green sunrise with a howling gale from the north blowing an eagle a mile high down wind; gulls & wild ducks going the other way are caught in the teeth of it and a tern gives it up, is suddenly whirled a league to windward, considers joining the eagle. How the heagles fly in great circles. Nature is the most beautiful thing I ever saw in my life.[1] Then a gibbous moon, waning, oddly comes up over Barnet, accompanied by Venus, burning;[2] mystical and mad seascape. Eliot says – I just read in Axel's Castle – 'I confess my inability to understand the following stanza from Shelleys Skylark: Keen as are the arrows / Of that silver sphere / Whose intense lamp narrows / In the white dawn clear, / Until we hardly see who feel that it is there /. 'For the first time perhaps,' Eliot says, 'in verse of such eminence, sound exists without sense.'[3] Old fool. Too busy creaking around ruins (Margie said) the night before to know it was Venus as the morning star. It must be admitted however that some of his ruins are better than some of Shelley. Thanks most awfully writing Margie at such length about the Horse:[4] it really is a frightfully good book – we were cheered up no end, & now everything

seems taking a turn for the better with Duell Sloan & Pearce enthusiastic & almost publishing it and others interested . . . Some
notes on Conrad, Joseph; & second thinkings; having sailed right
through him recently. First a bit destructive. The first long chapter
of the Nigger is absolutely the greatest thing of its kind in literature;
but the rest falls off; he might compel a landsman to take it for
granted but it is not right & doesn't even stand up with a much
cruder but somehow more human thing like Dauber.[5] Noone could
find their way around that ship, he seems to have forgotten they are
rounding the Cape of Good Hope too; the very end is a horrible
mixture of sentimentality & veiled contempt for humanity coming
strictly out of the quarter deck. I think it's a failure on the whole, in
spite of titanic bits. I feel that perhaps *Typhoon* ought to have been
The Nigger: in spite of the fact that it's an unparalleled typhoon, I
somehow wanted it to go on longer; which I never should have
thought I would.[6] For as he says himself the worst of the typhoon
comes at the end. This is true of the story too. The end seems a bit
feeble, & he obviously didn't like it much himself, for here he informs us carelessly that all the while it was Christmas Eve, which as
any sailor would tell you must have produced at the beginning quite
different moral obliquities among the largely English crew. The first
time old MacWhirr feels 'I shouldn't like to lose her' or something, it
is moving: the second time hokum. It's wonderful in the engine
room: not so good in the stokehold. Of course it seems inevitable he
would have all the firemen passed out & the second engineer & don-
keyman doing the work; it isn't quite right just the same. The watch
couldn't have been achieved it is true, but there would have been at
least two stokers and a trimmer down there, one of whom surely
would have hung on. And if not, where were they? Captain Mac-
Whirr is based I think – believe it or not – partly on Captain Cook.[7] I
suppose it is still one of the best stories one would read in a lifetime. I
love The Shadow Line still & the Secret Sharer; though Freya of the
Seven Isles is another disappointment.[8] On the other hand The Secret
Agent is a surprise, an absolutely marvellous book.[9] There is a cab-
drive I might mention that is like nothing on earth had not Hugh
Walpole or somebody anticipated one.[10] But yet another surprise is a
thing I'd never heard of, a short novel called The Point of Honour.
(or, I think, The Duel.) If you have not read this you must do so.
Dealing with a period of history that usually bores me, the
Napoleonic wars, it is nevertheless Conrad at his very best; he has
been reading Flaubert or someone & the effect is astonishing & profound.[11] It is also frightfully funny, which I never should have
thought of Conrad. Let us see Teresina. Let us see Branches. We

watch the post. Let us see you. Let us see you both. God bless you. God bless Betty. God bless Nick. And now the Sun, terrific, a sign!

love from us both – Margie sends –

Malcolm

Annotations:

1 The 'heagles' and the comment about nature are attributed to 'Sam' in 'The Forest Path to the Spring' and are quotations from conversations with Sam Miller, one of the Lowrys' Dollarton friends.

2 Barnet is a small geographical area near Burnaby, across Burrard Inlet to the south-east of Dollarton.

3 In Edmond Wilson's *Axel's Castle* (1931; New York: Charles Scribner's Sons, 1954), pp. 117-18, it is *Wilson* who claims that 'Eliot . . . has confessed, with a certain superciliousness, his inability to understand' the fifth stanza of Percy Bysshe Shelley's 'To a Skylark' (1820). Wilson has quoted Eliot's remark about Shelley from Eliot's 'Note On Richard Crashaw,' which appeared in *For Lancelot Andrewes: Essays on Style and Order* (London: Faber & Faber, 1928), p. 96. Lowry has repeated Eliot verbatim. William Empson also comments upon Eliot's response to Shelley's poem in his 1930 study *Seven Types of Ambiguity* (197-98), and notes that Shelley's poem has been receiving 'much discussion recently.' Empson's reference is to Eliot's *Lancelot Andrewes* collection, if not also to Eliot's 1926 unpublished Clark Lectures at Trinity College, from which the essays in the collection were drawn. See Lowry's comments about Empson in his 29 October 1942 letter (**178**) to Gerald Noxon.

4 Noxon wrote to Margerie on 13 December with a detailed commentary on her book but generally reconfirming his earlier estimation of it.

5 Joseph Conrad's early novel *The Nigger of the 'Narcissus'* (1897) is a tale of sailing life and the sea. *Dauber: A Poem* (1913) is a narrative poem about the sea by John Masefield (1878-1967), who was England's poet laureate from 1930 to 1967.

6 *Typhoon* (1902) is one of Conrad's stories of the sea.

7 Captain James Cook (1728-79), the English sea captain, navigator, cartographer, and explorer, is especially famous for his voyages in the Pacific, Antarctic, and Arctic oceans. The notion that Captain Mac-Whirr from *Typhoon* is based on Cook seems to be a Lowry invention.

8 These are all long stories by Conrad.

9 Conrad's novel *The Secret Agent* was first published in 1907.

10 Hugh Walpole (1884-1941) was an English writer of stories, novels, plays, travel books, and a study of Conrad.

11 Conrad's story 'The Duel' (1908), called 'Point of Honor: A Military Tale' in the American edition of *A Set of Six* (1908), is about the antagonism between two calvary officers in Napoleon's army; it is also one of

Conrad's earliest studies of opposites who are in a sense doubles. Gustave Flaubert (1821-80) was indeed an important influence on Conrad, and Lowry may have picked up the idea from reading Hugh Walpole's 1915 monograph *Joseph Conrad*.

Editorial Notes:

a. This two-page pencil holograph has drafts of paragraphs for chapter 5 of *Under the Volcano* on the verso of each page. It can be dated with certainty because of the references to Margerie's work and to Gerald Noxon's comments on *Horse in the Sky* in his 13 December 1943 letter; see *Letters of Malcolm Lowry and Gerald Noxon* (63-68, 68-70) for Margerie's reply.

187: To Conrad Aiken

P: H(ts)
PP: *LAL* 176-78

> Dollarton, B.C.,
> Canada
> 4 March 1944

Dear old bird:

Thanks very much for your letter, am very proud and flattered to help if I can – hope not too tardy, your letter of February 20 took ten days arriving[1] – don't know if such ideas as I have any good but trot them out for what they're worth, my reader of most anthologies is a questing chap; poor, not knowing much, student and haunter of libraries, who though he may have read through many anthologies always feels like Stout Cortez on opening another one, but stares at Killarney instead of Pacific, is delighted he understands but invariably disappointed, often for the wrong reasons, but at the bottom full of love persists, by the age of forty when he has read Marvell's Coy Mistress and Munro's Cat for the five thousandth time may get a glimmering,[2] and by the time he is so old and shaky he can't turn the pages, may even be looking for some poem of his own in one, which has been put in, however, only in the belief that he is dead. Which, you may say, he was all the time. I am trying to be funny and I don't mean your anthologies. One of my most treasured possessions was your red companion book for the Squire one put out by Secker[3] and I have owned and lost and owned again your other many times. However I seem to see this reader somewhere, and feel the nice old chap should be treated sternly; though slightly humored perhaps in this one particular; for some reason he isn't over fond of too many *long* poems in his anthologies. Let's face it, he reads in the jakes, which, since they are outdoors in a forest perhaps, seems to him poetic justice; nothing will cure him of constipation, it is true, but he reads slowly and likes to finish a Poem at a sitting. However, down to tacks: – 25-30 pages of Aiken. I think your second idea the best, a scattering from all the poems, but with more form in the scattering than there seems at present and more poems; a progression, or parabola, of them which taken together would give more effect of your development as an artist, even if imperfectly, or something of the effect designed by the scrapped 'Divine Pilgrim' idea, only with many short poems instead at the beginning and end, of not much more than a page each, a gradual ascent, then leaving a sizeable stretch of arc at the summit for you to Landscape or Jones it or even slice-of-John Deth it in or otherwise go to town;[4] the decline of the parabola wouldn't be a Wordsworthian decline, on the contrary, you would end in a blaze of glory, at the same time finally a dying fall, not necessarily chronological, shading off via the Temptation at the end of the middle, into, say, the first and last sonnets of And In The Human Heart to a contrast of shorter eclogues like Who Shapes a Balustrade? and Anaesthesia, ending on a simple note, like The Sounding.[5] For the very beginning I would suggest all short and something like (1) From House of Dust – the exquisite passage: 'Sunlight roared them like a dark invisible sea' 'dark blue pools of magic' (2) the Three Pale Beautiful Pilgrims (3) Rye sunset 'Here by the wall of the ancient town I lean' (4) The Room (5) Sound of Breaking.[6] Thenceforward the sound of breaking would go on getting considerably louder, (rising to a climax, I was going to suggest, at Goya, sandwiched in between two longer things, in its original prose form; I never liked it – er – as well in verse,[7] but perhaps this would not do) and using preludes (though you might culminate at a longer one, cold but shattering, like 'at the dark's edge how great the darkness is'[8] from both groups as sort of buffer states between attitudes, dark or bitter preludes on the upgrade, brightening on the down. My parabola should perhaps have been the other way up, but never mind. I have said nothing of Tetelestai or And In the Hanging Gardens or King Borborigmi,[9] or one of my favorite parts, which is the very end of Punch[10] – as became of recent years the whole of John Deth – perhaps the motion too jaunty altogether however, if *cut into*????) – one would like to see The Four Appearances, many preludes that will not be in, and a hell of a lot beside; (Margie puts in a strong last plea for the Morning Song from Senlin,[11] feeling something also powerful and scientific beneath that song, and perhaps it might go well as number 3 instead of Rye Sunset, though the equivalence seems unfair); but you can't have everything, as the Elephant said to the woodpecker, and I feel you ought to give previously unanthologised poems a chance where possible: the ones you cut out will go on ringing all right.

I wish I had time to be more detailed but it seems if I don't get this off right away it won't be any good to you anyhow. I hope there maybe a good idea at the bottom of this somewhere and anyhow it's the best I can manage and me with a stomach ache. I think some of the Eclogues among the greatest things you've written.

Margie sends love as I do to you both –

Malc

Annotations:

1 According to Sugars (176), this letter is missing, but it is clear from the context that Aiken has asked Lowry's advice about which poems he should include in the anthology he is editing, *Twentieth-Century American Poetry* (New York: Modern Library, 1944).

2 Lowry is referring to Andrew Marvell's 'To His Coy Mistress' and to the frequently anthologized poem 'Milk for the Cat' (1914) by British poet Harold Monro (1879-1932). Aiken, like Lowry, was a lover of cats and certain to catch the allusion.

3 Aiken selected the poetry for *Modern American Poets* (London: Martin Secker, 1922).

4 Lowry's references here are to Aiken's *Landscape West of Eden* (1935), *The Coming Forth by Day of Osiris Jones* (1931), and *John Deth* (1930).

5 These are all poems in Aiken's *Brownstone Eclogues* (1942).

6 Lowry's suggestions (2) through (5) are all from Aiken's *Priapus and the Pool* (1925).

7 'Goya' was published in prose form in *Blue Voyage* (142-43), and in verse form in Aiken's *Selected Poems* (1929).

8 See the last line to prelude 'XXXIII' in Aiken's *Preludes for Memnon* (1931).

9 All three poems are from *Priapus and the Pool*.

10 Aiken published *Punch: The Immortal Liar, Documents in His History* in 1921.

11 'The Four Appearances' is from *Brownstone Eclogues*, and the 'Morning Song of Senlin' forms part of *Senlin: A Biography* (1925).

188: To James Craige
p: UBC(ms,phc)

[Dollarton, B.C.]
[1944][a]

– My very dear Jimmy:[1]
   I'm sorry I can't get in to-day – but will be with you in spirit &
come as soon as I can. Hope all went & goes well: your boat etc has
been drawn up & all is well, safe, & happy here, though of course
everything misses you[b]

God bless.

Malcolm

Annotations:

1 'Jimmy' (James) Craige (1879-1966), a Manx boatbuilder and one of
   Lowry's dearest friends at Dollarton, helped the Lowrys with all aspects
   of practical life on the beach. Craige's friends and family recall that
   Jimmy admired Margerie's ability to cope with their primitive life-style.
   For anecdotes of the Lowrys' friendship with Craige and his family, see
   Day and Salloum; see also photographs 28 and 29.

Editorial Notes:

a. No originals of Lowry's cards and letters to Craige appear to have
   survived. From the photocopy this note appears to be written on a 7.5-
   by-12-cm piece of paper, and there is no date or inside address. It has
   been copied together with a postcard dated 26 June 1944, but there is no
   other reason for dating and cataloguing it in 1944.
b. A line and an asterisk have been inserted in the left margin at this point.
   At the top of the page someone has drawn an asterisk and written the
   following remark: 'Ruskin's term is "*pathetic fallacy*" see Benét's *Readers
   Encyclopedia*, p. 828.'

189: To Gerald Noxon
p: Texas(ts)
pp: *LLN* 76-83

Dollarton, B.C.
24 April 1944

Dear Gerald:
   First of all let us say we both thought T.M. [*Teresina Maria*] absolutely first rate and read it with much excitement and enjoyment and

profit. We should have answered long before but the Lowry menage has had a slightly disrupting time of it lately and we weren't in the best form and we wanted to *be* in the best form when we got down to the serious business of criticism and appreciation. (Nothing serious wrong with us, just minor harrassments like dentists, colds in the head, etc.) We read it separately, without discussing, and made our notes separately, so as to give you two different opinions. Possibly the most helpful thing would be to give you our notes, made while reading it, and let you see what you make of them. Remember that while we were reading with pleasure, we were doing what we do between ourselves, that is, being hypercritical and looking for everything we could find to pick on.

[Margerie Lowry's notes omitted][a]

Malcolm's notes

The book should push on to very grand things: Teresina herself is an enormous success throughout. The style seems to arise naturally out of the material and is in itself a real achievement; original and uninfluenced – on first reading it seemed a little monotonous but it is somehow just right – recapitulatory, doubling back on itself, its final effect is poetical and the perfect medium for the unfolding of the story, which afterwards you are scarcely aware has not been proceeding straight ahead, so buried was the authors touch that, so to speak, 'fled and pursued transverse the resonant fugue.'[1]

Piddling criticisms; and genuflections.

8. Do not like the dots or asterisks; nothing will persuade me they are not a weakness. So suggest you begin Chap II with They drank the real soft wines etc which is better musically, too.

13. type error: Poussin.[2]

14. Beautiful and subtle description here.

20-21. Admirable echoing stuff in the garage. Giacomo done excellently.

24. Very piddling criticism: a slight feeling of too many gots and gets, though you need got rather drunk.

Note Teresina, Roberto, Signora Bicci, all unqualified successes. Chap VII Beautifully done! Likewise Chap VIII

60. Type error: instinctively.

Enrico Pezzoni is introduced brilliantly.

The tennis game is a delight, and I'm very glad you used it.[3] The drive towards Naples after the game is particu-

larly good; and everything proceeds with excellent architec-
tonic balance and swing; no criticism here – it's fine.
101. But I have a criticism of your handling of the Enrico
Pezzoni scene; I feel you want a little more subtlety.
One feels a little dubious about the key business; on second
reading you see it is probably O.K. after all, but a doubt
sticks. The propositioning seems a little bit too true to
type, and that it probably would be, doesn't seem to help
artistically. At first I wrote: One solution to it might be
to cut (top of 100) 'If we can hit on some arrangement
suitable to everyone concerned', keeping the rest of Pezzoni's sentence in. Keep all Teresina's thoughts as they
are, and the key incident as it is, only when you get to
Enrico threatening her outside, at the very bottom of 102,
take what seems to be a curse off the passage by saying
something like: She could hear every word he said. Pezzoni
had drunk heavily at dinner, and he was threatening them
both now. Then 'what he and the others *could* do' rather
than *would*. Now I feel this is a pretty lousy suggestion,
but still it may suggest something to you. Or it might help
if you said there, or earlier, something of this nature:
There seems, in all Italians of Enrico Pezzoni's stamp, some
inner compulsion to behave at given moments like Baron Scarpia in Giacomo Puccini's Tosca.[4]
    But the last words of the close of this chapter XV are
really beautiful and moving.
104. All the business in the Continental excellent and exciting.
108. But I am not sure technique is right at bottom (see
later) and I object to the asterisks. Better change chapter. Roberto's drive becomes wildly exciting.
    'I hope that Roberto does what I told him . . . that
and nothing more.' – 'This may be the chance you're waiting
for, Roberto,' happily as they balance each other, seem
slightly what one might call 'cartoon technique' – I think
that such complete simplicity can indeed come off: but here
it started up at me. I do not see what would be wrong with:
And he almost persuaded himself ducking under the shower
that everything else would be easy, so long as Roberto did
what he was told, and nothing more.
    And: In fact it was perhaps the chance he'd been wait-
ing for, he thought as he reached into his pocket for the
door-key. Or at any rate just one of them in monologue.
The rest is splendid.

122. passim: I do not agree with Margie's criticism of this
though perhaps it would be a good idea to see something out
of the window – perhaps a Roman movie house or something,
with what is showing there – and a few more of your pet
trams, the Monte Sacro one far from home? – if this is
impossible at any rate a brief sense of Rome again, striking
the chord of the opening chapter. The best of literature is
like Flash Gordon[5] at times, as this must be here,
unavoidably, if you are to keep it simple. I think,
however, you could take any curse off that, or of possibly
too blatant radio technique off it by opening Chap XVIII as
follows: a la Dostoevsky.

> It is a fact, however, that the following scene took
> place: – Dino Maccari, etc. . . . .

130. All this is then fine until we come to Maria's last
speech, which I question.

This too struck me as very fine when I first read it, but on second
thoughts perhaps it is a little too fine. Certainly you need something
of the kind thematically, and its ironic contrast with the brothel
owners ideas of America is very great; though you don't get this immediately. I'm not sure that it is right aesthetically; on the other hand
it might seem quite different in the light of the whole book. Quite
apart from this I don't think Maria would *say* all of it; that doesn't
necessarily matter and perhaps its due to my ignorance of Italians and
of the country anyway. I think one good answer to the problem
might be along these lines: have Maria make her dying speech all
right, but not quite so strong on liberty, though there must be the
wish, of course, that Teresina should leave. etc. Then have Signora
Bicci carry the burden of the thematic business; after all we have been
aware from Chapter I of Signora Bicci and the Fascists and what she
feels in regard to them, and we also know her much better than we
do Maria. One becomes very fond of Signora Bicci almost anything
you want to make her say will be O.K. with the reader. But I admit I
would have none of this criticism myself. I would tell me to go to
hell here. But let a doubt stick because of our mutual reaction to the
scene; perhaps a slight cut in Maria's speech would do the trick. . .
Altogether a swell job, Gerald, a beautiful story, beautifully and
originally told, and we are all impatience to see the end of it; a swell
and I believe eminently saleable and profitable job too. Some of our
suggestions will be lousy so chuck them out. You know what you
need for the book as a whole; whereas in spite of your having told us
the general broad outline – so that we know to some extent what

you're building towards – we still of necessity can't see it *all* and therefore may make some stupid criticisms which we wouldn't make reading the whole thing.

Only further suggestions I have that may be worth considering, if not already considered:

A. Have a short scene of sea and darkness on board the ship; and possible one of dawn too. (By the way, I can't forget that Joe Venuti – who's record Ragging the Scale you used in Storm over Asia once – was born in mid-Atlantic.[6] Somehow that man's violin makes the freest most joyous and liberty sounding music of anything I ever heard except a lark. I can't help thinking that Venuti records say something about an Italian's dreams of America; I feel somewhere later, very tiny, Joe Venuti's violin might be heard off stage, furious and nostalgic. . .)

B. Have the wheel come full circle at the end, with a vision or panorama of Rome again, if only in someone's imagination, with the Monte Sacro tram, etc., as before.

Thank you very much also for the radio script, the Pillars of Hercules[7] which was very amusing, and also really touching; did you send it to us to use as a model if and when we might want to try to write some radio scripts; if so thank you very much again; if not, and you want it back will you please say so? We would like so much to have heard it or hear it. You didn't tell us times or name of your Easter play and we couldn't find out when it was; we turned the radio off and on all day but with no luck.

We wish you could be here – and please come soon. The spring is not so good right at the moment and the black nights are Eridanus[8] from pole to pole. But pretty soon bright days will be arriving again, we hope, with the White Man.

Have you read a novel the Lost Week End by one Charles Jackson a radioman from New York?[9] It is perhaps not a very fine novel but admirably about a drunkard and hangovers and alcoholic wards as they have never been done (save by me of course) it struck a somewhat shrewd psychic blow that has rendered it discouraging to work on such for some weeks. But one plods on hopefully – I'd like to know what you thought however, if it has seriously undercut my delowryiums.

All the very best to Betty and Nick,

Love

Malcolm & Margerie

P.S. We were just about to mail this when Percy[10] told us he heard you broadcasting from Frisco last night with William Winter, that you've just come back from England again! We are mailing this to Ontario, hoping though that you have to stop over at Vancouver and will have time to see us!! Many happy returns of a day.

Annotations:

1 Lowry's quotation is from Milton; see *Paradise Lost* XI.563.
2 Nicolas Poussin (1594?-1665) is a French painter known for large canvases of mythological and historical subjects.
3 See Lowry's 15 June 1943 letter (**182**), in which he urges Noxon to include this tennis game.
4 Baron Scarpia is the villain and lecher in Puccini's opera *Tosca* (1900).
5 *Flash Gordon* is the title of a popular, futuristic cartoon series in the Superman mode created by American cartoonist Alexander Raymond in 1934 and introduced as a daily newspaper strip in 1940.
6 Lowry mentions Noxon's choice of Venuti's music for *Storm over Asia* in almost the same words in his 21 September 1940 letter (**151**).
7 'Pillars of Hercules' was a thirty-minute radio drama written by Gerald Noxon and broadcast for the CBC program 'Stage' on 5 March 1944.
8 Eridanus, known in astronomy as the River Eridanus, is a large southern constellation between Cetus and Orion and contains the bright star Archenar. Eridanus was also Lowry's name for his Dollarton paradise.
9 Charles R. Jackson (1903-68) was an American writer who worked for the Columbia Broadcasting Company for two years in the thirties and then as a freelancer. His first novel, *The Lost Weekend* (1944), became a best-seller and was made into a movie starring Ray Milland in 1945. Both novel and movie haunted Lowry, who felt that Jackson's portrayal of an alcoholic's five-day binge robbed *Under the Volcano* of its novelty. Moreover Lowry, always fearing charges of plagiarism, was certain he would be accused of copying Jackson; see, for example, his 6 June 1945 letter (**202**) to Harold Matson. Apart from the similarity of theme, *The Lost Weekend* and *Under the Volcano* have little in common. Nevertheless, Lowry must have been struck by the fact that Jackson's hero, the alcoholic, writer, and intellectual Don Birnam, is given to quoting Shakespeare, Dostoevsky, Joyce, and Thomas Mann and refers to Poe, Keats, Byron, Dowson, and Chatterton as his boyhood idols, because these writers are also among Lowry's favourites. Jackson published three more novels and several stories, articles, and reviews before his death from a combination of drugs and alcohol in 1968.
10 Percy Cummins owned the store in Dollarton where the Lowrys purchased their supplies.

Editorial Notes:

a. In the original typescript 'Margie's notes' appear before Lowry's. These are included in *Letters of Malcolm Lowry and Gerald Noxon* (76-79).

⌒⌒

This letter, described so aptly by Lowry as 'a brand from the burning,' is to his friend Charles Stansfeld-Jones, and it is one of the few items to survive the fire that destroyed the Lowrys' Dollarton home in June 1944. All that survived of Lowry's manuscript of 'In Ballast to the White Sea' are some charred fragments, now stored with his papers at UBC. But if the physical reminders of that terrible day are few, the literary ones are many and important. So profound was the psychological impact of this fire on Lowry that it would become a recurring theme in his letters and a central topos *in* October Ferry to Gabriola. *Fortunately the Lowrys rescued the manuscript of* Under the Volcano *from the flames and fled east with it to the sanctuary of Gerald Noxon's home in Ontario.*

190: To Charles Stansfeld-Jones

P: UBC(ms)

[Dollarton, B.C.]
[post 7 June 1944][a]

Well meaning bollocks.[1]

Having a bloody painful time with back & must get packed so
can't come this aftn

A letter – I send it you just as I was composing it from time
to time by my desk – a brand from the burning now.

Decipher it if you can; it isn't altogether nonesense;
though in my callousness it rather underestimates you.

You won't read any of the books of course, & most of them
you've read anyway, & nearly all of them were unreadable. . .
You are ahead. You may have missed something in passing
something by however though it adds up to this : nada.

An expert as no one on this (this is not a dirty crack) how
the hell can any or many of these books mean much to you.

But they might be read (but of course you have surpassed
them anyway so my letter is absolute nonesense) *in the long
interval You will have to wait for everyone else to catch up:*

I don't hear anything about God save that he's good
which means his sense of humour is good too. May he bless
you. Will be back in 2 or 3 months Thanks for all *your*
help, I shall miss trips & teas & Islands & You three will
write Rubina & Deadre[2]

A brand from the burning: the commentary on this side I
can't understand, & should probably count off as delirious:
the notes for the letter on the other side I can't
understand either, but at any rate shows I was thinking of
you. We saved the paper by the way not, alas, alas, so far
can I find Rubina's Tarot.

Malc

[Lowry's 'notes for the letter'][b]

1. a touchstone. What is a touchstone? Looked up. You have
it. Parzival will do. Parzival, Pilgrims' Progress, Don
Quixote, Ulysses, [several words illegible] Aeschylus – (the
same is not true of later drama Moby Dick, Faust – but what
can we do – all of them are fairly lousy, even when great.[3]

2. Personal identification. Start on a contemporary.

3. the immediate identification will not live up to the
touchstone: but you will pretend it does for the time being

4. the, a certain identity of Poetic diction with mystical
cliché. (You might have taken something from Uzell here but
I doubt it)[4] Mystical clichés, I appreciate, may only seem
so when given to the world: to the mystic they have a different value. But since it produces the wrong evocations to
a worldly mind & [word illegible] as it were [several words
illegible] why use them?

5. During wartime no magazine or paper whatever will serve
as any hint of or guide & scarcely in peace. But the more
intellectual & clique & 'insane' ones are often for some
reason the more reliable. Even communist ones. Horizon in
England. New Republic. New Statesman. Throw the Atlantic
Monthly far out of the window & these other magazines too
after them. Or keep for other use.

6. Vaughn, Donne, the Metaphysicals.[5]

7. Kafka, the Castle.[6]

7. Yeats: Modern Poetry. More because Yeats is your man ('The Tower' The Vision – virtually unprocurable but you would be the man to understand it)[7] eventually who has edited, also to convince you that all modern poetry is not insane, that there are many kindred spirits there.

8. Throw all historical estimates out of the window at the beginning. For the beginning consider that all the poets & writers are writing in one room.

9. Many chaps such as TS Eliot [are] your meat to some extent. Symbolism of the Tarot Pack etc in Waste [Land] The birds that you call insane.[8] But leave them for the time being.

10. In the end throw everything out of the window but what seems to contribute to your 'harmony' etc. God is a great artist surely – & how else can you appear before him with your instrument in tune unless you have encompassed and used great art – you cannot use all of it or you would go cuckoo like Faust – a danger; which in measure you have to enrich your life but beware of a priori assumptions stock response, & Uzells. Else a great (price is [word illegible]).

11. I have the key & here it is & there is [word illegible] your room. But beyond the first room is another door to which you have the key & I haven't, then many others, like a Chinese puzzle.

12. Only the perception that these people are so to speak kindred spirits working towards the same goal keeps me from the sense of working without a tradition at all & in this sense I am as poor Parzival, an ignorant fellow.

13. I got an honours degree just but not a first class one at St Cathr Cambridge. I am not in any sense a clever or a brilliant man but feel that I am a probably nevertheless [word illegible] a writer [word illegible] to be reckoned with. & I feel there may be some [several words illegible] in which I say Though this is scarcely the first.

11. There is a book in the Public Library of all Greek

drama the Oresteia of Aeschylus, & two Oedipuses the
Antigone & Euripides the Trojan Women & the introductions
translated by [word illegible] Read it: do not be put off
by the style. You will get a kick out of the [word
illegible] Aristophanes but be sure not to get the wrong
kind of book.[9]

12. Put this away for the time being & get hold of Powys &
perhaps thence [. . .]ᶜ yourself. Powys as a [. . .] is far
from a first or even second [. . .] except in spots. But
what [. . .] I think will move you probably. He is a
descendant of Donne. A flash [two words illegible] Maiden
Castle [two words illegible] In defence of sexuality etc.[10]

[marginalia]ᵈ

Poems need not all go de bump de bump de bump. Air need not
be zephyr-like. The relation of Poetic Diction to mystical
cliche & hence to [Elphanstone] & hence to life.

Tolstoys: War & Peace.

Reading a good [word illegible] books is not quite the same
as being an analytical chemist: poetry is, of course, a form
of magic Invention etc. All that. If you like poetry has
become debased; as science has: its function is no longer
within the magic circle. Try to think that good poetry may
exist exclusive of that function. You are still using
words. Shakespeare for instance, without stretching a
point. But perhaps the other great point to be made here is
that of all the great dramatists Shakespeare alone is not a
moralist [as it were amoral] in some sort.

Annotations:

1 'Well meaning bollocks' refers to the contents of Lowry's letter rather
   than to his addressee, Charles Stansfeld-Jones; 'bollocks' is a British vul-
   garism meaning rubbish or nonsense. That the letter and notes were for
   Stansfeld-Jones is clear from internal evidence.
2 Rubina was Stansfeld-Jones's wife and Deirdre their thirty-two-year-old
   adopted daughter. 'Rubina' was the name that Stansfeld-Jones gave his
   wife, Prudence Wratten Stansfeld-Jones, presumably because he found
   Prudence inelegant and inappropriate.
3 Lowry's list of 'touchstones' includes several major texts of Western

literature. *Parzival* is the early thirteenth century German verse epic by Wolfram von Eschenbach, adapted from the *Percival* of Chrétien de Troyes. Parsifal (or Percival, from Arthurian legend) is the pure knight who wins the Holy Grail and cures the wounded king. Richard Wagner (1813-83) wrote a major opera, *Parsifal* (1882) on the subject. *Pilgrim's Progress* (1678) is the Christian allegory by John Bunyan, from which Lowry chose an epigraph for *Under the Volcano*; *Don Quixote* (1605; 1615) is Cervantes' romance and another Lowry favourite; *Ulysses* is either a reference to the hero of Homer's *Odyssey* or, more likely, to James Joyce's novel *Ulysses* (1922); *Faust* (1808; 1833) is Johann Wolfgang von Goethe's (1749-1832) dramatic poem, which provided Lowry with another epigraph for his novel; *Moby-Dick* (1851) is Herman Melville's masterpiece and one of Lowry's favourite novels. Aeschylus (525-456 BC), an Athenian poet and founder of Greek tragic drama, wrote the trilogy on the story of Orestes that Lowry mentions in his eleventh point.

4 Lowry's reference here and in his tenth point is probably to Thomas H. Uzzell's *Narrative Technique: A Practical Course in Literary Psychology* (New York: Harcourt Brace, 1934). First published in 1923, Uzzell's book on the literary and psychological principles for good writing became very popular. He recommended the short story as the best preparation and discipline for the aspiring writer.

5 'Metaphysical poets' is the term, coined by John Dryden and adopted by Samuel Johnson, for a group of seventeenth-century English poets noted for their complex conceits and imagery. Chief among these poets is John Donne, but some of the others are Henry Vaughan (1621-95), Abraham Cowley (1618-67), and Richard Crashaw (1612?-49). In his 1921 essay 'The Metaphysical Poets' T.S. Eliot focused attention on this type of poetry and on new editions of the poets' work.

6 Franz Kafka's novel *Das Schloss* (1926), translated into English as *The Castle* in 1930, is a fine example of the novelist's disturbing treatment of the themes of terror, searching, and judgement. Lowry may be suggesting it to Stansfeld-Jones because of its cabbalistic and gnostic qualities – though Kafka was neither a cabbalist nor a gnostic.

7 William Butler Yeats's *A Vision* (1925) is his mystical interpretation of mind, being, and cosmology based on a system of actively related opposites. This extraordinary book resulted from Mrs Yeats's automatic writing down of the speech and images revealed to her by 'presences' who had 'come to give [Yeats] metaphors for poetry.' *The Tower* (1929) is a volume of his poetry characterized by his mysticism and symbolism, and it contains some of his best-known poems, such as 'Sailing to Byzantium,' 'Leda and the Swan,' and 'All Soul's Night,' the epilogue to *A Vision*.

8 T.S. Eliot refers to the Tarot in *The Waste Land* (1922); see I.43-57.

9 Aristophanes (ca 448-ca 380 BC) was an Athenian comic poet famous for his plays. Since the name of the translator of the volume in question is illegible, I cannot confirm which collection Lowry is refering to.

10 John Cowper Powys (1872-1962), an English educator, critic, poet, and prolific novelist, is known for long novels that deal with myth, cosmic fantasies, and the elemental forces in nature; for example, *A Glastonbury Romance* (1933) treats the Grail legend in a modern context. *Maiden Castle* (1936), however, is a particularly interesting Lowry recommendation. It opens on the morning of All Souls', 2 November 1935, and closes, after coming 'Full Circle,' twelve months later. The story is an exploration of the elemental and spiritual forces of femininity through a hero, 'Noman,' who has been deeply scarred by the deaths of his mother and wife. The novel also contains a character whom Lowry may be thinking of in connection with his friend Stansfeld-Jones. Powys describes him thus: 'Mr Enoch Quirm . . . is a mysterious and rather sinister figure (of Welsh origin) who desires to get into touch with the old gods of *Mai-dun*, or "Maiden Castle," the great neolithic earth-work near Dorchester.'

Editorial Notes:

a. This is the date, in pencil, at the top right of the holograph, which consists of a single 21.5-by-26.5-cm sheet of torn brownish paper with pencilled text on both sides. In transcribing the text, I have taken as the recto the side that carries the complimentary close and signature; the so-called notes on the verso follow.
b. The first twelve notes are included, without explanation, in Kilgallin (49-51); see also his discussion of Lowry's friendship with Stansfeld-Jones (46-52).
c. The lower left-hand corner of the page has been torn off, causing gaps in the transcription of the first three sentences of the second point 12.
d. The following marginalia include the apparently random comments that Lowry squeezed into any available space on the verso. Those marginalia that he marked for insertion at a particular point have been incorporated into the text or notes as Lowry indicated.

191: To Betty and Gerald Noxon

P: UBC(ms)
PP: *LLN* 92; *CP* 362

[Dollarton, B.C.]
[June 1944][a]

Betty & Gerald Noxon.

Delighted excited journeying youward[1]	4
tourist arriving Oakville eight thirty a.m. Monday	7
Margie unhurt myself fit	5

though back fried no 5
stiff upper lips or Nordic 5
glooms saved Branches Detectives Volcano Purgatorio 6
Noxon photos alas Betty's picture whole thousand 8
pages Paradiso lost will reimburse 5
gently you are saints please 5
do not dread 3

Malcolm

Annotations:

1 When Gerald Noxon learned of the Lowrys' 7 June 1944 fire, he invited them to stay with him and his wife in Oakville, and he sent them the money for the trip.

Editorial Notes:

a. A date of June 1944 has been written at the top of this holograph, which would have been written sometime between 19 June 1944, when Noxon instructed his bank to wire two hundred dollars to Margerie Lowry, and the time when the Lowrys began their train trip east early in July; see Day (301). This note to the Noxons is almost certainly a draft telegram. It has been written in pencil on half a sheet of 26.5-by-21.5-cm paper and corrected in black ink. At the end of each line there is a number, and each number has been changed or rewritten in ink in the right margin. The version transcribed here follows the ink changes.

192: To Mr and Mrs James Craige

P: UBC(pcard phc)

[Winnipeg, Manitoba]
[26 June 1944][a]

[Message May Be Written On This Side][1]
It might be, but for a certain inarticulacy.
Will write to you both later.[2]
Meantime, are enjoying the Rockies.
Many thanks for the many lifts once more

Malcolm & Margerie Lowry

Annotations:

1 This instruction appears on the left side of the card, the right being reserved for the addressee's name and address.

2 This card was sent to Jimmy Craige, Lowry's Manx boat-builder friend and neighbour on the beach, and his wife, Elizabeth (1878-1953), during the Lowrys' trip to Ontario, where they were to stay with Gerald and Betty Noxon. Craige had arranged for the Lowrys to stay at his son-in-law's (Downie Kirk) cabin after their fire, and in February 1945 Craige picked them up when they returned to Dollarton to begin rebuilding their own place. Lowry was especially fond of 'old Jimmy.'

Editorial Notes:

a. This is the postmark date on the card, which is addressed to 'Mr & Mrs James Craig [sic].' Although the correct Manx spelling of the name is with a final *e*, the Craiges accepted this spelling.

193: To Margerie Bonner Lowry

P: UBC(ms)

Rural Route **2**,
[Oakville, Ontario]
[July 1944]^a

Darling, sweetheart: –
– I write this in the Oakville of nostalgic memory on one of its Tuesday half shut or shot matinees at 4 o'clock on the way to send you the telegram I didn't send you when you left, at the station office,[1] – on Geraldo's advice, for with [illegible] still absent it would have been phoned to an empty apartment – and write it smoking the pipe you gave me, which I have bent a paper clip to clean very admirably, – with the pencil you used to love in its little improvised brass case, wearing the Hawaiian shirt you gave me; so, with all these things that, as it were, *are* you, I don't feel *so* lonesome. Or rather I do feel abominably lonesome without you: but these objects mitigate, if slightly. I (– we), have thought of you at St Catherine's[2] crossing the border, and later at the border itself – will you get past, would you, we watched the clock, of course you would, how could you not? Yet the mere *fact* of parting to some extent overwhelmed these anxieties. The pubs were shut but Gerald & I sat till quite late, melan-

choly without you, but happy drinking your health, not with such disastrous fulsomeness in the physical sense that we were not able to get in many good hours work to-day, however, in spite of the bloody kids, who have gone slightly haywire in your absence and ping out of one door only to pong in at another. Basta, but as D.H.L. says – pazienza![3] This must be short, to catch the macabre inconveniences of the post; but god bless you – be happy – make the most (it has, too much, of itself) of New York – you are a writer of real genius capable of great things – both of us think that – bear up, look to your gods even when you imagine there aren't any – and to God, who will help – You have already done great things, all the forces of construction I feel will help you now willy nilly – you have gone perhaps to look for some asses, you will certainly speak to some, but you will find a kingdom.[4] I said it.

God bless you, my wife-sweetheart

Your husband, with love

Malcolm

Annotations:

1 Shortly after the Lowrys arrived in Oakville, Margerie made a short trip to New York to see her publishers, Scribner's, and Harold Matson in the hope of sorting out what was happening to her two mystery novels.
2 The small southern Ontario town of St Catharines is near the Canadian-United States border, and there is an official border-crossing at this point. Lowry, who had been turned back at the border-crossing in British Columbia in 1939 when he was trying to visit Margerie in Los Angeles, was always alarmed by these formalities.
3 *Basta, pazienza* means literally 'enough, patience' in Italian, and D.H.L. is the English writer D.H. Lawrence, an early favourite of Lowry's. Lawrence did often use the expletive 'basta!' but not the word 'pazienza,' unless Lowry has a particular quotation in mind.
4 Lowry's ironic allusion is to Christ's entry into Jerusalem; see Matthew 21:5.

Editorial Notes:

a. This letter, like the three to Margerie that follow, was written in pencil and lacks a date or inside address, but it is clear from the contents that all four were written during Margerie's trip to New York in July 1944; see also Lowry's 15 September 1946 letter (246) to Maxwell Perkins at Scribner's.

194: To Margerie Bonner Lowry

P: UBC(ms)

Rural Route **2**,
[Oakville, Ontario]
[July 1944]

My own:
– Found myself waiting all day yesterday like the man in the song
Just another day Wasted Away[1] so that when, at seven pm, which
seemed the likeliest time you would call (but it is expensive), Nick
tried out his new bicycle bell outside, my heart nearly stopped beating. Yesterday I led a hell of a healthy life until about 8:30 pm
without a drink, exercised, sweated, walked, ran about, swam,
worked (though I've suddenly become completely fed up with the
bull chapter,[2] which merely seems to me to be well named!); and at
8:30 pm I set out by myself to walk to Oakville, with the hope perhaps of a couple of beers before closing time; alas, it was a gala
occasion of some sort and it seems to me I drank about fifty, the pub
nere seemed to close, nor my thirst to be assuaged: I returned sober
after the others had gone to bed, & rose at ten to-day, pretending that
I had slept that long, though actually I woke at six or seven, and
merely sweltered in a delirium of acousticsgly thisgly peacefulgly
placegly hygly the larkegly beingly the mostgly absolutelygly bloo-
dyglyawfulgly noiseygly havengly lgly evengly struckgly sothatgly
I findgly itgly wellnighimpossiblegly to workgly longhandgly
thoughgly lgly shallgly continue to try. I myself am fighting against
one of my periodic lapses into a deep silence embarrassing and hurt-
ful to all around me, and all the stranger since it coincides with our,
with your, great triumph; verily the flowers came up while Parsifal
inc. suffered but perhaps I am Amfortas and cannot recover quite
until you return wth certain news of spear and cup:[3] what a muddled
thought! – But then my soul is plunged in chaos without you so how
may it rejoice on all eight cylinders continuously? The other day I
found myself with, in my pockets, two pipes, two pencils, two
boxes of matches, two packages of crumpled cigarettes, two letters
to you, one gloomy, one gay, and at the same time wearing two
pairs of trousers, and two shirts: I should have mentioned the two
cents – I only wasn't wearing two pairs of shoes because: – (couldn't
be a case of double personality by any chance?)
    In the Oakville Inn sits an idiot: 'If you only kept quiet nobody'd
know your crazy' someone said to him brutally, so I was kind to

him. Now he says nothing but, when one comes in and periodically for the rest of the evening:

> 'I'm watching you.' or:
> 'I can see you.'
> 'You won't escape me.'

(He doesn't know it but he's going into the Volcano.)[4]

Last night a roof shingler told me of a fire in his shack which he put out; three times people have told me about fires, and there has been one fire outside the Oakville (where I would almost live if I had my way); and there is also a goat tethered near the road that came from nowhere. The Qliphoth[5] recognises its old champion but daren't come too close, especially as I found in the grass a message: *Fresh new Crackerjack.*[6]

I would like to 'get' the shadows when you walk home at night – I have been walking tremendously – they are beautiful and terrifying these shadows of cars that creep down the fences and sweep zebra like across the grass path in the avenue of dark oaks under the moon; a single shadow like an umbrella on rails travelling down the fence . . . Gone.

I have a feeling now for this country that is of your blood[7] and feel if you will play the angel that we could be happy here in our old rythyms & harmony of work & love: and though I am unhappy here at the moment with these good people with whom I tragically feel I have nothing now in common – but have I with anyone save yourself, & demons, & certain kinds of fish? – I sense that all this may be altered by your triumphal return and accomplishment, friendship sweet and, once more, rebirth, and the case altered.

God bless you my darling.

Your husband

Malcolm

Annotations:

1 'Just Another Day Wasted Away' (1927) was an American popular song, with words by Charles Tobias and music by Roy Turk.
2 Lowry is referring to chapter 9 of *Under the Volcano*.
3 Lowry's references here are to the story of the Holy Grail as portrayed in Wagner's opera *Parsifal* (1882). Amfortas, the son of Titurel, King of the Holy Grail, has received a wound that will not heal and lost the Sacred Spear in the garden of Klingsor, the Magician. He can only be healed by a 'Pure Fool made wise by pity' who can resist the temptation of Kundry in the magic garden and return with the Sacred Spear. Parsifal is, of

course, that 'Pure Fool,' and he returns to heal Amfortas. Lowry's thought here may be muddled, but it is interesting in so far as *Parsifal* was an important source of imagery and myth for him. Parsifal's suffering amidst the flowers is a specific reference to the scene between Parsifal and Kundry in act 2 of Wagner's opera. Here Kundry reminds Parsifal of his childhood and his mother, whom he has forgotten and for whom he now grieves.

4 Lowry uses these stray remarks effectively in chapter 10 of *Under the Volcano*.

5 The Qliphoth, the realm of evil spirits or Shells, is a cabbalistic term for the world of matter, the place in which Geoffrey Firmin finds himself in *Under the Volcano*; see his unsent letter to Yvonne in chapter one.

6 'Crackerjack' is the trade name of an American sticky sweet popular with children or spectators at baseball games, but the term 'crackerjack' denotes something wonderful or remarkable. Crackerjack is also nautical slang for a pounded biscuit with minced salted meat.

7 Margerie Bonner was born and spent her childhood in Adrian, Michigan, which lies to the west of the province of Ontario on the American side of Lake Huron. Although west and somewhat south of Oakville, Adrian has a similar topography.

195: To Margerie Bonner Lowry

P: UBC(ms)

[Rural Route 2,]
[Oakville, Ontario]
[July 1944]
etc./date?

My darling sweetheart
– it made me so happy to hear you on the phone last night so happy sounding; I still can't make out precisely what must have happened but I feel in my bones that it is good, even with the proviso: be happy, but don't be too doggone happy. I can't quite understand it, I feel that whatever the good news may be it doesn't altogether excuse Hal or Weber:[1] they had no *damn right* to make you suffer like that; on the other hand, and *at the same time* . . . Obviously the business is spiritual, largely, produce valid explanations though they indeed may. . . I know that you are on the threshold of something great, of the fulfilment you deserve, though you meet with minor oblique disappointment. At this or if so, don't worry; for 'crackerjack New York', was, I feel, the prophesy . . .[2]

To-day, after cleaning house till 2 o'clock in the morning – Gerald turned in at about one – got up at six to meet Betty coming back from Virginia on a train arriving Oakville 7:40 – so said Geraldo, baffled by timetables. The train did not arrive till 9 o'clock odd. We paced the platform with beer-cigarette-coffee hangovers. Five thousand times, it seemed we met the train, ran to meet Betty. The lines went on into the far distance uphill. A bird would fly across the lines, far away. To the right was a tree like a green exploding sea-mine, frozen. The onion factory got into gear [two words illegible], the coal companies: quasi-trimmers wheeled barrows at a little distance, or were screening coal. Rows of lamps like erect snakes stood along the platform. On the other side were cornflowers and dandelions, a garbage can like a brazier blazing burning furiously red all by itself among meadowsweet. One after one the terrible trains appeared on the horizon, first the distant wail, then the frightful spouting & spindling of smoke over [word illegible] then a round hull, as if not on the lines, as if going the other way, as if stopping, as if not stopping, or as if slipping away over the fields, Oh God, not stopping – & the lines shaking, the station flying, the coal dust, black bituminous, on *clippertyclipticlipticlipteclackletecluckletewheeeeeeee!* (not mine) & then another train, clipperty one clipperty one coming in the other direction, clipperty two clipperty two with one light burning against the morning,[3] clipperty three clipperty three a single useless strange eye . . . Trains, trains, trains: whizz, bang, crash; *not his train* cruel.

I picked flowers for Betty, conquered apprehension, decay of the societal instinct: helped, I hope, to give her a glad homecoming, sent your thanks & love: appraised, at breakfast, with intelligence & genuine enthusiasm, & on your behalf, her pictures.

God bless you my sweetheart my sweetheart – I am working – but blimey, that bed is lonely.

hasta la vista,[4] my wife,

Your loving husband

Malcolm

Good luck.[a]

Annotations:

1 Harold Matson, Lowry's literary agent in New York, was also handling Margerie's manuscript; William Weber was the editor at Scribner's with whom she was having difficulty corresponding.
2 Lowry's reference to 'crackerjack New York' is an allusion to his previous letter in which he tells her that he found a message in the grass: '*Fresh new Crackerjack.*' The prophecy, or so Lowry suggests, is that New York will prove lucky and lucrative for her.

3 Parts of this description of waiting at the train station as trains whizz
 through found their way verbatim into chapter 10 of *Under the Volcano.*
4 The Spanish form of farewell means 'until we meet again.'

Editorial Notes:

a. Above 'Good luck' Lowry has drawn a seagull, which he and Margerie
 frequently used as a sign of hope, affection, and good cheer. This is the
 first instance of a practice that is increasingly common in later letters.

196: To Margerie Bonner Lowry
P: UBC(ms)

Rural Route **2**,
[Oakville, Ontario]
[July 1944]

Letter no 2/
My own darling; –
 I have just received two more of your precious letters[1] which
brings us up to about your second telephone conversation; your
letters arrived however just after I had finished the letter I am sending
at the same time as this – so this one is written later. The other one is
a bit gloomy, so pay no attention to it, where it *is* gloomy.
 I had not intended it to be, where there was such good news, but
there *is* such a sense of unreality here – What on earth *is* happening?
I am so proud of you but on the other hand so afraid of your being let
down again and distrustful of these people (all their explanations
seem totally inadequate) that every now & then I don't know what to
think.
 At the same time I do have faith, I believe in you, & the power of
your constructive abilities to have wrought the miracle.
 But perhaps we existed on another plane altogether in Dollarton –
as if we were dead or alive in a higher sense, or what?
 How I long to be *alone together* with you again. Gerald & Betty are
very proud & glad for you. Come home soon.
 All love from your husband

Malcolm

Annotations:

1 Unfortunately, very few of Margerie Lowry's letters to her husband
 appear to have survived, and nothing is extant from her trip to New
 York in July of 1944.

197: To Gerald and Betty Noxon

p: Texas(ms)
pp: *LLN* 92–93

Snider.
[Rural Route **2**,]
[Oakville, Ontario]
[early September 1944]^a

Dear folks:–
– phantom ping pong balls, an unaccounted for bicycle that rushes through the forest, & a broken sailing ship that sails eternally through a sea of green grass. A newspaper that, strangely, delivers itself.

We think of your pictures.

Broke down toward the end and produced some Blue Top for Hill the Mover[1] in his last throes (while with heroic abnegation still re-serving 4 bottles for Margerie & I to drink when she came back, at which time they were all largely consumed by myself) – explained you would have done, of course, had the beer been, as it were, yours: but knew I should not have done, as I saw Hill the Mover moving in-exorably straight through the forest – none of this nonsense about roads: – 'Boy, you're speaking my language!' the driver, who hailed from Vancouver, said as I was producing it, and I suspected at that time how fluently that language would be spoken by the time H the M reached Niagara. . .

We think of Cleo.

Working *very* hard here; Volcano seems, actually, almost finished. We had an Earthquake. We hear finally about house in N-in-the-L to-day, & if all O.K., we will stuff all our triumphs horrors and angels into our bags, strap them up tight, and so be seeing you again soon:[2] we wld arrive in a barrel, at least bring one, but for the regula-tions, & certain memories of one Capt. Webb.[3]

We swim in the lake, which is still very fine indeed – the heck with these bacteria boys; can't you see them, on the Caribbean, say, on holidays: 'Although marvellous weather we were forced to spend most of our time in the stuffy cabin down below because of the tons of coloric bacteria (wrongly called spray) being flung to leeward up on deck. – A gull visited us, but on being disturbed, crashed straight down through the bushes into the lake, & sank for a while, so full of pickerel he couldn't clear the trees, presumably . . . I had a con-tretemps with the chinless wonder in the bank, the asst. mgr. who discovered himself insulted, Gerald, because he hadn't been introduced to you. I thought of saying to him that that was because he *was* only the asst. mgr. He managed however to be quite offensive which makes me think there must be something about me which arouses antagonism: don't I know who have to shave every 3 days . . . We owe you money, will repay, – also Nick – Thanks a million for everything: sorry, I was probably a loathsome guest, a sloth or mud lark might have been better. But I myself am marvellously benefited: as also Margie: can only hope I didn't spoil your summer too much. Mushrooms of fabulous size & destructive appearance have sprung up each morning & ourselves with them, discovering they are edible; delicious, though we have not yet tried Destroying Angel bordelaise! My mother has sent me The British Weekly which contains News of the Churches, Across Asia Minor in an Araba by Annie C. Burt, Ruby Ferguson's columns, and an article on the Robomb.[4] 'By this we mean that we must not be satisfied with arrangements & precautions such as the punctuation of our sky with interfering objects. We must beat it at its own game . . . in a fair field . . . from the very outset. We modestly but firmly believe that this can be done. Our conviction rests finally upon what might even be called a theological prejudice or conviction!'[5] . . God bless – love to Nick.

Malc

Annotations:

1 'Blue Top' was a brand of Canadian beer manufactured by the southern Ontario company called Blue Top Brewing, and 'Hill the Mover' is a southern Ontario transportation company that featured its name prominently on its vans.
2 The Lowrys stayed in the Oakville house until October first when they joined the Noxons in Niagara-on-the-Lake; on the fifteenth they moved into their own rented house close to the Noxons.
3 Captain Matthew Webb (1848-83) had been a master of a British sailing ship and a famous swimmer. He successfully swam the English Channel, but was killed on 24 July 1883 when he attempted to swim the rapids at Niagara.
4 The *British Weekly: A Journal of Social and Christian Progress*, a weekly newspaper published in London and sent regularly to Canada, was primarily devoted to the views and news of the Protestant sects and churches in England. Two of its regular features were 'News of the Churches' and 'Ruby Ferguson's Column,' the latter dealing with letters from readers seeking Mrs Ferguson's advice. Annie C. Burt's memoir about her 1914 journey from Tarsus to Marsovan and back, called 'Across Asia Minor in an Araba,' appeared in four instalments: 13 and 20

July and 7 and 14 September 1944. An araba is a native horse-drawn, covered spring wagon, 'primitive but comfortable,' according to Mrs Burt.

5 The 'article on the Robomb' is in fact a section of the regular editorial front-page feature called 'Commentary on the Week.' The term 'Robomb' is not used in the article, but Lowry is referring to the 'pilot-less plane or robot-bomber' being used by the Germans, and he is quoting verbatim from a subsection of the 'Commentary' headed 'Our Light Travels,' the *British Weekly*, 20 July 1944, 185.

Editorial Notes:

a. Lowry has written 'Snider' at the top right of the recto of this single-page pencil holograph. The name refers to a Judge Snider, the former owner of the Noxons' Oakville house, but it is also a joke shared with the Noxons; see Lowry's September 1944 letter (**198**) to them. There is no date on this letter, but in the late summer of 1944 the Noxons moved from Oakville to their new home in Niagara-on-the-Lake, and Lowry is writing to them shortly after their move.

198: To Gerald and Betty Noxon

P: Texas(ms)
PP: *LLN* 95–98

c/o Noxon,
Wynwood,
Judge Snider's Estate,[1]
Rural Route #2,
Oakville, Ontario
[September 1944][a]

My dear Gerald and Betty:

The house, without the Red Dragon, and the Silver Flagon,[2] and all, is emptied of itself, and its beauty, somewhat like a body from which the spirit has fled: the body I am thinking of I saw, one late December, in a Crux Roza in the Palace of Cortes:[3] it lay there, whole and uninjured, in its feet and a small boy jumped over it gaily, twice, in and out of its arms, to get to the phone while the doctor thumped it on its chest, once, as if greeting a boon companion. Its owner was not there, it seemed, but still alive and gay somewhere, perhaps gone to have a drink.

It is a very gay carcase too, to wrap ourselves in which we are endlessly grateful (I also wrap myself up sometimes in the cold abandoned oilskin of Justice, when Mrs Young[4] is not looking, and go out looking for toadstools in the rain) never more so than late last night after returning from Toronto whither, in order to reestablish our awareness of reality, we had made an enormous pilgrimage to see – what but Pelleas and Melisande?[5]

You do not think that is funny? But that is very funny. That's so, gentlemans:

For perhaps one way of reestablishing ones awareness of reality is not to go to Toronto on a Friday night which, although beautiful, is not unlike Liverpool on a Sunday night, and listen, in the middle of a dark wood, in the Massey Hall, in Shuter street,[6] to Debussey's whole tone harmonies, expressing such words as:

GOLAUD
Pourquoi avez-vous l'air si etonne?

MÉLISANDE
Vous êtes un géant

GOLAUD
Je suis un homme comme les autres . . .

MÉLISANDE
Pourqoui êtes-vous venu ici?

GOLAUD
Je n'en sais rien moi-même. Je chassais dans la
forêt. Je poursuivais un sanglier. Je me suis trompé
de chemin. – Vous l'avez l'air tres jeune. Quel âge
avez-vous?

MÉLISANDE
Je commence à avoir froid . . .

or   MÉLISANDE
Oh! do not touch me . . .

GOLAUD
Do not cry out . . . I will not touch you. But
come with me. The night is very dark and very cold.
Come with me.

MÉLISANDE
Where are you going?

GOLAUD
I do not know. . . I am lost also.[7]

Toronto frightened me, my first experience of a city since Vancouver; the pubs were shut, we took a Flash Gordon experiment to the Royal York Hotel & found a catacomb:[8] the gigantic chained doors of a Bastille informed us, in a kind of underground Picadilly-Circus of the soul, that the ladies' beverage room was closed: Margie had to escort me, gibbering, across the street, where we were unable to purchase a chocolate soda.

In all this darkness the supramodern building of Brights Wines in Yonge Street gleamed brightly; shut too, however.[9]

I was shaved by my barber who after four weeks is still humming Moonlight and Roses,[10] now in whole tone harmonies: 'Everything must have its opposite, light dark, good bad: now take some of these old civilisations, some of these statues these old ducks put up, the Egyptians or were they the Chinese, I dunno, these statues there, in the desert: their enemy is deterioration: yes, deterioration: they say the noses of some of them old ducks fell off, of these statues there; in the desert, I dunno. . . Ha ha! May I ask you one thing: you are not a catholic? Then I tell you something – moonlight and roses – This war – moonlight and roses – is a war between the Catholics and the Protestants. The Catholics is the bad; sir, I dunno. Perhaps you would know?'

I have met too, having a hot dog, the Mad Fisherman of Oakville. He says he was not a friend of Captain Webb's.[11] His proudest boast is that he built the barrel with his own hands in which his friend Bobby Leach went over Niagara Falls three times.[12] The barrel was made of steel hoops with red plush inside. Later Bobby Leach slipped on an orange peel in Niagara and died at three o'clock in the morning in the Station Hotel, with the Mad Fisherman at his side. He is a great man, I think.

The lake this morning is radiant molten cobalt to the horizon and flowing fast in every direction; there is an endless white Alaskan mountain range of clouds, above which is a blue sky, and below which the coast line is clear, with Niagara Falls an approaching train.

The other day we turned left toward the railway and found ourselves in fields of flowers and butterflies up to our necks, seven different kinds of daisies, purple wild asters, goldenrod, wild primroses, milkweed blowing, and locusts and dandelion colored butterflies (so that it was like walking in a lilliputian airport)[13] lilac mushrooms and, on the horizon, under the trees, a single blue green white horse, stamping . . .

The day was blue and hot, the railway lines ran into mirage at both ends, and the firemen of the trains were practising Mood Indigo on the Wurlitzer organ[14] or perhaps, it was the Golaud theme from Pelleas.

We are doing well on our works and eating your corn and peppers and your wonderful tomatoes (and they say there is not immortality!) – and even beans. – Teresina has a front seat here, however, and we are reading same with renewed enthusiasm. I think also of the Inspector of Signs. What a wonderful opportunity you have to do a more than Dead Souls of England here![15]

.There was a very strange noise outside last night and the Asst. Bank Manager has grovelled before us on his nose in the ante-room of the Halton – drunk as a lark! The lease has arrived and we are very excited.

Best love to Nick and you both,

from

Malc

P.S.[b] Margie will have written re arrival etc: your hospitality is deeply appreciated: hope we will not be too much trouble, Betty, – certainly we are in much better fettle!

P.P.S. Extract, Betty, from This Indenture.
... C M. Lowry, hereinafter called the Lessee of the Second Party Witnesseth that in Consideration of the Rents Covenants & Agreements respectively reserved and contained on the part of the said Lessee his Executors administrators & Assigns to be respectively paid observed & performed the said Lessee has demised & leased and by these present DOTH demise & LEASE with the said Lessee, his executors, administrators & assigns, ALL THAT messuage or tenement situate lying and being in the town of Niagara, County of Lincoln, & Province of Ontario, composed of Lot Number Twenty-five (25), known as the Misses WINTERBOTTOM lot . . . . .

Annotations:

1 According to Noxon, Judge Snider was the former owner of the Noxons' house in Oakville, and on occasion Noxon gave his address as the 'Snider Estate, R.R. #2, Oakville, Ontario.' See his 6 June 1943 and 5 January 1947 letters to the Lowrys in the *Letters of Malcolm Lowry and Gerald Noxon*; in the latter he describes using Judge Snider as a character in a novel he is writing.
2 Lowry's mention of the dragon and the flagon may be an allusion, shared with Noxon, to G.K. Chesterton's poem 'The Englishman' (1914), the first stanza of which reads:

> St George he was for England,
> And before he killed the dragon
> He drank a pint of English ale
> Out of an English flagon.
> For though he fast right readily
> In hair-shirt or in mail,
> It isn't safe to give him cakes
> Unless you give him ale.

3 The Crux Roja, or the Red Cross, may have had an office in the six-teenth-century Palace of Cortes in Cuernavaca, Mexico, which now houses the administration of the state of Morelos.

4 Mrs Young was an Oakville neighbour.

5 *Pelléas et Mélisande* (1902), a musical drama by the French composer Claude Debussy (1862-1918), is based upon a symbolic play by Maurice Maeterlinck. The irony of Lowry's point about reality arises from the fact that neither the story nor Debussy's harmonic system (using dis-sonance and the whole tone scale) is 'realistic.'

6 Massey Hall, on Shuter Street in downtown Toronto, was built by Hart A. Massey and opened in 1894. It was designed primarily for musical performances and concerts, and it is still in use today. Lowry's reference to being in a dark wood is an allusion to Dante's *Inferno* and to *Under the Volcano*, but also to act I.iv of Debussy's 'drame lyrique,' in which Golaud finds Mélisande lost in the forest.

7 Debussy's opera opens as Golaud (the baritone), the grandson of a king, finds the mysterious maiden, Mélisande (the soprano), weeping in the forest. He brings her to the castle and they marry, but Mélisande falls in love with Golaud's half-brother, Pelléas (the tenor), and the story ends with the death of the lovers. Lowry's quotations from the French (and the English translation) of the libretto for act I.i are accurate, although he has slightly scrambled the order of the lines. The similarities between the opera and *Under the Volcano* would not have escaped Lowry.

8 The Royal York Hotel, built by the Canadian National Railway in 1929 and named for Frederick, Duke of York, the son of George III, domi-nated the Toronto skyline in the forties. It still stands on Front Street across from Union Station, and it still has an underground gallery of stores and restaurants.

9 Brights Wines is the name of a major southern Ontario winery. Built in 1795, Yonge Street is the oldest and still one of the major thoroughfares running north-south through central Toronto.

10 'Moonlight and Roses' (1925) was written by Ben Black and Neil Monet and based upon Edwin H. Lemare's 'Andantino in D' (1892); it was re-vived as a popular song in 1928.

11 Captain Matthew Webb died in his attempt to swim the rapids in the Niagara River below Niagara Falls.

12 Bobby Leach (?-1926), a professional stuntman from London, England,

went through the rapids once and over the Niagara Falls once in a steel drum in July 1911. According to Gordon Donaldson in *Niagara: The Eternal Circus* (Toronto: Doubleday, 1979), p. 194, Leach died in Christchurch, New Zealand (not the Station Hotel in Niagara), as a result of an infection that set in after he slipped on an orange peel and broke his leg.

13 In part 1 of Jonathan Swift's (1607-1745) *Gulliver's Travels* (1726), the hero, Lemuel Gulliver, is shipwrecked and swims to shore in the country of Lilliput, where everything is of a most diminutive size; hence, 'lilliputian' denotes something very small.

14 'Mood Indigo' is a short, instrumental jazz composition created in 1930 by Duke Ellington (1899-1974) in collaboration with Barney Bigard. A Wurlitzer organ is a key-board instrument made by the Wurlitzer Company of the United States.

15 Lowry's reference here, and in the preceding sentence, is not entirely clear. He may be thinking, however, of the manuscript of a novel on which Noxon was working at this time, parts of which have been published as 'Clegg's Wall' in *On Malcolm Lowry and Other Writings by Gerald Noxon*, edited by Miguel Mota and Paul Tiessen (Waterloo, Ont.: *Malcolm Lowry Review*, 1987), pp. 111-46. This novel about a strange Englishman is set in Toronto and, as far as one can tell from the published fragments, was promising to be a gruesome story; hence, Lowry may have thought of it as a kind of local *Dead Souls*. The novel *Dead Souls* (1842) by Nikolai Gogol was never finished, but the first part displays the mixture of caricature, fantasy, and the grotesque for which the Russian writer is famous. Judging from the context, 'Clegg's Wall' may have been called 'The Inspector of Signs' at one point, or Lowry may simply be making a joking allusion to the sinister signs, gardens, and inspectors in *Under the Volcano*. In a 29 May 1989 letter to me, Paul Tiessen notes that in the thirties Noxon worked for a short time in London as an 'inspector of signs' or billboards.

Editorial Notes:

a. This letter is undated, but the context confirms that it was written in early September, shortly after the Noxons had moved to their new home in Niagara-on-the-Lake at the beginning of the month.

b. Both postscripts are squeezed into the top left corner of the recto of the first page of this four-page holograph. Lowry has written in pencil on the rectos only, and he has used the cheap canary second-cut paper that he usually used for drafts. A separate sheet of this paper, filed with the letter, has a list of instructions, written by Margerie, for operating the stove, and on the verso Lowry has drafted a passage for chapter 4 of *Under the Volcano*. The letter by Margerie, referred to in this postscript, informs the Noxons that they expect to arrive in Niagara-on-the-Lake on 1 October; see *Letters of Malcolm Lowry and Gerald Noxon* (99-100).

199: To Conrad Aiken

P: H(ms)
PP: *LAL* 181–82

Write Dollarton P.O.,
Dollarton, B.C., Canada
[December 1944]^a

As from Niagara.[1]

– Dear old Conrad: Thanks immensely for The Soldier,[2] which I have read 5 or 6 times straight through and am about to read a 7th. I was extraordinarily sensitive to the honour of receiving it at the time to the extent that I almost felt I had been rewarded with some cross, of another nature, of course, to the one one bears. I think it contains some of your absolutely finest & purest & most richly poetic & greatest work, which is to say, the finest being done to-day. It is of course enormously well thought out. Some of it should be engraved on stone & I doubt not will be, when you will perhaps be there, or will no longer care. For the rest I do not know: your daemon has led you into a strange path indeed, & after all, what can you do but obey? Myself my non-conformist sympathy is somewhat for the outlaw or dissenter but it would be more than superficial & irrelevant to deduce from such music of more than facts accepted that yours was not too, or was. Be that as it may, it is with renewed courage that we shall travel 4000 miles toward our burned house to rebuild it (& how I understand now your feelings now for some loved houses – & may God spare Jeakes!)[3] remembering that, before we left, we ran up Tashtego-wise on all that remained, the flag . . . Which reminds me that the Canadian Broadcasting Company has invited me to do Moby Dick for them, in 13 installments.[4]

God bless & a happy Xmas & sincerely thank you, again Conrad – love from us both to you & Mary – – Malc.

– Afraid that my writing (see over) is not much better than my telephone voice. (What I said over the phone was the prayer Tagore liked, meaning: With Thy Graciousness, Oh Thou Terrible, forever save us! – so no wonder you said What?) – Just finished today after 3 yrs & 3 months revision 8 hours a day approx, soberly Under the Volcano . . . The old man dying, Nordahl dead.[5] In Ballast is no more.[6] Brother Wilfrid in the Royal Artillery, Russell in the police.[7] Saved Brownstone – Brimstone! – Elegies[8] from the fire, slightly scorched. – But keep working & keep your pecker up – the birds, as you say, endure . . .[9]

Love   Malc

Annotations:

1 The Lowrys stayed in Niagara-on-the-Lake until February, when they
   returned to Dollarton; thus Lowry is writing from Niagara-on-the-Lake
   but reminding Aiken of the Dollarton address.
2 Aiken published *The Soldier: A Poem* in November of 1944.
3 Lowry fears for the safety of Jeakes House, the Aikens' home in Rye,
   England, because of the war.
4 Malcolm and Margerie worked together on a radio version of *Moby-
   Dick*, but it was neither completed nor broadcast. Tashtego is the har-
   pooner in *Moby-Dick* who first sights the whale, and the Lowrys
   planned to bring the third episode of their radio play to its climax with
   his 'wild cry': 'There she blows!'
5 Lowry's father, who was seriously ill with cancer (see Bradbrook, 29),
   died on 11 February 1945, and Nordahl Grieg (1902-43) was killed on 2
   December when the bomber in which he was flying did not return from
   an attack on Berlin.
6 Lowry's copy of the manuscript for his novel 'In Ballast to the White
   Sea,' based in part upon his 1931 visit to Nordahl Grieg in Norway, was
   destroyed when the Lowrys' shack burned down on 7 June 1944. Only
   sixteen pages of typescript and manuscript, some charred fragments,
   and two notebooks survived the fire; see UBC 12:14-15.
7 Lowry's two elder brothers are Wilfrid Malbon (1900-74) and Arthur
   Russell Lowry (1905-). The eldest brother is Stuart Lowry.
8 Here Aiken's *Eclogues* becomes 'Elegies,' but in a letter written to Aiken
   in October 1945 (**205**) Lowry explains his mistake.
9 Aiken's 'The Sounding,' the eighth poem in *Brownstone Eclogues* (1942),
   concludes with the line: 'man kills his children. But the birds endure.'

Editorial Notes:

a. This letter is written on the back of a Christmas card that is signed 'from
    Malc & Margie' on the inside right-hand page beneath the inscribed
    greetings. An addendum is written on the inside left-hand page of the
    card.

200: To James Craige

P: UBC(card, phc)

> [Niagara-on-the-Lake,]
> [Ontario,]
> [Canada]
> [December 1944]

Dear Jimmy:–
     We shall be thinking of you at Xmas & this is just a note to remind

you that we shall be drinking your health then. I hope that 'Nunki' hasn't played you false & our heartfelt thanks for undertaking to look after her.[1] We shall be seeing you soon in four or five weeks when we are returning to Dollarton & hope to rebuild our ruin so please keep an eye out for any old lumber. As I say we shall be thinking of you, thanks again for looking after things while we rounded our spiritual Point of Eyre,[2] & a very Merry Xmas to you and Mrs Craig
from
Malcolm & Margerie Lowry

Annotations:

1 ''Nunki' was one of the Lowrys' cats.
2 By their 'spiritual Point of Eyre' Lowry clearly means the trauma of their 7 June fire, but he may also be thinking of the Point of Eyre on the Isle of Man. As a boy Lowry had spent family holidays on the Isle of Man and Jimmy Craige was a Manxman, so this reference would have a special resonance.

201: To Gerald and Betty Noxon

P: Texas(ms)
PP: *LLN* 108-12

Dollarton P.O.,
Dollarton, B.C.
14 May 1945

Dear Gerald & Betty –
    I must apologise for not having written long ago, but what with this & that, I haven't had much time, or my hands have been covered with mud, or there was a creosote post we needed drifting out to sea, or we were finishing the benighted Volcano – we still are, really are, this time: Margie's just finishing typing the tenth chapter – or, we had an accident. We had, in fact, a bad accident – precisely the same thing you did, Betty – Margie ran a nail in her foot, but with near disastrous results. I couldn't get a doctor (it was a Saturday afternoon) to come out, or, for that matter, contact one to get her to; the situation didn't seem to warrant hospitals & stretcher bearers, it wasn't, at first, too painful, so we first-aided it ourselves, feeling the chances of tetanus were slight: we had overlooked blood-poisoning, & the next morning that was what she found herself with; result, hospital, a temperature of 105, and an extremely foul time for Margie.[1] All this a month ago – she came out a fortnight ago, but can

still hardly walk, though she's very much better & will be about sprightly as ever in a week or so: it was the first day we got the lumber for the house (we already had the foundations in) so work on it has been held up, & the lumber – when last looked at – was still lying near the Dollarton wharf with all its innocent looking nails in it. All this has been pretty grim, though we contrived some fun out of it here & there, & I have become, at least, what she last expected, a pretty good cook. Margie was under morphia alot of the time when I went to see her at the hospital – the way there being past a movie showing Lon Chaney Jr in Calling Mr Death,[2] a funeral parlour, and a Fire station – in a semi-private room with an old lady of 94 who had broken her hip, also under morphia, in the next bed. Margie would say, over & over again, 'Blank pages, millions of blank pages, to which the old lady would reply 'oh, oh, what shall I do is that you Ada 3 bedposts is 4 I'm stuck now' 'No, blank pages,' Margie would say, and the poor old lady: 'What shall I do, I'm done up, I'm done up, Peg, are you there? I've got this wolf and I've pulled it down . . . Who has come in downstairs – oh, it's hard, it's hard – alas for those sweeps, is Mr Way there? I jumped up from the chair & I tried to get to the bathroom – I jumped up from the – ' 'Not at all! Blank pages! millions of blank pages!' 'Oh gran you've wet the bed again – what's that my garter? your doctor? No, my garter. Your daughter – ? No no, my garter.' 'Blank pages, that's what!' 'Give me the scissors, please, to-morrow I'll be washing and shaving. I want the scissors to cut it off to-day. Who are those four? Come in, come in . . . I can see you. But I can't see who you are. What happened downstairs?' 'Blank pages.' 'I know you're there, but I can't see you. There was such a noise, a noise – what happened? it was a noise like tin.' 'Only blank pages.' 'Stop moving that furniture! They were all moving furniture . . . Nurse! Nurse! help! help! *The moon's coming in the window!* – – – –

I'm sorry to hear about Nick's having had bronchial pneumonia, & hope that he is quite ok now. I expect also that you will have spring by now; if so, that is more than we have, save for the rain part of it, though the woods are very fine and lush and full of wild bleeding heart. I have begun to swim, tentatively – Margie not yet; but she probably will when her foot's better –

I hope sincerely, Betty, that the water-color show at Eaton's was a great success, as also the oils & water colors show, later, in Montreal: you certainly *deserve* great success, by God – the Great Face behind sometimes seems to have oddly delayed plans, though, in regard to the careers of artists. If I ever make any cash myself that has not the mark of evanescence upon it one of my first actions will certainly be to buy one of your pictures. Margie's proofs arrived – the first half in two batches, one batch uncorrected by the proof reader, the other corrected: she was instructed to look out for another similar two batches, comprising the last part, but only one batch arrived, the uncorrected section: reluctant to send this back corrected by her, contrary to Webers instructions,[3] she has held on to it, awaiting the corrected portion, but it has still not arrived: meantime there is every reason to suppose that the book had been already sent out in some prepublication form without Margie's corrections at all: Weber has once more resumed his perplexing Castellan silence, but there is cause to hope that owing to 'certain auxiliary circumstances'[4] things are looking up a bit, from what they were: in fact, since Scribners cannot bring out her second book later than November, under contract, it appears at the moment that she may have two books coming out at once. I hope, Gerald, that T.M. [*Teresina Maria*] clicked with Quincy Howe[5] – what is the news on this? If there are any initial disappointments, which I sincerely hope not, you must brush them away and get on with the second part, while they iron themselves out into encouragements. But I wouldn't have thought you'd be having much trouble in getting it placed – perhaps Simon & Shuster are bringing it out now, as I write: I hope so. Matson would be glad to handle the book, I know, if you require an agent: his address is 30 Rockerfeller Plaza, New York 20, N.Y: but then, of course, perhaps you might not be glad to handle Matson. We have no radio as yet so haven't heard you recently on the air – . I suppose you must have been pretty busy with V.E day:[6] We like to hear your broadcasts, though, very much indeed (Vancouver's local efforts are not very high class) – tell us when we may hear another drama from your pen, for we may be getting a radio soon. We have listened under poor circumstances to the remaining Margie's and Margie's-&-my efforts: Maria Chapedelaine came through pretty well, though poorly produced, & Grey Owl very well, I thought. Sunshine Sketches of a Little Town, the one in which I had the largest hand, had the distinction of being the worst thing I've ever listened to in any medium whatsoever:[7] however, just as you told us they wouldn't, they didn't use ¼ of our script. I think they were quite foolish not to, since under your tutelage, the difficulties in the way had been adequately smoothed out, I thought: as it was, they achieved something really awful, and even stuffed in a gruesome joke about a drowned man turning green, as presumably more suitable for children. We were hurt since even Whitey,[8] whose radio we were listening to, thought we must be morons for having written it. Re Moby Dick we are a bit bewildered and wish you could find out for us how the land lies, if at all.[9] We have written twice to [Andrew] Allan[10] but so far got no reply, in spite of the comparitive urgency, several months ago, of our request for one of some sort. I suppose he has been busy with V.E. day – or teeth-troubles – still & all – dying though we are to do it, it's a bit hard to go on with a project of that kind as we'd like to do it without some kind of further say-so on the subject, as you intimated yourself: the result has been that in watching the post each day we've been discouraged from proceeding further, though it's all planned out, & with the Volc almost completely done, we're rarin' to go. We have had also some heartrendering moments re the house: people have built a bloody great babel on our old bedroom, they tore down our flags and our stakes, & repellant infants dance upon our pier. Nevertheless, we're still building it, & by expanding on the other side, we'll have a nicer place than before eventually. We are in our right minds again, at all events; so that I see my lugubriousness as your guest in sad perspective, though it was very fine to be with you all at that & a much appreciated privilege – as also to know the unique Niagara. Well, perhaps I shall do best to cull some advice for us all from an obscure book of Melville's – 'Never wait for calm water, which never was & never will be, but dash with all your derangements at your object, leaving the rest to fortune' – [11]

Best love to Nick & yourselves from us both, as to Mrs Lane & Mrs Noxon –

affectionately

Malc

Annotations:

1 In April, during the reconstruction of their cabin, Margerie had stepped on a nail. Infection set in and she had to be taken to hospital in North Vancouver, where she spent several unpleasant days. Lowry later transcribed his journal notes on her accident and his visits to the hospital (including fragments of the morphine-induced chatter reported to the Noxons in this letter) into drafts of 'Eridanus.'

2 Lon Chaney Jr (1906-73), an American stage and screen actor, played the role of the doctor in the murder-thriller *Calling Mr Death* (1943), directed by Reginald Le Borg.

3 William C. Weber was Margerie Bonner's editor at Scribner's, but he did not see her novel *The Last Twist of the Knife* through the publishing process properly. The ongoing saga with Scribner's is documented in several of Lowry's letters, but see in particular his 15 September 1946 letter (**246**) to Maxwell Perkins.

4 'Owing to auxiliary circumstances' is a phrase from chapter 5 of Kafka's

Castle, and one that Lowry enjoyed quoting; see his 5 June 1951 letter (**459**) to Albert Erskine.

5 Quincey Howe (1900–77) was editor-in-chief with the New York publishing house of Simon & Schuster during the thirties and forties.

6 V.E. Day stands for 'Victory in Europe' and signifies the Allied victory at the end of the Second World War on 8 May 1945.

6 Margerie Lowry (with Malcolm's help) had prepared dramatic scripts for Andrew Allan's Canadian Broadcasting Corporation (CBC) 'Stage' series. The three scripts mentioned here were produced for 'Stage 45.' 'Maria Chapdelaine' was based on Louis Hémon's 1916 novel of the same name; 'Grey Owl' was about the life of Archibald Belaney (1888–1938), alias Grey Owl, the English writer and conservationist who claimed to be part Indian and lived most of his life in Canada. 'Sunshine Sketches of a Little Town' was adapted from Canadian humorist Stephen Leacock's (1869–1944) 1912 satire of a small Ontario town.

8 Whitey, Miles Went, was one of Lowry's closest friends. As a character called Kristbjorg, Whitey and his tales appear in such Lowry stories as 'The Forest Path to the Spring' from *Hear us Oh Lord* and 'Kristbjorg's Story: In the Black Hills' from *Psalms and Songs*.

9 The Lowrys were hoping to complete a radio adaptation of Melville's novel for Andrew Allan's 'Stage,' but the project was never completed. The surviving holograph draft and typescripts of the radio script are in UBC 16:1–5.

10 Andrew Allan (1907–74), for many years a radio producer with the Canadian Broadcasting Corporation (CBC), is best known for his pioneer developments in radio drama. From 1940 to 1943 he produced plays for CBC in Vancouver, and from 1943, when he moved to Toronto, he produced many fine radio dramas, including the excellent adaptation of Conrad Aiken's story *Mr Arcularis* (1934), broadcast on 28 November 1948.

11 Lowry is quoting from Melville's romance *Israel Potter: His Fifty Years of Exile* (1855), included in the 1931 edition of *Romances of Herman Melville* that Lowry probably owned. The second paragraph of chapter 18 reads as follows: 'The career of this stubborn adventurer signally illustrates the idea that since all human affairs are subject to organic disorder, since they are created in and sustained by a sort of half-disciplined chaos, hence he who in great things seeks success must never wait for smooth water, which never was and never will be, but, with what straggling method he can, dash with all his derangements at his object, leaving the rest to Fortune.' This Melville quotation became a Lowry favourite.

202: To Harold Matson

P: Matson(ms); UBC(phc)
PP: *SL* 45-47

Dollarton P.O.,
Dollarton B.C.,
Canada
6 June 1945

My dear Hal:

Several days [ago] I dispatched, after taking some thought, the m.ss. of the new Under the Volcano to you: it may take some time to reach you, therefore I am writing this letter now in the hope it may arrive more or less coincident with it.

I took thought – & also extraordinary liberty, for which I hope you will forgive me, of sending it at all – because of the trouble & patience you have had with it in its former state: my idea had been, after all that (to say nothing of the expense you must have undergone on its behalf) to send it round myself in its revised version, & if anyone took it, then to ask you the favour of acting for it & me again, if it seemed worth your while.

I felt, however, that it ought to be in your hands, & so sent it feeling that this time there was perhaps a fairly substantial chance it might click with somebody without so much trouble, and also, whether this be so or not, because I very much wanted your opinion and value that.

The book was to be have been the first part of a trilogy: the third part is a dead loss, utterly consumed, (save for a tattered circle of three or four burned pages all of which more or less concern fire, for some reason), in a holocaust that took our house a year ago to-morrow, which had to be the seventh;[1] but doubtless this can be re-written in time and the second part is still, happily, extant; I feel that I have about ten such books in me, if & when I can get around to writing them. As it stands, the book requires a short preface, & some notes, and if it seems worth it, these will follow in due course. Of course, it may not be any good at all: five years ago I deceived myself into thinking I had pulled it off, as of course I had not done: however I feel now it may be a pretty good job & myself justified in sending it you, since my impression is that the majority of its faults in the older version have been done away with, at least, as well as some of the objections which various publishers raised as to its publication.

The Lost Week End was a considerable blow to me and I do not know how far the success of that book would militate against the success of this: I suppose there will be people who will say it is nothing but a pale reflection of that excellent study, for the fact that nearly all the alcoholic part was written before I had even heard of that book can weigh but little with the reader; having read, finally, the horrible thing I did my very utmost not to be influenced by it and even hoiked out what I thought to be a quite fine passage because on reconsideration, it seemed to possess something of the other books rythm; on my side I can say that Under the Volcano begins, so to speak, whether the other leaves off, and after all the former is about lots of other things as well. Even more damaging to me was the impact of The Lost Week End upon the second part of the trilogy which is based upon the novella I had called The Last Address: however in the final analysis I am up to something quite different and all this probably will turn out not to matter, when I have got over my unworthy professional jealousy on the score. (The Lost Week End is not be confused with The *Last* Week End, by my friend John Sommerfield, author of Volunteer in Spain, written ten years ago & I believe published by Wishart in London, in which no less a figure than poor old ex-Malcolm plays a part not wholly unlike that of the hapless Birnam in The Lost W.E. However.)[2]

As for Margie, while delighted with her new contract etc, she has so far failed to receive the corrected proofs of the second part of The Shapes from Weber, as per his promise; whether she is right or wrong, for her part, in not sending back the uncorrected proofs of the second part (i.e. corrected only by her) – I don't know any better than she; but doubtless some light will dawn again soon from the inscrutable Scribners; which will make it all more clear. She has just got over a bad session in hospital with blood-poisoning, contracted while rebuilding our house, from a rusty nail in the foot. She is now getting on well again, however, as is the new house which we are building literally ourselves – someone agonizingly built *over* our old bedroom, in spite of our stakes left there on the site, but we have transcended all this & are making a very fine place indeed, which will be even better than the old one.

A great friend of mine who was at college with me – a well-known radioman in Canada, ex-editor of Experiment etc & ex-assistant director with Lubitsch[3] in Hollywood – has written, (which is more to the point,) a very interesting & moving novel centred in pre-war Italy entitled Teresina Maria: I told him he could not do better than send it to you and I hope he has done so & if so that it will meet with your approval. Whit [Burnett] published some of his early work: he is also an excellent poet, & has lots of things boiling, including two other novels, & many short stories. I think he would be a very good venture if he could get restarted in the literary field, which he was away from to some extent while concerned in radio, movies etc, not to say the English blitz. His name is Gerald Noxon – very familiar here, as I say, on the air.

I was very touched indeed by your kind remembrances of me, which was relayed to me by Margie, and this is indeed sincerely reciprocated.[4] I thank you also for the suggestion concerning the extraordinary experiments that were being carried out by your acquaintance in tapping the memory and indeed had I not had on my mind at that time so much that I wanted to forget I should have come immediately to New York and availed myself of the offices of your friend; perhaps at some later date it would not be too late to attempt something of the sort but at that period I was not sufficiently in balance, I think. Meantime both Margie & I are continuing to work hard. I thank you for everything you have done for her, & again, for me, though I have not yet rung the bell.[5]

I enclose a short note from Duell Sloan & Pearce that may or may not be of some use now.[6]

With very kindest regards, believe me,

Yours sincerely,

Malcolm

Annotations:

1 When the Lowrys' Dollarton shack burned down on 7 June 1944, his entire manuscript for 'In Ballast to the White Sea' was destroyed. The 'tattered circle' of a few pages (UBC 12:14) is all that remains.
2 The publication of Charles Jackson's novel *The Lost Weekend* (1944) was, as has been seen, a continuing source of anxiety for Lowry. John Sommerfield (1908-91), the English writer, was a close friend of Lowry's in London during the summer and fall of 1932. *Volunteer in Spain* was published in 1937, but 'The Last Week End,' whose protagonist, David Nordall, is modelled on Lowry, has never, to my knowledge, been published. See Day's description (152-55) of the Lowry character.
3 Ernst Lubitsch (1892-1947), an actor with Max Reinhardt's company and a famous German film director, went to the United States in 1923, where he worked with various Hollywood studios and became director of production at Paramount.
4 Lowry may be referring to conversations between Margerie and Harold Matson when she visited New York in July 1944.
5 Two letters from Matson to Lowry, 22 June and 31 July 1945, have survived with the Matson papers, and in them he expresses his interest in and fascination with *Under the Volcano* but goes on to say that he fears it is 'much too long, and much too full of talk.'
6 There is no note from the publisher extant with this letter.

203: To Jonathan Cape

P: Harvard(ms)

[Dollarton, B.C.,]
[June 1945][a]

Dear Jonathan Cape: herewith the mss of a novel which I hope fulfills
to some extent the promise you saw in me when, with that promise
in mind, you published, many years ago, Ultramarine.[1]
I realise I am still in some debt to your firm, & to past improvidence
in these matters, the breakdown of the author at that time must be
counted as the cause: and I am hoping that this book, should you find
it publishable, may make amends.
I have lost touch with my agent & I do not know if Mr Miles is still
with you so I am sending the mss in accordance with the terms of the
contract that gave you the first refusal of my second book, straight
to yourself.[2] My agent used to be Farquaharson of Red Lion Square;
A.J. Rose used to act for me there; as I say I do not know any present
address, but if they are still in the land of the living, & you still get
work from them, perhaps it would not be too much to ask you to
pass the mss on to them, after you have read it yourself, & come to
some decision, favourable or other wise. A.C.M. [Arthur Calder-
Marshall] was in Mexico with me & encouraged me very much with
the book in its initial stages; should you find an extra opinion worth
your while I know he would be interested to see the manuscript,
since he knows better than anyone the circumstances that gave it
birth.
I know he would be pleased also to help with any alterations or corrections, should you like the book, & should these be necessary, &
myself too far away. I hope to God he is well: & you too. Under the
Volcano, though complete in itself, was the first volume of a trilogy
to be called The Voyage That Never Ends – the Volcano being a kind
of inferno part. I had the two other volumes almost ready when the
theme stepped outside of my book and demolished my house by fire,
leaving only what I send you, a shorter version of the Purgatorio
volume, which I am developing now, and about 200 poems, of all I
have written in twelve years.
I was badly burned & went away, but have now returned & rebuilt
the house with my own hands; in fact I am sitting at this moment,
where the flames once raged the fiercest, as the saying is, looking
at the sea, & writing this letter. Similarly that lost work will be
rewritten in due course – With best wishes, yours v sincerely

Malcolm Lowry

Annotations:

1 Jonathan Cape published *Ultramarine* in 1933, and this letter appears to be the cover letter that accompanied the manuscript of *Under the Volcano*, which Lowry sent to him in June.
2 Hamish Miles, the editor at Cape who had handled *Ultramarine*, died in 1938.

Editorial Notes:

a. The transcription of this letter has been made from the 'Eridanus' manuscript housed with the Malcolm Lowry papers in the Houghton Library, Harvard. This manuscript is remarkable in a number of ways. It comprises thirty-five folio (seventy numbered) pages torn from a 15-by-25-cm notebook covered in Lowry's extremely small but clear, orderly pencil script with frequent marginalia at the tops of the pages and to the left of the red-ruled margin line.

The manuscript includes many different types of material, such as drafts for the novel in progress about the 'Trumbaughs' experiences in Mexico; passages of 'Margie's notes' copied by Lowry from Margerie's journal for their trip to Mexico in 1946; descriptive passages for 'Notes at the Wicket Gate' dated 'Friday: Dec. 10/43'; many references to the rebuilding of their shack during the summer of 1945, copied by Lowry from his own journals; two poems (one, called 'A Note,' about an injured bat, the other, untitled, about being an unsuccessful 'middleaged' writer; see Scherf [391]); and this letter to Cape, which appears on pages 55-56, squeezed between the second poem and draft passages for the fiction.

Although the letter has been signed, it carries no inside address or date, and it appears that Lowry intended the letter to be incorporated into the 'Eridanus' fiction. Internal evidence, such as the references to his fire, confirm a summer 1945 date, especially in light of the fact that he had sent a copy of the revised *Under the Volcano* to Harold Matson at the beginning of June. No separate holograph or typescript original letter appears to have survived, but it is unlikely that Lowry would have sent his manuscript to Cape without a covering letter such as this.

In order to preserve the original character of this letter, which is squeezed into a notebook draft for a novel, I have retained the spacing of the holograph throughout.

204: To Trustees, Westminster Bank, Liverpool

P: UBC(ms,tsc)

[Dollarton P.O.,]
[Dollarton, B.C.]
[July 1945]ᵃ

Dear Sir:[1]

.I wish to acknowledge with thanks your courteous letter of the
13th July in which you outline my present financial position, so far as
that pertains to the conditions of my father's will.[2]

Needless to say, these conditions affecting myself strike me as
extraordinarily generous but it has added to my distress at my
father's death that he never lived to see the proof that I had become
capable of supporting myself by my own pen independently of any
income or allowance he might grant me, for this I know would have
gladened him.ᵇ

I mention this because I feel it incumbent on myself to say that my
father had already more than adequately provided for me during his
lifetime and that I certainly saw no reason why such provisions
should continue; and was so far from looking for it to do so that
I have been making my own arrangements as if the income I was
receiving might cease.

Consequently by my own efforts and by saving I had by June 1944
amassed a quite considerable sum. At this time a house – a small cottage I had bought in the country in 1941 – burned down (uninsured
because the fire hazard was too extreme) and left me without a roof
over my head.ᶜ I saved about two fifths of my work but suffered an
enormous and irreparable loss.

With these things I did not worry my father nor shall I inflict them
upon you, in case I be led into some form of what I believe your profession terms ignoratio elenchi.ᵈ

Suffice it that after a journey East[3] I returned here to Dollarton
where I have been engaged for the past six months in rebuilding the
house with my own hands – an occupation that has not been rendered any more simple by shortage of lumber [& by the fact that in
my absence some nice fellow had built upon half my site. Having
rendered the house livable in (which it is not yet though I live in it) it
was my intention – keeping the place as a kind of sheetanchor – to do
some travelling But – though I am still perfectly solvent – doctor's
bills and so forth have made a hole in my savings so that I am no
longer able to do this]

[With all this in mind it struck me as reasonable to make the inquiry if,] So, since my gross annual income is, according to your communication, in the neighbourhood of £100, or about 33:6:8 per month, and I have been since September 1940 receiving the amount regulated by the provisions of the Defense Finance regulations, namely £25 per month, if there is not [now (in the event of these regulations being modified or lifted)] some [sum technically] part of my income that would be recoverable on retroactive grounds at the discretion of the Trustees of course, but this not having relation to whatever amount should determine as my income for this year.

So far as I am concerned, it would be a relief at this tentative period to have money, if it exists, in the bank here, where I could either keep it or draw on it at my discretion rather than have it accumulating in the fund, even if that meant some increase in my future monthly income.[4]

I note that the settlement was made in 1938 but prior to 1940 it is more than likely that this could not pertain, and after September 1940 possible that such a hypothetical surplus should be fairly considered as payment or part payment for prior expenses on my behalf made by my father.

On the other hand I thought it worth while to ask since virtually famine prices here, as with you, make living an expensive project, no matter how frugally you may organize your affairs, and though those prices will, I think, come down, they will probably get worse before they get better; in addition to which, such a sum in the bank would give me a breathing spell from the retrenchments that I shall have otherwise to make at the expense of the work I want to do and the freedom of movement I require to do it in. [At the moment, for the first time in many years, I am unprepared, as it were, for a crisis: –]

Thank you again for your letter and your consideration of this matter.

Yours very truly

[unsigned]

Annotations:

1 In 1968 the Westminster Banks combined with the National Provincial Banks to form the National Westminster Banks, but at the time of Lowry's letter the bank was called simply Westminster Bank.

2 This letter does not appear to have survived.

3 Lowry is referring to the time he and Margerie spent with Gerald and

Betty Noxon in Oakville and Niagara-on-the-Lake; they returned to
Dollarton in February 1945.

4 Lowry was still receiving installments from these funds well into the
fifties; see his 25 January 1954 letter (**602**) to Harold Matson.

Editorial Notes:

a. The copy-text for this letter presents some special difficulties. The
signed letter sent to the Westminster Bank does not appear to have survived, but the Lowry collection holds two versions of the letter: one is
an unsigned pencil holograph on five sheets of lined 18-by-23-cm paper,
torn from a scribbler, with several marginal additions, deletions, and
interlineations; the other is an unsigned two-page carbon with neither an
inside address nor a date. July 1945 has been written in pencil at the top
right of the carbon.

The carbon differs from the holograph in certain ways. First, several
passages from the holograph are not included in the carbon, whether the
holograph shows them as deleted or not; second, there are variations in
spellings that are interesting; for example, the holograph has 'defense'
where the carbon has 'defence,' the latter spelling being more commonly British. It is possible, therefore, that Lowry typed this letter
himself, instead of having Margerie do so, as was usual with important
letters; however, it is more likely that there was at least one further typescript version of this letter, typed by Margerie and sent to the bank, that
has not yet been discovered. In the absence of such a text the transcription presented here follows Lowry's holograph, with Lowry's deleted
passages included in editorial notes and with those passages that are deleted in the carbon but not marked for deletion in the holograph retained
in square brackets.

b. The following completion of this sentence has been crossed out: 'the
more so since circumstances are not more adverse to a writer anywhere
in the world than here. Canada, for instance, does not support one single
intelligent magazine – practically her sole outlet for her original writers
is radio – & America, which demands a 50% tax on your earnings: nonetheless all this offers a challenge & a pioneer opportunity'.

c. The following passage has been crossed out: 'through no fault of my
own unless it can be called a fault to occupy a place at all where the fire
hazard is so extreme noone will insure it [. . .] became rather more difficult, the more especially since at that period I had just been recovering
from a long & serious illness:'

d. The typescript of this letter has 'ignoratis elenchi,' but Lowry has clearly
written 'ignoratio elenchi.' The term is one of his favourite Latin expressions, meaning literally an ignorant or ill-informed critical inquiry,
but in legal practice referring more specifically to the logical fallacy of
failing to refute an opponent's argument or failing to understand and
address the argument in question.

205: To Conrad Aiken

p: UBC(ms); H(ts)
pp: *SL* 47-52; *LAL* 186-93

[Dollarton, B.C.]
[mid-October 1945]ᵃ

Dear old Conrad:

Thanks awfully for yours & have been meaning to write a really fat informative & diverting letter – in fact, made all the notes for same, but I want to get this letter off now so it will be in time to wish you bon voyage, therefore I must make a sacrifice of the other for the time being. Yes, the phoenix clapped its wings all right all right, in fact gave such a bloody great resounding clap that the poor bird nearly broke its neck and had to be immolated all over again. As you know we went East after the fire. The grave preceded us however. The interminable golden bittersweet awful beautiful Eastern autumn (which I'd never experienced) restored Margie, (whose childhood was in Michigan) to *some* extent, but me it almost slew. It had a worse effect upon me, in fact, than on Henry Adams,[1] though the Noxon's Niagara-on-the-Lake is something to see: really beautiful. I was in shocking bad form, & worse company so all in all, though I was very disappointed not to see you, – albeit I *heard* you – it was perhaps just as well I didn't. How the Noxon's put with me – if they really did – I don't know. Actually the business of the fire seemed to drive us both slightly cuckoo. Its traumatic result alone was shattering. We had to live through the bloody fire all over again every night. I would wake to find Margie screaming or she would wake to find me yelling and gnashing my teeth; that is to say, what teeth I have left to gnash. Apart from these diversions (fortunately the Noxon's were sound sleepers, but when we moved to a house of our own, it grew much worse) fire itself seemed to follow us around in a fashion nothing short of diabolical. Betty had painted a picture of a neighbouring house in Oakville that Margie & I had thought of renting for the winter because it vaguely resembled our old one and one day when everyone was out I sat in the attic studying this picture which I liked very much. My concentration on the picture was somewhat marred by the fact that in my imagination the house kept bursting into flame and sure enough, about a week later, that's precisely what the house did; they couldn't get the fire engines through the woods, nothing of the kind had happened for fifty years in that rural route, and there was terrific to-do, through all of which Margie & I, for once, calmly slept. Then when we went down to Niagara the house next door to ours, one night while we [were] over at the Nox-ons, went up in a blaze: we heard the shouts & bells & saw the awful sun, (E.d. again) – I don't know why so much Emily Dickinson[2] to-day – & of course thought it was *our* house and ran over in a panic, so much so that Margie was not even convinced it was *not* our house by the time we had got there & took all our manuscripts out into the street. And to cap everything, when we returned here, it turned out that the house where someone had been good enough to let us store our bedding & some few things we had left after *our* fire, had in our absence itself been burned down, totally demolished, and our bed-ding & stuff with it, the house mysteriously bursting into flame for no reason at all apparently, one calm mild evening when the owners weren't even there. Margie & I had invented, in a horror story, a murderer, a black magician one of whose specialties was the starting of fires by means of incomprehensible talismans.[3] This fictitious gent's name was Pell & the m.s. concerning him I had happened to rescue from our fire. Swelp me bob if the owners of this house don't to be called Pell too, though there had been no connection at all originally. And so forth; altogether about fifty other odd senseless sad terrifying & curiously related things that make me sometimes think (taking it all in all!) that maybe I am the chap chosen of God or the devil to elucidate the Law of Series.[4] Unfortunately it would seem to involve one in such rotten bad art: or need it not? At all events, I have been reading Kant's Critique of Pure Reason to see if that would help. Or perhaps Bergson's [and] Osbert Sitwell – & some of James Joyce's experiences seem to tie up.[5]

When we arrived back here too it was to find that someone, strangers & vultures, had disregarded our burned stakes & notices and built smack on half our old site, blocking our southerly view, a great tall ugly erection to be full in the summer of rackety rickety children & hysterical fat women, who meantime had pulled down the flags we had left – perhaps too dramatically – flying on our poor old ruin thrown dead mice down our well and shat – even on the walls – all over the toilet. This of course is a crime, according to the local folkways, the mores, or whatever, though we had no legal toe-hold in the matter, – one incidentally of the prime causes of jungle warfare – pioneer's and squatters rights having been abolished: our few fishermen friends – with ourselves the only permanent inhabi-tants – arrived back too late from Alaska to prevent it & our local Manx boat builder only got insulted and nearly beaten up when he tried to put a stop to it. They had no excuse, knew we were coming back. We could have knocked their house down ourselves & had the support of even most of the summer community but like a fool or not I decided to be Christlike about it with the result that we had them in our hair all summer while we were building on what space was left for us, our new neighbours even calling us greedy because we made the most of that, until one day the owner came over and asked why we wouldn't speak to them more often and accused me of putting a curse on them and on their house, that they'd couldn't be happy there, that the youngest child, for instance, had almost drowned the day before, & so on, and that they'd had one misfortune after another, ever since they'd built there, to which I replied that while we forgave them all right, they had never had the charity to perceive that there was anything to forgive, moreover if you built on top of a guy's soul, you couldn't be sure what would happen, and if something you didn't like did happen, it was no use coming round complaining to us and looking as if they'd swallowed Paddy Murphy's goat and the horns were sticking out of their arse. All round, quite an ethical problem.

To be frank, it is ourselves who have had a share of the misfortunes. Margie ran a nail through her foot the first day we got the lumber in – cellulitis set in – then blood poisoning, shortage of doctors, and finally hospital and probings, and a horrible anxious awful time that was. Meanwhile she received the first part of her proofs for her novel but we are still waiting for the promised proofreaders copy of the second part, Scribners having held her first novel now for over four years (it is getting into the fifth year) without publishing it and although they signed a contract for a second novel[6] with a time limit set for publication date at this fall it is already this fall and still Margerie hasn't had so much as a smell of the proofs of this second novel, which was supposed to be at the printers last Xmas, so it looks as though a breach of contract looms with what small comfort that is for the poor author. Scribners have proved the worlds most undependable and unscrupulous people to deal with and you are certainly well rid of their new outfit. Granted they dared not behave like that with someone like you, but what the hell. I then proceeded to cut off the end of my thumb while doing some ripsawing with an ordinary saw, which set us back with the building and for the last two months I have been in bed practically unable to move with a toxalmia caused by an osteomyelitis due to an abcessed tooth that became abcessed and had to be removed owing to malpractice. There is a shortage of dentists – they will not take new patients, even if you are hopping with agony as I was, and on V.J. day[7] too, with the drugstores all shut. But on the other hand there is apparently also a surplus of dentists: they are threatening to open offices on the street, because of the housing shortage. But I myself have not been able to find a trace of these dentists. Meantime there has been an average of two murders a week here, most of them by or of children: a pet slayer likewise is at large who has disembowelled thirteen goats, several sailors' monkeys, twelve pet rabbits, and is doubtless also somewise responsible for the apparition of half a cocker spaniel in a lane near West Vancouver. On the other hand a murderer – no relative but embarrassingly also of the name Trumbaugh[8] – has shot a policeman that was several months ago, but was reminded of it for at time of writing he has just received a reprieve & wondered if that were a good omen. Just the same we have built our house and paradise has been regained. I forgot to say that no sooner had paradise been regained that we received the notice that a new law had gone through and that all our lovely forest was to be torn down and ourselves with it within a year and turned into 'autocamps of the better class.' This placed our new house – which, by the way has the distinction of being the last example of such pioneer activity on Vancouver waterfront property – under a sentence of death that was finally too much for our sense of humour and my temperature went up within a quarter of an hour to 103. A sad story, you say, almost as poignant as The Triumph of Egg??[9] Not a bit of it. Reprieve has come for the Trumbaughs also. There will be no autocamps of the better class, and no neighbours either, of the worst class. We may live here for three years at least as we are doing without molestation or paying any rent at all and then buy the land too, that is the part we want & we are being given first choice – for a reasonable price. Thus does your old Malc, if still a conservative-Christian-anarchist at heart, at last join the ranks of the petty bourgeoisie. I feel somewhat like a Prometheus who became interested in real estate & decided to buy up his Caucasian ravine. At the moment we are living in the house, without inside walls. It's pouring with rain, & it doesn't leak. What triumph. Herewith our handiwork – also the pier we built ourselves, all that was left of our old house – it used to come out of our front door – the vultures wedged themselves in just beyond, hoping to use our pier too, not to say our well.!

My novel – the Volcano – , seems to have gone smack into the void – no intelligent comments so far, or encouragement. I think it is really good, though The Lost Week End[10] may have deprived it of some of its impact – alack – prosaic justice? – if not to be confused with The *Last* Week End, by J. Sommerfield, in which it actually is old Malc who goes all too recognizably down the drain, and pretty feeble too. I was planning to send you the Volcano in some trepidation but with some pride too but I don't like to saddle you with the only copy in my possession at present and I don't see how I can get

back the only available other one before you sail. So please take the
will for the deed for the time being. I'll learn 'em eventually, as Mr
Wolfe once said, I feel.

The only difference in my present status since I wrote the above is
that while we are still living in the house without inside walls the
roof is leaking in six different places. But now your letter about the
Collected Poems has arrived and I hasten to make some reply in
time, though please forgive me if what I say seems hastily digested.[11]
In brief, these are the ideas which immediately occur to me and I
hope they are not merely confusing. I think the idea of reversing the
chronological order is a very good one, in fact as good as can be, –
though I think perhaps The Soldier might profit by being dislocated
out of the new order and being placed, if not actually among the
symphonies somewhere near them in the second volume. What I
mean is, if the poem does not belong to the symphonies, The Soldier
does to the notion of The Divine Pilgrim. Houston Peterson or
somebody once put the possibly erroneous idea in my head that you
had once thought of including Tetelestai also under The Divine Pilgrim heading and even if this is erroneous and Tetelestai not a
symphony this is worth thinking of if you haven't already rejected
it.[12] As for the early poems I would certainly put in every thing that
can possibly be of use to the fellow-poet and student of your work,
Discordants with Youth that's now so bravely spending and as many
of the actual Cats & Rats Turns & Movies[13] as you have space for.
The latterly certainly stay with me as unique & powerful work,
whatever you may think of them. I would also take the opportunity
of exhuming from undeserved limbo such pieces as 'Red petals in the
dust under a tree,'[14] Asphalt 'tossing our tortured hands to no escape'
(though not very early, 1925 model?), but very fine, and even the
'succubus you kissed' lampoon you wrote agin the Imagists, which
has a historical interest, & giving the dates of all these. I don't know
about a selection from Earth Triumphant, but I would be inclined to
make a short one: – possibly you are right to disown it, but I myself
cannot forget the 'unaccustomed wetness in my trousers' with which
I read it at Your Uncle Potters.[15] The only other departure that
comes to me would be to start the whole collected poems with the
Morning Song of Senlin and end them with The Coming Forth by
Day of Osiris Jones. I must say I like this notion per se exceedingly,
if it would not play too much hob with your reversed chronology.
Whatever you do, I am very glad a Collected Poems is coming out
and the very best luck with them.

If by the way you have any old Harpers Bazzaars, Vice Versas,
Southern Reviews or what not you are thinking of throwing away –

no old Dials, alack? – we would be immensely beholden if you would wrap a paper around them and shoot them in this direction C.O.D. or something for we are absolutely stuck here for such reading matter, all intelligent American magazines having been unprocurable for donkeys years: on the other hand it occurs to me it is probably a poor time to ask what with you packing & all: so if it's too much trouble, just forget it.

Well, bon voyage, old fellow and our very best love to you both and best wishes for Mary's success & our very best again to her and you and also to Jeakes[16]

πασα θαηασσα θαηασσα – [17]

Malc

J.L.D's [John Davenport] address – last I heard – was I think The Malting House, Chippenham, Wilts.

P.S. When I suggested starting with the Morning Song of Senlin I wasn't of course forgetting that the Morning Song was only part of Senlin: a biography. My idea, possibly rather naïve, was that the Poems should start with Senlin rising in the morning & close with the comment of the grass in The Coming forth, which I felt would rather beautifully *enclose* the Pilgrim theme running throughout your work. Possibly the idea would be better if there were just one volume. However, perhaps it was a good one. I just send this p.s because such things can be irritating; almost as irritating – perhaps you say – as when I once referred to Brownstone Eclogues as Brownstone Elegies, a stupid mistake that I saw too late & was doubtless due to a state of mind: I was thinking of them as *Brimstone* Eclogues, & the correction got off on the wrong foot. I am now almost better of the toxalmia & the roof-leaks are mysteriously healing of themselves. At high tide you can dive out of our casement windows into perilous seas forlorn[18] – very useful. Jesus, this is a beautiful place. We are thinking of travelling for six months, however, into the sun – Haiti, or a freighter to Samoa.[19] Do you know any new magazines friendly to more or less original or experimental short stories that do not have to start: 'I was just leaving Oliphant & Company's offices when I saw Mike.'? Please give my love to the drugstore where the [mouthesills] were bought, the pirates pushing trucks, Mr Smith, Malvolio, Silberstein, the engineer with long-beaked oilcan, the shipboys, & of course the Kraken & any pynters & gilders who have been to Vancouver, likewise the tarred seams, the Silurian (if seen) & don't forget the sea.[20]

Best love & success to Mary & yourself from us both & again Bon

Voyage – & to Jeakes, John & Jan [Aiken], The Ship, Mermaid St & the Burra [Ed Burra]

Malc

Annotations:

1 Henry Adams (1838-1918) was an American historian, philosopher, and author. He is best known today for *The Education of Henry Adams* (1918).

2 Lowry's reference is to the American poet Emily Dickinson (1830-86); however, he is thinking not of a poem but of a 4 July 1879 letter she wrote to her cousins Louisa and Fannie Norcross. Dickinson describes being awakened by a nearby fire thus: 'We were waked by the ticking of bells, . . . I sprang to the window, and each side of the curtain saw that awful sun.' By 1945 Lowry could have read this letter in either Martha Dickinson Bianchi's *The Life and Letters of Emily Dickinson* (Boston: Houghton Mifflin, 1924), p. 320, or *Letters of Emily Dickinson*, ed. Mabel Loomis Todd (New York: Harper & Brothers, 1931), p. 258.

3 *The Shapes That Creep* (New York: Charles Scribner's Sons, 1946).

4 Lowry had long been interested in the law of series, more particularly the way it is used by J.W. Dunne to describe 'serial time' in *An Experiment with Time* (London: Faber and Faber, 1927), pp. 132-96. He was sensitive about the effect of Dunne's theories upon his art because, in her criticism of the 1940 version of *Under the Volcano*, Martha Foley had noted that it suffered from the influence of Dunne's theory of serial time. See Lowry's 4 March 1941 letter (**163**) to Harold Matson, and Appendix 2.

5 This sentence is difficult to transcribe with absolute certainty due to the illegibility of the superscript insertion '[and] Osbert Sitwell.' From the context it would appear that Lowry could be thinking of Henri Bergson's discussion of 'planes of consciousness' in *Matter and Memory*, first translated into English in 1911, or of his discussion of psychic phenomena in *Mind-Energy* (1920). Certainly, many of Sitwell's stories turn upon coincidence and uncanny phenomena, and his 1929 novel, *The Man Who Lost Himself*, is the story of an artist's disturbed psyche and his prophetic dreams or hallucinations. See Lowry's 3 March 1940 letter (**128**) to Aiken for his comments upon Joyce and superstitious coincidences.

6 Although in previous letters Lowry suggests that *The Last Twist of the Knife* was the *first* detective novel written by Margerie, *The Shapes That Creep* was actually the first to be published.

7 V.J. (Victory over Japan) Day, 15 August 1945, formally marked the end of the Second World War in the Pacific. It was on the fifteenth that the Allies declared their victory and that Emperor Hirohito announced the Japanese surrender over the radio.

8 Martin Trumbaugh is the protagonist in Lowry's early drafts of *Dark as the Grave*, 'La Mordida,' and 'Through the Panama,' and he was named

after the jazz musician Frankie Trumbauer (see 'Through the Panama,' 34); the protagonist's name was later changed to Sigbjørn Wilderness.

9 Lowry is thinking of Sherwood Anderson, *The Triumph of the Egg: A Book of Impressions from American Life in Tales and Poems* (New York: B.W. Huebsch, 1921).

10 See Lowry's comments on *The Lost Weekend* in his 6 June 1945 letter (202) to Harold Matson.

11 In a 16 October 1945 letter, which reached Lowry before he had finished this letter to Aiken, Aiken explained that Duell, Sloan and Pearce were planning a two-volume edition of his collected poems, and he asked Lowry for 'a few Helpful Hints and Suggestions, and especially about the whole question of what if any of the earlier things to include.' Aiken ends his request by saying: 'I value your judgement more highly than any other, and will listen intently to whatever you say' (Sugars 185).

12 Houston Peterson wrote the first critical book on Aiken, *The Melody of Chaos* (1931), and 'Tetelestai,' originally in Aiken's *Priapus and the Pool*, appears in 'The Divine Pilgrim' section of *Collected Poems*.

13 Aiken took Lowry's advice on 'Discordants' and 'Bain's Cats and Rats,' both of which appear in *Collected Poems*.

14 Lowry quotes from this poem in his 27 October 1930 letter (25) to John Davenport.

15 Aiken's uncle, his mother's brother, was Alfred Claghorn Potter (1867-1940), and he was assistant University Librarian at Harvard in 1929. Aiken became very close to this interesting uncle during his years at Harvard, and Lowry may have met Alfred Potter during his visit with Aiken in the summer of 1929. For a description of Uncle Alfred, see Edward Butscher's *Conrad Aiken: Poet of White Horse Vale*, pp. 174-75.

16 The Aikens sailed from Halifax to Liverpool in November 1945 en route to their house in Rye, where they hoped to have the peace and quiet to paint and write. According to Aiken's 14 September 1945 letter to Lowry, Jeake's House was threatened with seizure by the authorities.

17 Lowry is quoting the Greek used by Aiken in *Blue Voyage* (245) which means 'the whole sea, the sea.'

18 Lowry is echoing the last line of stanza 7 of John Keats's 'Ode to a Nightingale' (1819): 'Of perilous seas, in faery lands forlorn.'

19 On 28 November 1945 the Lowrys flew to Mexico via Los Angeles and stayed in Cuernavaca; both *Dark as the Grave* and the unpublished 'La Mordida' are based on this trip. Their trip by freighter to Haiti did not take place until December 1947.

20 Lowry is stringing together allusions to Aiken's *Blue Voyage*.

Editorial Notes:

a. The Huntington library has a variant typescript of this letter labelled 'a copy' and dated 24 October 1945 by Aiken. The present transcription follows the holograph pencil draft (UBC 2:2), which includes marginalia and other material not included either in Aiken's 'copy' or in the different version published in *Selected Letters*. The letter on which Aiken's 'copy' is presumably based has not been located. The postscript is filed separately from the rest of the letter in the Aiken collection. Lowry may have sent it along after he had mailed the main letter, but it is clearly meant as a continuation and clarification of points in the letter.

Lowry scholars have long known that Margerie helped her husband with the drafting of his fiction and letters, but as this letter makes clear, Lowry also helped with hers. Lowry has written this version of her letter to Harold Matson, and I have included it in the collection to demonstrate this collateral help.

206: To Harold Matson

P: UBC(ms)

[Dollarton, B.C.]
[25 October 1945]

Dear Hal

About two months ago I wrote you a long letter with several questions in it of some import to me, but not having had any reply, save a rejection slip on the Horse, I've finally come to the conclusion you probably didn't get it, either due to the dishevelled state of the mails these days, or because you were away on your vacation or something.[1]

Since the questions are still of some import, though since writing I have got down to another mystery, I thought the most sensible thing was to send you a copy of it I happened to have, which herewith –

With very best wishes

[unsigned]

Annotations:

1 A very rough draft of another letter from Margerie to Matson exists in the Lowry collection (UBC 2:2), but no fair copy appears to have survived in Matson's files. This four-page draft letter, comprising a typescript with major holograph additions by Lowry and one holograph section by Margerie, contains several questions regarding Margerie's work and Scribner's behaviour. It is clearly Margerie's letter to be sent over her signature, but it is one that Lowry helped her to compose. On

the versos of the letter are Lowry's holograph drafts of sections of *Under the Volcano*.

207: To Mrs Anna Mabelle [John Stuart] Bonner

p: UBC(ms)
pp: *SL* 53-54

[Cuernavaca,]
[Mexico]
[19 December 1945][a]

My very dearest Mother –

I was so proud and so delighted to meet you, and traces of your kindness, thoughtfulness and sensitivity were so much everywhere in the house, even to the books at one's bedside, that I was very chagrined to think how inadequately I must have expressed my appreciation: but it was wonderful having the privilege at last of seeing you and talking to you and I enormously enjoyed my visit.[1] We had a very fine trip here and I have described this in part to Priscilla and Bert, who will doubtless relay it to you.[2] The night before last Margie saw Achernar and Canopus for the first time; and how thrilling that was! (I should have said just Achernar in Eridanus for the first time, for of course you can see Canopus sometimes in Los Angeles.) Last night we ran into something that would have interested you. We went to see an old friend of mine, previously having observed the full moon rise over the volcano Ixtaccihuatl, then came out into the street to find a lunar eclipse in progress which became total as we walked back toward the pension.[3] At each gap between the walls, through a vista of trees, we had a strangely beautiful glimpse of the increasing eclipse until finally, round a turn, it was total, and the moon turned a rusty brown. After dinner we had to pay some more visits in total darkness but when we finally got home & we climbed to our balcony the moon was out of her eclipse, and the stars were shining. They were winking like jewels out of white fleecy clouds and high up the brilliant normal full moon was sliding down a wide sapphire night sky into a kind of white ocean of fleece. We both thought of you and wished you were here to share it all. A Mexican was singing away to himself at the other end of our verandah, and we wondered if he were not singing half from relief that the world had not come to an end after all and the moon was with us as usual! (I must admit to being pretty relieved that the world had relinquished its shadow because for some reason I had never seen previously even a partial eclipse of the moon and so had been feeling

definitely uneasy all evening.) Well, mother, this is just a little note
to tell you that we are thinking of you often and also to say how
enormously I appreciate how much trouble and work Priscilla and
you went to to make me feel at home and happy with you, which I
certainly was!

Now hasta la vista, & God bless you –

Till the next time, your affectionate son

Malcolm

Annotations:

1 The Lowrys left Dollarton on 28 November 1945 for a trip to Mexico
via Los Angeles, where they spent almost two weeks with Margerie's
family. They flew to Mexico City on 11 December.
2 A separate letter addressed to both the Woolfans does not appear to have
survived. Lowry may be referring to a single page of lined notebook
paper that has the complete text of the December 1945 letter to his sister-
in-law, Priscilla Woolfan, and the last part of a letter (**209**) to 'Bert',
Priscilla's husband Dr E. Bertrand Woolfan (1894-1961).
3 A full lunar eclipse visible in North and South America occurred on
Tuesday evening, 18 December 1945.

Editorial Notes:

a. Lowry has not written an inside address or date on this fine holograph
letter, and Margerie Lowry has dated it 'November 1945' in *Selected
Letters*. However, the letter must have been written on the day after the
lunar eclipse described here, which occurred on 18 December.

208: To Gerald, Betty & Nick Noxon

P: Texas(pcard)
PP: *LLN* 118

[Mexico]
December 1945[a]

... of an overloaded style;[1] we just dropped in here on the way –
where? Feliz Ano Nuevo y Feliz Navidad[2] – we think of last year –
best wishes for T.M. [*Teresina Maria*] & Works address: Wells Fargo,
Mexico City, Mexico D.F.

Malc & Margie

Annotations:

1 An 'overloaded' or 'churrigueresque' style is the word Lowry used to
  describe *Under the Volcano* in his 2 January 1946 letter (**210**) to Jonathan
  Cape (see his comments on chapter 10). This postcard shows a black and
  white photograph of the highly ornate interior of a church in Tlaxcala,
  and the term 'churrigueresque' comes from the name of the Spanish
  baroque architect and sculptor José Churriguera (1650-1725).
2 *Feliz Ano Nuevo y Feliz Navidad* is Spanish for 'Happy New Year and
  Happy Christmas.'

Editorial Notes:

a. The postmark on this card is virtually illegible. It was mailed in Cuerna-
    vaca on what appears to be 26 December, and Lowry has written 'Dec
    1945' in pencil at the top. Like most of his holograph letters to Noxon,
    the message and address on this card are in pencil.

209: To Priscilla Woolfan

P: UBC(ms)
PP: *SL* 53

[Cuernavaca,]
[Mexico]
[December 1945][a]

My very dear sister Priscilla:
    I have temporarily written myself out of news – Waiving the
formal, this note comes from the heart, with real love & gratitude.
Were I to attempt to say all that I feel for the way you opened your
home & your hearts to me it would take another novel as long as the
Volcano. But I know that being muy simpatico[1] you will take a likewise simpatico attitude to my inarticulacy & will understand. I had
long looked forward to meeting you but it rarely if ever happens that
the reality exceeds the anticipation as it did with you: I was proud,
grateful and charmed, all at once. There are many things here that
would interest & amuse you & also give you the creeps – things wonderful, things horrible, things wonderful-horrible – especially some
of the new houses. What do you think of our living in M. Laruelle's
house, & all by accident, the only one we could get – chevron-shaped
windows and all:[2] it gives us an odd feeling of living *inside* a book, a
kind of intra-dimensional life. We walked out of a house the other
night into a full eclipse of the moon[3] – there was the moon, looking

incredibly near & spherical, & apparently coming nearer: we thought it was some terrestial visitor and that we had gone completely cuckoo. – Give Mother our best love & tell her we are writing her together today.

Adios, God bless,

Your brother,

Malcolm

[P.S.] Well Bert, my very deep gratitude for all you did for me in Los Angeles, such incredible kindness on your part and Priscilla's & Mother's as I cannot hope to repay and in fact can scarcely begin to itemize. I cherish the very fondest memories of my visit, and shall not among other things, ever forget my first American football game. Please remember me kindly to all your good friends whom I met and who were so hospitable: – once more my deepest gratitude to you,

With love & sincerest friendship

Your brother

Malcolm

Annotations:

1 The Spanish expression *muy simpatico* suggests 'very genial' or 'understanding.'
2 Jacques Laruelle's house in *Under the Volcano* (see especially chapter 7) was based upon the house at 24 Calle Humboldt in Cuernavaca (see Figure 11), where the Lowrys stayed during this visit to Mexico.
3 See Lowry's December 1945 letter (**207**) to Margerie's mother and its annotation 3.

Editorial Notes:

a. A postmarked original of this letter does not appear to have survived, but what may be a draft exists on both sides of an 18-by-22-cm page of lined paper torn from a notebook, and the transcription reproduced here has been made from the draft (UBC 2:3). On the recto, above the first few lines of this letter, is the last part of a letter Lowry wrote to his brother-in-law Dr E.B. Woolfan, and the page has clearly been folded three times in Lowry's characteristic manner. The date in *Selected Letters* (November 1945) is incorrect because the Lowrys did not arrive in Cuernavaca until 11 December. The same error in dating occurs with Lowry's letter (**207**) to his mother-in-law (see *Selected Letters*, 53–54). The last few lines and complimentary close of the letter to E.B. Woolfan are included here as a postscript because the main part of the letter, presumably written on a separate page, does not appear to have survived.

Figure 11: *Laruelle's tower
in Cuernavaca.*

On *28 November 1945 the Lowrys left Dollarton for a holiday in Mexico.
Margerie wanted to see the scene of the book she had helped to create, and
Malcolm hoped that by visiting these scenes with her he could lay the ghosts
of 1937-38. They left in good spirits and with a sense of achievement:* Under
the Volcano *had been sent to Harold Matson and Jonathan Cape; they had
rebuilt their Dollarton home, and, most important, three weeks before their
departure they had received a letter from Cape, who sounded impressed with*
Volcano.

*They arrived in Mexico City on 11 December, and a week later they
moved to Cuernavaca, where, to Lowry's grim delight, they rented rooms in
the very house he had given to Laruelle in the novel. For the moment the
signs seemed propitious. It was there, however, in Laruelle's tower, on New
Year's Eve that he received a second letter from his British publisher. This
time Jonathan Cape explained that one of the firm's readers had questioned
several aspects of the novel and recommended major changes. Cape wanted
Lowry to consider these criticisms and, in essence, defend his work. 'So that
my letter should not appear ambiguous,' Cape wrote, 'let me say that if you
decide to implement the suggestions contained in the report . . . I will publish
it.' However, if Lowry refused to change anything, Cape explained that he
was not necessarily going to reject the manuscript because he believed that the
book had 'integrity and importance.'*

*The reader's report, submitted by trusted Cape reader William Plomer,
criticized the lack of action, the weak character drawing, the initial 'tedium,'
and several other features of the text; in short, Plomer was not enthusiastic.
Lowry, of course, was devastated. His first response was a despairing and
half-hearted attempt to slash his wrists, but he quickly rallied and sat down to
compose what is now seen as one of the most extraordinary documents in
modern literary history. Lowry's 2 January 1946 letter (**210**) to Jonathan
Cape is both apologia and exegesis. It demonstrates Lowry's keen insight
into his own work and psyche, and it is written with a passion, humility,
intelligence, and humour that make it a powerful literary text in its own
right.*

210: To Jonathan Cape

p: UBC(ts)
pp: *SL* 57-88; *MLJC*

> 24 Calle de Humboldt,
> Cuernavaca, Morelos,
> Mexico
> [2 January 1946]ᵃ

Dear Mr Cape:

Thank you very much indeed for yours of the 29th November, which did not reach me, however, until New Years Eve, and moreover reached me here, in Cuernavaca, where completely by chance, I happen to be living in the very tower which was the original of the house of M. Laruelle, which I had only seen previously from the outside, and that ten years ago, but which is the very place where as it happens the Consul in the Volcano also had a little complication with some delayed correspondence.

Passing over my feelings, which you can readily imagine, of involved triumph, I will, lest these should crystallise into a complete agraphia, get down immediately to the business in hand.[1]

My first feeling is that the reader, a copy of whose report you sent me, could not have been (to judge from your first letter to me) as sympathetic as the reader to whom you first gave it.

On the other hand, while I distinctly agree with much this second reader very intelligently says, and while in his place I might have said much the same by way of criticism, he puts me somewhat at a loss to reply definitely to your questions re revisions, for reasons which I shall try to set forth, and which I am sure both you and he would agree are valid, at least for the author.

It is true that the novel gets off to a slow start, and while he is right to regard this as a fault (and while in general this may be certainly a fault in any novel) I think it possible for various human reasons that its gravity might have weighed upon him more heavily than it would weigh upon the reader per se, certain provisions for him having first been made. If the book anyhow were already in print and its pages not wearing the dumb pleading disperate and desperate look of the unpublished manuscript, I feel a reader's interest would tend to be very much more engaged at the outset just as, were the book already, say, an established classic, a reader's feelings would be most different: albeit he might say God this is tough going, he would plod gamely on through the dark morass – indeed he might feel ashamed not to – because of the reports which had already reached his ears of the rewarding vistas further on.

Using the word reader in the more general sense, I suggest that whether or not the Volcano as it is seems tedious at the beginning, depends somewhat upon that reader's state of mind and how prepared he is to grapple with the form of the book and the author's true intention. Since while he may be prepared and equipped to do both he cannot *know* the nature of either of these things at the start I suggest that a little subtle but solid elucidation in a preface or a blurb might negate very largely or modify the reaction you fear: (that it was your first reaction, and might well have been mine in your place I am asking you for the moment to be generous enough to consider beside the point) if he were *conditioned*, I say, ever so slightly towards the acceptance of that slow beginning as inevitable, supposing I convince you it is – slow, but perhaps not necessarily so tedious after all – the results might be surprising. If you say, well, a good wine needs no bush, all I can reply is: well, I am not talking of good wine but mescal, & quite apart from the bush, once inside the cantina, mescal needs salt and lemon to get it down, and perhaps you would not drink it at all if it were not in such an enticing bottle. If that seems beside the point too, then let me ask who would have felt encouraged to venture into the draught of The Waste Land without some anterior knowledge and anticipation of its poetic cases?[2]

Some of the difficulties of approach having been cleared away therefore, I feel the first chapter for example, much as it stands, is necessary since it sets, even without the reader's knowledge, the mood and tone of the book as well as the slow melancholy tragic rhythm of Mexico itself, its sadness, and above all establishes the *terrain*: if anything here finally looks to everyone just too feeble for words I would be only too delighted to cut it, but how can you be sure that by any really serious cutting here, especially any that radically alters the form, you are not undermining the foundations of the book, the basic structure, without which your reader might not have read it at all?

I venture to suggest finally that the book is a good deal thicker, deeper, better, and a great deal more carefully planned and executed than he suspects and that if your reader is not at fault in not spotting some of its deeper meanings or in dismissing them as pretentious or irrelevant or uninteresting where they erupt on to the surface of the book, that is at least partly because of what may be a virtue and not a fault on my side, namely that the top level of the book, for all its longeurs, has been by and large so compellingly designed that the reader does not want to take time off to stop and plunge beneath the surface. If this is in fact true, of how many books can you say it? And how many books of which you can say it can you say also that you were not, somewhere along the line the first time you read it, bored because you wanted to 'get on.' I do not want to make childish comparisons, but to go to the obvious classics what about The Idiot? The Possessed? What about the beginning of Moby Dick? To say nothing of Wuthering Heights.[3] E.M. Forster, I think, says somewhere that it [is] more of a feat to get by with the end,[4] and in the Volcano at least I claim I have done this, but without the beginning, or rather the first chapter, which as it were answers it, echoes back to it over the bridge of the intervening chapters, the end – and without it the book – would lose much of its meaning.

Since I am pleading for a rereading of Under the Volcano in the light of certain aspects of it which may not perhaps have struck you at all, with a view to any possible alterations, and not making a defense of its every word, I had better say that for my part I feel that the main defect of Under the Volcano, from which the others spring, comes from something irremediable. It is that the author's equipment, such as it is, is subjective rather than objective, a better equipment, in short, for a certain kind of poet than a novelist. On the other hand I claim that just as a tailor will try to conceal the deformities of his client so I have tried, aware of this defect, to conceal in the Volcano as well as possible the deformities of my own mind, taking heart from the fact that since the conception of the whole thing was essentially poetical, perhaps these deformities don't matter so very much after all, even when they show! But poems often have to be read several times before their full meaning will reveal itself, explode in the mind, and it is precisely this poetical conception of the *whole* that I suggest has been, if understandably, missed. But to be more specific: your reader's main objections to the book are:

1. The long initial tedium, which I have discussed in part but will take up again later.

2. The weakness of the character drawing. This is a valid criticism. But I have not exactly attempted to draw characters in the normal sense – though swelp me bob it's only Aristotle who thought character counted least.[5] But here, as I shall say somewhere else, there just isn't *room*: the characters will have to wait for another book, though I did go to incredible trouble to make my major characters seem adequate on the most *superficial* plane on which this book can be read, and I believe in some eyes the character drawing will appear the reverse of weak. (What about female readers?) The truth is that the character drawing is not only weak but virtually nonexistent, save with certain minor characters, the four main characters being intended, in one of the book's meanings, to be

aspects of the same man, or of the human spirit, and two of them, Hugh and the Consul, more obviously are. I suggest that here and there what may look like unsuccessful attempts at character drawing may only be the concrete bases to the creature's lives without which again the book could not be read at all. But weak or no there is nothing I can do to improve it without reconceiving or rewriting the book, unless it is to take something out – but then, as I say, one might be thereby only removing a prop which while it perhaps looked vexing to you in passing, was actually holding something important up.

3. 'The author has spread himself too much. The book is *much too long* and over elaborate for its content, and could have been much more effective if only half or two thirds its present length. The author has overreached himself and is given to eccentric word-spinning and too much stream-of-consciousness stuff.' This may well be so, but I think the author may be forgiven if he asks for a fuller appraisal of that content – I say it all again – in terms of the author's intention as a whole and chapter by chapter before he can reach any agreement with anyone as to what precisely renders it over-elaborate and should therefore be cut to render that whole more effective. If the reader has not got hold of the content at first go how can he decide then what makes it much too long, especially since his reactions may turn out to be quite different on a second reading? And not only authors perhaps but readers can overreach themselves, by reading too fast however carefully they think they are going – and what tedious book is this one has to read so fast? I believe there is such a thing as wandering attention that is the fault neither of reader nor writer: though more of this later. As for the eccentric word-spinning, I honestly don't think there is much that is not in some way thematic. As for the 'stream-of-consciousness stuff', many techniques have been employed, and while I did try to cut mere 'stuff' to a minimum, I suspect that your reader would finally agree, if confronted with the same problems, that most of it could be done in no other way: a lot of the so-called 'stuff' I feel to be justified simply on poetical or dramatic grounds: and I think you would be surprised to find how much of what at first sight seems unnecessary even in this 'stuff' is simply disguised, honest-to-God, exposition, the author trying to proceed on Henry James dictum that what is not vivid is not represented, what is not represented is not art.[6]

To return to the criticisms on the first and second page of your reader's report:

1. 'Flashbacks of the character's past lives and past and present

thoughts and emotions . . . (these) are often tedious and unconvincing.' These flashbacks are necessary however, I feel: where they are really tedious or unconvincing, I should be glad to cut of course, but I feel it only fair to the book that this should be done only after what I shall say later (and have already said) has been taken into account. That which may seem inorganic in itself might prove right in terms of the whole churrigueresque structure I conceived and which I hope may begin soon to loom out of the fog for you like Borda's horrible-beautiful cathedral in Taxco.[7]

2. 'Mexican local colour heaped on in shovelfuls – is very well done and gives one an astonishing sense of the place and the atmosphere.' Thank you very much, but if you will excuse my saying so I did not heap the local colour, whatever that is, on in shovelfuls. I am delighted he likes it, but take issue because what he says implies carelessness. I hope to convince you that, just as I said in my first letter, all that is there is there for a reason. – And what about the use of Nature, of which he says nothing??

3. 'The mescal-inspired phantasmagoria, or heebie-jeebies to which Geoffrey has succumbed . . . is impressive but I think too long, wayward and elaborate – on account of (3) the book inevitably recalls The Lost Weekend.' I will take this in combination with your reader's last and welcome remarks re the books virtues, and the last sentence of the report in which he says: 'Everything should be concentrated on the drunk's inability to rise to the occasion of Yvonne's return, on his delirious consciousness (which is very well done) and on the local colour, which is excellent throughout.' I do not want to quibble – but I do seem to detect something like a contradiction here. Here is my mescal-inspired phantasmagoria, which is impressive but already too long wayward and elaborate, – to say nothing of too much eccentric word-spinning and stream of consciousness stuff – and yet on the other hand, I am invited to concentrate still *more* upon it, since all this can be after all nothing but the delirious consciousness (which is very well done) – and I would like very much to know how I can concentrate still more upon a delirious consciousness without making it still more long wayward elaborate, and since that is the way of delirious consciousnesses, without investing it with still more stream of consciousness stuff: moreover here too is my local colour, and although this is already 'heaped on in shovelfuls' (if excellent throughout) I am invited to concentrate still more upon it and this without calling in the aid of some yet large long-handled scoop-like implement used to lift and throw earth, coal, grain and so forth: nor do I see either how I can very well concentrate very much more than I have on the drunk's inability to rise

to the occasion of Yvonne's return without incurring the risk of being accused of heaping on the mescal inspired phantasmagoria with – at least! – a snow plough. Having let me have my fun, I must say that I admit the critical probity in your reader's last remarks but that it would be impossible to act on his suggestions without writing another book, possibly a better one, but still, another. I respect what he says, for what he seems to be saying is (like Yeats, when he cut nearly all the famous but irrelevant lines out of the Ballad of Reading Gaol and thereby, unfortunately for my thesis, much improved it): a work of art should have but one subject.[8] Perhaps it will be seen that the Volcano, after all, *has* but one subject. This brings me to the unhappy (for me) subject of the Lost Weekend. Mr Jackson likewise obeys your reader's aesthetic and does to my mind an excellent job within the limits he set himself. Your reader could not know, of course that it should have been the other way round – that it was the Lost Weekend that should have inevitably recalled the Volcano, whether this matters or not in the long run it happens to have a very desiccating effect on me. I began the Volcano in 1936, the same year having written, in New York, a novelette of about 100 pages about an alcoholic entitled The Last Address, which takes place mostly in the same hospital ward where Don Birnam spends an interesting afternoon. This – it was too short I thought to publish separately or I would have sent it to you for it was and is, I believe, remarkably good – was accepted and paid for by Story Magazine, who were publishing novelettes at that time, but was never published because they had meantime changed their policy back to shorter things again.[9] It was however, in spite of Zola, accepted as more or less pioneer work in that field, and nine years and two months ago when I was here in this same town in Mexico I conceived the Volcano and I decided really to go to town on the poetical possibilities of that subject.[10] I had written a 40,000-word version by 1937 that Arthur Calder-Marshall liked, but it was not thorough or honest enough. In 1939 I volunteered to come to England but was told to remain in Canada and in 1940, while waiting to be called up, I rewrote the entire book in six months, but it was no damn good, a failure, except for the drunk passages about the Consul but even some of them did not seem to me good enough. I also rewrote The Last Address in 1940-41 and rechristened it Lunar Caustic, and conceived the idea of a trilogy entitled The Voyage That Never Ends for your firm (nothing less than a trilogy would do) with the Volcano as the first, infernal part, a much amplified Lunar Caustic as the second, purgatorial part and an enormous novel I was also working on called In Ballast to the White Sea (which I lost when my house burned down

as I believe I wrote you) as the paradisal third part, the whole to concern the battering the human spirit takes (doubtless because it is
overreaching itself) in its ascent towards its true purpose. At the end
of 1941 I laid aside In Ballast – of which there were 1000 pages of
eccentric word-spinning by this time – and decided to take this mescal-inspired phantasmagoria the Volcano by the throat and really do
something about it, it having become a spiritual thing by this time. I
also told my wife that I would probably cut my throat if during this
period of the world's drunkenness someone else had the same sober
idea. I worked for two more years, eight hours a day, and had just
ascetically completed all the drunken parts to my satisfaction and
there were but three other chapters to rewrite when one day round
about New Years '44, I picked up an American review of The Lost
Weekend. At first I thought it must be The *Last* Weekend, by my
old pal John (Volunteer in Spain) Summerfield, a very strange book
in which figured in some decline no less a person than myself,[11] and I
am still wondering what John thinks about this: but doubtless the
old boy ascribes it to the capitalist system. The Lost Weekend did
not appear in Canada till about April '44 and after reading the book
it became extremely hard for the time being to go on writing and
having faith in mine. I could still congratulate myself upon having In
Ballast up my sleeve however, but only a month or so later that
went completely west with my house. My wife saved the MSS. of the
Volcano, God knows how, while I was doing something about the
forest, and the book was finished over a year ago in Niagara-on-the-
Lake Ontario. We returned to British Columbia to rebuild our
house and since we had some serious setbacks and accidents in doing
so it took some time to get the typescript in order. Meantime, however this Lost Weekend business on top of everything else had
somewhat got me down. The only way I can look upon it is as a
form of punishment. My own worst fault in the past has been precisely lack of integrity and that is particularly hard to face in one's
own work. Youth plus booze plus hysterical identifications plus
vanity plus self-deception plus no work plus more booze. But now
when this ex-psuedo author climbs down from his cross in his little
Oberammergau[12] where he has been hibernating all these years to
offer something really original and terrific to atone for his sins, it
turns out that somebody from Brooklyn has just done the same
thing better. Or has he not?? And how many times has this author
not been told that *that* theme of all themes couldn't sell, that nothing
was duller than dipsomania! Anyway Papa Henry James would certainly have agreed that all this was a turn of the screw.[13] But I think
it not unreasonable to suppose either that he might have added that,

for that matter, the Volcano was, so to say, a couple of turns of the screw on The Lost Weekend anyway. At all events I've tried to give you some of the reasons why I can't turn the Volcano into simply a kind of quid pro quo[14] of the thing, which is what your reader's suggestions would tend to make it, or, if that's unfair to your reader, what I would then tend to make it. These reasons may be briefly crystallized. 1. Your reader wants me to do what I wanted to do myself (and still sometimes regret not having done) but did not do because 2. Under the Volcano, such as it is, is better. After this long digression, to return to the last page of your reader's report: I agree:

A. It is worth my while – and I am anxious – to make the book as effective as possible. But I think it only fair to the book that the lengths which have been gone to already to make it effective as possible *in its own terms* should be appreciated by someone who sees the whole.

B. Cuts should possibly be made in some of the passages indicated, but with the same reservations: I disagree that:

A. Hugh's past is of little interest,

B. or relevance

for reasons I shall set forth. One, which may seem odd, is: There is not a single part of this book I have not submitted to Flaubert's acid test of reading aloud or having read aloud,[15] frequently to the kind of people one would expect to loathe it, and nearly always to people who were not afraid of speaking their minds. Chapter VI – which concerns Hugh's past life – always convulsed people with laughter so much so that often the reader could not go on. Apart from anything else then, and there is much else – what about its humour? This does not take care of its relevance, which I shall point out: but to refer back to something I said before, I submit that the real reason why your reader found this chapter of no interest or relevance was perhaps that I had built better than I knew in the previous chapter, and he wanted to skip and get on to the Consul again. Actually this chapter is the heart of the book and if cuts are to be made in it they should be made on the advice of someone who having seen what the author is driving at has at least an inspiration equivalent to that of the author who created it.

I had wanted to give in the following pages a kind of synopsis of the Volcano chapter by chapter, but since my spare copy of the mss. has not reached me from Canada I will simply suggest as well as I can some of its deeper meanings, and something of the form and intention that was in the author's mind, and that which he feels should be taken into account, should alterations be necessary. The twelve chapters should be considered as twelve blocks, to each of which I have devoted over a period of years a great deal of labour, and I hope to convince you that whatever cuts may be made there must still be twelve chapters. Each chapter is a unity in itself and all are related and interrelated. Twelve is a universal unit. To say nothing of the 12 labours of Hercules,[16] there are 12 hours in a day, and the book is concerned with a single day as well as, though very incidentally, with time: there are 12 months in a year, and the novel is enclosed by a year: while the deeply buried layer of the novel or poem that attaches itself to myth, does so to the Jewish Cabbala where the number 12 is of the highest symbolic importance. The Cabbala is used for poetical purposes because it represents man's spiritual aspiration. The Tree of Life, which is its emblem, is a kind of complicated ladder with Kether, or Light, at the top and an extremely unpleasant abyss some way above the middle.[17] The Consul's spiritual domain in this regard is probably the Qliphoth, the world of shells and demons, represented by the Tree of Life upside down – all this is not important at all to the understanding of the book, I just mention it in passing to hint that, as Henry James says, 'There are depths.'[18] But also, because I have to have my 12: it is as if I hear a clock slowly striking midnight for Faust;[19] as I think of the slow progression of the chapters, I feel it destined to have 12 chapters and nothing more nor less will satisfy me. For the rest the book is written on numerous planes with provision made, it was my fond hope, for almost every kind of reader, my approach with all humility being opposite, I felt, to that of Mr Joyce, i.e., a simplyfy-ing, as far as possible, of what originally suggested itself in far more baffling, complex and esoteric terms, rather than the other way round.[20] The novel can be read simply as a story which you can skip if you want. It can be read as a story you will get more out of if you don't skip. It can be regarded as a kind of symphony, or in another way as a kind of opera – or even a horse opera. It is hot music, a poem, a song, a tragedy, a comedy, a farce, and so forth. It is super-ficial, profound, entertaining and boring, according to taste. It is a prophecy, a political warning, a cryptogram, a preposterous movie, and a writing on the wall. It can even be regarded as a sort of machine: it works too, believe me, as I have found out. In case you think I mean it to be everything but a novel I better say that after all that is all it is intended to be and, though I say so myself, a deeply serious one too. But it is also I claim a work of art somewhat different from the one you suspected it was, and more successful too, even though according to its own lights.

This novel then is concerned principally, in Edmund Wilson's words, (speaking of Gogol) with the forces in man which cause him to be terrified of himself.[21] It is also concerned with the guilt of man, with his remorse, with his ceaseless struggling toward the light under the weight of the past, and with his doom. The allegory is that of the Garden of Eden, the Garden representing the world, from which we ourselves run perhaps slightly more danger of being ejected than when I wrote the book. The drunkenness of the Consul is used on one plane to symbolise the universal drunkenness of mankind during the war, or during the period immediately preceding it, which is almost the same thing, and what profundity and final meaning there is in his fate should be seen also in its universal relationship to the ultimate fate of mankind.

Since it is Chapter I that I believe to be chiefly responsible for your reader's charge of tedium, and since, as I've said, I believe that a reader needs only a little flying start for this apparent tedium to be turned into an increasing suspense from the outset, I will devote more space to this first chapter than to any other, unless it is the sixth, saying also in passing that I believe it will become clear on a second reading that nearly all the material in I is necessary, and if one should try to eliminate this chapter entirely, or chop up all the material in it and stuff it in here and there into the book in wedges and blocks – I even tried it once – it would not only take a very long time but the results would be nowhere near as effective, while it would moreover buckle the very form of the book, which is to be considered like that of a wheel, with 12 spokes, the motion of which is something like that, conceivably, of time itself.

Under the Volcano

(*Note*: the book opens in the Casino de la Selva. Selva means wood and this strikes the opening chord of the Inferno – (remember, the book was planned and still is a kind of Inferno, with Purgatorio and Paradiso to follow, the tragic protagonist in each, like Tchitchikov in Dead Souls,[22] becoming slightly better) in the middle of our life . . . in a dark wood, etc., this chord being struck again in VI, the middle and heart of the book where Hugh, in the middle of his life, recalls at the beginning of that chapter Dante's words: the chord is struck again remotely toward the end of VII where the Consul enters a gloomy cantina called El Bosque, which also means the wood (both of these places being by the way real, one here, the other in Oaxaca) while the chord is resolved in XI, in the chapter concerning Yvonne's death, where the wood becomes real, and dark.)

I*

The scene is Mexico, the meeting place, according to some, of mankind itself, pyre of Bierce and springboard of Hart Crane,[23] the age-old arena of racial and political conflicts of every nature, and where a colorful native people of genius have a religion that we can roughly describe as one of death, so that it is a good place, at least [as good as] Lancashire or Yorkshire, to set our drama of a man's struggle between the powers of darkness and light. Its geographical remoteness from us, as well as the closeness of its problems to our own, will assist the tragedy each in its own way. We can see it as the world itself, or the Garden of Eden, or both at once. Or we can see it as a kind of timeless symbol of the world on which we can place the Garden of Eden, the Tower of Babel and indeed anything else we please. It is paradisal: it is unquestionably infernal. It is, in fact, Mexico, the place of the pulques and chinches,[24] and it is important to remember that when the story opens it is November 1939, not November 1938, the Day of the Dead,[25] and precisely one year after the Consul has gone down the barranca, the ravine, the abyss that man finds himself looking into now (to quote the Archbishop of York) the worse one in the Cabbala, the still unmentionably worse one in the Qliphoth, or simply down the drain, according to taste.

I have spoken already of one reason why I consider this chapter necessary more or less as it is, for the terrain, the mood, the sadness of Mexico, etc., but before I go on to mention any more I must say I fail to see what is wrong with this opening, as Dr Vigil and M. Laruelle, on the latter's last day in the country, discuss the Consul. After their parting the ensuing exposition is perhaps hard to follow and you can say that it is a melodramatic fault that by concealing the true nature of the death of Yvonne and the Consul I have created suspense by false means: myself, I believe the concealment is organic, but even were it not the criterion by which most critics condemn such devices seems to me to be that of pure reporting, and against the kind of novel they admire I am in rebellion, both revolutionary and reactionary at once. You can say too that it is a gamey and outworn trick to begin at the end of the book: it certainly is: I like it in this case and there is moreover a deep motive for it, as I have partially explained, and as I think you will see shortly. During Laruelle's walk we have to give some account of who he is, this is done as clearly as

* [For the following, chapter by chapter, explanation of *Under the Volcano*, annotations have been kept to a minimum. Readers should consult *A Companion to 'Under the Volcano'*.]

possible and if it could be achieved in a shorter or more masterly fashion I would be only too willing to take advice: a second reading however will show you what thematic problems we are also solving on the way, not to say what hams, that have to be there, are being hung in the window. Meanwhile the story is unfolding as the Mexican evening deepens into night: the reader is told of the love of M. Laruelle for Yvonne, the chord of tragic love is struck in the farewell visit at sunset to the Palace of Maximilian,[26] where Hugh and Yvonne are to stand (or have stood) in the noonday in Chapter IV and while M. Laruelle leans over the fateful ravine we have, in his memory, the Taskerson episode. (Taskerson crops up again in V, in VII the Consul sings the Taskerson song to himself, and even in XII he is still trying to walk with the Taskerson 'erect manly carriage.') The Taskerson episode in this Chapter I – damned by implication by your reader – may be unsound if considered seriously in the light of a psychological etiology for the Consul's drinking or downfall, but I have a sincere and not unjustified conviction that it is very funny in itself, and justified in itself musically and artistically at this point as relief, as also for another reason: is it not precisely in this particular passage that your reader may have acquired the necessary *sympathy* with Geoffrey Firmin that enabled him to read past Chapter II and into III without being beset by the tedium there instead – and hence to become much more interested as he went on? – Your reader has omitted the possibility of the poor author's having any wit anywhere. If you do not believe this Taskerson incident is funny, try reading it aloud. I think that wit might seem slightly larger on a second reading, also the drunken man on horseback, who now appears to interrupt M. Laruelle's reverie, by hurtling on up the Calle Nicaragua, might have a larger significance: and still more on a third reading. This drunken horseman is by implication the first appearance of the Consul himself as a symbol of mankind. Here also, as if tangentially (even if your reader saw it as but another shovelful of local colour) is also struck the chord of Yvonne's death in XI; true, this horse is not riderless as yet, but it may well be soon: here man and the force he will release are for the moment fused. (Since by the way there is no suggestion in your reader's report that he has read the rather important Chapter XI, in which there is incidentally some of the action he misses, I had better say at this point that Yvonne is finally killed by a panic stricken horse in XI that the Consul drunkenly releases in a thunderstorm in XII, (the 2 chapters overlapping in time at this juncture) in the erroneous fuddled yet almost praiseworthy belief he is doing somebody a good turn). M. Laruelle now, avoiding the house where I am writing this letter (which is one thing that must certainly be cut if I am not to spend my patrimony sending it airmail) goes gloomily toward the local movie. In the cinema and the bar people are taking refuge from the storm as in the world they are creeping into bomb shelters, and the lights have gone out as they have gone out in the world. The movie playing is Las Manos de Orlac,[27] the same film that had been playing exactly a year before when the Consul was killed, but the man with the bloody hands in the poster, via the German origin on the picture, symbolizes the *guilt* of mankind, which relates him also to M. Laruelle and the Consul again, while he is also more particularly a foreshadowing of the thief who takes the money from the dying man by the roadside in chapter VIII, and whose hands are also covered with blood. Inside the cinema cantina we hear more of the Consul from the cinema manager, Bustamente, much of which again may engage our sympathy for the Consul and our interest in him. It should not be forgotten that it is the Day of the Dead and that on that day in Mexico the dead are supposed to commune with the living. Life however is omnipresent: but meantime there have been both political (the German film star Maria Landrock) and historical (Cortez and Moctezuma) notes being sounded in the background;[28] and while the story itself is being unfolded, the themes and counterthemes of the book are being stated. Finally Bustamente comes back with the book of Elizabethan plays M. Laruelle has left there 18 months before and the theme of Faust is struck. Laruelle had been planning to make a modern movie of Faust but for a moment the Consul himself seems like his Faust, who had sold his soul to the devil. We now hear more of the Consul, his gallant war record, & of a war crime he has possibly committed against some German submarine officers, – whether he is really as much to blame as he tells himself, he is, in a sense, paid back in coin for it at the end of the book and you may say that here the Consul is merely being established in the Grecian manner as a fellow of some stature, so that his fall may be tragic: it could be cut, I suppose, even though this is exactly as I see the Consul – but do we not look at him with more interest thereafter? We also hear that the Consul has been suspected of being an English spy, or 'espider', and though he suffers dreadfully from the mania of persecution, and you feel sometimes, quite objectively, that he is indeed being followed throughout the book, it is as if the Consul himself is not aware of this and is afraid of something quite different: for lack of an object therefore it was the writer's reasonable hope that this first sense of being followed might settle on the reader and haunt him instead. At the moment however Bustamente's sympathy for him should arouse *our* sympathy. This sympathy I feel should be very considerably increased by the Consul's letter which Laruelle reads, and which was never posted, and this letter I believe important: his tortured cry is not answered until in the last chapter, XII, when in the Farolito, the Consul finds Yvonne's letters he has lost and never really read, until this time just before his death. M. Laruelle burns the Consul's letter, the act of which is poetically balanced by the flight of vultures ('like burnt paper floating from a fire') at the end of III, and also by the burning of the Consul's MSS. in Yvonne's dying dream in XI: the storm is over: and –

Outside in the dark tempestuous night backwards revolved the luminous wheel.

This wheel is of course the Ferris wheel in the square, but it is, if you like, also many other things: it is Buddha's wheel of the law (see VII) it is eternity, it is the instrument of eternal recurrence, the eternal return, and it is the form of the book; or superficially it can be seen simply in an obvious movie sense as the wheel of time whirling backwards until we have reached the year before and Chapter II and in this sense, if we like, we can look at the rest of the book through Laruelle's eyes, as if it were his creation.

(*Note*: In the Cabbala, the misuse of magical powers is compared to drunkenness or the misuse of wine, and termed, if I remember rightly, in Hebrew *sod*, which gives us our parallel.[29] There is a kind of attribute of the word *sod* also which implies garden or a neglected garden, I seem to recall too, for the Cabbala is sometimes considered as the garden itself, with the Tree of Life, which is related of course to that Tree the forbidden fruit of which gave one the knowledge of good and evil, and ourselves the legend of Adam and Eve, planted within it. Be these things as they may – and they are certainly at the root of most of our knowledge, the wisdom of our religious thought, and most of our inborn superstitions as to the origin of man, William James if not Freud would certainly agree with me when I say that the agonies of the drunkard find their most accurate poetic analogue in the agonies of the mystic who has abused his powers.[30] The Consul here of course has the whole thing wonderfully and drunkenly mixed up: mescal in Mexico is a hell of a drink but it is still a drink you can get at any cantina, more readily I dare say than Scotch these days at the dear old Horseshoe. But mescal is also a drug, taken in the form of buttons and the transcending of its effects is one of the well-known ordeals that occultists have to go through.[31] It would appear that the Consul has fuddledly come to confuse the two and he is perhaps not far wrong.)

Final note on Chapter I: If this chapter is to be cut can it not be done then with such wisdom as to make the chapter and the book itself better? I feel the chapter makes a wonderful entity and must be cut if at all by someone who at least sees its potentialities in terms of the whole book. I myself don't see much wrong with it. Against the charge of appalling pretentiousness, which is the most obvious one to be made by anyone who has read this letter, I feel I go clear; because these other meanings and danks and darks are not stressed at all: it is only if the reader himself, prompted by instinct or curiosity, cares to invoke them that they will raise their demonic heads from the abyss, or peer at him from above. But even if he is not prompted by anything, new meanings will certainly reveal themselves if he reads this book again. I hope you will be good enough not to remind me that the same might be said of Orphan Annie or Jemima Puddle-duck.[32]

II

You are now back on exactly the same day the year before – the Day of the Dead 1938 – and the story of Yvonne's and the Consul's last day begins at 7 o'clock in the morning on her arrival. I do not see any difficulties here. The mysterious contrapuntal dialogue in the Bella Vista bar you hear is supplied by Weber, you will later see if you watch and listen carefully, the smuggler who flew Hugh down to Mexico, and who is mixed up with the local thugs – as your reader calls them – and Sinarchistas in the Farolito in Parian who finally shoot the Consul. The chord of no se puede vivir sin amar,[33] the writing in gold leaf outside M. Laruelle's house (where I am writing this letter, with my back to the degenerate machicolation, and even if you do not believe in my wheels – the wheel shows up in this chapter in the flywheel in the printer's shop – and so on, you must admit this is funny, as also that it is quite funny that the same movie happens to be playing in town as was playing here nine years ago – not Las Manos de Orlac as it happens but La Tragedia de Mayerling,)[34] is struck ironically by the bartender with his 'absolutamente necessario', the recurring notices for the boxing match symbolise the conflict between Yvonne and the Consul. The chapter is a sort of bridge, it was written with extreme care; it too is absolutemente necessario, I think you would agree yourself on a second reading: it is an entity, a unity in itself, as are all the other chapters; it is, I claim, dramatic, amusing, and within its limits I think is entirely successful. I don't see any opportunity for cuts either.

III

I think will improve on a second reading and still more on a third. But since I believe your reader was impressed by it I will pass over it quickly. Word-spinning flashback while the Consul is lying down flat on his face in the Calle Nicaragua is really very careful exposition. This chapter was first written in 1940, and completed in 1942 long before Jackson went Lostweekending. Cuts should be made with great sympathy ('compliments of the Venezuelan Government' bit might go for instance) by someone – or by the author in conjunction with someone – who is prepared for the book to sink slowly at a not distant date into the action of the mind, and who is not necessarily put off by this. The scene between the Consul and Yvonne where he is impotent is balanced by scene between Consul and Maria in the last chapter: meanings of the Consul's impotence are practically inexhaustible. The dead man with hat over head the Consul sees in the garden is man by the wayside in Chapter VIII. This can happen in really super d.t.s. Paracelsus will bear me out.[35]

IV

Necessary, I feel, much as it is, especially in view of my last sentence re III about the action of the mind. In this there is another kind of action. There is movement and swiftness, it is a contrast, it supplies a needed *ozone*. It gives a needed, also, sympathy and understanding of Mexico and her problems and people from a *material* viewpoint. If the very beginning seems slightly ridiculous you can read it as satire but on a second reading I think the whole will improve vastly. We have now the countermovement of the Battle of the Ebro being lost, while no one does anything about it, which is a kind of correlative of the scene by the roadside in VIII, the victim of which here first makes his appearance outside the cantina La Sepultura, with his horse tethered near, that will kill Yvonne. Man's political aspirations, as opposed to his spiritual, come into view, and Hugh's sense of guilt balances the Consul's. If part of it must be cut, let it be done with a view to the whole – and with genius at least, I feel like saying, – and let it not be cut so that it bleeds. Almost everything in it is relevant even down to the horses, the dogs, the river, and the small talk about the local movie. And what is not, as I say, supplies a needed ozone. For myself I think this ride through the Mexican morning sunlight is one of the best things in the book, and if Hugh strikes you as himself slightly preposterous, there is importance to the theme in the passage re his passionate desire for *goodness* at the close.

V

Is a contrast in the reverse direction, the opening words having an ironic bearing on the last words of IV. The book is now fast sinking into the action of the mind, and away from normal action, and yet I believe that by now your reader was really interested, *too* interested in fact here in the Consul to be able to cope with VI. Here at all events the most important theme of the book appears: 'Le gusta esta jardin?' on the sign. The Consul slightly mistranslates this sign, but – 'You like this garden? Why is it yours? We evict those who destroy!' will have to stand (while we will point out else where that the real translation can be in a certain sense even more more horrifying).[36] The garden is the Garden of Eden, which he even discusses with Mr Quincey. It is the world too. It also has all the cabbalistic attributes of 'garden'. (Though all this is buried far down in the book, so that if you don't want to bother about it, you needn't. I wish that Hugh I'Anson Fausset, however, one of your own writers, one whose writings I very much admire and some of whose writings have had a very formative influence on my own life, could read the Volcano.)[37] On the surface I am going to town here on the subject of the drunkard and I hope do well and amusingly. Parian again is death. Word-spinning phantasmagoria somewhere toward end of first part is necessary. It should be clear that the Consul has a blackout and that the second part in the bathroom is concerned with what he remembers half deliriously of the missing hour. Most of what he remembers is again disguised exposition and drama which carries on the story to the question: shall they go to Guanajuato (life) or Tomalin, which of course involves Parian (death). For the rest the Consul at one point identifies himself with the infant Horus, about which or whom the less said the better; some mystics believe him responsible for this last war, but I need another language I guess to explain what I mean. Perhaps Mr Fausset would explain, but at all events you don't have to think about it because the passage is only short, and reads like quite good lunacy. The rest I think is perfectly good clean d.t.s such as your reader would approve of. This was first written in 1937. Final revision was made in March 1943. This too is an entity in itself. Possible objection could be to the technique of the second part but I believe it is a subtle way to do a difficult thing. Cuts might be made here, I guess, but they would have to be inspired at least as much as the chapter was.

VI

Here we come to the heart of the book which, instead of going into high delirious gear of the Consul returns instead, surprisingly although inevitably if you reflect, to the uneasy, but healthy, systole-diastole of Hugh. In the middle of our life . . . and the theme of the Inferno is stated again, then follows the enormously long *straight* passage. This passage is the one your reader claims has little or no interest or relevance and I maintain he skipped because of a virtue on my side, namely he was more interested in the Consul himself. But here the guilt theme, and the theme of man's guilt, takes on a new shade of meaning. Hugh may be a bit of a fool but he none the less typifies the sort of person who may make or break our future: in fact he *is* the future in a certain sense. He is everyman tightened up a screw, for he is just beyond being mediocre. And he is the youth of everyman. Moreover his frustrations with his music, with the sea, in his desire to be good and decent, his self-deceptions, triumphs, defeats and dishonesties (and once more I point out that a much needed ozone blows into the book here with the sea air) his troubles with his guitar, are everyone's frustrations, triumphs, defeats, dishonesties and troubles with their quid pro quo of a guitar. And his desire to be a composer or musician is everyone's innate desire to be a poet of life in some way, while his desire to be accepted at sea is everyone's desire, conscious or unconscious, to be a part – even if it doesn't exist – of the brotherhood of man. He is revealed as a frustrated fellow whose frustrations might just as well have made him a drunk too, just like the Consul, (who was frustrated as a poet – as who is not? – this indeed is another thing that binds us all together – but for whose drunkenness no satisfactory etiology is ever given unless it is in VII. 'But the cold world shall not know.') Hugh feels he has betrayed himself by betraying his brother and also betrayed the brotherhood of man by having been at one time an anti-Semite. But when, in the middle of the chapter, which is also the middle of the book, his thoughts are interrupted by Geoffrey's call of 'Help', you can receive, I claim, upon rereading, a frisson of a quite different calibre to that received when reading such pieces as William Wilson or other stories about dopplegangers.[38] Hugh and the Consul are the same person, but within a book which obeys not the laws of other books, but those it creates as it goes along. I have reason to believe that much of this long straight passage is extremely funny anyway and will cause people to laugh aloud. We now proceed into the still greater nonsense and at the same time far more desperate seriousness of the shaving scene. Hugh shaves the corpse – but I cannot be persuaded that nonetheless much of this is not very hilarious indeed. We are then introduced to Geoffrey's room, with his picture of his old ship the Samaritan (and the theme is struck remotely again of the man by the wayside in VIII) upon which ship it has been mentioned before in I etc. that he either has committed or imagines he has but was certainly made in part responsible for, a crime against a number of German submarine officers – valid at least as any crime we may have committed in the past against Germany in general, that ugsome child of Europe whose evil and destructive energy is so much responsible for all our progress. At the same time he shows Hugh his alchemistic books, and we are for a moment, if in a psuedo-farcical situation, standing before the evidence of what is no less than the magical basis of the world. You do not believe the world has a magical basis, especially while the Battle of the Ebro is going on, or worse, bombs are dropping in Bedford Square?[39] Well, perhaps I don't either. But the point is that Hitler *did*. And Hitler was another psuedo black magician out of the same drawer as Amfortas in the Parsifal he so much admired, and who has had the same inevitable fate.[40] And if you don't believe that a British general actually told me that the real reason why Hitler destroyed the Polish Jews was to prevent their cabbalistic knowledge being used against *him* you can let me have my point on poetical grounds, I repeat, since it is made at a very sunken level of the book and is not very important here anyway. Saturn lives at 63, and Bahomet lives next door, however, and don't say I didn't tell you![41] – The rest of the chapter, and all this is probably too long, takes Hugh and the Consul and Yvonne, meeting Laruelle on the way (I hope dramatically) up to the house where I am now writing you this letter: the point about the postcard the Consul receives (from the same tiny bearded postman who delivered your delayed letter to me on New Years Eve) is that it was posted about a year before in 1937 not long after she left, or was sent away by the Consul (following her affair with Laruelle but probably so that the Consul could drink in peace) and that its tone would seem to suggest that her going away was only a final thing in the Consul's mind, that really they loved each other all the time, had just had a lover's quarrel, and in spite of M. Laruelle, the whole thing was absolutely unnecessary. The chapter closes with a dying fall, like the end of some guitar piece of Ed Lang's,[42] or conceivably Hugh's (and in this respect the brackets earlier might represent the 'breaks') oddly but rightly, I felt, the path theme of Dante, however, reappearing and fading with the vanishing road.

I believe on rereading this chapter it will seem to have much more relevance than before and its humor will appear as more considerable. On the other hand this is undoubtedly the juiciest area for your surgeon's knife. The middle part of the shaving scene was written in 1937, as was the very end, that much comprising the whole chapter then. The new version was done in 1943 but I had not quite finally revised it in 1944 when my house burned down. The final revisions I made later in 1944 comprised the first work I had been able to do since the fire, in which several pages of this chapter and notes for cuts were lost, and it well may be the job is shaky or forced here and there. This is the first point in the book where I can be persuaded to share your reader's objections, I think, to any extent. Some of it may be in a kind of bad taste. On the other hand I feel it deserves a careful rereading – I say again and again – in the light of the form and intention I have indicated, bearing in mind that the journalistic style of the first part is intended to represent Hugh himself. In brief, I could stand even slashing cuts were your surgeon to say 'This would be more effective if such and such were done' – and I saw he was taking everything into account. If a major operation by a sympathetic surgeon will save the patient's life, O.K., but, even though I do live in Mexico, I'm damned if I'm going to help him cut out his heart. (And then, when he's dead, 'just flop it back in again anyway,' as the nurse said to me having just attended the post mortem.)

VII

Here we come to seven, the fateful, the magic, the lucky good-bad number and the scene in the tower, where I write this letter. By a coincidence I moved to the tower on January 7 – I was living in another apartment in the same house, but downstairs, when I got your letter. My house burned down on June 7, when I returned to the burned site someone had branded, for some reason, the number 7 on a burned tree; why was I not a philosopher? Philosophy has been dying since the days of Duns Scotus,[43] though it continues underground, if quacking slightly. Boehme would support me when I speak of the passion for order even in the smallest things that exist in the universe.[44] 7 too is the number on the horse that will kill Yvonne and 7 the hour when the Consul will die. – I believe the intention of this chapter to be quite clear and that it is one your reader approves of and I think too it is probably one of the best in the book. It was first written in 1936, rewritten in 1937, 1940, 1941, 1943, and finally 1944. Parallels with the Lost Weekend I think are most in evidence in this chapter. One long one that does not appear and which was written long before the L.W.E. I hoiked out with a heavy heart, but imbued with the spirit of competition, then added something else to my telephone scene to outdo him. I was particularly annoyed because my telephone scene in III and this one before I revised it, as I have said, were written long before Jackson's book appeared. Another parallel toward the end where when he had his drink before him he doesn't pick it up will have to stand: it was written in 1937 anyway. I allowed myself also in the conversation in the middle with Laruelle a little of the Consul's professional contempt for the belief that the d.t.s is the end of everything and I think if you ever publish the book you might do me justice by saying that this begins where Jackson leaves off. If there must be cuts here again I say they should be made by someone who appreciates this chapter as an entity right down to the bit about Samaritana mia and with reference to the whole book. There are the usual thicknesses and obliquities, stray cards from the Tarot pack, and odd political and mystical chords and dissonances being sounded here and there in this chapter but I won't go into them: but there is also, above all, the continued attention to the *story*. The horseman, first seen in IV and who is to be the man by the roadside, is seen again going up the hill, and whose horse, with the number 7 on it, will kill Yvonne. This chapter constitutes almost the Consul's last chance and if the book has been read carefully I feel you should have a fine sense of doom by this time. Es inevitable la muerte del Papa is quite possibly just an anachronism, but I feel it must stand for I hold this a fine ending.

(Notes re local color heaped on in shovelfuls: this chapter is a good example and every damn thing in it is organic. The madman futilely and endlessly throwing a bicycle tire in front of him, the man stuck half way up the slippery pole – these are projections of the Consul and of the futility of his life, and at the same time are *right*, are *true*, are what one sees here. Life is a forest of symbols, as Baudelaire said, but I won't be told you can't see the wood for the trees here!)[45]

VIII

Here the book, so to speak, goes into reverse – or more strictly speaking, it begins to go downhill, though not, by any means, I hope, in the sense of deteriorating! (the first word) toward the abyss I think it one of the better chapters though it needs reading carefully, I feel the reader will be well rewarded. Man dying by the roadside with his horse branded No. 7 near is, of course, the chap who'd been sitting outside the pulqueria in IV, had appeared singing in VII when the Consul identified himself with him. He is, obviously, mankind himself, mankind dying, then, – in the Battle of the Ebro, or now, in Europe, while we do nothing, or if we would, have put ourselves in a position where we *can* do nothing, but talk, while he goes on dying – in another sense he is the Consul too. I claim the chapter proceeds well on its own account while these meanings are revealed without

being too much laboured. I think the meaning is obvious, intentionally so, almost, in a sense, like a cartoon, and on one plane as
oversimplified as journalism, intentionally too, for it is through
Hugh's eyes. The story on the top plane is being carried on normally
however, and while the local political significance would be clear to
anyone who knows Mexico, the wider political and religious significance must be self-evident to anyone. It was the first chapter written
in the book; the incident by the roadside, based on a personal experience, was the germ of the book. I feel that some wag not too
unlike your reader might tell me at this point that I would do better
to reduce the book back to this original germ so that we could all
have it printed in O'Brien's Best Short Stories of 1956,[46] with luck,
instead of as a novel, and against this resourceful notion I can only
cite the example of Beethoven, who also was somewhat inclined to
overspread himself I seem to think, even though most of his themes
are actually so simple they could be played by just rolling an orange
down the black keys.[47] The chapter is more apropos now than then,
in 1936: then there were no deputies – though I invented them in
1941: now there are; in fact one is living in an apartment downstairs. I
don't think it can be cut: but if it must be, it should be done with the
same reservations I have made elsewhere. As for the xopilotes, the
vultures, I should add that they are more than merely cartoon birds:
they are real in these parts, in fact one is looking at me as I write,
none too pleasantly either: they fly through the whole book and in
XI become as it were archetypal, Promethean fowl. Once considered
by ornithologists the first of birds all I can say is that they are more
than likely to be the last.

IX

This chapter was originally written in 1937 but then it was through
Hugh's eyes. Then it was rewritten as through the Consul's eyes.
And now – as it must be for the sake of balance if you reflect – it is
through Yvonne's eyes. Possibly it could have been seen just as well
through the bull's eyes, but it reads very well aloud and I think is
among other things a successful and colorful entity in itself and
musically speaking ought to be an exceedingly good contrast to VIII
and X. Readers might disagree about flashbacks here, some think it
good, others suspecting a belated attempt to draw character and at
that a meretricious one – though I feel many of your *feminine* readers
might approve. The flashbacks are not here though either for their
own sake, or particularly for the sake of character, which as I said
was my last consideration as it was Aristotle's – since there isn't *room*

for one thing. (It was, I think, one of your own writers, and a magnificent one, Sean O'Faolain, who put this heretical notion even further into my headpiece about the comparative unimportance of character anyway.[48] Since he is a wonderful character drawer himself his words bore weight with me. Were not Hamlet and Laertes, he says, at the final moment, almost the same person? The novel then, he went on to argue, should reform itself by drawing upon its ancient Aeschylean and tragic heritage. There are a thousand writers who can draw adequate characters till all is blue for one who can tell you anything new about hell fire. And I am telling you something new about hell fire. I see the pitfalls – it can be an easy way out of hard work, an invitation to eccentric word spinning, and labored phantasmagorias, and subjective inferior masterpieces that on closer investigation turn out not even to be bonafide documents but like my own Ultramarine, to be apparently translated with a windmill out of the unoriginal Latvian, but just the same in our Elizabethan days we used to have at least passionate poetic writing about things that will always mean something and not just silly ass style and semicolon technique: and in this sense I am trying to remedy a deficiency, to strike a blow, to fire a shot for you as it were, roughly in the direction, say, of another Renaissance: it will probably go straight through my brain but that is another matter. Possibly too the Renaissance is already in full swing but if so I have heard nothing of this in Canada.) No, the real point of this chapter is Hope, with a capital H, for this note must be struck in order to stress the later downfall. Though even the capacity of the intelligent reader for suspending his disbelief is enormous I didn't intend that this feeling of hope should be experienced by the reader in quite the ordinary way, though he can if he wants to. I intended somehow the feeling of hope per se to transcend even one's interest in the characters. Since these characters are in one way 'Things,' as that French philosopher of the Absurd fellow has it,[49] or even if you believe in them you know perfectly well that they are ditched anyhow, this hope should be, rather, a transcendent, a universal hope. The novel meanwhile is, as it were, teetering between past and future – between despair (the past) and hope – hence these flashbacks (some of them could doubtless be cut slightly but I don't think I could do it). Shall the Consul, once more, go forward and be reborn -- as if previously to Guanajuato – is there a chance that he may be, at any rate on the top level? – or shall he sink back into degeneracy and Parian and extinction. He is one aspect of Everyman (just as Yvonne is so to speak the eternal woman, as in Parsifal, Kundry, whoever she was, angel and destroyer both).[50] The other aspect of Everyman is of course Hugh who all this time is somewhat preposterously subduing the bull: in short, though with intentional absurdity – the whole book for that matter can be seen as a kind of gruesome and serious absurdity, just like the world in fact – he conquers the animal forces of nature which the Consul later lets loose. The threads of the various themes of the book begin to be drawn together. The close of the chapter, with the Indian carrying his father, is a restatement and universalising of the theme of humanity struggling on under the eternal tragic weight of the past. But it is also Freudian (man eternally carrying the psychological burden of his father) Sophoclean, Oedipean, what have you, which relates the Indian to the Consul again.

If cuts are made those things and the fact that it is a unity in itself, as usual, should be taken into account. It was finally completed as it stands in 1944.

X

This was first written in '36-'37 and rewritten at various periods up to 1943. This final version was written after my fire, in the summer and fall of 1944, and I dare say this is another obvious candidate for your surgeon's knife. Nothing I wrote after the fire save most of XI has quite the integrity of what I wrote before it but though this chapter seems absolutely interminable, indeed intolerable, when read aloud, I submit it to be a considerable inspiration and one of the best of the lot. The opening train theme is related to Freudian death dreams and also to 'A corpse will be transported by express' of the beginning of II and I can't see that it is not extremely thrilling in its gruesome fashion. Passage that follows re the 'virgin for those who have nobody with' ties up with opening pages of Chapter I and were written previously – as was the humorous menu section. I can see valid objections though to the great length of some of the Tlaxcala stuff from the folder: but I was absolutely unable to resist it. I cut and cut as it was, I even sacrificed two good points, namely that Tlaxcala is probably the only capital in the world where black magic is still a working proposition, and that it is also the easiest place in the world to get a divorce in, and then could cut no more: I thought it too good, while the constant repetition of churrigueresque 'of an overloaded style' seemed to be a suggestion that the book was satirizing itself. This Tlaxcala folder part has a quite different effect when read with the eyes, as it will be (I hope) – then you can of course get it much more swiftly; and I had originally thought it would possibly go quicker still if some experiment were made with the typesetting such as the occasional use of black letter for the headings juxtaposed with anything from cursive down to diamond type for the rest and back again according to the reader's interest or the Consul's state of delirium: some simplification of this suggestion might be extremely effective but I do not see how it can be very popular with you and is perhaps a little much anyway. At all events I believe there are strange evocations and explosions here that have merit in themselves even if you are not closely following what is happening, much as, even if you can't make out what Harpo is saying, the sound of the words themselves may be funny.[51] Revelations such as that Pulqueria, which is a kind of Mexican pub, is also the name of Raskolnikov's mother should doubtless not be taken too seriously, but the whole Tlaxcala business *does* have an underlying deep seriousness. Tlaxcala, of course, just like Parian, is death: but the Tlaxcalans were Mexico's traitors – here the Consul is giving way to the forces within him that are betraying himself, that indeed have now finally betrayed him, and the general plan of the whole phantasmagoric thing seems to me to be right. Dialogue here brings in the theme of war, which is of course related to the Consul's self-destruction. This chapter was finally completed about a year before atom bombs, etc. But if it does so happen that man is now in danger of finding himself in the evil position of the black magician of old who discovered suddenly that all the elements of the universe were against him, the old Consul might be given credit for pointing out as much in a crazy passage where he even names the elements uranium plutonium, and so forth; undoubtedly it is of no interest as prophecy any more, but I can't say it dates! This little bit is, of course, thematic, if you reflect. At the end of this chapter the volcanoes, which have been getting closer throughout, are used as a symbol of approaching war. In spite of its apparent chaos this chapter has been written very carefully and with attention to every word. It too, is an entity in itself, and if it must be cut I ask that the cutter see it also as an entity and in its place in the book. Though I suggest it is dramatically extremely powerful regarded in a certain light, I am more disposed to have this chapter and chapter VI cut than any other, if cuts there must be, and if in the case of this chapter it is merely rendered more dramatic and more powerful.

XI

This was the last chapter I wrote and was completed in late 1944, though I had had its conception in mind for a long time. My object was to pull out here all the stops of Nature, to go to town, as it were, on the natural elemental beauty of the world and the stars, and through the latter to relate the book, as it was related through the wheel at the end of Chapter I, to eternity. Here the wheel appears in another guise, the wheel of the motion of the stars and constellations themselves through the universe. And here again appears the dark wood of Dante, this time as a real wood and not just a cantina or the name of one. Here again too appears the theme of the Day of the Dead, the scene in the cemetery balancing the scene of the mourners at the opening of the book, but this time it has tremendously more human emphasis. The chapter again acts as a double contrast to the lesser horrors of X and the worse ones of XII. On the surface Hugh and Yvonne are simply searching for the Consul, but such a search would have added meaning to anyone who knows anything of the Eleusinian mysteries, and the same esoteric idea of this kind of search also appears in Shakespeare's Tempest.[52] Here however all the meanings of the book have to be blended somehow in an unpretentious and organic manner in the interest of the tale itself and this was no mean task, especially as Yvonne had to be killed by a horse in a thunderstorm, and Hugh left holding a guitar in a dark wood, singing drunken songs of revolutionary Spain. Could Thomas Hardy do as much?[53] I suspect your reader, who doesn't even mention the very important fact of Yvonne's death, of not reading this chapter at all – and I take this again as a compliment that he was too interested in what happened to the Consul to do more than glance at it. Be that as it may, I feel passionately that the chapter comes off, partly because I came to believe so absolutely in it. Actually someone being killed by a horse in a thunderstorm is nothing like so unusual an occurrence as you might suppose in these parts, where the paths in the forests are narrow and horses when they do get frightened become more wildly panic-stricken than did the ancestors of their riders who thought the horses Cortez sent against them were supernatural beings. I feel that this chapter like all the rest calls for a sympathetic rereading. It is quite short and I don't think can be cut at all and is *absolutely necessary*. Yvonne's dying visions hark back to her first thoughts at the beginning of chapter II and also to Chapter IX, but the very end of the chapter has practically stepped outside the bounds of the book altogether. Yvonne imagines herself gathered up and swept up to the stars: a not dissimilar idea appears at the end of one of Julian Green's books, but my notion came obviously enough from Faust, where Marguerite is hauled up to heaven on pulleys, while the devil hauls Faust down to hell.[54] Here Yvonne imagines herself voyaging straight up through the stars to the Pleiades, while the Consul is, simultaneously and incidentally, being cast straight down the abyss. The horse of course is the evil force that the Consul has released. But by this time you know the humbler aspect of this horse. It is no less than the horse you last heard of in X and that first appeared in IV, likewise riderless, during Hugh and Yvonne's ride, outside the pulqueria La Sepultura.

(*Note*: Is it too much to say that all these chords, struck and resolved, while no reader can possibly apprehend them on first or even fourth reading, consciously, nevertheless vastly contribute *unconsciously* to the final weight of the book?)

XII

This chapter was first written at the beginning of 1937 and I think is definitely the best of the lot. I have scarcely changed it since 1940 – though I made some slight additions and subtractions in 1942 and substituted the passage 'How like are the groans of love to the groans of the dying' etc. in 1944 – for another one not so good. I do think it deserves more than rereading carefully and that it is not only not fair to say it merely recalls The Lost Weekend but ridiculous. In any event, I believe, it goes even on the superficial plane a good deal further than that in terms of human agony, and, as his book does, it can widen, I think, one's knowledge of hell. In fact the feeling you are supposed to get from this chapter is an almost biblical one. Hasn't the guy had enough suffering? Surely we've reached the end now. But no. Apparently it's only just starting. All the strands of the book, political, esoteric, tragical, comical, religious, and what not are here gathered together and in the Farolito in Parian we are standing amid the confusion of tongues of Biblical prophecy. Parian, as I have said, has represented death all along, but this, I would like the reader to feel, is far worse than that. This chapter is the easterly tower, Chapter I being the westerly, at each end of my churrigueresque Mexican cathedral, and all the gargoyles of the latter are repeated with interest in this. While the doleful bells of one echo the doleful bells of the other, just as the hopeless letters of Yvonne the Consul finally finds here answer the hopeless letter of the Consul M. Laruelle reads precisely a year later in Chapter I. Possibly you did not find much to criticise in this chapter but I believe it will immeasurably improve when the whole is taken into account. The slightly ridiculous horse that the Consul releases and which kills Yvonne is of course the destructive force we have heard of before, some fifteen times, I am afraid, in this letter and suggested first in I, and which his own final absorption by the powers of evil releases. There was a half-humorous foreshadowing of his action in VII, in terms of a quotation from Goethe, when Laruelle and he were passed by the horse and its rider, who waved at them and rode off singing. There still remain passages of humour in this chapter and they are necessary because after all we are expected to believe and not believe and then again to believe: the humour is a kind of bridge between the naturalistic and the transcendental and then back to the naturalistic again, though that humour I feel always remains true to the special reality created by the chapter itself. I am so inordinately proud of this chapter that you will be surprised when I say that I think it possible that it too can be cut here and there, though the deadly flat tempo of the beginning seems to me essential and important. I don't think the chapter's final effect should be depressing: I feel you should most definitely get your katharsis, while there is even a hint of redemption for the poor old Consul at the end, who realises that he is after all part of humanity: and indeed, as I have said before, what profundity and final meaning there is in his fate should be seen also in its universal relationship to the ultimate fate of mankind.

> You like this garden?
> Why is it yours?
> We evict those who destroy!

Reading all this over I am struck among other things such as that writers can always grow fancy and learned about their books and say almost anything at all, as Sherwood Anderson once said in another context, by how much stress is laid on the esoteric element.[55] This does not of course matter two hoots in a hollow if the whole thing is not good art, and to make it such was the whole of my labour. The esoteric business was only a deep laid anchor anyway but I think I may be forgiven for bringing it in evidence since your reader never saw that the book had any such significance at all. That is right too; I don't care whether the reader does or doesn't see it, but the meaning is there just the same and I might have stressed another element of the book just as well. For they are all involved with each other and their fusion is the book. I believe it more than comes off, on the whole, and because of this belief I am asking you for this revaluation of it as it was conceived and upon its own terms. Though I would be grievously disappointed were you not to publish it I can scarcely do otherwise than this, believing as I do that the things that stand in the way of its appreciation are largely superficial. On the other hand I am extremely sensible of the honour you do me by considering it and I do not wish to be vain or stubborn about cuts, even large ones, where a more piercing and maturer eye than mine can see the advantage to the *whole*, the wound being drawn together. I can hope only that I have made some case for a further look at the thing being worth while. Whether it sells or not seems to me either way a risk. But there is something about the destiny of the creation of the book that seems to tell me it just might go *on* selling a very long time. Whether this is the same kind of delusion, at best, that beset another of your authors, Herman Melville, when he wrote such berserk pieces as Pierre remains to be seen, but certain it is in that case that no major alterations could have altered its destiny, prevented its plates from being burned, or its author from becoming a customs inspector.[56] I was reading somewhere of that internal basic use of time which makes or breaks a motion picture, and which is the work of the director or cutter. It depends on the speed at which one scene moves and on the amount of footage devoted to another: and it depends also on what sequences are placed between others, because that way movies are made allows you to shift whole sequences about. I believe that the reader whose report you sent me was at least impressed to the extent that he read the book creatively, but too much so, as if he were already a director and cutter combined of some *potential* work, without stopping to ask himself how far it had already been directed and cut, and what internal basic use of time and so on, was making him as interested as he was.

But what, I repeat, of the reaction of your first reader? There is a certain disparity in tone between your letters of October 15 (received in Canada Nov. 2) and that of 29th Nov. (received here in Mexico Dec. 31) i.e. in your first one you do not mention any criticisms but simply say that your reader was greatly impressed and that it was a long time since you had begun to read a book with such hope and expectation as in reading Under the Volcano and seizing, perhaps too hastily, on this, I can deduce only that your first reader was tremendously more sympathetic towards it??? You also said 'I will send you a cable when I have finished reading it so it is possible you may get a cable before receiving this letter.' Of course I now see why you found this extremely difficult or impossible but at that time I waited and waited in vain for that cable as you can only wait in winter in the Canadian Wilderness, unless it is in Heckmondwike, Yorks.[57] When therefore I received your letter of 29th Nov. here on New Year's Eve, with your second reader's report, it produced, together with the sense of triumph, one of those barranca–like drops in spirits peculiar to authors and it is to this I must attribute the time I've taken to reply. Talk about turning the accomplishment of many years into an hour glass – but I never heard of it being turned into a mescal glass before, and a small one at that! – However after puzzling my brains, I decided that however your own feelings might lean x–ward or y–ward of the crystallization of reaction, you were putting me, as you had every right to do, on the spot. In short, you were saying: 'If this book is any damn good as it is he'll explain why!' I was being invited, I thought, if necessary, to do battle. So here is the battle. For taking such a long time about it I sincerely apologise but it has been a difficult letter to write.

I have now received your second letter with a copy of the report and I thank you for this. On your twenty-fifth anniversary I heartily congratulate you. It seems to me that among other things your firm has done more international good than any other. For myself, my first school prize was the Hairy Ape, ourselves being allowed to choose our own prizes when they were books, so with your volume of O'Neill's plays containing the Hairy Ape, complete with Latin inscription inside, I was therefore presented by the Headmaster on Prize Day. Those O'Neill volumes with the labels, I guess, sent me to sea and everywhere else, but also for the Melville volumes, the O'Brien books, Hugh I'Anson Fausset, and among lesser known things the strange Leo Steni novels, and Calder-Marshall's About Levy, for these and hundreds of other things besides I am eternally grateful.[58] When I was looking in '28 or '29 for some work in England by the American Conrad Aiken sure enough I found Costumes by Eros published by your firm and this led to a lasting and valuable friendship. (I believe him indisputably one of the world's nine or ten greatest living writers and I mention in passing that 2/3 of his stuff has never had a fair hearing in England and is probably just lying around somewhere. I believe him to be living now at his old English home again at Jeakes House, Rye, Sussex.) All this by the way.

I have spoken of thinking of the book as like some Mexican churrigueresque cathedral: but that is probably just confusing, the more especially since I have been quoting Aristotle at you, and the book has in its odd way a severe classical pattern – you can even see the German submarine officers taking revenge on the Consul in the form of the sinarquistas and semi-fascist brutos at the end, as I said before. No – please put all that down to the local tropic fever which just recently has been sending my temperature up too far. No. The book should be seen as essentially *trochal*, I repeat, the form of it as a wheel so that, when you get to the end, if you have read carefully, you should want to turn back to the beginning again, where it is not impossible, too, that your eye might alight once more upon Sophocles' Wonders are many, and none is more wonderful than man – just to cheer you up. For the book was so designed, counterdesigned and interwelded that it could be read an indefinite number of times and still not have yielded all its meanings or its drama or its poetry: and it is upon this fact that I base my hope in it, and in that hope that, with all its faults, and now with all the redundancies of my letter, I have offered it to you.

Yours very sincerely,

Malcolm Lowry

Annotations:

1 Jonathan Cape's 29 November 1945 letter to Lowry, with William Plomer's report, are in the Lowry collection (UBC 1:11). Although Plomer praised the book, he recommended that it be 'drastically shortened.'

2 T.S. Eliot's poem *The Waste Land* (1922) had a marked influence on Lowry, which is particularly evident in the 1933 edition of *Ultramarine*.

3 *The Idiot* (*Idiot* 1866; trans. 1914) and *The Possessed* (*Besy* 1871-72; trans. 1931) are novels by Feodor Dostoevsky; *Moby-Dick* (1851) is Herman Melville's American classic; and *Wuthering Heights* (1847) is Emily Brontë's novel; all were Lowry favourites.

4 Edward Morgan Forster (1879-1970), the English novelist and Fellow of King's College, Cambridge, makes this point more than once in his 1926-27 Clark Lectures at Trinity College, Cambridge, which were published as *Aspects of the Novel* (1927). For example, in his discussion of plot he warns that 'the inherent defect of novels [is that] they go off at the end.'

5 In his *Poetics* the Greek philosopher Aristotle (384-322 BC) argues that plot, not character, is the 'soul' of drama, and he focuses critical and artistic attention upon dramatic form and structure.

6 Henry James (1843-1916), the American novelist, also wrote critical prefaces to his novels, essays, and many letters in which he discusses art in terms very like these, but, although both the idea and the language are Jamesian, the words Lowry is quoting are Richard P. Blackmur's, from his introduction to James's *The Art of the Novel* (New York: Scribner's Sons, 1934), p. xi: 'The argument which runs throughout the Prefaces, [is] that in art what is merely stated is not presented, what is not presented is not vivid, what is not vivid is not represented, and what is not represented is not art.' As Frederick Asals has noted (*Swinging the Maelstrom*, 95) this 'dictum' meant a great deal to Lowry, who printed it on a piece of paper in large capitals and kept it by his desk as a motto.

7 Lowry is referring to the remarkable church of Santa Prisca in the Mexican town of Taxco. The church was built by José de la Borda between 1748 and 1758 in the ornate baroque style known as churrigueresque, after the Spanish architect José Churriguera. See Lowry's reference to Taxco in his 1950 letter (**433**) to Viking Press, the publisher of Samuel Putnam's translations of Cervantes.

8 When W.B. Yeats prepared *The Oxford Book of Modern Verse, 1892-1935* (Oxford: Clarendon, 1936), he decided to edit Oscar Wilde's poem *The*

Ballad of Reading Gaol (1898) severely. In his Introduction Yeats boasted that he had 'plucked out even famous lines because, effective in themselves, put into the Ballad they became artificial, trivial, arbitrary; a work of art can have but one subject' (p. vii). Margerie had given Malcolm a copy of the *Oxford Book of Modern Verse* for his birthday in 1941, and he has paraphrased Yeats's remark from memory.

9   I have not been able to confirm this version of events surrounding Lowry, Whit Burnett, and *Story* magazine; see Day (197-98).

10 Lowry is no doubt thinking of *d'Assommoir* (1877), a grim naturalist novel about life in the bars and taverns of a city, by the French writer Émile Zola (1840-1902).

11 Lowry speaks of his old friend in the same terms in his 6 June 1945 letter (**202**) to Harold Matson; 'The Last Week End' has not been published.

12 Oberammergau is the Bavarian town in the foothills of the Alps where the famous Passion-Play Festival has been held every ten years since 1634.

13 Lowry's image here is an allusion to Henry James's famous story 'The Turn of the Screw' (1898).

14 *Quid pro quo* is the Latin expression meaning 'this for that.'

15 The French novelist Gustave Flaubert (1821-80), author of *Madame Bovary* (1857), frequently read aloud from his work to his friends or at the top of his voice when alone in his study, which he called his *gueuloir* (place for shouting aloud).

16 Hercules (the Roman name for the Greek hero Heracles) was renowned for his feats of courage and strength. His twelve labours, for which he was armed by the gods, included slaying or capturing dangerous beasts, and other less bloody tasks, such as cleaning the stables of Augeas.

17 Lowry had learned about the cabbala from Charles Stansfeld-Jones, and his description of the Tree of Life closely follows that offered by Stansfeld-Jones in *Q.B.L. or The Bride's Reception*, first published in the twenties and reprinted by Samuel Weiser in 1972.

18 I have not found an exact source for this familiar Jamesian idea.

19 The Faust story plays a key role in *Under the Volcano* from the earliest drafts. Here Lowry is referring specifically to scene 19 of Christopher Marlowe's tragedy *Doctor Faustus* (ca 1592), when the clock strikes twelve and the desperate Faustus is carried off to hell by devils.

20 There has been considerable debate about the degree to which Lowry was influenced by James Joyce, but in all his extant references to Joyce, Lowry dismisses any direct influence and often seems critical of Joyce's style and methods.

21 In his essay 'A Treatise on Tales of Horror,' first published in the *New Yorker*, 27 May 1944, Edmund Wilson sees Gogol, Poe, and Kafka as the three greatest writers of tales of horror that 'lay hold on the terrors that lie deep in the human psyche and that cause man to fear himself.'

22 Nikolai Gogol (1809-52) published part 1 of *Dead Souls* in 1842. The hero, Tchitchikov, travels about the neighbourhood of a Russian town

buying the peasants who have died but still appear on the register for tax purposes. This charming buyer of 'dead souls' is exposed as a fraud but continues on his way; Gogol did not live to complete part 2 of the novel, in which he had planned to bring his hero to judgement.

23 Ambrose Bierce (1842-1914?) was an American journalist known for his acerbic wit and his tales of the American Civil War. He became disillusioned with contemporary society and in 1913 disappeared into Mexico, which was in the midst of revolutionary struggles. Hart Crane (1899-1932), an American poet best remembered for his long poem *The Bridge* (1930), committed suicide by jumping from the ship that was bringing him back to the United States after a year in Mexico.

24 These are Mexican-Spanish words; *pulque* is the alcoholic milky pulp from the agave cactus, and *chinches* are bedbugs.

25 The Mexican Day of the Dead (*el Día de los Difuntos*) or All Souls Day is 2 November, but the festival begins with candlelight processions and graveside vigils on the night of 1 November.

26 The Austrian Archduke Maximilian, who tried to rule Mexico from 1864 to 1867, and his wife Carlota had a summer residence on the outskirts of Cuernavaca; it was restored in 1960 and is now called the 'Casa de Maximilian.'

27 *Las Manos de Orlac* is the Spanish title for *The Hands of Orlac* (*Orlacs Hände*), a German expressionist film made by Robert Wiene in 1925. The Hollywood version of the film, *Mad Love* (1935), starred Peter Lorre as the mad doctor.

28 Maria Landrock (1922-), who had a brief career as a skater, culminating in the 1936 Olympics in Berlin, switched to a career in the theatre and appeared in German films between 1940 and 1944. In chapter I of the *Volcano* Laruelle notices a 'garish three-sheet of a German film star [. . .] hanging behind the bar' (32). This star is Maria Landrock, but Lowry could not have seen a poster with her picture and name advertising a film between 1937 and 1939; therefore, he must have picked up this reference during his later visit to Mexico in 1945-46 or on some other occasion. The political associations of her name, given her work with the Nazi film industry, strike a minor but sinister note consistent with Lowry's text. Hernán Cortés (ca 1485-1547) led the Spanish invasion of Mexico, and Moctezuma II (1502-18) was the Aztec king overthrown by the Spaniards.

29 The Hebrew word *sod* means mystery or secret. Lowry's brief description of the associations of the word, however, warrant further comment because they suggest that his familiarity with Jewish cabbala has some real depth. The Hebrew word for garden is 'pardes' (*prds*), and, although there is no etymological or exegetical connection between *sod* and *prds*, there is an important mystical link well known amongst cabbalists. *Sod* is a mystic acronym (a *notarikon*) for *prds*, and in the cabbala the garden is a metaphor for mystical speculation, which can be successful or not, depending upon the skill and behaviour of the initiate. Lowry always

took these kinds of mystical and metaphorical connections and associations very seriously, so it is not difficult to appreciate the relevance of cabbala to the Consul's dilemma and the wider symbolic purposes of *Under the Volcano*.

30 William James (1842-1910), the brother of Henry James, was an American philosopher and psychologist, and Lowry valued his views on religion as psychological fact in *The Varieties of Religious Experience* (1902), a book that he owned and read often. Both James and Sigmund Freud (1856-1939) commented upon psychological aspects of alcoholism and religion, and Lowry could be thinking here of a number of general sources in their works, but for a particular linking of alcohol with mysticism see *The Varieties of Religious Experience* (New York: Modern Library, 1902), pp. 377-78; both pages have been marked in Lowry's copy of the text.

31 Mescal is a strong Mexican drink distilled from the fermented juice of agave cactus. It is the hallucinogenic drug mescaline that is taken in the form of 'buttons.'

32 The American comic strip 'Little Orphan Annie' was created in 1924 by Harold Gray (1894-1968). It became a regular and popular feature in the *New York Daily News*, the *Chicago Tribune*, and other newspapers. *The Tale of Jemima Puddleduck* (1908) is by the English writer of children's stories Beatrix Potter (1866-1943), who also created *Peter Rabbit*.

33 This important theme and motif means 'One cannot live without loving,' and the original phrase is from *De los nombres de Christo* (1583) by the Augustinian monk Fray Luis Ponce de León (1528-91).

34 'La Tragedia de Mayerling' is probably the 1935 French film *Mayerling* directed by Anatole Litvak and starring Charles Boyer in what has been described as 'one of the most famous and poignant of romantic tragedies in history.' In the film a prince trapped in a loveless marriage flees for a night of love with his sweetheart, after which they die in a suicide pact.

35 Philippus Aureolus Paracelsus (1493-1541), the Swiss physician and alchemist, discusses the hallucinations resulting from delirium tremens, poisons, and fevers at several points in his collected works, notably in the *Philosophia occulta*.

36 This important sign caused Lowry considerable trouble during the editing of his novel; see the notes to his 22 June 1946 letter (**226**) and his 16 July 1946 letter (**237**) to Albert Erskine.

37 Hugh I'Anson Fausset (1895-1965) was an English poet, novelist, and critic of such writers as Keats, Donne, and Whitman. He was deeply influenced, in his own poetry and fiction, by his study of Eastern philosophies. Lowry had read at least two books by Fausset, both of which were published by Cape: *The Proving of Psyche* (1929) and *A Modern Prelude* (1933). There are some striking parallels between Fausset's description of his own life in *A Modern Prelude* and the background Lowry gives to Geoffrey in *Under the Volcano*; there are also similarities between Fausset's personal life and Lowry's that the latter could not

have missed. Fausset's books are permeated with his spiritualist beliefs, his mysticism, and his profound belief in the redemptive capacity of great art. He warns against excessive self-consciousness and links his argument to many of the writers who were important to Lowry.

38 Edgar Allan Poe, one of Lowry's great favourites, wrote 'William Wilson' (1839), a story about doubles (*Doppelgänger*) that Lowry admired.

39 From their opening on 1 January 1921 until their move in 1990, Jonathan Cape's offices were in Bedford Square, a fashionable area of Blooms-bury not far from the British Museum.

40 Adolf Hitler's (1889-1945) admiration for Wagner and Wagnerian opera is legendary. Amfortas, the son of Titurel and the Keeper of the Holy Grail in Wagner's opera *Parsifal* (1882), has betrayed his sacred trust and received a wound that can only be healed by the services of a 'Pure Fool,' the young knight Parsifal, who retrieves the Sacred Spear. Although Amfortas is healed at the end of the opera, it is Parsifal who is hailed as the new king when Titurel dies. Lowry, who knew this opera well, seems none the less to be confusing or conflating Amfortas with the magician Klingsor, who wounds Amfortas and seizes the Sacred Spear.

41 Saturn (closely identified with the Greek god Cronos) is the classical and Persian god associated with time and misfortune; he is famous in myth-ology for having devoured his sons. In numerology and the occult Saturn's malevolent qualities are stressed, and the number sixty-three is held to be fatal because that year in a person's life was viewed super-stitiously as the grand climacteric of ancient medicine. Bahomet, or Baphomet, is a devil worshipped, according to legend, in the secret ceremonies of Freemasons and is said to be the 'god' of the Knights Templar.

42 Eddie Lang, the pseudonym for Salvatore Massaro (1902-33), was an American jazz guitarist who worked with Joe Venuti and Paul White-man. At the time of his early death he was the accompanist for Bing Crosby.

43 Johannes Duns Scotus (1265?-1308?), a Scots Franciscan and philosopher who lectured at Oxford University, was an extreme philosophical real-ist, and his followers, called Scotists, were an influential scholastic sect until the sixteenth century.

44 Jacob Boehme (1575-1624) was a German mystic whose works, first translated into English in the mid-seventeenth century, were reprinted in 1910-24, and they had considerable influence in literary and occult circles of the day.

45 Lowry's joking reference is, in part, to the poem 'Correspondences' from the famous collection of poems *Les Fleurs du Mal* (1857) by Charles Baudelaire. The first four lines are:

> La Nature est un temple où de vivants piliers
> Laissent parfois sortir de confuses paroles;
> L'homme y passe à travers des forêts de symboles
> Qui l'observent avec des regards familiers.

Baudelaire's third line, loosely translated as 'Man wanders through a forest of symbols,' gives Lowry his allusion, which he completes with the familiar image for ignorance or the confusion of a part with the whole: the inability to distinguish a forest from its trees.

46 After Edward J. O'Brien's death in 1941, Martha Foley edited *Best American Short Stories* for many years. When one remembers that at the beginning of his career Lowry had been very proud to have an early short story accepted by O'Brien, and that Martha Foley had not liked an earlier version of *Volcano*, the complex irony implied by this remark at this stage in his life is perhaps easier to appreciate.

47 Ludwig Van Beethoven (1770–1827) was one of Germany's greatest classical composers.

48 Sean O'Faolain (1900–91) was a prolific Irish writer of novels, stories, screenplays, and a wide range of non-fiction. Lowry may be thinking here of O'Faolain's advice to young writers in his occassional essays for the *Bell*, a monthly literary magazine published in Dublin from 1940 to 1954. Using one of the stories published in an issue of the magazine, O'Faolain would write a critique of the piece and offer advice. For example, in the 'New Writers' essay for the February 1941 issue of the *Bell*, O'Faolain warned that an author 'must never [sell] himself to his characters' but must 'keep apart' from them (61).

49 The 'French philosopher of the Absurd fellow' is probably Jean-Paul Sartre (1905–80), the French phenomenologist and existentialist philosopher, critic, novelist, and playwright, who often classified people, characters, and consciousness as things, though Lowry may also be thinking of the French writer Albert Camus (1913–60), who is closely associated with the 'philosophy of the absurd' and more loosely with existentialism.

50 Kundry is the enchantress in Wagner's *Parsifal*. It is Kundry who tries to seduce Parsifal in the magic garden of the magician, Klingsor, but when she fails she becomes a supplicant in search of salvation, and she dies at the end of the opera when Amfortas is healed and Parsifal raises the Grail on high.

51 Harpo Marx (1893–1964) was one of the three Marx brothers' comedy team, which performed on screen and stage and in vaudeville.

52 The Eleusinian mysteries, associated with the town of Eleusis, which is some twenty-one km west of Athens, are the most famous religious mysteries of ancient Greece. The religious rites involved fasting, purification, and dramas portraying the story of Demeter and Persephone, and the successful completion of the rituals insured the soul's safe passage to a future world of happiness. Shakespeare's late romance *The Tempest* (1611), which turns upon the metaphors of alchemical theatre and marriage, concerns the struggle of the exiled Duke of Milan and magician, Prospero, to maintain control over his daughter and his island and to facilitate the symbolic, restorative marriage of Miranda and Ferdinand. Lowry's choice of *The Tempest* in this context is interesting, not

because Shakespeare is using Eleusinian mysteries but because this play has a magus as its hero and a successfully completed ritual as its plot; the contrast with *Under the Volcano* is striking.

53 The English writer Thomas Hardy is especially praised for the handling of natural effects in his novels and for his dark, fatalistic vision of human life.

54 Julien Green had been a favourite of Lowry's since his reading of *The Dark Journey* (New York: Harper & Brothers, 1929; French orig. *Leviathan*, 1929) in the early thirties. The novel he has in mind here could be *The Dark Journey*, a story of doomed love, betrayal, and murder in which the young heroine, Angèle, dies at the end in circumstances that echo Yvonne's death in chapter eleven of *Under the Volcano*. Or he might be thinking of *Midnight* (1936; *Minuit*, 1936), which ends with the death of another of Green's heroines, who, while dying, sees a vision of a man who lifts her away from the earth up towards the heaven 'with an irresistible force.' See also Ackerley/Clipper, 414, and Lowry's 15 July 1946 letter (**236**) to Albert Erskine.

55 Sherwood Anderson (1876-1941), a prolific American novelist, short story writer, poet, and editor, wrote about contemporary life and modernization in the American midwest in a straightforward style. *Winesburg, Ohio* (1919) is one of his most important works and is considered a classic of its type.

56 Herman Melville's *Pierre* (1852), usually considered to be semi-autobiographical, follows the rather convoluted fate of a hero who commits suicide at the end.

57 The word Lowry has written is *Heckmondwike*, not 'Reckmondwike,' as shown in *Selected Letters*. Heckmondwike is a town on the Yorkshire moors in the area associated with Charlotte Brontë's novel *Shirley* (1849).

58 Leo Steni published three books with Cape: *Afternoon and Twilight of Vanda Pinelli* (1926), *Prelude to a Rope for Myer* (1928), and *Sailor in a Whirlpool* (1930). All three were unsuccessful, and Cape has no surviving record of their dealings with this author. The name may be a pseudonym. Arthur Calder-Marshall published *About Levy* with Cape in 1933.

Editorial Notes:

a. This transcription has been made from what appears to be the original typescript (UBC 2:3) that was sent to Jonathan Cape from Mexico; no other copy has survived with the Cape archive at the University of Reading in England. It comprises eleven 16-by-28-cm sheets of paper with single-spaced typing on verso and recto of each sheet and with minor changes in pencil; it is signed in pencil. The date appears to have been added, in pencil, by Margerie. Differences between this copy-text and the version published in *Selected Letters* are confined to matters of spelling, punctuation, and typography. The former editors

Americanized Lowry's British spelling (where he had not already done so himself), tidied up his idiosyncratic punctuation *passim*, underlined all titles (Lowry rarely underlines them), and inserted accents where Lowry neglected them. Filed with the copy-text is a partial pencil draft with notes on lined paper torn from a notebook and a complete draft comprising a foliation of twelve pages of typescript with two pages of pencil draft and nine pages of inserts.

211: To James Craige

P: UBC(pcard phc)

[Mexico]
[5 January 1946]

My dear Jimmy!

Picture of one of the finest one way streets:[1] i.e, the victim goes up, but – . . . . – Much love, happiest of Xmases & New Years to you & Mrs Craig

Affectionately from,

Malc & Margie

Annotations:

1 The card shows a photograph of the thirty-two-metre-wide stairway leading up the pyramid of Teopanzolco ('the abandoned temple') on the eastern outskirts of Cuernavaca. The pyramid was built in the Aztec period, and Lowry's reference is to the victims who were ritually sacrificed there; they went up the one-way street alive, but not down. The postcard, mailed from Mexico, is postmarked 5 January 1946.

212: To Harold Matson

P: Matson(telegram)

RCA Communications,
Cuernavaca,
[Mexico]
12 April 1946

MARGIE AND SELF IN MEXICO IMPERATIVE LEAVE IN TEN DAYS DELIGHTED COME NEW YORK IF MY EXPENSES PAID[1] RATHER COME FROM MEXICO OTHERWISE RETURNING CANADA VIA LOS ANGELES MUST KNOW

IMMEDIATELY FOR RESERVATIONS VOLCANO JUST ACCEPTED CAPE
LONDON PLEASE REPLY HUMBOLDT 24 CUERNAVACA MORELOS MEXICO
AND ADVISE MANY THANKS

MALCOLM LOWRY

Annotations:

1 *Under the Volcano* was accepted in London and New York simultaneously, with both Cape and Reynal & Hitchcock sending telegrams to
Lowry dated 6 April 1946. By April, however, events in Mexico were
becoming unpleasant for the Lowrys so that, when Curtice Hitchcock
suggested Lowry come to New York to help with the editing of *Under
the Volcano*, Lowry seized upon the idea as a way of getting out of
Mexico quickly. As it turned out, Hitchcock changed his mind about
the need for this visit, and Lowry went to New York in February 1947
for the publication of his novel.

213: To Harold Matson

P: Matson(telegram)

RCA Communications,
Cuernavaca,
[Mexico]
14 April 1946

PLEASE WIRE EXPENSE MONEY BANCO NACIONAL DE MEXICO
CUERNAVACA WILL MAKE RESERVATIONS IMMEDIATELY HAVE VISITORS
VISA TILL NOVEMBER AMERICA SALE OF BOOK MAY REQUIRE SLIGHT
CHANGE OF STATUS LET YOU KNOW DATE OF ARRIVAL SOON AS POSSIBLE
FELICIDAD TUSEN TAK SKOAL[1]

MALCOLM LOWRY

Annotations:

1 *Felicidad* is Spanish for 'happiness,' but what Lowry needs here is *Fel-
icidades*, for 'best wishes'; *tusen tak* is Norwegian for 'a thousand thanks,'
and *skoal* is a Scandinavian drinking toast. Lowry particularly liked to
use the latter terms with Matson, who was of Norwegian descent.

*Apart from his telegram (**212**) to Matson, this telegram to Gerald Noxon is Lowry's first announcement of the news of* Under the Volcano's *acceptance for publication. Given Noxon's interest in the novel and his support of Lowry during the difficult months after the fire, it seems only fitting that Lowry would first want to share this news with his friend.*

214: To Gerald Noxon

P: Texas(telegram)
PP: *LLN* 120

> Canadian Pacific,
> via Mextel,
> Cuernavaca, Morelos,
> [Mexico]
> 15 April 1946

VOLCANO ACCEPTED LONDON NEW YORK SAME DAY NEWS RECEIVED
LARUELLES TOWER[1] HUMBOLDT 24 CUERNAVACA MORELOS WHERE
LIVING YOUR LETTER RECEIVED DEAR FRIEND CONGRATULATIONS
BRANCHES[2] LEAVING SOON NEW YORK HITCHCOCKS EXPENSE LOVE
SPEND FEW DAYS NIAGARA BEFORE RETURNING DOLLARTON IF YOU CAN
STAND ME LOVE BETTY NICK FROM MARGIE AND

> MALCOLM LOWRY

Annotations:

1 'Laruelle's tower' on Calle Humboldt is the house with a tower and chevron-shaped windows that Lowry used in *Under the Volcano*; see Figure 11 on page 497. Lowry was deeply impressed by the fact that he and Margerie were actually staying in this house during their Mexican trip.

2 In his 18 January 1946 letter to Lowry, the letter to which this telegram is the reply, Noxon writes that 'Branches of the Night' are being published first, in periodical form here in Toronto . . . and eventually in book form in the same place' (*Letters of Malcolm Lowry and Gerald Noxon*, 119-20). One of Noxon's verses, called simply 'Poem,' did indeed appear in *Canadian Poetry Magazine* 12, 1 (1948): 13, and Paul Tiessen describes it as 'an excerpt from . . . 'Branches of the Night'' (*Letters of Malcolm Lowry and Gerald Noxon*, 4n). Noxon's entire long poem has not been published to date.

215: To Harold Matson

P: Matson(telegram)

RCA Communications,
Cuernavaca,
[Mexico]
19 April 1946

LETTER RECEIVED TERMS FINE[1] WILL LEAVE FOR CANADA BEFORE MAY
FIRST PLEASE IF POSSIBLE SEND CONTRACT AND FIRST ADVANCE MEXICO
IMMEDIATELY SO I RECEIVE BEFORE LEAVING AS WE WILL NOT REACH
CANADA FOR FEW WEEKS AND OWING AUXILIARY CIRCUMSTANCES
REALLY NEED READY CASH PLEASE WIRE IF THIS POSSIBLE MANY THANKS

MALCOLM LOWRY

Annotations:

1 In a 13 April 1946 telegram Matson explained Curtice Hitchcock's terms
   for bringing Lowry to New York to edit *Under the Volcano*, but in his 16
   April 1946 letter to Lowry, Matson informed him that Hitchcock had
   changed his mind, believing it better to spend the money on promotion
   or on bringing Lowry to New York for publication. It is not clear from
   Lowry's telegram, however, just what 'terms' he is referring to, and the
   confusion over this early idea of a possible trip to New York to edit the
   manuscript would lead to later misunderstandings between Lowry and
   Albert Erskine.

216: To Dr E.B. Woolfan

P: UBC(ts)
PP: *SL* 88–89

[Cuernavaca,]
[Mexico]
[19 April 1946][a]

Dear old Bert:
   Margie, I see, (see above)[1] is her old ebullient self. What she means
by fanfare I don't know. Though I'm sure the darling thinks she
knows. What it probably will amount to is a few bad cocktails and
some publicity the book and I could do well without. The truth is the
terms Reynal and Hitchcock have offered in New York were super
excellent but today they have suddenly capitulated and the terms

have become more so. They too, like Cape, will let me have my every holy word and won't tamper with a line. They also suggest I come to New York at publication time instead of right now. For myself, I have forgotten already completely what the book is about, the double success on the same day being like receiving an atom bomb between Rolando's fissure and the Island of Reil.[2] I don't even walk today which is Good Friday, and though I am quite harmless and cheery you can imagine where I think I am. Since the book will probably kill my English mother stone dead if she ever reads it (which she undoubtedly won't, just like my American brother)[3] I am going to ask you if you will be so good as to send the following cables (a) to my mother (b) to my eldest brother, to whom owing to some gentile limey priority I ought to break the news first. Will reimburse of course, as for the others, when get to Los Angeles. All thanks again to my sister Priscilla for her faith in that book and to my American mother for hers and also say I will answer her marvellous and beautiful letter to me when I have dealt with this and to her all love. I hope I can stay with you – or near – when we come to L.A. I am a burden I know, but I could live in the garage or even with Ichabod[4] in his cage, preferably if he is on the bourbon. We would gnatter harmlessly to each other.

Best love,

Malcolm

Evelyn Lowry, Inglewood, Caldy, Cheshire, England.
delay writing due most excellent news regards work dearest love writing   Malcolm Lowry

Stuart Lowry, Corvalley, Upton, Cheshire, England.
Book accepted England America simultaneously forgive silence heretofore thanks Donald[5] degree writing.   love   Malcolm Lowry

P.S. These can go what I think they call Night Letter Cable or some such which allows 20 words including address and signature. Thank you again for your trouble.

Annotations:

1 Lowry's letter to his brother-in-law begins on the lower half of the recto of the page. 'Above' it is Margerie's letter to her family.
2 Both 'Rolando's fissure' and the 'Island of Reil' are names for specific parts of the brain. The former, named after the nineteenth-century

anatomist Luigi Rolando, is in the cerebral cortex; the latter, named after the nineteenth-century physician Johann C. Reil, is in the cerebral hemisphere.

3 By his 'American brother' Lowry could mean Bert himself or Harold Matson, who, he feared, had never read the manuscript; see his April 1946 letter (**219**) to Gerald Noxon.

4 Ichabod was the Woolfans' pet bird, but the name also recalls Ichabod Crane, a character in the American classic short story 'The Legend of Sleepy Hollow' (1820) by Washington Irving (1783-1859).

5 Donald Lowry, Stuart's son, was one of Lowry's nephews.

Editorial Notes:

a. This letter is undated, but Lowry says that he is writing on Good Friday, which fell on 19 April in 1946.

217: To Harold Matson

P: Matson(telegram); UBC(phc)

RCA Communications,
Cuernavaca,
[Mexico]
20 April 1946

HAVE CAPE CONTRACT BUT HAVE NOT SIGNED OR TAKEN MONEY WILL BEAR IN MIND WHAT YOU SAY CANADIAN RIGHTS ETC FEEL NEED LEGAL ADVICE BEFORE SIGNING ONE CONTRACT POSSIBLY ABROGATING OTHER ABSOLUTELY MUST LEAVE MEXICO[1] WILL SEE LAWYER LOS ANGELES IS SOME ADVANCE POSSIBLE THESE TERMS QUICK SOS MANY THANKS

MALCOLM LOWRY

Annotations:

1 By this time the Lowrys were having considerable difficulty with the Mexican authorities; see his 15 June 1946 letter (**224**) to A. Ronald Button.

218: To Harold Matson

P: Matson(telegram)

> RCA Communications,
> Cuernavaca,
> [Mexico]
> 28 April 1946

THANKS TREMENDOUSLY FOR CASH WILL EXPLAIN DELAY IN
ACKNOWLEDGEMENT LATER SENDING YOU COPY CAPE CONTRACT
WHICH WILL NOT SIGN WITHOUT YOUR SAYSO FLYING LOS ANGELES
ABOUT MAY FIFTH[1] THANKS AGAIN LIKE WISE HITCHCOCK REGARDS
FROM MARGIE AND SELF COME TO SUNNY ACAPULCO FOR VACATION
TRULY DIFFERENT WRITING

> MALCOLM LOWRY

Annotations:

1 The Lowrys were deported from Mexico on 4 May 1946.

219: To Gerald Noxon

P: Texas(ms)
PP: *LLN* 122

> [Mexico]
> [April 1946][a]

Dear old Gerald: –

This is just a short note – thanks awfully for your two letters – will
reply, but this is to say in a hurry that we won't be coming to New
York until fall – Reynal & Hitchcock having decided that they'll
publish the book as it stands if I wish, without much editing – but
probably it can stand a few cuts, or even more than a few, have you
any suggestions – you know how I value your opinion – Chap VI too
long, some of the Spanish is haywire too of course – am very disappointed won't see you this summer think it would have been a
good thing for Margie go New York Niagara too – I got the
Jonathan Cape contract on same day after battling with them for
months – they will publish it as it stands too, if I wish – Cape
contract slightly contradicts Hitchcock one who want Canadian
rights,[1] so I haven't signed it yet (couldn't, for physical reasons, even
if I wanted to) – have had terrific battle likewise with the Mexican

authorities here also that has completely worn us out, they forbade me to write another line – but what if should write to my mother in the excusado? – And what if *we* set a trap! Grand opera but bad for us both: will write more later.[2] British Consul virtually refused to help at all – who shall blame him? We triumphed in the end ourselves but at an awful cost both in cash & nerves. Reynal & Hitchcock apparently mean to go to town on the book however: far too much dough is already sitting in the post office here, – will sit there forever so far as I can see unless I can sign my name to it, at the moment can't, not even with a cross.

All best love to Betty & Nick from us both

Malcolm[3]

[P.S.] Advice to authors. Believe Matson OK: the first 150 years are the worst. He had no belief in the Volcano had not even read it – we both told him to go to hell, then he sold it.

Annotations:

1 Jonathan Cape wished to retain Canadian rights, but since Reynal & Hitchcock also wanted the Canadian market, there was some delay and further negotiation before a contract leaving Canadian rights to the American publisher was signed. Lowry discusses this in several letters to Harold Matson; see especially his letter of 15 June 1946 (**225**).
2 Lowry did indeed 'write more later' regarding this disastrous trip to Mexico. It became the basis of his unfinished and (to date) unpublished novel 'La Mordida' and the subject of several letters; see his 15 June 1946 letter (**224**) to A. Ronald Button.
3 Despite his claim above that he cannot sign anything, Lowry has signed this letter.

Editorial Notes:

a. This holograph letter has been written in pencil on the recto of a single sheet of 16-by-28-cm paper. There is no inside address or date. Margerie has written her own letter to 'Dear Betty & Gerald & Nick' on the verso with a marginal addition by Lowry; see *Letters of Malcolm Lowry and Gerald Noxon* (123). I have shown Lowry's marginal addition, which he has keyed to Margerie's mention of Harold Matson, as a postscript.

220: To Harold Matson

P: Matson(ts); UBC(phc)

c/o Dr E.B. Woolfan,
1643 Queens Road,
Hollywood 46,
California
8 May 1946

Dear Hal:

Herewith a copy of the Cape contract,[1] which I conclude to be of a stock printed variety, but which naturally remains still unsigned: I have already cabled him that of course the clause that places him as my American agent, and possibly other clauses too, are invalid and am writing him to ask him if we cannot come to some arrangement whereby you may have the Canadian rights. But possibly there are other clauses which are too ambiguous and on these I would like your advice. As I said before, I won't sign without your say-so, and perhaps also you could suggest to me in what manner I should cancel these clauses, whether by brackets, pasting paper over them, crossing them out or whatever. I would send you the original but for the fact that I would like to retain it with the Hitchcock telegram in order to do some bragging to some friends of my wife's who are throwing me a party the day after tomorrow: but if you want it you shall have it, quam celerrime.

If this letter seems to be a little erratic I should add, in a bracket, that we have ourselves just been through the most godawful experience of our lives.

On account of my poor, or too potent writings (Chapter XII of the Volcano we think), after seven weeks of pure unadulterated hell during which they took away all of our papers and identification, after their having violated the Mexican constitution and admitting it themselves, we were suddenly & without warning driven 1000 miles at the point of a gun out of Mexico – I just escaped the Consul's ultimate fate by three minutes, outwitted the Dostoiveskien Inspector at 2 in the morning, got Margie and self across the border, where Texas gave me legal sanctuary, as of course her.[2]

I shall be in Hollywood at the above address until about the 15th if you want to wire me here for any urgent reason, and back in Dollarton at my old address approximately a week later, and am naturally awaiting your reply with anxiety.[3]

As for the Mexican thing, more later. I feel like turning Zola[4] on it at the moment and have been strongly advised to do so for the sake of others as well – but for the while I am holding myself in. Their government at the moment, easy going on the surface, is the evillest thing I ever saw.[5] Mexico seems to me now likewise predominantly Nazi. I had no idea how near I had hit the truth in Chapter XII – whatever good that did me.

Thank you again for everything – you literally saved our lives with the 500 for they stole damn near everything else and we never would have got out of the country without it. With all best wishes from us both, bloodily yet sincerely yours,

Malcolm

Annotations:

1 Lowry's final contract does not appear to have survived, but three pages (twenty-one clauses) of a 'Memorandum of Agreement' between Cape and Lowry are extant with the Matson Lowry file; see Lowry's 15 June 1946 letter (**225**) to Matson.

2 The 'Dostoievskian Inspector' is the infamous Porfiry in *Crime and Punishment*.

3 A railway strike forced the Lowrys to begin the trip from Los Angeles to Vancouver by bus on 12 May.

4 Émile Zola, one of the foremost French writers of the nineteenth century, received considerable negative attention for his championing of Alfred Dreyfus, the young Jewish captain in the French army who had been wrongly accused and convicted of spying. It was Zola's famous open letter called 'J'accuse' on the front page of the newspaper *L'Aurore* for 13 January 1898 that led to riots, official review of the Dreyfus case, exposure of corruption, and continued scandal. Zola's letter has since become synonymous with the individual's fight to preserve the truth in the face of official corruption and abuse of political power; therefore, Lowry's idea here is that, like Zola, he should take up the cause of his and Margerie's treatment in Mexico.

5 The government in power in Mexico during the months of the Lowrys' ordeal was the Partido Revolucionario Institucional (PRI: Institutional Revolutionary Party), headed by the newly appointed civilian and lawyer Miguel Alemán Valdés, who was president of Mexico from 1946 to 1952. Although Alemán was successful in developing the country, corruption was widespread, and popular faith in the principles of the Mexican Revolution was seriously eroded during these years.

221: To Harold Matson

P: Matson(ts); UBC(phc)

> Dollarton P.O.,
> Dollarton, B.C.,
> Canada
> 28 May 1946

Dear Hal:

I am terribly sorry for any delay in my reply but this was unavoidable: I only just got home and am answering your letter immediately as possible.

The contract from Reynal and Hitchcock is fine, in fact very fine indeed and for this I thank you. I have no objection to clause 16 re motion picture rights – to the contrary I think you acted very wisely here. I am herewith returning it duly signed, but with the clause re Canadian rights still hanging fire until I hear from Cape. I am also writing him re the clause concerning territory outside the British Empire and the United States to be an open market.

As to having Mr Peters[1] act for me I am afraid I should not do this now as I have already told Cape I would deal with him directly in England and considering the various other changes I am asking him to make, I feel it would be better not to repudiate this. Needless to say I see the advantages of having Mr Peters act as my agent and I thank you for bringing this up, and possibly in the course of my correspondence with Mr Cape this can be worked out.

I thank you also for your advice on the other clauses in the Cape contract which I shall accept as far as possible. To itemize:

Clause 9 is eliminated.

Clause 11 would be eliminated if I had Mr Peters as an agent, but since I have not, Cape might as well have this, as I see it, partly in recompense should he give us Canadian rights etc.

Clause 12 ditto.

Clause 18 – I shall mention as you suggest and thank you again for watching out for my interests.

I was very sorry indeed to hear of Curtice Hitchcock's death, which is indeed a tragedy, and please convey my deepest sympathy to his co-founder.[2] I am also deeply appreciative of the fact that he liked my book.

Coincidentally it was almost paralleled by this author's death too, if not both these authors, but I must keep this Mexican experience for another letter. At all events it was horrendous, I have no notion how we survived it, if indeed we did; all delays and S.O.S.'s were due to it: your letter and Cape's arrived in the middle of it – delivered to the tower in chapter 7 (by the postman in chapter 7.)

Can you send Mr Hitchcock's notes and suggestions to me as quickly as possible so that I may get down to them, as if they plan fall publication time is indeed of the essence. Unfortunately I was forced to leave my copy of the Volcano in Mexico and do not know when, if ever, I'll get it. So if Mr Hitchcock's and the editor's notes simply refer to page numbers I am on the spot. I have a working copy here but the page numbers are different. I am very reluctant to ask for their copy, but since I know the book so well the slightest extra suggestion such as we think the scene between so and so, chapter so and so, should be shortened, or Spanish here seems haywire, would be enough.

Thank you again for everything. With all the very best to you from Margerie and myself,

Malcolm

Annotations:

1 A.D. Peters, of A.D. Peters and W.N. Roughead, was a literary agent in London who represented Harold Matson's clients in England. Peters' address appears at the top right of the Matson Company letterhead.
2 Curtice Hitchcock's sudden death in May 1946 troubled Lowry, in part because he felt that Hitchcock had been his chief supporter and that Eugene Reynal was not as favourably disposed to *Under the Volcano* as his partner had been.

222: To Jonathan Cape

P: UBC(ts)

Dollarton P.O.,
Dollarton, B.C.,
Canada
30 May 1946

Dear Mr Cape:

This is about the 50th time in the course of the last weeks that this letter has been written in one form or another.[1]

My wife and I returned to Cuernavaca from an extremely grim experience in Acapulco to discover your letter and your contract, which I couldn't sign as it stood then for the reason suggested in my cable. Although I had previously told you I would prefer you to act as my American agent, who is also my wife's agent, it turned out that my New York agent, had sold it in America, and all this news I received on the same day. I had not heard from my agent since he wrote me an extremely disappointing letter saying that he did not believe in the book as it stood, that while it had possibilities it should be largely rewritten, etc. All this was about the time, as I recall, that I replied to your first letter, when I said I was not altogether satisfied with my American connection and the time also when I was awaiting your cable which did not – for reasons I could only see clearly much later – come. My wife was meanwhile having trouble with her publishers, Scribner's, who were under contract to have brought out a book of hers last fall, and no reply or explanation was forthcoming on this: we hadn't indeed had a word from our agent save this discouraging one for months and months and when we left for Mexico, though your letter had given me hope of another kind, it was with the assumption that the copy of Under the Volcano I'd sent to our agent in America would undoubtedly be returned to our Canadian address. Indeed a letter had been sent to him by my wife, who sometimes acts as my secretary, telling him to return it, if that was all he thought about it, and hence my say-so to you on this matter. Instead of doing this however he went right ahead and sold it to the firm of Reynal and Hitchcock, who had only had it since the middle of February I now learn, and the curious thing about this firm is that they apparently think it a masterpiece, to a man. They want to bring it out this fall exactly as it stands, or with any changes I myself wish to make. Since the agent in question didn't even know we were in Mexico, the New York acceptance was finally forwarded to Mexico from Canada, and this news, I repeat, arrived upon precisely the same day as yours, after the aforesaid grim experience.

I should have said in the middle of the experience, for the Consul, or something worse, now stuck another claw out of the abyss at us right at this moment of doubly complicated triumph. To cut a very long story short – for the experience lasted nearly 2 months – the Mexican government (and it is now probably the worst since Diaz)[2] discovered a slight flaw in our papers: that it was the fault of their own Consul in Los Angeles made no difference. And then they discovered, or invented, another one: our tourist cards gave our occupation as writers, therefore, they decided, we were 'working' in Mexico, therefore we must put up a large bond, in Holy Week with all the bonding companies closed, therefore they must confiscate all our papers, therefore we must not write another word, not even letters to our mothers, let alone publishers. Due to war regulations, Canada had only allowed us a certain amount of money for our trip, and as by now these brutos had done us out of all we had, it was therefore necessary to get some money at once from somewhere. Meantime I had cabled you that I could not sign all clauses in your contract because of the Reynal and Hitchcock one, and the New York agent ditto because of yours, but at this point the Mexican difficulties reached their crisis, my New York agent wired me that Hitchcock offered a free trip to New York, as well as more spot cash instantly than would otherwise be perhaps good for one at one time, and, our situation having now become desperate, not to say melodramatic, I had very little choice but to accept this money. Whereupon, the Mexican government, having set their trap, promptly stole our bond, held my wife and I incommunicado so that our Consuls – Consuls! – should not be able to interfere in their illegal treatment of us, and then found it necessary to take us, at the point of a gun, 1500 miles across Mexico with the disturbing yet patent object, since they were terrified lest we get out with the story, of shooting us in Nuevo Laredo.[3] However (doubtless because I had seen too many Russian or French films) I somehow or other outwitted the Dostoievskian Inspector at 2 A.M., and, with the connivance of yet other peculiar Mexican officials, we escaped across the border, papers and all, where Texas gave us legal sanctuary. You can possibly understand however, that I have been under some slight strain.

I had written this much of this letter in Los Angeles, where we were staying with my wife's family hoping to have a rest and get our affairs in order before finishing the long trip back home. But we were forced to leave Los Angeles overnight in order to avoid a threatened general railroad strike which would tie up all communications and leave us stranded there indefinitely, and so traveled by any means we could get, as quickly as possible back here, where we are once more at our old address in Dollarton.

Taking the money bound me to the Reynal and Hitchcock contract. It also gives me a time limit in which to do my editing. So with certain provisos I have now signed it. They are fully informed of your rights in the matter, and know that you may insist, for instance, upon Canadian rights. (see clause 1 below) So far as I can see the following are the only points of difference.

Clause 1. My American publishers would like the Canadian rights – or at any rate they feel that such could be handled better at this end than yours should you plan publication *next* year, their feeling being it would greatly benefit the sale in Canada to take advantage of the publicity and exploitation they plan *this fall*[4] when the book is published in America, and the question might arise what good the Canadian rights would do yourself if you were to bring it out in

Canada much later. I don't know what to do about this so perhaps you would (a) give me some fatherly advice or (b) suggest some terms by which they could bring it out simultaneously in Canada and America with a certain percentage of Canadian publication going to you.

Clause 1. Also it seems to me more fair if this would be changed so that you would have exclusive rights throughout the British Empire (except as above), Reynal and Hitchcock be given exclusive rights in the United States, and other territories should be an open market in which the English and American publishers can sell the book in the English language. Please advise me about this as Reynal and Hitchcock will accept this compromise.

Clause 9 will now have to be eliminated entirely and I must hereby rescind and revoke it as I am not now, as I was last fall, when I replied to your first letter, able to give you authority to negotiate for any American publication.

Clause 11 and 12 – I do not believe that these conflict in any way with the American contract. They do not demand any percentage on first serial rights and since that, I understand, usually is handled by one's agent, and since I am dealing directly with you, this seems O.K. They ask the usual percentage on second serial rights, etc., but only demand their 10% of any motion picture rights if they have sold more than 25,000 copies the first year of publication.

Everything else seems in order.

Thank you for your letter and needless to say I am very happy and proud to have you publish the book, and that you finally consider it publishable as it stands. I shall make certain cuts in the final editing and will indicate these cuts as you suggest. I shall also be happy to write the preface of 1000 words and also the blurb of 150-200 words.[5]

I am frightfully sorry to have been so long answering but what with the near disastrous experience in Mexico, the arrival of the other contract, and the difficulties involved in the long journey back here I found it impossible. All this may seem likewise a lot of fuss and feathers about a book that may sell only one copy. I cannot account for Reynal and Hitchcock being unanimously agreed that the thing was not only good but even as it stood a potential big money-maker. It seems just one of those things. I would have liked you to have published the book first, but you see the position I am in. I have tried to be as ethical as possible in the most complicated spiritual onslaught that ever hit me. I would have felt I had some obligation to [Innes] Rose but I could not see Farquarson as interested in this kind of thing, at least as things stood formerly.[6] I am a bad negotiator and a poor business man and if you feel that for your own protection the thing should be handled through one channel, my New York agent suggested his London representative, Mr A.D. Peters, might take on the job of adjusting any differences or conflicts between the two contracts, but having told you I would prefer to deal with you directly I see no reason why such differences cannot be settled between us since as I have indicated they are not of a serious nature and concern only a few clauses. If however I seem to be doing you down, which may be the case, the Peters idea may be a good one, because I understand you know each other well. From this you may gather that my New York agent is Harold Matson. Actually the best of agents, he is a great personal friend of very long standing and it would have been the ultima thule of ingratitude to have denied him now he had at long last sold something of mine and apparently persevered on my behalf even in the face of his own disbelief.

In any event I would be most grateful if you would be generous enough to waive my own delays and reply to this by airmail to Dollarton, as the R. and H. contract is held up in New York for final filing until we hear from you about the above, and as I have said they plan fall publication and now the time is short.

Thank you again for everything.

Yours very faithfully,

[unsigned]

Annotations:

1 In addition to this final typescript carbon of the letter, there are two holograph versions (one in Margerie's hand), the other heavily corrected, a partial holograph, and a partial typescript, both with some deletions and additions. This textual evidence certainly corroborates Lowry's difficulty with this letter.

2 Porfiro Díaz (1828-1915) was the dictatorial president of Mexico from 1876 to 1910. His overthrow in 1910 marked the beginning of the revolution, which in turn led to civil war and to the rise of worse dictators, such as General Victoriano Huerta. In 1946 the president of Mexico was Miguel Alemán, who is remembered for his buildings and industrialization efforts.

3 Nuevo Laredo, on the Mexican border with the United States, is the twin city of Laredo in Texas. It was from here that the Lowrys were deported on 4 May 1946.

4 The original plan had been to publish *Under the Volcano* in the fall of 1946, but delays over the contracts and with the editing caused a postponement of the American publication until 19 February 1947. The Cape edition was published on 1 September 1947.

5 The agreement with Cape stipulated that Lowry would write a preface
and 'blurb,' but these proved painfully difficult for him to produce. He
did finally send something to Cape with his 10 January 1947 letter.
6 Innes Rose had been Lowry's literary agent with the London firm of
John Farquharson and had placed *Ultramarine* with Cape in 1932; see
Lowry's 1936 letter (**68**) to Rose.

223: To Mrs Anna Mabelle [John Stuart] Bonner
      and Dr and Mrs E.B. Woolfan

P: UBC(ts)
PP: *SL* 90–91

Dollarton, B.C.,
Canada
7 June 1946

Dear Mother, Priscilla and Bert:

Just a line to thank you enormously for all your kindness and
hospitality toward me.[1]

I know that you went to no end of trouble on my account to make
me comfortable happy and at home, which I was, and though in return my contribution was precisely naught, that did not mean I did
not deeply appreciate everything in my sloth-like manner: nor can I
think of you all without a deeply heart-warming feeling.

Thank you very much indeed, Bert, for the typewriter. I think it
a much better typewriter than Margie's and no, please do not give
the shoes you gave me away to anyone else. Instead allow my spirit
to walk about the house in them, which has the added advantage
that the spirit in question will not fill every nook and craney with
cigarette smoke.

Our house is still here but civilization, so-called, is closing in upon
us a little too much for our liking: there is another Englishman here
who lives up a tree and perhaps he has the right idea, or at any rate a
cunning perception of man's place in relation to the world.

I think we might buy an island: live half each year on it and work,
and travel the other half.

I dare say you saw in the papers, or Time, (issue May 13) and were
trying kindly to conceal from me, the fact that Curtice Hitchcock
dropped dead of coronary thrombosis.[2] Apart from all my other feelings I did not know how far this was going to effect matters since he
was the one originally mainly interested in the Volcano: my agent
has assured me that all the editors are equally enthusiastic, but it was
an eerie coincidence, remembering the Volcano's theme (only

against death does man cry in vain) and eerie too to find his signature on my contract awaiting us here, suggesting that it must have been about the last thing he did.

In San Francisco we saw, hard by the Matson Line sheds, two freighters moored: one named Cape Friendship, the other Hitchcock Victory, and one may be pardoned if this too gave one something of a start.

Well, we are very happy here except that I am distressed to think that our preoccupation with my work is interfering with Margie's but I guess it will all come even in the end.

I cannot believe that our manuscripts will not arrive from Mexico eventually, so do not worry about that on our account. Please give our kindest regards to Edna and her Husband. And with fondest love to you all,

Malcolm

Annotations:

1 After the Lowrys were deported from Mexico on 4 May 1946, they went to Los Angeles for a brief rest with Margerie's family.
2 Curtice Hitchcock (1892-1946) had established the New York publishing firm of Reynal & Hitchcock with Eugene Reynal in 1933. Lowry believed that Hitchcock had liked the *Volcano* but that Reynal did not, despite Harold Matson's assurances to the contrary.

⌒

When Lowry set out for his Mexican holiday in November 1945, he intended to lay the ghosts of 1937-38. In this he may have succeeded, but those ghosts were quickly replaced by a new set that was equally persistent and recalcitrant. Lowry's long letter to Los Angeles attorney Ronald Button is his formal statement describing the persecution he and Margerie suffered in Mexico between 14 March and 4 May 1946. Just what he hoped to achieve by writing to Button is unclear, but he may have been partially motivated by Zola's example (see letter 220) to set the record straight and to warn others. Whether or not it served any practical purpose, this letter provides a factual account – in excruciating detail – *of the experiences that form the basis of his manuscript 'La Mordida.'*

224: To A. Ronald Button

P: UBC(tsc)
PP: *SL* 91–112

Dollarton, B.C.,
Canada
15 June 1946[a]

The following is a statement of what happened to my wife and I in Mexico and wherever possible is verified by dates, names and places.[1]

I am an Englishman, resident in Canada. My wife is American. We left Canada on November 28, 1945, and flew to Los Angeles via United Air Lines, for the purpose of visiting my wife's mother, Mrs J.S. Bonner, and her sister and brother-in-law, Dr and Mrs E.B. Woolfan of 1643 Queens Road, Hollywood, California. From there we proposed to go on to Mexico to spend the winter for purposes of travel and health. At the Mexican consulate in Los Angeles, after making application and waiting the required 24 hours, I obtained a visa on my English passport and we were both given Tourist Cards. These would expire June 10, but we were at that time planning to return to Canada not later than the end of April. I was carrying two passports, my old one, which would expire the end of December but on which I had received my American visa from the American Consulate in Vancouver, B.C., Canada which was good for one year, and my new one, procured from the British Consulate in Los Angeles, on which I was given the Mexican visa. We also carried my birth certificate, my wife's birth certificate proving her American citizenship, our marriage license, and letters from our bank in Vancouver. At the Mexican Consulate in Los Angeles I produced both my passports and pointed out to them that I had been in Mexico from November 1936 to July 1938. I was not at all sure that I, being English, did not require to go through even further formalities: but I was assured that all regulations had been complied with and that all was satisfactory.

After visiting my wife's family we departed by American Airlines and arrived in Mexico City on approximately December 12, 1945. A few days later we left for Cuernavaca, Morelos, where we rented an apartment at 24 Calle de Humboldt, the proprietor of which is Senora Maria Luisa Blanco de Arriola. We lived in this apartment in Cuernavaca with the exception of a few trips to Oaxaca, Puebla, Tlaxcala, etc.

Certain explanations are necessary at this point. I had written a

novel set in Mexico called Under the Volcano and had received a virtual acceptance of it (later verified) by my publishers, Jonathan Cape,
in London. A subsidiary reason for voting for the trip was that it
would be a possible opportunity to correct, if necessary, some of the
idiomatic Spanish and possibly make a few notes for a preface to the
book of a friendly nature to Mexico. Not that the book should be
construed as unfriendly: to the contrary. On the other hand I felt it
might be misunderstood in Mexico, since many shades of opinion
are reflected in it, which is not surprising since that country is used as
an analogue of the world itself. But there is no political resolution,
other, that is to say, than a democratic one: in fact no resolution at all
unless it is, perhaps, moral. On our Tourist Cards we gave our occu-
pations as writers (escritores) but we entered as tourists and remained
as tourists with no intention of 'working' in Mexico, or taking any
money from Mexico for any work done while there, and in fact we
did no work while there with the exception of a few notes.

On Friday the 8th of March, 1946, after several happy months, we
left Cuernavaca for another brief trip, stopping in Taxco and Iguala,
and arrived in Acapulco on Sunday the 10th of March, 1946. We
stayed at the Hotel Quinta Eugenia at Caleta Beach. On the following Thursday, March 14, two men from the Office of Migracion
came to the hotel and asked to see our papers. It should be pointed
out that Acapulco is a port of entry and as a consequence all names of
tourists are sent into this office as a matter of course. My wife had
packed our bags while I was attending to reservations, etc., and since
we only intended to be away a week at most and she was afraid of
theft (we had had many things stolen) she unfortunately left our
papers in the apartment in Cuernavaca. Needless to say I knew by
experience how important it is to have one's papers with one when
travelling in a foreign country. But a new policy of sympathetic
attitude toward tourists that pertained in the state of Morelos
(superficially at least) did not incline one to take a serious view of our
omission. We had never been once asked for our papers since check-
ing in at the airport in Mexico City. I believe it is not, by the way,
illegal not to have your papers with you as long as you have them at
your place of residence. We therefore explained to the men from the
Migracion where our papers were and asked them what the trouble
was. They announced that we would have to remain in Acapulco, at
the hotel, until they checked on our Tourist Cards with Mexico City
and said they would send a wire that day regarding this. They also
told me that they had an unpaid fine against me to the amount of 50
pesos for having overstayed my leave in 1938 and further, because
they had pursued this fine until 1943, apparently not aware I had left

the country in July 1938, that they had in their files a letter saying that I was not allowed to enter Mexico without permission of the Chief of Migracion. This latter injunction I knew nothing about whatsoever. As to the 50-peso fine for having overstayed my leave, I must now make a further statement regarding that.

In November of 1936 I had originally entered Mexico through Acapulco, arriving by boat, and had returned to Acapulco again in the early spring of 1938. Since I had then a 'rentista's' status[2] I had had already further extensions on my original visa or card or whatever but at this time I required a further extension and had been wrongly advised, so far as I can recall, that I could get it there in Acapulco, since that had been my original port of entry; and I was also planning to leave from here by the Panama Pacific line. I applied for this extension and was then told, after many delays, that it was necessary to go to Mexico City to procure it. Very possibly there were other factors that I have forgotten, such as the possible defection of the Panama Pacific itself: I have a vague recollection that they suddenly stopped running their ships at a time when I could have left Mexico within the period then allotted me. Either that or my money was delayed in arriving through the American Express in New York. At all events I went to Mexico City, in company with the then Chief of Migracion in Acapulco, whose fare I paid to and probably from Mexico City, and also his hotel room at the Biltmore Hotel, and various expenses. I had by now overstayed my leave by, I think, not more than a few days. I cannot, however, swear to this. In Mexico City I went with this Chief of Migracion, a man by the name of Guyou (I cannot recall the exact spelling) to the main office of Migracion on Bucarelli St and was given, to the best of my knowledge, a further extension of six months. At any rate I certainly left Mexico well within the new time given me with no further difficulty that I can remember over my papers at any point, though I had other difficulties, chiefly personal. My first wife had returned to America in December 1937 and I had been, and still was, to some extent, very ill, the consequence of dysentery, malaria and rheumatic fever. Also there had been, as I said, some confusion about my income arriving, due to my changes of address or other misunderstanding, and as a result I had become somewhat in debt. My parents having become anxious about my health put a lawyer at my disposal and my income was paid through him, and before I left Mexico any and all debts were paid in full.[3] I am certain that if any fine was imposed it was also paid at that time – indeed it *must* have been or I should certainly not have been allowed to leave. I left Mexico in July 1938 and was admitted to America at Nogales. I was not aware, I repeat, of any unpaid fine nor of any such letter from the Chief of Migracion. Utterly oblivious that there might be anything held against me I applied for my visa and Tourist Card to enter Mexico in 1946 in good faith, and was given them by the Mexican Consulate in Los Angeles as stated.

To return to Acapulco and my statement of what happened there in March 1946: my wife, who was still not in the best of health, and I, went every day into the office of Migracion and waited some hours but no word from Mexico City was forthcoming. Meantime I was racking my brains to discover if anything else could possibly have caused this injunction against me and I remembered this: in 1937 my first wife and I had put a bond as 'rentistas.' This had been mainly arranged through her and a friend and when she left in 1937 she took the papers concerning this bond with her.[4] So far as I know I was still within the time limit of this bond when in Acapulco in 1938 and do not believe I could have got an extension if the bond had run out. But late in 1939, or early in 1940, when I was in Canada, I received word through my father's lawyer that the man who had underwritten this bond had been intimidated by the authorities for a whole year on the false grounds that I had not left the country at all.[5] To straighten up this matter I immediately went to the acting Mexican Consul here in Vancouver, produced proof that I had indeed left in July 1938 and this proof was forwarded to the necessary authorities so that they would cease intimidating this man, whose name I cannot now recall. I am certain also that if any compensation was due him it was paid, via funds at my disposal in America, since I believe it was then impossible to send funds out of this country.

Anxious to discover the precise truth with a view to remedying matters I now asked the Sub-Chief of Migracion in Acapulco to show my wife and I what was against me in his file and he was generous enough to do this. He only gave us a short while to look and the Spanish was too complicated to take in at a glance. I ascertained however that there was nothing about any bond whatsoever and that the file was mainly concerned with the government's unsuccessful attempt to recover this 50 peso fine. Guyou, however was mentioned, as was my trip to Mexico City with him, and since he was the only one directly concerned with my having overstayed my leave, and the intermediary between myself and the Mexican Government, and since, moreover, he would hardly have returned to Acapulco (we were staying at the same hotel in Mexico City) without having seen to it first that the fine was paid, either to the head office or to himself, the obvious implication is that something mysterious happened to this fine, as a consequence of which it was never crossed off the books at Acapulco. I could not help noting that the excuse he had given [for my not having paid the fine, which of course I *had* paid,]^b was that I was too *ebriadad* to do business with. If this were so it seems peculiar that I was not too *ebriadad* to make the trip to Mexico City, not to say to remember over eight years afterwards the hotel I put him up at, or to spend one whole afternoon with him at the head office, and stranger still, perhaps, that I was never arrested for being so *ebriadad*, if it was serious enough to put on a file against me as a matter of character. The fact is I was making many notes at that time in the cantinas or sidewalk taverns I imagined one protagonist of my forthcoming novel to be frequenting and these notes taken at this time make an important part of it. Doubtless this habit counted against me, though no one ever objected to it overtly. I was also, for that matter, making notes for a long dramatic poem entitled The Cantinas.[6]

I ascertained two facts of importance however from this file. First that the edict forbidding me to reenter the country without special permission was filed two months after I had left it, in September 1938, which explained why there was nothing about the bond. For they could scarcely forbid me to reenter the country without having prior knowledge of my having left it, and if they possessed this knowledge, what right had they to persecute the underwriter of my bond for a year on the grounds that I was still in Mexico? The second fact was that my date of entry into Mexico was wrongly given as September 1936. Actually it was November, 1936: apparently an innocent mistake, this could nevertheless make it appear that I had overstayed my leave that much longer, for here were two months extra credited to me when I had never been in the country at all. I have gone into all this as fully as possible because this was the only time I was ever allowed a glimpse of what purported to be held against me. When the British Consulate inquired, they were never informed but were merely told somewhat vaguely that 'there had been some trouble.' Later, when my wife and I were in Mexico City with an interpreter and witness we made every effort, as will be seen, to discover the reason for the treatment we received, but by this time they had emphatically denied that they had anything against me at all.

I now observed something else. The Sub-Chief of Migracion showed me the telegram he had sent to Mexico City explaining that we did not have our Tourist Cards with us, etc., and asking for instructions. In this telegram he had given the name of my *first* wife as being here with me in Acapulco, although we had repeatedly explained the situation to him. My wife had given him her name, stated that she was *not* with me in Mexico in 1938, had never been in Mexico at all before, and that she was, as a matter of fact, in Los Angeles in 1938 and completely unaware of my existence. He replied that he had looked in my old file and found out what my wife's name was and we needn't try to tell him it was something else. In the end I believe we convinced him of the truth. He was himself going to Mexico City the following day and he stated that he would go himself and correct this error. I do not know whether this mistake on the part of the Sub-Chief of Migracion in Acapulco was ever cleared up or not, despite repeated efforts, for later on, in Mexico City, if not Sr Corunna, someone in his office still seemed under the impression that my present wife was indeed my first wife who had entered under a false name for some obscure purpose of her own and for all I know nothing ever really convinced them to the contrary.

On Wednesday, March 20, 1946, a man from the Oficina Federal de Hacienda came to our hotel. He refused to come into our room but stood on the porch, having called the manager and several of the employees of the hotel also, he threatened us, using abusive terms in a loud voice, demanding instant payment of the same 50 peso fine. It was very difficult to understand him as he became quite incoherent in the end, but we finally persuaded him to meet us that afternoon at 4 o'clock in the office of the Department of Turista, where there would be a man who would interpret and act as witness for us. We therefore met at this office, where a man who is second in command at the office, Senor Obregon, interpreted for us and said that unless the fine was paid at once I would be taken to jail. It must be repeated that our papers and money were in Cuernavaca, we had only taken a limited amount with us for the trip and had already paid for telegrams, long distance phone calls, et al to Mexico City in an effort to expedite the matter, our hotel bill was running on in Acapulco and our rent was now due in Cuernavaca, and all this we had explained fully without the slightest sympathy toward our plight being forthcoming. They merely said they would doubtless hear from Mexico City tomorrow, or 'Mexico City is very slow.' The man from the Hacienda said finally that he would give me until Saturday morning to pay the fine and would take my watch (or something else) as security. Senor Obregon, who was most kind throughout, therefore said that if such procedure was necessary he would himself keep the watch as security and this he did. The Chief of the Department of Turistas had meantime telephoned the Department of Migracion and was, at our request, inquiring about a long distance call purported to have been put through at our expense that day to Mexico City regarding our case. He reported that they had been told in Mexico City that they had no knowledge of the case at all and knew nothing about me whatsoever, but that still they would not release us. I protested that since there was absolutely nothing against my wife it was wrong to hold her and she went on to add that she should be allowed to go to Cuernavaca and get our papers and money, and that if she was not allowed to go she or I would call the American Consul long distance to Mexico City and apply for aid. This was relayed by phone and the Chief of Turista told us that the Chief of Migracion had now said that my wife would be allowed to go to Cuernavaca but that she must leave at once and be back by Saturday. It was impossible at such short notice to get reservations and she was forced to leave on a second class bus to make a night trip alone across Mexico. I will not go into the obvious dangers of such a trip. She arrived in Cuernavaca at 5 A.M., got our papers and money and proceeded to Mexico City where she appealed to the British Consulate. She went to the British Consulate since I am, as stated, an Englishman and it was I and the 50 peso fine etc. against me that was, or seemed to be, the trouble. Moreover as a British subject herself by marriage she was entitled to his protection. She was unable to see the Consul General but presented our case to Mr Percival Hughes, the Vice Consul. He looked through our papers carefully, said that they were in perfect order, was most sympathetic, made notes of the numbers of our Tourist Cards, my passport, all dates concerning the matter, etc., etc. She told him of the fine and all that she knew concerning the reason for it and he said that if she would stay over night in Mexico City he would go with her the following morning to the Department of Migracion and straighten the whole matter out. The following morning, Friday March 22, he informed her that the Consul General had ordered her to return to Acapulco and pay the fine there. He said that they would go, however, to the Migracion office that morning and see that we were released at once. She returned to Acapulco by bus and on Saturday morning we went, together with a Mr W. Hudson, who acted as interpreter and witness, to the Oficina Federal de Hacienda. There we paid the fine. We saw the man who had come to our hotel to demand payment and the Chief of Hacienda. We asked for the return of my watch and said that we objected to the manner in which this man had acted at our hotel as being totally unnecessary and embarrassing. He then denied threatening me with jail or having taken the watch. We asked that Senor Obregon be sent for which was done. He arrived, very graciously returned my watch, and entirely corroborated our statement as to threats, etc. The Chief of Hacienda then informed us that their man had no right to make threats or to take the watch, that all he was empowered to do was quietly to present me with a bill. He further offered an apology, said that the Constitution of Mexico had been breached by this action and that we could make a complaint if we wished and that we had two witnesses. This we declined to do out of a reciprocal courtesy to the courtesy which was being shown us at this point by the Office of Hacienda. Mr Hudson, who had also been with us on one occasion to the Oficina of Migracion and had seen my file there, said that this was a mistake made in their own office and not my fault. The Chief of Hacienda, who was very courteous throughout this interview, agreed, while Senor Obregon expressed himself as dubious whether a fine of 50 pesos could be pursued for as long as 8 years anyway and sportingly promised to try and get it back for us if he could.

We then took the receipt for the fine, our papers, and went with Mr Hudson to the Office of Migracion, showed our papers and the receipt and asked if we were now free to leave. They said we could not leave until they heard from Mexico City. The British Vice Consul had promised to wire us at once if anything was wrong at his end: he did not wire us. He had also instructed us, if we were not immediately released upon my wife's return from Mexico City, to wire him. We did so and received no reply.

They kept us at Acapulco, where we were forced to come every day to the Office of Migracion, down into the town of Acapulco where the heat is extreme, and wait for hours, frequently in an empty office.

Meanwhile however the Sub-Chief of Migracion had returned from Mexico City and when we saw him delivered himself as follows: that in Mexico City they had, unfortunately, disclaimed any knowledge of receiving his wire, which might account for some of the delay. He said, however, that they had now found my file there, in which was a record of another fine, this time for 100 pesos, which had been paid. He also said that there was a photograph of me there with a beard. This was true, I had grown one for fun in 1937, and it was on the duplicate of my card or whatever as a 'rentista.' When I asked him if we could go now, he said that he had asked the Secretary of Migracion there if he would not let us go and the Secretary had said, 'No, don't do that.' When I asked him if there was anything further on the file, real or imaginary, which could account for this treatment he said, 'I don't know.' But he implied that the beard was a bad thing in itself, so bad indeed that my wife, in spite of her papers being in perfect order, in spite of there being nothing whatever against her, and her being an American citizen, could not go either. So we remained in Acapulco.

A statement of this kind is not the place to describe the feelings with which we received the news that Mexico had disclaimed all knowledge of receiving the wire. But we naturally wondered if it had not been sent very much later than stated, while we were kept waiting in the interim; just as we wondered if a phone call to Mexico that I had suspected the Chief of Turista (suspected because I recognized him as a friend of Guyou's who had formerly been in the Migracion) of only pretending was being put through by the Chief of Migracion while we waited in the former's office, had ever been put through at all.

So we waited in Acapulco.

About 10 days after my wife's return from Mexico City we received a letter from the British Consul General, Mr Rogers,[7] saying that the Mexican Authorities had decided to deport me and asking if my papers were in order to return to America, although my wife had shown these papers at the British Consulate to the Vice Consul, Mr Hughes who had written all this down, as before stated. We telephoned the Consulate long distance and spoke with Mr Hughes who could give absolutely no reason for this action by the Mexican Authorities and said they did not know why it was being done. He said he would talk to them further and wire me. This he did not do and I called him again some days later. He then said that I was not to be deported but might be asked to leave the country, but again could not say why as they had given him no reason. Finally, on Thursday, April 4th, the Office of Migracion in Acapulco, who themselves disclaimed all knowledge of this deportation order, said they had themselves decided we had been there too long and that they would give us a letter on the following day which would allow us to go, but made it obligatory that we appear at the office of Migracion in Mexico City on Monday, April 8th. The following day, 22 days after they first came to the hotel, they gave us this letter permitting us to leave.

We went to our apartment in Cuernavaca (where I promptly received the almost insane news that the book set in Mexico, for which I was proposing to write the friendly preface, had been accepted simultaneously in both England and America) and on Monday morning went to Mexico City with an interpreter, Mr Eduardo Ford, owner and proprietor of the restaurant 'Bahia,' 12 Jardin Morelos, Cuernavaca, Mexico. We were kept waiting in the office until it was too late to accomplish anything, and were told to return in a few days.

It should be said that it is about fifty miles from Cuernavaca to Mexico City but this gives no idea of the character of the trip. Though it only takes two to two and a half hours it is necessary to climb to an altitude of over 10,000 feet and one frequently arrives deafened. The climate likewise is completely different: one leaves Cuernavaca in tropical heat and you are likely at this time of year to run into a snow storm in the mountains: beautiful in itself, such a journey, endlessly repeated under such conditions becomes a nightmare, especially since it is difficult to make reservations either by car or bus, both are prone to break down on the way, and from all this my wife's health especially began to suffer. Despite this we managed to keep every appointment during the following four weeks punctually, yet we never waited less than three hours and usually four or five hours. We are far from wealthy people; had budgeted our vacation very carefully, and we were put to what was for us near fatal expense to make these frequent trips for ourselves and often an interpreter. For though we may specify only what happened during certain visits, it should be borne in mind that there were many more visits when despite promises nothing happened at all and we were kept waiting in a vacuum: we calculated that we travelled well over a thousand miles during those four weeks simply between Cuernavaca and Mexico City and probably it was more like twelve hundred.

To resume: we returned on Friday, April 12, and were informed that our case had been sent to the Office of Inspecion. We waited there the usual hours, finally saw an Inspector whose name I do not know but who was in charge of our case and whom I shall have reason to refer to many times more, simply as the Inspector. He took all our papers, (including the receipt for the fine which was incidentally never returned to us) and our identification and consulted with the Chief of the Office of Inspeccion one Sr Corunna. The fine had been paid and our papers were in order. But the Inspector now noted that on our Tourist Cards we had given our occupation as writers. He then said that as writers we should not have been allowed to enter Mexico at all as tourists, and should have had a working permit or some other form of passport and asked if we would like immigration papers. Both we ourselves and our interpreter were astounded at this statement. Our interpreter remarked that there were thousands of writers, singers and painters, busily painting pictures all over Mexico, and inquired if all of them had entered the country on immigration or working papers, and if it was against the law for any artists to come to Mexico for a vacation. The inspector was himself somewhat taken aback but recovering himself stated that while it was true that they did not have immigration or working papers that actually they should have. Since we ourselves personally knew three artists who, on Tourist Cards only, were painting in Mexico and one of whom had been giving lessons to Mexicans and taking money for these lessons, besides writers who had certainly been writing articles for Magazines published in Mexico, such as *Modern Mexico* etc., and none of these people had been molested by the Government in any way, we were somewhat puzzled. We protested against what appeared to us to be discrimination, saying that if this were so it was not our fault but that of the Mexican Consulate in Los Angeles, but to no avail. I said that we were not working in Mexico, had taken no money in Mexico for any work done in Mexico nor had any intention of doing so; that we had, being writers, naturally taken some notes, mostly in the form of simply a day to day journal, or of the 'jot it down' variety, possibly to be transformed later into a short story or some travel articles my wife had thought of writing after our return to Canada, and so on. Whether or not I said anything about having taken notes for my proposed preface I don't remember. The Inspector admitted that the taking of such notes could hardly be called 'working' in Mexico. Nevertheless, he insisted that we *were* working, and demanded that we put up a bond of 500 pesos apiece and promise not to do any *more* work while we were in Mexico. We insisted that we had not done any work per se. He said that the bond would be necessary however, and gave us until Monday morning to produce the cash or the bond. This struck me as just possibly poetic justice in my case but our interpreter, Sr Ford, was highly indignant and said that the Inspector had just remarked to him that actually, of course, this was more or less extra-offical, and further that the Inspector said that if I had given the Chief of Migracion in Acapulco 50 pesos to put in his pocket that the whole thing would have been settled there and that the head office would never have heard of it. And this I was to hear repeated many times: that the defection was the original defection of my failing to pay the 'mordida.' The British Vice Consul himself said this to me openly later on in this same office and further advised me that it would be as well to offer the Inspector 100 pesos or so, and in fact it was impossible to sit in that office as long as we did without witnessing with one's own eyes the truth of this.

But somewhere, during the foregoing conversation, we did something in all innocence that doubtless complicated matters still further. In the belief that the Inspector doubted that we were who and what we said we were, or perhaps because by this time we were beginning to doubt our own identity, I showed him a copy of my wife's novel, (The Shapes That Creep, Scribner's, published January 14 of this year) my contract from Jonathan Cape of London, and also the telegram from Reynal and Hitchcock of New York re the acceptance of my book. The book had been finished in 1944 in Canada.

However, on this day, April 12, the Inspector said to our interpreter, Sr Ford, that if we put up this bond or the same amount of cash by Monday morning that our papers would be returned and that we would be free to stay in Mexico without any further molestation until the expiration of our Tourist Cards which would be on June 10th.

It is, of course, necessary to obtain someone with property to underwrite such a bond and this was difficult to do on such short notice because I knew no one in Mexico City who could do this and furthermore the following week was Holy Week and on Monday all bonding companies would be closed. However, our witness and interpreter, Sr Ford, was highly indignant at the procedure and offered (in spite of the fact that he was fully informed by myself of my previous error – if error it was – over just such a matter) to underwrite the bond himself, giving as security his own restaurant in Cuernavaca. He managed to obtain this bond for us and on the following Monday morning we presented it and asked for our papers. We were taken in to see the Chief of the department, Sr Corunna, who was very insulting to my wife, ordered her out of his office, and refused to give us our papers. We had said that we wished to leave Mexico as soon as possible and Corunna, whose technique is to shout, demanded the date of our leaving. I explained that we wished to fly as I did not feel the long train trip was good for my wife, and since Mexico was the port of exit when flying we could not possibly obtain our tickets without our papers. He then asked for the approximate date of our leaving and I told him as soon as we could possibly get reservations on the return of our papers. Calming down slightly he then told us to return again, as nearly as I can recall, about a week later when we would be given our papers, which were now in order. He assured us finally that all was well, that there was nothing to be concerned about, that it was a matter of no importance.

It may well be asked at this point why I did not appeal to the British Consulate again for help, or my wife did not go to her American Consul, although she is, as I have said, by virtue of marriage to myself, also a British subject and equally has a right to apply to the British Consulate. She did not go to the American Consul because it was my status that had precipitated the situation and she had only been drawn into it on that account and the American Consul could do nothing for me, and therefore nothing, we thought, would be achieved by this action. I did not appeal again to the British Consulate, save on one more occasion, because by this time I had lost faith in their ability, or willingness, to assist me. And finally, because we were continually assured, by everyone in the Office of

Inspeccion, despite the mental cruelty of this treatment, and right up to the very last moment, that our papers were in order, that they had absolutely nothing against us, and that there was nothing at all to worry about, and the various delays were simply a matter of Governmental red tape and slowness.

The day previous to our next appointment with Sr Corunna, we had Sr Ford telephone him long distance from Cuernavaca. Sr Ford talked with Corunna, who assured him that our papers were there, perfectly in order, and that we could now come and get them any time we wished. Therefore on or about April 23 we went to Mexico City to get our papers, intending immediately upon receipt of them to make application for airplane reservations. Meantime I had wired my bank in Canada to send money to the Banco Nacional de Mexico in Cuernavaca, and also received word that my agent in New York had wired me part of my advance money on my book to Cuerna-vaca. By this time we were running short of cash, because of all these extra expenses, but it was impossible to obtain either the money from the bank or the money from my agent at the telegraph office, as I was without any identification whatsoever, the Government having it all, so I was therefore also unable to buy tickets to leave the country, although I had several hundred dollars between the bank and the telegraph office. Sr Corunna once more refused to give us our papers, which, however, he repeated, were now in perfect order, and there was absolutely nothing for us to worry about. At that point Mr Hughes, the British Vice Consul, happened to come into the office on some other business and, since he was there, I did appeal to him again to try and get me some part of my papers, some identi-fication I could present in order to get my money, since the telegraph office would send the money back to New York if I did not claim it within a day or two more. Mr Hughes then spoke to Sr Corunna on our behalf and Corunna assured him that everything was all right, that the only reason we were not given our papers that day was because they had once more been sent back to the Office of Migra-cion where they were on the desk of a man who was not in his office that particular day. He said that if we would return on Friday he would have the papers for us and that there was no further question or delay. We therefore made a definite appointment for Friday morn-ing at 11:30 A.M., at which Mr Hughes also volunteered to be present. Mr Hughes further stated to us on that morning that it was he himself who had procured our release from Acapulco on the morning of Friday, April 9th, from the office of Migracion in Mexico City and had seen the telegram which had been sent. It seemed rather odd to us that it had been on Thursday, April 8th, that the office of Migracion in Acapulco had said that they themselves were letting us go, but we made no great issue of this. Mr Hughes further said that a week after they had first ordered my wife to return to Acapulco (on the promise that he or the Consul General would go that morning to the Migracion) they had sent the office boy over who returned with the report that I was to be deported. This trouble shooter, it will be shown, at least told part of the truth.

On Friday, April 26th, therefore, we returned once more to Mexico City to keep our appointment with Mr Hughes and Sr Corunna. When we arrived, on time, after a journey of more than usual difficulty during which our transportation twice broke down and which had required four cars to get us there, Mr Hughes was not there and my wife telephoned him while I sought an opportunity to speak again to Sr Corunna. Mr Hughes explained to my wife that he was too busy at the Consulate to keep his appointment with us but said, after my wife once more explained the need for identification so that I could get our money, and asked him for help, that he would telephone Sr Corunna regarding this matter. He asked her to call him back in ten minutes, which she did. Mr Hughes then said that he had spoken to Sr Corunna, who had told him that our papers were still on the desk in the department of Migracion, and that the man who had them was once more not in his office, or rather was there, but had simply made up his mind not to do any more work that day. Mr Hughes reiterated our plight, the necessity for some identification etc., but Sr Corunna replied that he was unable to give us anything. My wife appealed to Mr Hughes to make some further effort to help us, or to find out what, if anything, was wrong, but he replied that he could do no more for us at all.

I then spoke to Sr Corunna myself and was told to return the following morning. We returned once more to Mexico City the following morning and again I spoke to Sr Corunna. After some long discussion during which he repeatedly shouted at me as usual in an insulting manner – I kept my wife out of the conversations so far as possible because of his savagely hysterical method of conducting them – he went, in the end, to the Office of Migracion and procured my old, cancelled passport for me. He further told me to come once more to Mexico City on the following Tuesday, April 30th, when the man who had our papers would be there without fail and they would then definitely be returned to us. However he once more demanded when we intended to leave, and I once more explained that we could not make reservations without these papers or buy tickets until I could get my money.

We returned to Cuernavaca and I received the money from the

telegraph office that Saturday afternoon, just in time, as they were about to return it to New York. On Monday morning I went to the bank and received the money I had wired for to my Canadian bank.

On Tuesday morning we went once more to Mexico City and to the Office of Inspeccion. The Inspector then informed us that it was necessary for us to come with him and have some photographs taken for our Immigration papers. I think at this point my wife said, very understandably, that she didn't want Immigration papers but only wanted to leave Mexico, and if I did not say it myself it was only because I was engaged in keeping the temper which I knew it was their prime object for me to lose. I asked to be allowed to speak to Sr Corunna, saying that he had promised to give us back our papers without fail that morning. This was refused. I then inquired why they suddenly had decided to change our papers and my wife asked to be allowed to go to the department of Turista to obtain an interpreter who would explain more fully, since the Inspector was difficult to understand, our Spanish not being fluent, when he became excited. This was also refused and we were taken across the street where photographs were made under the assurance that these photographs were for Immigration papers. In them I look a criminal and my wife, (the Inspector rudely snatched off her hat at the moment they were taking the photograph and her hair was disarranged) like a madwoman. Anyone seeing these photographs would wonder not that we were to be deported but that such people could be at large at all, which I take it is the impression such pictures are designed to give. On the other hand, the strain was beginning to tell. Meantime we had been told that these photographs would be ready at 2 o'clock and that we must wait in the office of Inspeccion until that hour. We were refused permission to go to lunch, or even to go out for a cup of coffee, though I explained that as usual we had had to leave Cuernavaca very early in the morning and my wife was fatigued, or, in fact, to leave the office for any reason whatsoever, being assured, continually, however, that Sr Corunna would see me in a moment and that everything was quite in order. At 2 o'clock my wife went and got the photographs, which the Inspector regarded as being uproariously ridiculous and laughed at loudly and long. At 2:30 the Inspector suddenly informed us, after Sr Corunna had left and the office was just closing for the day, that it would be necessary for us to be at this office again on the morning of May 2 (May 1 being a holiday) at 12 noon, with all our luggage.

We protested that we could not understand the reason for this. We wished to remain in Cuernavaca, where we had paid the rent of our apartment, until leaving Mexico and did not wish to go to the further expense of living in Mexico City at an hotel. Also we did not understand why, after being assured, and the Consul likewise assured, that all our papers were in order, that there was nothing whatsoever against us, after we had put up the bond, etc. etc., why, we repeated, we were thus abruptly commanded to bring our luggage to Mexico City. The Inspector became very angry and seized my arm, said that if I did not understand I should come with him at once to jail. He further abused us for not living in Mexico City. When I explained hopelessly that we loved Cuernavcaca and wished to make the most of living there until our departure, he demanded to know the name of the hotel we were living at in Mexico City. He further said that if we were not in the office on May 2, at 12 noon, with our luggage, he would come to Cuernavaca and put us under arrest. The office was then closed, everyone had gone, there was nothing we could do that day. Once more therefore we returned to Cuernavaca. That evening we saw Sr Ford, who informed us that the bonding company, Central de Fianzas, S.A., Motolinia 20, Mexico City, had telephoned him long distance that afternoon to say that the Government had cashed in our bond, and required him, Sr Ford, to immediately make good the 1000 pesos or be jailed and his business confiscated. They had obviously cashed in this bond while keeping us waiting in the office insisting to us meanwhile that everything was quite all right. The following morning, May 1, Senor Ford received a telegram from the bonding company verifying the fact that the Government had cashed the bond the previous day. We have this telegram in our possession and I now quote it: *Hoy hizo efectivas secretarias Gobernacion fianzas esposos Lowry. Suplicamosle remitirnos inmediatamente un mil pesos importe garantias objeto no perjudicar intereses. Central de Fianzas, S.A.* We therefore paid Sr Ford the 1000 pesos and we have his receipt for the money.

On the following morning, Thursday May 2, we left Cuernavaca with our luggage in company with Sr Ford, who was going to the bonding company to pay them the 1000 pesos, and went to Mexico City. We arrived 2 hours ahead of time in the hope of finding out what the difficulty was and making some last effort to present our case to the authorities in its proper light. Also another Mexican citizen, sympathetic with our case and a man of some influence, had offered to meet us there at 10 A.M. and act as interpreter and witness for us. We waited for him until 10:45 but he did not arrive. We then went into the Department of Turista, where we had left our luggage for the time being, and saw Sr Buelna, the chief of that department. The time was short, as we had to appear in the office of Inspeccion with the luggage at 12 noon, but we explained our case and asked for help. At first he stated that he was unable to do anything at all since it was not in his department. However there were in his office at the time some American tourists who could not help hearing and in the end he kindly telephoned to someone in the office of the Sub-Secretario of the Interior and arranged for us to see the Sub-Secretario, Dr Perez-Martinez, in a few minutes, when he would be finished with his conference with the Secretario. Dr Martinez would, he said, at least give us a hearing. We went to the office of the Sub-Secretario, our names were sent in, we said the matter was urgent in the extreme, and waited over three quarters of an hour. By now it was nearly 12 o'clock and the Inspector came into the office and ordered us down to the office of Inspeccion. We explained that we were waiting to put our case before the Sub-Secretario, since we had been informed that he was the final authority in such matters. The Inspector again ordered us to come at once to the other office but still hoping for a hearing on our case we waited. We were eventually informed that the Sub-Secretario's secretary had refused to allow us to see Dr Martinez or inform him that we were waiting, on the following peculiar grounds: that since the Americans treated the Mexicans like dogs, in fact worse than dogs since Americans were kind to animals, why should we not be treated like dogs ourselves?

My wife, while I remained there still in hopes of obtaining a hearing at the last moment, then went back to see Sr Buelna to ask at least that we be given an interpreter and witness. Sr Buelna at first replied that this was impossible, but in the end was kind enough to provide us with one. In company with this witness we went to the office of Inspeccion. Here we waited, and asked to see Sr Corunna. We were informed that Sr Corunna had his orders from the Sub-Secretario regarding ourselves and that it would be impossible for us to see him. We tried once more to find out why we were being treated in this extraordinary manner and at this the Inspector became very angry and said that we had 'said bad things about Mexico.' This we denied – it could be called true only in the sense that we were objecting to this treatment now – stating as we had many times before that we loved Mexico and her people, which was so and still, despite this experience is so, and that we still wished to discover what was wrong, still wished a fair hearing, as we felt sure that there must be some final misunderstanding worse than all the others regarding our case. We were then told that we must accompany the Inspector to 113 Bucarelli, where we would be given our papers and allowed to go. Since we knew that this was (as it were) a jail and not a government office we protested. We asked for the British Consul. My wife asked for the American Consul. This was denied. We were told again that we were merely going to this 113 Bucarelli to get our papers, and were taken, under our protests, to this place. Once inside, we were forced to sign our names in a register. We once more protested and demanded to see our Consuls, asking what their intentions were regarding ourselves, if they meant to deport us, and if so, why? The Inspector denied emphatically that we were to be deported. We then asked the Interpreter, who was visibly wilting, to please telephone our Consuls immediately, and he replied that he would inform Sr Buelna of the situation.

My wife and I were then taken into a small barred room where there were already two other men in bed and no lavatory facilities for my wife, there being only one inordinately filthy lavatory for all four of us, which had no door and opened directly off the room where we were kept. We were informed that we were being held incommunicado, and locked in. The Chief of this place, however, was extremely courteous and was distressed by the lack of privacy for my wife. He also sent out for some food for us, at our expense naturally, saying that we could not possibly eat the prison food. This was true: there was no prison food. Or if so they were not going to provide us with any free. Everyone here was kind and sympathetic, and the Chief finally opened up another sort of room for us beyond the first one and brought us his own blanket which, he explained, was clean. It should be mentioned however that our luggage had meantime been brought to this place and deposited in an outer room. Later we discovered that our wardrobe trunk had been broken open and half of my wife's clothes were missing and also our camera. This theft can only have taken place at the Turista office or at 113 Bucarelli as there was no other opportunity. We had had nothing to eat all day and our food did not arrive until late afternoon, simultaneously with the Inspector. He gave us only five minutes to eat and then ordered us into a taxi in which we were taken to the railroad station and immediately put aboard the train. All further protestations or demands to see our Consuls were futile. Escape was impossible: the Inspector was armed.

Our train was a day coach with no berths and my wife and I were forced to sit up all that night and to stay within sight of the Inspector every minute. We both inquired of him several times the reason for this treatment. We asked if we were being deported and he replied definitely, no. He stated that his orders were to take us to Nuevo Laredo and there to give us our papers and allow us to cross the border to America alone and unmolested. We asked him why the bond had been cashed and he insisted that it had not been cashed. We then showed him the telegram proving that it had been cashed and he then said he had no knowledge of it at all. He, of course, had the tickets. He sat where he could watch our every movement, but apart from the sense of shame and embarassment it caused, he did not actively molest or persecute us and indeed allowed us to eat our meals in the dining car by ourselves. The stewards, conductor and train men were however left in no doubt as to our status and we were by and large made to feel like criminals.

When the train arrived in Nuevo Laredo it was after midnight of the second night: there was a severe thunderstorm and all the lights in the train had gone out. We then asked him for our papers, which he had promised, and with that he began throwing our luggage out of the window of the train and as the train began to pull out (it was a very brief stop) ordered us to get out, and in fact my wife, who had got off on the wrong side of the train had to cross back through the train while it was moving, narrowly escaping a serious accident.

We then all proceeded in a taxi, with our luggage, to the Mexican Immigration office, situated directly at the edge of the bridge across the Rio Grande River. There we waited again, watching the lights of Laredo on the American side of the bridge, while the Inspector conferred with a clerk whom he had ordered to write something on a typewriter. It was now about 2 o'clock in the morning. Presently this document which the clerk had been typing was presented to my wife to sign. When she read it she discovered it was a deportation order, stating that she admitted she was being deported for having broken the immigration laws of Mexico. Since they had all denied that we were being deported, and had never at any time given any reasons for this action, unless it was the Inspector's remark that we had said 'bad things about Mexico', and we had never at any time been given a fair hearing, and it was absolutely untrue in her case that she had broken any immigration laws whatsoever, and moreover I understand that you have to be given 24 hours notice in writing of any such impending deportation, my wife refused to sign. The clerk became very distressed and begged her to sign, implying grave danger to her if she did not. I told her not to sign and stated that I had no intention of signing any such order either. The Inspector became violently angry and incredibly insulting and since he had a gun and she was being threatened in no uncertain terms I finally told her to sign: there was no choice and in order to avoid being separated from her I then likewise signed, but we both stated that we completely repudiated the charge and that we were signing the document under pressure. They then told my wife that since she was an American she was free to go, and could walk across the bridge, but the American

Immigration office now being closed for the night I could not go until it opened in the morning. She refused to go without me and they then, curiously enough, urged her to go. I did not, by that time, trust their good will in the matter – if all this, why not ley fuga?[8] – and though I had at first told her to go I now felt it would be safer for her to remain with me. The Inspector then left, having given orders that we were both to be held in the office until the following morning. The clerk however, once the Inspector had left, took pity on my wife, who was utterly exhausted and in a condition of nervous shock, and arranged for us to go to an hotel, under guard, for a short time so that we might at least have a bath and a brief rest. At 5:30 A.M. another man from the Immigration office came to the hotel and took us back to the office.

Once more we waited in the Immigration office. We had been informed the night before that the American Immigration opened at 7 A.M. and that at that time we would be allowed to go. Therefore, shortly after 7, we asked if we could now leave and cross into America. We were informed that it would be necessary for us to see the Chief of this Immigration office and that he would be in between eight and nine o'clock. At nine o'clock the second in command of the office arrived and we presented our case to him as well as we could. We assured him that we were positive there had been some serious mistake, that we had been told over and over again that our papers were in order, that we had done nothing to provoke this peculiar treatment, that we had signed the paper the previous night under strong protest, and so on. He was courteous, but said we would have to wait for the Chief. Again we waited; a little later, while I was speaking to someone else in the office, my wife again spoke to the second in command. He informed her that the Inspector had left instructions that we were to be held there until he returned for us that morning. What disposition was then to be made of us we were never quite informed, but it was intimated that my wife was to be taken across the border by the Inspector and deported to America, since she had refused to leave without me the previous night. What they proposed to do with me I cannot make any sworn statement about, but the implications were not pleasant. We now once more briefly placed our case before this Sub-Chief, who took a most charitable and Christian attitude toward the whole thing. He very kindly allowed us to go and have a cup of coffee, saying he would speak to the Chief about us when he came in. These were moments of suspense. When we returned the Sub-Chief had spoken to the Chief and told us that we would be allowed to leave at once, as we had requested, before the onset of the Inspector, who was of course by now long overdue, it being after 10 A.M. I believe that we had convinced this Sub-Chief at least of our integrity, for he now returned our papers to us and made every effort to help us get away as quickly as possible. He procured a taxi for us, we were rushed through the Mexican customs without their even opening our luggage (while the Sub-Chief, as it were, stood guard outside, watching for the Inspector) and we swiftly crossed the bridge into America.

Our joy and relief at entering the United States were boundless.

While I was waiting in the office of Immigration in Laredo, Texas, as being a British subject my papers had to be inspected of course and my readmission card filled out, we saw the Inspector, who had apparently followed us right across the border, pass by in a towering temper, and that, I am glad to report, was the last we saw of this man. What he did or said I have no way of knowing. My papers being in order I was admitted that morning, Saturday the 4th of May, into the United States.

From Laredo we proceeded to Los Angeles, via Braniff, Continental and American Airlines, where we paid a visit to my wife's family and thence back here to our home in Canada. Immediately upon arriving in Los Angeles we consulted an attorney who advised us to prepare this statement and have it notarized.

To sum up our case my formulation of it would be something like the following:

That against my wife there was nothing whatsoever, that she had contravened no immigration regulations whatsoever, and that she was simply being made to suffer for being my wife. That against myself, setting aside such contributary factors as the 50 peso fine, there was against me fundamentally only the fact that I had entered a country that I was not permitted to enter without special permission of the Secretary of Gobernacion, my defense for such action being that I was unaware that any such injunction existed against me, and my proof that I was unaware of this injunction being in their own files, where it was stated that they had pursued an alleged unpaid fine against me until the year 1943 without being able to locate my address. If, since the injunction in question was placed in the files against me in September 1938, two months after I had left the country, they had made any communication at that early date re such an injunction to any second party such as a lawyer [Benjamin Parks] acting for my father in Mexico and Los Angeles who might know my address, I had to the very best of my knowledge and belief not been notified of this fact, and the proof that no such communication could have been made without double-dealing somewhere lay in the fact that the only further communication I ever received re my former visit to Mexico was in 1939 or 1940 when I heard something which is incompatible with any edict forbidding me to return: the Authorities claimed to believe I was still in the country. As before stated I then went to the acting Mexican Consul here in Vancouver and established the fact that I had left in July 1938. Furthermore, the Mexican Consulate in Los Angeles granted me my visa and Tourist Card although I told them I had been in Mexico before and waited 24 hours as previously stated. And finally, if Sr Corunna did not believe that I had acted in all good faith, why did he profess and reiterate for one month that all was well and my papers were in order and that we could depart unmolested? Why did they tell us the photographs were simply being made for Immigration papers, or insist until the last minute, at 2 o'clock in the morning at the border, that we would be given our papers back and allowed to leave? Why was it made impossible for us to obtain any basis for some proper accounting of what was being done with our 1000 peso bond, by giving us such short notice to leave our apartment in Cuernavaca, and by witholding Consular protection from us at the last moment by holding us incommunicado in 113 Bucarelli? Why, after having told the British Consulate I should be asked to leave the country, did they then require us to put up a bond, giving their solemn promise that if we did so we would be free to stay until the expiration of our Tourist Cards in June? Why, above all, if they sincerely wanted to get rid of us, didn't they simply let us go?

During the entire period of over 7 weeks we made every effort to cooperate with these Authorities in every way, to find out precisely what the difficulty was with a view, if possible, of straightening the matter out. But I was never told the precise reason for this injunction being issued in the first place, or allowed to present my case to anyone in authority who would listen to me. So far as the Gobernacion was concerned, we were never given a fair hearing. In fact we were never given a hearing of any sort by them. Whatever their motives in my case for this protracted persecution of the nationals of two friendly countries there seems no excuse nor warrant: and for my wife, an innocent American citizen, what was done to her amounts to a crime.

I swear that this statement is to the best of my knowledge and belief absolutely true.

[unsigned][c]

Annotations:

1 A. Ronald Button was an attorney in Los Angeles and a friend of the Woolfans, Lowry's in-laws. Lowry used the extraordinary events described in this letter and in his Mexican notebooks for the unfinished novel 'La Mordida.'

2 The Spanish legal term *rentista* means one who is a bondholder or who has independent financial means.

3 Lowry's first wife, Jan Gabrial, had gone to Los Angeles, where Lowry also went in July 1938, and where the lawyer in charge of his affairs was Benjamin Parks. Lowry is presenting a carefully edited and sanitized version of these details to Button.

4 In a letter to me of 9 December 1991, Jan Gabrial explains the couple's situation at the end of 1937 and Lowry's status in 1938. Apparently the Lowrys' Cuernavaca landlady, a Senora Baldwin, put Jan and Malcolm in touch with her lawyer in Mexico City, who drew up their *rentista* papers and 'went bond' for them as well. Jan did not take Lowry's papers with her to Los Angeles; she left them with friends (Marcia and Alfredo) in Mexico City for safe keeping because she feared that Lowry would lose them. She expected that he would collect them when he 'decided to rejoin me according to our plan.'

5 It is possible that the lawyer in Mexico City who had put up the bond was bothered by the authorities, but it is also possible that the trouble was caused by Malcolm himself. As Jan Gabrial explains, in every Oaxacan bar Lowry accused the young man he was travelling with (a friend of Marcia and Alfredo) of being a Communist. This man, whose name was Harry Mensch, helped to get Lowry out of jail in Oaxaca, but finally 'fled both Malcolm and Oaxaca.'

6 This long dramatic poem was never written, but ten poems about Mexico are listed under this general title in *Selected Poems* (34-44), and Scherf includes thirteen as 'The Cantinas' in part 3 of 'The Lighthouse Invites the Storm' (*CP*, 57-64).

7 There are transcriptions of several telegrams from the Mexican and British authorities kept with the drafts of Lowry's letter (UBC 2:4), and one of these, dated 5 April 1946, from D. Rogers, the British consul general, informs the Lowrys that they are free to return to the United States but that they must show the Mexican 'Ministerio de Gobernacion' both their reservations for the trip and their passports.

8 The Spanish phrase *ley de fuga* means 'escape from the law' and refers to a law-enforcement officer's right to shoot with impunity someone who is deemed to be attempting to escape legal confinement.

Editorial Notes:

a. There are two drafts and one clean carbon copy of this letter with the Lowry collection (UBC 2:4). The earliest is a heavily corrected manuscript and typescript foliation dated 'May 11, 1946,' with 'June 5' written in pencil and 'May 11' crossed out. The next one is a typescript on canary second-cut paper, with several holograph inserts, dated 'June 10.' The copy-text for this transcription is the thirty-four-page carbon copy of the letter, with address and full date of 15 June 1946. This copy, presumably the carbon of the letter sent to Button, has no name of addressee and no signature.

b. This interjection appears, without editorial comment, in *Selected Letters*, but not in the clean carbon copy from which this transcription has been made. Presumably Margerie added the phrases in order to clarify the context of Lowry's sentence.

c. In *Selected Letters* the letter closes with 'Very truly yours, / Malcolm Lowry.'

225: To Harold Matson

P: Matson(ts); UBC(phc)

> Dollarton P.O.,
> Dollarton, B.C.,
> Canada
> 15 June 1946

Dear Hal:

Thanks very much for your letter and here is a note in haste for I have just heard from Cape.

As you see he gives in on the matter of Canadian rights, but on condition that Hitchcock publishes it this year.

I enclose the memorandum and a copy of all the relevant excerpts from his letter.[a]

Against the context of the complete letter all this seems rather more amusingly put. If you like you can see this complete letter but I am keeping it for the moment because I have to answer that too.

I should say sadly put too, for it turns out that Cape was a close friend of Curtice Hitchcock.

Re Peters Cape seems to think that since we have now done all the business together why bring in an agent in England upon the question, but this by no means invalidates the idea from my point of view: however perhaps we could let this hang in the air for the moment and I will make it the subject of another letter.

Ironically I just received your copy of the refusal from Henry Holt[1] which, due to no fault of your own, has been chasing me from pillar to post since the lord knows when. I thought you'd given the

Volcano up. Incidentally this refusal represents the only really favorable itemized criticism from other than personal sources that I have seen.

I wish to thank you deeply for the masterly way in which you have handled the entire Hitchcock thing.

Sincerely,

Malcolm Lowry

Annotations:

1 On 11 January 1946 Helen K. Taylor, managing editor of the New York publisher Henry Holt and Company, wrote to Harold Matson explaining why Holt felt they must reject *Under the Volcano*. Despite its brilliance and the fact that it makes '*The Lost Weekend* look like a Sunday school picnic,' they felt the book lacked balance and discipline.

Editorial Notes:

a. Lowry has enclosed with this letter the following excerpts from Cape's letter to him and the memorandum of agreement that Cape mentions having sent for Matson:

Herewith a copy of all the excerpts from Cape's letter which have any bearing on the contract:

Now as to the Agreement: Clause 1. 'If Reynal and Hitchcock will publish soon for you, then we will let them sell their edition in Canada without let or hindrance. This however does not mean that if they do a cheap edition it can circulate there unreservedly like R. & H.'s original edition. The matter will have to be raised again with us.' It is in your interest that you should hold on to Canada and not let the Yanks have it as a piece of makeweight. Their methods of selling in Canada are salutary and somewhat abrupt. After the book has been published a month or two the Canadian jobber has sold out what he bought and doesn't bother about the title anymore, unless there is such a pronounced demand that orders keep coming to him, whereas if *we* publish the book in Canada, and I say publish, which means travelling it and sending out review copies and perhaps doing some advertising, the eventual result is likely to be more satisfactory. And above all, usually so long as we have stock of the book here, there is stock of it available in Toronto, so that orders can be filled and the book obtained in the Dominion. Of course, things at the present time are not running in the same orderly way as used to be the case, but our method has always been to *publish* the book in Canada and to maintain a stock in Toronto.

We are therefore quite prepared for Reynal and Hitchcock to have the right of entry for their edition into the Dominion of Canada, and also South America. We however do not want their edition competing with ours on the Continent of Europe. We go to considerable expense to send travellers and representatives to certain of the European countries regularly. Our representative is at present in France, and only two weeks ago our representative returned from a business tour in Sweden, Norway, Denmark and Finland. So far as the Far East is concerned, Reynal and Hitchcock can sell any copies there if they wish to – it can be an open market.

I have deleted clause 9 from the agreement. Clauses 11 and 12 should not conflict with anything in your American contract.

So as to make it quite clear, I attach a memorandum which you can send to Matson for his guidance in the matter of drawing the contract with Reynal and Hitchcock.

$\frown$

In June of 1946 Lowry first established contact with the man who would be his editor for the rest of his life. Albert Erskine prepared Under the Volcano *for its February 1947 publication by Reynal & Hitchcock, and in the process he became fascinated by the novel and captivated by its author. Lowry's friendship with Erskine existed through and in the written word – they only met a few times. But in the close to one hundred letters that he wrote to Erskine between 1946 and 1956, Lowry grew to depend enormously on his epistolary presence and emotional and psychological support. After Reynal & Hitchcock was dissolved, Erskine moved to Random House, and for about three years Lowry did not know whether he could keep Erskine as his editor. The uncertainty caused him considerable anguish, as the letters from 1949 to 1952 make clear. When Random House suspended their contract with him in 1954, Lowry was bereft, as much by the realization that he had 'let Albert down' as by the loss of the publisher's support. But to the end of his life Lowry thought of Erskine as 'Brother Albert.'*

226: To Albert Erskine

p: UBC(ts)
pp: *SL* 112-14

> Dollarton P.O.,
> Dollarton, B.C.,
> Canada
> 22 June 1946

Dear Mr Erskine:

Thank you very much indeed for your letter and your more than heartening words and I am replying as quickly as I can.[1]

My carbon copy of Under the Volcano was left behind in Mexico itself, to be sent on (together with many notes, and a draft of another novel) but it hasn't arrived yet, after 7 weeks, so I have only a working copy with different page numbers from yours to go by. Of course I can locate myself by simply a word or two and I think I've done all right here where're you've mentioned a specific sentence.

I've brought up a few more points in addition to yours while I'm at it and since I'm in a hurry to get this off air mail please forgive me for putting them in here instead of in the notes.

Can La Despedida be used to mean The Parting in the sense that I've used it for the name of the picture of the split rock in II? If not it should be simple to find the right word. I meant to verify all such points in Mexico but it turned out I didn't have time to do them all. Los Manos de Orlac should of course be Las Manos de Orlac throughout. There are liable to be a few other such mistakes in Spanish, typographical errors or whatnot where the Spanish is used conventionally and meant to be correct. Cervantes' remark in X (¾ way through) for instance, where they are discussing lighting 3 cigarettes with one match and which begins: La supersticion dice. . . perhaps should be checked. On the barrels at Senora Gregorio's (end of VII) manzanillo should be manzanilla, rumpopo, rumpope. (I met her a month or two ago by the way, still doing fine. I said 'Goodbye'. She said 'The same to you.' The character named Juan Cerillo in IV – also Dr Vigil – had been, alas, murdered, after too much mescal.) I may have spelt some of the perfectamentes and excelentisimos wrong too, in spite of all care, in I and V. The picture of the demons and drunks I call Los Borracheros in VII (at the beginning in Laruelle's house) I could swear *was* called Los Borracheros in fact: but I have not been able to verify the existence of such a word at all so maybe we'll have to think of something else.

I'm very flattered you ask about Ultramarine.[2] I have a copy but I think the book, which set out to be good, is an inexcusable mess of which I've been very ashamed for 13 years. The first and only real version was lost by Chatto and Windus and I rewrote it in two months from notes salvaged from a waste paper basket and a few published bits.[3] I wouldn't like to send you my copy without first having crossed out about half of it. That would leave about 125 pages of good, original work, however, and I've always wanted to redo it. But it is essentially a short novel. There are no short cuts for getting it except from me, I hope: it is, thank God, out of print.

I wrote another short novel called Lunar Caustic in 1936 (rewritten in 1940) which has never seen the light. Under the Volcano was orginally planned as the inferno part of a Dantesque trilogy to be called The Voyage That Never Ends. Lunar Caustic was the purgatorial part, but was to be much expanded. I lost all the notes for its expansion in a fire, but though rather unmotivated, it's probably better as it stands, though it might need a month or two's work on it. The Paradiso part was called In Ballast to the White Sea, was a good deal longer than the Volcano and was completely destroyed in the fire here which took our house and all our books. We rebuilt the house.

I've got masses of poems left, (one of which was published by the Atlantic Monthly)[4] enough to make two volumes, I'd thought of calling The Lighthouse Invites the Storm and Wild Bleeding Hearts. But otherwise I'm more or less in the position of having to start again.

I'm absolutely so delighted you are publishing the Volcano you will forgive me rambling on.

Answers to your notes follow.

Yours sincerely and most gratefully,

Malcolm Lowry

P.S. By the way, two other books called 'Volcano' (just like that) have to go and get themselves published within the last year – one about Paricutin, the other a mystery by Hugh somebody, published in the American Magazine.[5] Does that make any difference? I'd loathe to change the title after so long. The Day of the Dead is my only alternative but it's not half so good. And besides it's bad luck, like changing the name of a ship.

Answers to your notes.[a]

Page 7 – also Page 328.
If nothing is gained by the border around Quauhnahuac in the

light of my intention below, then I suggest you drop it down to a separate line without the rules around it, just as you say.

I felt Quauhnahuac was rather an esoteric name and that the border round it sort of universalised it, by relating it to any wayside station anywhere. I also feel that this probably looks more eccentric in type-script than it would in print. But let me yield to your judgement on this. However it is done though, it should be done the same in both Chapters I and VIII: the evocation should be the same, and the evo-cation was meant to be primarily that of 'station' and 'parting.' I wasn't trying to emphasize the name itself.

Re the name itself though I have this to say. Quauhnahuac was the Aztec name for Cuernavaca. Very few people seemed to know this in 1938: but now they've got a great sign in the suburbs saying so. The Quauhnahuac of the book is not Cuernavaca, however, so much as Cuernavaca a few feet in the air, with a bit of Oaxaca etc. thrown in. I suppose I ought to make a note to that effect. However, on a visit to Mexico from which I have just returned I made a somewhat sinister discovery. Quauhnahuac used to be translated, I always understood, as 'Where the Eagle Stops.' But now it turns out that it doesn't mean that at all and it says so now on this sign. I should say at this point that Under the Volcano was originally part of a trilogy – roughly the inferno part, with purgatorio and paradiso to follow – the protago-nist would get a little better throughout, like Tchitchikov[6] – but anyhow hence the Casino de la Selva, and the quotation from the beginning of the Inferno 'In the middle of my life I found my self in a dark wood' etc. at the beginning of Chapter VI in the middle of the book (The Consul also finds himself in a pub called El Bosque, or the wood) and so on: the theme turns up again in XI. Now I discover that Quauhnahuac actually means in Aztec 'Near the Wood.' and I feel this is too good a point to miss and should be brought in some-where, very tiny. Perhaps you could make a suggestion.

Page 16.
Sentence: 'His love had brought a peace' etc. – was sweated upon, and I don't think can be improved (even though it may not be so hot) on reflection, if it still runs thus, which I have in my version:

> His love had brought a peace, for all too short a while, that was strangely like the enchantment, the spell, of Chartres itself, long ago, whose every sidestreet he had come to love and cafe where he could gaze at the cathedral eternally sailing against the clouds, the spell not even the fact he was scandalously in debt there, could break.

My reasons: all one could do to improve it, unless one rewrote it, would be to put:

(a) a comma after the second love (which would spoil the rhythm).

(b) 'he had come to love' after cafe (which would confuse the sense).

But if you see any way of clarifying it by rearrangement you have my blessing.

Page 56.

I absolutely see your point but I think, for reasons I'll state here and later, it would be undesirable to have Prologue or call Chapter II Chapter I. But since it's equally undesirable to have people reading on into the book thinking they're still in 1939, I feel this might be cleared up conveniently in the usual kind of italicised note at the beginning of the book where one says that characters are imaginary, that Cuckoldshaven is not necessarily to be identified with Cuernavaca because it means Cow's Horn, or that all applications by the W.C.T.U.[7] for use as propaganda material should be accompanied by a case of Scotch addressed to the author – and so forth. The reason why I am against I (1939), II (1938), is that it somehow spoils the uniformity. There are also – to refer back to your former suggestion – definite reasons why there should be *twelve* chapters in the sense I, II, III, IV, V etc. and I'll come to that when I answer your last observation in your letter. Moreover I don't think we want any more gargoyles on our already rather too churrigueresque structure.

Page 58.

Re sentence beginning 'Ashamed, numb. . .' Yes, you're right. However the overlapping style at this point is necessary. I suggest a second 'Yvonne' before 'glanced defensively.'

Page 71.

– Born in Hawaii. . . You're probably right, but I can't make out what to do about it by crikey. The sentence isn't quite objective, but a sort of half-afterthought on Yvonne's part, if that excuses it. Thus it almost belongs parenthetically to the former sentence. I think I may originally have written: Having been born in Hawaii (leaving the she understood.) and cut the 'having been' then so as not to have two 'beens.' Therefore all I can think of is to reinstate this to read: 'Having been born in Hawaii, there'd been volcanoes in her life before, however.' Which is pretty horrible too. And probably ungrammatical too. Though a semicolon after 'look at them now' binding the two sentences together might help.

Page 162 – line 18.

Yes, avuncular baffles me also, when I think about it too much. I meant that he said it with a kind of relish that one somehow associates with uncles at Christmas, as also with a kind of avuncular familiarity toward Yvonne (other things lacking) and perhaps even a kind of rather avuncular look on his face. But if it rings no bells at all, why not just 'with relish.'

Page 184.

J'adoube. . . Yes, I agree. Out with the parenthesis.

Page 221 ff.

I fear – yes – this chapter, or the first part of it, may be too long. But I have different page numbers to you and a very imperfect and underscored copy of this chapter to work on so I can't locate myself from 221 ff without something more specific to guide me. On the other hand since I felt rather that the second half might strike as too long perhaps we are both wrong. For one thing it is Chapter VI in a unit of twelve chapters and we are here at the heart of the book. I think the detail re life on cargo vessel is too meticulously woven to cut. That is to say, it has already been cut to the bone. And I think the book can support the chapter's great length. Perhaps there are too many names of magical books though and if you have any specific suggestions re cuts on the sea part I'll take them to heart. But I feel this supplies, like Chapter IV, a needed ozone, among other things. The style was supposed to be appropriate to Hugh himself, half journalism, half a kind of swing, with the brackets the hot guitar breaks. Dantesque theme reappears at the very end.

News of your acceptance of the book – likewise Cape's – was delivered at M. Laruelle's house, where I was living quite by accident in the tower, never having set foot in it before, by the little postman at the end of this chapter. This of course is the house also in Chapter 7. I went to live in the tower on January 7.

Page 236.

Yes, brug was a typographical error, but I thought it a rather expressive word and let it stand. If it expresses nothing let us by all means restore it to grub without further brugging around.

Page 244.

My version has: . . . seemed part, less (of) the loud mosaic of one's stupid life there. . . . than the strange dream of some old monk etc. Possibly you have '*but* the strange dream' etc. instead of 'than.' This would be caused by my having written originally: '*Not* (of) the loud mosaic of etc. . . *but* the strange dream etc.' And the 'but' has wrongly survived when it should be 'than.' The 'of' before 'loud mosaic' is cut out in either case to avoid Flaubert's crime of two 'ofs' in one clause:[8] but if it is too obscure perhaps we should reinstate it; sentence therefore would read:

> (Cambridge)! Whose fountains in moonlight and closed courts and cloisters, whose enduring beauty in its virtuous remote self-assurance, seemed part, less of the loud mosaic of one's stupid life there, though maintained perhaps by the countless deceitful memories of such lives, than the strange dream of some old monk, eight hundred years dead, whose forbidding house, reared upon piles and stakes driven into the marshy ground, had once shone like a beacon out of the mysterious silence, and solitude of the fens.

In the clause 'than the strange dream of some old monk' part of, between 'than' and 'the' is understood. 'Whose,' as I have indicated refers to Cambridge University itself, which sprang out of those old monasteries built on the fens.

Page 256.
Anti-aircraft guns. Yes, they did: some kind anyhow, even if just Lewis or Maxim.[9] I may be a bit screwy on my German at one point here though, when they are looking at the Q ship.

Page 350 (cf. 339)
I see your point, which is a good one, though I think a practised thief could have done it. In fact I was trying to describe something of which I was an eye witness. I will have a shot at rewriting it if it really does seem impossible, but I would greatly welcome a suggestion here. Also I cannot quite locate myself because of the different page numbers. So if you would just specify – – sentence beginning so and so, it would help greatly.

Other things bother me slightly in this chapter. I would like to call in a Mexican expert's opinion on the word pelado. I make excuse for Hugh's relative ignorance, but am still not quite certain I am not stretching a point in regard to this, and also the use of gachupiné here.[10] These terms are of course mutually contradictory in one way: what bothers me is whether my irony is on a sound enough basis to mean something while the reader accepts Hugh's fumbling at the same time. I am not quite certain whether gachupiné can apply to *any* Spanish born Spaniard or not. It might be better to use the Spanish word. I am also slightly uneasy about the word chingarn. (When they are arguing by the side of the road.) I'm not sure that it can be characterized precisely as a word expressing merely obscene contempt. Impugning one's mother, in Oaxaca it conveys a whole phrase so obscene that I was not able to find an opportunity on my recent visit to Mexico to inquire tactfully whether I had its meaning quite correctly without loss of life in the meantime.

Pge 414 ff.

Yes I daresay you're right, that there are too many excerpts from the folder. It seems much too long read aloud. On the other hand the eye passes quickly over these things and the very look of the words is funny, even if you don't get the meaning. Though on rereading you might find ambiguities and relevancies everywhere. I had thought at one point of suggesting some kind of excursion into typographical genius: such as the use of pearl type or even diamond, or both (or occasionally extra-condensed) for some of the folder stuff, to compress it and heighten the feeling of delirium, combined with black letter for the headings by way of contrast. I can't think of a more maddening suggestion for an editor and it's probably lousy anyway. Or is it not? Have you any suggestions here for cuts? I find it hard to part with any of the quotations from the folder, having cut out many juicy bits, and impossibly hard to cut in my version, which looks as though it had been hit with an atom bomb already.

Page 476 – 477.

Le gusta esta Jardin? No sir. The little quotation slipped a bit. She drifted, in a difficult passage of time. She should not be in either place, neither between XI and XII nor at the head of Chapter XII, but at the *end* of chapter XII, on a separate page, at the very end of the book in fact. That is to say you read about the dog being thrown down the ravine after the Consul and you think you are at the end, then you turn over and find this looking at you. That is like those old swing tunes called Aunt Hagar Blues or what not of Ted Lewis[11] when the record ends and you are just about to take the record off, when it ends again, and you then proceed (one hopes as in this case) to put it on again.

But more about this quotation:

>?Le gusta esta Jardin?
>?Que es suyo?
>!Evite que hijos los destruyen!

It is not quite correct and since I haven't yet puzzled out what I finally ought to do about it perhaps you can give me some advice as it is important. I copied it down as above in 1938 from a sign in a little public garden in Oaxaca: whoever wrote it was probably Zapotecan.[12] There should not have been a question mark after Jardin because 'que' means 'that' and could hardly be used in the sense of 'porque' 'why?' Also hijos should strictly speaking be governed by something such as sus or los. But in one way it is immeasurably more dramatic as it is, even though wrong. Now the Consul has in V an hallucination about it – he refers it to himself and makes it still wronger (Do you like this garden? Why is it yours? We evict those who destroy!) Evite doesn't mean evict, but avoid or prevent: in this case 'evite que' means See to it that . . . not. But the Consul feels himself threatened with final eviction from the garden in V and indeed 'Evite' does *look* as if it meant 'evict,' even if not in the first person plural.

Whether later on the Consul should see it (in VII) in its correct form is what perplexes me – it stretches the imagination (even though it might be perfectly natural if the same person wrote it) that *both* signs should be wrong. On the other hand, if it is correct the second time he sees it, am I right to imply that he still translates it wrongly to himself, for most certainly he should still see his eviction in it? (Possibly somewhere else in the book, possibly in VIII, Hugh should see it in its correct form and translate it correctly: in fact that is what I shall have to do if I am to make my point at the very end.)

To me, both the sign as it appears in the book, incorrect as it is, and the Consul's hallucinatory translation of it, are of the utmost importance: I cannot think of the sign otherwise, I cannot put porque instead of que, I cannot sacrifice the erroneous question mark before the first que, I cannot see it otherwise than in three lines, nor translate the second line to myself other wise than 'Why is it yours?': that is what, having lived with it so long, it means to *me*.

But the question might rightly arise in the mind of some expert, irrespective of how the Consul translates it, as to whether such a mistake *could* be made in the Spanish on the sign. But granted he accepts that – if we make a little more subtle excuse than we have – I suppose the Spanish, as I said, will have to be correct at the *end*. This then there should read (still in three lines) I think:

> ?Le gusta esta Jardin
> Que es suyo?
> !Evite que sus hijos los destruyen!

This does not look anything like so good. But it *means* something even more terrifying and which could scarcely be more to the point, to wit:

> Do you like this garden
> That is yours?
> See to it that your *sons* do not destroy it!

Now to answer your final remarks re the disarticulation of XII. I had exactly the same idea as you and once tried to write it like that and I think it comes off better so far as the suspense is concerned. And if a movie were ever made of it, it ought to be done in that kind of D.W. Griffith manner. However here are the objections and I feel you will agree that they are sound ones, in fact insuperable, when seen in relation to the whole book. It does, on reflection, require not merely breaking up chapter XII, but XI too, for the reason that if XI is placed between two parts of XII, you would have two chapters in succession through the Consul's mind, which would spoil (a) the balance and uniformity of the book (b) the very necessary contrast between the end of X and the beginning of XI: and should you split up XI too, in order to get over this difficulty you would lose the equally important contrast between the end of XI and the beginning of XII. I feel that the flat white dead style and dead tempo of the beginning of XII would come off equally well, as you suggest yourself, against the feverish end of X, but unfortunately XII as a *whole* constitutes a kind of answer to I as a *whole* and our architechtonics would go west if we put it there. Moreover there are very good reasons, as I have said before, for having 12 chapters without any break in them, twelve solid blocks, or perhaps one should say spokes, for the form of the book is as it were trochal – as I see it, like a wheel, the image of which keeps recurring: I won't go into all these reasons here but I ask you to believe they exist. For instance there are 12 months in a year and the book is concerned with a year, twelve hours in a day, and the book is concerned with a day: 12 is a good sound universal unit anyhow, even if we say nothing about the 12 apostles, the 12 labors of Hercules, and all the cabbalistic attributes of 12, not to mention poor old Faust. It may be slightly childish of me but I would even like to see good big sinister looking Roman numerals at the beginning of each chapter.

That's all for the moment and quite enough too, I expect you are saying: I'll try not to be so long-winded next time,

M.L.

Annotations:

1 Albert Erskine (1911–93) was Lowry's editor with Reynal & Hitchcock
   and later with Random House, where he was also an editor for, among
   other contemporary authors, Ralph Ellison and William Faulkner.
   Erskine's 14 June 1946 letter to Lowry, with his notes and queries, is in
   the Lowry collection (UBC 1:20); further original letters from Erskine
   and some photocopies of his letters are also in the collection (UBC 1:20
   and 1:21). Most of the original Lowry letters to Erskine are with the
   Albert Erskine papers in Special Collections of the Alderman Library at
   the University of Virginia.
2 In a postscript to his letter Erskine asks how to get a copy of *Ultramarine*
   (1933), which he is 'extremely anxious to read.'
3 *Ultramarine* was formally accepted for publication by Chatto & Windus
   in December 1932. The firm wrote to Lowry's literary agency, John
   Farquharson, in Red Lion Square, London, on 21 December 1932 to
   negotiate a contract that included a 10% royalty on the first two thousand copies sold at 7.6s. with royalty increases after that. They requested
   world rights, exclusive of the United States, and they refused to grant an
   author's advance on the grounds that (as Ian Parsons, who was handling
   the manuscript at Chatto & Windus, noted in his 23 December 1932 letter to Farquharson) they liked the book but doubted that it would be a
   commercial success. The reader for Chatto & Windus, Oliver Warner,
   recommended publication in his 30 September 1932 report because he
   felt Lowry had a talent that warranted encouragement. Despite weakness in form, he described the manuscript as 'original' and 'poetic' with
   'brilliant' dialogue. Unfortunately, however, Parsons' copy of the
   manuscript was stolen from his car on 22 October, and this accident sent
   Lowry into a flurry of desperate activity. He had no carbon copy and so
   had to reassemble the novel from drafts and fragments retrieved from
   the waste-paper basket at the home of his Cambridge friend Dr Martin
   Case. When the novel was ready to deliver to Chatto & Windus, Lowry
   believed that they were not keen to publish it, so he withdrew it, and his
   agent, Innes Rose, placed the novel with Jonathan Cape, who published
   it on 12 June 1933. Lowry was never happy with *Ultramarine*, and he had
   plans to revise it extensively for his 1951 expanded version of *The
   Voyage That Never Ends*.
4 This poem is 'In Memoriam: Ingvald Bjorndal,' *Atlantic Monthly* 168, 4
   (1941): 501.
5 The book about the Mexican volcano, *El Volcán de Paricutin*, is by Eze-
   quiel Ordoñez and was first published in Mexico in 1947. The story
   called 'Volcano' by Hugh Pentecost (a name it is difficult to imagine
   Lowry forgetting) appeared in *American Magazine* (December 1945):
   161–86, where it was described as a 'complete American mystery
   novel.'

6 Tchitchikov is the hero of Nikolai Gogol's novel *Dead Souls* (1842).

7 W.C.T.U. are the initials of the Women's Christian Temperance Union, and the identity of the organization is essential to Lowry's joke.

8 I have not been able to identify a precise source in the letters or prose of Gustave Flaubert for Lowry's reference; however, he had read Flaubert's letters, and he may be thinking of a comment Flaubert made in an 1853 letter to his mother. See Lowry's 16 July 1946 letter (**237**) to Erskine, annotation 7.

9 Erskine has asked whether or not anti-aircraft guns had been mounted on Q-ships during the First World War. Lowry is correct; Q-ships (quiet ships), mainly disguised submarine destroyers, carried camouflaged weapons. The 'Lewis,' invented in 1911 by Isaac Newton Lewis, was basically an infantry weapon later modified for naval and air force combat; the 'Maxim,' invented in 1884 by Hiram Maxim, was the first successful portable machine-gun.

10 The Spanish word *gachupín* means literally 'a Spanish settler in Latin America,' but the connotation of the term is pejorative. Lowry dropped the word for the published text of chapter 8 in *Volcano*.

11 Ted Lewis (1891-1971), the American jazzman, band leader, and entertainer, gained international fame and popularized several jazz songs. In the mid-twenties he was instrumental in introducing American jazz to the British.

12 Oaxaca is the capital of the Mexican state of Oaxaca, where the indigenous people are Zapotecan and speak a number of Zapotecan dialects.

Editorial Notes:

a. I have included the notes, which comprise six pages of single-spaced typescript, enclosed with this letter to Erskine for several reasons. This set of 'Answers' provides the first and the best example of Lowry's editorial work with Erskine, and Lowry has concluded them with a brief holograph close followed by his initials, a form of signature he often uses with a postscript. Moreover, these notes do in fact continue the epistolary discourse of the letter in innumerable ways, from actual facts and comments to the conversational tone and allusions he is already weaving into a growing friendship with his editor. This first letter to Erskine illustrates the way in which Lowry 'built' the relationship. In subsequent letters dealing with the editorial work on the *Volcano* I have not included the accompanying notes and comments because, in them, Lowry becomes involved in editorial details quite separate from the covering letter. Annotations to the notes included with this letter have been kept to a minimum, and readers should consult *A Companion to 'Under the Volcano'* for information on the novel.

227: To Harold Matson

P: Matson(ts)

> Dollarton, B.C.,
> Canada
> 28 June 1946

Dear Hal:

I dashed off a letter to you a week or so ago to tell you immediately of my news from Cape, but I didn't say all I had on my mind.

Re your suggestion re Mr Peters. I think I mentioned that Cape seemed to think that since we had done all the business there was no point in calling in an agent at this late date: – but that by no means invalidates the idea from my point of view, especially so far as other works are concerned, and possibly so far as the Volcano itself may be concerned in England later. Incidentally, I just received the statement re my advance from Cape – I have to pay 9/- in the £ tax! On a £100 advance I only get 45 quid. Someone likewise forgot to enclose the cheque, which was kind of sad, unless it dropped out, which would be sadder still.

Mr Erskine of R.& H. wrote me a very grand letter about the Volcano, asking me also to reply to certain general questions re possible alterations etc. and this I did quam celerime: I had difficulty answering some of the questions because my working copy has different page numbers and is also rather imperfect. Should you happen to be in touch with him at the moment, could you mention that I have now got back my carbon copy with the same page numbers as his, so correspondence from now on should be that much simpler. I am going right through it with a fine tooth comb; errors seem mostly in Spanish, otherwise there are comparatively few. He also told me he had inquired of you re a copy of Ultramarine. I have one, and recently reread same with a good deal of embarrassment and loathing. I regret it was ever inflicted on you and would hate him to read it as it is. Some of the dialogue is hallucinating, but apart from that, and its form, it's impossible. I would like, however, as I've said before, to rewrite it. The result as I see it would be a stripped, honest, and much shorter novel – a novella in fact, that I believe would go in one volume with Lunar Caustic (The Last Address) – somewhat revised also, and a thing I recently blocked out in Mexico, entitled Dark as the Grave Wherein my Friend is Laid, potentially my best to date. This latter, apparently looking as if chewed by lions, has now got as far as Los Angeles and will shortly be progressing hither. Margie and I have another horror up our sleeves, however.[1]

As a matter of fact this letter mainly concerns Margie – who is still waiting to correct the proofread proofs of the second half of the Shapes That Creep. And what about The Last Twist – now some seven months overdue, for Scribner's contracted to bring it out not later than last fall. We've never had a word about this, let alone any proofs. I am taking up the cudgels on her behalf[2] because the said Scribner's, by dint of postponements, broken promises and un-answered letters have reduced the poor gal – who has had besides an awful lot of calamity befall her in the last years, to say nothing of being nearly murdered in Mexico (and we thought until just the other day all her notes taken there were lost too) – to a very under-standable state of mind in which she almost wishes not to write another line – and certainly not to Scribner's. I bought her a copy of the Shapes in Mexico (the last one they had) and it is in great demand here at the libraries, but Scribner's have never addressed a bloody word to her about it, nor has Weber ever deigned to explain why he didn't send those corrected proofs of the last half, nor has he replied to a single one of her letters for over a year now. It seems to me they owe her an apology at least. In fact their behaviour would seem to be almost incomprehensibly lousy. True, they brought the Shapes out eventually, but by that time the psychological damage had been done and the sight of it merely caused her anguish. It is true, also, that they paid her for The Last Twist, and so on, and that you have un-doubtedly done your bleeding best about the whole bloody thing – but this does not exempt Weber. I don't say this merely because she is my wife, but because she is a hell of a fine writer with lots of fine things in her to say and write and it is a shame that she should have been frustrated in this manner, which has incidentally finally affected her health, as it would of any other writer, male or female. A writer worth his or her salt can stand flat rejection and rebuffs of that kind ad infinitum, and so can she. It was those promises, followed by silence, followed by silence, the postponements followed by post-ponements, the post which was always going to bring word sometime within the next fortnight and then silence and no reply to letters or telegrams and then silence, and all this going on and on every day for years and years, that acted as a Chinese torture to her, which has now resulted in her own temporary silence. I imagine Scribner's has also exasperated you beyond measure and she is always eternally grateful to you for selling the two books – but would not some other publisher have taken them? She could and would have written half a dozen by now. I would be very grateful if you would direct a bazooka, even if for the umpteenth time, in Senor Weber's direction in regard to this. When I remind you that it is now half-a-decade since Scribner's first had the Shapes, and that the contract was signed over 4 years ago and with such high hopes by her, it can readily be seen that her patience can be matched only perhaps, say, by your own in regard to me. A word, an encouraging signal of some sort from them, just a reply to a letter once in a year to two or three, I feel would help a lot, if not from Weber, from someone in the firm. We have no idea how the Shapes went, the reviews seemed pretty good on the whole, and everyone I've spoken to liked it enormously, but if it didn't go as well as they thought it would they have only themselves to blame – not that it dates, on the contrary – but trends change in 4 years. And they should say something definite about The Last Twist. I don't know, by the way, if she rates some copies of the Shapes (as is the custom in England) but she certainly never got any, let alone any notice that the book had even been published. We found that out quite by accident.

And all this brings me to Horse in the Sky, which has presumably temporarily returned to the stable. I have a high regard for my critical faculty and all I can say about this book, having brought the best of that faculty unbiasedly to bear upon it, is that people are simply absolutely wrong about it and are foolish to reject it. It is a pure, spherical, cool, lovely and original piece of work, that has, moreoever, a certain stamp of the classic upon it. Indeed Emily Bronte herself would have been proud to have thought it up. The reports on this book were much more unfair than those upon the Volcano, where perhaps a charge of overreaching or tedium is a natural one. But nobody at all of the readers who have had the Horse so far have ever come to grips with it, and for a not dissimilar reason. They are already bring[ing] their own a priori ideas as to what such a book should be like to bear before finishing the first chapter. The apparent naivete, in this case, of the first chapter of the Horse gives little indication that the author is proposing to grapple with a drama of such extraordinary power and beauty as the one which emerges. When the drama begins to emerge they ask, at worst, why, therefore, being by a woman, it is not padded and dressed out like some preposterous and messy monstrosity like Forever Amber,[3] or conversely, if it has pretensions to art, why no kittens are put in the letter box, why none of the characters are Lesbians, or have their breasts cut off, or are ex-negro slaves, or reincarnations of Cockneys in Berkeley Square, and why anyway is not the style a mixture of Story Magazine, the Prairie Schooner, the Women's Home Journal, Eudora Welty Henry James and the medical section of Time.[4] Well, I wish to God I had written Horse in the Sky. Scribner's reasons for turning it down, so far as I could see, amounted simply to the fact that they didn't want an author with two kinds of career: well, she doesn't look yet as though she would get even one kind out of Scribner's. What about Reynal and Hitchcock? – even if they have already rejected it? Would my words – which are, believe me, objective – carry any weight with Mr Erskine? What do you think? We dream of having the same publisher, but the real point is, there is a book eating its heart out, that while utterly unpretentious, has some claim to being something rarer than first rate, namely, like Manon Lescaut (in French), on its own universal terms, perfect.[5] And those guys at R.& H. really do read. They are the answers to an author's prayer when I think what allowances they have made for the longeurs of the Volcano. Mind you, I feel they are right to have done so, but they don't have to make any such allowances for Horse in the Sky. The only hurdle they have to take is the one that looms as insurmountable and with such a big ditch on the other side: the hurdle of 'how can such a book of such ostensibly scant nature and character drawing be possibly so good as I say it is? Which means just as good in Hungarian or 1960 as it is now. Might it not be worth while, however, your having another shot, while the Lowry stock is, as it would appear, fairly high?

I'm sure I'm right, though, about Horse in the Sky and I have high hopes of Cape himself taking it. Perhaps that book really belongs in England first and would stand a better chance in America when in print and ratified?? At all events, this brings me back to the first part of my letter and Mr Peters. What about Margie's work in England? It seems to me that both the Shapes and The Last Twist stand a good chance of going well there: and I don't know of any such objection there – witness Graham Greene[6] – as exists in America to a writer having two careers. If Cape should take Horse in the Sky, may I ask him to refer to Mr Peters, as the one representing her work, and on the strength of that, likewise interest him in her other work. Cape doesn't publish detective stories, but I haven't a doubt that Gollancz or Collins or certainly somebody, would publish her mysteries there.[7] Only I wanted her to get a start on the serious side first over there and having battled with Cape's readers over the Volcano and succeeded I might as well take advantage of this flying start and see if I can't push her horse toward the winning post too: this is rather an illiterate letter, I see, but none the less sincere for all that.

As for myself, should the Volcano begin to rumble with any authority in Europe, I should likewise be glad of your English representative's services. But in the meantime, having settled with Cape (so to speak) I better let things hang fire, but with sincere thanks to yourself for the suggestion: I must say that nine bob in the pound tax doesn't sound so good for any of us in them parts.

Re Mexico: yes, I'll postpone that too again, in fact we need a drink to swallow it and I look forward to same with you in the not too distant future. There is one of the best stories in that that ever came a writer's way only it was exceptionally dreadful to be in the middle of it.

And we've got the notes: and what notes – such as were never heard of on land or sea, we hope. I hope they're all there: the Volcano has arrived here intact so there's no reason why they shouldn't be, in spite of the reported chewings. Margie's very bucked at this because what we were having to face was another couple of novels down the drain, but until she gets on her writer's feet again, quill in hand, I'm writing her letters for her. She'd be even more bucked if you wrote her one, however.

Thank you a million for everything. With kindest regards from us both,

Skoal,

Malcolm

Annotations:

1 This new 'horror' is almost certainly 'La Mordida,' which deals with their recent torments in Mexico.

2 See Lowry's 15 September 1946 letter (**246**) to Maxwell Perkins.

3 *Forever Amber* (1944) is a fast-paced, sensational story of Restoration England by the American novelist Kathleen Winsor. At 972 pages of faulty dialogue and 'astounding fakery' (as one contemporary reviewer put it), it provides Lowry with an apt contrast to Margerie's novel.

4 Lowry's sarcasm here includes two serious American writers: Henry James and Eudora Welty (1909–), a Mississippi writer of excellent short stories and novels.

5 *Manon Lescaut* is the title of Abbé Prévost's 1731 novel, which inspired Jules Massenet's opera *Manon* (1884) and Giacomo Puccini's 1893 opera *Manon Lescaut*. Lowry appears to be thinking of Prévost's novel or Massenet's French opera, which are certainly the more tragic treatments of the story.

6 The English author Graham Greene (1904–91) was a prolific writer of fiction, non-fiction, and drama.

7 Gollanz (Victor) Ltd is a London publishing house that handles all types of books, and Collins is another London publisher of a wide range of books.

228: To Albert Erskine

P: UBC(ts)
PP: *SL* 114-17

Dollarton, B.C.,
Canada
30 June 1946

Dear Mr Erskine:

I have now got back my carbon copy of the Volcano with the same page numbers as yourself and I am going through it with a fine tooth comb with an eye on your own notes again and I will whizz my results to you airmail chapter by chapter, or sometimes two or three chapters at a time, as they are finished anyhow, and with a view of saving you as much trouble as possible. If I get long winded or ask irrelevant questions which cannot possibly be answered please pay no attention, time being of the essence, I will not stop to revise, and by formulating certain questions I may be answering them for myself as I go along, and in this category is probably the question about 'Le Gusta Este Jardin' etc. though of course I shall always be glad of your advice and when I remain in doubt, your final word.

Not in this category is the following question. I had at one time thought of appending a list of notes to the book, which would help to elucidate such matters in the deeper layers as that the garden can be seen not only as the world, or the Garden of Eden, but legitimately as the Cabbala itself, and that the abuse of wine (sōd) is identified in the Cabbala with the abuse of magical powers, and so forth, à la Childe Harolde.[1] It was also my intention to acknowledge in these notes any borrowings, echoes, design-governing postures, and so on, as used to be the custom with poets, and might well be the custom with novelists. Of these there are remarkably few, and they became less and less as I carved and hacked away at the book down to its final form, so that of design-governing postures, for instance, there remain virtually none. A few echoes still survive, however, nearly all deliberate. The question is whether they are still worth while acknowledging in notes at the end, as a matter of interest if for nothing else, if I have time for that, or whether, failing that, they should be altered, which would be a grief, and probably unnecessary. Since the book was written with enormous care and meticulousness, and its integrity is not in doubt from my point of view, you must put this down to a slight neurosis of mine on this particular subject, due doubtless to an Elizabethan unscrupulousness in my evil youth in other works mercifully forgotten save by the author's mediaeval conscience.

These echoes are mostly all in the first chapter, and here only one seems worth bothering about (page 16) where I am uncertain of my reference. I will cite them in order however: P. 3 the single phrase 'bangs and cries' (of the fiesta) – though nothing else in the passage – is lifted from a rather stupid story by J.C. Squire, chiefly about duck shooting, though also in relation to a fair, but for all that I cannot improve on those words and won't alter them either, unless I have to.[2] P. 11 the words 'personal battle' occur somewhere in D.H. Lawrence's letters where he is discussing the first World War and saying something to the effect that it was the 'personal battle' that should be carried into the soul of every man in England, a similar thought, but I hate to put it in inverted commas and my wife says Lawrence did not originate it. P. 16 There is another echo of Lawrence's letters, I think, in the passage beginning 'And now M. Laruelle could feel their burden pressing on him from outside. . .' and this I would be extremely obliged if you would look up for me, if you have the Letters to hand, because I cannot do it myself: I can't get the book here. It is a nuisance if I am right too, for the sentence took a long while to write: the echo would seem to inhere in the phrase 'with their secret mines of silver,' and not elsewhere: this could thus only be from one of Lawrence's letters when he was living at the Hotel Francia, Oaxaca, circa 1924 (as I myself did in 1938 and 1946) at the time he was excoriating Murry, so it should be easy to check – what I wish to know is whether the similarity requires any slight alteration or further attention on my part, or whether it is justified as it is: I know he speaks of the Oaxaquenian hills 'standing round, inhuman', and of the hidden (or secret) silver mines, and of course I was thinking of the same hills and the same mines, in spite of the fact that I had transferred them to Quauhnahuac – alack, having written this, which I cannot well cross out, my wife now says that the passage I mean re the 'secret mines of silver' – if it indeed is phrased at all like that – is not to be found when Lawrence was writing from or of Oaxaca, but from some desolate place further north in Mexico, like Chihuahua or Sonora – The Woman Who Rode Away country in short – but in the Letters at a date not far off from the one I've mentioned.[3] P. 19 'There was always the abyss' a similar thought occurs in Julian Green's Personal Record – [4] God knows where and it is almost too banal to mention, but it was in my mind that M. Laruelle might have read that book, and I had originally tried to get in, 'As Julian Green had suggested' or something, but found it too difficult to compound with Quauhnahuac. P. 46 'unbandaging of great giants' – there is a not dissimilar image in Virginia Woolf's To the Lighthouse for noises at night in a deserted house, but I had not read that book when I wrote this passage.[5] P. 47 'jonquil' in relation to dawn is unfortunately one of Faulkner's favorite adjectives too in that connection.[6] It is of course just right here and I have done my damndest to get away from it elsewhere though I have needed it badly in both VII and XII, neither violet nor lilac nor anything else having precisely what I wanted. There are very few such things in any of the other chapters that I can think of at the moment, save the repeated 'Companero' in VIII and XII, which was vaguely suggested by something in The Rainbow Fields by Ralph Bates,[7] though there are plenty of obscure points, which combined with such as the above, would make for an interesting page or two of notes. I never read a novel with notes at the end before but I don't see why it should not be done. I've certainly read plenty that need them. The objections here are (a) time (b) that they may interfere with the purity of the general format. But I would like your advice on the subject.

My sincerest apologies if I am putting you to undue trouble over this but we live under tough conditions here and my wish is only to be as helpful as possible in the briefest possible time.

With kindest regards,

Malcolm Lowry

P.S. By the way, are you going to send the proofs all at once, or in batches? It matters not but I am excited to know.

Annotations:

1 The Hebrew word *sod* means 'secret' or 'mystery,' but it also has important mystical associations in cabbala; see annotation 29 in Lowry's 2 January 1946 letter (**210**) to Jonathan Cape. The autobiographical poem *Childe Harold's Pilgrimage* (1812-18) by the English romantic poet Lord Byron presents the hero as an eternal wanderer in search of some way to heal his spiritual stagnation and his disillusionment with the world. Lowry may be thinking of the famous stanza 90 from canto 3, in which Harold discovers mystical truth, or of Harold's profligate behaviour and self-exile from England, as described in the opening stanzas of canto 1, or he may simply be thinking more generally of Harold's symbolic significance as a questor.

2 John Collins Squire (1884-1958) was an English writer of short stories and poetry, and the story in question is 'The Alibi,' from his collection *Outside Eden* (1933); see Ackerley/Clipper (9).

3 In his 15 November 1924 letter to John Middleton Murray from Hotel Francia, Oaxaca, Mexico, D.H. Lawrence describes the 'unventured

hills . . . already like an illusion, standing round inhuman,' and in a 5 October 1923 letter to Witter Bynner he speaks of 'lost, motionless silver-mines.' Lawrence's story 'The Woman Who Rode Away' first appeared in *Dial* (July-August 1925) and was included by E.J. O'Brien in *Best British Short Stories of 1926.*

4 Lowry had read Green's *Personal Record* shortly after it was published in 1939; see his 6 September 1940 letter (**149**) to Harold Matson. Green makes numerous references to the abyss in *Personal Record*, and he often speaks of life, people, or things as sliding 'into the abyss.'

5 In the central section of Virginia Woolf's *To the Lighthouse* (1927), 'Time Passes,' there are several fine images of the Ramsays' deserted house at night. Lowry might be thinking of the following: 'Now and again some glass tinkled in the cupboard as if a giant voice had shrieked so loud in its agony that tumblers stood inside a cupboard vibrated too.'

6 William Faulkner (1897-1962), a leading American novelist whose work Lowry admired, does indeed use the word 'jonquil' to describe the dawn; see, for example, book 3 of *The Hamlet*, published by Random House in 1940, where dawn 'upward bursts and fills night's globed negation with jonquil thunder.' Lowry was bothered by what he felt were certain echoes of Faulkner in *Under the Volcano.*

7 Ralph Bates (1899-), a seldom-remembered English novelist who fought in the Spanish Civil War, published short novels with Jonathan Cape in the late thirties and early forties. Lowry appears to be conflating two of Bates's titles: *Rainbow Fish* (1937) and *The Fields of Paradise* (1941); the former is about the sea, the latter about a Mexican *ejido* (an area of communal land controlled by local farmers). Bates uses the word *compañero* in both *The Fields of Paradise* and *The Olive Field* (1936).

229: To Albert Erskine

P: UBC(ms)
PP: *MLMW* 110-12

Dollarton, B.C.,
Canada
[5 July 1946]²

Dear Mr Erskine:

Well, every man his own Laocoon!¹

Concerning a letter forwarded me by Hal Matson,² about your having postponed the Volcano I wrote you one asking if it was still not too late to change your mind without doubtless taking fully into account that it was the amount of research I seemed calmly suggesting you do, quite apart from the number of corrections I was making myself, not to say insertions, many of which may have appeared to

you quite negligible, that had been responsible for the postponement.

On top of these items I perceive clearly the paradox of Cape tying
up the Canadian rights with the obligation of your bringing the
book out this year while your author meantime makes it quietly and
maddeningly impossible for you to do this.

I did not of course make any such suggestion to Cape myself but
so far as that goes I'm writing him anyhow on the subject & I'm sure
he will waive that stipulation. I have no British agent at present; I
should have had Hal's representative act for me over there, but the
insane coincidence of getting the news of the books acceptance on the
same day in two countries was enough to ravel any author into
knots.

For myself the delay has been caused by the arrival of the ms from
Mexico, as well by second thoughts due to my recent visit there, the
awful difficulty of getting books here, the non–existence of our own
owing to the fire, and numerous other difficulties I won't go into,
but which, all piling on at once at this point, make me believe in
Cocteau's remark: Truly our books hate us!³

[As regards the book itself 'Le guste esta jardin'] & the Spanish
seem to me the only real difficulty & the former I have already
solved.

There are really no echoes etc that I do not myself really consider
to be absolutely justifiable & assimilated, *absorbed*, & I have mentioned them to you partly for my own psychological benefit & partly
in case you might somewhere disagree.

I will not now make these the subject of a separate appendix to my
notes but when I come to any either coincidental or otherwise will
simply mention it and the page in question, since I feel you should
know of their existence.

Enclosed are notes to IV.⁴ There is nothing in V to speak of save
the Jardin problem, already solved, nothing in VI *I* can see now save
the German to be verified, nothing in VII save a little Spanish & the
garden again, in VIII little, IX nothing unless you can see something,
X I'll try to cut somewhat, & nothing to speak of in XI or XII.

This may still, I am aware, leave too much for you to do to get it
out by October, but I hate to let you down, if that is what I seem to
be doing, & [am willing & ready to cooperate wherever & however I
can. In either case, would you give me a deadline? I seem to remember there is one in the contract but have no copy of it.]ᵇ

For the rest, while I am proud of having written Under the
Volcano, I must confess to being slightly timorous of it. I have not
been very fortunate, to say the least, in my works so far, and it

would distress me to think you were losing interest in it so so soon after you had seemed to have such high hopes for it.[5]

[unsigned]

Annotations:

1 Laocoön, the Trojan priest of Greek mythology, was strangled by sea serpents for having offended the gods. Lowry liked this image of his own self-inflicted suffering.
2 This letter does not appear to have survived.
3 Jean Cocteau (1889-1963) was greatly admired by Lowry all his life, principally for his play *La Machine infernale*, for which Cocteau gave him tickets for two nights' performances in Paris in 1934; see the production photograph in Volume II. The remark that Lowry attributes to Cocteau may in fact have come from Julien Green's *Personal Record* (1939); see Lowry's 9 April 1940 letter (133) to Conrad Aiken.
4 The only 'notes to IV' that appear to be extant are the pencil notes found with this holograph. One is of particular interest with regard to Hugh's telegram at the beginning of this chapter in *Volcano*. Lowry writes: 'Significance of intelube has passed from my mind. But it might have something to do with the London Daily Herald or the United Press, if that matters. Cable is based on real one & used by permission of the reporter who sent it, I having sat in at the concoction thereof. Cable was, till lately, in my possession.' See the 25 June 1937 telegram (70) to the *Daily Herald*.
5 Erskine concludes his 8 July 1946 letter as follows: 'I'd like to remark on the concluding paragraph of your July 5 letter (about our "losing interest").' He then goes on to assure Lowry that, short of sleeping with the manuscript, his interest continues to grow. For some reason George Woodcock omitted Lowry's final paragraph when he published the letter in *Malcolm Lowry: The Man and His Work*; however, he did include Lowry's notes for chapter 4 (not chapter 5, as Woodcock has it).

Editorial Notes:

a. This letter has been transcribed from a holograph draft (UBC 2:7); a final holograph or typescript text does not appear to have survived. The draft is undated and unsigned, and pencil corrections for chapter 4 are with it. 'July 5' has been written at the top of the recto of the first page in what may be Margerie's writing, and this seems an appropriate date on the basis of the sequence of letters to Erskine, the progress of revisions to *Volcano*, and the news of the postponed publication date. Furthermore, in his 8 July 1946 letter to Lowry, Erskine mentions receiving one from Lowry dated 5 July, and he appears to be responding to comments made by Lowry in the letter transcribed here. This further corroborates a date of 5 July; see annotation 5.
b. The completion of this paragraph is in Margerie's hand.

230: To Jonathan Cape

P: UBC(ms)

[Dollarton, B.C.]
[July 1946]

Dear Mr Cape:–[a]

Sad story.

I have received one of those thingamagigs from you which looks as though it were intended to be accompanied by a cheque: perhaps not, because it says '*due* to author' etc: but if so, I have to inform you that the said cheque, to the best of my knowledge, was not there.[1]

I opened the letter in the forest; in a storm, with my arms full of groceries, & there is one chance in a thousand that it blew away without my knowledge: I sought everywhere, but found naught, & arrived home with a stoop in my soul.

However if it *was* there originally, either that is the explanation, or it was pinched out of the envelope, and in either case therefore, I suppose I have reluctantly to ask you to stop payment on the said cheque, though how that can be done, if at all, I have no notion.

If it was not there originally, all is well, save the 9/- in the £ tax, which I take to be the common crucifixion of us all: anyhow I must owe you 45 quid, if not 55 quid, so I deeply appreciate the fact that you as it were intimated you were not going to send me nothing: if that was not intended to be the case, all is likewise well & just, though I cannot help likewise appreciating the fact that had I had an agent you would have had then to send me, so to speak, less than nothing.

While specie of any kind is almost more than welcome to members, like myself, of the lumpenproletariat,[2] I feel to bound to point out that if you for your part have to pay a nine bob in the pound tax on anything I pay back to you from Canada it might be as well not merely to stop payment on the said cheque but to withold it altogether.

If on the other hand you are allowing me somehow or other to pay my debt back bit by bit in some other fashion, that would work out fine too, because I could then buy some lumber to make inside walls for our house, which would enable me to survive the winter & then get down to finishing a new novel that much sooner.

In this regard I should say my carbon of Under the Volcano, looking as if chewed by lions, & covered with chile, & even shot full of bullet holes, has arrived from Mexico:[3] my notes have apparently now got as far as America & are being forwarded, & this is a tremendous relief, because therein is a novel much better than the Volcano, concerning which the former arrival will greatly facilitate correspondence with yourself.[4]

I am sending you, under separate cover, so that it may be some-time before it arrives, a novel entitled Horse in the Sky, as yet unpublished, by Margerie Bonner, and I beg of you to give this book your most earnest consideration, since I believe it a first rate piece of work, or even something rarer, and what is more, there is much in the future that might come from the same stable, if this be given a chance. This I doubt whether it will get in America, unless it were given in England first, partly because the novel, although written by a middle westerner, albeit of English descent, seems to belong to a stream essentially English, and partly because the author is likewise already a successful writer of mystery stories, whose publisher Scribners is extremely reluctant that she have another 'serious' career. She isn't, however quite successful enough as yet to claim Graham Greene's kind of prerogative, but is too much poten-tially of a winner from Scribners point of view for them to encourage this other more important aspect of her talent: and for cognate reasons she is, in America, therefore unable to interest an-other publisher in herself as a serious long-term venture, because they come smack up against the fact that Scribners is grooming her for a career of crime. They published a book by her called The Shapes That Creep, this year, which has gone well, and are doing another one called The Last Twist of the Knife this autumn. And there is yet another one; & so forth. When you have swallowed the fact that this inside knowledge of the lady's work is due to the co-incidence of her having been my wife for some six years I hope you can believe me when I say that I am being absolutely objective, which I am, in recommending Horse in the Sky for your most serious attention. It is an extraordinarily beautiful and powerful book, set in Devonshire & in the Irish Hills of Michigan. There are things about it that you may not like, but over elaborateness is not one of them. It is quite short, 250 pages or so, and a criticism might be that, unlike the Volcano, it is not elaborate enough. This criti-cism would be unjust, I believe, for it makes its effect by powerful juxtapositions and understatement, with an extraordinary economy of words, though it contains a story which is by implication quite as complicated as Rosamond Lehmann's The Ballad & the Source.[5] In fact, at first, it seems even a bit naïve. Then, in spite of its apparent simplicity, you are threatened with what seems too much 'white-napery', the feeling that you might be in for just another period-regional piece about the Middle west, but these threats once

removed by the short dramatic chapters and mounting tempo the Strinbergian story begins to emerge.[6]
It is told swiftly and beautifully, and in a manner uninfluenced by any writer I know of. In fact it never seems to have occurred to any writer to tell a story in this way, though its manner is simplicity itself. The story, which as you soon begin to realise, concerns fate more than the Middle West, has finally a quality of inevitableness and absolute truth that Emily Bronte herself would have been proud to achieve. And in its quality of wildness and storm and poetic beauty it may also recall that writer. But there are few inventories, and it is sparing of involutions. It moves like a swiftly flowing river in spring; – I should say in spate almost: yet it is clear & pure, & sweeps little debris along with it. In a curious way, vengeful though its resolution is, it seems to transcend itself, so that when you have finished it you find yourself poetically & imaginatively enriched & its song does not leave you. In short, I believe you would never be sorry if you published this book. It could, by the way, be very easily translated, and in French especially it would go excellently. In short, I believe you would never be sorry if you published this book.

At all events I am sending it to you for your yea or nay with a proud sense as of discovery.

I despatched immediately your terms to R & H, & thank you very much for replying so quickly.

With kind regards –

Malcolm Lowry

Annotations:

1 No 'thingamagig' or other correspondence from Cape concerning the cheque appears to have survived.
2 The term 'lumpenproletariat,' especially in Marxist theory, refers to the lowest level of the proletariat, comprising unskilled workers and vagrants.
3 When the Lowrys were deported from Mexico on 4 May 1946 they had to leave their manuscripts and other belongings behind.
4 Lowry could be thinking here of *Dark as the Grave* or 'La Mordida.'
5 Rosamond Lehmann (1901-90), an English novelist and translator, wrote several novels in the thirties from which she gained a reputation as a 'feminine' writer. *The Ballad and the Source* (1945) is usually seen as one of her better novels due to the complex portrait of its heroine.
6 Margerie's novel bears a certain resemblance to the Swedish playwright August Strindberg's (1849-1912) dark play about a sexual liaison between a lady and her servant, *Miss Julie* (1888).

Editorial Notes:

a. This transcription has been made from an undated pencil holograph on three sheets of cheap paper. Although it is probably only a draft, it carries relatively few deletions, interlineations, and additions; it has been signed.

231: To Albert Erskine

P: UBC(ts)

Dollarton, B.C.,
Canada
6 July 1946

Dear Mr Erskine:

Herewith the notes on V. I carefully considered the problem of the garden and have solved it so far very simply as indicated in the enclosed by leaving it as it is, but adding a couple of natural qualifications through the Consul's mind.[1]

Este would be more correct than esta, but esta is better poetically and I feel the mistake might easily be made by an Indian as indeed it was.

I think the Consul's feeling about there being too many question marks is right too and in keeping with his visual heebie-jeebies.

So unless you, or anyone's, suspension of disbelief is troubled I'm satisfied on this point until we get to VII where as things stand at the moment I'm going to cut 2/3 of the quotation altogether.

I am trying to make these corrections of a final kind, in order to obviate corrections on the proofs as far as possible.

If it is of any interest to you the passage on 201 was written early in 1943, considerably before the advent of the atom bomb, and the same goes for another passage in Chapter X re the elements.

Page 206, the last page of Chapter V, rather reminds me of The Lost Week End. It was written in 1937. 98% of the Volcano was indeed written before the publication of that opus. The latter event made this author swim six miles straight. And back.

Yours sincerely,

Malcolm Lowry

P.S. Part of my anxiety over your postponement of the book, if that is finally settled upon, is that at my back I seem to hear Charles Jackson's chariot hurrying near with yet another book on the same subject.[2]

Annotations:

1 Lowry makes some suggestions regarding the sign, but Erskine raises further concerns about the accuracy of the Spanish in his 8 July 1946 letter to Lowry.

2 There are some gaps in the correspondence between Lowry and Erskine during the mid-June to early July period. As a result, the letter in which Erskine announces a postponement of publication date does not appear to have survived, and the reasons for the postponement are not clear. In his 8 July 1946 letter to Lowry, Erskine claims he is relieved by the post-ponement and now plans to have advance copies for reviewers by 1 November. It is also clear from Erskine's letter that there were other letters from Lowry (such as the one dated 5 July 1946) that have not survived with Erskine's papers.

232: To Albert Erskine

P: UBC(ts)

Dollarton, B.C.,
Canada
8 July 1946

Dear Mr Erskine:

Herewith the corrections on VI. I considered carefully about there being too much in the sea part, and decided it was too integrated to cut, or rather it already has been cut to the bone.

There are however a few homeward bound stitches elsewhere and these I have fixed as indicated in the enclosed, cutting wherever possible.[1]

I decided against making a whopping great cut at one point of six or seven pages because it gave the thing on rereading a kind of arrhythmia.

I have tried to eliminate dubious points so far as possible and ask you to forgive me once more that I have to bother you with such things as the translation of El Redondillo that I am not in a position to verify myself.

I have another apology to make re my first letter to you. There are certain questions I asked you re pelado etc. in VIII that on the arrival of my carbon copy from Mexico it would seem I had dealt with myself, if not quite to one's final satisfaction.

This was due to our fire. I was working partly on the revision of this chapter when that happened, and it seemed to burn my memory a little around the edges, so that later, whenever I have thought of

VIII, I have thought of an earlier version of it, that wasn't being worked on at such a grim moment.

I have now finished with VII and VIII, save for the typing, and am on to IX so that I'm nearly ¾ way through.

Rain – rain – rain here, Vancouver's Jubilee,[2] and the city full of wild Indians.

Yours sincerely,
Malcolm Lowry

Annotations:

1 Lowry's changes to chapter 6 consist mainly of punctuation and Spanish corrections.
2 On 6 April 1886 the town of Granville was incorporated into the city of Vancouver; therefore, 1946 was the city's Diamond Jubilee.

233: To Albert Erskine

P: UBC(ms)

[Dollarton, B.C.]
[ca 9 July 1946][a]

Dear Mr Erskine:

I thought I'd thrown everything into this book except the kitchen stove and Les 10 Frattelinis.

Now I see that I have the 10 Frattelinis.[1]

With best wishes,
Malcolm Lowry

P.S. And the kitchen stove.

– We're in the channel &
full steam ahead!

Annotations:

1 'Les 10 Frattelinis' (see also *Under the Volcano*, 268) is a reference to the famous group of Italian clowns called 'Les Trois Fratellinis.' The three Fratellini brothers, Paul, Albert, and François, settled in Paris and by 1922 had joined the Comédie-Française. They often appeared with other members of their circus family, which may explain Lowry's number of ten. The group was much loved in France and travelled widely between the wars. In 1951 the surviving brother, Albert, tried to form a new troupe of Fratellinis with his nephews, but he was not successful.

Editorial Notes:

a. This holograph note has been written on the verso of a page of notes and corrections for chapter 9 of the *Volcano*. It bears neither inside address nor date, but was certainly written in sequence with the chapter-by-chapter corrections Lowry was working on in July.

234: To Albert Erskine

P: UBC(ms)

[Dollarton, B.C.]
[ca 10 July 1946][a]

Dear Mr Erskine:

I got your excellent letter yesterday[1] for which I thank you sincerely – my wife & I went over it betweentimes watching the windjammer Pamin unload: a grand sight.

I will answer in detail *quam celerrime*.

With best wishes

Malcolm Lowry

Poem for Mr Erskine as from one correcting mss to another

How are we off for awares?
And how are we off for despairs?
How, oh Lord, for wives?
And how, oh God, for lives?
How are we off for not?
And how many deaths have we got?[2]

Annotations:

1 This letter does not appear to have survived.
2 See 'Correcting Manuscript' (*CP*, 167).

Editorial Notes:

a. This brief holograph letter has been written on the verso of the fourth and final page of the corrections to chapter 10 of *Volcano*. It is possible that, rather than typing a separate covering letter for each set of corrections, Lowry has included his letter in this informal manner. These letters show how the relationship between the men was growing rapidly into one of friendship and, on Lowry's side, trust.

235: To Albert Erskine

P: UBC(ms)

[Dollarton, B.C.]
[early July 1946]ᵃ

Dear Mr Erskine: –

I'm awfully sorry if its my fault about the postponement, but circumstances were agin me.

Of course I certainly don't think you should be penalised about the Canadian rights under the circumstances, but I have no English agent & have to write Cape myself about this, which I shall of course immediately do.[1]

However here is another Chapter corrected – I have practically finished 4 & 5 – & I think I will be as far as 7 by the end of the week & probably could finish the whole thing in two weeks.

The apparent plethora of alterations in I & the number of questions there I think gives an unfortunate impression. There are no more inserts to speak of: from now they will mostly be cuts though of course the Jardin thing has to be fixed.

If it were important for it to be published in October & you stand to lose by not publishing it then I am quite prepared to make some financial sacrifice myself on the matter.

Could you please let me know before I write Cape if it is not too late for you to change your mind, if I keep to some date line you set me.

Yours sincerely

Malcolm Lowry

Annotations:

1 Lowry had lost touch with Innes Rose, his former Cambridge friend and literary agent from the thirties, and did not hear from him again until the fall of 1946; see Lowry's November 1946 letter (**257**) to Jonathan Cape.

Editorial Notes:

a. This transcription has been made from a rough pencil draft (UBC 2:7) for which a typed final letter does not appear to have survived. Margerie has written some revisions in the left margin.

236: To Albert Erskine

P: UBC(ts)
PP: *Lln* 5. 184–85

Dollarton, B.C.,
Canada
15 July 1946

Dear Mr Erskine:

Herewith Chapter XI. The object of this chapter was, so to speak, to pull out all the stops of nature and the universe. The 'search' for the Consul is not unrelated to the Eleusinian mysteries.[1] The vultures here have in part flapped vaguely out of Nuttall's Ornithology (circa 1880) and the soulful eagle may seem to bear some bedraggled resemblance to Yeats or even Walter Van Tilburg Clark's Hawk, though I believe this to be remote.[2] Euzakadi (p. 458) refers to Bilbao. The culmination of the Pleiades, back to Chapter I again: the Pleiades are associated with this particular day. The dark wood harks back to Dante (El Bosque, Casino de la Selva, Quauhnahuac etc.) P. 464: 'Throw the bloody little man in the river', 'Set Barrabas free!' These two remarks, but nothing else, are quotations or near quotations from two personal friends of mine: the first Tom ('Savage Civilizations' 'Letter to Oxford' 'Mass Observation') Harrison, the second Nordahl Grieg.[3] They both refer to what the world tends to do to the poet type of fellow and there is something like the first remark in Harrison's iconoclastic Letter to Oxford. 'Gi os Barabbas frei – ' are the last words of Grieg's play 'Barabbas', which has never been translated into English and which ran for one night at the National Theatret Oslo, circa '29. (It was indeed hooted off the stage by schnappes-drinking Lutherans who objected to seeing Christ where Oswald was wont to roam. Sibelius offered to write some music for this but both Grieg and Sibelius got slightly plasterado on that occasion so he never did.)[4]

Re the last page 476. Somewhere in Julian Green's 'Personal Record' he notes that he would like to end a book with his heroine soaring straight aloft, and in one of his perhaps more cheery works, some female does just that, though not without some assistance from an admirer, and not toward the Pleiades, and indeed you are not quite sure at that point whether the lady has not been dead for some time, or is just getting ready to sup some more horrors.[5] Possibly I was thinking of that too, but what I really had in mind was Faust, (the opera) where Marguerite is hauled up to heaven with pulleys, while the old boy goes down the drain:[6] this, and of course, the picture in VII and XII, Los Borracheros, I mean Los Borrachones, I mean Los Borrachonazos (what about borracho*nazis* for XII? – better resist the temptation) where there is similar soaring and spiralling.[7]

The only other brilliant thing worthy of note as regards this chapter is that I have cut out from the beginning five of the better lines in the whole book under the impression that they were familiar and possibly echoed Katherine Anne Porter. They were familiar all right, but did not echo Katherine Anne Porter or anybody else, their familiarity being merely due to the fact that I had rewritten them myself some 50 times. Doubtless to the chapter's advantage, however, these lines are now gone beyond precise recall.

I am in process of replying to your letter and the questions therein, and will get the result off to you airmail at the earliest opportunity, probably to-morrow.

With best wishes,

Malcolm Lowry

P.S. In fact, since my replies may be holding you up, I'll get those off to-morrow, & XII by Wednesday. This by the way is written with an eagle's feather, washed up on the beach.[8]

Annotations:

1 Lowry makes a similar claim in his 2 January 1946 letter (**210**) to Jonathan Cape.

2 Thomas Nuttall is well known for his books on birds. The first such is *A Manual of Ornithology of the United States and of Canada* (1832). Lowry is thinking of American writer Walter van Tilburg Clark's animal story called 'Hook,' which first appeared in the *Atlantic Monthly* 2, 166 (August 1940): 223-34. The story is about the suffering and death of a hawk.

3 See Ackerley/Clipper (407) for comments on both of these 'quotations.' Grieg's play *Barrabas* (1927) was the first of six plays by Lowry's Norwegian hero, of which only one, *Nederlagst* (1937; *Defeat* 1945), has been translated into English to date.

4 I have not been able to confirm Lowry's description, either of the play's reception or of Grieg and Sibelius (the Finnish composer) getting 'plasterado' together. However, both men were heavy drinkers, so Lowry *may* be right. The last line of Grieg's play is 'Gi os Barrabas fri.'

5 Green does not make this comment in *Personal Record* (1939), but he does often end his novels with the death of his heroine. For example, *Midnight* (1936) ends with the dying heroine, Elisabeth, being lifted up from the earth towards the heavens.

6 Lowry is referring to Charles Gounod's *Faust* (1859).

7 In the notes with his 8 July 1946 letter to Lowry, Erskine explains that

the Spanish dictionary offers *los borrachones* and *los borrachonazos*, but not 'borracheros.' He recommends *borrachones*. Lowry continues to have fun with 'borrochonazi' in subsequent letters.

8 Lowry's signature and postscript have been written in black ink that is a bit thick and blotchy at points. The eagle's feather pen was, in fact, given to Lowry by Jimmy Craige, and the pen still exists.

237: To Albert Erskine

P: UBC(ts)

Dollarton, B.C.,
Canada
16 July 1946

Dear Mr Erskine:

Re your letter July 8, in haste.

(a) Der Englishe dampfer tragt Schutzfarben gegen deutche U-boote.

(b) Go verlies ich der Wellteil unserer Antipoden. . .

The original note of this, together with the translation, has been lost, but these were in the beginning literal captions to two photographs, the first of a British Q ship, the second of the Emden, in a book printed in Gothic German dealing with the exploits of Captain Müller,[1] which were shown me in a German restaurant in Mexico where I was eating (with, as I recall, a member – or one invalided out – of the International Brigade likewise strangely named Muller) a hamburger bifsteak mit zwei eier mit cerveza Munchener grande,[2] by the proprietor, whom I now suspect of having been a borrachonazi. I regret, so far as regards (a), dampf if I know now what tragt Schutzfarben means, but (a) should *mean* something like: The English steamer (i.e. Q boat) goes – er – to do something or other against the German U boat. Whereas on the other hand (b) – well now, as for (b) – though I know of no word 'Go' in the German language, so it may be So, and ich which means 'I' looks a bit equivocal and may really be 'in', in which case 'der' may be, for all I know, 'den' – (b) should *mean*, as if Muller perhaps had said this, something like: And so I go to seek in the watery world at large *our* Antipodes . . . I'm awfully sorry to be putting you to extra trouble about these sentences, I don't think they need much fixing, but my German is rotten and ohne ein German dictionary al stereless within a boote am I (amid the sea betwexen windes two)[3] in regard to them myself.

Re punctuation.[4]

Examples: from your letter.

   1. p. 65. re nonrestrictive clauses. She was watching the Consul, who seemed, etc. Yes, by all means I agree there should be a comma after Consul and in similar cases. I'm sure I meant to put one here and probably didn't only because Consul was on the end of a line and I didn't notice it.

   2. re commas and dashes. Yes, I agree with you. Out with the commas. The very idea of them is horrible, in fact, as you put it, hanging in space.

   3. p. 5. re commas before and/or after parenthesis: Yes again. Ignorance, sir, pure ignorance, though in the main I've tried to punctuate carefully, except of course where there isn't any punctuation, or where there isn't any room, and demons have got into the machinery, and so on.

My answers to your answers to my answers to your notes re my letter of June 22nd and your letter of July 8 period:

   p. 58. 'Have you anything to declare? . .' 'Butterflies.' (See Sorrow in Sunlight.)[5] Yes, the butterflies. Well, as you see it, 'commotion' refers merely to butterflies, at least is meant to syntactically, i.e. this commotion of butterflies etc. so that there is a mistake about the comma.

   But the comma was purposely placed after 'commotion' precisely in order that it should not mean *merely* 'commotion of butterflies.'

   Commotion in fact is used – as I.A. Richards somewhere suggests it should be used – to mean, rather, *e*motion;[6] so that while the commotion does indeed include that of the butterflies, it also refers back to Yvonne's whole state of mind, i.e. her consciousness so lashed by wind and air and voyage she still seemed to be travelling etc., and taken like this you can neither remove the comma after commotion nor put the said butterflies in parenthesis, brackets, nor yet in any other nets or even boxes.

   The question of a second 'Yvonne' before 'glanced defensively' etc. still remains but if you don't like it don't put it there. Possibly I suggested it because, in the version I was then working on, the sentence started on the previous page, so that one rather lost 'Yvonne'. To refer back to the other: your suggestion of the bracket is very good in itself and on second thoughts, to contradict myself, possibly brings out my meaning even better, by blocking the word commotion in such a way that it calls more attention to its ambiguity: but no, on third thoughts, I think it, respectfully, a mistake.

Page 71. Born in Hawaii, she had had volcanoes etc. Yes, that's fine – though wouldn't 'she'd had' be even better?

Page 224 (you mean 244) Yes – Flaubert was referring to des. I think he said, To say 'of the kingdom of France' is a crime. He also said: 'Follow out your metaphors.' 'Purple passages are futile,' and 'Ah, the ands, the buts, the ifs, the howevers – is there never an end to this murderous prose!' And, falling on his desk, died, being murdered thereby.[7]

Page 350 (cf. 339) I reorganized the passage you mentioned about the pelado and the hat, and kicked out gachupin altogether, re which apologies for your trouble: pelado I think is O.K. now – most of its meanings were given me by them who ought to know, and I don't think I'm loading the dice too much now by taking advantage of Hugh's relative ignorance of Mexico, if not, quite so much as before, of Spanish.

Page 476. (cf. new passage beginning of VIII, middle of VII, and V) Le gusta este jardin? . . .

Oh God our help in ages past our hope in years to come.[8] Destruyen I know for certain is right and evite is right. And you too are right. The original notice was wrong in 1938. And now in 1946 is wronger still. I agree with everything you say, but with two small reservations. The Spanish of the notice should be correct in all 3½ places where it appears but in V, where the Consul first sees it, it should be printed thus:

> ?LE GUSTA ESTE JARDIN?
> ?QUE ES SUYO?
> !EVITE QUE SUS HIJOS LO DESTRUYEN!

with two erroneous question marks as above, one after jardin and one before Que – else how is the reader who knows Spanish going to believe that the Consul reads que on the second line as por qué, even though the reader makes allowance for his other mistakes: we have now made excuse ourselves for the thing in V, which allows us some small margin for error, the Consul himself feels here that there may be too many question marks, so that I don't think anyone will feel a proof reader has slipped merely, as long as the Spanish itself is correct: as for those who don't understand the Spanish they can carry the Consul's mistranslation along with them so far as VIII, page 324, where the notice appears correctly and Hugh translates it accurately, though here in order to avoid emphasis among other reasons it is printed horizontally and not even italicised: at the end of the book, the thing should be printed again, as it really appears, in caps, and in 3 lines, but with the extra question marks excised, viz:

?LE GUSTA ESTE JARDIN
QUE ES SUYO?
!EVITE QUE SUS HIJOS LO DESTRUYEN!

when the two meanings should explode simultaneously.

What remains for me to ask you is:

(a) do you *agree* with cutting it down in VII, page 305, and if so is it cricket to print a question mark after jardin there, which, though the rest is missing, implies the same hallucination as in V?

(b) Is my horizontal unitalicised rendering of it in VIII, page 324, a sound scheme – if you think it should appear there precisely as it does at the end, that's O.K. by me, but it turns up at a rather inconvenient point for one thing, where I am (I'm afraid rather typically) already rather bogged down with the notices Inhumaciones and Quo Vadis?[9] But I thought I got round the problem well and may even have solved it, at that.

In short, is this arrangement O.K. or have you a better idea?

If you have it has my blessing. My wife tells me I suddenly sat up in bed in the middle of last night saying grimly: 'My God, I can't cut *that*, or if I do, *it* will cut *me!*'

La Despedida – yes, let's keep it.

And let's have Los Borrachones in VI, keeping the Consul's question why not Los Borrachos the same. (Whether or not I can keep Los Borrachonazos – wonderful word – out of XII remains to be seen in what goes by to-morrow's post to you.)[a]

Finally, thanks most awfully for all the trouble you've gone to, as also for your encouragement: I will write in reply to the rest of your letter by another post, but I think I have answered all the main points that were holding you up. I must catch the mail with this and then, for an hour or two, since our house still has no inside walls, I must, with my wife, saw up a semicolon or two and place them beside a bracket upon a non-restrictive stud accompanied by two exclamation posts upside down, –

With best wishes,

Malcolm Lowry

Annotations:

1 Karl von Müller (1873-1923) was the famous commander of the SMS *Emden*, one of the most celebrated light cruisers of the German Imperial Navy during the First World War. Using camouflage and disguise, the cruiser enjoyed a great deal of success in its operations in the Indian Ocean before being trapped by the British and beached on a coral reef in November 1914, with a loss of most of her men. To date four more

German ships have born the famous name. I have not been able to locate the book that Lowry describes here, but in earlier drafts of *Volcano* (for example, UBC 30: 1,15) there are references that suggest the captions came from a German newspaper article on the *Emden*. The first quotation ('The British steamship has been camouflaged for protection against German submarines') is factual and could well have appeared in a newspaper; the second sounds more like a formal quotation ('Thus I left the continent of our Antipodes'). In the drafts for chapter 6, Lowry has misspelt the German just as he has here, but Erskine has corrected it for the published text.

2 Lowry's German-Spanish description of his meal amounts to 'a beef hamburger with two eggs with a large Munich beer.'

3 Lowry's quotation is from Geoffrey Chaucer's *Troilus and Criseyde* (ca 1386): 'Al stereless within a boat am I / Amidde the sea, bitwixen windes two, / That in contrarye stonden evermo' (Book 1, 416-18). This passage is also used as an epigraph for *October Ferry to Gabriola*.

4 Lowry's punctuation is highly idiosyncratic, so that it is not surprising that the American university-educated Erskine would challenge him on it. For example, as these letters demonstrate so clearly, Lowry loved commas before parentheses, and Erskine goes to considerable, good-humoured pains in his 8 July 1946 letter to explain and demonstrate why and how not to do this. Dashes and colons (more common in British than in North American usage) are sprinkled liberally through Lowry's prose, and Erskine struggles to reduce these as well. This business of punctuation became a source of jokes between the two men.

5 *Sorrow in Sunlight*, a 1924 novel by Ronald Firbank, was published by Brentano's in London in an edition of one thousand copies. The story is set in Haiti and the characters speak in the local patois. An unusual but by no means especially good novel, *Sorrow in Sunlight* clearly stayed in Lowry's memory, for phrases from it recur in his work. Here, he is remembering the following passage:

> 'Have you nothing, young man, to declare?'
> '. . . Butterflies!'
> 'Exempt of duty.   Pass.'   (p. 56)

But Hugh's healthy 'systole and diastole' may also be an echo of Firbank's novel (p. 69), and see annotation 11 for Lowry's June 1931 letter (**33**) to Conrad Aiken.

6 In his *Coleridge on the Imagination* (London: Kegan Paul, 1934), I.A. Richards comments that a 'good general prescription wherever we meet with this word [emotion] in critical prose, is to try replacing it with *commotion* – a word which very commonly will have the same *sense* with different emotive accompaniments' (p. 36). Richards goes on to discuss the sense of the word *emotion* in psychology, with a view to reconsidering Coleridge's theory of the imagination.

7 Lowry seems to be thinking of Gustave Flaubert's remarks in a 28-29

June 1853 letter to his mother: 'Que de répétitions de mots je viens de surprendre! Que de *tout*, de *mais*, de *car*, de *cependant*! Voilà ce que la prose a de diabolique, c'est qu'elle n'est jamais finie.' See *Oeuvres Complètes de Gustave Flaubert: Corréspondance (1852-1854)*, p. 252. Lowry, who had read Flaubert's letters in the early forties, was fond of quoting and alluding to his comments about good prose.

8 'Oh God our help in ages past, / Our hope for years to come' are the opening lines of the hymn based on Psalm 90; see, for example, the Church of England's *Hymn Book to Music* or the *Methodist Hymn and Tune Book*.

9 *Inhumaciones* means 'burials' in Spanish, but see Ackerley/Clipper (310-11). *Quo vadis* is Latin for 'Where are you going?' but it is also the title of Henrik Sienkiewicz's (1848-1916) novel *Quo Vadis?* (1896) about the early Christians in ancient Rome.

Editorial Notes:

a. The typed notes to chapter 12 (UBC 2:6) do not appear to have an extant covering letter; however, at the end of the third page, after a final question about the word 'foisting' (see *Volcano*, 375), Lowry has written in pencil: 'Well – ! we got here! – just under the gun – I have to rush for the post – I have two page 511's – I hope you have *one* – some slight changes here may seem unnecessary, but all have a reason – detritus of other chapters seems to wash up on the beach of the last – letter follows – With best wishes Malcolm Lowry.'

238: To Harold Matson

P: Matson(ts); UBC(phc)

Dollarton, B.C.,
Canada
29 July 1946

Dear Hal:

In haste to catch mail: thanks awfully for yours of July 23. Yes, my status is as stated: I am still English, on a visitor's permit, though I now have the right to become Canadian any time I wish. I was recently advised against this move for my own financial protection by the Immigration themselves, and also in order to facilitate travel. It looks as though they were right: but on the other hand this 30% deduction also would appear right pro tem, and on top of this I now perceive I owe you some $100. Perhaps you will advise me on this point: I could pay this back right off, or rather in two or three installments, on the other hand by that time the proofs would probably be out – for I have now finished all my corrections, subject only to Erskine's final say-so – and consequently the second batch of advance money would by that time have been paid to you, from which you could deduct. Please tell me what is your wish. I am harrowed to think you have done so much for me and now I still owe you money, but maybe the Volcano will actually be a success or something. I also wish to express again my great appreciation of your generosity in having sent that money to Mexico, about which adventure more later. Such a phenomenal drama out of such a top drawer was this indeed that I verily believe you would think your friend had finally and absolutely gone cuckoo were I just to set down the bare facts here. But if I *can* only write it – gawdblimey! The notes should be arriving today, the Volcano itself having proceeded them.

I wrote to Cape again a week or two back re Canadian rights and postponement of the Volcano and cannot see he will raise any objection to this.[1]

Re Margie: There is only *one* final copy of The Last Twist of the Knife, which is with Scribner's.[2] Any other previous versions you may have a copy of she considers impossible, so please don't send Peters such of that book – better wait for the proofs: she'd like to see these too, she feels, quite naturally, what if they're printing the wrong version? And anyhow, she has a right to see the proofs??? Re her corrections on the proofs of the Shapes for which she is charged $44.21. Only the first half of the proofs were sent her, she made no corrections for which she could be possibly indemnified for that amount, so far as I can see none of the ones she made were used anyhow. She never saw the proofs of the second half of the book at all: they were never sent as promised, nor has she ever received any of her author's copies. Apart from that she never received a bill, as stated, for these excess corrections, and the item which concerns 'purchases' likewise is obscure to her.

Otherwise, all is well. We are finishing our house and I'm hoping greatly to get down and see you before the snow flies or at least is frozen. Best Wishes, from us both

(Excuse pencil) – Malcolm[a]

Annotations:

1 This letter to Cape does not appear to have survived.
2 The existence of this single copy would later become a problem for

Margerie when Scribner's published her novel without its final chapter; see Lowry's 20 September 1946 letter (**247**) to Maxwell Perkins.

Editorial Notes:

a. Although the letter is typed, the complimentary close and signature are written in pencil.

239: To Gerald Noxon

p: Texas(ts)
pp: *LLN* 125-26

Dollarton, B.C.
29 July 1946

Dear old Gerald:

Well, I guess you may have been a bit anxious about us after our odd letter from Nuevo Espana but here we are, back in the old homestead again. Or rather, new homestead. On the whole it is beginning to look better than the old one though we are still doing a lot of carpentering. I am sitting in one of your favorite chairs and the washing is blowing on the old pier – we still sing 'When Gerald comes to town' and everything in fact is as it was, only better. It is only recently we have been able to sing the said song again without mingled feelings of sadness and disaster and in a minor key but now the house and everything else is getting on so well the song is once more gay and we can even look forward once more to the visit of the White Man without agonizing over the burned posts. It is true we were nearly murdered in Mexico not long ago and in fact only just escaped with our lives across the border: but that is another story for a winter evening and una botella. Fortunately it is such a good story that all that experience now seems very much worth while to both of us. It is, however, disarming to be as it were *inside* a novel, the prota-gonist, or protagonists, rather than the author; but fate was such an extraordinarily good artist in this case that one forgives it for having seemed capable of stopping at nothing at all in order to gain its ends: besides, one now has been given the chance of stepping into fate's shoes for a while and writing it up oneself, as indeed one is planning to do.[1]

News from here is all bright. Margie got so fed up with Scribner's that I have been doing her letter writing for her but to-day we got the first Scribner statement from Hal re the Shapes which is in the 5000 sale class and has even run into a second edition apparently, which is damn good and encouraging news albeit she is charged for corrections on proofs she never made, never, indeed, for that matter received. The Last Twist is coming out shortly, we hear, but not from Scribner's, via her press clipping bureau and a review in the Retail Bookseller:[2] she has never seen the proofs and does not know what version they are printing. And I have high hopes of the Horse [in the Sky] in England.

Reynal and Hitchcock seem to be planning to go to town on the Volcano and re this publishers they have proved such swell people to deal with that I do not hesitate to suggest you get in touch with them yourself, specifically with one Albert Erskine, who has in addition to the work involved maintained such a hilarious, if scholarly, correspondence on the subject that one cannot but conclude him to be a kindred spirit of a kind you would find most understanding in regard to your own works. As for Hal I would, in spite of his faults, stick to him: he shows up trumps particularly as a business agent. In the field of royalties, etc. – in short, after the event – you will find him tops: he is very slow at precipitating that event however and I would not put it past him not to read one's books at all: his judgement seems better of 'writer' rather than 'book'. I have had to get through with the Volcano in somewhat of a hurry in regard to Hitchcock: I would have been better off for your advice re possible cuts etc. They gave me carte blanche and I made very few. A crashing thematic mistake in Spanish held me up for a while but I think I solved it satisfactorily.[3] But with Cape though I have contracted to write a preface of 1000 words and also a blurb! – Can you help? I am in a considerable stew about what to say.[4] Unlike Hitchcock, the readers of whom (all 7, as Erskine remarked) seemed to think it the berries, Cape's readers, all save I, appeared to think the thing rather a bloody bore and wanted me to rewrite it. I refused to do this but had to battle literally for every chapter. Though I convinced them in the end there may be something in what they say, namely that the reader may be put off by the slow moving beginning unless he has some intimation of the reasons for this and the gruesomes and/or profundities in store for him and so on. I await your advice. I need scarcely add how much I thank you for your own part in and encouragement re the book. All your suggestions turned out right, and the parts you sat on, such as Chapter II, and which I rewrote with Margie's and your help until they got your O.K. have become the strongest.

We went to – where, you seem destined not to find out since the last pages of this letter have mysteriously disappeared.[a] However this is more or less the final bits and pieces of news etc: Please tell us when the Branches are blossoming forth. The Volc is coming out sometime around the first of the year and Hitchcock's want me to be in N.Y. on publication date so we plan to come east somewhere round that time and are very much looking forward to stopping in Niagara and seeing you all. Our very best love to you and Betty and Nick – God bless

from

Malc

Annotations:

1 After his return to Dollarton in May, Lowry began to incorporate his and Margerie's experiences in Mexico into his work-in-progress. The initial weeks of the trip became the basis for *Dark as the Grave Wherein My Friend Is Laid*, and the nightmarish persecutions of the final weeks provided the plot for 'La Mordida.'
2 Margerie's novel was announced in several places during July 1946, and the *Retail Bookseller*, a monthly magazine for the book trade that carries brief reviews, describes her novel in a few lines (July 1946): 55[B]. However, Scribner's does not appear to have made any effort to advertize the book.
3 Lowry is probably referring to his difficulty with the 'Le gusta este jardin' sign and epigraph in *Under the Volcano*. During July 1946 he was sending Albert Erskine chapter-by-chapter notes and corrections for the novel and wrestling with the Spanish for this important sign.
4 See Lowry's 10 January 1947 letter (**272**) to Jonathan Cape.

Editorial Notes:

a. The typescript sent to Noxon appears in the form transcribed here, and I have not located a draft of this letter with the 'last pages.'

240: To Evelyn Boden Lowry

P: UBC(ms)

Dollarton P.O.,
Dollarton, B.C.
[Summer 1946]

My very dearest Mum:[1]

I regret deeply I have become such a rotten letter writer recently, but I have had & have almost more work at the moment than I can cope with & at the same time even write to you, let alone anybody else.

In short, both my American & my English publisher & my agent are all keeping me at it: I have to get the book ready for American publication by the end of this year or America loses the Canadian rights to England & it's all a very complicated problem at such a long distance: I believe I shall probably go to New York in the fall for a while to facilitate matters.

That I have some insight into your own problems over there is shown by the fact in the last two months I have made out of my brain about as much as my entire yearly income, a considerable sum in normal times but which is taxed so heavily I don't expect to see half of it, if that: I have to pay 9/- in the £ on everything I earn in England, there is a similarly cracking great tax in America, & things have not been improved for me by the Canadian dollar going on a parity with the American one so that my excursion into the capitalist class, if brilliant, is liable to be rather brief: on the other hand of course I may be in for making more cash still, but the world as it is I fail to see what it will do me.

It all goes to show though what happens when you stick to what you are doing if you believe in it in the face of discouragement; I must have been told a hundred thousand times that there was no market at all for the kind of thing I was doing, & indeed the book in question was turned down in the original form by every publisher in New York six years ago,[2] including the very famous ones who say it is one of the most interesting books they have ever had in the whole history of their publishing. Well, well, well; one seems to have heard it all before, of the life of many writers who were worthwhile, & even of those who weren't very good. It [is] as though such writers have unconsciously anticipated events or the public taste & have to bide their time in patience until suddenly they find a public or in my case a publisher at least, as if ready made for them. For my own part I am somewhat indifferent to the fate of the book & I am certainly fed up with all the time it takes negotiating when I want to get down to simply creative work again. You are often in my thoughts – thank you very much for the pressed flowers – & the papers – yes indeed I believe in the hereafter – who wouldn't, since it seems sometimes as though it's just around the corner for everybody. Meantime America seems to be going cuckoo & the condition here of Canada is – as a radio writer put it – something like being one Siamese twin when the other is bent on committing suicide. But the birds, as Conrad said, endure. God bless you my darling & be happy & try & keep your heart in the highlands.[3] That's where mine is anyhow – right smack in the highlands. Heaps of love from your most affectionate son

Malcolm

P.S. I will try & send you a little present out of season.

Annotations:

1 Lowry's mother, Evelyn Boden Lowry (1873-1950), remains a very shadowy figure in Lowry's biography. Day's references to her are few and ambiguous; Margerie repeated stories of her neglect of her youngest son, but friends from Lowry's youth suggest that he was close to his mother. Russell Lowry has refused to discuss his mother. What little evidence survives, however, suggests that Lowry was in regular correspondence with his mother through much of his life and that she was, in fact, interested in his work and his general welfare. There are seven extant letters from Mrs Lowry to her 'darling boy' in the Lowry collection (UBC 1:39), and they span the years from 1937 to 1950. The tone, subject-matter, and questions in these letters all suggest a rather simple, straightforward, domestic woman who lacks intellectual interests but none the less displays sincere warmth and affection for her absent, youngest son. Only two of Lowry's letters to his mother appear to have survived, this one and his late 1949 letter (376). See Bowker (1-9).
2 Lowry is remembering the rejection of *Under the Volcano* by twelve New York publishers in 1940-41.
3 'My Heart's in the Highlands,' is the title of Robert Burns's 1798 poem and William Saroyan's play.

241: To Conrad Aiken

P: H(ts)
PP: *LAL* 194-95

> Dollarton, B.C.,
> Canada
> 5 August 1946

Dear old Conrad:
   I hope you and Mary are by now ensconced in Jeakes House, Rye, and that the sea-poppies and Camber Castle, not to say tram, and the ships blithely sailing down the meadows are still there, and that that which was once the province of the sea is not now too much a province of the same again by virtue of being a navel base.
   As for myself we are still living in the same place with rather more side walls, and suffering from success slightly, the Volcano having being accepted in England and America upon the same day, ourselves curiously having been in Mexico itself, in your wedding place, at that time, whither we went because of climate.[1] But I was not convinced and said so too, there among marigolds, with Easter coming:

however it is apparently *so*, and in America at least (Reynal and Hitchcock) has even gone to the printers. I delayed telling you this for Hitchcock had no sooner signed the contract than he dropped dead etc. and there were other delays. I hope to God you will like this work by your old pupil a little though, which Cape brings out in England, and I shall send you as soon as I get any copies. Margie's first detective story [*The Shapes That Creep*] came out finally after Scribner's kept it nearly 5 years; it has sold five thousand copies, and is still selling. They brought out her second the other day, The Last Twist of the Knife, but without having sent her any proofs and according to a letter received from a reader (the first she'd even heard of its publication) minus its last chapter: so that there are no explanations of the murder etc.[2] Scribner's are really the limit. Our correspondence is equalled only by Joyce's with Grant Richards.[3] Margie has written a damn good serious novel entitled Horse in the Sky which is with Cape: while flapping incompetently about and just about driving poor Margie cockoo with delays and lies and non-answered letters Scribner's had meantime tried even to prevent her publishing this book, since it would 'interfere' with the 'career' which they had anyway at every point done their level best to bitch. She thrives however, as do I.

Well, all my very best love to you and Mary from us both – remember me to the Burra and the Nashes and all[4] – and John – I see Jane's name on the editorial board of Time?[5] – and Jane – should the grandfather clock still be there please give him a friendly tug of the bollocks from me – and the Ship.

– from love fifteen to vantage out to back again to love –[6]

Malc

– I have been rereading the Eclogues: wonderful.

Annotations:

1 The Aikens were married in Mexico in July 1937 while staying with Malcolm and Jan; see Lowry's letter 50 to Aiken.

2 *The Last Twist of the Knife* was reissued by Scribner's later in 1946 with its last chapter. See Lowry's 15 September 1946 letter (246) to Maxwell Perkins.

3 Grant Richards (1872-1948) was the publisher to whom Joyce first sent *Dubliners* in 1905. Richards accepted the book in February 1906, refused it in September 1907, and finally published it in June 1914; see Lowry's 15 September 1946 letter (246) to Maxwell Perkins.

4 Shortly after his move to Winchelsea (near Rye) in 1922, Aiken met the English surrealist painter Paul Nash (1889-1946) and his wife Margaret.

They remained friends, with visits back and forth whenever Aiken was
in Rye; see Edward Butscher's description of this relationship in *Conrad
Aiken: Poet of White Horse Vale*, pp. 360-61. 'The Burra' is the English
painter Ed Burra.
5 Jane Aiken's name appears on the masthead of *Time* as an editorial researcher from 4 February 1946 to 25 November 1946.
6 'Love fifteen' and 'advantage out' are scoring terms in tennis.

242: To Harold Matson

P: Columbia(ts); UBC(phc)

Dollarton, B.C.,
Canada
14 August 1946

Dear Hal:
Cape compromises with February 1947 as a deadline – is this
O.K.? I myself think this is reasonable since I got all my alterations
in by the middle of July. But please tell me if this is agreeable with
R. & H.
The first Margie heard of the publication of The Last Twist of the
Knife was a dubious fan letter from one Myrtle Van Court, Santa
Monica Calif. (of whom neither of us have ever heard before) which
says in part . . . I am writing to protest the abrupt ending . . . We are
left with no explanation of Turgeon's motives in murdering Paul . . .
I have read a number of books lately in which several pages were
missing and am wondering if this happened in The Last Twist of the
Knife as I can't feel that the story is complete . . . and so on, ending:
If you really finished your story with Turgeon's confession I apologise to the publishers, but if they *left out* the final pages I shall not
forgive them for ruining a good story . . .
Well, (you guessed it) that's exactly what Scribner's have done,
left out, or lost, the ending, and I think you will agree with me that
on top of everything else that is the limit for the omission seems to
have also a rather deleterious effect on the reviews, since all so far
mention the incomplete and poor quality of the detection. And while
I don't think the book was as good as The Shapes, the detection per
se was actually better.
Now in spite of repeated requests to Scribner's for the proofs, as I
said, Margie was never sent them (in fact she is still waiting for the
proofread ones of the second half of The Shapes); if Scribner's *lost*
that ending, of which there was no copy since they had the only final

version, they must have been at least *aware* of it and they should have given her a chance to write another ending; if they didn't lose it but just left it out by mistake there is even less excuse, and if they left it out on *purpose*, they surely owe her an explanation.

This, since they have already breached their contract with that work, it would seem they owe her anyhow: but I can't feel they should be allowed to get away with this. For one thing it makes Margie guilty of one of the unpardonable sins in detective story writing and may considerably queer her reputation.

You can imagine how tantalizing it is, to say the least, when it is impossible to buy the book here, and we would be very obliged if you would look into the matter.

At all events, if you are sending her work to Peters, I think some note should be made to the effect that it is incomplete, which, from the only evidence at my disposal, it certainly and disastrously is.

I would like to know how it is possible that two such different people as Weber and Erskine should be in the publishing business.

I am afraid I put the latter to a lot of work but he is a delight to do business with. R. & H. would seem the tops. It is hard for me to believe that Scribner's, in spite of all their dough, are not the bottom. At all events you would think that Margie was a personal enemy rather than a promising author from the cynical slipshod and heartless way they have treated her.

We look forward to seeing you. Tell Erskine, him likewise. I expect you are in your holidays: if so, curse me not. This is a wonderful country to live, swim, work and bite trees in, but boy is it gloomy from the human point of view. I have yet to hear a remark that even deviated into humour. By their cafes shall ye know them, as Margie says. And as I say:

> Old Blake was right, he got down to the hub
> When he said we should worship in the pub,
> Save only in Canada, where I'm told
> The churches and the taverns both are cold.[1]

Thanks for everything and all the best from Margie and

Malcolm

Annotations:

1 William Blake (1757-1827), the visionary English poet and artist, is remembered here by Lowry for his lighter lyric verse. In particular Lowry has devised a playful allusion to the message and metre of Blake's 'The Little Vagabond' from *Songs of Experience*:

Dear Mother, dear Mother, the Church is cold,
But the Ale-house is healthy & pleasant & warm;
[. . .]
But if at the Church they would give us some Ale,
And a pleasant fire our souls to regale,
We'd sing and we'd pray all the live long day,
Nor ever once wish from the Church to stray.

243: To Carolyn Stagg

P : UBC(ts)

Dollarton, B.C.,
Canada
14 August 1946

Dear Mrs Stagg:[1]

I hope I may not be impugned for lack of courtesy in my failure to reply to your questions hitherto re biographical details etc. but the book's postponement perhaps rendered this less urgent and there was a lot of work on the book itself that had to be done immediately. So please forgive me; I am attending to this matter now and will send you the result to-morrow.

I did not, by the way, ever get the copy of the same questionnaire you mentioned having sent to Hal Matson.[2] With kind regards

Sincerely,

Malcolm Lowry

Annotations:

1 Carolyn Willyoung Stagg, of the publications department at Reynal & Hitchcock, had written to Harold Matson on 1 May 1946 requesting biographical information on Lowry for use in preparing the publishers' catalogue that would announce the forthcoming publication of *Under the Volcano*.

2 She had also sent a biographical information form to Matson with her 1 May 1946 letter, for forwarding to Lowry.

244: To Mrs Anna Mabelle [John Stuart] Bonner and Dr and
      Mrs E.B. Woolfan

P: UBC(ts)

Dollarton, B.C.,
Canada
28 August 1946

My very dear Mother, Priscilla and Bert:
  – A more than unusually foul correspondent, I hope I can be forgiven just sending this note. Thank you very deeply for your very
sweet cards on my birthday: all the sentiments therein are more than
reciprocated.

My life is at the moment almost entirely taken up with work and
the house, as you must realise. Scribner's has been giving us our
usual bad moments, but otherwise all is fine.

In the latter connection poor Margie hasn't even seen a copy of the
Last Twist of the Knife yet: a fan letter has informed us that the so
and so's have missed out or lost the last chapter but since we haven't
seen it we don't know if there may be a reason for this or if it is not as
bad as we suspect from the reviews, which are certainly not as good
as they should be.

It doesn't come out in Canada for another month or two at least,
so I wonder if you could be good enough to send Margie a copy after
you have read it. I never heard of an author going through the hoop
like her, unless it was me: however, I have her work out on the line
in England now and I expect bright news from there.[1] I am informed
that Scribner's could be sued for about all they have, taking it all and
all, and that they also could be made to withdraw this version of The
Last Twist, if incomplete. The trouble with all this is, it involves a
writer in anxieties that greatly interfere with the business of writing,
it's true that she might make enough out of it to live on for a year, or
buy a couple of fur coats, but only at the expense of her peace of
mind and another book she might have written: besides, whatever
you do these days the government takes it, so what?

I have to pay 9/– in the £ income tax on my earnings from
Jonathan Cape, England: 45%. Oh boy. And it would be 55% if I
had an agent. As it is, I am my own agent, in England and since my
efforts are about equivalent in time wasted to that 55% the net result
is, as the Yorkshiremen say, nowt.[2] A new law is shortly going to
make this state of affairs, at least as regards my income tax in
America, which is also terrific, better, I believe.

I hope all your ventures may prosper – my love to all – your affectionate brother, son –

Malcolm

Annotations:

1 Lowry had asked Jonathan Cape to consider Margerie's novel *Horse in the Sky*; see his July 1946 letter (**230**) to Cape.
2 The words 'nowt' or 'nouth' are Yorkshire dialect and obsolete forms of nought, meaning nothing.

245: To Albert Erskine

P: UBC(ts)
PP: *SL* 118

Dollarton, B.C.,
Canada
28 August 1946[a]

Dear Mr Erskine:

Just a note to inform you I'm still extant and to say how much I enjoyed our correspondence and appreciated the trouble you have gone to and were going to on my behalf.

I hope I got you the corrections in in time.

The reason I haven't written in further reply is that I became suddenly seized with an indescribable loathing at the mere sight of my prose, at the mere sight of anything I write, in fact, even a cheque (perhaps particularly a cheque.)

I acquired a baby seal and same swam out to sea: doubtless a good thing. Our cat went up a tree and we got that down. My wife has recently had a detective story [*The Last Twist of the Knife*] published, minus the last chapter: since the explanation of the murders is in there, this must be something unique in literary history. Only we don't know, since we can't get the book. In fact, we didn't even get the proofs. It is raining. My uncle is in the garden with his good strong stout stick. I hope all is well.

Yours very sincerely,

Malcolm Lowry

September 1946 629

Editorial Notes:

a. The date given for this letter in *Selected Letters*, 17 August 1946, is incorrect. The typescript is clearly dated 28 August.

246: To Maxwell Perkins

P: UBC(ts, phc)
PP: *SL* 118–26

Dollarton, B.C.,
Canada
15 September 1946[a]

Dear Mr Perkins:[1]
I wish to call your attention to a crashing and cynical injustice perpetrated by your firm. Knowing of you as a man of integrity, I should be extremely obliged if you will bear with me and not immediately refer this to what you conceive to be the proper department, a quite futile procedure in this case, as I hope you will shortly be convinced.

As for myself, I am a writer, my publishers are Reynal and Hitchcock, New York, and Jonathan Cape, London, and my name Malcolm Lowry (not to be confused with Malcolm Cowley, who once wrote an article about you and Scribner's in which he mentioned that you rather missed the old type of villain in business, or words to that effect).[2] The injustice in question however, concerns one of your own authors, Margerie Bonner, and myself only in that she is my wife. I am writing this letter for her since she is, at the moment, sick and unable to cope with it herself. She has had two books published by your firm this year, both mystery novels: The Shapes That Creep, which received good reviews and which, according to a recent statement of royalties due her, has had a good sale, and The Last Twist of the Knife.

The Shapes That Creep was submitted to your firm precisely half a decade ago, was kept for nine months, and in June of 1942 was accepted. The contract was signed, publication for fall of that year was indicated, (although there was no time clause in the contract) and she was told she would receive the galley proofs shortly.

I should mention here that at that time the person handling, so to say, my wife's work for Scribner's was (I say 'was' advisedly because it quite patently is not now being 'handled' by anyone that I know of) a Mr W.C. Weber,[3] and no doubt he also had his difficulties during these years and I feel certain he is an excellent, likeable and capable fellow. This would seem to be less the point than precisely what this excellent, likeable and capable fellow achieved or failed to achieve in relation to my wife's work. Here, then, are the facts.

The Shapes That Creep was, first of all, according to Mr Weber, coming out, as stated, in the fall of 1942 – this being relayed through her agent for she had no direct word from Weber at this time. Over a period of six months, from, say, August 1942 to January 1943, my wife was promised, periodically, that she would have the proofs in 'about a fortnight.' We live in the wilderness of British Columbia where a letter is somewhat of an event, (that of course is not your fault) and this was to be her first published novel. Every day she would go up to meet the post, and every day be disappointed and this went on for another six months when she was informed through her agent that the book had been postponed again till the winter of 1944: once more she began to expect the proofs, once more the daily ordeal of the post and once more, every day, the disappointment.

You have doubtless experienced such disappointments yourself, every writer has to take them: but please wait a moment, for I believe what follows to be almost unique in the annals of publishing. This kind of thing: proofs the next fortnight, postponement, no word at all for months, the daily crucifixion of the post, and so on, began again in 1944 and went on right through 1944.

At this point, to be perfectly fair to your firm, there were, of course, any number of good reasons that could be brought forward for these postponements: the war, paper shortages, etc. etc. Many well known writers were having their books postponed as we well knew. By March of 1944 my wife asked her agent if possibly she herself should write your firm in an attempt to ascertain what the status of her novel was, feeling that some sort of contact might be established that would give her some encouragement. Her agent replied that anything was worth trying: that he himself – even at this comparatively early date in the long history of her difficulties with Scribner's – had never had such an experience with a reputable firm like yourselves and did not know what more to do. He gave her Weber's name and she immediately wrote him. There was no reply. She wrote again, sending the letter registered mail: no reply. She telegraphed: no reply. All this complete lack of contact with one's publisher was not exactly stimulating or helpful to a young American author just starting out but I should say here that she had not been idle in the meantime. She had completely rewritten and revised her first book, the recently published Last Twist of the Knife, and had written a serious novel, Horse in the Sky. She had also nearly completed another mystery novel entitled The Moon Saw Him Murdered,[4] when – (again through no fault of yours) our house burned down.

This was bad, but chiefly, as it happened, for me. She lost no work except her spare copies of The Last Twist of the Knife, the only one being with her agent in New York, awaiting publication of The Shapes That Creep, before being submitted to your firm. However, after we lost our home, we went east where we stayed, near Toronto, with the news commentator, Gerald Noxon.

By this time my wife was almost reconciled to the postponements; the paper shortage was certainly a real thing and it was more the cynical manner with which the whole thing seemed to be conducted, or not conducted, that made it intolerable, especially in the light of those articles about yourself in the New Yorker by Malcolm Cowley, in which Scribner's appeared to be sitting very pretty indeed and were a firm by which any author would be tickled pink to be published.

Besides, Noxon and myself read my wife passages from Kafka's The Castle and also extracts from Joyce's correspondence with Grant Richards, to help her to take 'the long view.'[5] She had, however, quite given up hope of ever seeing her work in print, and her agent having also been thinking the blackest thoughts was just on the point of demanding the return of her manuscript from Scribner's when on my advice my wife herself went, in July 1944, to New York.

Here she encountered the business-like, erudite and amiable Mr Weber who assured her – astoundingly! – that Scribner's would be very sorry to lose her, that The Shapes That Creep had already gone to press, was scheduled for October publication of that year, and that the galleys would be along in 'about a fortnight.' He further inquired if she had any other books to follow up The Shapes That Creep and my wife had her agent send him the copy (the only copy extant because of our fire: Weber was informed of this fact) of The Last Twist of the Knife. Indeed, the only disappointing news she brought back was that Mr Weber would not consider reading her serious novel because it had been found that it didn't pay for a writer to have 'two' careers, i.e., a serious, and a mystery one. Since my wife had not yet begun to have one career, and The Shapes That Creep was already becoming somewhat out of date to her mind, Noxon and I graduated her from Kafka's Castle to his The Trial, in hopes that she might, in case of accident, take a longer view still.[6]

For now once more began the waiting for the proofs which were, definitely this time, Weber said, to arrive 'in a fortnight.' September, October, November and December came and went, with no proofs, but meanwhile Weber notified her that Scribner's had accepted The Last Twist of the Knife. After a month or six weeks – this is mentioned not because it normally would be a long time but simply because it involved another broken promise – the contract arrived and an advance was paid of $350, only this time there was a time limit in the contract: The Last Twist of the Knife was to be published not later than Fall, 1945. Weber said that Scribner's wished her to make certain alterations and additions, to which she agreed, and stated that he *had mailed* the MSS to her for these corrections, together with his notes, and she should receive it within a day or two. Now she had two things to watch the post for; neither arrived. Time went by, and she became more and more anxious about the MSS, since it was the only one. We were attempting to trace it through the post, when, finally, various long distance phone calls and telegrams elicited the news from Weber that the manuscript had *not*, after all, been mailed, but had been 'mislaid.' Also it developed that Scribner's had changed their minds regarding the additions and alterations they had requested her to make. I quote from a telegram of Weber's dated January 12, 1945, in my possession: 'Have recalled Last Twist and sent to press you can make minor corrections in galley sheet due any day now scheduling for fall publication – Bill Weber.'[7]

In February, 1945, we returned to British Columbia to rebuild our burned house and the situation was now this: The Shapes That Creep was scheduled for Spring publication and the proofs were due 'within a fortnight.' The Last Twist of the Knife was scheduled for Fall publication and the proofs of that also would be along 'any day now', so as to give her time for these (now) minor corrections your firm wished her to make. This was naturally of equal importance to her since she also wished her book to be as good as she could possibly make it.

In April of that year, 1945, an astounding thing happened. The proofs of The Shapes actually *did* turn up.[8] That is, the *proof read* proofs of the first half: with these proofs came a letter from Weber stating that the similarly *proof read* proofs of the second half would be turning up 'within a fortnight,' and Weber had also promised to read these proofs himself before they were dispatched to her, as he had kindly done in the first half. Sure enough, a second batch of proofs arrived, but not proof read, so that the situation was not clear: my wife for her part made her corrections on the proof read galleys of the first part and returned them promptly, but she didn't want to correct the second batch because according to Weber's advice she would then be correcting the wrong proofs and would have to do the work all over again. She wrote Weber asking what he desired her to do regarding these un-proof read galleys of the second half: there was no reply, and she never received the promised proof read galleys, in spite of writing again and again, or any further word regarding them. She has not, in fact, from that day to this, ever had one more line or word from him or any member of your firm. So that, when the Shapes finally was published, it was without her corrections on the last half and not merely this, but with many corrections she did make on the first half completely ignored. It should also be mentioned that in addition to the letters she wrote in regard to The Shapes she wrote continually and anxiously about The Last Twist, which, you perhaps remember, was reported to have gone to press in January 1945. But she has never had one more word regarding The Last Twist either, from your firm. However, in October of last year, 1945, my wife, with the actual intention of being sporting, wrote her agent asking him to intimate to Weber that he was taking you into breach of contract, in case the terms of the contract had been forgotten. Hal Matson, who is her agent and also mine, was away on holiday, but his secretary, on receiving my wife's letter, answered at once, reporting that she had telephoned Mr Weber in regard to The Last Twist of the Knife and that he stated that he had written, or was writing, my wife and that the galley proofs were in the mail, or would be shortly. Needless to say neither letter or proofs or any further explanation were forthcoming.

In December of last year, having given up all hopes for both books, we took a trip to California and hence to Mexico – by which time you had already broken your contract for The Last Twist of the Knife. When we reached Los Angeles we discovered, via the Booksellers Journals, that The Shapes had actually been twice announced for publication: in June, 1945 and October 1945, postponed again, and now was announced a third time, while The Last Twist of the Knife had also been announced, without a date given.

No replies being forthcoming to any letters, as usual, and her agent being in as great a state of bewilderment as she, she arrived in Mexico equally concerned about both books. True, they seemed a little *nearer* to coming out, but there was a really agonizing question (to the author) in regard to the Last Twist – why had she never received the proofs? Perhaps the MSS had actually been lost and never found. And then, perhaps she still might receive the promised proofs – and the proof read proofs of the last half of The Shapes That Creep.

In order to give no chance for any of these Utopian[9] proofs to miscarry, my wife wrote Weber in January 1946, registered mail, giving our address in Mexico. This letter was couched in extremely stinging terms: every other human approach having failed, she thought

perhaps this might bring some result. As regards the Last Twist she
said that if she did not hear from Scribner's soon she would put the
whole business, as she had, and still has, a perfect right to do, in the
hands of a lawyer, reluctant as she was to become involved in this
sort of thing. But even this brought no reply.

Then, sometime in February, quite by accident, I came across a
copy of The Shapes That Creep in the American Book Store in
Mexico City and bought it for her.

So there it was at last, published. She had not, of course, received
her promised author's copies, (she still has not received them) but as
a consequence of its publication she wrote again to Scribner's, re-
scinding her previous letter, reminding them, once more, of her
address, and asking if some new start could not be made, upon an
honourable and decent basis, even complimenting them upon the
good taste shown in the general format, etc., and trying also once
more, since everything cannot be done through one's agent, to establish a friendly relationship with her publisher. She also asked, for the
umpteenth time, for some news of The Last Twist of the Knife and
about the proofs of this book.

There was, God help you, no reply.

On returning to Canada in May of this year she wrote again, this
time to our agent, about The Last Twist of the Knife, the proofs of
which she was still somehow expecting to arrive. The only reply he
could give was that he had 'no reason to believe that any new
methods would change the habits of certain people at Scribner's.'

Then, at the beginning of August, my wife received a fan letter,
forwarded her from Scribner's, which reads as follows: 'I have just
finished reading, and enjoying, your mystery story The Last Twist
of the Knife, and I am writing to protest its abrupt ending. The book
ends with Turgeon confessing to the two killings, and we are left
with no explanation of his motive in murdering Paul, even if we
accept the supposition that Delight was blackmailing Turgeon. I
have read a number of books lately in which several pages were missing, and am wondering if this happened in The Last Twist of the
Knife as I can't feel that the story is complete. We, readers, cheerfully
accepted books with poor print, many typographical errors, and the
subject matter spoiled by sheets missing, during the war – but we *are*
complaining that it continues as of this date. If you really finished
your story with Turgeon's confession I apologize to the publishers
but if they *left out* the final pages I shall not forgive them for ruining a
good story.'[10]

This letter was her first knowledge of the book's publication, and
suggests, as you see, that this book, of which she has never – I have

to repeat myself – seen the proofs, and still to this day has not seen as a book, has been published without its last chapter. Subsequent reviews, received through her clipping service (...'Motive and solution are just too nebulous for this mystery fan.'... the solution, which is sudden and without adequate explanation'.... so incredibly badly ended that it seems as though it could never possibly have come from the author of the delightful 'Shapes That Creep.') substantiate this and testify to the weakness of the ending, and the detection. We are unable to obtain a copy of this book here in Canada so far, but my wife wrote to someone in Los Angeles, who bought and read the book and sent her a report on it which leaves no possible doubt in our minds: the book has been published without its last chapter. On top of everything else, this puts my wife very unfairly into the position of having committed, from the mystery writer's point of view, an unforgiveable crime, a crime which she did not commit, for though I don't think the book as a whole was so good as The Shapes, it was excellently complete and the detection, per se, was actually better than that in The Shapes. But the omission of the last chapter, with its all-important tying up of motives and clues and the rest has done her, she feels, considerable damage as a writer of mystery stories, for as the book stands, we are told, there is absolutely no reason given for the murders at all.

I can testify to the fact that when this book was sent to our agent the last chapter was there, intact and complete, and my wife can testify to the fact that when she was in New York she saw this copy in the office of her agent, just before it was sent to Mr Weber, and looked it through to be sure it was the correct version, since, you will remember, she had rewritten this book, and that it was complete at that time.

It is possible that somebody at Scribner's might have lost this chapter and your firm would not be responsible for it, or it might have been mislaid in some other way for which your firm still would not be responsible, but in this case somebody at Scribner's must have *known* that it was lost and my wife should have been given a chance to write that part again. And if the book had gone to press, as Mr Weber stated in his wire of Janurary 12, 1945, how could he be unaware, as a mystery expert, that it lacked a last chapter? If my wife had ever been sent the proofs she would of course have seen at once that it was lacking, and perhaps – who knows? – that is why she never *was* sent the proofs. I am so disgusted when I think of this that I scarcely have the heart to recapitulate all the unnecessary lies, the carelessnesses the complete protracted cynical disregard for human feelings and common forthrightness that has permeated Scribner's dealings with my wife's work and which makes this last incident a more than last straw. The whole thing strikes me as shameful and unspeakable, and at the same time so utterly senseless – what is your motive? And if the thing is motiveless, as it would appear, how can you continue to employ such irresponsible people and maintain your reputation, or indeed any reputation at all?

Writers often tend to be high strung creatures and my wife is no exception: she has been so continually tormented and worried by this damned thing for so many years now that this last discouragement has actually affected her health. From one standpoint, looked at with a bleak abstracted relative eye, it all may not seem so much, yet it is impossible to convey in a letter such as this the anguish and strain, for a *writer*, of such an experience.

It is true we shall probably be going east again this winter, as Reynal and Hitchcock have invited me to be in New York at publication time of my novel; perhaps this time Noxon and I will entertain my wife with selections from Crime and Punishment . . .[11] It may be that such ordeals and disappointments may come to have in time a positive value to one who is essentially a serious artist. That does not make Scribner's blame – or Weber's – any the less. After all, mystery story writers also have souls and possibly even destinies.

Personally, I do not believe that all this should be taken lying down. In fact I'm sure it should not. For whatever your legal position in the matter, your ethical position deserves your attention. So, I respectfully ask you, what, in her position, would you do?

I am sending this letter by registered mail to be sure that you, or someone at Scribner's, will receive it.

Yours very truly,

Malcolm Lowry

Annotations:

1 Maxwell Perkins (1884-1947), one of the greatest of American editors, was with Charles Scribner's Sons publishing house for most of his career and handled the work of such writers as F. Scott Fitzgerald, Ernest Hemingway, and Thomas Wolfe.

2 Malcolm Cowley (1898-1989), an American literary historian, critic, and editor, is especially remembered for his first book, *Exile's Return* (1934), and his long association with Viking Press, which published his collections of the works of such American writers as William Faulkner, Ernest Hemingway, and F. Scott Fitzgerald. Cowley's two-part article on Maxwell Perkins, 'Unshaken Friend,' appeared in the *New Yorker* for 8 April and 15 April 1944.

3 In his 2 October 1946 letter to Margerie, Charles Scribner explains that Mr Weber had been 'laboring under an intense nervous strain' in recent

years, but apart from that excuse of personal difficulty, there now seems no way of determining precisely how and why *The Last Twist of the Knife* was published without its final chapter.

4 A manuscript with this title does not appear to have survived.

5 The Grant Richards/James Joyce tangle over *Dubliners* had become an infamous example (at least among writers) of a publisher's mistreatment of an author. Richards, the publisher of *Dubliners* (1914), delayed publication for eight years.

6 Franz Kafka's novels *The Castle* and *The Trial* were favourites of Lowry's, and he no doubt appreciated the parallels between the fate of Kafka's characters and Margerie's dilemma of endless waiting in the face of silence, anxiety, doubt, and hopelessness.

7 Neither this telegram nor any other correspondence from Mr Weber appears to have survived.

8 To clarify Lowry's references in this letter, the following distinctions should be noted: Galley proofs, which are, by custom, proof-read by a publisher's in-house editor, are sent to an author for further proof-reading. Page proofs are the final pre-publication text of a book, and may also be sent to an author for last-minute corrections. It is also customary to make changes on the manuscript copy of a book before sending it to a printer for the preparation of galleys. Margerie's final chapter must have gone astray at the manuscript stage; thus, the omission would have shown up in the galleys.

9 The proofs were 'Utopian' in the sense that they did not appear to exist in reality.

10 This 'fan' letter does not appear to have survived.

11 Dostoevsky's novel *Crime and Punishment* (1866) was a Lowry favourite.

Editorial Notes:

a. This transcription has been made from a photocopy (UBC 2:8) of the final version of the letter. However, the provenance of the original letter, if still extant, has not been confirmed. The photocopy carries two errors in dating that are accidentals; the typescript draft (UBC 2:8) has the correct dates, which are shown here.

247: To Maxwell Perkins

P: UBC(phc)
PP: *SL* 126-27

Dollarton, B.C.,
Canada
20 September 1946

Dear Mr Perkins:

Thank you very much indeed for your prompt and kindly wire.[1]

Simply as a signal from the beyond I may say its therapeutic value
was prodigious, for I think you can understand how one can come to
doubt, over such a long period, not only one's achievement, but
one's very existence.

Re your request for my wife to furnish a last chapter for The Last
Twist of the Knife: we assume from this that the chapter in question
has been, in some way, mislaid or cannot be found at present. She'd
been considering the possibility that whoever edited that suitably
named book had simply put it out without this chapter for some
reason of his own, and that it would still be in your files with the
MSS. However, she certainly could rewrite the last chapter soon if
only she had a copy of the book itself. I think I mentioned that she
hadn't yet even seen it (or the proofs) and all we had to go on were a
'fan' letter, some reviews, and a report from Los Angeles, to establish that it doesn't *have* an ending, though there seems no doubt this
is so. We have tried to get a copy here in Vancouver several times
without success, (you should know that it is considered definitely
low-minded to try and buy any kind of a book in Canada, even from
a bookseller: 'Have you a copy of the Last Twist of the Knife?' 'No,
all last week's copies of Life are sold out.') and since she wrote it so
long ago, she can hardly pick up the threads now without something
to start from – and I think I mentioned that the MSS your firm had
was her only one due to our fire.

Thank you again for your courtesy in replying so promptly; we
shall be awaiting your letter with the greatest interest and, on my
wife's part, renewed hope that at last all this may be resolved in a
friendly and civilized manner,

Yours very sincerely,

Malcolm Lowry

Annotations:

1 Perkins' wire does not appear to have survived, but in his 24 September
  1946 letter to Lowry he proffers his and the firm's apologies, reports that
  Mr Weber claims never to have seen the missing chapter, and offers
  other possible explanations for the situation. He then suggests various
  ways of rectifying the problem, once Margerie supplies the missing
  chapter.

248: To Harold Matson

P: Matson(ms)

> Dollarton P.O.,
> Dollarton, B.C.,
> Canada
> [24 September 1946]

Querido Hal:[1]

In tremendous haste –

I have cheque from you for $280.48, for which many thanks, this being the $500 less commission & a couple of *Canadian* taxes.

Am I entitled to this?[2] I think I mentioned to you I was still technically English (though I can change my status, not so very easily, it appears now, & not at once.) The English tax, I think you said, was 30%, in which case I'd get $150 less, *alas*; so I am holding on to the cheque for the time being without cashing it until I hear further from you. You said the law might change in the case of the 30% tax?? While the 15% looks like a fixture.

Anyhow, I'm quite in the dark about it here.

> Best wishes from us both
> Malcolm

Annotations:

1 *Querido* is Spanish for 'dear.'
2 On 30 August 1946 George J. McDermott, treasurer with Reynal & Hitchcock, advised Harold Matson that on making the second $500 payment on *Under the Volcano* (for delivery of the completed manuscript), they had deducted 15 per cent, instead of the usual 30 per cent for British authors, because Lowry lived in Canada and was subject to Canadian taxes only. Lowry was entitled to the sum of $280.48.

249: To Albert Erskine

P: UBC(telegram)

> Western Union,
> Vancouver, B.C.
> 24 September 1946

[ACCENTS] OK[1] ZACUALI IS AZTEC STOP MEANING TOWER[2] GOD BLESS

MALCOLM LOWRY

Annotations:

1 Lowry's telegram in response to Erskine's 20 September 1946 letter actually has 'accepts' for 'accents,' but Erksine has asked Lowry to wire him with regard to the correct accents on words like Parián and Tomalín.

2 In the same letter Erskine has asked Lowry where he found the word 'zacuali,' since he cannot 'find it in any dictionary.'

250: To Maxwell Perkins

P: UBC(phc)
PP: *SL* 127-28

Dollarton, B.C.,
Canada
30 September 1946

Dear Mr Perkins:

I am much beholden to you for your understanding letter and also for your second telegram and all this of course goes for Mrs Lowry too.[1]

My statement re Canadian bookstores here was no exaggeration: we had had The Last Twist on order here for some time but there was no telling whether the order ever went through, though they said yes.

Considering the number of crossed purposes, telephones off the hook, and inexplicable confusions in this episode – for example, we arrived back in Canada from Mexico in May, we were in touch with Hal Matson, so I don't see why she didn't get her author's copies – I was beginning to think that the explanation if any might more fairly lie in a metaphysical direction; and my inclination towards such an explanation – in part at least – was strengthened rather than otherwise when upon opening your kindly-meant special delivery parcel – the brave man does it with a knife! – we discovered that while the jacket of my wife's book was all right, in fact excellent, and what was within was all right too, it wasn't Margerie Bonner's The Last Twist, but Marion Strobel's Kiss and Kill![2]

I am afraid, though it verges upon unsportmanship, if not sadism, that I have been unable to resist telling you this, but perhaps the curse is taken off by the information that as a result of this innocent error we were unable to stop laughing for twenty minutes.

The other volume was O.K. and was indeed The Last Twist of the

Knife for which many thanks; or rather was, sure enough, merely the Knife without the Last Twist, and somewhat bloodstained as to proof-reading at that – however, my wife has now read it, certain old notes for the last chapter have been found, and though the job seemed at first something like putting a linoleum on an engine room floor, I think I can safely say you'll have the copy for the last chapter within the week.

My wife has been somewhat under the weather recently, as I think I said, but is considerably better, and will write you herself when she sends off the copy.

Yes, it has been a pleasure hearing from you too, this in strong distinction from the always uniquely horrible experience of being in the right, only less horrible indeed an experience than being in the wrong, unless it is more so.

Well, I must stop, for I'm off to the movies to see Murnau's Last Laugh – true, it's taken rather a long time to get here – to be closely followed next week by the Fall of the House of Usher – perhaps I shall take Kant's Critique of Pure Reason with me to read on the bus –[3]

With kind regards from us both,

Yours sincerely

Malcolm Lowry

Annotations:

1 See Lowry's 20 September 1946 letter (**247**) to Perkins, annotation 3.
2 Marion Strobel (1895-1966), an American writer of poetry and fiction, published *Kiss and Kill* in 1946. She was associate editor of *Poetry* magazine from 1920 to 1924, and thereafter until her death she was actively involved with the magazine.
3 F.W. Murnau's classic film *The Last Laugh* (1924) was a Lowry favourite, as was Jean Epstein's black and white silent version of Edgar Allan Poe's story 'The Fall of the House of Usher' (1928). It is a typical stroke of Lowryan humour to add to these references something of the nature of Kant's *Critique of Pure Reason*. Immanuel Kant (1724-1804), the German philosopher, developed a critical philosophy in which he challenged contemporary faith in reason; therefore, Lowry's suggestion that he take Kant's major treatise (*Kritik der reinen Vernunft*, 1781) 'to read on the bus' is a delightful reflection on the absurd, irrational events surrounding Margerie's relations with Scribner's.

251: To Gerald Noxon

P: Texas(ts)
PP: *LLN* 127–28

Dollarton, B.C.
15 October 1946

Dear old Gerald:

This is a kind of interim letter soliciting some advice, suggestions, or failing that simply some moral support for one Vernon Van Sickle, a very good fellow who is by the way of carrying on bravely here in Vancouver certain works bravely started by yourself in Cambridge with the Film Society, etc.[1]

For my part I took the liberty of advising him to write you and this he is doing; as I see it his problems – apart from the usual ones of finances and the stupidity of other groups etc. – arise mainly from the difficulty of getting hold of good films, many of which are tied up, I understand, by the British Institute on the one hand, and on the other by American organizations that won't let go of them.[2] I thought by virtue of your experience in both hemispheres you might be able to point a way of prying them loose or suggest at least some direction or possible liaison with any other group in Toronto or elsewhere that might make this easier.

So far he has done very well: Sunrise, The Baker's Wife, Crime and Punishment, Fall of the House of Usher, The Last Laugh, Cyprus is an Island, Night Mail and so on: and such things as Greed, The Loves of Jeanne Ney, Joan of Arc, The Italian Straw Hat, and 'M' are being shown during the winter.[3] He shows the silent classics for the most part at a studio on Saturday, and has the Paradise theatre on Sunday nights every fortnight, much as you had the Tivoli, for the others.[4]

It is with the others curiously that he chiefly gets let down: he will have been promised, say, La Bete Humaine, but then at the last moment will be sent something dull like Veille d'Armes that no one would much want to see. Or the Song of Ceylon simply vanishes in transit.[5]

Many films he can't get hold of at all unless he buys them outright – and this is impossible because they haven't much capital: or since it's a non-profit business, all they have goes on the various aspects of rentals. Naturally he wants to get hold of as many of the finer French modern films as he can while some of his other difficulties would seem to be due to certain films still being with the Custodians of Enemy Property. But the main difficulty would seem to be with the

British Institute and the virtual impossiblity of establishing any clear contact or arriving at any clear understanding with them: I feel you might know somebody there who would make dealings with them easier.

At all events I hope you will write him as this kind of work is important and can only lead to a Better Thing.

I'll reserve other news for another letter – some of it absolutely staggering – among other things, Margie's second book [*The Last Twist of the Knife*], of which she never received the proofs, published without a last chapter and eight months after the time limit on her contract had elapsed: I finally wrote itemizing the whole bloody business to [Maxwell] Perkins – result: Scribner's has been turned upside down: expressions of horror, the book withdrawn and to be published again, apologies from Charles Scribner himself – the cause, unknown to the rest of the firm until now, Margie's editor there, Weber, had gone mad –

All best love to Betty Nick and yourself from us both

Malcolm[a]

Annotations:

1 Vernon Van Sickle was a programmer with the Vancouver branch of the National Film Society of Canada in the late forties. The National Society was inactive from 1941 to 1945 because of the war, but they began to screen contemporary foreign films and older silent films again in 1946; Van Sickle was one of those in charge of ordering films until sometime in 1948, when he left Vancouver. In 1950 the name was changed to the Vancouver Film Society. I would like to thank Dennis Duffy, who has made a video documentary about the period, and Stanley Fox for this information on the society; see also annotations 4 and 5. In 1929 Noxon had been the founding president of the Cambridge Film Guild, and for several years thereafter he wrote film reviews and essays on the cinema, and worked on documentary films. He was responsible for bringing many experimental avant-garde foreign films to Cambridge audiences – thus Lowry's appeal to him for practical advice.

2 The British Film Institute in London was founded in 1933 to encourage the development and appreciation of cinema. It houses the National Film Archive and the National Film Theatre. Restrictions put in place during the war and still in effect made obtaining films, especially from Germany, very difficult.

3 Lowry's list of films includes a number of silent classics and documentaries: F.W. Murnau's *Sunrise* (1927) was one of his special favourites (see his 23 April 1951 letter [**455**] to Clemens ten Holder); *The Baker's Wife* (1938), directed by Marcel Pagnol, was a popular comedy; there have been several versions of Dostoevsky's novel, but Lowry may

be thinking of *Crime and Punishment* (1935), directed by Josef Von Stern-berg with Peter Lorre; Jean Epstein's *The Fall of the House of Usher* (1928) was another Lowry favourite; *The Last Laugh* (1924) was also directed by Murnau; *Cyprus Is an Island* (1946) is a British documentary about the history and culture of Cyprus; *Night Mail* (1936) was an influential British documentary made by John Grierson; *Greed* (1923) is one of Erich Von Stroheim's great films; *The Love of Jeanne Ney* (1927), G.W. Pabst's silent classic, starred such famous actors as Uno Henning and Brigitte Helm; *Joan of Arc* could be one or another of several famous films on the subject, such as George Méliès' in 1900 or Carl Dreyer's in 1928; *The Italian Straw Hat* (1927) is a French classic directed by René Clair, and Fritz Lang's famous *M* (1931) stars Peter Lorre.

4 Contemporary foreign films were screened at the downtown Vancouver Paradise Theatre and silent films were shown at John Goss's Studio Theatre. Society members also held private screenings in their homes, and the Lowrys sometimes attended these as well as the theatre screen-ings.

5 *La Bête humaine* (1938) by Jean Renoir is another film classic, and *Song of Ceylon* (1934) is a British documentary. *Veille d'Armes*, a 1935 film by Marcel L'Herbier, was screened at the Paradise Cinema; according to Stanley Fox, who, together with Allan King, ran the film society, 'the film was one of those tedious French farces that were turned out in great quantity in the thirties. The Film Society audience was quite bored with the thing.'

Editorial Notes:

a. Margerie Lowry has added a note to Betty Noxon after Lowry's signa-ture on the verso of the typescript; see *Letters of Malcolm Lowry and Gerald Noxon* (128).

252: To Albert Erskine

P: UBC(ms)

Dollarton P.O.,
Dollarton, B.C.
[ca 28 October 1946]ª

Dear Albert Erskine:

Well, the proofs arrived safely, (complete with an enormous 7 stamped on the envelope by the Canadian Postal Revenue Dept.), and coincidentally by the same post as some proofs, anxiously awaited by my wife, arrived for *her*.[1] Before I go on to express my

(and for that matter my wife's too.) complete admiration for everything you have done I feel I better say that I am working under more
difficulties than usual; not that I think we can't make port by your
scheduled date, but that I'd feel better if you knew that we were beating up the coast with a pronounced list to starboard and quite alot of
our tophamper lying about on the deck for the crew to fall over. In
order to get a picture of where & how we live you have to think of
Epstein's Fall of the House of Usher (the movie) only more so – at all
events in winter. My wife fell badly ill that night of the proofs & required a doctor – but noone would come (they are totally cynical in
this part of the world). The hospitals were full too. There had to be a
tremendous storm and when I found a sort of doctor, after breaking
into his house, which was quite dark, it was to find him also utterly
plasterando[2] & indeed completely Consular on the kitchen floor with
his wife. He nobly pulled himself together, however, and staggered
through the forest, set fire to our house with a cigarette (I put this
one out), left his stethescope & 3 chrysanthemums behind, but otherwise acquitted himself well. But the result is – though it all has a
happy ending – that I am nursing my wife with one hand, and correcting the proofs with the other, while my wife for her part is, so to
speak, nursing my proofs with one hand and correcting my cooking
efforts with the other. (Cooking here is on a stove like the one in
Charlie Chaplin's Gold Rush)[3] I note your letter was written on the
23rd; that means it took 5 days to get here. Thus if I am to get the
proofs back to you by Wednesday I must send them by this Saturday
at the latest; airmail, spec. deliv – & I'm sure this can be done, though
I've missed a few valuable days (somewhere around that time is the
Mexican Day of the Dead, by the way).[4]
– Now, to answer as many questions as I can. First, the 'hand': we're
both delighted with the black sinister hand you have, so unless you
really have a better one, I suggest we stick to it: perhaps the open one
will be better?? but at all events I shall have to make a slight change in
the text.[5] I didn't mean the words should come *inside* the hand,
though I see that that is what I have conveyed. I agree with you re
Chapter X, phonetic renderings & also about the dashes: there *can* be
a difference of value in their length i.e.

> '—— going down to Halifax – '
> '—— What did you say? Engine-room! . . . Well,
> let me tell you something. I was in a bloody ship once
> that really did have an engine-room to write bloody
> home about. It had triple expansion bloody engines,
> but the funny thing about it was that the steam ——'

'Hey, no stewards in here!'

'No stewards in here ———'

'This mates a bloody man; he's got me weighed up,
like *that*.'

'—— went through the bloody high pressure
cylinder, and then went through a bloody sort of
electrical superheater bloody fancy thing etc.

This is from Ultramarine: if you have 1500 pages of that kind of
thing – or what seems like it – length of dashes becomes important;
but I don't think it matters here.[6]

I agree, hands down, re Chapter I; also with your suggested cut.[7] I
felt I had to have *some* hams in the window: but I think these are
pretty gamy, even in these days of meat shortages. The chapter
meets with my objection to some extent to, now I can *see* it. All I can
say is, as the greatgrandson of the stonemason remarked, regarding,
from a height on the cathedral, several hundred feet below, his for-
bear's gargoyle: 'It's immature.' Or somewhat so. I love the *very*
beginning. But it does get a bit contrived & heavy. But I don't see
what I can do about it. Your cut will help, though that will make it
even more crepuscular: also I shall have to make it clear that Laruelle
is going back to *France*.

Don't think I agree re cuts in Chapter II: flying voice is not only
Weber's but also serves to disguise the banality of the other dialogue:
moreover there's some good double-entend if you read it one way:
but I might have to italicise here.

Don't think I agree re cuts in XII: though I agree with you: & also
with Coleridge.[8] (If you get me.)

One sometimes cannot be sure that one is not cutting the very
thing that, upon reading it the first time, produced the final verisi-
militude, & the compulsion to read it a second.

I agree re cutting the two lines of song under the hand in XI.[9]

Concerning the whole proofs I am inarticulate with gratitude &
admiration for what you have done. In fact we are yammering. The
whole thing seems to have been mysteriously improved 100% by the
general arrangement: even the insuperable X seems to come off
admirably. The two greatest surprises, with myself, were V and XI.
I thought XI had been a let down but I see it is far from it: in fact one
of the best.

Toward the end of IX it looks as though the author was actually
out of touch with his material at one point: round about where
the Consul says he had a dream about 23 nuns.[10] I'll have to make a

slight cut round there, even if it does send another thirty bucks spiralling down the drain.

We now have the jacket sketch & are gloating over that. But more of this later. It's a fine job, but my wife & [I] slightly disagree. I would have been all for your wife's squiggly line Miroish background [11] that made it look like a book about shooting tigers in Burma, which sounds marvellous, with this color background: but if it be better to hold to the stripped & the pure, which it well may be, we're going to suggest the same type & colors for that, but a different color background, say wine-red or purple: anyhow we'll shoot in the suggestion when we return the sketches though I must say it's very fine as it is. [12]

Not much sleep these last few nights what with one thing & the other & when I do sleep I am pursued through the heavens by vast billowing galleyproofs that emit a strange sound of singing *downwards* instead of across (if you follow me): moreover last night the galleyproofs were playing like a record, not only the words on them, but all the possibilities of all the other words – rather a strain. Perhaps the strain will excuse my asking a favour, even though late in the day.

In the midst of more important things I start bothering about supertrivia, my wife assures me for no reason & for god's sake not to put you to more trouble.

'Bangs & cries' in I etc we will let pass without a qualm: but a vexing devil in my subconscious makes me continue to be uneasy about a/ the passage middle of p 2 (galleys) Chapter I where Vigil brings out his cigarette lighter b/ passage top of p 9 (galleys) Chapter I where the manager strikes a match with that same lightning-swift fumbling-thwarting courtesy etc.

My wife says she remembers my writing these passages before I read Faulkner's 'Wild Palms.'[13] I'm not so sure. I have a feeling that certain phrases in a/ & in b/ may be the result of other phrases in Wild Palms adhering to my subconscious like flies to flypaper. I don't know if it is important but if you have a copy to hand would you glance through the part where the interne first comes on the scene?

I think all we will discover is that he too strikes a match with a certain gesture, that he too has black hair on his wrists, or that he too has hair stiff, shining with brilliantine. Or that Faulkner describes some gesture of his with some similar portmanteau phrases.

It's intolerable of me to ask you, but though I've had a copy on order a long while it hasn't come: & it is amazing how exacerbated one can get at times like this, so that I may even end by changing one or other of these passages. Even though it will cause you unnecessary trouble, send another 50 bucks down the drain, & even though I wrote them myself.[14]

God bless.

Malcolm L.

Annotations:

1 Lowry developed a particular fascination with the number seven, which is the number branded on the horse in *Volcano*. Dramatic things seemed to happen to him on this day, such as the 7 June 1944 fire that destroyed his cabin and, with it, many of his papers. The seven stamped on this envelope containing the delayed galley proofs would be a clear sign to Lowry of malevolent influences at work in his life.

2 Though scarcely correct Spanish, 'plasterando,' like his earlier neologism 'plasterado,' is an evocative rendering of the English colloquialism for being very drunk: plastered.

3 In one of his most famous films, *The Gold Rush* (1924), Chaplin (1889–1977) has more than a little trouble cooking on a wood stove.

4 The timing here is as follows: Erskine's letter was written on Wednesday, 23 October, and did not arrive in Dollarton until Monday, 28 October, five days being longer than was usual at that time for mail to travel from New York to Vancouver. Lowry reckons that he must finish the proofs and mail them back to Erskine by Saturday, 2 November, if Erskine is to receive them by his deadline of Wednesday, 6 November. The Mexican Day of the Dead is celebrated on 2 November, but there are candle-light vigils that begin on the first.

5 The galleys showed a small, solid black hand pointing 'A Parián,' but as Erskine explains in his letter of 23 October 1946, he prefers an open hand with the writing inside it. Lowry finally chose the solid black hand for chapter 10 of *Under the Volcano*.

6 In the same letter Erskine questions Lowry about his use of dashes because he has not, he says, the 'foggiest idea of how to arrange a logical scheme' for them. Lowry was greatly attached to dashes (as his letters alone show); therefore, in defence of them he offers Erskine this section of dialogue from *Ultramarine* (254). It is worth noting, however, that in the published text of *Ultramarine* Cape did not make the alterations to the length of the dashes that Lowry has indicated here. For the final text of *Volcano* Lowry accepted Erskine's advice, so that the dashes in chapter 10 are standardized.

7 Erskine has suggested cutting a section from the description of Laruelle because he feels that it makes the character seem more important than he is and consequently unbalances the chapter with non-essential detail.

8 Erskine has asked Lowry to consider reducing a little some of the babble by the sailor and the pimp that surrounds Geoffrey in the Farolito of chapter 12 because it becomes too much, thereby weakening its effectiveness in creating an oppressive atmosphere. Erskine then paraphrases

Coleridge's criticism of Wordsworth, who he felt had lapsed into 'a laborious minuteness and fidelity in the representation of reality . . . and . . . the insertion of accidental circumstances [which] appear superfluous in poetry.' See Samuel T. Coleridge, *Biographia Literaria*, vol. 2 (London: Oxford University Press, 1962), pp. 101-02.

9 For reasons of layout and visual impact, Erskine has suggested cutting a fragment of Hugh's song that Lowry had originally placed beneath the 'A Parián' sign.

10 Lowry cut this dream about the nuns from chapter 9 when the novel was already in galley proof.

11 The 'Miroish' line is a reference to the characteristic work of the Spanish surrealist painter Joan Miró (1893-1983).

12 The dust-jacket on the first American publication of the novel shows an all-over sworl of thin black lines on a white ground, which creates the visual effect of a spider web or of eddying ripples on the surface of water. The lettering is in pink and yellow.

13 Lowry's uneasiness about phrases from William Faulkner's *The Wild Palms* (New York: Random House, 1939) is unnecessary, and Erskine assures him of this in his 7 November 1946 letter. It would hardly be surprising, however, if *The Wild Palms* did impress Lowry because it portrays an adulterous love that ends in tragedy for all concerned, and it is set in 1938, a year (as Lowry also knew) that 'has no place in it for love' (p. 140). The man who 'fumble[s] a match' is Rittenmeyer, the abandoned husband who wants his wife back, in the scene where he confronts his wife's lover (pp. 56-58).

14 If an author makes changes (other than correction of typographical errors) at the galley- or page-proof stage, the cost of these changes is usually borne by the author.

Editorial Notes:

a. This nine-page pencil draft letter has an inside address and signature but no date. It is clear from internal references to Erskine's 23 October 1946 letter and to the Mexican Day of the Dead (the first and second of November) that Lowry is writing on or close to 28 October, the day he received Erskine's letter.

253: To Albert Erskine

P: UBC(telegram)

Western Union,
Deep Cove, B.C.
4 November 1946

STORMS HOLDING AIR MAIL NO DUPLICATE PROOFS[1] TAKEN YOUR [ADVICE] TWELVE[2] GOD BLESS

MALCOLM LOWRY

Annotations:

1 In his 23 October 1946 letter Erskine announced that he was sending a duplicate set of galleys to Lowry, and he also made a number of suggestions for small cuts.
2 The telegram has 'advise' for 'advice,' and the advice Lowry is accepting regarding chapter 12 of *Under the Volcano* is to reconsider the length of the intrusions by the sailor and the pimp as they stand, with Geoffrey, at the bar of El Farolito; see his decision on these in his 28 October 1946 letter (252) to Erskine.

254: To Albert Erskine

P: UBC(telegram)

> Western Union,
> Vancouver, B.C.
> 5 November 1946

MS AND DUPLICATE PROOFS HELD BY CUSTOMS OFFICE AS PER USUAL
ANYTHING SENT BY EXPRESS RECEIVED BY ME TODAY AND WILL BE
CHECKED AND DISPATCHED BACK TO YOU AT ONCE REGARDS

MALCOLM LOWRY

255: To Albert Erskine

P: UBC(ms)
PP: *SL* 117–18

> [Dollarton, B.C.]
> [early November 1946][a]

Dear Albert Erskine:

I have received the first batch of manuscript up to & including Chap VI, but not yet the second half of the manuscript, & not yet the duplicate proofs. However we have been working night and day and have nearly finished corrections so when the rest of the stuff arrives I shall get it back to you sine mora.[1] On the other hand to-day is Friday, my own dead line for getting it all to you by Wednesday, & the duplicate proofs have still not arrived: para consequencia[2] unless I should send it by V2 rocket or by space ship I don't see how you will get it by that day. It's true they may be waiting for me up at the post office now but it'll still take me at least a day to transfer everything from one proofs to another so that even at best I won't be able to get it off to-morrow: & the P.O is shut Sunday. I hope this will not throw us back; they have suddenly become slow here about air mail & books and things even get hung up at the border or the customs.

Meantime I have run into an infatuation with sound of own words dept: (incredibly, indescribably), & infatuation with other peoples' words dept. unusual (E.A. Poe) supplication (Nordahl Grieg) seeth-ing (Conrad Aiken).

I hope I won't be too trying. At least I haven't wired you (yet) to put the whole thing in the first person at the last moment. Nor yet put in an S.O.S. for Napier's Peninsular War or Cicero's Epistles without which it could not be corrected at all.[3] You have done an absolutely marvellous job on the proofs, the typography et al & I feel so moved by this, as well as by your understanding of the book, which is better than my own, that I feel the words all ought to be better somehow to live up to it.

hasta la vista

Malcolm L.

Annotations:

1 The Latin phrase *sine mora* means 'without delay.'
2 Lowry's conflation of Spanish (*por consiguiente*) and Latin (*per consequen-tias*) suggests 'consequently.'
3 Sir William Francis Napier (1785-1860), an English soldier and histor-ian, published his six-volume *History of War in the Peninsula* between 1828 and 1840. Marcus Tullius Cicero (106-43 BC), the Roman orator and writer, composed two sets of epistles, *Epistulae ad familiares* and *Epistulae ad Atticum*, in several volumes. After his many requests that Erskine look things up for him in books that he could not get in Dollar-ton (or Vancouver), Lowry's joke here is to the point.

Editorial Notes:

a. This transcription has been made from a pencil holograph on a single page of Lowry's cheap canary second-cut paper. It has been folded three times in Lowry's characteristic way, so it is possible that this copy is the one sent to Erskine. Lowry often wrote to Erskine using cheap paper and pencil in what look like little more than draft letters.

256: To Albert Erskine

P: UBC(ms)
PP: *SL* 128-29

[Dollarton. B.C.]
[6 November 1946]

Dear Albert Erskine:

   My god, how does one survive it, if indeed one does survive it. Why are there not stained glass windows in memory of all the authors, & all the publishers too. Oh god, St Erskine. Oh Christ, St Lowry. Last night I was haunted by an individual, not a hollow man,[1] much worse than that, but a man who had been absolutely crushed flat by a book, flat as one of those pressed Canterbury bells that one's mother sends one from England now and then; and this man, believe it or not, was me. Meantime my wife, having happily recovered otherwise in health, is troubled at night by commas wiggling around her ankles, like tadpoles, but that bite and even *sting* her: by colons that swell up like canonballs: and *ghosts* of galleys that try to wrap themselves round her in the manner [of] a winding sheet. (The day after to-morrow we're going to see The Pirates of Penzance.)[2] The day after to-morrow we are not going to see the Pirates of Penzance. At least, I don't think so. (For that read, now, to-morrow.) The reason is the galley-proofs – duplicate. Yesterday I sent a wire re their non-arrival: to-day I got your wire (wrongly relayed over the phone) & also a notice from the Canadian National Railway Express (in spite of your having it sent Air Express.) dated November 4th. And in spite of your having sent it Special Deliv. Snag is neatly expressed in remark on red label on package which so far as I can read it says:

Canadian National Express
IN BOND
From Tomb   to Maul

Deliver to Collector of Custom & Excise
Vancouver

Important Notice – Agent at Destination must not Deliver This Shipment unless he has evidence that clearance through customs has been arranged when released by Customs Officer. The agent at customs port should affix a 'Cleared Customs sticker' (Form 5246.)

All this in spite of Air Express Prepaid waybill numbers & God knows what trouble you went to: I'd have warned you if I'd remembered that nothing but straight airmail or post goes straight through but I'd forgotten we were a foreign country: at all events I've got it, which is the main thing, after a nightmarish day in Vancouver chasing from office to office & giving them hell to no avail: it is now 7 o'clock Wednesday night November 6th – your parcel is dated Oct 31 – to-day is the day you should have had it back; to-morrow – **Nov 7** – the day you mentioned it should go to the printers: – so I better see how fast I can work, – and how. Well, here goes: occasionally an asterisk on proofs will refer you to a letter, – & what is opposite there you will find, in the following pages, somewhere among the other remarks pertinent to the particular chapter.

N.B. Extra note
Re dedication, somewhere.

 To Margerie, my wife.

[unsigned]^a

Annotations:

1 Lowry's reference is to T.S. Eliot's poem 'The Hollow Men' (1925).
2 *The Pirates of Penzance* (1879) is a popular comic opera by the English composers Sir William Schwenck Gilbert (1836-1911) and Sir Arthur Sullivan (1842-1900).

Editorial Notes:

a. This pencil holograph letter, on 7.5-by-12-cm pages torn from a pocket notebook, is unsigned and carries no complimentary close; the editors of *Selected Letters* either added these details or were working from a copy that appears not to have survived.

257: To Jonathan Cape

P: UBC(ts)
PP: *SL* 130-31

[Dollarton, B.C.]
[November 1946]^a

Dear Mr Cape:
 Absolutely up to the eyes in proofs – will you do me an enormous favour in the interests of God, literature, and one of your writers; I speak of the late-lamented Mr Melville.

A year or so ago my wife and I were hitting the high places in radio – we even got written up in Time as having achieved some of the best in radio. To cut a long story short, we did finally a serious radio dramatization of Moby Dick, of a character completely to revolutionize radio.

While most people in the CBC agreed it was the most magnificent script they'd ever had, they achieved a change of heart at the last moment, said the public wouldn't stand for it, would we change it, and we said no.

We also gave up radio, this being indeed a job worse than driving geese to water, even at its highest, or at any rate you can't mix it with serious writing too strenuously.

However now we read that Barnes[1] is doing a serious dramatization of Moby Dick and I will bet my bottom dollar that that idea came via us through the radio grape-vine.

That is not the point so much as that no one else *could* do Moby Dick as we have done it – it is too damned hard and too many problems to be solved – [so we want to] shoot our script in to him quam celerime, in the certain knowledge that when he sees *our* script he'll have to haul whatever else he has cooking out of production, if he's got that far.[2]

But even, at worst, our script cannot fail to be a help: it's consummate of its kind.

Since I don't know the address of the BBC [British Broadcasting Corporation] would you kindly send this thither by space rocket and a bevy of messengers, or at least by the next post, this being the favour, though I may say I would have taken the liberty of asking you to forward it anyhow, since it will have far more authority as arriving from Melville's publisher, or as if from H.M. himself, whose ghost we like to think we can hear saying, 'Save me.'

You only haven't got my wife's book [*Horse in the Sky*] because she hasn't got it yet from the agent.

You will have my proofs soon.

We are wallowing in success, feeling in fact like starving men whose eyes are being stuffed with potatoes.

I had a letter from Innes Rose who has returned from the wars, I am relieved to hear; should you encounter him would you tell him I will write him as soon as I can.

Happy Haloween, Happy Xmas, and also Happy New Year –

Ever sincerely yours,

[unsigned]

P.S. I find myself making some of the cuts intimated by your reader, in spite of all the hubbub I made.

Annotations:

1 George Reginald Barnes (1904-60) joined the British Broadcasting Corporation (BBC) in 1935 and became the first Head of the Third Programme which produced Henry Reed's radio-play adaptation of *Moby-Dick* in 1947. This adaptation, published by Cape in 1947, was a critical success and earned Reed considerable praise.
2 The only extant 'script' of the Lowrys' adaptation of *Moby-Dick* is the synopsis in the UBC Malcolm Lowry collection, 16:1-5. If they sent a full script to Jonathan Cape, it does not appear to have survived, but it is probable that what Lowry describes here as a 'script' is, in fact, the synopsis. There is no record of Cape's response to any *Moby-Dick* material sent to him by Lowry.

Editorial Notes:

a. This transcription has been made from an undated typescript that is unsigned; the original letter appears not to have survived.

258: To Albert Erskine

P: UBC(ts)

Dollarton, B.C.,
Canada
21 November 1946

Dear Albert Erskine:

Thanks awfully for reading Wild Palms and for your letter on that subject: I changed an extra passage or two however, where there seemed Faulkner's, or another's, influence, too much in the machinery, largely in that of 'stage directions.'[1]

I hope my cuts in the last chapter were O.K. I can't bear to look, but I sort of feel they are right. I went there rather beyond your advice, which I took also in I, but not in II, for reasons which do not seem to me particularly well founded either. I glowered over it with the knife, but it uttered such a disheartening yelp at the feeble nick I made, that I let the poor thing be.

At this point I went on and wrote an enormously long letter[2] which brought in everything from the evils of the Canadian Customs to the local murder, but fearing you would never get to the end of this, I have – since I'm still in that groove – cut this too, for I have an important question to ask.

The weather is so inconceivably dreadful here that we intend to take a trip by bus as soon as possible to New Orleans. Para consequencia, since we are trying to get away by the 26th or 27th, could you wire me (collect) on receiving this letter, what is the status of the page proofs, the point being that if you have already sent them, or if they are practically ready to send, we will wait here and correct them, so as not to lose any time, but if they won't be ready for another 10 days or two weeks or longer, they could be sent to New Orleans and I can correct them there. But in any event please wire so we'll know whether to go or stay:[3] when we go I'll keep in touch with you, so you'll know my address, but I don't foresee any difficulty of communication, since as between New Orleans and New York it will be easier than between New York and Dollarton.

From New Orleans we are intending eventually to try and come to New York (in 2 months or so?) – but more of that later.

Ever sincerely yours,

Malcolm Lowry

Annotations:

1 Lowry continued to be troubled by what he thought were echoes of Faulkner's *The Wild Palms*; see his 28 October 1946 letter (**252**) to Erskine and Erskine's assurances that he 'forget all about it' (annotation 13).

2 See Lowry's 21 November 1946 letter (**259**) to Erskine; the section in which he 'went on and wrote an enormously long letter' is in braces.

3 No wire from Erskine is extant with the UBC Lowry collection or the Erskine papers at the University of Virginia, but the Lowrys left for the trip, flying from Vancouver to Seattle, on 30 November 1946; from Seattle they took a bus south and east to New Orleans, where they arrived on 6 December.

259: To Albert Erskine

P: UBC(ms)

Dollarton P.O.,
Dollarton, B.C.
[21 November 1946][a]

– Dear Albert Erskine: –

Thanks awfully for reading Wild Palms & for your letter on that subject: I changed [an] extra passage or two, however, where there seemed Faulkner's, or another's influence, too much in the machinery, largely in that of 'stage directions.'

I hope my cuts in the last chapter were o.k: I can't bear to look, but I sort of feel they are right. I went there rather beyond your advice, which I took also in I, but not in II, for reasons which do not seem to me particularly well founded either. I glowered over it with the knife, but it uttered such a disheartening yelp at the feeble nick I made, that I let the poor thing be.

{I hope also that you got the corrected proofs not too late for your plans. We were delayed by these estupidos in the Air Express & the Customs. Vancouver is some 15 miles from here, & none too easy to reach, there being an irregular bus service. I didn't get the card from the Express till the forenoon of Nov 5, I went into town right off, but the place where they had the stuff wouldn't give it me till I'd checked in my card with another office in the Canadian National Railway station some 4 miles away. I had to get there & back within half an hour or not only would the former office close but I'd miss my bus home too. So it was a rush, not helped by the fact that when I did return to the Customs my place had been taken by apparently the entire chorus of a local revue, who had likewise chosen that time to get parcels. I noted you'd sent it Special Delivery but in spite of that I gathered they hadn't the slightest intention of delivering it at all. It would seem that the only Customs dodging method is straight air mail, & even that is not absolutely certain. I was relieved to discover that the next day was the 6th, not the 7th, as I said in my letter, so if mine got through to you without a hitch, you may not have received it more than two or three days late anyhow.}

Meantime the cold here is terrific; even the sea is beginning to freeze, & though I swam in it yesterday, it is getting a bit much. When the cold hits here it *seems* worse than in the east, because noone is properly prepared for it. It is true we have no taps to freeze: which is a comfort. We have a murder, however, out here, uncomfortably like one dreamed-up by my wife for literary purposes, & in the same primeval spot, which is a bit odd, though they haven't yet called on us to solve it. 'What a pretty little boat' 'How happy he looks scudding along all by himself out there! says my wife the other day, when in fact it was undoubtedly the murderer making his get-away.[1]

In short, what with the freezing, & the homicides, and the wolves, and the bears, & the cougars, we are contemplating rather shamefacedly (shamefacedly because when 3 years ago there was similar weather we were the only pioneers who didn't move into town, so that we were the sole population of Dollarton, in fact we *were* Dollarton) a trip, by bus, to New Orleans.

We then thought we'd come to New York, but somewhat oddly, via Haiti, before returning to the cougars, the bears, the wolves, the homicides, & the freezings again in early spring.

Para consequencia, since it will be necessary that I don't go out of touch, perhaps I may ask you a few questions the answers to which may have some bearing on the date of our setting forth, not to say our subsequent movements.

First: When do you expect the page proofs – or rather when, approximately, would I get them?

We aim to take work & a typewriter with us, & to be working in New Orleans for 2 or 3 weeks: & if possible, I'd like to correct the page proofs there, rather than here: (in fact, we are getting such terrific onshore winds with high smashing tides – our house is built actually in the sea, it's right under the floor as I write, or more accurately, do not write but digress, – that you might as well correct proofs going round the horn before the mast as here: love it though we do, the sheer noise is sometimes titanic, & chores take on an epic aspect & worse, swallow up the whole day, & we'd both like a slight rest from that:) so, as I say, I'd rather do the page proofs in New Orleans. But if they were coming soon – say within a week or two – perhaps it would be better to stay here until they arrive: on the other hand, we would be in closer touch in New Orleans (if not in Haiti, but we wouldn't in that case move from New Orleans till that was done.)

As things stand at the moment, Cape shifted the deadline to February re Canadian rights. I take it that that means till the 1st of March but since by now what with all my alterations & digressions & questions it would be about the ultima thule of ingratitude on my part if you were to be penalised for my apparent strange inability to know what I'm talking about at the right moment do you want me to write him again; if it still seems too close a margin for you?? I am so far dealing with Cape direct and since I don't want to be unfair to him either I am quite willing to be penalised myself if you can't bring it out at the time you thought. Actually I don't know how much it matters to Cape, who, if you have truck strikes, has apparently so many obstacles in the old country in the way of publishing anything that he may not be able to bring it out till heaven knows when, or if (for I've known him for years & he was also a great friend of Mr Hitchcock's) the good man may not be having some kind of joke with me, as to say, 'Let us see, my boy, if you may be business-like, if only for 5 minutes.'

Well, I've tried: but theres a clause in the contract that says I must write both a preface & the blurb, which indeed is a joke, because I can't do it at all: so far as the former is concerned I've got as far as 'I like prefaces, I read them' for the opening, & 'Now put it back in the 3-d shelf where you found it' for the end. That seems pretty good: but as for the middle: and the blurb. Jesus Murphy as they say in the Yukon. The inhibition isn't due to false modesty either because one must have written some hundreds in daydreams. '. . . These significant pages' . . . 'trenchent style' 'notable achievement.' Or as Max Beerbohm says somewhere . . . those tripping numbers . . .'[2] Ah well

It looks however as though I may, with your permission have to perpetrate a slightly dirty trick which is, to send him the proofs you sent me, that is, *after* I've corrected your page proofs on their basis: may I have your permission to do this? I don't know what the moral aspect of this would be at all, if any, but it would certainly save me & him no end of trouble & since I could scarcely do other than crib the corrected passages on to the copy I now have (which I don't want to trust to the post since it's the sole one in my possession) perhaps you'll allow me to do just this; so long of course as we don't crib the format & everything else too: the strongest point I have is that I would that much sooner be able to get down to the work in progress; this is very complicated & I want enormously to discuss it with you, which is indeed the chief reason I want to come to N.Y.

I have drafted out 25 chapters of a novel to be called La Mordida – but actually there are 4 short novels in progress (La Mordida should be shortish finally) – the other three being Dark as the Grave wherein my friend is laid, Lunar Caustic, & a revised version of the at present unspeakable loathsome Ultramarine: however in La Mordida we are really, I think, out in the cold beyond Pierre,[3] so to speak, at the Pole & among the undiscovered Arctic explorers, where the needle respects every point of the compass at once: but fortunately we are in the Tropic of Capricorn too.

(There should also be a fifth: but that is more than enough for the present.)
Re New York per se. I certainly wished I could have been there & seen you within the last few months: my wife wished to go New Yorkwards too, but health prevented.

Previous to that, when Hal Matson had transmitted, to me in Mexico, from you, the question was I contemplating a trip to New York in the near future, & if so, the situation was with yourselves such & so, I had replied that I would be delighted to come; later, however, he said that you'd decided I needn't come, so for me not to come, unless I insisted.

Once back here again, I felt that I should have come: & then that I should go: then, on receiving one of your letters, that it would be better to go: but by this time the state of my wife's health wld have prevented it anyway; I think I kept Hal informed about this. There was some item in some previous exchange of letters, however, that intimated that it might be better, or that it might still be good to come at publication time, but possibly this is no longer so.

I am saying all this mostly because of the financial angle, & because I would have indeed liked to have come before, when I could, namely from Mexico. There was something or other in some clause, or in some stipulation that is no longer a clause, that anyhow seemed to suggest that you would, should I come, credit me with some sum or abbreviate some other sum, from future royalties, I forget precisely what because I haven't the correspondence bearing upon it to hand:[4] what I am driving at is that it may be you are not willing to do this any longer but in any event, so far as I know, I am coming to New York.

I am not, by the way, by any means broke, though I was pretty low financially at the time of your acceptance: in fact I have been lately fallen heir to quite a considerable sum of money, or what would be in England, in the early 20th century, such: on the other hand I am murderously taxed & find it pretty difficult under our government to get any proportion of what in normal times would supposedly be transmitted easily at any time I want it: for this reason if the previous arrangement has not fallen through it would be highly convenient for me if you would reconsider some such arrangement, or a modification of it, for it would make all the difference in N. York, where I understand prices are high & we have at present no way of knowing where we should stay: a lo contrario,[5] if that all seems to you now utterly impossible – & I perfectly understand how it might – we are intending to come to New York anyway & such may be done well under one's own steam, though I'd like to know when is the best time, so not to miss you – anyhow

We shall be arriving from Haiti, possibly even travelling hence with a barrel of rum (though not, I hope, like Lord Nelson, in one).[6]

Ever sincerely yours –

Malcolm Lowry

Annotations:

1 On 15 November 1946 the Vancouver newspapers were all reporting the case of 'A Deep Cove Man Shot to Death.' The murder took place in

a small hamlet to the east of the Lowrys' Dollarton cabin on the four-teenth of the month, and it is possible that the murderer could have fled the isolated spot by boat. Reports continued to appear in the news-papers, and a suspect was arrested on 23 November. Margerie's mystery novel *The Shapes That Creep* (1946) contains a local murder.

2 Sir Max Beerbohm (1872-1956), the English essayist, critic, and carica-turist, wrote several volumes of essays, stories, and parodies and was dramatic critic for the *Saturday Review* for many years. The phrase 'those tripping numbers' certainly sounds like Beerbohm, but I have not located Lowry's source.

3 This is Herman Melville's *Pierre; or, The Ambiguities* (1852), a novel Lowry frequently refers to in his letters. This autobiographical novel was a publishing disaster for its author, and Lowry may be thinking of that or of its autobiographical hero, who becomes the victim of his own ideals, in his implied comparison with 'La Mordida.'

4 In April 1946 Curtice Hitchcock had thought it might be necessary to bring Lowry to New York for the editing of *Under the Volcano*, but he changed his mind about the need for extensive editing. On 13 April 1946 Matson telegraphed Lowry in Mexico to say that 'Hitchcock offers to put up five hundred dollars toward expenses [for a trip to New York], half of which would be later deducted from royalties.' Three days later, however, Matson wrote to Lowry explaining that Hitchcock no longer felt that the revisions he had wanted were sufficient to warrant bringing Lowry to New York and 'that he would rather spend the transportation money on editorial advertising and promotion, or . . . in connection with a trip . . . East at the time of publication.'

5 Lowry has deleted 'on the other hand' and inserted his Spanish in a superscript; the correct Spanish, however, is *de lo contrario*, which means 'otherwise.'

6 Viscount Horatio Nelson (1785-1805), the famous British admiral, was shot and killed on board the *Victory* after the Battle of Trafalgar. Because an airtight coffin could not be made aboard ship for the return voyage to England, Lord Nelson's body was placed in a large barrel of brandy.

Editorial Notes:

a. This six-page pencil holograph is the 'enormously long letter' referred to in Lowry's 21 November 1946 typescript letter (**258**) to Erskine; this version was, of course, not sent to Erskine, but it is a complete letter, and I have included it here because of the information it provides about the progress of Lowry's work and the developing friendship with his editor, which would become crucial to Lowry in the coming years.

260: To Albert Erskine

P: UBC(telegram)

Western Union,
Vancouver, B.C.
25 November 1946

MANY THANKS YOUR WIRE[1] ABSOLUTELY DONT NEED TO SEE PAGE
PROOFS HOWEVER ANXIOUS KNOW HOW CORRECTIONS LOOK TO YOUR
EYE ESPECIALLY CHAPTER TWELVE WILL KEEP YOU POSTED MY ADDRESS
AS MATTERS STAND WILL BE CANADA TILL THURSDAY[2] THEN LEAVE FOR
NEW ORLEANS GOD AND JOHN LEWIS[3] WILLING BLESSINGS FROM FORMER

MALCOLM LOWRY

Annotations:

1 This wire does not appear to have survived.
2 Thursday is 28 November, and according to Day (369) the Lowrys left
  Dollarton for Seattle on 30 November to begin their complicated
  journey south.
3 John Lewis (1880–1969), president of the United Mine Workers of
  America from 1920 to 1960, called a halt to a coal strike in the United
  States on 7 December 1946, just in time to avoid heavy government
  fines and rationing. Threats of the strike had begun as early as 15
  November.

261: To John Davenport

P: UBC(pcard)

[Saint Louis,]
[Missouri]
[6 December 1946]

However this may be, I meant to post this in Wyoming;[1] & I am
writing it in smoky old St Louis, drinking claret with my wife & eating Leiderkranz,[2] in the middle of a coal strike, in a horrible-beautiful
hotelroom. Marvellous to hear from you but you never seemed very
far away; what could one have done without your laughter? R[eynal]
& Hitchcock invited me to N.Y for publication of book [*Under the
Volcano*] there Feb. but for next two months my address will be Gen.
Delivery, New Orleans, whence I will write at more length. My

Margerie sends love to yours, as do I, & to the children. 'ave a good time. God bless you.

Malc

Annotations:

1 The picture on this postcard, after the oil painting 'A Drink of Water' (1939) by the American artist Lewis H. 'Dude' Larsen (1909-), shows a cowboy and a horse drinking from a mountain stream. Larsen's poem is printed on the back of the card, and some of its lines must have struck Lowry as especially appropriate for one of his oldest drinking companions:

> Now I have drank at cocktail parties,
> Whiskey, wine, and all the rest,
> But when I'm tired, hot and sweaty,
> I like my mountain water best.

Lowry also sent a Larsen postcard (**262**) to Gerald Noxon.

2 The correct spelling of the name of this pungent American beer cheese is Liederkranz. It was created in 1895 by Emil Frey, who owned a delicatessen in New York and was trying to imitate a famous German cheese called Schlosskäse Bismarck.

262: To Gerald Noxon

P: Texas(pcard]
PP: *LLN* 131

[Saint Louis,]
[Missouri]
[6 December 1946]^a

Dear old Gerald:
meant to post this in Wyoming, then thought (in honor of the Blues) wd do so in St Louis, where we sit in a smoky hotel-room, (in the middle of a coal strike), drinking claret & eating Liederkranz; our address for next 6 weeks will be *Gen Delivery, New Orleans*: afterwards we hope to go to Haiti for a bit; then N.Y (Volc comes out Feb.) & so home, via Canada, hoping to see *you* on way. Nothing but good news from our end. Both hard at work at new works. All fondest love to Betty Nick & yourself – Ever

Malc

P.S. In Wyoming we saw some *live* penguins; also dinosaur's bones.

Editorial Notes:

a. This is the postmark date on the card, which shows a reproduction of a painting of a stallion by Lewis H. 'Dude' Larsen called 'Freedom' (1943). The message on the card has been written by Lowry, but the address is in Margerie's hand.

263: To Albert Erskine

P: UBC(ms)
PP: *SL* 132-34

[New Orleans,]
[Louisiana]
[ca 15 December 1946]ᵃ

Dear Mr Erskine:

We went over the page proofs in the back room of a brawling New Orleans bar hard by the p. office, drinking very good beer out of fine copper tankards, but to-day when we went back they threw us out. 'This is a bar, not an office.' Apparently you can gamble, play confidence tricks, & even murder in these joints, and you can listen to the thrice god-awful shindy coming out of juke boxes or the sextuply beyond god-awful hillbilly music that seems to have put a stop here to jazz – of which I am both a passionate admirer and an ancient aficionado, & of which this is the home – but a fellow can't look at his proofs. 'We don't know what kind of a thing it is you're doing, & the boys are asking questions.' I spoke to an old guy who'd once played with [Joe] Venuti & he said: 'Boy I like to play like you say, but nobody asks for it any more, & what the hell can I do with a guitarist like I got.' So I'm feeling pretty hurt this morning – but apart from that New Orleans is superlatively wonderful; moreover I've got to do something about that Spanish moss before I die.

Well, I've got your list & I've checked the names of the people I know. I'm a bit dubious about my list, however: I've no way of knowing how interested some of them would be, friends or no, & I'm not sure if Conrad Aiken, for example, is in England or America. The Jane Aiken I mentioned is an editorial researcher on Time, & is Aiken's daughter whom I knew as a child. I'd like a review copy to go to Conrad A. though. I'm not very clear about those to whom review copies might be sent with any profit; but these I have marked anyway with a tick & a star; those whom I merely *know* simply with a tick. But there's one name I missed & should put in; that is Michael Redgrave, the actor, an old & good college friend of mine who is at present in America making a movie, I believe, for Fritz Lang.[1] So far as I know his address is Diana Productions, Universal City, Calif, & I certainly would like if possible a review copy to be sent to him.

For the rest; thank you again for everything. Re coming to New York I feel I ought to have explained before to you that I very much wanted to do this when I was originally asked by your firm through my agent if I could – this was way back in April & my plan was at that time to proceed straight from Mexico to N.Y; but then I was informed by my agent that you didn't want me to do this, & that it might be better for me to come at publication time. Between May & October it would have been very difficult for me to come anyway but I would have made it if I had been informed by my agent of any change of plans – for my part I would have preferred being in New York during the period of editing; feeling that that was when I could have been the most help. But the final word I had from my agent was that Mr Hitchcock had decided that my trip was unnecessary until perhaps publication time, and there the matter still rests.

Since I want to get this back to you by return mail & am in fact finishing it in the p.o itself – Loitering in this building prohibited – I'll keep anything further for another letter – hope my telegram was comprehensible,

very best wishes

Malcolm Lowry

Annotations:

1 Michael Redgrave (1908–85) did star in Fritz Lang's film *The Secret beyond the Door* (1948). Shooting for this film did not begin in Hollywood until 1 February 1947, and Redgrave did not reach the United States until some time in January.

Editorial Notes:

a. Lowry's pencil holograph is on both sides of a single 21-by-27.5-cm sheet of cheap typewriter paper. There is no date or inside address, and the paper shows several stains from what Lowry describes as beer in his 17 December 1946 letter (264) to Erskine.

264: To Albert Erskine

P: UBC(ts)

> 622 Saint Ann Street,
> New Orleans, Louisiana,
> 17 December 1946

Deart Albert Erskine:

I hope you got my somewhat beerstained letter O.K. and that it was legible and also my wire.[1] The Postoffice is way up town, we are living miles deep in the French quarter, so the only thing for it was to work in a cafe or pub up town if we didn't want to lose valuable time.

I have today received the bound proof copy of the Volcano for which many thanks indeed. Both of us think it looks very fine and we are lost in admiration of your whole creative job in editing it. It must have been a terrible bore and sweat for you at times and I can only hope that the book in some way proves worthy of your trouble.

New Orleans, for all its beauty, interest and marvellous food is getting us down slightly; it is, by the way, absolutely wide open, in fact Babylonian and we fear we shall die, like half the English kings, of some kind of surfeit of lampreys absinthe or what not, if we do not do something vigorous soon. Also it is enormously expensive. We long to see the rest of the South but Missouri seems the only state within our means.

So we thought to move to Haiti for some 30 days, and the only original thing about this is we are going on a Liberty Ship carrying bauxite to Trinidad and which does not carry passengers. How, if at all, we shall get from there to New York, I don't know but that is still our aim. Re New York, what I wanted to say was that I believe there was some kind of clause in the contract, or if not in the contract, hovering in the air, or if not still hovering in the air, that once hovered in the air, which intimated that your firm might be willing to pay something or other + or − something else or other to be deducted from later royalties, if any, towards my expenses in N.Y.[2] What I meant was, I was intending to try and come quite regardless of whether this arrangement still stood. For one thing I appreciate that it is quite unfair to you, if you had wanted me to come at another time, why you should pay anything towards any such expenses for my coming at some other time, when you may not particularly want me to come but which happens to suit me fine. (But I do repeat that I myself wanted to come straight from Mexico.) On the other hand I did get the impression that some such arrangement still stood re the time of publication, and I wouldn't say it wouldn't help if I ever get there. But on the other hand too I realise you may well have been put to other quite unforseen expenses as a consequence of my general dillying and Spanish incompetence and I don't want you to feel that I would just arrive and then start holding you up for something you may have meantime decided was unfeasible. You never know with these blasted limeys. We have a bit – I think I also get another instalment of advance when the book comes out – so one should get by. But please let me know about this.

What I was hoping to do was while in Haiti to get my work in progress into some sort of shape where I might be able to discuss it with you in N.Y.

We are planning to sail next Monday, the 23rd I think, on the s.s. Donald Wright for Port au Prince;[3] there will then be a hiatus of some 5 days or so while we wallow in the Sargasso Sea[4] or wherever, but I can be reached at this address safely this week and I'll let you know by the end of the week what my address will be in Haiti, I think airmail communication is fairly easy. A very merry Christmas from us both to you and Mrs Erskine and a very happy New Year.

Sincerely,

Malcolm Lowry

P.S. Can you draw cartoons? If so, let us collaborate and make a lot of money. Here is my first idea, and I'm afraid somebody else is going to think of it. A steamer is docked in port, the passengers are all standing lined up, while the crew solemnly tips them.

Annotations:

1 Lowry's wire (**260**) was sent from Vancouver on 25 November 1946, and the 'beerstained letter' (**263**) is the one dated ca 15 December 1946.
2 Lowry is recalling Matson's 13 April 1946 telegram and his 16 April 1946 letter describing and then cancelling Curtice Hitchcock's plan for bringing Lowry to New York; see Lowry's 21 November 1946 letter (**259**) to Erskine, annotation 4.
3 In 1946, 23 December was a Monday, but the ss *Donald Wright* did not leave for Haiti until 26 December.
4 The Sargasso Sea, a relatively calm area of water, lies well to the north-east of Haiti, and there seems little reason for a ship going south to Haiti and Trinidad to go near it.

265: To Albert Erskine

P: UBC(ms)
PP: *SL* 131-32

[New Orleans,]
[Louisiana]
[ca 20 December 1946]

Dear Erskine:

(In dear old Ultima thule that is a rather stern form of address, so that whenever I am addressed as Lowry, courteous though it be, I always quail slightly, feeling that it is immediately going to be followed by a formal invitation to be thrashed within an inch of one's life by the Headmaster, or by some such remark as: For Christ sake didn't I tell you ten minutes to go down to that Chief Engineer & fetch up a bucket of steam! But my wife tells me that in these states its implications – as of course I knew, nor are they, obviously, here, – are not so. Please enjoy a quiet laugh here at my expense. I have just spent a wonderful afternoon with my wife wandering round old New Orleans, visiting the pirate Lafitte's dens,[1] observing certain relics of tortures, & also apprehending a delicate panorama of certain redcoats – of course not limeys – lying flat on their face, slaughtered, in what looked to me – though could it be? – a hailstorm.[2] You'd polished them off anyway. I was also so fascinated by the history of the riverboat Robert E. Lee[3] in the museum I had to be dragged away by main force, not however, before having learned the following:

EXTRA!
Lee arrived at St Louis at 11.20
Time out from New Orleans, 3 days
18 hours, & 19 minutes.
Natchez not in sight.
Natchez old time – 3 days, 21 hours
& 58 minutes.
EXTRA!)   Please notice I closed
                                   the bracket.[a]

In haste.

Reactions re cover etc – & far more than cover. Before I go on to that, re the book, the 'everything in it,' as you have presented it, is a marvellous creative job.

Re the cover – I like everything about it; here is, verbatim, my wife, and a very knowledgeable early friend of hers – reaction; – as accurately as I can get it down on the spot:

– 'really a work of genius, if you stare at it long enough, you're down through into the ultimate Pit of blackness; not only is it the vortex, but the SHAKY vortex, – (note comma & dash) – not only from the point of view of salesmanship: – *right*, from the point of view of the book – sinister quality, quality of horror, & yet great dignity.'

That is what they say; & I agree.

Re Jimmy Stern – he is an old pal, the best & most amusing of fellows, as also of writers – but he really hated all but one poem of all my past work; quite deservedly too: I felt, if anyone would give the Volcano the brush-off, though it hurt him, it would be Jimmy. Have you read The Heartless Land? I am tickled pink he liked the Volcano.

Re – the parcel you have so generously sent me, containing the other book, I don't know what to say; a thousand thanks – but if it shouldn't arrive to-morrow, I may indeed should it prove impossible to cope with the ad Haitian postal arrangements, have to do as you suggest –

God bless & a Merry Xmas all over again to you & Mrs Erskine from us both.

Malcolm Lowry

P.S. Although we are now leaving, like the Pequod, on Christmas Eve.[4]

Annotations:

1 Jean Lafitte (ca 1780-1826) was a Louisiana privateer and smuggler who fought with the Americans against the British in the 1812 Battle of New Orleans and again in 1815. He settled near the town, in a spot from which he could carry out raids on Spanish ships in the Gulf of Mexico.

2 The 'delicate panorama' of slaughtered redcoats to which Lowry is referring is probably Hyacinthe Laclotte's painting 'The Battle of New Orleans' (1815), in the Isaac Delgado Museum of Art in New Orleans. Andrew Jackson's army defeated the British, killing more than two thousand men, in this celebrated battle.

3 The *Robert E. Lee II* is perhaps the most famous riverboat in American history. In June 1870 it raced another paddle-wheeler, the *Natchez*, upriver from New Orleans to St Louis, reaching speeds of up to fifteen miles per hour, and the race made international headlines. The *Robert E. Lee* won, leaving the *Natchez* far behind.

4 The *Pequod*, Captain Ahab's ship in Melville's *Moby-Dick*, sets sail from Nantucket on Christmas Day.

Editorial Notes:

a. The opening bracket appears at the beginning of the letter. During the editing process Erskine had chided Lowry about his punctuation.

266: To James Stern

P: Texas(card)

[New Orleans,]
[Louisiana]
[21 December 1946]

Dear old Jimmy:

It was lovely of you to wire me so generously your appreciation of the Volcano, which wire I received with delight this morning and I can't say how much that meant to me.[1]

(– Er – you will perhaps recognise the phrase 'hangover thunder-clapping about his skull' Chap V, the opening: it comes out of a letter from you to me from some years back, in which kittens were also boxing.)[2]

It was also marvellous to get in touch with you again. We aim to come to New York in February – is there anywhere to live? And can you be seen then?

We are sailing for Port-au-Prince, Haiti, on Monday, on a bauxite freighter on which we are the sole passengers, the s.s. Donald Wright.

I don't know when, if ever, the thing will reach port, but I'll write you again from Haiti, anyhow, where our address is:

c/o Anton Kneer,
Agent Alcoa S.S. Co.
Port-au-Prince.

Meantime many congratulations upon your *own* work: also The Woman who was loved? I was just about to buy, on receiving your wire, the volume that contains it someone having told me it was the best short story they ever read. Although it would be extraordinarily hard for anyone to beat The Man who was Loved.[3]

Well – thank you again from my heart – my dear fellow, and since almost immediately we must be 'Gone mit de vind' –[4] God bless to you and yours and hasta la vista,

from

Malcolm

Annotations:

1 In his wire (UBC 1:64), sent to Lowry at 622 St Anne Street, New Orleans, on 19 December, Stern says: 'Am lying under the Volcano consumed with excitement jealousy gratitude and indescribable praise.'

2 Stern's letter with the hangover phrase does not appear to have survived, but in his 17 September 1940 letter to Lowry (UBC 1:64) Stern does mention 'kittens . . . ready to shake their fists in welcome.'

3 Both stories appeared in the collection called *The Man Who Was Loved* (1951), but 'The Woman Who Was Loved' was first published in *Harper's Bazaar* (January 1945): 63ff, and later in *The Best American Short Stories of 1946*, edited by Martha Foley.

4 Lowry's Germanic joke is an allusion to Margaret Mitchell's Pulitzer Prize-winning novel about the American Civil War called *Gone with the Wind* (1936).

267: To Conrad Aiken

P: H(card)
PP: *LAL* 199

New Orleans
[Louisiana]
[21 December 1946]ᵃ

My very dear old Conrad:

I owe you a letter, in reply to your marvellous one – but please forgive my not replying & now I must reply from Haiti where our address will be:

c/o Anton Kneer
Agent – S.S. Alcoa Co.
Port-au-Prince –   We sail day after tomorrow, the 23rd, on a bauxite freighter on which we are the only passengers, the s.s. *Donald Wright*.

Margie has a book reissued by Scribners, of which more later, I tried to have a proof copy of the Volcano sent you, as I don't know where you are, nor D. S & Pearce's[1] address, so in case *you're* at sea too, I'm sending this c/o New Directions, to save time (I hope): we are coming to N.Y. in Feb – & I hope to God I can see you then.

If you hate the Volcano, don't let that embarrass you, or fear it will break one's heart; it will, of course, but doubtless that would be all to the good, too. Actually I submit it is pretty good work from your old – & new – pupil.

God bless to Mary & yourself.

Malc

The Merriest of Xmases & the Happiest of New Years to you, Mary,
& Conrad: also love to John & Jane –

from Malcolm &

Margerie

Annotations:

1   Aiken's publisher was Duell, Sloan and Pearce.

Editorial Notes:

a. This letter was written by Lowry on the inside of a Christmas card
    and in the margins around the season's greetings. Lowry's reference to a
    sailing date of 23 December means this card must have been written
    on the twenty-first.

268: To Albert Erskine

P: UBC(card)

[New Orleans,]
[Louisiana]
[December 1946][a]

My address in Haiti will be:

c/o Mr Anton Kneer
Agent-Alcoa S.S. Co.
Port-au-Prince.
Haiti

until one gets there, it is somewhere amidships, or even aloft, on
board *s.s. Donald Wright.* The Xmas card comes all the way from
New York. (I received a tremendously enthusiastic wire from Jimmy
Stern re the Volcano this morning, which meant alot to me, because
he is damned hard to please: I hope that may bode well.)

All the best again

M.L.

Editorial Notes:

a. Although there is no addressee named on this card, the contents suggest
    that Lowry is writing to Albert Erskine in New York. Moreover, it is
    clear from the complimentary close – 'All the best *again*' – that this note
    inside the card is an addendum to something else, such as an enclosed
    letter or a letter sent shortly before the card, for example, the December
    1946 letter (**265**).

269: To Gerald, Betty and Nick Noxon

P: Texas(card)
PP: *LLN* 131-32

[New Orleans,]
[Louisiana]
[December 1946]ᵃ

to Betty & Gerald & Nick with best love & best wishes for a Merry
Xmas – & a Happy New Year – when we shall be thinking of you, as
do you please think of us (we are spending ours at sea, on board a
bauxite freighter the s.s. Donald Wright, outward bound from New
Orleans to Haiti, & we are the only passengers)

from

Malcolm [& Margerie]

Best love & every Christmas wish & hoping with all our hearts to see
you on our way home our address in Haiti –

    c/o Anton Kneer
    Agent – Alcoa S.S. Co.
    Port-au-Prince.

Cheerio!

Margie

(see note by Malcolm inside G.F.N.)[1]

This is the second Christmas card I got for you – I wrote you all a
long letter on the first one, but suddenly decided the next morning it
was too sentimental, & might put you off; more fool I – so please
take the deed for the deed.

Malc

Annotations:

1 This parenthetical remark is in Margerie's hand; G.F.N. are Noxon's
  initials: Gerald Forbes Noxon.

Editorial Notes:

a. This Christmas card, sent from New Orleans sometime in December
   1946, has three separate messages. Together with the formal card greetings is the first note from Lowry, who has signed for himself and
   Margerie. Margerie has added her own note and their Haiti address, and
   Lowry has added a further note inside the card. They have signed the
   card separately.

270: To Albert Erskine

P: UBC(pcard)
PP: *SL* 134

New Orleans,
Louisiana
26 December 1946[a]

Just like the old days of my grandpappy – the crew got so perfecta-
mente borracho they couldn't (& finally wouldn't) take the ship out –
(I don't blame them, I think it will sink at the dock before we get
aboard, which ought to be 5 minutes ago) *argal*,[1] we spent a wonderful Xmas Eve & day reading & *eating* your wonderful edition of
Daumier,[2] though have to send it back c/o you – all thanks to you &
Mr [Frank] Taylor[3] – God bless you.

Lowry

Annotations:

1 'Argal' is a literary adverb, probably a modern British pronunciation of
the Latin *ergo* (therefore), used facetiously to indicate specious or absurd
reasoning.
2 Albert Erskine and Frank Taylor had sent the Lowrys Reynal & Hitchcock's new edition of Honoré Daumier's *124 Lithographs* (1946); this
book is now with Lowry's library at UBC.
3 Lowry met Frank Taylor (1916–), editor-in-chief at Reynal & Hitchcock, when he was in New York for the publication of *Under the Volcano*
in February 1947, and the two became friends; see Lowry's Spring 1947
letter (**296**) to Taylor.

Editorial Notes:

a. The postcard shows a colour drawing of the Old Absinthe House on
Bourbon Street at Bienville in New Orleans.

Selected Bibliography

This bibliography contains items that are cited frequently or have been of general use in preparing the edition. All other reference materials are cited in the annotations, and works by and about Lowry are listed separately at the beginning of the volume.

Aiken, Conrad. *Priapus and the Pool and Other Poems*. New York: Boni & Liveright, 1925.

—. *Blue Voyage*. New York: Scribner's Sons, 1927.

—. *Preludes for Memnon*. New York: Scribner's, 1931.

—. *Great Circle*. London: Wishart, 1933.

Altman, Janet Gurkin. *Epistolarity: Approaches to a Form*. Columbus: Ohio State University Press, 1982.

Aubert, Jacques. 'D'éthique et de lettres.' *Pas tant* 21 (1989): 11-17.

Baker, Derek. *Partnership in Excellence: A Late-Victorian Education Venture: The Leys School, Cambridge 1875-1975*. Cambridge: Governors of the Leys School, 1975.

Beebe, Maurice. *Ivory Towers and Sacred Founts: The Artist as Hero in Fiction from Goethe to Joyce*. New York: New York University Press, 1964.

Bonner, Margerie. *The Last Twist of the Knife*. New York: Scribner's Sons, 1946.

—. *The Shapes That Creep*. New York: Scribner's Sons, 1946.

—. *Horse in the Sky*. New York: Scribner's Sons, 1947.

Bowker, Gordon & Paul Tiessen, ed. *Proceedings of the London Conference on Malcolm Lowry, 1984*. London: Goldsmiths' College, 1985.

Bradbrook, Muriel. 'Lowry and Some Cambridge Literary Friends.' In *Proceedings of the London Conference on Malcolm Lowry, 1984*, ed. Gordon Bowker and Paul Tiessen. 12-13.

675

Burnett, Whit. *The Literary Life and the Hell with It.* New York: Harper, 1939.

Butscher, Edward. *Conrad Aiken: Poet of White Horse Vale.* Athens: University of Georgia Press, 1988.

Byatt, A.S. *Possession: A Romance.* London: Chatto & Windus, 1990.

Churchill, Victor. *All My Sins Remembered.* London: Heinemann, 1964.

Clunn, Harold. *The Face of London.* London: Simpkin Marshall, 1932.

Committee of the General Synod, ed. *The Book of Common Praise: Being the Hymn Book of the Church of England in Canada.* London: Oxford University Press, 1938.

Dainard, J.A., ed. *Editing Correspondence.* Papers Given at the Fourteenth Annual Conference on Editorial Problems, University of Toronto, 3-4 Nov. 1978. New York: Garland, 1979.

Day, Douglas. 'Malcolm Lowry: Letters to an Editor,' *Shenandoah* 15,3 (1964): 3-15.

Derrida, Jacques. *La Carte postale de Socrate à Freud et au-delà.* Paris: Flammarion, 1980.

Donaldson, Gordon. *Niagara: The Eternal Circus.* Toronto: Doubleday, 1979.

Foley, Martha. *The Story of STORY Magazine: A Memoir.* Ed. Jay Neugeboren. London: W.W. Norton, 1980.

Fowler, Carolyn. *Philippe Thoby-Marcelin, écrivain haïtien et Pierre Marcelin, romancier haïtien.* Sherbrooke, Quebec: Éditions Naaman, 1985.

Freud, Sigmund. *The Standard Edition of the Complete Psychological Works of Sigmund Freud.* Trans. James Strachey, Anna Freud, Alix Strachey, Alan Tyson. Vol. 12. London: Hogarth Press, 1958.

Furness, N.H. 'The Dramatist as Exile: Ernst Toller and the English Theatre.' In *Theatre and Film in Exile: German Artists in Britain, 1933-1945,* ed. Gunter Berghaus. Oxford: Berg Oswald Wolff, 1989. 121-34.

Genette, Gérard. *Palimpsestes: La Littérature au second degré.* Paris: Éditions du Seuil, 1982.

Grace, Sherrill. 'The "Asperin Tree" and the Volcano: Carol Phillips and Malcolm Lowry.' *Journal of Modern Literature* 17,4 (1991): 509-20.

—. '"The Daily Crucifixion of the Post": Editing and Theorizing the Lowry Letters.' In *Challenges, Projects, Texts: Canadian Editing,* ed. John Lennox and Janet Peterson. New York: AMS Press, 1993. 26-53.

—. 'Respecting Plagiarism: Tradition, Guilt, and Malcolm Lowry's 'pelagiarist pen'.' *English Studies in Canada* 28,4 (1993): 461-82.

Green, Julien. *Personal Record 1928-1939*. Trans. Jocelyn Godefroi. New York: Harper & Brothers, 1939.

Grieg, Nordahl. *The Ship Sails On*. Trans. A.G. Chater. New York: Knopf, 1927.

Howard, Michael S. *Jonathan Cape, Publisher*. London: Cape, 1971.

Howarth, T.E.B. *Cambridge Between Two Wars*. London: Collins, 1978.

James, Henry. *The Aspern Papers*. London: Macmillan, 1911.

Jung, Carl. *Psychology of the Unconscious*. Trans. Beatrice M. Hinkle. London: Kegan Paul, Trench, Trubner, 1916.

Killorin, Joseph, ed. *Selected Letters of Conrad Aiken*. New Haven: Yale University Press, 1978.

Kim, Suzanne. 'Les Lettres de Malcolm Lowry.' *Études anglaises* 22,1 (1969): 58-61.

Koss, Stephen. *The Rise and Fall of the Political Press in Britain*. 2 vols. London: Hamish Hamilton, 1981-84.

Levine, Herbert S. *Hitler's Free City: A History of the Nazi Party in Danzig, 1925-39*. Chicago: University of Chiago Press, 1970.

Leys Fortnightly: The Magazine of Leys School, Cambridge. Vol. 51. Cambridge: R.J. Severs, 1927.

Lochner, R.K. *The Last Gentleman-of-War: The Raider Exploits of the Cruiser Emden*. Trans. Thea and Harry Lindauer. Annapolis, Maryland: Naval Institute Press, 1988.

Lorenz, Clarissa. *Lorelei Two: My Life with Conrad Aiken*. Athens: University of Georgia Press, 1983.

Lowry, Malcolm. 'Hollywood and the War.' *Vancouver Daily Province* 12 Dec. 1939: 4.

—. 'The Real Mr Chips.' *Vancouver Daily Province* 13 Dec. 1939: 4.

—. 'Where Did That One Go To 'Erbert?' *Vancouver Daily Province* 29 Dec. 1939: 4.

—. 'Garden of Etla.' *United Nations World* 4,6 (1950): 44-47.

McKenzie, D.F. *Bibliography and the Sociology of Texts*. London: British Library, 1986.

McLeish, Kenneth. *The Penguin Companion to the Arts in the 20th Century*. Harmondsworth: Penguin, 1986.

McMillan, Dougald. *Transition: The History of a Literary Era, 1927-1938*. London: Calder and Boyars, 1975.

Mota, Miguel, and Paul Tiessen, eds. *The Cinema of Malcolm Lowry: A Scholarly Edition of 'Tender is the Night.'* Vancouver: UBC Press, 1990.

New, William H.. *Malcolm Lowry: A Reference Guide*. Boston: G.K. Hall, 1978.

Pawley, Edward. *BBC Engineering 1922-1972*. London: BBC Publications, 1972.

Price, R.G.G. *A History of Punch*. London: Collins, 1957.

Redgrave, Michael. *In My Mind's Eye: An Autobiography*. London: Weidenfeld & Nicolson, 1983.

Schneider, Michel. *Voleurs de mots: Essai sur le plagiat, la psychanalyse et la pensée*. Paris: Gallimard, 1985.

Stern, James. 'Malcolm Lowry: A First Impression.' *Encounter* 29,3 (1967): 58-68.

Tebbel, John W. *A History of Book Publishing in the United States*. 4 vols. New York: R.R. Bowker, 1972-81.

Tillet, Beverly, ed. *Jerry Silverman's Folk Song Encyclopedia*. 2 vols. New York: Chappell Music, 1975.

Watkins, Ernest. *R.B. Bennett: A Biography*. Toronto: Kingswood House, 1963.

Wilber, Richard. *H.H. Stevens, 1878-1973*. Toronto: University of Toronto Press, 1977.

Wilson, Edmond. *Classics and Commercials: A Literary Chronicle of the Forties*. New York: Farrar, Straus, 1950.

Index

Index to Addressees giving letter number

General Reference Index